Malay

Singapore
& Brunei

Tony Wheeler
Hugh Finlay
Peter Turner
Geoff Crowther

Malaysia, Singapore & Brunei – a travel survival kit

4th edition

Published by
Lonely Planet Publications Pty Ltd (ACN 005 607 983)
PO Box 617, Hawthorn, Vic 3122, Australia
Lonely Planet Publications, Inc
PO Box 2001A, Berkeley, CA 94702, USA

Printed by
Singapore National Printers Ltd, Singapore

Photographs by
Brendon Hyde (BH), Charlotte Hindle (CH), David Ross (DR), Geoff Crowther (GC),
Hugh Finlay (HF), Joe Cummings (JC), Mark Lightbody (ML), Paul Steel (PS),
Peter Turner (PT), Sue Tan (ST), Tony Wheeler (TW), Vicki Beale (VB)

Front cover: Kek Lok Si Temple, Penang, Malaysia (D & J Heaton), Scoopix Photo Library

First Published
1982

This Edition
August 1991

> **Singapore**
> The 'nuts and bolts' information about Singapore in this book is identical to the information in
> *Singapore - city guide*

Although the authors and publisher have tried to make the information as
accurate as possible, they accept no responsibility for any loss, injury or
inconvenience sustained by any person using this book.

National Library of Australia Cataloguing in Publication Data

Wheeler, Tony, 1946- .
    Malaysia, Singapore & Brunei: a travel survival kit.

    4th ed.
    Includes index.
    ISBN 0 86442 113 3.

    1. Malaysia – Description and travel – Guide-books.
    2. Singapore – Description and travel – Guide- books.
    3. Brunei – Description and travel – Guide-books.
    I. Crowther, Geoff, 1944- . Malaysia, Singapore & Brunei. II. Title.

915.95

Tony Wheeler

Tony Wheeler was born in England, but spent most of his youth overseas due to his father's occupation with British Airways. He returned to England to do a university degree in engineering, worked for a short time as an automotive design engineer, returned to university again and did an MBA then dropped out on the Asian overland trail with his wife Maureen. They've been travelling, writing and publishing guidebooks ever since having set up Lonely Planet Publications in the mid-70s. Travel for the Wheelers is now considerably enlivened by their daughter Tashi and son Kieran.

Hugh Finlay

After deciding there must be more to life than a career in civil engineering, Hugh first took off around Australia in the mid-'70s, working at everything from parking cars to prospecting for diamonds in the back blocks of South Australia, before heading further afield. He spent three years travelling and working in three continents, including a stint on an irrigation project in Saudi Arabia, before joining Lonely Planet in 1985.

Hugh has also written the Lonely Planet guide *Jordan & Syria – a travel survival kit*, co-authored *Morocco, Algeria & Tunisia – a travel survival kit*, and has contributed to others including *Africa on a shoestring* and *India – a travel survival kit*.

Peter Turner

Peter was born in Melbourne and studied Asian studies, politics and English at university before setting off on the Asian trail. His long-held interest in South-East Asia has seen him make numerous trips to the region, and he has also travelled further afield in Asia, the Pacific, North America and Europe. He joined Lonely Planet as an editor in 1986 and has also worked on Lonely Planet's Australia guide and *Singapore – city guide*.

Geoff Crowther

Born in Yorkshire, England, Geoff took to his heels early on in the search for the miraculous. The lure of the unknown took him to Kabul, Kathmandu and Lamu in the days before the overland bus companies began digging up the dirt along the tracks of Africa. His experiences led him to join the now legendary but sadly defunct alternative information centre BIT in the late '60s.

In 1977, he wrote his first guide for Lonely Planet – *Africa on the cheap*. He has also written LP's *South America on a shoestring*, travel survival kits to *Korea* and *East Africa* and has co-authored LP's guides to *India, Kenya* and *Morocco, Algeria & Tunisia*.

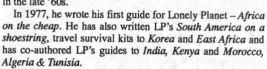

From the Publisher

This book was edited by Sharan Kaur and Alan Tiller edited LP's *Singapore – city guide* which forms the Singapore chapter in this book. Tamsin Wilson was responsible for the design, illustrations and cover design; Tamsin Wilson, Valerie Tellini and Ann Jeffree updated the maps and Margaret Jung, Tracey O'Mara, Chris Lee-Ack and Vicki Beale helped with the last-minute corrections.

Thanks must also go to Dan Levin for fixing computer problems and Sharon Wertheim for indexing.

Acknowledgments

Hugh would like to thank Dennis Pile and the MTDC staff in both Sydney and KL for their assistance to him while undertaking this trip, and Patrick Chee for risking life and limb to check out the logging route from Belaga to Bintulu in Sarawak.

Peter would like to thank Kevin Dragon of the Singapore Tourist Promotion Board, Alex 'Hilton' Ping, Sugiman, Karsten Mack and, above all, Lorraine for her support and endurance.

Producing this Book

Researching the first edition of this guide was originally a two-part operation. While Geoff Crowther covered East Malaysia and Brunei, Tony and Maureen Wheeler roamed around Singapore and up and down the Malay peninsula.

Researching the second edition was handled by Mark Lightbody author of Lonely Planet's *Canada - a travel survival kit* and updater of several LP guidebooks. The third edition was again a joint effort. Sue Tan tackled the east coast of the peninsula along with East Malaysia and Brunei. Joe Cummings covered the west coast and Singapore.

For this edition, Hugh Finlay undertook the bulk of the work and covered the west coast of Peninsular Malaysia, Sabah, Sarawak and Brunei, while Peter Turner did Singapore and the east coast of the peninsula. Tony Wheeler made a last-minute visit to note the latest changes in Singapore, Melaka, KL and Penang.

Last, but not least, a special thanks to those readers who took the time and energy to write to us from places large and small all over the region. These people's names appear at the back of the book on page 420.

Warning & Request

Things change – prices go up, schedules change, good places go bad and bad places go bankrupt – nothing stays the same. So if you find things better or worse, recently opened or long since closed, please write and tell us and help make the next edition better!

Your letters will be used to help update future editions and, where possible, important changes will also be included as a Stop Press section in reprints.

All information is greatly appreciated and the best letters will receive a free copy of the next edition, or any other Lonely Planet book of your choice.

Contents

MAP LEGEND

BOUNDARIES

▪–▪–▪–▪–	International Boundaries
▪▪–▪▪–▪▪–	Internal Boundaries
–▪–▪–▪–	National Parks, Reserves
– – – –	The Equator
··············	The Tropics

SYMBOLS

◉ NEW DELHI	National Capital
● BOMBAY	Provincial or State Capital
● Pune	Major Town
• Barsi	Minor Town
▣	Post Office
✈	Airport
i	Tourist Information
●	Bus Station, Terminal
66	Highway Route Number
☪ ✝ ⛪	Mosque, Church, Cathedral
∴	Temple, Ruin or Archaeological Site
▬	Hostel
✚	Hospital
✳	Lookout
⛛	Camping Areas
⌐	Picnic Areas
⌂	Hut or Chalet
▲	Mountain
⊬⊬	Railway Station
⟋⟋	Road Bridge
⊬⊬⊬	Road Rail Bridge
)(	Road Tunnel
)( )(	Railway Tunnel
⌒⌒	Escarpment or Cliff
⊃⊂	Pass
∿	Ancient or Historic Wall

ROUTES

——————	Major Roads and Highways
– – – –	Unsealed Major Roads
——————	Sealed Roads
– – – –	Unsealed Roads, Tracks
————	City Streets
+++++++++++++	Railways
▬●▬	Subways
················	Walking Tracks
– – – – –	Ferry Routes
⊣⊣ ⊣⊣ ⊣⊣ ⊣⊣	Cable Car or Chair Lift

HYDROGRAPHIC FEATURES

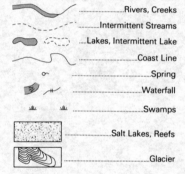

	Rivers, Creeks
	Intermittent Streams
	Lakes, Intermittent Lake
	Coast Line
	Spring
	Waterfall
	Swamps
	Salt Lakes, Reefs
	Glacier

OTHER FEATURES

	Parks, Gardens and National Parks
	Built Up Area
	Market Place and Pedestrian Mall
	Plaza and Town Square
	Cemetery

Note: Not all the symbols displayed above will necessarily appear in this book

Introduction

Malaysia, Singapore and Brunei are three independent South-East Asian nations offering the visitor a taste of Asia at its most accessible. In all of Asia only Japan has a higher per capita income than these countries so, as you might expect, they are relatively prosperous and forward looking. Transport facilities are good, accommodation standards are high, the food excellent (often amazingly good in fact) and for the visitor there are very few problems to be faced.

Yet despite these high standards these are not expensive countries - Singapore may be able to offer all the air-conditioned comforts your credit cards can handle and East Malaysia may at times be a little pricey due to its jungle-frontier situation, but in Peninsular Malaysia the costs can be absurdly cheap if you want them to be.

More important than simple ease of travel this region offers amazing variety both geographically and culturally. If you want beaches and tropical islands it's hard to beat the east coast of the peninsula. If you want mountains, parks and wildlife then you can climb Mt Kinabalu, explore the rivers of Sarawak or watch for wildlife in the huge Taman Negara (national park) on the peninsula.

If you want city life then you can try the historic old port of Melaka, the easy going back streets of Georgetown in Penang or the modern-as-tomorrow city of Singapore. When it comes to people you've got Malays, Chinese, Indians and a whole host of indigenous tribes in Sabah and Sarawak. Last, but far from least, you've got a choice of food which alone brings people back to the region over and over again; there's no question in many people's minds that Singapore is deservedly the food capital of Asia.

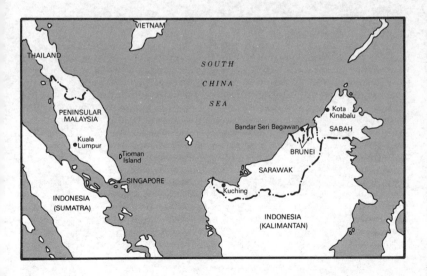

SINGAPORE

Facts about the Country

HISTORY

Today, Singapore is one of the great modern city-states, yet in the 14th century Chinese traders described Singapore, or Temasek as it was then known, as a barren, pirate-infested island.

According to Malay legend, a Sumatran prince encountered a lion on Temasek and this good omen prompted him to found Singapura, or 'Lion City'. Although lions have never inhabited Singapore and there is no evidence of any early city, it was likely that Singapore was a small trading outpost of the powerful Sumatran Srivijaya Empire before it became a vassal state of the Javanese Majapahit Empire in the mid-13th century.

In the early 1390s, Parameswara, a prince from Palembang, threw off allegiance to the Majapahit Empire and fled to Temasek. Although Parameswara and his party were well received, they promptly murdered their host and used the island as a pirate base. In 1398, the Thais attacked Temasek, and

Parameswara fled to Malacca (Melaka). It was a propitious move, for he went on to found one of the great trading ports of the East.

Singapore again became a quiet backwater, but during the 15th century in the nearby Straits of Malacca, the Portuguese and their cannons came to contest the Arab monopoly on the lucrative spice and China trades. The Portuguese seized Malacca in 1511 but their dominance was short-lived. The Dutch undermined their trade by founding Batavia (now Jakarta), allowing ships to use the Sunda Straits to Europe and to avoid the Straits of Malacca altogether. The Dutch then seized Malacca in 1641 and became the dominant European power in the region.

The Arrival of Raffles

The British became interested in the Straits of Malacca in the 18th century when the East India Company set out to establish a port to secure and protect its line of trade from China to the colonies in India. In 1786, Captain Francis Light founded a settlement on Penang Island.

The second of the Straits Settlements was Malacca. In 1795, Holland and her colonies were annexed by France. Britain, at war with the French, then seized all Dutch possessions in South-East Asia and ruled them for the duration of the war.

Sir Stamford Raffles was lieutenant-governor of Java from 1811 to 1816. Raffles, a great believer in the British Empire's right to rule, was also an admirer and scholar of ways of the East. Although a far-sighted, progressive thinker, he proved to be an impractical and overzealous administrator. He was recalled to Britain in disgrace after heavy financial losses, but returned to the East in 1817 to become lieutenant-governor of Bencoolen, an insignificant British trading post in Sumatra.

With the end of the Napoleonic wars and the defeat of France, Britain returned Dutch territories. Raffles, fearing a resurgence of the Dutch trading monopoly, argued strongly for an increased British influence in the Straits of Malacca.

After petitioning the Governor-General of India, Raffles set forth to establish a settlement in Riau with Colonel William Farquhar, the former Resident of Malacca. Farquhar had married a Malay woman and was well versed in local politics.

On 29 January 1819, Raffles landed on the island of Singapore. He reached agreement to found a settlement with the local ruler, the Temenggong, and with Sultan Hussein, a contender to the fragmented Malay court. Raffles promptly left Singapore to return to Bencoolen, leaving Farquhar as Resident.

The Dutch were furious at this incursion into their territory and the fledging colony lived under constant fear of attack, but the Dutch did not intervene. Farquhar quickly set about establishing a trading post. The port was declared free of tariffs and Farquhar used his influence to attract Malaccan traders.

Raffles briefly visited Singapore in May 1819 to find a thriving town, and by 1821 Singapore's population had grown to 5000, including 1000 Chinese. The Temenggong established his settlement on the Singapore River, while Sultan Hussein built his palace at Kampong Glam.

Raffles, who had little direct involvement in Singapore's early development, returned in 1822. After illness and the death of three of his children, Raffles was a broken man but the sight of his thriving colony revived his spirits. Raffles delayed his return to England and set about running Singapore.

He moved the commercial district across the river to its present site and levelled a hill to form Raffles Place. The government area was allocated around Forbidden Hill (now Fort Canning Hill) and the east bank of the river. Chinatown was divided among the various Chinese groups, and Raffles himself moved to Forbidden Hill.

By the time Raffles left in 1823, he had laid the foundations of the city, but more importantly he had firmly established Singapore as a free port – something that Singapore traders have vehemently fought for ever since.

By 1824, the Temenggong and Sultan Hussein were living beyond their stipends and agreed to be bought out in one payment. Singapore and the surrounding islands were seceded to the British.

The Early Years

In 1826, Singapore became part of the Straits Settlements with Penang and Malacca, which had been swapped with the Dutch for Bencoolen. The Straits Settlements came under the authority of Calcutta, which allocated few funds to running these areas. While commerce boomed, the judiciary and bureaucracy were hopelessly underfunded and social services were nonexistent.

By all accounts, Singapore was a fetid, stinking, disease-ridden colony. Piracy remained a problem and was not eliminated until the 1870s. While merchants petitioned Calcutta for more services, at the same time they recoiled at any suggestions of increased taxes. Singapore's revenue was derived mostly from gambling, opium and *arak* (the local firewater, or spirit).

Despite Singapore's problems, migrants came in their thousands. Singapore became the major port in the region, and its population – Bugis, Javanese, Arab, Indian and Chinese – reflected its trade. The Chinese, who were soon the largest group, comprised mostly of immigrants from the southern provinces – Hokkien, Teochew, Cantonese and Hakka.

The hard-working, resourceful Chinese migrants formed guilds, but they also joined the Triad, a secret society dedicated to overthrowing the Manchu Dynasty in China. The Triad, and other secret societies, were responsible for much of Singapore's crime, yet they also provided the social framework that the government neglected. The societies provided housing and jobs, and settled disputes within the communities.

Singapore's trade went through boom and bust periods in the early days and depended on uncertain entrepôt trade. It was controlled by European trading houses, while the Chinese acted as intermediaries, dealing with Chinese and other Asian traders.

Early attempts at agriculture were a disaster and crops failed because of disease and poor soil. Gambier and pepper had some success, but the push to establish plantations in the island's interior exposed another threat – tigers.

Tigers killed many labourers and one village had to be abandoned. A tiger was even found in the well-to-do residential district of Orchard Rd, and this prompted the government to place a bounty on tigers. Tiger hunting became a fashionable pastime and many were killed in the 1860s. The last tiger on Singapore was shot in 1904.

Laissez-faire Singapore continued to grow with little or no social, educational or medical services, but by the 1860s Calcutta began to provide more funds and many of Singapore's grand colonial buildings date from this period.

A Thriving Colony

On 1 April 1867, the Straits Settlements became a fully fledged crown colony, run from Singapore. Singapore was a key link in the chain of British ports, especially with the opening of the Suez Canal, and a full army regiment was stationed there.

Chinese migration continued and in the 1870s massive numbers came to Singapore. Many of the Chinese were now wealthy in their own right and owned trading houses. Indian migration had also increased steadily from the mid-19th century.

Trade with the Malay Peninsula had been going on for years, but Singaporean merchants pressed for a greater government presence to enforce contracts and control the autonomous sultanates. The government began to install British Residents and advisers on the peninsula.

Peninsular trade, most of which was exported through Singapore, grew dramatically at the end of the 19th century. Tin mines dotted Malaya and in 1877, rubber seeds, originally smuggled out of Brazil, were sent to Singapore. A year later, the pneumatic tyre was invented and the rubber trade boomed.

All the while, Singapore came to take on the appearance of a cosmopolitan city. Tennis was played on the Padang, and in the evening it was a favourite strolling ground for British gentlefolk. The manually-drawn rickshaw was imported into Singapore during 1880, the first car arrived in 1896 and Raffles Hotel opened in 1899.

The government also registered the Chinese organisations and attempted to control the secret societies. Opium addiction was rife and in an attempt to control it, the government manufactured and sold opium in 1910, which provided almost half of the government's revenue.

Singapore was also a centre for South-East Asian studies and thought. Muslim thought and literature blossomed, and Singapore was a major staging point for the Hajj, or pilgrimage to Mecca. The Arab St area was, and still is, a popular place for pilgrims to stay.

The 1920s witnessed another boom, despite a massive fall in rubber prices in 1920, and immigration soared. Millionaires, including a number of Chinese migrants such as Aw Boon Haw, the 'Tiger Balm King', were made overnight.

The Chinese were by far the greatest immigrant group and Chinese immigration peaked in 1930 when 250,000 Chinese came to Singapore. The upheavals in China were played out in Singapore with the establishment of the Kuomintang party, which had a very active communist faction.

The Chinese secret societies were allied with political factions, and gunmen and street gangs made headlines. The colonial government attempted to control the Chinese community, but it was mainland politics which provided the greatest sway and inspiration.

The communists played a dominant role in the trade unions and the mainland controlled parties fostered anticolonial sentiments. In 1929, the government was faced with the twin problems of controlling subversive forces and shoring up an economy battered by the great depression.

Its answers lay in banning the Kuomintang, censoring the Chinese press, withdrawing funds for Chinese education and establishing strict immigration quotas. Chinese immigration was cut to a tenth of its previous levels, and Singapore would never again witness the massive migration that had played such a large part in its development. Yet by the 1930s, Singapore was undeniably and irrevocably a Chinese city.

Singapore's inexorable economic growth continued after the depression, and the well-to-do prospered. The 1930s were a time of greater public works and social amenities. Though the Malayan Communist Party was well established and the seeds of independence grew in the community, the colonial government was firmly ensconced, convinced of its right to rule and looking forward to a long and prosperous reign.

The Japanese Invasion

The Japanese brutally destroyed the complacency of British rule and forever laid to rest notions of European superiority and British military might.

On 7 December 1941, the Japanese bombed Pearl Harbour and invaded the Malay Peninsula. In less than two months, they routed ill-prepared British and Commonwealth forces and stormed down the peninsula, conquering all before them. By 31 January, they were in Johore Bahru, massing in preparation for an assault on Singapore.

The Japanese commander, General Yamashita, was already a national hero but his rapid successes had left his supply lines overextended, and his troops were outnumbered. Nonetheless, he decided to attack before the retreating forces regrouped and reinforcements could arrive.

The Japanese invaded Singapore from the north-west on 8 February 1941. They met fierce resistance but over the next week they slowly advanced towards the city. Churchill sent word to hold Singapore at all cost but the pessimistic military command led by Lieutenant-General Arthur Percival feared a bloodbath of Singapore's citizens.

On 15 February, with the city in range of Japanese artillery, Percival called upon the Japanese to discuss peace terms.

Yamashita was stunned. With only a few days of ammunition and supplies left, he feared that continued resistance would force him to call off the attack. Percival, unaware of the Japanese position, saw no way out and surrendered unconditionally.

It was one of the worst defeats in the history of the British Empire. The European population was herded onto the Padang and then marched away for internment, many of them at the infamous Changi Prison.

Singapore was renamed Syonan (Light of the South) and the Japanese quickly set about establishing order. Anti-Chinese sentiment was unleashed and Japanese troops started a massacre. Communists and intellectuals were singled out, but there was no method in the ensuing slaughter. In one week, thousands were executed and the Japanese lost any chance to gain the respect and cooperation of the people.

Though the Japanese ruled harshly, life in Singapore was tolerable while the war went well for Japan. As the war progressed, however, inflation skyrocketed and food, medicines and other essentials were in short supply.

Conditions were appalling during the last phase of the war, and many died of malnutrition and disease. The war ended suddenly with Japan's surrender, and Singapore was spared the agony of recapture.

Post War & the Road to Independence

After the suffering experienced under the Japanese, the British were welcomed back to Singapore but their right to rule was now in question. Plans for limited self-government and a Malayan Union were drawn up, uniting the Malay states of the peninsula with British possessions in Borneo. Singapore was excluded, largely because of Malay fears of Chinese Singapore's dominance.

Singapore was run-down and its services neglected after the war. Poverty, unemployment and shortages provided fuel for the Malayan Communist Party, whose freedom fighters had emerged as the heroes of the war.

The General Labour Union, the communist labour organisation, had a huge following and in 1946 and 1947 Singapore was crippled by strikes.

Meanwhile, new political opportunities in Malaya saw the rapid development of Malay nationalism. The United Malays National Organisation (UMNO) was the dominant Malay party and presented strong opposition to the Malay Union. UMNO argued for a federation, based on the Malay sultanates, and opposed citizenship laws which gave equal rights to all races, thereby undermining the special status of Malays.

Singapore moved slowly to self-government. The socialist Malayan Democratic Union was the first real political party, but it became increasingly radical and boycotted the first elections in 1947, leaving the conservative Progressive Party as the only party to contest the election.

After early successes, the communists realised that they were not going to gain power under the colonial government's political agenda and they began a campaign of armed struggle in Malaya. In 1948, the Emergency was declared. The communists were outlawed and a guerrilla war was waged on the peninsula for 12 years. There was no fighting in Singapore but left-wing politics languished under the political repression of Emergency regulations.

The Rise of the PAP & Lee Kuan Yew
By the early 1950s, the communist threat waned and left-wing activity again surfaced into the open. The centre-left Labour Front was active, and student and union movements were at the forefront of communist and socialist activity.

One of the rising stars of this era was Lee Kuan Yew, a third generation Straits-born Chinese who had studied law at Cambridge. Lee Kuan Yew had good contacts with the elite and British-educated intellectuals. He became involved with the Progressive Party, but grew dissatisfied with their conservative politics. Lee then became a legal adviser to several unions where he became acquainted with the left and the power of union politics.

Most importantly, he realised the need to be aligned with the forces that appealed to the Chinese-educated majority.

The People's Action Party (PAP) was founded in 1954 with Lee Kuan Yew as secretary-general. The PAP was an uneasy alliance − Lee Kuan Yew led the noncommunist faction, but the party's main power base was communist. Lee, always a pragmatic and shrewd politician, realised that power in Singapore was impossible without communist support.

With the easing of the Emergency and the 1955 elections, Singaporean politics came of age. A spirited campaign saw the right-wing parties trounced and David Marshall's Labour Front form a coalition government. The PAP was vocal in opposition, competing with the Labour Front for the left position.

PAP's influence continued to grow; although a noncommunal party, it appealed to the majority Chinese and attracted the strong left-wing vote. The PAP contested all seats in the 1959 elections and it was swept to power with an overwhelming majority. Lew Kuan Yew became prime minister.

The establishment was shocked. The PAP's left-wing image sent a wave of fear through the business community. Foreign companies moved their headquarters and there was a flight of capital from Singapore. The government embarked on an anti-Western campaign, but it was anticolonial rather than anticapitalist.

The radical PAP leadership had, in fact, been replaced by moderates after the Internal Security Council, comprised of British, Singaporean and Malaysian representatives, had ordered the arrest of the extreme left of the party in a communist crackdown in 1958. The PAP found votes in fiery speeches but their socialist policies were in fact quite temperate.

The Federation of Malaya had already achieved independence in 1957, and the PAP's aim was for full independence and union with the federation. The British agreed, but Malaya had no desire for union with a left-wing Singapore. The PAP government took a strongly pro-Malay stance to appease Malaya, and introduced Malay as the national language. It tried to woo foreign capital to bolster the ailing economy, much to the disgust of the extreme-left faction.

A split was inevitable. In 1961, the PAP was torn asunder by the wholesale defection of the left to form the Barisan Sosialis.

The PAP was one short of a majority in parliament and they held precariously onto power with the help of the right-wing Alliance party. The position of the PAP strengthened after February 1963 when 100 left-wing leaders, including half of the Barisan Sosialis leadership, were arrested under Operation Cold Store for supporting a rebellion in Brunei.

Independence

Full independence and union with Malaya was now firmly back on the agenda. Thinking in Malaya had also turned around, with Malaya preferring to have a moderate Singapore within a union rather than a communist Singapore outside it. The Federation of Malaysia came into being in September 1963, and at the same time Lee Kuan Yew held a snap election.

The government campaigned on its already impressive list of achievements – increases in public housing, health standards and education spending were dramatic. Crime was down and the government used its powers under the Emergency to arrest secret-society members. The PAP won 37 of the 51 seats, while the Barisan Sosialis won 13.

The Malaysian union was never going to be easy and the PAP made a grave mistake in contesting the 1964 federal elections, even though it had earlier promised not to stand. Its social democrat platform was soundly rejected by the conservative Malaysian electorate, and its campaign had only aroused suspicions of a Singaporean takeover.

Tension mounted when Singapore refused to extend the privileged position held by Malays in Malaya to the Malays in Singapore. Communal violence broke out in the Malay Geylang district of Singapore in 1964 and more than 20 people were killed. To add to these problems, Indonesia embarked on a campaign of confrontation against Malaysia, and Singapore became a target of Indonesian bombings.

By 1965, Singapore was expelled and the union was over. A tearful Lee Kuan Yew likened Singapore to a head without a body, and feared that Singapore, with no natural resources, would not survive.

The Republic of Singapore

Singapore became independent on 9 August 1965. Lee's fears proved to be unfounded, and Singapore boomed and became the success story of the region. Rapid industrialisation and large foreign investment helped give Singapore full employment and a rising standard of living. In 1968, the PAP won every parliamentary seat after the Barisan Sosialis boycotted the election.

Gross domestic product expanded at nearly 10% per year and Singapore, through a program of government-planned economic expansion, rapidly developed its industry and became a centre of Asian finance. Stable government, industrial calm and previously unknown political quiet prompted further foreign investment. Lee Kuan Yew presided over an economic miracle and Singapore's international standing grew.

The face of Singapore changed dramatically with modernisation. Slum clearance and new building projects were the order in Singapore's brave new world, and many old buildings fell to the wreckers. The Housing Development Board's new estates were a huge success as more and more Singaporeans had decent housing.

Singapore's government was talented, free of corruption and enjoyed popular support. However, opposition to the Government was viewed harshly. The media was the instrument of government campaigns and national objectives; in 1971 the government closed the *Nanyang Siang Pau* after its criticism of government education policy, and attacked the *Eastern Sun* and the *Singapore Herald*. Further laws to control the media were introduced in 1974 and 1977. Government control over student groups and labour organisations also increased.

The PAP believed its benign dictatorship was the only way to secure peace and prosperity for Singapore, and Lee Kuan Yew remains staunchly unrepentant, convinced that his tough measures were necessary to develop Singapore. By the 1970s, Singapore was the wealthiest country in Asia behind Japan.

The PAP won every seat in each election held until 1981 when J B Jeyaretnam of the Workers' Party won a seat at a by-election. The government was shocked and undertook even greater control of the press.

A second opposition member was elected in the 1984 elections, and the government decided that if the electorate wanted an opposition voice then the government would supply it. The government instituted a system where it could appoint its own non-elected opposition members. The 1984 election also saw the election of Lee Hsien Loong, Lee Kuan Yew's son, who became a rising star in cabinet.

By the 1980s, the second tier of PAP leaders came to the fore and Lee Kuan Yew handed over greater responsibility to his juniors. Goh Chok Tong became deputy prime minister and Lee Kuan Yew's designated successor. Singapore's economic miracle continued, despite a hiccup in the mid-80s, and the country possessed a diversified economic base and a literate, skilled population.

Lee Kuan Yew resigned as prime minister in November 1990 and Goh Chok Tong took over. Lee Hsien Loong, or B G (for Brigadier General) as he is affectionately known, is widely touted as a future leader. He possesses his father's oratory skills and stubbornness, though Lee Kuan Yew seems keen to distance himself from a political dynasty.

Lee's resignation coincided with the completion of the Mass Rapid Transit subway system, an impressive testament to Singapore's modernisation and technological achievements. Though Lee has detractors, especially in the Western media, his achievements are undeniable. He transformed Singapore from a poverty-stricken, run-down city with no natural resources and an uncertain future, to a great city-state where its citizens enjoy a safe and prosperous existence. A shrewd politician, brilliant orator and astute leader, he remains the father of modern Singapore and his popularity is as high as ever.

Lee Kuan Yew remains in cabinet and there are plans to give more power to the largely ceremonial president's role, no doubt to accommodate Lee. It is difficult to imagine Lee relinquishing power and allowing Singapore to depart from the course he has steered since 1959. In fact, Lee has even promised to return from the grave if things go wrong in Singapore.

Yet Singaporeans are demanding change. The new generation, which has not lived through the hardships of the past, are seeking liberalisation and increased freedom. There are calls for the repeal of the Internal Security Act which was used to detain nearly 100 activists without trial in 1987.

In January 1991, the new government showed signs of change by allowing previous political exiles to return to Singapore, but it remains to be seen if Goh Chock Tong's government will plot a new path in Singaporean politics, or simply deliver more of the same. The next elections, due in 1993, promise to be even closer with the opposition parties hoping to increase their 36% share of the vote.

GEOGRAPHY

Singapore is a low-lying island of 616 sq km, just over 100 km north of the equator. Apart from the main island, there are also about 50 smaller islands. Singapore is connected with Peninsular Malaysia by a km-long causeway. Bukit Timah (Hill of Tin) is the highest point on the island at an altitude of 162 metres.

CLIMATE

Singapore has a typically tropical climate – it's hot and humid year round. Once you've got used to the tropics, however, it never strikes you as too uncomfortable. The temperature rarely drops below 20°C (68°F), even at night, and usually climbs to 30°C (86°F) or more during the day. Humidity tends to hover around the 90% mark.

Rain, when it comes, tends to be short and sharp and is soon replaced by more of that ever-present sunshine. At certain times of the year, it may rain every day but it's rare that it rains all day. Singapore is at its wettest from November to January.

ECONOMY

Singapore is one of Asia's four 'dragons' – the Asian economic boom countries of Taiwan, Korea, Hong Kong and Singapore. Singapore's gross domestic product is currently growing at around 8%, an annual growth rate that Singapore has averaged for more than 20 years. Singapore has a current account surplus of over US$1500 million, it is a net creditor, inflation is low and unemployment is virtually nonexistent.

Singapore's economy is based on trade, shipping, banking and tourism, with a growing programme of light industrialisation. It also has a major oil refining business producing much of the petroleum for the South-East Asian region. Other important industries include ship building and maintenance, and electronics. Singapore's port is the fourth busiest in the world.

For many Western countries with mounting foreign debt, declining exports and increasing imports, Singapore is seen as a model free-market economy. A model economy it may be, but its approach is not free market.

While tariffs are low or nonexistent and foreign capital is encouraged with minimal restrictions, Singapore is very definitely a managed economy in the Japanese mould. It is the government that provides direction by targeting industries for development and offering tax incentives. Unions and the labour market are controlled by the government, and there is tough legislation against strikes.

While the government promotes free trade, it always reserves the right to intervene, as it did in 1985 when it closed the stock exchange for three days after a major Singaporean company, Pan Electric Industries, went into receivership.

The Monetary Authority of Singapore (MAS) is a good example of government involvement in the economy. It acts as a central bank and powerful financial market regulator to promote sustained economic growth and provide stability in the financial services sector. Singapore's finance market is one of the largest in Asia and provides 25% of the country's income – to a large degree this is because of the investment stability provided by the MAS.

Singapore does have its share of free marketeers though, and many in the business community want less government involvement in the economy. Singapore wants to assume the role of Asia's finance centre, especially with Hong Kong's changeover to the mainland in 1997, but investors in 'anything goes' Hong Kong are wary of more regulated Singaporean markets. Singapore's restrictive society is also a problem, and Singapore suffers from a brain drain that sees it lose many of its skilled professionals.

Singapore is no welfare state but it does guarantee its citizens decent housing, health care, high standards of education and superannuation. There are no unemployment payments or programmes, but unemployment is negligible and the government insists that anyone who wants to work can find it. In fact, Singapore has to import workers from neighbouring countries, particularly to do the hard, dirty work which Singaporeans no longer want any part of.

All workers and their employers make sizeable contributions to the Central Provident Fund (CPF), a form of superannuation that is returned on retirement. Some CPF savings, however, can be used in the purchase of government housing.

POPULATION

Singapore's polyglot population numbers 2.7 million. It's made up of 76% Chinese, 15% Malay, 7% Indian and 2% from a variety of races.

Singapore's population density is high but the government waged a particularly successful birth control campaign in the 1970s and early 1980s. In fact, it was so successful that the birth rate dropped off alarmingly, especially in the Chinese community. To reverse the trend, tax incentives were introduced for university-educated women who had children, although at the same time rewards of S$10,000 were offered to those willing to undergo sterilisation.

Under new policies, there are now tax rebates of up to S$20,000 for couples who have a third and fourth child. In another move, government-sponsored marriage brokers are teaching social skills to hardworking Singaporeans who are so dedicated to their work that they don't know how to woo the opposite sex.

Singapore has also relaxed its immigration laws to allow 25,000 Hong Kong Chinese and their dependents into Singapore each year. This concession to 'Honkies' (as Singaporeans call the citizens of Hong Kong) is a controversial move that is seen by some as an attempt to swell the Chinese population.

PEOPLE

Singapore's character, and the main interest for the visitor, lies in the diversity of its population. Chinatown still thrives with the sights, sounds and rituals of a Chinese city, Little India is a microcosm of the subcontinent, and Malay traditions and culture are still practised in the Geylang and Katong districts. But modern Singapore is essentially a Chinese city with strong Western influences, and the old ways are dying.

The growing Westernisation of Singapore is a cause of concern for the government. English is the principal language of education, and growing prosperity sees Singaporeans consuming Western values along with Western goods. For the government, this divergence from traditional values threatens to undermine the spirit – essentially the work-oriented Chinese spirit – that built Singapore.

In an attempt to reverse the new ways of the young, the government runs campaigns to develop awareness of traditional culture and values. These include cultural exhibitions, the compulsory study of the mother tongue in schools and attempts to instil moral training in schools through religious instruction.

The government's guiding philosophy is Confucian, and its ideal society is based on the Confucian values of devotion to parents and family, loyalty to friends, and the emphasis on education, justice and good government. It is a secular, pragmatic society instilled with a healthy dose of materialism. However, there is little place for the individual, and responsibility for social welfare lies with the family, not government.

The most recent government publicity campaign is based on the officially adopted philosophy of 'shared values' in an attempt to counteract Western ideology. The Confucian shared values are: nation before community and society above self; respect and community support for the individual; consensus instead of conflict; and, racial and religious harmony. The campaign is viewed with suspicion by non-Chinese Singaporeans.

Government policy has always been to promote Singapore as a multicultural nation where the three main racial groups can live in equality and harmony, while still maintaining their own cultural identities. The government strives hard to unite Singaporeans and promote equality, though there are imbalances in the distribution of wealth and power amongst the racial groups. For the most part, the government is successful in promoting racial harmony, a not-always-easy task in multiracial Singapore.

Chinese

The Chinese first settled in the Nanyang, as South-East Asia is known in China, as far back as the 14th century. In the 19th and 20th centuries, waves of Chinese migrants in search of a better life poured into Singapore and provided the labour that ran the colony.

The migrants came mostly from the southern provinces: Hokkien Chinese from the vicinity of Amoy in Fukien province; the Teochew from Swatow in eastern Kwangtung; Hakka from Kwangtung and Fukien; and Cantonese from Canton. Hokkiens and Teochews enjoyed an affinity in dialect and customs, but the Cantonese and Hakkas may as well have come from opposite ends of the earth. The Chinese settlers soon established their own areas in Singapore, and the divisions along dialect lines still exists to some extent in the older areas of town.

Settlement for the immigrants was made easier by Chinese organisations based on clan, dialect and occupation. Upon arrival, immigrants were taken in by the various communities and given work and housing. The secret societies were particularly prevalent in Singapore in the 19th century and, while they eventually became nothing more than criminal gangs, they provided many useful social functions and were more powerful than the colonial government in the life of the Chinese.

Most Chinese living in Singapore today were born here. The campaign to speak Mandarin has given the Chinese a common dialect, but English is also a unifying tongue. Increasing Westernisation and English education still have some way to go to totally undermine traditional Chinese customs and beliefs.

Traditional Chinese thought is a rich blend of religion and philosophy. Taoism, Buddhism and Confucianism often come as a package religion and many Chinese temples accommodate all three.

Ancestor worship plays a large part in Chinese life, and children are expected to provide for their parents in life, and after death with offerings and ritual veneration. The Chinese funeral is an important event and one of the most colourful and expensive ceremonies. At a traditional funeral, paper houses, cars, television sets and even paper servants are offered and burnt so that the deceased can enjoy all these material benefits in the next life.

Feng Shui is another Chinese belief that is actually gaining popularity in Singapore. Feng Shui is the art of placing and orienting furniture, houses, HDB housing estates – whatever – to repel *chi*, or negative energy. Lee Kuan Yew regularly consulted Feng Shui experts; it is said his luck declined when he continued with badly sited land reclamation.

Luck is a Chinese preoccupation, and fortune telling via palm reading and the *I Ching* is very popular. Astrology and the Chinese zodiac also play a large role. Based on the lunar calendar, each year in the Chinese zodiac is designated by an animal.

The zodiac chart supposedly originated when the Buddha commanded the beasts of the earth to assemble before him. Only 12 turned up and hence there are only twelve zodiac signs – the snake, horse, monkey, rooster etc. Your sign is based on the year in which you were born. The year of the dragon is particularly propitious, and the birth rate jumps dramatically when it occurs (the last one was 1988). The Chinese New Year falls in January or February and is the major Chinese celebration.

Malays

The Malays are the original inhabitants of Singapore. They are the main racial group throughout the region stretching from the Malay Peninsula across Indonesia to the Philippines. Many Malays migrated to Singapore from the peninsula, and large numbers of Javanese and Bugis (from Riau and Sulawesi) also settled in Singapore.

Malays in Singapore are Muslim. Islam provides the major influence in everyday life and is the rallying point of Malay society. The month of Ramadan, when Muslims fast from sunrise to sunset, is the most important month of the Islamic year. Hari Raya Puasa, the end of the fast, is the major Malay celebration.

Islam was brought to the region by Arab and Indian traders and adopted in the 15th century, but traditional Malay culture still owes much to pre-Islamic Hindu and animist beliefs. For example, *wayang kulit*, the Malay shadow puppet play, portrays tales from the Hindu epics of the *Ramayana* and *Mahabharata*.

In Malay society, harmony is the guiding principle, and it is the duty of the individual to make sure peace and harmony is maintained. A Malay is expected to be courteous and avoid conflict, and by promoting the wellbeing of others, all of society benefits.

Malays have a strong sense of community and hospitality, and the *kampong*, or village, is at the centre of Malay life. The kampong still exists in some urban areas of Singapore, where it has become something like a very strong neighbourhood watch committee. It looks after the rights and needs of the inhabitants in a small area, and elders may be called upon to provide moral and spiritual guidance, and settle disputes within the community.

The Malay language is still the primary language of Malays in Singapore and it holds its own against English. However, traditional Malay culture is not much in evidence. The majority of Malays live in high-rise districts such as Geylang, but in fast-diminishing rural Singapore and the islands to the north, traditional Malay kampongs still exist.

Indians

Indian migration dates mostly from the middle of the 19th century when the British recruited labour for the plantations of Malaya. While many Indians arrived in Singapore, most passed through and eventually settled in Malaya.

In Singapore, approximately 60% of the Indian population are Tamil and a further 20% are Malayalis from the southern Indian state of Kerala. The rest come from all over India – Bengalis, Punjabis and Kashmiris. The majority of Indians are Hindu, but a large number are Muslim and there are also Sikhs, Parsis, Christians and Buddhists.

The Indian communities still stick very closely together and Indian culture shows the greatest resilience. Major Indian celebrations are Thaipusam and Deepavali.

LANGUAGE

The four official languages of Singapore are Chinese, Malay, Tamil and English. Malay is the national language and English is the main language of business and administration. English is the linking language between the various ethnic groups and spoken almost everywhere. The only communication problems you may have is with older Singaporeans who did not learn English at school.

Chinese dialects are still widely spoken, especially amongst the older Chinese. The most common dialects are Hakka, Hokkien, Teochew and Cantonese. However, the government's long-standing campaign to promote Mandarin, the main nondialectal Chinese language, has been quite successful.

Tamil is the main Indian dialect, but other dialects include Malayalam and Hindi.

Bahasa Malaysia (Malay language) is the national language. It was adopted as a gesture of goodwill towards the original inhabitants of Singapore, and as a sign of appeasement to Malaysia. Nonetheless English is the dominate language.

After independence, the government had a bi-lingual education policy that attempted to develop the vernacular languages and lessen the use of English. This was in contrast to British education policy which promoted English while trying to discourage Chinese education.

However, Chinese graduates found that they had less opportunities for higher education and greater difficulties in finding a job. English was the language of business and united the various ethnic groups, and the government eventually had to give it more priority. It officially became the first language of instruction in schools in 1987.

All children are also taught their mother tongue at school, which in the case of the Chinese is Mandarin. This policy is largely designed to unite the various Chinese groups and to make sure Chinese Singaporeans don't lose contact with their traditions.

However, this language policy does not please all Singaporeans. Many young Chinese prefer English education and do not want to be forced to study Mandarin, which plays a prominent part in overall school marks. The Malays are generally in favour of learning Malay, but many in the Indian community would prefer to concentrate on English, given the limited use of Indian dialects.

The Peranankans have been hardest hit by this policy, as many align themselves more closely with Malay culture and language but have been forced to study Mandarin.

Facts for the Visitor

VISAS & EMBASSIES

Most nationalities, including Commonwealth citizens, western Europeans and
Americans, do not require a visa to visit
Singapore. Upon arrival you are issued with
a 14-day stay permit. You can easily extend
this for another two weeks as long as you can
show that you have an air ticket out of Singapore and/or sufficient funds to stay.
Further extensions are more difficult but in
theory most nationalities can extend for up
to 90 days. The Immigration Department (tel
532 2877) is in the South Bridge Centre, 95
South Bridge Rd, on the corner of Pickering
St.

Singaporean Embassies

Some Singaporean embassies and high com-
missions overseas include:

Australia
    17 Forster Crescent, Yarralumla, Canberra ACT
    2600 (tel (062) 733 3944)
Germany
    Substrasse 133, 5300 Bonn 2 (tel (0228) 31-20-
    07)
Hong Kong
    17th floor, United Centre, 95 Queensway (tel (5)
    27 2212)
India
    E6 Chandragupta Marg, Chanakyapuri, New
    Delhi 110021 (tel 60 4162)
Indonesia
    Jalan H R Rasuna Said, Kuningan, Jakarta 12950
    (tel (21) 52 1489)
Japan
    12-3 Roppongi, 5 Chome, Minato-ku, Tokyo (tel
    3585 9111)
Malaysia
    290 Jalan Tun Razak, 50400 Kuala Lumpur (tel
    (03) 261 6404)
New Zealand
    17 Kabul St, Khandallah, Wellington (tel 79
    2076)
Philippines
    6th Floor, ODC International Plaza, 217-219
    Salcedo St, Legaspi Village, Makati, Metro
    Manila (tel 816 1764)

Thailand
    129 Sathorn Tai Rd, Bangkok (tel (2) 286 2111)
UK
    2 Wilton Crescent, London SW1X 8RW (tel
    (071) 235 8135)
USA
    1824 R St NW, Washington DC 20009-1691 (tel
    (202) 667 7555)

Consulates & Embassies in Singapore

Many foreign consulates and embassies are
conveniently located around Orchard Rd.
Addresses for some of them include:

Australia
    25 Napier Rd (tel 737 9311)
Bangladesh
    United Square, 101 Thomson Rd (tel 255 0075)
Brunei
    7A Tanglin Hill (tel 474 3393)
Burma
    15 St Martin's Drive (tel 235 8704)
Canada
    IBM Towers, 80 Anson Rd (tel 225 6363)
Denmark
    United Square, 101 Thomson Rd (tel 250 3383)
Germany
    Far East Shopping Centre, 545 Orchard Rd (tel
    737 1355)
India
    31 Grange Rd (tel 737 6777)
Indonesia
    7 Chatsworth Rd (tel 737 7422)
Japan
    16 Nassim Rd (tel 235 8855)
Republic of Korea
    United Square, 101 Thomson Rd (tel 256 1188)
Malaysia
    301 Jervois Rd (tel 235 0111)
Netherlands
    Liat Towers, 541 Orchard Rd (tel 737 1155)
New Zealand
    13 Nassim Rd (tel 235 9966)
Norway
    Hong Leong Building, 16 Raffles Quay (tel 220
    7122)
Pakistan
    20A Nassim Rd (tel 737 6988)
Philippines
    20 Nassim Rd (tel 737 3977)
Sri Lanka
    Goldhill Plaza, 51 Newton Rd (tel 254 4595)

Sweden
    PUB Building, 111 Somerset Rd (tel 734 2771)
Thailand
    370 Orchard Rd (tel 737 2644)
UK
    Tanglin Rd (tel 473 9333)
USA
    30 Hill St (tel 338 0251)
USSR
    51 Nassim Rd (tel 235 1834)

MONEY
Exchange Rates

A$1	=	S$1.34
C$1	=	S$1.48
HK$1	=	S$0.21
NZ$1	=	S$1.02
UK£1	=	S$3.35
US$1	=	S$1.71

Currency
Singapore uses 1c, 5c, 10c, 20c, 50c and S$1 coins, while notes are in denominations of S$1, S$5, S$10, S$50, S$100 and S$1000; Singapore also has a S$10,000 note – not that you'll see too many. Brunei notes are interchangeable with Singapore notes, but Malaysian notes are no longer interchangeable.

All major credit cards are widely accepted, although you're not going to make yourself too popular after a hard bargaining session for a new camera if you then try to pay for it with your Amex card.

Banks
Most of the major banks are in the Central Business District, although there are also a number of banks along Orchard Rd and local banks all over the city. Exchange rates tend to vary from bank to bank and some even have a service charge on each exchange transaction – this is usually S$2 to S$3, so ask first. Banks are open from 10 am to 3 pm weekdays and from 11 am to 4.30 pm on Saturdays; the Orchard Rd branches of the major banks are open on Sundays from 9.30 am to 3 pm.

Moneychangers do not charge fees, so you will usually get a better exchange rate for cash and travellers' cheques than at the banks. You will find moneychangers in just about every shopping centre in Singapore. Indeed, most of the shops will accept foreign cash and travellers' cheques at a slightly lower rate.

The traditional home of moneychangers is Change Alley, the small lane sandwiched between the buildings of Asia's banking giants, where Indian moneychangers with fists full of foreign notes sidle up to you whispering, 'change money, change money'. Change Alley has undergone a number of alterations and is a shadow of its former self but you can still be exhorted to change money.

Apart from changing other currencies to Singapore dollars, moneychangers also offer a wide variety of other currencies for sale and will do amazing multiple currency transactions in the blink of an eye. Some travellers report that you can even get good rates for some restricted currencies – if you want to arrive (illegally) in India with a pocketful of rupees, for example.

Costs
Singapore is much more expensive than other South-East Asian countries but there are good deals to be had no matter what your budget.

If you are travelling on a shoestring budget, prices will come as a shock but you can still stay in Singapore without spending too much money. The great temptation is to run amok in the shops and blow your budget on electrical goods or indulge in all the luxuries you may have craved for while travelling in less-developed Asian countries.

Expect to pay a minimum of US$3 per night for a dorm bed and from US$10 to US$25 for a double room in a cheap hotel or crash pad. You can also eat well in Singapore for a reasonable price. A good meal at a food centre or small coffee shop can cost less than US$3. Transport is cheap in Singapore and many of the island's attractions are free. So it is possible to stay in Singapore for US$10 per day, though US$15 is more realistic.

If you have more to spend, then most of your cash will be absorbed in hotel bills. Mid-range, second-string hotels cost from US$30 to US$60, while international-standard hotels cost from US$70 and go way up to exorbitant prices. Restaurants will cost from US$10, though you can spend hundreds of dollars if you want to. Taxis are quite cheap in Singapore, as are most other nonessentials and luxuries.

Tipping
Tipping is not usual in Singapore. The most expensive hotels and restaurants have a 10% service charge – if the charge is paid, tipping is actually prohibited.

TOURIST OFFICES
The Tourist Information Centre (tel 330 0431), 01-19 Raffles City Tower, is beside the Singapore Airlines office on the North Bridge Rd side of the Raffles City complex. It is open from 8.30 am to 5 pm Monday to Friday and from 8.30 am to 1 pm on Saturdays. They can answer most of your queries and have an excellent selection of hand-outs, though not all are displayed.

Pick up a copy of the *Singapore Official Guide* and the *See Singapore by Bus* pamphlet which lists all major destinations and how they can be reached by bus. *Tour it Yourself* is an excellent, detailed guide for independent exploration of the major tourist attractions as well as some little-known areas.

The hotels and Changi Airport also stock a range of tourist leaflets and free tourist maps. There is a hotel booking desk at the airport but the cheapest rooms they have are S$60; it doesn't cover any of the bottom-end places to stay.

Singapore Tourist Promotion Board
The Singapore Tourist Promotion Board offices in Singapore and overseas include:

Australia
    Suite 1604, Level 16, Westpac Plaza, 60 Margaret St, Sydney 2000 (tel (02) 241 3771)
    8th floor, St George's Crt, 16 St George's Terrace, Perth 6000 (tel (06) 221 3864)
Germany
    Poststrasse 2-4, D-6000 Frankfurt/Main (tel (069) 23 1456)
Hong Kong
    1-3, D'Aguilar St, Central, Hong Kong (tel (5) 22 4052)
New Zealand
    c/o Walshes World, 2nd floor, Dingwall Building, 87 Queen St, Auckland 1 (tel (9) 79 3708)
Singapore
    36-04 Raffles City Tower, 250 North Bridge Rd (tel 339 6622)
UK
    1st Floor Carrington House, 126-130 Regent St, London W1R 5FE (tel (071) 437 0033)
USA
    NBR 12th Floor, 590 Fifth Ave, New York, NY 10036 (tel (212) 302 4861)
    Suite 510, 8484 Wilshire Blvd, Beverly Hills, California 90211 (tel (213) 852 1901)

BUSINESS HOURS & HOLIDAYS
In Singapore, government offices are usually open from Monday to Friday and Saturday mornings. Hours vary, starting around 7.30 to 9.30 am and closing between 4 and 6 pm. On Saturdays, closing time is between 11.30 am and 1 pm. Shop hours are also variable, although Monday to Saturday from 9 am to 8 or 9 pm is a good rule of thumb.

The following days are public holidays in Singapore. For those days not based on the Western calendar, the months they are likely to fall are:

January
   New Year's Day
January or February
   Chinese New Year
April
   Good Friday, Hari Raya Puasa
April or May
   Vesak Day
1 May
   Labour Day
June or July
   Hari Raya Haji
9 August
   National Day
November
   Deepavali
25 December
   Christmas Day

CULTURAL EVENTS

With so many cultures and religions, there is an amazing number of festivals and events to celebrate in Singapore. Although some of them have a fixed date, the Hindus, Muslims and Chinese all follow a lunar calendar which results in the dates for many events varying from year to year. In particular, the Muslim festivals can change enormously over a period of years. Each year, the tourist office puts out a *Calendar of Festivals & Events* leaflet with specific dates and venues of various festivals and events.

January-February

Ponggal – Ponggal is a harvest festival and the time for thanksgiving. Celebrated by south Indians, they offer rice, vegetables, sugar cane and spices to the gods. It is celebrated at the Sri Srinivasa Perumal Temple on Serangoon Rd.

Chinese New Year – Dragon dances and pedestrian parades mark the start of the new year. Families hold open house, unmarried relatives (especially children) receive *ang pows* (money in red packets), businesses traditionally clear their debts and everybody wishes you a Kong Hee Fatt Choy (a happy and prosperous new year). Chinatown is lit up, especially along Eu Tong Sen St and New Bridge Rd, and the *Singapore River Hong Bao Special* features *pasar malam* (night market) stalls, variety shows and fireworks.

Chingay – Processions of Chinese flag bearers down Orchard Rd, balancing bamboo flag poles six to 12-metres long, can be seen on the 22nd day after the Chinese New Year.

Thaipusam – One of the most dramatic Hindu festivals in which devotees honour Lord Subramaniam with acts of amazing masochism. In Singapore, they march in a procession to the Chettiar Temple carrying *kavadis*, heavy metal frames decorated with peacock feathers, fruit and flowers. The kavadis are hung from their bodies with metal hooks and spikes driven into the flesh. Other devotees pierce their cheeks and tongues with metal skewers or walk on sandals of nails. Along the procession route, the kavadi carriers dance to the drum beat while spectators urge them on with shouts of 'Vel, Vel'. In the evening, the procession continues with an image of Subramaniam in a temple car. This festival is now officially banned in India.

March-April

Cheng Beng – On All Soul's Day, Chinese traditionally visit the tombs of their ancestors to clean and repair them and make offerings.

Birthday of the Monkey God – The birthday of T'se Tien Tai Seng Yeh is celebrated twice a year at the Monkey God Temple in Seng Poh Rd opposite the Tiong Bahru Market. Mediums pierce their cheeks and tongues with skewers and go into a trance during which they write special charms in blood.

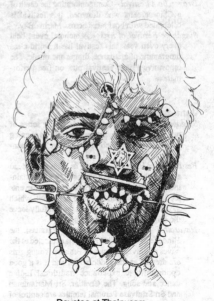

Devotee at Thaipusam

Hari Raya Puasa – The major Muslim events each year are connected with Ramadan, the month during which Muslims cannot eat or drink from sunrise to sunset. Hari Raya Puasa marks the end of the month-long fast with three days of joyful celebration. It is most noticeable in the Malay areas, when Geylang Serai and the surroundings roads are draped in lights for the occasion.

April-May

Vesak Day – Buddha's birth, enlightenment and death are celebrated by various events, including the release of caged birds to symbolise the setting free of captive souls. Temples such as Thian Hock Keng Temple on Telok Ayer St and the Temple of 1000 Lights on Serangoon Rd are thronged with worshippers.

May-June

Birthday of the Third Prince – The child-god is honoured with processions, and devotees go into a trance and spear themselves with spikes and swords. Celebrations, if you can call them that, are held at various temples and in Queen St, near Bencoolen St.

Dragon Boat Festival – Commemorating the death of a Chinese saint who drowned, this festival is celebrated with boat races across Marina Bay.

Singapore Festival of Arts – A biennial event held every even year, this festival has a world-class programme of art, dance, drama and music. The innovative Fringe Festival puts on free performances.

June-September

Singapore National Day – On 9 August, a series of military and civilian processions and an evening firework display celebrate Singapore's independence in 1965.

Festival of the Hungry Ghosts – The souls of the dead are released for one day of feasting and entertainment on earth. Chinese operas and other events are laid on for them and food is put out, which the ghosts eat the spirit of but thoughtfully leave the substance for mortal celebrants.

Navarathri – In the Tamil month of Purattasi, the Hindu festival of 'Nine Nights' is dedicated to the wives of Shiva, Vishnu and Brahma. Young girls are dressed as the goddess Kali and it is a good opportunity to experience traditional Indian dance and song. The Chettiar, Sri Mariamman and Sri Srinivasa Perumal temples are centres of activity.

September-October

Thimithi (Fire Walking Ceremony) – Hindu devotees prove their faith by walking across glowing coals at the Sri Mariamman Temple.

Moon Cake Festival – The overthrow of the Mongol warlords in ancient China is celebrated by eating moon cakes and lighting colourful paper lanterns. Moon cakes are made with bean paste, lotus seeds and sometimes a duck egg.

October-November

Pilgrimage to Kusu Island – Tua Pek Kong, the God of Prosperity, is honoured by Taoists in Singapore by making a pilgrimage to the shrine on Kusu Island.

Deepavali – Rama's victory over the demon King Ravana is celebrated with the 'Festival of Lights', where tiny oil lamps are lit outside Hindu homes. The Hindu Temples on Serangoon Rd are draped in lights.

Festival of the Nine Emperor Gods – Nine days of Chinese operas, processions and other events honour the nine emperor gods.

December

Christmas – Orchard Rd celebrates Christmas with shopfront displays and the Christmas light-up, another of the illuminations that Singapore is so fond of.

POST & TELECOMMUNICATIONS
Post

The GPO, with its efficient poste restante service, is on Fullerton Rd, close to the Singapore River. It's open from 8.30 am to 5 pm weekdays and till 1 pm on Saturday. The post offices at the airport and Orchard Point, 160 Orchard Rd, are open from 8 am to 8 pm every day.

Telephone

Local phone calls from private homes, hotels and Changi Airport are free. From telephone booths, the cost of a call is 10c for three minutes.

Overseas telephone calls can be made 24 hours a day and the service is very efficient. As well as hotels, you can make international phone calls at a Telecom centre like the ones at 15 Hill St or 71 Robinson Rd, or selected post offices such as the GPO or Orchard Point post office.

At the phone centres, there are also Direct

Home phones (press a country button to contact the operator, then reverse the charges) and credit-card phones (just swipe your Amex, Diners, Mastercard or Visa card through the slot).

You can also dial international calls yourself from public pay phones but you'll need a phone which takes 50c or, preferably, S$1 coins. Or, buy a phonecard and use one of the phones which accept these cards (many pay phones will now only operate with phonecards – not coins). Phonecards, which cost from S$2, are available at Telecom centres, 7-Eleven stores, Times bookstores and Guardian pharmacies. For directory information call 03; the emergency number is 999.

TIME
Singapore is two hours behind Australian Eastern Standard Time (Sydney and Melbourne), eight hours ahead of Greenwich Mean Time (London), 13 hours ahead of American Eastern Standard Time (New York) and 16 hours ahead of American Western Standard Time (San Francisco and Los Angeles). Thus, when it is noon in Singapore, it is 2 pm in Sydney, 4 am in London, 11 pm in New York and 8 pm the previous day in Los Angeles.

ELECTRICITY
Electricity supplies are dependable and run at 220-240 volts and 50 cycles. Plugs are of the two, round-pin type.

LAUNDRY
Singapore has a few self-service laundries, though they are rare compared to services offered by regular laundries. The only one anywhere near the Bencoolen St area is the Washy Washy Laundromat on the 1st floor of Orchard Plaza, 150 Orchard Rd, next to the Meridien Hotel. A wash is S$3.50, drying S$3.50 or it's S$9 for the drop-off and collect service.

BOOKS & MAPS
People & Society
Tales of Chinatown by Sit Yin Fong is a readable and informative piece on Chinese life. Fong was a journalist in Singapore for many years and writes anecdotal short stories about Chinese customs and beliefs.

Living in Singapore by the American Association of Singapore is handy for Westerners planning to set up house in Singapore. This is a useful introduction to life in the tropical city-state.

Son of Singapore by Tan Kok Seng is the fascinating autobiography of a labourer who grew up in Singapore in the 1950s.

History
There are a great number of books dealing with various events in Singapore's history.

A History of Singapore by C M Turnball is the best choice for a detailed overview of Singapore's history from prehistory to the present. It is an excellent scholarly work which is also very readable and a mine of interesting information. The author has also written *A Short History of Malaysia, Singapore & Brunei*.

Singapore: Its Past, Present and Future by Alex Josey deals mostly with Singapore's later history and is very pro-People's Action Party (PAP).

Raffles by Maurice Collins is the story of the man who founded Singapore.

Recently, there has been a great deal of interest in the fall of Singapore, the subsequent Japanese occupation and the internal and external struggles of the '50s and '60s. *Sinister Twilight – The Fall of Singapore* by Noel Barber recounts the bunglings, underestimations and final heroics that culminated in the rapid collapse of Singapore.

Out in the Midday Sun by Kate Caffrey tells of the hardships of those who were captured and spent the rest of the war years in prison camps like the notorious Changi camp.

Politics
Lee Kuan Yew – The Struggle for Singapore by Alex Josey covers all the twists and turns of Lee Kuan Yew's rise to power and the successful path which his People's Action Party has piloted Singapore along.

Governing Singapore by Raj Vasil is available in almost every bookshop in Singapore and is as close as you'll get to the official PAP line. It includes interviews with Lee Kuan Yew and Goh Tok Chong.

Fiction

Singapore and Malaysia have always provided a fertile setting for novelists, and Joseph Conrad's *The Shadow Line* and *Lord Jim* both use the region as a backdrop. Somerset Maugham spent time in Singapore writing his classic short stories, many of which were set in Malaya – look for the *Borneo Stories*.

Saint Jack by Paul Theroux is the story of an American pimp in Singapore, and *King Rat* by James Clavell is based on the experiences of POWs in Changi Prison.

The Singapore Grip by J G Farrell was a local bestseller and provides an almost surreal view of life in Singapore as the Japanese stormed down the peninsula in WW II. A certain amount of 'fiddling while Rome burned' appeared to be going on.

Tanamera: A Novel of Singapore by Noel Barber is the story of two families in Singapore. The author was a journalist who lived in Singapore before the war.

Travel Guides

Insight Singapore, part of the Insight guide series, features their usual collection of text and photographs.

South-East Asia on a Shoestring (Lonely Planet) is our overall guidebook to the region. If you're travelling further afield, there are other LP guides to most South-East and North-East Asian countries, including Malaysia and Indonesia. Lonely Planet's *Singapore City Guide* is available for travellers who are just going to Singapore. Other series guides to Singapore include: Baedeker's, Papineau's, Berlitz and Fodor's.

General

Singapore: a Guide to Buildings, Streets, Places by Norman Edwards & Peter Keys is a wonderful architectural guide to Singapore. It has photographs and discussions of Singapore's major buildings and streetscapes, but it also includes a number of interesting titbits on Singapore's history and culture.

Bookshops

Singapore's main bookshop chains are MPH and Times. In the Orchard Rd area, Centrepoint and Plaza Singapura shopping centres have a good selection of bookshops.

MPH's main shop at 71-77 Stamford Rd, which was extensively renovated in 1991, is probably the best general bookshop in the region. MPH also has other stores on Robinson Rd, at Changi Airport, at Dhoby Ghaut and Orchard MRT stations, and in the basement level and on the 4th floor of Centre- point on Orchard Rd.

Centrepoint also has a large Times store on the 4th level. Other Times bookshops include those at Lucky Plaza and Plaza Singapura on Orchard Rd, Holland Village, the World Trade Centre and a large store at Raffles City.

Select Books on the 3rd floor of the Tanglin Shopping Centre, 19 Tanglin Rd, has an excellent collection specialising in South-East Asia.

Kinokuniya has some interesting collections and good books on the region. Their shops are at Plaza Singapura and Wisma Atria on Orchard Rd, and Raffles City. There are also book and magazine stalls in many of the larger hotels.

Maps

The American Express/STPB *Map of Singapore* is an excellent free map; it is available at the airport on arrival, at most middle and top-end hotels and at some shopping centres. *The Singapore Visitor Map*, another giveaway, is in Japanese as well as English and is especially good for shopping centres.

There are a number of commercial maps available, of which the *Nelles Singapore Map* (S$8.50) is one of the best. The best reference of all if you plan on spending any length of time in Singapore or want to rent a car is the *Singapore Street Directory*, a bargain at S$6 and available at most bookshops.

MEDIA

Newspapers & Magazines

Singapore has three Chinese daily newspapers with a combined circulation of over 350,000 and three English newspapers with a similar circulation. There is also a Malay daily and an Indian daily.

The English daily newspapers are the establishment *Straits Times* and the *Business Times*, and *The New Paper*, an evening tabloid which started in 1988. *The New Paper* is a long way behind in circulation but it is giving the *Straits Times* a run for its money. It's in the tits-on-page-three mould but without the tits (this is staid Singapore after all), and is seen as the fun alternative.

The press in Singapore knows its limits and you will find very little criticism of the government. The foreign media sometimes doesn't know its limits, and the government has been known to bring pressure to bear on those that do not report to its liking, as the *Far Eastern Economic Review* found out. A few newsstands in Singapore still stock the Review, under the counter with all advertising blacked out. *Times*, *Newsweek* and many other foreign magazines are readily available.

Radio & TV

The government-run Singapore Broadcasting Corporation controls broadcasting.

Singapore has seven radio stations transmitting in four languages – Malay, Chinese, Tamil and English – on the AM, FM and short-wave bands. A pirate station also transmits from Batam Island in the Riau Archipelago and is proving very popular.

Singapore has three TV channels, 5 and 8 which transmit in all the four languages, and 12 which transmits mostly in English. Singaporeans can also pick up Malaysian television.

HEALTH

In Singapore, you can eat virtually anywhere and not worry, and the tap water is safe to drink. Vaccinations are required only if you come from a yellow fever area, and Singapore is not a malarial area. The main health concern is the heat, it is important to avoid dehydration by drinking plenty of fluids.

Dehydration or salt deficiency can cause heat exhaustion. Take time to acclimatise to high temperatures and make sure you get sufficient liquids. Salt defficiency is characterised by fatigue, lethargy, headaches, giddiness and muscle cramps, and in this case salt tablets may help.

Medical facilities are of a high standard, readily available and reasonably priced. In fact, if you need dental work done, Singapore is a root-canal discount centre compared to most Western countries.

A visit to a general practitioner costs from S$20 to S$40. Singapore's public hospitals will accept self-referred patients. Singapore General Hospital (tel 222 3322) is on Outram Rd, near Chinatown and the Outram Park MRT station. A consultation with a senior nurse is S$30, a specialist S$45 or a senior consultant S$60.

Health Insurance

A travel insurance policy to cover theft, loss and medical problems is a wise idea. There are a wide variety of policies and your travel agent will have recommendations. Check the small print: some policies specifically exclude 'dangerous activities' such as scuba diving; you may prefer a policy which pays doctors or hospitals direct rather than you having to pay on the spot and claim later; and check if the policy covers ambulances or an emergency flight home.

WOMEN TRAVELLERS

Singapore is probably the safest Asian country to travel in and sexual harassment is very rare. Women are not cloistered in Singaporean society and enjoy much more freedom and equality than in the rest of Asia. Government policy favours sexual equality, and abortion is available on request but not for 'foreign' pregnancies.

FINES

Singapore has a number of frowned-upon activities, and the sometimes draconian methods of dealing with minor transgressions has caused both mirth and dread amongst visitors. The famous anti-long-hair campaign is pretty much a thing of the past. You're unlikely to be turned away on arrival or given a short back and sides on the spot, though some Malaysians have been known to receive the treatment in recent times.

Singapore remains tough on a number of other minor issues, however, and the standard way of stamping out un-Singaporean activities is to slap a S$500 fine on any offender. Actually, it is very rare that anybody does get fined that amount, but the severity of the fines is enough to ensure compliance.

Smoking in a public place – buses, lifts, cinemas, restaurants, air-conditioned shopping centres and government offices – is hit with a S$500 fine. You can smoke at food stalls and on the street (as long as you dispose of your butt, of course). The move to ban smoking in private cars was eventually quashed because of the difficulty in enforcing it.

Jaywalking is a relatively minor crime – walk across the road within 50 metres of a designated crossing and it could cost you S$50. The successful antilittering campaign continues – up to S$1000 fine for dropping even a cigarette butt on the street – and, not surprisingly, Singapore is amazingly clean.

The MRT, Singapore's pride and joy, attracts some particularly heavy fines. As you wait for a train, you can have them explained to you in four languages by the droning monotone voice that is unerringly like something out of '1984'. Eating, drinking and smoking are forbidden, and if you use the MRT toilet and don't flush it, the fine is S$1000. In fact, the 'flush or fine' campaign applies all over Singapore and has prompted apocryphal reports of flush sensors in the toilets to detect offenders.

WORK

Work opportunities for foreigners are limited in Singapore, and while Singapore does have a fairly large expatriate European community, this is a reflection of the large representation of overseas companies rather than a shortage of skills in the Singaporean labour market.

In almost all cases, foreign workers obtain employment before they come to Singapore. There is a slight demand in some professions but Singapore is attempting to fill labour shortages by attracting Hong Kong professionals wanting out before 1997. The overwhelming majority of jobs are for domestic servants (newspapers are full of agencies advertising Filipino house maids) and unskilled labourers.

Top: Singapore by day (PS)
Bottom: Singapore by night (PS)

Top: Sri Vadapathira Kaliamman Temple, Singapore (CH)
Left: Singapore National Museum & Art Gallery, Singapore (TW)
Right: Tiger Balm Gardens, Singapore (TW)

Getting There & Away

AIR

To/From the USA

Tickets from the US west coast to Singapore cost from US$550 one way or US$900 return. Scan the Sunday travel section of west coast newspapers like the *LA Times* or the *San Francisco Chronicle-Examiner* for agents handling discount tickets. Some cheap fares include a stopover in Hong Kong. Similar deals from the US east coast can be found in the Sunday newspapers there.

To/From Europe

Discount tickets to Singapore are available at London travel agents from around £250 one way and £500 return. It's also possible to get flights from London to Australia with stopovers in Singapore from around £750 to £900 return, depending on the season of travel. A ticket from London to Auckland with a Singapore stopover costs around £510 one way. For more information, check the travel-ad pages in the weekly London 'what's on' magazine *Time Out*, daily newspapers or the various giveaway papers. Two good agents for cheap airline tickets are Trailfinders (tel (071) 938 3444) at 46 Earls Court Rd and 194 Kensington High St, London W8, or STA (tel (071) 937 9962) at 74 Old Brompton Rd, London SW7.

To/From Australia

Advance purchase fares from the Australian east coast to Singapore vary from around A$600 to A$800 one way and A$900 to A$1000 return, depending on the season of travel.

Many of the airlines that fly from Australia to Europe stop over in Singapore. Alitalia often has cheap tickets to Singapore if it can't fill all its seats to Europe, but it is difficult to get confirmation on tickets until the last minute.

To/From New Zealand

A number of airlines fly from Auckland to Singapore. If you shop around, you can get discount fares between Auckland and Singapore from around NZ$750 one way and NZ$1300 return. Some fares will allow you to stopover in Australia on the way.

To/From Malaysia

Malaysian Airline System (MAS) is the main carrier between Malaysia and Singapore with direct flights from Kuala Lumpur (M$130, M$100 shuttle), Kuantan (M$120), Langkawi (M$180) and Penang (M$150) in Peninsular Malaysia, and Kuching and Kota Kinabalu (M$346) in East Malaysia. Pelangi Air has direct flights to Singapore from Melaka and Tioman Island (M$100). Tradewinds also flies between Singapore and Tioman.

Return fares are double the single fares quoted here; one-way fares from Singapore to Malaysia are the same price but in Singapore dollars and therefore more expensive.

Going to Malaysia, you can save quite a few dollars if you fly from Johore Bahru (JB) rather than Singapore. For example, to Kota Kinabalu the fares are M$301 from JB but S$346 from Singapore. To persuade travellers to take advantage of these lower fares, MAS offers a bus service directly from their Singapore city-centre office to the JB airport.

To/From Indonesia

A number of airlines fly from Singapore to Jakarta for S$180 to S$200 one way and around S$250 return. You can buy a ticket with Garuda direct to Bali for S$420 one way or with stops in Jakarta and Yogyakarta for S$660. Garuda also have flights between Singapore and the Sumatran cities of Medan, Padang, Palembang and Pekanbaru.

From Jakarta to Singapore, expect to pay US$125. Some good agents to try in Jakarta are Kaliman Travel (tel 33 0101) in the President Hotel on Jalan Thamrin and, next door, Vayatour (tel 33 6640). Indo Shangrila Travel (tel 63 2703), 219G Jalan Gajah Mada, is the agent for STA Travel. There are also plenty of travel agents at Kuta and Ubud on Bali.

To/From Thailand

You can fly from Bangkok to Singapore for about 3500 baht. STA Travel (tel 281 5314) in Bangkok is at the Thai Hotel, 78 Prachatpatai Rd.

From Singapore to Bangkok, fares range from S$185 to S$220 one way and from S$350 return. For southern Thailand, you have to fly first to Penang, and then from Penang to Hat Yai for M$80 or Phuket for slightly more.

Airline Offices

Singapore is a major international crossroad and a great number of airlines fly there. Offices of some of the most frequently used airlines include:

Aeroflot
  02-15 Meridien Shopping Centre, 100 Orchard Rd (tel 235 5252)
Air Canada
  02-43 Meridien Shopping Centre, 100 Orchard Rd (tel 732 8555)
Air India
  UIC Building, 5 Shenton Way (tel 225 9411)
Air Lanka
  02-00/B PIL Building, 140 Cecil St (tel 223 6026)
Air Mauritius
  01-00 LKN Building, 135 Cecil St (tel 222 3033)
Air Nauru
  01-57 International Plaza, 10 Anson Rd (tel 222 6738)
Air New Zealand
  13-06 Ocean Building, 10 Collyer Quay (tel 535 8266)
Alitalia
  15-05 Wisma Atria, 435 Orchard Rd (tel 737 3166)
American Airlines
  11-02 Natwest Centre, 15 McCallum St (tel 221 6988)
Bangladesh Biman
  01-100 Fidvi Building, 97-99 Market St (tel 535 2155)

British Airways
  02-16 The Paragon, 290 Orchard Rd (tel 253 8444)
Cathay Pacific
  16-01 Ocean Building, 10 Collyer Quay (tel 533 1333)
China Airlines
  08-02 Orchard Towers, 400 Orchard Rd (tel 737 2211)
El Al
  06-00 Thong Sia Building, 30 Bideford Rd (tel 733 8433)
Garuda
  01-68 United Square, 101 Thomson Rd (tel 250 2888)
Indian Airlines
  01-03 Marina House, 70 Shenton Way (tel 225 4949)
Japan Air Lines
  01-01 Hong Leong Building, 16 Raffles Quay (tel 221 0522)
KLM
  01-02 Mandarin Hotel, 333 Orchard Rd (tel 737 7622)
Korean Air Lines
  07-08 Ocean Building, 10 Collyer Quay (tel 534 2111)
Lufthansa
  03-01 Tanglin Shopping Centre, 19 Tanglin Rd (tel 737 9222)
MAS
  02-09 Singapore Shopping Centre, 190 Clemenceau Ave (tel 336 6777)
Olympic Airways
  15-04 Hong Leong Building, 16 Raffles Quay (tel 225 8877)
Pakistan International Airlines
  01-01 Ming Court Hotel, 1 Tanglin Rd (tel 737 3233)
Philippine Airlines
  01-022 Parklane Shopping Mall, 35 Selegie Rd (tel 336 1611)
Qantas
  01-05 Mandarin Hotel, 333 Orchard Rd (tel 737 3744)
Royal Brunei Airlines
  01-4/5 Royal Holiday Inn Shopping Centre, 25 Scotts Rd (tel 235 4672)
Royal Nepal Airlines
  09-00 SIA Building, 77 Robinson Rd (tel 225 7575)
Scandinavian Airlines System
  01-00 Finlayson House, 4 Raffles Quay (tel 225 1333)
Singapore Airlines
  77 Robinson Rd (tel 223 8888)
  Mandarin Hotel, Orchard Rd (tel 229 7293)
  Raffles City, North Bridge Rd (tel 229 7274)

Swiss Air
    18-01 Wisma Atria, 435 Orchard Rd (tel 737 8133)
Thai International
    08-01 Keck Seng Towers, 133 Cecil St (tel 224 9977)
TWA
    02-00 Thong Sia Building, 30 Bideford Rd (tel 734 8911)
United Airlines
    01-03 Hong Leong Buiding, 16 Raffles Quay (tel 220 0711)
UTA
    14-05 Orchard Towers, 400 Orchard Rd (tel 737 6355)

Singapore Airport

Singapore's ultramodern Changi International Airport is another of those miracles that Singapore specialises in. It's vast, efficient, organised and was built in record time. At the airport, there are banking and money-changing facilities, a post office and telephone facilities (open 24 hours), a free hotel reservation service from 8 am to 11.30 pm, left luggage facilities (S$2 per bag for the first day and S$1.50 per day thereafter), a variety of shops in the boarding area and a supermarket in the basement.

On your way through the arrivals concourse, pick up the free booklets, maps and other guides which are available from stands. They give you a lot of useful information and good-quality colour maps of Singapore island and the city centre. There's even a free booklet listing all flights to and from Singapore, a guide to the airport and the glossy monthly travel rag *Changi*.

If you need a place to rest, there are day rooms in the transit lounge which cost from S$15 to S$22 per six hours. Or, if you just need a shower, you can have one for S$5, including towel and soap. You can get your haircut while you wait for your flight too, and there are audio-visual shows. There's even a two-hour tour of Singapore for transit passengers. Kids are also catered for with an imaginative play area in the transit lounge.

There are plenty of places to eat at the airport (this is Singapore after all, food capital of South-East Asia), including a Swensen's ice-cream bar upstairs, a Chinese restaurant, a Japanese restaurant, a cafe serving Malay, Nonya and Indian food, and the Transit 'Buffeteria' and Wing's Cafeteria both open 24 hours.

If you are one of the millions of air travellers fed up with overpriced and terrible food at airports, then Changi Airport has the answer for that too – there is a McDonald's at one end of the arrival hall and a Noodle Restaurant at the other end; both charge normal prices. To find even cheaper food, just take the elevator beside McDonald's on the arrival level to the basement 1 'Food Centre', where you'll find a typical Singapore hawkers' food centre! It's essentially the staff cafeteria but the public are quite welcome.

The airport tax (Passenger Service Charge) from Singapore is S$5 to Malaysia and Brunei, and S$12 further afield. You can purchase PSC coupons in advance at airline offices, travel agencies and major hotels if you don't want to fiddle with Singapore currency at the airport. You don't have to pay the charge if you're just in transit – as long as you don't leave the transit lounge.

Changi Airport continues to poll in the various travel-trade magazines as one of the best airports in the world (along with Amsterdam's Schipol Airport). You'll understand why when you arrive and are whisked through immigration to find your bags waiting on the other side.

Changi has recently been extended with the building of Terminal 2, in itself an international terminal to match the world's best. It has duty-free shops, restaurants, day rooms, a fitness centre, a business centre etc – all that Terminal 1 has and more. The two terminals are connected by the Changi Skytrain, a monorail that runs every 1½ minutes.

Terminal 2 is expected to handle Singapore's increasing air traffic well into the 21st century but Terminal 1 still has the bulk of arrivals and departures. The following airlines use Terminal 2: Finnair, Malaysia Airlines, Myanma Airways, Olympic Airways, Philippine Airlines, Royal Brunei Airlines, Sabena World Airlines, Singapore Airlines and Tradewinds. All other airlines use Terminal 1.

Airport Transport Singapore's Changi International Airport is at the extreme eastern end of the island, about 20 km from the city centre. There is no problem in getting into the city because, with typical Singaporean efficiency, an expressway was built along reclaimed land.

You've got the choice of a very convenient public bus, taxis or the more expensive limousine services. For the public buses, follow the signs in the airport terminal to the basement bus stop.

For travellers heading to Orchard Rd or the Beach Rd/Bencoolen St cheap accommodation enclave, by far the best bus service is No 390, which costs S$1.20. Bus drivers don't give change so make sure you get some coins when you change money. Bus No 390 operates every 10 to 12 minutes from 6 am to midnight daily, and takes about half an hour to reach the city.

As this bus approaches the city, it comes off the flyover into Raffles Blvd and then Stamford Rd. For Beach Rd, get off when you see the round towers of the Raffles City skyscraper on your right, just past the open playing fields of the Padang on your left. A half km further along is the National Museum and the stop for Bencoolen St. The bus then continues up Penang Rd, Somerset Rd and Orchard Blvd (which all run parallel to Orchard Rd) and then comes back along Tanglin Rd and Orchard Rd. When heading out to the airport, catch bus No 390 on Orchard or Bras Basah roads.

Other buses to/from the airport include bus No 24 to the Ang Mo Kio interchange, No 27 to the Tampines interchange and No 149 to the Tao Payoh interchange.

Taxis from the airport are subject to a S$3 supplementary charge on top of the meter fare, which will probably be from S$10 to S$15 to most places. Note: this charge only applies to taxis from the airport, not from the city.

LAND
To/From Malaysia
Bus For Johore Bahru, you can take SBS bus No 170 for 80c. It leaves from the Ban San terminal at the corner of Queen and Arab streets; the Bugis MRT is within walking distance. You can also catch the bus on Rochor Rd, Rochor Canal Rd or Bukit Timah Rd. For S$1.50, you can take the express bus to Johore Bahru operated by Singapore-Johore Express Ltd (tel 292 8149) which departs every 10 minutes, also from the Ban San terminal.

The bus stops at the Singapore checkpoint, but don't worry if it leaves while you clear immigration – keep your ticket and you can just hop on the next one that comes along. The bus then stops at Malaysian immigration and customs at the other end of the Causeway, one km away. After clearing the Malaysian checkpoint, you can then catch the bus again (your ticket is still valid) to the Johore Bahru bus terminus, or you can walk to town.

You will be approached by moneychangers, whose first offer will usually be less than the going rate. There is no shortage of banks and official moneychangers in Johore Bahru, or you can change money in Singapore before you leave.

If you are travelling beyond Johore Bahru, it is much easier to catch a long-distance bus straight from Singapore, but there is a greater variety of bus services from Johore Bahru. The majority of buses from Johore Bahru to other parts of Malaysia leave in the morning and early afternoon.

In Singapore, most of the long-distance buses to Malaysia leave from the bus terminal at the corner of Lavender St and Kallang Bahru, opposite the large Kallang Bahru complex. It is to the north-east of Bencoolen St, near the top end of Jalan Besar. Take bus Nos 122, 133, 145 or 147 from Victoria St or take the MRT to Lavender station, then one of these buses from the Kallang Rd bus stop. It's a hot half-km walk from the Lavender MRT station to the bus station.

Masmara (tel 732 6555) is the main agent for buses to Malaysia and has an office at the bus station (tel 294 7034) and at 05-53 Far East Plaza, 14 Scotts Rd. Also at the bus station, Ekoba-Hasry-Hosni Express (tel

296 3164) has buses to Kuala Lumpur and Penang, and Melacca-Singapore Express (tel 293 5915) has buses to Melaka at 8, 9, 10, 11 am, 1, 2, 3 and 4 pm. The fare is S$11 for an air-con bus and the trip takes six hours. Most travel agents sell bus tickets to Malaysia.

You can also catch buses to Kuala Lumpur (KL) from the Ban San terminal at the corner of Queen and Arab streets. Kuala Lumpur-Singapore Express (tel 292 8254) have buses to KL at 9am, 1 and 10 pm for S$16.10.

Masmara Travel can tell you about other buses within Malaysia. Some fares and times for air-con buses from Singapore to Malaysia include:

Destination	Departure Time	Fare
Kuala Lumpur	9 am or 9 pm	S$17
Ipoh	6.30 pm	S$25
Butterworth	6.30 pm	S$30
Penang	6.30 pm	S$31
Alor Setar	5 pm	S$36
Mersing	8, 9 & 10 am, 9 & 10 pm	S$11
Kuantan	9 & 10 am, 10 pm	S$16
Kuala Terengganu	8 am, 8 pm	S$23
Kota Bharu	7.30 pm	S$30

Most of the buses are new and in immaculate condition with mod-cons such as radio, TV and a toilet. To Kuala Lumpur takes about eight hours, mainly because the road is very busy in both directions. There's also a lunch and snack break on the way. If you want to hitchhike into Malaysia, go to Johore Bahru before starting.

Train Singapore is the southern termination point for the Malaysian railway system. Malaysia has two main rail lines: the primary line going from Singapore to Kuala Lumpur, Butterworth, Alor Setar and then into Thailand; and a second line branching off at Gemas and going right up through the centre of the country to Tumpat, near Kota Bharu on the east coast.

The Singapore Railway Station (tel 222 5165 for fare and schedule information) is on Keppel Rd, south-west of Chinatown, about one km from the Tanjong Pagar MRT station. From Bencoolen St, take bus Nos 97, 100, 125, 146 or 163. From Orchard Rd, take bus No 167.

Five trains per day go to Kuala Lumpur. The Ekspres Rakyat leaves at 7.45 am (arrives 2.30 pm), the mail train at 8.30 am (arrives 5.50 pm), the Ekspres Sinaran at 2.45 pm (arrives 9.25 pm), an ordinary train at 8.35 pm (arrives 6.15 am) and the night mail train leaves at 10 pm (arrives 7 am).

All trains are efficient, well-maintained and comfortable, but ordinary and mail trains stop at all stations and are slow. The express trains are well worth the extra money, and the Ekspres Rakyat continues on to Butterworth, arriving at 9.10 pm. There is also an ordinary train to Gemas at 3.20 pm.

While there is a noticeable jump in comfort from 3rd to 2nd class, 1st class is not much better than 2nd class and considerably more expensive. Rail passes are available to foreign tourists.

From Singapore, there is also a *relbas* service to Kulai, just past Johore Bahru. This train is useful for getting to Johore Bahru, but you should allow up to an hour to buy your ticket and clear customs. Trains leave at 7 and 10 am, 12.30 and 5 pm, take 20 minutes and cost S$1.50.

For full details of train fares and schedules see the Malaysia Getting Around chapter.

Taxi Malaysia has a cheap, well-developed, long-distance taxi system that makes Malaysian travel a real breeze. A long-distance taxi is usually a Mercedes, Peugeot or, more recently, a Japanese car that plies between set destinations. As soon as a full complement of four passengers turns up, off you go.

Singapore also has such taxis to destinations in Malaysia. For Johore Bahru, taxis leave from the Ban San terminal at the corner of Queen and Arab streets. They cost S$4 per person. Foreigners are likely to have to pay more or hire a whole taxi for S$16 since they take longer to clear the border than Singaporeans or Malaysians, or so the taxi drivers claim. On weekends and holidays, you are better off taking a bus because the taxis may well get stuck in the traffic while the buses sail on past in the express lane.

You can get taxis into Malaysia from Singapore without going to Johore Bahru first. Try the Malaysia Taxi Service (tel 298 3831) at 290 Jalan Besar for all places in Malaysia. Another is the Kuala Lumpur Taxi Service (tel 223 1889) at 191 New Bridge Rd.

To/From Thailand
If you want to go direct from Singapore to Thailand overland, the quickest and cheapest way is by bus. You must have a visa to enter Thailand overland. See the Visas section in the Malaysia Facts for the Visitor chapter.

Bus The main terminal for buses to and from Thailand is at the Golden Mile Complex, 5001 Beach Rd. It's at the north-eastern end of Beach Rd, where it meets Crawford St; the Lavender MRT station is nearby. A number of travel agents specialising in buses and tours to Thailand operate from there. They include: Singthai Tour (tel 293 2222), Phya Travel Service (tel 294 5415) and Singapore Comfort Travel (tel 297 2910). Fares start from S$23 to Hat Yai and S$55 to Bangkok.

Train The rail route into Thailand is on the Butterworth-Alor Setar-Hat Yai route which crosses into Thailand at Padang Besar. You can take the International Express from Butterworth in Malaysia all the way to Bangkok with connections from Singapore. The International Express leaves Butterworth at 1.30 pm, so if you want to go from Singapore it involves an overnight stop in Butterworth. The train arrives in Hat Yai at 4.40 pm and in Bangkok at 8.35 am the following morning. From Singapore to Bangkok costs S$175.60 (1st class) and S$80.30 (2nd class).

SEA
To/From Indonesia
Curiously, there is no direct shipping service between the main ports in Indonesia and near neighbour Singapore but it is possible to travel between the two nations via the islands of the Riau Archipelago. Most nationalities are issued a tourist pass, valid for two months, upon arrival in Indonesia but only at major air and sea ports. At other ports, visas are required.

The Riau Archipelago is the cluster of Indonesian islands immediately south of Singapore. The two most visited islands are Batam and Bintan, both of which can be reached by ferry services from Singapore. The ferries are modern, fast, air-conditioned and show movies. From Tanjung Pinang on Bintan, you can catch boats to Java and Sumatra.

Batam Island is a major resort and very popular with Singaporeans. It only takes half an hour to reach Sekupang on Batam Island from Singapore. Some ferries continue on to Tanjung Pinang, or there are direct ferries from Singapore to Tanjung Pinang taking 2½ hours.

Departures are from Finger Pier at the end of Prince Edward Rd off Shenton Way. Yang Passenger Ferry Service (tel 223 9902, 222 6178) and Dino Shipping (tel 221 4916) between them have more than 20 departures per day to Batam, from 7.40 am to 6 pm. The cost is S$16 one way and S$30 return. Inasco Enterprises (tel 224 9797) has three boats per day to Batam (S$20 one way, S$30 return).

Dino Shipping has boats to Tanjung Pinang, via Batam, departing Singapore at 10.20 am and 3 pm. The cost is S$45 one way and S$80 return. These boats stop at Batam for two hours. Direct boats to Tanjung Pinang leave at 10 and 10.30 am and cost S$50 one way and S$80 return.

Once you get to these islands, there is a variety of ways of continuing to other parts of Indonesia. By far the easiest way is to fly. Merpati has flights between Tanjung Pinang and Jakarta, Pekanbaru or Palembang with connections to Batam and a number of other cities. Flights from Tanjung Pinang to Jakarta cost 105,000 rp.

A more time-consuming way to travel is to take the *Indah Putra* between Tanjung Pinang and Pekanbaru, a 32-hour boat trip costing 15,000 rp deck class or 20,000 rp for a cabin. There are other possibilities if you're willing to wait, including irregular ships to ports in Java or Sumatra. Pelni's *KM Lawit* stops at Tanjung Pinang every second week on its way to either Jakarta or Sumatra. The fare to Jakarta costs 30,000 rp economy, 64,000 2nd class and 81,000 rp 1st class, but check with travel agents in Singapore to book a passage on this boat – otherwise you could miss it and have to wait a month.

To/From India

After five years out of operation, the shipping service between Singapore, Penang and Madras in India recommenced in late 1990. It's operated by the 800-passenger MV *Vignesswara*.

LEAVING SINGAPORE
Departure Tax

From Singapore, the departure tax is S$5 on flights to Malaysia and S$12 on longer international flights.

Travel Agents/Airline Tickets

Singapore is also a good place to look for cheap plane tickets, though Bangkok and Penang have been slightly cheaper than Singapore recently. Airmaster Travel (tel 338 3942) at 36B Prinsep St is a long-running, reliable agent, and in the same building, Airpower Travel (tel 337 1392), 36C Prinsep St, has received glowing recommendations from many travellers. STA (Student Travel) (tel 734 5681) in the Ming Court Hotel is also worth trying. Many others advertise in the *Straits Times'* classified columns.

Fares vary with when you want to fly and who you want to fly with. The cheapest fares are likely to be with the least loved airlines

(various Eastern European ones, Bangladesh Biman etc), via inconvenient routes (you're forced to make stopovers on the way) at awkward times (they only fly every other Tuesday at 3 am).

Some typical discount fares being quoted in Singapore include South-East Asian destinations like Bangkok from S$185 to S$220 one way, Denpasar from S$420 one way or S$550 excursion return, Jakarta S$180 one way or S$300 return and Hong Kong S$550 one way or S$750 return. To the subcontinent, you can fly to Madras or Bombay for S$550 and Kathmandu for S$600.

Fares to Australia or New Zealand include Sydney or Melbourne for S$720 one way or S$1200 return, Auckland S$900 one way via Indonesia or S$1000 via Australia, Perth S$620 one way and Darwin S$510 one way or S$710 return.

London, or other European destinations, costs from S$750 one way with the Eastern European airlines and from S$850 one way with the better airlines. With a stopover in India or Nepal, the fare is around S$1100.

One-way fares to the US west coast are around S$900 direct or with a stop in Manila, S$1050 via Indonesia and S$1500 via Australia or New Zealand.

There are always some special multistop deals on offer such as Singapore-Bangkok-Hong Kong-Taipei-US west coast for S$1000 with China Airlines. You can add Tokyo and Honolulu to that route for a few dollars more, and there are similar fares which terminate in Europe instead of the USA.

Getting Around

BUS

Singapore has an extremely frequent and comprehensive bus network. While the Mass Rapid Transit (MRT) subway system is easy and convenient to use, for door-to-door public transport it is hard to beat the buses. You rarely have to wait more than a few minutes for a bus and they will get you almost anywhere you want to go. The Singapore Tourist Promotion Board's *See Singapore by Bus*, available free from the tourist office, is an excellent pamphlet that lists all Singapore's major destinations and the buses that go to them. It includes maps of bus stops for the Bencoolen St, Orchard Rd, Havelock Rd and Raffles City areas.

If you intend to do a lot of travelling by bus in Singapore, a copy of the *Bus Guide* is a worthwhile investment. It costs 70c at bookshops, but shoestring travellers may well find that their hotel has a supply left behind by departing visitors. The guide lists all bus routes in a convenient pocket-size guide. Best of all is the street index that gives the numbers of all the bus lines going to each of the listed streets.

The buses follow the same route into and out of the city, and fares start from 50c and go up in 10c increments to a maximum of 80c. There are also four air-con bus services where the fares range from 60c to S$1.20. Almost all buses are OMO (one-man operated) buses, and when you board you have to drop the exact fare into the change box. No change is given.

There are two types of OMO bus. One charges a flat rate (like the airport bus No 390) and displays the OMO logo and the fare. The other operates a step fare system where you pay between 50c and 80c depending on where you board. These display the OTS logo, or are marked 'OMO DRF'. Ask the driver for the fare if you are not sure. For information on buses call 287 2727.

For those with limited time in Singapore who still want to see as much of the island as possible for as cheaply as possible, there are the Singapore Explorer bus tickets. These provide unlimited travel to anywhere on the island with either Singapore Bus Service or Trans-Island Bus Service buses.

Six different routes have been named – Historic Singapore, the Temple Route, the Flora & Fauna Route, Island of Contrasts, the Food Trail and the Chinese Touch. You can break your journey wherever you like. One-day Explorer tickets cost S$5 or a three-day ticket is S$12. They are available from many hotels, including the YMCAs, and travel agents, or phone 287 2727 for more details. With the Explorer ticket, you also get a bus map showing the bus stops and points of interest.

MASS RAPID TRANSIT (MRT)

Singapore's ultra modern Mass Rapid Transit (MRT) system started limited operation in late '87 and is now complete. It is the pride of Singapore and Lee Kuan Yew's swan song – the crowning achievement of the many achievements he presided over. His resignation as prime minister coincided with the completion of the MRT. The MRT is the easiest, quickest and most comfortable way of getting around Singapore, and it can transport you across town in air-conditioned comfort in a matter of minutes. However, many of Singapore's attractions are not on the MRT lines and buses are often the best mode of transport to reach them.

The MRT was primarily designed to provide cheap, reliable transport from the housing estates to the city and industrial estates. Most of the 44 km of underground track is in the inner-city area, but out towards the housing estates the MRT runs above ground.

The Orchard Rd tourist hotel area is well serviced by the Somerset, Orchard and Newton MRT stations. Dhoby Ghaut is the closest station to Bencoolen St, while the Beach Rd accommodation area is between City Hall and Bugis stations. Raffles Place MRT station is right in the heart of the Central Business District and Outram Park is the closest station to Chinatown.

The excellent *MRT Guide* is available from newsstands and bookstores for 80c. It lists places of interest, government offices and shows the nearest station and connecting bus services if they are needed. Maps show the surrounding areas for all stations, including bus stops and taxi ranks.

Using the subway system is extremely simple. You check the map showing fares from your station, put money in the slot and press the button for the fare you want. You can get a single-trip ticket (green) or a stored-value ticket (blue) that is valid until you've used up the value of the ticket. You insert the ticket into the entry gate to enter and on departure the ticket is retained by the exit gate unless it still has 'stored value'.

Single-trip tickets cost from 50c to S$1.40. Ticket machines take 10c, 20c, 50c and S$1 coins; they also give change. There are even note-changing machines which change S$1 notes to coins. Store-value tickets cost S$10 and are purchased from the ticket offices found at all MRT stations.

The trains run from around 6 am to midnight, and the last trains pass the inner-city stations at roughly 11.45 pm. At peak times, there is a train every four to five minutes, and at off-peak periods every six to eight minutes.

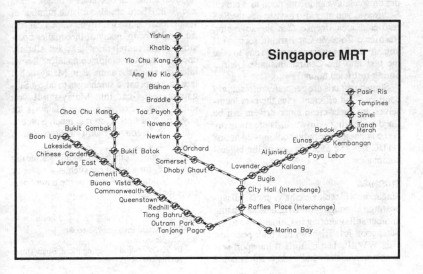

Singapore MRT

TAXI

Singapore has a good supply of taxis – 12,500 of them – and it's usually not too difficult to find one. The exceptions may include rush hours, trips out to the airport (which taxi drivers are sometimes reluctant to make) or at meal times (Singaporeans are not at all enthusiastic about missing a meal).

It is quite easy to recognise Singapore taxis although they come in several varieties – most common being black with a yellow roof or pale blue. Taxis are all metered and although you should ensure the meter is flagged down, there's usually no problem – unlike some Asian countries where the meters always seem to be 'broken'. Flagfall is S$2.20 for the first 1½ km then 10c for each additional 275 metres up to 10 km. Beyond 10 km, the charge is 10c per 250 metres.

From midnight to 6 am, there is a 50% surcharge over the meter fare. From the airport, there is a surcharge of S$3 for each journey – but not to the airport. Radio bookings cost an additional S$2, or only S$1 if you book 30 minutes in advance. There is also a S$1 surcharge on all trips from the Central Business District between 4 and 7 pm on weekdays and from noon to 3 pm on Saturdays. You may also have to pay the S$3 restricted area licence (see the following Restricted Zone & Car Parking section) if you are the first passenger of the day to take the taxi into the Central Business District during restricted hours.

Singapore taxis are generally refreshingly courteous and efficient, plus the cars themselves are super-clean since drivers can be fined for driving a dirty cab. There are many taxi companies; for radio bookings 24 hours, NTUC (tel 452 5555) is one of the biggest companies.

TRISHAW

Singapore's bicycle rickshaws are fast disappearing, although you'll find a surprising number still operating in Chinatown and off Serangoon Rd. Trishaws had their peak just after WW II when motorised transport was almost nonexistent and trishaw riders could make a very healthy income. Today, they are mainly used for local shopping trips or to transport articles too heavy to carry. They rarely venture on to Singapore's heavily trafficked main streets.

There are, however, trishaws at many tourist centres in case you really have to try one out. Always agree on the fare beforehand. On the street, a very short ride is S$2 and the price goes up from there.

Night-time trishaw tours of Chinatown and Little India are operated from a number of the larger hotels.

CAR

Singaporeans drive on the left-hand side of the road and the wearing of seat belts is compulsory. Unlike in most Asian countries, traffic is orderly, but the profusion of one-way streets and streets that change names can make driving difficult for the uninitiated. The *Singapore Street Directory*, a bargain at S$6, is essential for negotiating Singapore's streets.

Rent-a-Car

Singapore has branches of the three major regional rent-a-car operators – Sintat, Hertz and Avis. There are also a large number of small, local operators. If you want a car just for local driving, many of the smaller operators quote rental rates that are slightly cheaper than the major companies. Rental rates are about the same as in Malaysia but there are expensive surcharges to take a Singapore rent-a-car into Malaysia. If you intend renting a car to drive in Malaysia for any length of time, then it is much better to rent a car in Johore Bahru or elsewhere in Malaysia.

Rates start from S$90 a day, including insurance, for a small car such as a Laser or Sunny. Addresses of some of the main operators include:

Avis
    200 Orchard Blvd (tel 737 1668)
Best Car Rental
    03-20 Coronation Shopping Plaza, Bukit Timah Rd (tel 469 4411)

Blue Star Car Rental
  02-19 Balestier Complex, Balestier Rd (tel 253 4661)
Budget Enterprise
  8 Sixth Ave (tel 469 0111)
Hertz Rent-a-Car
  19 Tanglin Rd (tel 734 4646)
Ken-Air Rent-a-Car
  01-41 Specialists Centre, Orchard Rd (tel 737 8282)
Sime Darby Services
  280 Kampong Arang Rd (tel 447 3388)
Sintat Rent-a-Car
  320 Orchard Rd (tel 235 5855)

Restricted Zone & Car Parking

From 7.30 to 10.15 am each morning, the area encompassing the Central Business District, Chinatown and Orchard Rd is a restricted zone where cars may only enter with an area licence sticker or if they carry at least four people. A daily licence costs S$3 per day or S$60 per month – not surprisingly this has dramatically reduced traffic problems in the rush hour! The licence requirement also applies to taxis, so if you want to take a taxi into the CBD during these hours you must pay for the taxi licence which costs S$3 – unless somebody else has already done so of course. The licence stickers are sold at booths just outside the district boundaries, or you can buy them at some post offices.

And if you should carelessly enter the CBD without a licence? There may well be inspectors standing by the roadside noting down the number plates of unlicensed cars as they enter the CBD. A S$50 fine will soon arrive at the car owner's address.

Parking in many places in Singapore is operated by a coupon system. You can buy a booklet of coupons at parking kiosks and post offices. You must display a coupon in your car window with holes punched out to indicate the time, day and date your car was parked.

BICYCLE

Singapore's heavy traffic and good public transport system does not make bicycling such an attractive proposition. Bicycles can be hired at a number of places on the East Coast Parkway, but they are intended mostly for weekend jaunts along the foreshore. Try the East Coast Recreation Centre next to McDonald's or the bicycle centre next to the food centre at East Coast Park.

WALKING

Getting around Singapore on foot has one small problem – apart from the heat and humidity that is. The problem, in old Singapore only, is the 'five-foot ways' instead of sidewalks or pavements. A five-foot way, which takes its name from the fact that it is roughly five-feet wide, is a walkway at the front of the traditional Chinese shop-houses, but enclosed, verandah-like, in the front of the building.

The difficulty with them is that every shop's walkway is individual. It may well be higher or lower than the shop next door or closer to or further from the street. Walking thus becomes a constant up and down and side to side, further complicated by the fact that half the shops seem to overflow right across the walkway forcing you to venture into the street.

As well as people parking their bikes or motorcycles across them, you are likely to trip over the odd *chowkidar* asleep on his *charpoy* at night. (A chowkidar is an Indian nightwatchman and a charpoy is the traditional rope-strung bed which chowkidars seem to spend most of their time horizontal upon.) To further add to the joys of walking in Singapore, there are open drains waiting to catch the unwary.

Still, if you can drag your eyes away from where your feet are going, there is plenty to see as you stroll the five-foot ways.

BOAT & FERRY

There is a wide variety of boating possibilities in Singapore. You can charter a bumboat (motorised sampan) to take a tour up the Singapore River or to go to the islands around Singapore. Speedboats can be hired from Ponggol Boatel to go across to the northern islands or for water skiing. There are regular ferry services from Clifford Pier or the World Trade Centre to Sentosa and the other southern islands. There are also Port of Singapore Authority ferry tours or you can take more luxurious junk tours around the harbour either by daylight or as an evening dinner cruise with operators like Fairwind or Watertours.

Singapore

Lying almost on the equator, Singapore is a prosperous city-state that has overcome its lack of natural resources to become one of the powerhouse economies of Asia. In less than 200 years, Singapore has been transformed from a swampy island into a modern industrial nation.

Modern Singapore is a city of concrete, glass, freeways and shopping centres. You can stay in fashionable Orchard Rd at a luxury hotel, eat Italian food, drink Californian wine, buy European designer-label clothes and never know you were in the East at all. But for those who wish to do a little exploring, Singapore offers a taste of the great Asian cultures in a small, easy-to-get-around package.

In the crowded streets of Chinatown, fortune tellers, calligraphers and temple worshippers are still a part of everyday Singapore. In Little India, you can buy the best sari material, freshly ground spices or a picture of your favourite Hindu god. In the small shops of Arab St, the cry of the imam can be heard from the nearby Sultan Mosque.

Singapore may no longer be the rough and ready port of rickshaws, opium dens, pearl luggers and pirates, but you can still recapture the colonial era with a gin sling under the flashing ceiling fans at Raffles Hotel. Many other fine reminders of Singapore's colonial past remain, despite Singapore's relentless development.

THINGS TO SEE

Singapore's greatest attraction is its ability to offer a taste of Asian culture in a small, easy-to-get-around package. Minutes from the modern business centre with its towering air-conditioned office blocks are the narrow streets of Chinatown where the bicycle rickshaw is still the best way to get around. Meanwhile, across the river there is Little India (Serangoon Rd) and the Muslim centre of Arab St, while even further out of the city are the new housing complexes and industrial centres.

City, River & Harbour

The Singapore River has always been the centre of Singapore and its history. The river no longer thrives with commerce, yet the surrounding area does – namely the Central Business District, the commercial heart south of the river that borders on to Chinatown and the harbour. To the north of the river is colonial Singapore where you'll find the imposing monuments of British rule – the stone grey edifices of the town hall, parliament and museum, the churches and Victorian architecture.

Singapore River Singapore's city centre straddles the Singapore River and runs parallel to the waterfront along Raffles Quay, Shenton Way, Robinson Rd and Cecil St (see the City Centre map). The Singapore River, with old shops and houses along the river bank and soaring office buildings right behind them, is one of the most picturesque areas of Singapore. The river was once the thriving heart of Singapore, and up to a few years ago you could still see bustling activity along this stretch of river. The loading and unloading of sampans and bumboats, the cranes, and the yelling, sweating labourers have all gone. All boats have been kicked out of the area and relocated to the Pasir Panjang wharves west of the city centre.

At the mouth of the river, or at least what used to be the mouth before the most recent bout of land reclamation, stands Singapore's symbol of tourism, the Merlion (a water spouting half-lion, half-fish statue).

The river area around the business district still thrives but with the bustling of office workers, and it's a pleasant walk further west along the river to the surviving old godowns (warehouses) around Clarke Quay that await redevelopment. A good way to see the river

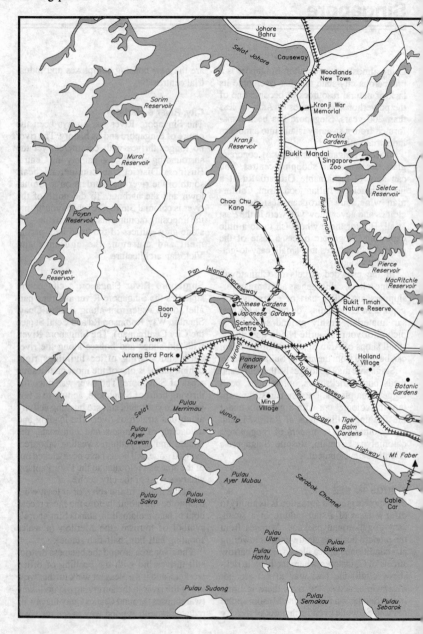

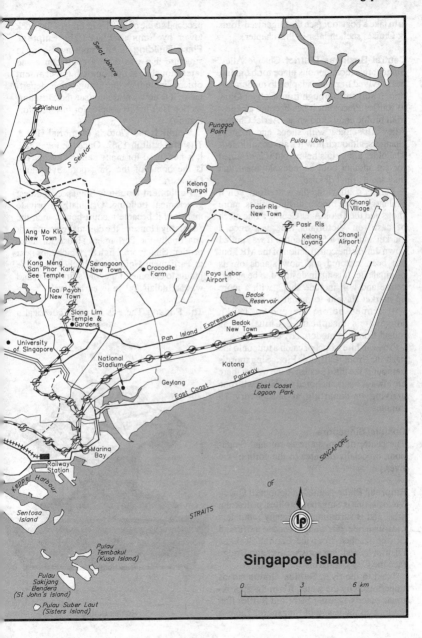

Singapore Island

is to take a boat tour (see the Organised Tours & Cruises section later in this chapter).

Central Business District Change Alley, Singapore's most famous place for bargains, has survived or rather adapted to modernisation. It still cuts through from Collyer Quay to Raffles Place, but it has become a pedestrian bridge and is known as 'Aerial Change Alley'. It's lined with shops and money-changers, although now it's air-conditioned! The older alley runs below but it is destined for yet another bout of redevelopment that may see its final demise.

Further south along the waterfront, you'll find large office blocks, airline offices, more shops and the Telok Ayer Centre, a fine piece of cast-iron Victoriana that was once a market and then a food centre. It was pulled down during the construction of the MRT but has been restored and now stands on its original site. It is again destined to be a food centre and will include shops with a more up-market flavour to match its face-lift (it will reopen before the end of 1991). Singapore's disappearing Chinatown is inland from this modern city centre.

You can hire a boat or catch a tour onto the harbour from Clifford Pier. Singapore's harbour is the third busiest in the world; there are always boats anchored offshore, with one arriving or departing at least every 15 minutes.

Colonial Singapore

The centre of Singapore is colonial Singapore, especially the area to the north of the river.

Empress Place Named in honour of Queen Victoria, this is Singapore's oldest pedestrian area, and is surrounded by many reminders of British rule. It remains closed to traffic and can be reached from the Central Business District by walking across Cavenagh Bridge (see the City Centre map).

Next to the river, **Raffles' Statue** stands imperiously by the water. It's in the approximate place where Sir Stamford Raffles first set foot on the island of Singapore. There is

a second statue of Raffles in front of the clock tower by Empress Place. The **Empress Place Building** is an imposing Georgian structure that was once a court house and later housed a number of government offices, including the immigration department. It is now a museum (see the Museums section later in this chapter for further information).

Nearby is the **Victoria Memorial Hall & Theatre**, built in 1862. Once the town hall, it is now used for many cultural events and is the home of the Singapore Symphony Orchestra.

Parliament House is Singapore's oldest government building. Originally a private mansion, it became a court house, then the Assembly House of the colonial government and finally the Parliament House for independent Singapore. High St, which runs next to Parliament House, was hacked from the jungle to become Singapore's first street and was an Indian area in its early days.

The Padang There is no more quizzical a

Raffles Statue

symbol of British colonialism than the open field of the Padang, north of Empress Place. It is here that flannelled fools played cricket in the tropical heat, cheered on by the members in the Singapore Cricket Club pavilion at one end of the Padang. At the other end of the field is the Singapore Recreation Club, which was set up for the Eurasian community. Cricket is still played on the weekends; segregation is, officially, no longer practised.

The Padang was a centre for colonial life and a place to promenade in the evenings. Things haven't changed all that drastically, and the Esplanade Park opposite the Padang on the foreshore is still the place for an evening stroll. The Padang also witnessed the beginning of the end of colonial rule, for it was here that the invading Japanese herded the European community together, before marching them off to Changi Prison.

The **Supreme Court** and **City Hall** are two imposing colonial buildings across from the Padang on St Andrews Rd.

Raffles Hotel The Raffles Hotel on Beach Rd (see the Around Bencoolen St map) is far more than just an expensive place to stay or the best known hotel in Singapore. It's a Singapore institution, an architectural landmark which has been classified by the government as a part of Singapore's 'cultural heritage', and a place that virtually oozes the old-fashioned atmosphere of the East as Somerset Maugham would have known it.

Originally, the Raffles started as a tiffin house run by Captain Dare. Later he expanded it into a hotel which in 1886 was taken over by the Sarkies brothers, three Armenians who built a string of hotels which were to become famous throughout the East. They include the Strand in Rangoon and the E&O in Penang as well as the Raffles.

The Raffles soon became a byword for oriental luxury and was featured in novels by Joseph Conrad and Somerset Maugham. It was also recommended by Rudyard Kipling as the place to 'feed at' when in Singapore (but stay elsewhere he added!), and in its Long Bar, Ngiam Tong Boon created the

Singapore Sling in 1915. You can still front the bar and order a Singapore Sling – the Raffles orders gin by the truckload.

More recently, the Raffles was threatened by redevelopment. It had lost its waterfront location to land reclamation and more modern hotels could offer better facilities and far lower running costs. The Raffles has been closed for two years while it undergoes extensive renovations and extensions which are faithful to the original structure. It will reopen by the end of 1991.

A visit to the Raffles is well worthwhile even if you're not staying there. You can sip a drink in the bar or order tea on the immaculate lawn – and turn the clock back a century.

Churches The most imposing examples of colonial architecture between Bras Basah Rd and Coleman St are the churches (see the Around Bencoolen St map). Many are run-down and their congregations depleted or nonexistent, but the Urban Redevelopment Authority has most of them earmarked for restoration.

St Andrew's Cathedral is Singapore's Anglican cathedral, built in Gothic style between 1856 and 1863. It's in the block surrounded by North Bridge Rd, Coleman St, Stamford Rd and St Andrews Rd. The Catholic **Cathedral of the Good Shepherd** on Queen St is a stolid neo-classical edifice built between 1843 and 1846 and is a Singapore historic monument. The best examples of religious buildings, however, are **St Joseph's Institution,** a former Catholic boys school near the corner of Bras Basah Rd and Queen St, and the **Convent of the Holy Infant Jesus** on the corner of Bras Basah Rd and Victoria St.

The oldest church in Singapore is the Armenian **Church of St Gregory the Illuminator** on Hill St which is no longer used for services.

Fort Canning If you continue north-west up Coleman St from the Padang, you pass the Armenian Church and come to Fort Canning Hill, a good viewpoint over Singapore. Once

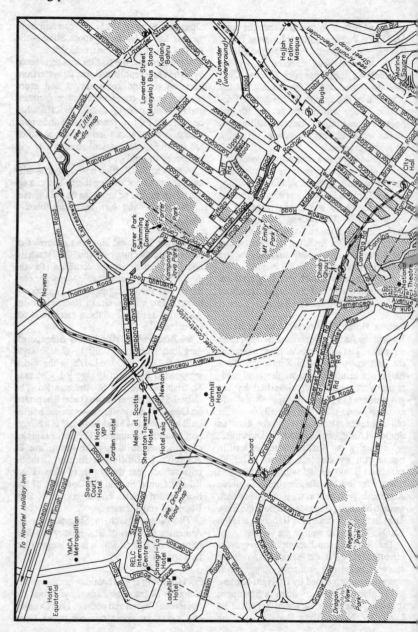

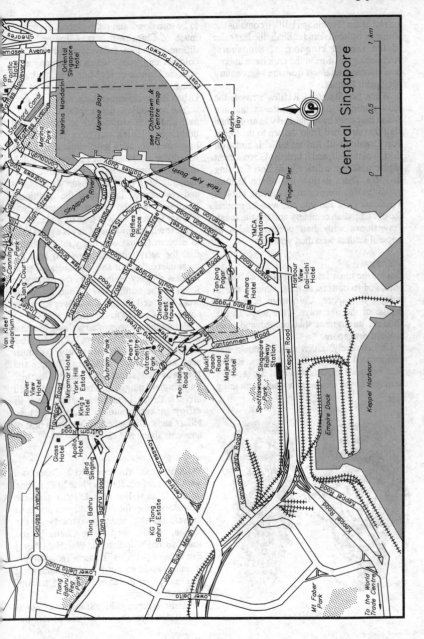

Central Singapore

known as the 'Forbidden Hill', it contains the shrine of Sultan Iskander Shah, the last ruler of the ancient kingdom of Singapura. Archaeological digs in the park have uncovered Javanese artefacts from the 14th century Majapahit Empire.

When Sir Stamford Raffles arrived, the only reminder of any greatness that the island may once have claimed was an earthen wall that stretched from the sea to the top of Fort Canning Hill. Raffles built his house on the top of the hill, and it became Government House until the military built Fort Canning in 1860. There is little left of the historic buildings that were once on the hill, but it is a pleasant park and you can wander around the old Christian cemetery and see the many gravestones with their poignant tales of hopeful settlers who died young.

Chinatown

One of the most fascinating areas of Singapore, and its cultural heart, is Chinatown. In today's Singapore, Chinatown is the last refuge of the old ways – the ways of the Chinese immigrants that shaped and built modern Singapore.

Unfortunately, much of Chinatown has disappeared over the last 30 years. Rather than being an important part of Singapore's heritage, it was viewed as a slum, something to be torn down and redeveloped. However, much of Chinatown is now destined for a different kind of redevelopment. The old colonial shopfronts, which are synonymous with the Chinese on the Malay Peninsula, are being restored under the direction of the Urban Redevelopment Authority.

The restorations are faithful to the original, and it is wonderful to see the old buildings winning out over the concrete high-rises, but such redevelopments pose a new threat to Chinatown. The restored buildings are now desirable properties commanding high rents for townhouses, shops and restaurants. Inevitably, the traditional businesses will be forced out and a new touristy Chinatown will take its place.

Meanwhile, any time of day is a good time to explore Chinatown, but you'll probably find the early morning hours not only the most interesting but also the coolest. Chinatown is roughly bounded by the Singapore River to the north, New Bridge Rd to the west, Maxwell Rd and Kreta Ayer Rd to the south and Cecil St to the east.

Following is a suggested walking tour that takes in most of Chinatown, but if your time is limited or your feet are weary, the 'must sees' are the Thian Hock Keng Temple and the crowded streets of Smith, Temple, Pagoda and Trengganu. These streets are still alive with traditional businesses such as effigy makers, outdoor barbers, fortune tellers and calligraphers, as well as a host of souvenir shops and eateries.

Painted Masks

Walking Tour You can start a Chinatown walking tour from Raffles Place MRT station in the Central Business District (see the Chinatown map for the location of points of interest on this walking tour). From the station, wander west along Chulia St and south down Philip St to the **Wak Hai Cheng Bio Temple (A)**. This Teochew Taoist temple is quite run-down but has some interesting scenes depicted under, and on top of, the roof of the main temple.

Continue down Phillip St and over Church St to Telok Ayer St, where the real clamour

■ PLACES TO STAY

1   New Otani Hotel
3   Excelsior Hotel
4   Peninsula Hotel
18 Furama Hotel
20 Great Southern Hotel
39 New Asia Hotel
40 Air View Hotel

▼ PLACES TO EAT

2   Hill Street Food Centre
21 Food Centre
26 Food Centre
34 Chinatown Complex - Market & Food Place
36 Maxwell Food Centre
37 Moti Mahal
38 Beng Hiang
41 Amoy Street Food Centre
42 Market/Food Centre
46 Telok Ayer Centre

OTHER

5   Funan Centre
6   Peninsula Plaza
7   High Street Centre
8   Tan Si Chong Su Temple
9   Melaka Mosque
10 Supreme Court
11 Singapore Cricket Club
12 Esplanade Park
13 Queen Elizabeth Walk
14 Parliament House

15 Victoria Concert Hall & Victoria Theatre
16 Empress Place
17 Furama Shopping Centre
19 People's Park Centre
22 People's Park Complex
23 Jamae Mosque
24 South Bridge Centre
25 OCBC Centre
27 Fullerton Building
28 GPO
29 Hong Kong Bank Building
30 Clifford Centre & Change Alley
31 Clifford Pier
32 Ocean Building
33 Overseas Union Shopping Centre
35 Kreta Ayer People's Theatre
43 International Plaza
44 DBS Building
45 Hong Leong Building
47 Shenton House
48 UIC Building
49 Chinese Methodist Church

Ⓐ WALKING TOUR

A Wak Hai Cheng Bio Temple
B Fuk Yak Ch'i Temple
C Nagore Durgha Shrine
D Thian Hock Keng Temple
E Al-Abrar Mosque
F Temple Carvers
G Lion Dance Masks
H Tanjong Pagar
I Funeral Paraphernalia Dealers
J Sri Mariamman Temple
K Tong Chai Medical Institute

of Chinatown begins. Telok Ayer St was once on the seashore in Singapore's early days and was something of a brawling area frequented by sailors, but despite this it has a profusion of temples and mosques representing Singapore's major faiths.

The **Fuk Tak Ch'i Temple (B)** is hidden away at 76 Telok Ayer St, and at first glance it looks like a shop. It is a Hakka temple, noted for statues of the God of Wealth and his horse, which attract worshipping gamblers. Just before the temple is a shop devoted almost entirely to selling incense – from small packets to huge pillars.

At the junction with Boon Tat St, you'll find the **Nagore Durgha Shrine (C)**, an old mosque built by Muslims from south India during 1829 and 1830. It's not that interesting, but just a little south-west down the street is the Chinese **Thian Hock Keng Temple (D)**, or Temple of Heavenly Happiness, one of the most interesting temples in Singapore (see the Temples, Mosques & Churches section later in this chapter for more details).

Continue walking along Telok Ayer St and you'll soon come to the **Al-Abrar Mosque (E)** which was originally built in 1827 and rebuilt in its present form from 1850 to 1855. A right turn and then another right turn will

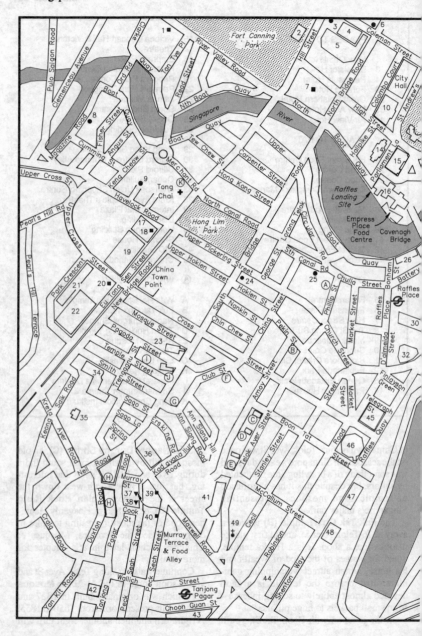

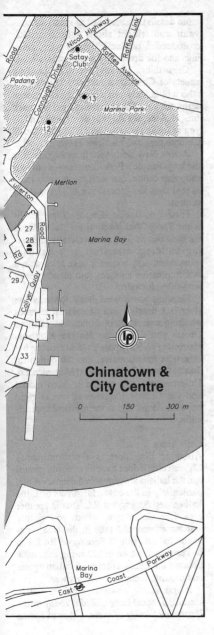

Chinatown & City Centre

bring you into Amoy St, a Hokkien area that once catered to sailors and the sea trade, as evidenced by the sign at No 89: 'Kwong Thye Hin, Native Passenger Lodging House'. Once again there are rows of typical Chinese shopfronts with their convoluted 'five-foot ways'.

Walking on these covered walkways is always a continuous obstacle course. It's amazing how on many of these old Chinese houses, bushes and even large trees seem to sprout straight out of the walls – an indication of the amazing fertility which Singapore's steamy climate seems to engender.

Continue up Amoy St over Cross St, a wide new road which has been ruthlessly pushed right through the middle of Chinatown, and then turn left (north-west) up Pekin St to China St. This whole street is a fascinating conglomeration of shops and shopfront activity, and the bicycle rickshaw is still the main form of transport for goods.

If you walk south-west on China St and cross back over Cross St, the name changes to Club St, a curious street because it seems to go steeply uphill when you would think this part of Singapore was as flat as a pancake. On the corner with Gemmill Lane are the shops of the Chinese **temple carvers (F)** which produce religious figures and temple furniture.

The quiet area around Club St, Ann Siang Rd and Ann Siang Hill was once a clove and nutmeg plantation until it became a prime residential area for Hokkien merchants. There are some particularly good examples of highly decorated terraces, a number of which house the old Chinese guilds. These include the gold and silver workers guild, the Chinese mechanics and even a restaurant guild.

On the corner of Club St and Ann Siang Hill is the Lee Kun Store, which specialises in the intricate **lion dance masks (G)** made from paper and bamboo.

Continue north-east up to South Bridge Rd and you enter the real heart of Chinatown. Although the street hawkers have gone and many shops now cater to the tourist trade, there is plenty of the old atmosphere of Chinatown.

But before you delve into this area, wander down South Bridge Rd to the new **Tanjong Pagar (H)** development, wedged between Neil and Tanjong Pagar roads, to see the eventual fate of Chinatown. The beautifully restored terraces accommodate a variety of restaurants, craft and antique shops. Attempts have been made to house traditional businesses here, but this is a touristy recreation of Chinatown, not the real thing.

Heading back to the centre of Chinatown, go up Sago St, which runs north-west off South Bridge Rd, to Trengganu St. Until recently, Sago St had the last of the old 'death houses' where old folk were once packed off towards the end of their lives, thus avoiding the possible bad luck of a death in the home. Along Temple St, look for the **funeral paraphernalia dealers (I)** who turn out paper cars, houses, ships, and other equipment just in case you can take it with you.

Also in this area is the **Sri Mariamman Temple (J)**, Singapore's oldest Hindu temple (see the Temples, Mosques & Churches section later in this chapter for more details). Pagoda St has plenty of souvenir and trinket shops selling masks, reproduction bronzes, bamboo ware, carvings and silk dressing gowns. Bargain hard.

Other things you may see in the bustling streets of Chinatown include calligraphers who will quickly pen a message in Chinese script for you; Chinese delicacies like shark fins, abalone, sea slugs or deer horns; and, if you're feeling poorly, there is no shortage of Chinese herb and medicine shops.

Across New Bridge Rd from Pagoda St is the huge People's Park Complex – a modern shopping centre, but with much more local appeal than the general run of Orchard Rd centres.

Further north-east along Eu Tong Sen St is the **Tong Chai Medical Institute (K)** on Eu Tong Sen St. This architecturally interesting building, classified as a national monument, now houses a large shop with a few impressive antiques (but mostly cheap souvenirs) for sale.

Heading north-west back towards the river is a derelict area of colonial terraces awaiting renovation or demolition. In these streets you'll find the **Melaka Mosque**, claimed to be Singapore's oldest mosque but otherwise unimpressive, and the delightful **Tan Si Chong Su Temple** on Magazine Rd. Unfortunately, this temple is often closed and the Central Expressway works right opposite do not add to the mystical appreciation.

Little India

Although Singapore is a predominantly Chinese city, it does have its minority groups and the Indians are probably the most visible, particularly in the colourful streets of Little India along Serangoon Rd. This is another area, like Chinatown, where you simply wander around and take in the area's flavours. Indeed, around Serangoon Rd it can be very much a case of following your nose because the heady aromas of Indian spices and cooking seem to be everywhere.

If you want a new sari, a pair of Indian sandals, a recent issue of *India Today* or the *Illustrated Weekly of India*, a tape of Indian

Lion Dance Mask

music or a framed portrait of your favourite Hindu god, then Little India is the place to go.

It's also, not surprisingly, a good place to eat, and you'll see streetside cooks frying chapattis at all times of the day. Since many of Singapore's Indians are Tamils from the south of India, the accent on food is mainly vegetarian, and there are some superb places to eat vegetarian food – number one being the well known Komala Vilas restaurant.

Walking Tour Little India is not very extensive, and you can sample its sights, scents and sounds in an hour or two (see the Little India map for the location of points of interest on this walking tour). Little India is roughly the area bounded by Bukit Timah Rd to the south, Lavender St to the north, Race Course Rd to the west and Jalan Besar to the east. The real centre of Little India is at the southern end of Serangoon Rd and the small streets that run off it. Here, the shops are wall-to-wall Indian, but only a hundred metres or so away the Chinese influence reappears.

Unfortunately, much of the western side of Serangoon Rd has been flattened and consists of open paddocks but there are interesting temples further north. Race Course Rd has a few shops and some good restaurants down its southern end, but the housing estates have made an unmistakable contribution to its atmosphere.

The **Zhujiao Centre (A)** on Serangoon Rd near Buffalo Rd is Little India's market. It is also known as the KK (Kandang Kerbau) market, its old name before it was rehoused in this modern building. Downstairs is a 'wet market', the Singaporean term for a produce market, and upstairs is a hawkers' centre where Indian food is well represented. On the 2nd floor, stalls sell a variety of everyday goods but you can also buy brassware and Indian textiles.

Across Serangoon Rd are sari shops such as the Govindasamy store, and nearby are **spice shops (B)** that sell fresh spices ground daily on their mills. Wander around the backstreets with the names of imperial India such

as Clive, Hastings and Campbell. This is the heart of Little India with a variety of shops selling spices, Indian music cassettes, saris, religious artefacts and everyday goods for the Indian household.

This is also a restaurant area and the best place to sample south Indian vegetarian food. At 76 Serangoon Rd is the famous Komala Vilas restaurant and around the corner in Upper Dickson Rd is the equally good New Woodlands restaurant.

Apart from the ubiquitous gold shops (gold is a girl's best friend in Asia), there are a few interesting **jewellers (C)** on Serangoon and Buffalo roads that make jewellery crafted with traditional designs.

The southern end of Race Course Rd has the best collection of restaurants in Little India, from the tandoori food of north India to Singapore's famous fish-head curry (sounds and looks terrible, tastes delicious).

On the corner of Belilios and Serangoon roads is the **Veerama Kali Amman Temple (D)**, a Shaivite temple dedicated to Kali. It is always popular with worshippers, especially at dusk.

Further north-east along Serangoon Rd is the Serangoon Plaza. Architecturally, historically and culturally it's a write-off, but the department stores here are good places for bargains. The range may not be extensive, but the prices for electrical goods and other household items are usually as good as you'll find anywhere in Singapore.

The **Sri Srinivasa Perumal Temple (E)** is an extensive temple dedicated to Vishnu. The temple dates from 1855 but the impressive *gopuram* (gateway) is a relatively recent addition, built in 1966. Inside the temple, you will find a statue of Perumal, or Vishnu, and his consorts Lakshmi and Andal, as well as his bird-mount Garuda. This temple is the starting point for devotees who make the walk to the Chettiar Hindu Temple during the Thaipusam festival.

Not far from the Sri Srinivasa Temple is the Sakya Muni Buddha Gaya Temple, better known as the **Temple of 1000 Lights (F)** (see the Temples, Mosques & Churches section later in this chapter for more

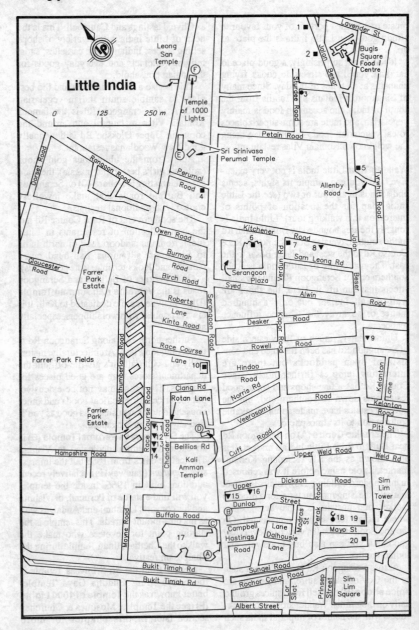

Little India

0 125 250 m

1 ■
2 ■
3 ●

Leong San Temple

F

Temple of 1000 Lights

Sri Srinivasa Perumal Temple

E

Perumal Road
4 ■

5 ■

Allenby Road

Dorset Road
Rangoon Road

Gloucester Road

Farrer Park Estate

Owen Road
Burmah Road
Birch Road
Roberts Lane
Kinta Road
Race Course Lane

Farrer Park Fields

Northumberland Road

Farrier Park Estate

Hampshire Road

Race Course Road

1 ▼
2 ▼
3 ▼
14 ▼

Chander Road

10 ■

Clang Rd
Rotan Lane

D

Belilios Rd

Kali Amman Temple

Kitchener Road

6 ■

Serangoon Plaza

Syed

7 ■ 8 ▼
Sam Leong Rd

Verdun Rd

Alwin Road

Desker Road

Kapor Rd

Rowell Road

Hindoo Road

Norris Rd

Veerasamy Road

Cuff Road

Serangoon Road

Jalan Besar
Sturdee Road
Petain Road

Tyrwhitt Road

9 ▼

Kelantan Lane

Kelantan Road

Pitt St

Upper Weld Road

Dickson Road

Upper Dunlop Street
15 ▼ 16 ▼

B

Campbell Lane
Hastings Road
Dalhousie Lane

Buffalo Road

C

17

A

Bukit Timah Rd
Bukit Timah Rd

Mayne Road

Madras St
Perak Road

Sungei Road

Rochor Canal Road

Albert Street

Lavender St

Bugis Square Food Centre

Weld Rd

Sim Lim Tower

18 ● 19 ■
Mayo St
20 ■

Sim Lim Square

Lor Silat
Prinsep Street

■ PLACES TO STAY

1 Palace Hotel
2 Kam Leng Hotel
4 Friendly Rest House
5 International Hotel
6 New Park Hotel
7 Tai Hoe Hotel
10 Broadway Hotel
19 Sim Lim Lodging House
   & Tower
20 South Seas Hotel

▼ PLACES TO EAT

8 Fut Sai Kai Restaurant
9 Berseh Food Centre
11 Muthu's Curry Restaurant
12 Nur Jehan
13 Delhi Restaurant
14 Banana Leaf Apolo
15 Komala Vilas
16 Madras New
   Woodlands Cafe
17 Zhujiao Centre

   OTHER

3 Sunday Morning Bird Singing
18 Abdul Gaffoor Mosque

Ⓐ WALKING TOUR

A Zhujiao Centre
B Spice Shops
C Jewellers
D Veerama Kali Amman Temple
E Sri SrinivasaPerumal Temple
F Temple of 1000 Lights

---

information). It's a glitzy, slightly tacky Thai-influenced temple, but one of Singapore's best known. A far more beautiful temple is the small Leong San Temple across the road. This Buddhist and Taoist temple has some fine ceramic carvings inside.

From Little India, you can wander across to Jalan Besar. The Indian influence is not so noticeable here; the fine old pastel-coloured terraces are Peranakan in style. There are a number of traditional businesses on and around Jalan Besar, and Kelantan Lane is a good place for antiques. The area around

Jalan Besar and Petain Rd is popular with bird-lovers, especially on Sunday mornings when the birds often sing in competition. At night, this area is noted for far less wholesome activities. Just off Jalan Besar on Dunlop St, down towards Rochor Canal Rd, is the Abdul Gaffoor Mosque. It's an intriguing fairy-tale blend of Arabic and Victorian architecture.

Arab Street

While Chinatown provides Singapore with a Chinese flavour and Serangoon Rd is where you head to for the tastes and smells of India, Arab St is the Muslim centre (see the Around Bencoolen St map). Along this street, and especially along North Bridge Rd and adjoining side streets with Malay names like Pahang Rd, Aliwal St, Jalan Pisang and Jalan Sultan, you'll find batiks from Indonesia and sarongs, hookahs, rosaries, flower essences, hajj caps, songkok hats, basket-ware and rattan goods.

Sultan Mosque, the focus for Singapore's Muslim community, is near the corner of Arab St and North Bridge Rd. You'll also find good Indian Muslim food at restaurants along North Bridge Rd. During the month of Ramadan, when Muslims fast from sunrise to sunset, the area is alive with foodstalls, especially in Bussorah St where the faithful come to buy food at dusk.

If you head north-east up Baghdad St, you come to Sultan Gate, which leads to the Istana Kampong Glam. The *istana* (palace) was the residence of Sultan Ali Iskander Shah and was built around 1840. The Kampong Glam area is the historic seat of the Malay royalty, resident here before the arrival of Sir Stamford Raffles. In the early days of Singapore, it was allocated not only to the original Malays but also to Javanese, Bugis and Arab merchants and residents.

On the corner of Jalan Sultan and Victoria St is the old Kampong Glam cemetery, where it is said that the Malay royalty is buried among the frangipani trees. Adjoining it is the Malabar Muslim Jama-Ath Mosque, a beautiful little mosque that is at its fairy-tale best when lit up in the evening.

Another interesting mosque in this area is the Hajjah Fatimah Mosque on Beach Rd. A national monument, it was built by a Malaccan-born Malay woman, Hajjah Fatimah, on the site of her home.

Other Areas
Orchard Rd Singapore's international tourists and its wealthy residents also have whole areas of Singapore to themselves. Orchard Rd is where the high-class hotels predominate and beyond it you enter the area of the Singapore elite (see the Orchard Rd map). Prior to independence, the mansions of the colonial rulers were built there, and today Singapore's wealthy elite, as well as many expatriate personnel, live in these fine old houses.

Orchard Rd itself is mostly a place to shop. Its rows of modern shopping centres hold a variety of stores selling everything from the latest in Japanese gadgetry to the antiques of the East. Here you'll also find the majority of Singapore's international hotels, many of Singapore's nightspots and a whole host of restaurants, bars and lounges. This area is a showcase for modern Singapore and an impressive row of the delights of capitalism. However, it has little to offer in the way of historical or cultural interest.

One exception is Peranakan Place, an old row of colonial shopfronts that houses a museum dedicated to Peranakan culture (see the Museums section later in this chapter for more information). The Peranakans are the descendants of Chinese and Malay marriages and exhibit a fascinating blend of both cultures. From Peranakan Place, wander north up Emerald Hill Rd, where some fine terrace houses remain. This whole area was once a nutmeg plantation owned by William Cuppage, an early Singapore settler. At the turn of the century, much of it was subdivided and it became a fashionable residential area for Peranakan and Straits-born Chinese merchants.

Little Malaysia? If Singapore has a Chinese, Indian and Muslim area – where is Singapore's Malay area? If you want to experience Malaysia, the real thing is just across the Causeway. However, there are Malay areas in Singapore, though Malay culture is not so

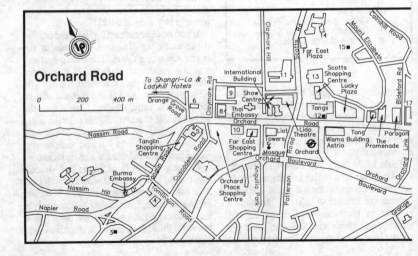

obvious and easily marketed as a tourist attraction.

Geylang Serai is a popular Malay residential area, though you are not going to see traditional *attap* houses and sarong-clad cottage industry workers. The area has plenty of high-rise buildings, though there are some older buildings around, especially on the *lorong* (alleys) that run off Geylang Rd.

To experience a traditional market that hasn't yet been rebuilt as a concrete box, take the MRT to the Paya Lebar station and then walk along Sims Ave to the Geylang Serai market. From the market you can head down Joo Chiat Rd to the East Coast Rd and explore the Katong district. You will pass a row of fine Peranakan-style terraces, and the East Coast Rd shopping centre has some interesting antique shops. The walk takes a couple of hours.

HOTELS

1	Hotel Premier	14	Goodward Park Hotel
2	ANA	15	York Hotel
3	Omni Marco Polo	16	Mandarin Singapore
4	Regent Hotel	17	Crown Prince Hotel
5	Orchard Parade Hotel	18	Phoenix Hotel Singapore
6	Orchard Hotel	19	Holiday Inn Park View
7	Boulevard Hotel	20	Mitre Hotel
8	Orchard Towers	21	Grand Central Hotel
9	Negara Hotel	22	Supreme Hotel
10	Singapore Hilton	23	Meridien Singapore Hotel
11	Royal Holiday Inn Singapore	24	Cockpit Hotel International
12	Dynasty Hotel	25	Lloyd's Inn
13	Hyatt Regency Singapore	26	Imperial Hotel
		27	Bay View Inn
		28	New Mayfair Hotel

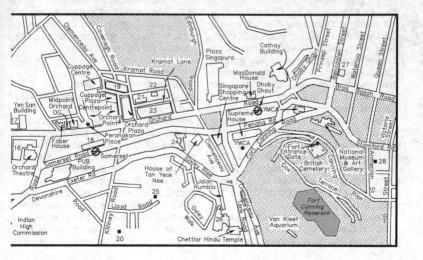

There are still *kampong* (villages) in Singapore that appear to have missed the modern age. If you drive out along Sembawang Rd or Punggol Rd, you can still come across surprisingly rural scenes. The islands of the north-east, such as Pulau Ubin and Pulau Tekong are also rural and very Malay in character.

Holland Village If you're thinking of settling in Singapore and wonder what the life of an expatriate is like, head for Holland Village, an expat shopping centre. It's on Holland Rd, a westerly continuation of Orchard Rd, and services the garden belt suburbs of the well-to-do.

Holland Village is, in fact, just a suburban shopping centre where foreigners can shop, sip coffee and feel at home. However, there are a few good restaurants and watering holes, and the Holland Shopping Centre is a modern complex and one of the best places to buy antiques, furnishings and crafts such as porcelain ware, batik, wood carvings, etc.

Changi Village Changi, on the east coast of Singapore, is a pleasant escape from the hubbub of downtown Singapore. Don't expect to find traditional kampong houses, the buildings are modern, but Changi does have a village atmosphere. Changi's beach is not exactly a tropical paradise but it has a good stretch of sand and offers safe swimming. It's popular on weekends but almost deserted during the week. The food in Changi is an attraction, and there are some good seafood restaurants and foodstalls near the beach. A visit to Changi Village can be included with a trip to Changi Prison.

From Changi, you can catch ferries to Pulau Ubin and Pulau Tekong (see the Islands, Beaches & Water Sports section later in this chapter). Ferries also go to Pengerang across the strait in Malaysia. This is an interesting back-door route into Malaysia; ferries leave Changi from 7 am to 4 pm and cost S$4.

You can reach Changi on bus Nos 1 and 2 from the Bencoolen St/Raffles City area. If you have a few hours to kill at the airport,

you can reach Changi Village in about half an hour; take bus No 24 to Upper Changi Rd, after you turn off the expressway, and then take bus Nos 2 or 14.

Housing Estates Still another side of Singapore is found in the modern HDB (Housing & Development Board) satellite cities like Toa Payoh, Pasir Ris, Tampines and Bukit Panjang. Around 87% of Singaporeans live in these government housing blocks and once again it's a programme that Singapore manages to make work.

While high-rise housing has become a dirty word in many countries, in Singapore they're almost universally popular. It is a resounding success as a public housing programme and many of the residents own their own flats, with subsidised interest rates (currently around 3%) provided by the HDB. It is possible to take a tour of a housing estate (see the Organised Tours & Cruises section later in this chapter).

Jurong Jurong Town, west of the city centre, is more than just a new housing area. A huge industrial complex has been built from the ground up on land that was still a swamp at the end of WW II. Today, it is the power house of Singapore's economic success story. The Jurong area also has a number of tourist attractions, such as the Jurong Bird Park, the Singapore Science Centre, and the Chinese and Japanese Gardens.

Temples, Mosques & Churches

Singapore's polyglot population has resulted in an equally varied collection of places of worship. There are mosques, churches and Hindu, Taoist and Buddhist temples. The churches chiefly date from the English colonial period (see the Colonial Singapore section earlier in this chapter), though Singapore's oldest church is Armenian, as Armenian traders were visiting Singapore at about the same time as Sir Stamford Raffles. The Hindu temples are basically of the south Indian Dravidian style since many of Singapore's Indian settlers are Tamils from that region. The most notable temples are listed here; others are also mentioned in the Chinatown and Little India sections in this chapter.

Thian Hock Keng The Temple of Heavenly Happiness on Telok Ayer St in Chinatown is the oldest and one of the most colourful temples in Singapore – in part due to restoration work in 1979. The temple was originally built in 1840 and dedicated to Ma-Cho-Po, the Queen of Heaven and protector of sailors.

At that time it was on the waterfront and since many Chinese settlers were arriving in Singapore by sea it was inevitable that a joss house be built where they could offer thanks for a safe voyage. As you wander through the courtyards of the temple, look for the rooftop dragons, the intricately decorated beams, the burning joss sticks, the gold-leafed panels and, best of all, the beautifully painted doors.

Sri Mariamman Temple The Sri Mariamman Temple on South Bridge Rd, right in the heart of Chinatown, is the oldest Hindu temple in Singapore. It was originally built in 1827, but its present form dates from 1862 when the original wooden temple was rebuilt. With its colourful gopuram, or tower, over the entrance gate, this is clearly a temple in the south Indian Dravidian style. A superb collection of colourfully painted Hindu figures gaze out from the gopuram.

Around October each year, the temple is the scene for the Thimithi festival during which devotees walk barefoot over burning coals – supposedly feeling no pain, although spectators report that quite a few hotfoot it over the final few steps!

Temple of 1000 Lights Towards the north-eastern end of Race Course Rd at No 366, close to the corner of Serangoon Rd and Lavender St, is the Sakaya Muni Buddha Gaya Temple, or the Temple of 1000 Lights. This Buddhist temple is dominated by a brightly painted 15-metre-high seated figure of the Buddha. The temple was inspired by a Thai monk named Vutthisasara. Although it is a Thai-style temple, it's actually very Chinese in its technicolour decoration.

Apart from the huge Buddha image, the temple includes oddities like a wax model of Gandhi and a figure of Ganesh, the elephant-headed Hindu god. A huge mother-of-pearl footprint, complete with the 108 auspicious marks which distinguish a Buddha foot from any other two-metre-long foot, is said to be a replica of the footprint on top of Adam's Peak in Sri Lanka.

Behind and inside the giant statue is a smaller image of the reclining Buddha in the act of entering nirvana. Around the base, models tell the story of the Buddha's life, and, of course, there are the 1000 lights which give the temple its name.

Any bus going north-east down Serangoon Rd will take you to the temple.

Sultan Mosque The Sultan Mosque on North Bridge Rd near Arab St is the biggest mosque in Singapore. It was originally built in 1825 with the aid of a grant from Sir Stamford Raffles and the East India Company as a result of Raffles' treaty with the Sultan of Johore. A hundred years later, the original mosque was replaced by a magnificent gold-domed building. The mosque is open to visitors from 5 am to 8.30 pm daily, and the best time to visit is during a religious ceremony.

Siong Lim Temple At 184E Jalan Toa Payoh, north of the city centre and out towards Paya Lebar Airport, this temple is one of the largest in Singapore and includes a Chinese rock garden. It was built in 1908 but includes more recent additions. This Buddhist temple features Thai Buddha statues and 2000 kg incense burners.

The temple is about one km east from the Toa Payoh MRT station.

Other Temples & Mosques Singapore has many other Chinese and Indian temples and mosques. On Tank Rd, near the intersection of Clemenceau Ave and River Valley Rd, the **Chettiar Hindu Temple** was completed in 1984 and replaces a much earlier temple built by Indian chettiars, or money lenders. It is dedicated to the six-headed Lord Subramaniam and is at its most active during the festival of Thaipusam.

The Islamic **Nagore Durgha Shrine** and **Al-Abrar Mosque** are on Telok Ayer St in Chinatown. The **Hajjah Fatimah Mosque** on Java Rd is near the Crawford St (northeastern) end of Beach Rd. It's a picturesque, small mosque built around 1845 and has a leaning minaret. The **Jamae (or Chulia) Mosque** on South Bridge Rd is only a short distance from the Sri Mariamman Temple in Chinatown. It was built by Muslim Indians from the Coromandel Coast of Tamil Nadu between 1830 and 1855.

On Magazine Rd, near Clemenceau Ave and the Singapore River, the **Tan Si Chong Su Temple** is a temple and ancestral hall built in 1876 for the Tan clan. The **Kuan Yin Temple** on Waterloo St is one of the most popular Chinese temples – after all Kuan Yin is one of the most popular goddesses. This temple was rebuilt in 1982, but the flower sellers and fortune tellers out the front make it one of the liveliest temples in Singapore. On top of Mt Faber on Pender Rd stands the **1000 Buddhas Hilltop Temple**.

The **Kong Meng San Phor Kark See Temple** on Bright Hill Drive is the largest temple in Singapore and covers 12 hectares. A modern temple, it is impressive in its size and design, though its main function is as a crematorium where funerals, complete with paper effigies, are frequent. The attached old people's home is reminiscent of the old death houses.

Museums
National Museum & Art Gallery The National Museum on Stamford Rd traces its ancestry back to Mr Raffles himself who first brought up the idea of a museum for Singapore in 1823. The original museum, which finally opened in 1849, then moved to another location in 1862 before being rehoused at the present building in 1887.

Exhibits include archaeological artefacts from the Asia region, articles relating to Chinese trade and settlement in the region, Malaysian and Indonesian arts and crafts, and a wide collection of items relating to Sir Stamford Raffles. These include his manuscripts plus maps and paintings of old Singapore.

The art gallery includes contemporary paintings from both Singaporean and other South-East Asian artists. Particularly interesting is the superb jade collection from Haw Par House which has now been closed. The Aw brothers, of Tiger Balm fame, amassed not only this priceless collection of jade pieces but also a variety of other valuable pieces of art. The museum is open from 9 am to 4.30 pm daily and admission is S$1. There is a museum bookshop, and tours of the museum leave from the information counter at 11 am from Tuesdays to Saturdays.

Empress Place Museum The Empress Place building has been recently restored and turned into a repository of Chinese culture. It is part of the government's drive to make Singaporeans more aware of their Chinese heritage, and features exhibitions, regularly rotated, from the People's Republic of China focusing on various Chinese dynasties. The building itself, built in 1865, is a fine example of colonial architecture, and you can wander around and explore the vaults.

Yuan Dynasty Vase

Top: Raffles Hotel, Singapore (PS)
Bottom: Chinatown Renovations, Singapore (TW)

Top: Pottery Stalls near Melaka, Malaysia (HF)
Left: Singapore Street Calligrapher (PS)
Right: Shopfront in Kuching, Sarawak (GC)

There are shops on the ground floor and other small exhibitions are held here. Empress Place is open daily from 9.30 am to 9.30 pm, and entry is S$6 for adults and S$3 for children when a major exhibition is showing.

Changi Prison Museum Changi is still used as a prison but within the main gate is a museum and a replica of the prison chapel used by Allied prisoners of war during their horrendous internment at the hands of the Japanese during WW II. Among the displays are a number of sometimes shocking photographs taken secretly by Australian POW George Aspinal. Popular with relatives who lost love ones in Changi, a visit can be a moving experience. Changi Prison Museum is open Monday to Friday from 8.30 am to 12.30 pm and from 2 to 4.45 pm. It is also open on Saturday mornings.

Changi Prison can be reached by bus Nos 1 and 2 from Victoria St, near Bencoolen St and Raffles City.

Peranakan Place Museum Amongst the glass and chrome of modern Orchard Rd is Peranakan Place, a complex of old Nonya-Baba shop-houses on the corner of Orchard and Emerald Hill roads.

Peranakan culture is that of the Straits-born Chinese who spoke a Malay dialect and developed their own customs which were a hybrid of Chinese and Malay. 'Nonya' is the word for an adult Peranakan woman, 'Baba' her male counterpart. There is a restaurant, a small museum and a coffee shop which exhibit Peranakan culture. Due to its location on Orchard Rd, it tends to be a bit touristy, but if traditional Straits Chinese culture interests you, it shouldn't be missed. Tours of the museum go on demand and cost S$4 for adults and S$2 for children.

Peranakan Place is just north of the Somerset MRT station.

Singapore Science Centre On Science Centre Rd, off Jurong Town Hall Rd, the Science Centre is great fun. It attempts to make science come alive by providing

countless opportunities to try things out for yourself. There are handles to crank, buttons to push, levers to pull, microscopes to look through and films to watch. The centre is open from 10 am to 6 pm Tuesday to Sunday and admission is S$2 (children 50c).

One of the main attractions is the three-dimensional Omni-theatre with full-blown whizz-bang movies covering topics from space flights to journeys inside the atom. Movies are screened every day except Monday from 3 to 8 pm with extra screenings on weekends at noon and 2 pm. The cost is S$6 for adults and S$4 for children. There is also a planetarium at the centre.

The easiest way to get there is to take the MRT to Jurong East station and then walk half a km west or take bus No 335 from the station. Otherwise, take a bus to Jurong East bus interchange and then take bus No 335, or, take a bus to Jurong bus interchange and then take bus Nos 157 or 178 to the centre.

Parks, Gardens & Wildlife
Singapore has been dubbed the Garden City and with good reason – it's green, lush and parks and gardens are scattered everywhere. In part, this fertility is a factor of the climate; you only have to stick a twig in the ground for it to become a tree in weeks! The government has backed up this natural advantage with a concentrated programme that has even turned the dividing strip on highways into flourishing gardens – you notice it even as you drive into Singapore from the Causeway.

The Chinese predilection for wildlife extends beyond eating it, and there are a number of wildlife parks and gardens. Singapore's Zoological Gardens are the best in Asia and the equal of most in the world.

Botanic Gardens Singapore's 127-year-old Botanic Gardens are on the corner of Cluny and Holland roads, not far from Tanglin Rd and the tourist office. They are a popular and peaceful retreat for Singaporeans.

The Botanic Gardens also house the herbarium where much work has been done on breeding the orchids for which Singapore is famous. The orchid enclosure contains over 2500 examples of orchids representing 250 species and hybrids in all. In an earlier era, the gardens pioneered the development of Brazilian rubber plants that were to spread all over South-East Asia.

The 47-hectare gardens are open from 5 am to 11 pm on weekdays and until midnight on weekends; admission is free. Early in the morning, you'll see hundreds of Singaporeans jogging there.

The gardens can be reached on bus Nos 7, 14 or 174, which run along Stamford Rd and Orchard Rd. Bus No 106, which runs along Bencoolen St and Orchard Rd, also goes to the zoo.

Tiger Balm Gardens About 10 km west from the city centre on Pasir Panjang Rd, the Tiger Balm Gardens are a magnificent tribute to bad taste. An exotic collection of concrete and plaster figures cover the hillside park. Also known as Haw Par Villa, it's a delight to children of all ages. It includes a gaudy grotesquerie of statues illustrating the pleasures and punishments of this life and the next, scenes from Chinese legends, and a whole series of 'international displays'.

The gardens are financed by the fortune the Aw brothers made from their miracle cure-all Tiger Balm, and the odd bottle of Tiger Oil duly makes its appearance in some displays. Recent major renovations have turned the gardens into a bit of a fun park (a couple of rides and theatre-style performances); there are far fewer of the quirky figures and scenes which made it so much fun. At S$16 for admission, the gardens are not good value.

The gardens are open from 8 am to 6 pm

daily. To get there, take bus No 97 from Bencoolen St and bus No 143 from Orchard Rd.

Chinese & Japanese Gardens Off Yuan Ching Rd at Jurong Park, the adjoining Chinese and Japanese gardens each cover 13.5 hectares. The Japanese gardens, known as Seiwaen, are calm and reflective while the Chinese gardens (Yu Hwa Yuan), which occupy an island by the Jurong Lake, are exuberant and colourful with attractions like the 'Cloud-Piercing Pagoda' and the 'White Rainbow Bridge'. The Chinese and Japanese gardens are linked by a 65-metre bridge.

The gardens are open from 9 am to 7 pm Monday to Saturday and from 8.30 am to 7 pm on Sundays and holidays. Admission to the gardens is S$2.50 for adults and S$1.20 for children.

The Chinese Garden MRT station is right by Jurong Lake. For most of the journey, the MRT runs above ground and travels through the suburbs and housing estates that are the reality of modern Singapore.

Jurong Bird Park The bird park is on Jalan Ahmad Ibrahim. This 20-hectare park has over 3000 birds and includes a two-hectare walk-in aviary with an artificial waterfall at one end. This aviary is the largest in the world. Exhibits include everything from cassowaries, birds of paradise, eagles and cockatoos to parrots, macaws and even penguins in air-conditioned comfort. The nocturnal house includes owls, kiwis and night herons.

You can walk around the park or take the tram service that shuttles around the park dropping off people and picking them up. The park is open daily from 9 am to 6 pm. It's suggested that you visit the park early in the morning or late in the afternoon since the birds tend to be less active during the heat of the day.

There are also a number of special shows held throughout the day, including 'King of the Skies' at 10 am and 4 pm which feature birds of prey and includes a condor. Admission to the park is S$5 for adults and

S$2.50 for children, and the tram service costs an additional S$1.

You can get there by taxi or by any of the many buses that run to the Jurong bus interchange from where bus Nos 250, 252 and 253 will take you to the bird park. You can climb up Jurong Hill, beside the park, from where there is a good view over Jurong.

Sunday Morning Bird Singing One of the nicest things to do on a Sunday morning in Singapore is to go and hear the birds sing. The Chinese love caged birds as their beautifully ornate bird cages indicate. The birds – thrushes, merboks, sharmas and mata putehs – are treasured for their singing ability. To ensure the quality of their song, the doting owner will feed his bird a carefully prepared diet and once a week crowds of bird fanciers get together for a bird song session.

The bird cages are hung up on wires strung between trees or under verandahs. They're not mixed indiscriminately – sharmas sing with sharmas, merboks with merboks – and each type of bird has its own design of cage. Tall pointy ones for tall pointy birds, short and squat ones for short squat birds.

Having assembled the birds, the proud owners then congregate around tables, sip coffee and listen to their birds go through their paces. It's a delightful scene both musically and visually.

The main bird-concert venue is on Sunday mornings from around 8 to 11 am at the junction of Tiong Bahru and Seng Poh roads, only a few hundred metres from the Havelock Rd hotel enclave.

To get there take the MRT to Tiong Bahru station, then walk east half a km. By bus, take No 123 from Orchard Rd, No 103 from Bencoolen St or Nos 33, 41, 62, 90, 103 from Raffles City to Tiong Bahru Rd, then walk.

Zoological Gardens Located at 80 Mandai Lake Rd in the north of the island, Singapore's zoo has over 1600 animals on display in natural conditions. Wherever possible, moats replace bars and the zoo is spread out over 90 hectares of lush greenery. Exhibits of particular interest include the orang-utan colony (the largest zoo colony in the world) and the tiny mouse deer, the smallest hoofed animal in the world.

There is a breakfast programme at 9 am and high tea at 3 pm, where you are joined by one of the orang-utans! There is also a children's zoo and an elephant work performance. At most times of the day, you have a good chance of seeing one of the animal performances or one of the practice sessions in the zoo's outdoor theatre.

The Komodo dragons are another popular attraction and you can see their feeding frenzy on Sunday afternoons, though in fact they are not all that ferocious and need plenty more good feeds to reach full size.

The zoo is open daily from 8.30 am to 6 pm and admission is S$5 for adults and S$2 for kids. There is a zoo tram which runs from the main gate and costs S$1.50 for adults and S$1 for children.

To get to the zoo, take bus No 171 which runs along Stamford Rd and Orchard Rd. Several major hotels also have Zoo Express shuttle buses which go to the zoo and the Mandai Orchid Gardens for S$20 (adults) and S$14 (children) including entry – call 235 3111 for information. The Road Runner (tel 339 7738) also operates a return service to the zoo for S$10 (adults) and S$6 (children).

Mandai Orchid Gardens Singapore has a major business in cultivating orchids and the Mandai Orchid Gardens, beside the zoo on Mandai Lake Rd, is the best place to see them – four hectares of solid orchids! The gardens are open daily from 9 am to 6 pm and admission is S$1 for adults, 50c for children.

Crocodile Parks Crocodiles are definitely a boom industry in Singapore; there are three crocodile parks on the island.

Jurong Crocodile Paradise is next to the Jurong Bird Park and has the largest selection of these nasties. It is open Monday to Sunday from 9 am to 6 pm and costs S$4.40 for adults and S$2.50 for children. Get there from Orchard Rd and Bencoolen St by taking bus No 198 to Jurong bus interchange then bus Nos 250, 251 or 253.

The **Singapore Crocodilarium** is at 730 East Coast Parkway and puts on croc wrestling performances. It's open daily from 9 am to 5.30 pm and admission is S$2 for adults and $1 for children. The easiest way to get there from Orchard Rd and Bencoolen St is to take bus No 14 to the Katong shopping centre; it is then a 25-minute walk to the crocodilarium.

The **Singapore Crocodile Farm** on Upper Serangoon Rd takes the more commercial approach to crocodiles and turns them into handbags and other accessories. Check your government's customs regulations before you buy as some countries ban the import of crocodile skin products. Take bus Nos 81, 83, 97, 111 or 118A from Serangoon Rd.

The Singapore Zoo also has a good croc section, and a few restaurants, such as the open-air restaurants on Cuppage Rd (near Orchard Rd), even serve crocodile.

Van Kleef Aquarium On River Valley Rd in Fort Canning Park, the Van Kleef Aquarium has 71 tanks displaying nearly 5000 fish and other creatures including crocodiles and turtles. The aquarium is open daily from 10 am to 6 pm, and admission is S$1 for adults and 50c for children.

Other Parks Despite Singapore's dense population, there are many small parks and gardens, and every traffic island or highway divide is turned into a green plantation. **Fort Canning Park** off Clemenceau Ave provides 40 hectares of greenery right in the city – the National Theatre and the Van Kleef Aquarium are both here. Off Kampong Bahru Rd, the 116-metre-high **Mt Faber** provides fine views over the harbour and the city. To get there, take the cable car up from the World Trade Centre, it's conveniently visited in conjunction with a trip to Sentosa Island.

Bukit Timah Nature Reserve on the Upper Bukit Timah Rd boasts the highest point in Singapore, 162-metre Bukit Timah. **MacRitchie Reservoir** provides good walking tracks around the reservoir and is popular with joggers. Close to the city centre, there's **Elizabeth Walk**, across from the Padang, and the small **Merlion Park** at the mouth of Singapore River. There the merlion, symbol of Singapore, spouts a fountain of water out into the river.

The **East Coast Park**, east of the city centre toward the airport, is built on reclaimed land and has swimming, windsurfer and bike hire, a food centre and the Singapore Crocodilarium.

Other Attractions

House of Tan Yeok Nee On the corner of Clemenceau Ave and Penang Rd, near Orchard Rd, the House of Tan Yeok Nee is now the headquarters of the Salvation Army, but in 1885 it was built as the townhouse of a prosperous merchant in a style then common in the south of China.

It is open Monday to Friday from 8.30 am to 4.30 pm and Sunday from 9.30 am to 6 pm.

New Ming Village This pottery workshop at 32 Pandan Rd produces reproduction porcelain from the Ming and Qing dynasties. You can see the craftspeople create and, of course, buy their works. It is open every day from 9 am to 5 pm.

To get there, take a bus to Jurong bus interchange and then bus No 245 to Pandan Rd.

Singapore Mint Coin Gallery This gallery, on Jalan Boon Lay just east of Boon Lay MRT station, shows the minting process and exhibits coins and medals from Singapore and around the world. It is open Monday to Friday from 9.30 am to 4.30 pm and there is a shop.

War Memorials Near the Causeway off Woodlands Rd, the **Kranji War Memorial** includes the graves of thousands of Allied troops who died in the region during WW II. The walls are inscribed with the names of those who died and a register is available for inspection.

The **Singapore War Memorial** on Beach Rd near Raffles City is dedicated to the civilians of Singapore who died during the Japanese occupation. The Bukit Batok Memorial is now only a plaque to recognise the site of a Japanese memorial.

These sites, as well as Changi Prison Museum, can all be visited on a tour (see the Organised Tours & Cruises section later in this chapter).

Art Galleries There are a number of art galleries and displays apart from the major National Museum Art Gallery. On Clemenceau Ave, the National Theatre also has a gallery with paintings and ceramics. Exhibitions are listed in the newspapers. Some of the better known galleries featuring local artists and arts from South-East Asia include: Art Base, Art Focus, Clifford Gallery and Collector's Gallery.

Islands, Beaches & Water Sports
There are a number of islands around Singapore. The best known is Sentosa, meaning 'tranquillity' in Malay, which has been developed into a popular resort. Other islands include Kusu and St John's, the Sisters' Islands (south of Singapore), and islands such as Pulau Bukum, which are used as refineries and for other commercial purposes. South of Singapore's southern islands are many more islands – the scattered Indonesian islands of the Riau Archipelago.

There are other islands to the north and east between Singapore and Malaysia. There you will also find the *kelongs*, long arrow shaped fences erected to trap fish. The fish swim down the 'shaft' of the arrow into the 'arrowhead' from where they cannot find their way out. You can clearly see a number of these kelongs if your flight into Singapore approaches Changi Airport from the north. They're another disappearing sight since the Singapore government doesn't want any of these untidy things in the water. Permits for kelongs are not being renewed once they expire.

You don't have to leave the island of Singapore to find beaches and indulge in water sports. Although the construction of Changi Airport destroyed one of Singapore's favourite stretches of beach, there is still the huge East Coast Lagoon on the East Coast Parkway, not to mention the CN West Leisure Park at Jurong. Scuba diving enthusiasts will find coral reefs at Sisters' Islands and Pulau Semakan, while if you want to water ski, head to Punggol Point on the north coast.

Sentosa Island Sentosa Island, just off the south coast of Singapore, is a fun park with a whole host of activities and displays. It is directed mostly towards families – it's a good place to take the kids and has a few attractions to keep adults amused. There are sporting facilities here and you can spend a day at the beach, but as a tropical island it doesn't compare with the islands of Malaysia or the Riau Archipelago.

Sentosa is a big hit with Singaporeans, particularly on weekends when it can get very crowded. As with many Singapore attractions, Sentosa is up for refurbishment and new facilities will include a huge aquarium and extended hotel facilities.

Sentosa's attractions include the Surrender Chamber, with wax-work figures recreating the formal surrender by the Japanese forces in 1945, and the adjoining Pioneers of Singapore exhibit. The Maritime Museum has exhibits recording the history of Singapore and in the Coralarium there is, not surprisingly, a display of live corals.

At the Butterfly Park, you can walk among the butterflies, and there are over 4000 mounted specimens. Other attractions include the Mystery Maze Centre and the Rare Stone Museum. All of these charge entry fees and it can become quite expensive if you (or more likely the children) want to see the lot. Free attractions include the Musical Fountain and the nature walk.

Once used as a military base, the gun emplacements and underground tunnels of Sentosa's Fort Siloso, which date from the late 19th century, can be explored. The guns were all pointing in the wrong direction when the Japanese invaded in WW II and the island was then used by the victorious Japanese as a prisoner of war camp.

Whilst at Fort Siloso, you may bump into Sentosa's most unusual attraction, political prisoner Chia Thye Poh. Chia, arrested in 1966 under the Internal Security Act, served 23 years in jail before being banished to the Sentosa fun park. Branded a communist, Chia was a parliamentary member of the opposition Barisan Sosialis party before the PAP crackdown. Chia has never been tried and is something of an embarrassment to the government, which is still waiting for Chia to make a confession before it will release him. Chia refuses to confess to a crime he says he has never committed and serves out his bizarre sentence amongst the holiday delights of Sentosa Island.

There is a wide variety of sporting facilities on Sentosa, including an 18-hole golf course, a swimming lagoon, a canoeing centre, a roller-skating centre and grass ski slopes. Windsurfers, pedal boats and aquabikes can be hired.

The Rasa Sentosa Food Centre has a good selection of hawkers' food, and there is a night market from 6 pm to 10 pm, Friday to Sunday.

You can get around Sentosa by bicycle – rent a bike from the hire kiosk by the ferry terminal. The free bus service runs around the island roads with departures every 10 minutes, or you can take the five-stop monorail loop service.

Sentosa is open daily from 7.30 am until around 11 pm, or midnight from Friday to Sunday and on public holidays. Many of the attractions close at 7 pm but cultural shows, plays and discos are sometimes held in the evenings – check with the tourist office or ring the Sentosa Information Office (tel 270 7888).

Admission to Sentosa is S$3.50 for adults and S$2 for children for a normal ticket which covers the return ferry and transport on the monorail and buses. Most of the attractions cost extra, ranging from S$1 for Fort Siloso to S$3 for the Pioneers of Singapore and Surrender Chamber wax works. A composite ticket, which includes entry to the Pioneers of Singapore, Surrender Chamber, Fort Siloso and Coralarium, costs S$7 for adults and S$3.50 for children. After 5 pm, a normal ticket costs S$3 for adults and S$2 for children.

To get to Sentosa, take a bus or taxi to the World Trade Centre. From Orchard Rd or Havelock Rd take bus No 143; from the Bencoolen St area take bus Nos 97, 125, 146, 163 or 166. Ferries leave Jardine steps at the World Trade Centre every 15 minutes until around 11 pm.

The other alternative is to take the cable car. It leaves from the top of Mt Faber from 10 am to 7 pm, or you can board it next to the World Trade Centre. The return fare is S$6 for adults and S$3 for children, and you can buy tickets for separate stages. The cable-car ride, with its spectacular views, is the best part of a visit to Sentosa, so take it at least one way.

Accommodation is available on Sentosa at the camping site. Two luxury hotels are being built and the first is expected to open in late 1991.

St John's & Kusu Islands Although Sentosa is Singapore's best known island, there are two others which are also popular with locals as a city escape. On weekends, they can become rather crowded but during the week you'll find St John's and Kusu fairly quiet and good places for a peaceful swim. Both islands have changing rooms, toilet facilities, grassy picnic areas and swimming areas.

St John's Island is much bigger than Kusu, which you can walk around in 10 minutes. Kusu has a Chinese temple and a Malay shrine.

To get to these islands, take a ferry from the World Trade Centre (WTC). It costs S$5 for the round trip and takes 30 minutes to reach Kusu and then another 30 minutes to St John's. On weekdays, it is only feasible to visit one island as there are only two boats per day and the last boat from St John's leaves at 2.45 pm. There are many more departures on weekends:

Mondays to Saturdays

WTC	Kusu	St John's
10.00 am	10.45 am	11.15 am
1.30 pm	2.15 pm	2.45 pm

Sundays & Public Holidays

WTC	Kusu	St John's
9.00 am	10.00 am	10.20 am
10.00 am	11.00 am	11.20 am
11.20 am	12.20 pm	12.40 pm
12.20 pm	1.20 pm	1.40 pm
1.40 pm	2.40 pm	3.00 pm
2.40 pm	3.40 pm	4.00 pm
4.00 pm	5.00 pm	5.20 pm
5.00 pm	6.00 pm	6.20 pm
7.20 pm	8.00 pm	8.20 pm

Other Southern Islands Many of the islands on Singapore's southern shore accommodate the refineries that provide much of Singapore's export income. Others, such as Salu, Senang, Rawai and Sudong are live firing ranges. However, there are a few off-the-beaten-track islands where you can find a quiet beach.

Pulau Seking is one of the few places where you can still see a traditional Malay village. The kampong here remains intact, and the stilt houses are built over the sea. Many of the villagers work at nearby Pulau Bukum where the Shell refinery is located.

Pulau Hantu is one of Singapore's most popular diving spots with coral reefs nearby. The Sisters' Islands, a popular place for swimming, is also popular with divers. Other islands that can be visited include Lazarus Island (Pulau Sakijang Pelepah), Buran Darat, Terumbu Retan Laut and Pulau Renggit.

To reach these islands, you must rent a motorised 'bumboat' (sampan) from Clifford Pier or Jardine Steps at the World Trade Centre. Expect to pay at least S$25 per hour for a minimum of four hours, or S$200 per day. The boats will take six to 12 people. You can ask individual boat owners or contact the Singapore Motor Launch Owners' Association on the 2nd floor at Clifford Pier, just east of the Raffles Place MRT station.

Northern Islands To get to the northern islands like Pulau Seletar, go to Punggol Boatel at Punggol Point or to Sembawang. The easiest northern islands to visit are Pulau Ubin and Pulau Tekong to the north-east; both can be visited from Changi Village.

Pulau Ubin From Changi Village, you can wander down to the ferry jetty and wait for a boat to take you across to Pulau Ubin. You can tell that this is a different side of Singapore as you wait for the ferry to fill up – they go when full and there is no fixed schedule. Pulau Ubin has quiet beaches and some popular seafood restaurants. There is also accommodation for budget travellers – see the Places to Stay – bottom end section. The ferry to Pulau Ubin costs S$1 (S$1.20 after 7 pm).

Pulau Tekong Off the eastern coast of Singapore, Pulau Tekong, Singapore's largest island, tends to be forgotten because it is often cut off the edge of Singapore maps (including the one in this book). To get there, take a ferry from Changi Point to the delightfully old-fashioned village of Kampung Salabin. There's great seafood at a dilapidated waterfront restaurant on stilts close to the dock.

The best way to get around the island is on a bicycle brought with you. There are no private cars here, just a few ancient and run-down unofficial taxis. See it while you can as there are plans to develop the island and build port facilities. Ferries depart from Changi Point for Pulau Tekong at 6.30 am and then every hour between 9 am and 7 pm from Monday to Saturday. The ferries run approximately every two hours on Sundays. The cost is S$1.

Organised Tours & Cruises

A wide variety of tours are available in Singapore. They can be booked at the desks of the big hotels, or the Singapore Tourist Promotion Board (tel 339 6622) can put you in touch with tour operators. Any of Singapore's travel agents can also book tours for you.

They include morning or afternoon tours around the city or to Jurong Bird Park, the east coast or the various parks and gardens in Singapore. These tours vary in price from around S$20 to S$40. To Jurong Bird Park is S$25, a 3½-hour city tour is S$21 and to Sentosa for a day is S$34. Nightly tours of Chinatown or Little India by bicycle trishaw cost S$35; the price includes a preliminary gin sling.

There are a number of historical tours, mostly tracing the settlement by Sir Stamford Raffles, as well as WW II tours on Wednesdays and Sundays from S$30 to S$40. Walking tours of Little India and Chinatown are available on Tuesdays, Thursdays and Saturdays for S$28.

Other tours include: Singapore by Night, Contrasting Cultures, Treasures in Singapore, Singapore Science Centre and the Horse Racing Tour. A new and different tour is a visit to an HDB (Housing & Development Board) housing estate to see how the majority of Singaporeans live.

Longer tours include a five-day Singapore Culinary Heritage Tour and the Singapore Golf Tour.

Licensed guides are available through the Registered Tourist Guides Association (tel 338 3441).

River Cruises One of the best ways to get a feel for central Singapore and its history is to take a river cruise. Lian Hup Choon Marine (tel 336 6119) operate a half-hour river tour for S$6 per adult and S$3 per child. It leaves from the Parliament House landing steps, not far from Empress Place. You can buy tickets at the booth there, and tours leave on the hour from 9 am to 7 pm. The tour goes upriver to the old godowns at Clarke Quay and then back down to the harbour.

Eastwind Organisation (tel 533 3432) operates a more leisurely one-hour cruise that stops at points of interest so you can wander around. It leaves Clifford Pier, near Raffles Place MRT station, every two hours between 10 am and 6 pm but it is subject to tide conditions. You can also catch it at the Clarke Quay landing site in front of the New Otani Hotel. The cost is S$15 for adults and S$9 for children.

Harbour Cruises A whole host of operators have harbour cruises departing from Clifford Pier. There is no shortage of touts trying to sell you tickets, or you can buy them at the Clifford Pier booking offices. Two companies offer 'tongkang' (Chinese junk) cruises and three main companies offer regular cruises as well as a number of lunch and dinner cruises. Most of them do the rounds of the harbour and visit the southern islands.

Eastwind Organisation (tel 533 3432) has two-hour junk tours at 10.30 am, 3 and 4 pm that cost S$20 for adults and S$10 for children. Water Tours (tel 533 9811) operates junk tours at the same times for the same price, as well as a dinner tour.

Island Cruises (tel 221 8333) has trips at 9.15 am and 4 pm costing S$23 for adults and S$15 for children. Raffles Cruises (tel 737 8778) leave Clifford Pier at 10 am and 2.30 pm, and cost S$30 for adults and S$15 for children. J&N Cruise (tel 223 8217) has a 1½-hour discovery cruise at 3 pm costing S$25 for adults and S$15 for children. All three companies also operate lunch, dinner and/or evening cruises.

It is also possible to charter boats – the Singapore Tourist Promotion Board (tel 339 6622) can put you in touch with charter-boat operators.

PLACES TO STAY

Singapore has a wide variety of accommodation in all price categories – you can get a dormitory bed in a 'crash pad' for S$6, a room in a cheap Chinese hotel for around S$25, pay over S$250 for a room in an 'international standard' hotel, or over S$1000 for some super-deluxe suites.

Hotels can be categorised into three groups. 'Top end' hotels are priced from around S$140 for a double. The main centre for these large hotels is along Orchard Rd. At the other end of the scale, most 'bottom end' hotels cost under S$50, and you can still find a room for under S$30. These cheaper places can mainly be found to the east of Bras Basah Rd, particularly along Beach Rd, Middle Rd and Bencoolen St.

'Mid-range' hotels cover the ever-shrinking middle ground – some of them are better cheap Chinese hotels but most of them are smaller, relatively newer air-con hotels. These hotels tend to be scattered throughout Singapore.

Over the last couple of years, Singapore's accommodation surplus has changed into an accommodation squeeze, and as a result prices have sky-rocketed. While the number of visitors has steadily increased by around 15% per year, the number of hotel rooms available has dropped due to the many top-end hotels undergoing renovation. While rising prices have mostly affected the top-end hotels, increases have also filtered down to the mid-range and bottom-end hotels.

In the major hotels, a 3% government tax and 10% service charge is added to your bill. The hotels stipulate that you should not tip. The 3% government tax also applies to the cheaper hotels but this is usually added to the quoted price.

For reservations, you can call Hotel Reservations Pty Ltd (tel 542 6955) which coordinates bookings for most middle and top-end hotels. They operate a stall at Changi Airport and keep an up-to-the-minute list of available rooms. You don't pay extra for the service, and you can sometimes get a better deal than the walk-in rates.

Sometimes, it can be difficult to find a hotel room; Chinese New Year is a particularly bad time of year when some places are also prone to sudden price increases.

Places to Stay – bottom end

The budget accommodation choice is between the cheap Chinese hotels and the 'crash pads' which are mainly concentrated in the area around Bencoolen St bounded by Bras Basah, Rochor, Beach and Selegie roads. There are other budget possibilities further north around Jalan Besar and in Chinatown.

Budget accommodation around Singapore can roughly be broken up into four areas – the Bencoolen St area, the Beach Rd area, the Jalan Besar area and Chinatown.

Bencoolen St has traditionally been the budget accommodation centre, and at almost any time of the night or day you can see travellers with backpacks seeking out a cheap hotel or crash pad. Bencoolen St itself is nothing special but it's within walking distance of the city centre, Orchard Rd and Little India. Nearby streets with cheap accommodation include Prinsep St, Middle Rd, Victoria St, and Selegie Rd, further towards Little India.

From Changi Airport, public bus No 390 will drop you on Stamford Rd. Get off near the National Museum, cross Stamford Rd and walk north through the small park to Bras Basah Rd and Bencoolen St. From the city centre and the railway station, bus Nos 10, 97, 100, 125 and 850 will drop you in this area. Bus Nos 100 and 125 will also drop you at Selegie Rd, and the nearest MRT station is Dhoby Ghaut, about 10 minutes' walk from Bencoolen St. From the Lavender St bus station, most buses on Jalan Besar go down Bencoolen St.

Beach Rd, a few blocks from Bencoolen St towards the (ever-receding) waterfront, is another centre for cheap hotels. If you aspire to the Raffles but can't afford the prices, at least you can stay nearby! Somehow, the several blocks north-east along Beach Rd from the Raffles have managed to stay a little enclave of old Singapore, unaffected by all the demolition around them. From the airport, bus No 390 can drop you near the towering Raffles City complex, opposite the Padang, from where it's a short walk to Beach Rd. From the railway station, bus Nos 10, 97, 100, 125 and 850 will drop you in this area. The cheap hotels around Beach Rd are about halfway between the City Hall and Bugis MRT stations.

Jalan Besar, near the Lavender St bus station, also has a number of cheap hotels. The area is close to Little India and Arab St, but otherwise it is a little inconvenient for most attractions.

Chinatown, one of the most interesting areas to stay, has a few cheap hotels, most of which are within walking distance of the railway station and the Outram Park and Tanjong Pagar MRT stations.

Crash Pads Singapore's crash pads are all mildly illegal since they're just residential flats or office space broken up into dormitories and cubicle-like rooms. But then this is Singapore and free enterprise is what counts! The trouble with them is that overcrowding tends to stretch the limited facilities, and the rooms really are small. In addition, everybody else there will be a traveller, just like yourself. On the other hand, they're good sources of information, good places to meet people and you won't find any cheaper accommodation in Singapore.

The crash pads, unlike the cheap hotels, are booming. New ones are constantly opening up, and the services they provide are improving. They offer the only really cheap accommodation in Singapore, with dormitory beds costing S$6 or S$7 and rooms starting from S$15. There is no official youth hotel in Singapore.

Crash pads do move around, usually in search of cheaper rents or under eviction notices initiated by other tenants in the building. The crash pads listed here are the more accessible and well-established ones. Others tend to come and go, so keep your eyes open, or just wander around Bencoolen St with a pack and you're sure to get plenty of offers.

Bencoolen St Area (See the Around Bencoolen St map.) At the Bras Basah Rd (south-western) end of Bencoolen St, you'll find *Peony Mansions*, the longest running crash pad. It's at 46-52 Bencoolen St, on top of a furniture store. There's no sign at all; go around the back and take the lift to the 6th floor and knock on the door at 50E.

Like all the crash pads, it's rather anonymous, and you can stay for as little as S$6 a night in simple dormitory-style accommodation that has seen better days; some private rooms are also available for around $20. There are other flats in the block, like *Latin House* (tel 339 6308) on the 3rd floor at No 46.

On the other side of Bencoolen St, between the Strand and Bencoolen hotels, is *Bencoolen House* (tel 338 1206) at No 27. The reception area is on the 7th floor. Dorm beds cost S$6 and rooms are available for S$25, ranging up to S$45 for an air-con room. It would be one of the better crash pads except for the bed bugs, which even the periodic dousings can't seem to eliminate.

At 173-175 Bencoolen St is another centre for crash pads in the newish Hong Guan Building. There are no signs here; go around the back and up the elevator by the parking lot.

The first crash pad you'll come to in this building is the *Hawaii Guest House* (tel 338 4817) on the 2nd floor. This is the biggest place here, and it has rooms on most of the floors. Dorm accommodation is S$7 and spartan rooms range from S$20 to S$30. The small *Goh's Homestay* (tel 339 6561) on the 6th floor of the Hong Guan Building is one of the best places in town. It has a relaxed atmosphere and is often run by travellers in return for free board. Dorms are S$7, or S$9 in smaller four-bed dorms, and there are a few rooms for around S$25. There is also a good eating/meeting area where you can get breakfast, snacks and drinks.

The *Why Not Homestay* (tel 338 0162, 338 6095) is one of the most popular and slickest of the crash pads. There are in fact two Why Nots – at 127 Bencoolen St next to the Sahib Restaurant, and in the Rainbow Building at 189 Selegie Rd, not far from Little India. The one in Bencoolen St has a popular bar cum travellers' meeting place downstairs. Dorm beds upstairs cost from S$8 to S$10 and there are a few rooms for S$20. Breakfast is available. The one in the Rainbow Building has more, and better, rooms from S$25 to S$40 and dorm beds from S$8 to S$10. Reception is on the 2nd floor (take the escalator) where there is also a good dining/bar area.

Just around the corner from the Why Not Homestay in Selegie Rd is the *Backpack Guest House* at 15 MacKenzie Rd. It's a friendly place and quieter than most. A bed in a large dorm costs S$5, or S$7 in a four-bed dorm. Rooms cost from S$25 to S$30.

Back towards Bras Basah Rd is another central crash pad, *Airmaster Travel Centre* (tel 338 3942) at 36B Prinsep St, a block

■ PLACES TO STAY

5	Plaza Hotel
6	Golden Landmark Hotel
8	Sim Lim Lodging House
10	South Seas Hotel
12	Backpack Guest House
14	Why Not Homestay (Rainbow Building)
17	New 7th Storey Hotel
18	Hawaii Guesthouse & Goh's Homestay
19	South-East Asia Hotel
21	Why Not Homestay (Bencoolen Street)
23	Sun Sun Hotel
24	Ah Chew Hotel
25	Das Travellers' Inn
26	Lido Hotel
27	Soon Seng Long Hotel
28	Tai Loke Hotel
32	Kian Hua Hotel
34	Shang Onn Hotel
35	Metropole Hotel
37	Allson's Hotel
38	Victoria Hotel
39	Hotel Bencoolen
40	Peony Mansions & Latin House
41	Airmaster Travel Centre & Airpower Travellers' Club
42	San Wah Hotel
43	Bencoolen House
45	Strand Hotel
44	Tiong Hoa Hotel
46	Bayview Inn
48	Carlton Hotel
50	Westin Plaza Hotel
52	YMCA
53	YWCA
54	Westin Stamford Hotel
55	New Mayfair Hotel

▼ PLACES TO EAT

3	Zam Zam Restaurant
7	Komala Vilas
15	Fatty's Chinese Restaurant
20	Sahib Restaurant
33	Swee Kee Restaurant
47	Rendezvouz Restaurant
57	Satay Club

OTHER

1	Kali Ammam Temple
2	Ban San Bus Terminal (for Johore Bahru)
4	Sultan Mosque
9	Sim Lim Tower
11	Mosque
13	Selegie Centre
16	Fu Lou Shou Complex
22	Selegie Complex
29	Peace Mansion
30	Peace Centre
31	Parklane Shopping Mall
36	Bras Basah Complex
49	Cathedral of the Good Shepherd
51	Singapore Tourist Promotions Board
56	MPH Bookshop
58	US Embassy
59	Church of St Gregory the Illuminator

north-west from Bencoolen St. Dorm beds are S$6 and rooms cost from S$20. On the 3rd floor is the *Airpower Travellers' Club* (tel 284 3700, 337 1392) with dorm beds for S$6 or S$7 air-con and rooms from S$15 to S$30. Both these places provide excellent information and are popular travel agents for cheap tickets to almost anywhere. They are of a similar, basic standard but Airpower gets the most travellers' recommendations.

Beach Rd Area The *Das Travellers' Inn* (tel 294 9740) on the 2nd floor (room 4) at 87 Beach Rd is a long-running place that has had more moves than the Israelites. A bed in a cramped dorm costs S$6, or S$8 in a seven-bed dorm. There are some private rooms for S$15.

Chinatown The only cheap place in Chinatown is the *Chinatown Guest House* (tel 220 0671), 5th floor, 325D New Bridge Rd, opposite Pearl's Centre. When it fills up, it's more reminiscent of a Calcutta slum than Chinatown, with wall-to-wall dorm beds for S$7 per person and inadequate bathroom facilities.

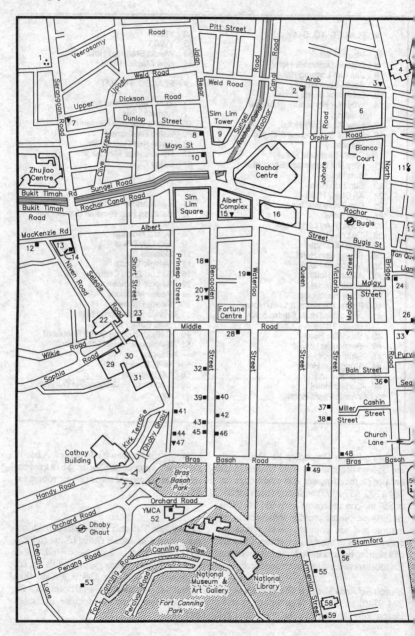

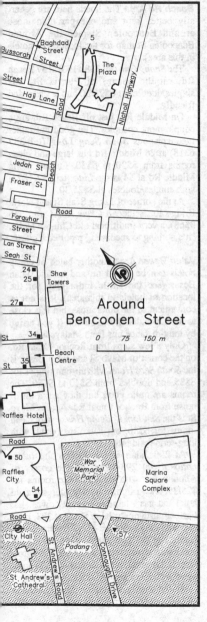

Around Bencoolen Street

0   75   150 m

Other Areas One of the most expensive, but best, crash pads is the *Sky-Scraper* (tel 737 4600) on the 3rd floor, Skyvilla, 376 Clemenceau Ave. It's right near the heart of Orchard Rd and a 10 minute walk to the Newton Circus Food Centre. The dormitories are closed-off balconies with two beds and cost S$10 per person including a cooked breakfast and free coffee and tea throughout the day. There is also a wide variety of private rooms ranging from S$25 for small partitioned rooms to S$50 for air-con rooms with bath.

The *Friendly Rest House* (tel 294 0847) is at 357A Serangoon Rd, just past Kitchener Rd, but the door is actually around the corner from Serangoon Rd on Perumal Rd. It's not very popular with travellers and inconvenient but the rooms are better than average and good value at S$14 and S$20.

Sandy's Place (tel 252 6711) on the 4th floor of the Goodwill Mansion at 355 Balestier Rd has mattresses on the floor for S$6 and beds for S$8. Rooms are available from S$20 to S$25. It's clean and the management are friendly.

If you really want to get away from it all, the *Nature Traveller House* (tel 542 6124) is on Pulau Ubin, an island off the north-east coast of Singapore; it can be reached by ferry from Changi Village. There are a number of dormitory beds from S$5 to S$7 and double rooms from S$12 to S$30 in this quiet retreat by the sea. From where the ferry docks at Pulau Ubin, it's a five-minute walk to the right past the police station.

Hotels Most of the cheap hotels have seen better days. They appear to be resigned to redevelopment and are, sadly, deteriorating each year. They are also declining in number, and you can be certain that there are no new hotels planned without air-con, bars, restaurants, high-speed lifts, swimming pools and all the other necessities of modern tourism. Rooms range from around S$25 to S$50.

These prices will get you a fairly spartan room with a bare floor, a few pieces of furniture, a sink and a fan. Toilets are usually shared but you may even get hot water in the showers. Couples should always ask for a single room – a single usually means just one double bed, whereas a double has two.

Bencoolen St Area (See the Around Bencoolen St map for the location of hotels in this area.) At 81 Bencoolen St, between Bras Basah and Middle roads, is the *Kian Hua Hotel* (tel 338 3492) with singles/doubles for S$27/35 (but they never seem to have any singles!). It's a typical old Chinese hotel but very run-down.

The *San Wah* (tel 336 2428) at 36 Bencoolen St is a little better than the cheapest Chinese hotels and many of the rooms are air-conditioned. They are certainly cashing in on the price rises and charge from S$45 to S$50 per room.

At 4 Prinsep St (one street north-west of Bencoolen St) is the *Tiong Hoa* (tel 338 4522). Rooms in this pleasantly run hotel are S$35 with fan or S$45 with air-con. It is better than most of the cheap hotels in this area and good value in comparison.

Just around the corner from Bencoolen St at 151 Middle Rd is the *Tai Loke* (tel 337 6209). Run-down rooms downstairs are S$28 but the large rooms upstairs for S$32 are better. At 260-262 Middle Rd, near the corner of Selegie Rd, is the clean *Sun Sun Hotel* (tel 338 4911). It's a reasonable place with singles/doubles at S$25/40, and there's a bar and restaurant downstairs.

The *Victoria Hotel* (tel 338 2381), in the shadow of Allson's Hotel (formerly the Tai-Pan Ramada) at 87 Victoria Street, is a faded place with air-con doubles with bath from S$40.

The *South-East Asia Hotel* (tel 338 2394) at 190 Waterloo St (which runs parallel to Bencoolen St) is a bit more costly, but it has air-con and is quiet and fairly new. Singles/doubles are S$50/55. This is the hotel for the lazy sightseer – within 200 metres of the hotel you'll find a Buddhist temple, Hindu temple, market, food stalls and shopping centre. The street is also alive with flower sellers and fortune tellers during the day.

Beach Rd Area The hotels here are generally better kept and cheaper than those around Bencoolen St (see the Around Bencoolen St map for the location of hotels in this area).

The *Shang Onn* (tel 338 4153) at 37 Beach Rd, on the corner of Purvis St, has singles/doubles at S$26/30 and is clean and friendly.

On Middle Rd, just off Beach Rd, are a couple more cheapies. The good but rather inconspicuous *Soon Seng Long* (tel 337 6318) at 26 Middle Rd has large and clean rooms from S$20 to S$30. Further along Middle Rd at 54 is the *Lido* (tel 337 1872) with singles/doubles at S$25/30.

At the corner of Liang Seah St and North Bridge Rd is the *Ah Chew Hotel* (tel 336 3563), a very traditional old Chinese Hotel. 'It's nothing to sneeze at,' reported a guest.

Jalan Besar Area Another batch of cheap hotels can be found on and around Jalan Besar (see the Little India map for the location of hotels in this area). It is not as convenient as the other areas, but it is close to the Lavender St bus station if you arrive by long-distance bus from Malaysia.

Only a few steps from Rochor Canal Rd, on the corner of Mayo St and Jalan Besar, is the *South Seas Hotel* with air-con singles for S$35 and doubles from S$40 to S$50. The rooms are quite good but they get a lot of noise from Rochor Canal Rd. Across Mayo St is the *Sim Lim Lodging House* with clean rooms for S$30, but it is usually full with long-term residents.

At 290 Jalan Besar, there's the *International* (tel 293 9238) on the corner of Allenby Rd, with single/double rooms for S$25/35. It's an architecturally interesting old hotel and has a large restaurant downstairs. Further north down Jalan Besar at 383, right opposite Bugis Square Food Centre, is the *Kam Leng* (tel 298 2289). It's a classic old hotel with wire-topped walls and old furniture. It has good, clean rooms at S$24 for a room with a fan and S$30 for air-con.

At the northern end of Jalan Besar at 407A-B, near Lavender St, is the spotlessly clean *Palace Hotel* (tel 298 3108) with singles/doubles at S$20/24. It's good for the price and only a short walk from the Lavender St bus station.

Another good, cheap hotel is the *Tai Hoe Hotel,* right near the New Park Hotel on the corner of Verdun and Kitchener roads. Rooms with fan cost S$20 and air-con rooms are S$30.

Chinatown Oddly, there are few hotels to speak of in Chinatown, nearly all are in the areas already mentioned north-east of Bras Basah Rd.

The *Great Southern* (tel 533 3223) at the corner of Eu Tong Sen and Upper Cross streets is opposite the People's Park shopping centre. It's nothing special and gets a lot of traffic noise, but it is right in the heart of Chinatown. Rooms with fan cost S$30 and air-con rooms are S$42.

Probably the best cheap hotel in all of Singapore is the *Majestic Hotel* (tel 222 3377) at 31 Bukit Pasoh Rd on the south-western edge of Chinatown. Bukit Pasoh Rd runs between New Bridge and Neil roads. It's a quiet street lined with traditional houses and buildings, but all are well maintained, in good condition and brightly painted. There's a pleasant park nearby where, in the morning and evening, people do tai chi and tai kuan do exercises. The hotel is immaculate and rooms are pleasant; many have a balcony. Singles/doubles are S$37/45 without bath, S$47/59 with bath.

Not far away on Peck Seah St are a couple of carpeted, air-con hotels with more pretensions than the Majestic but not nearly as good. The *New Asia* (tel 221 1861) is on Maxwell Rd at the corner of Peck Seah St. The rooms are pokey and overpriced at S$50/60 for singles/doubles. A couple of doors down at 10 Peck Seah St, the *Air View Hotel* (tel 225 7788) is slightly better than the New Asia and costs $36/55 for singles/doubles, or S$40/60 with TV (see the Chinatown map).

Other Areas The *New Mayfair Hotel* (tel 337 4542) is at 40-44 Armenian St near Orchard Rd, behind the National Museum. It's in one of Singapore's oldest streets and within walking distance of many attractions. Rooms with air-con and bath cost from S$45.

The *Mitre Hotel* (tel 737 3811), 145 Killeney Rd, is the cheapest hotel anywhere near Orchard Rd (half a km to the north). It's run-down but cheap with rooms for S$34 with air-con and bath.

The Ys

Singapore has a number of YMCAs and YWCAs. All of the YMCAs in Singapore take men, women and couples.

The *YMCA International House* (tel 337 3444) is at 1 Orchard Rd. It is more like a top mid-range hotel and has rooms for S$55 single, S$65 double, S$75 family and S$90 superior room, plus 10% service charge. All rooms have air-con, TV and telephone, and are very good value for what you get, so bookings are essential. A bed in the large dorm costs S$20, which isn't such good value.

The facilities at this YMCA are exceptionally good with a fitness centre, swimming pool (on the roof), squash and badminton courts, and a billiards room. There's also a restaurant which offers a cheap daily set meal and a McDonald's in the YMCA building which actually offers room service! You can phone down to have a Big Mac delivered to your room.

The *Metropolitan YMCA* (tel 737 7755) at 60 Stevens Rd has good rooms but is less conveniently located and lacks the facilities of the Orchard Rd YMCA. Singles/doubles with bathroom, TV and air-con cost S$62/72.50.

The *Metropolitan YMCA International Centre* (tel 222 4666), also called the Chinese YMCA, is at 70 Palmer Rd, near the railway station. If you want to be near Chinatown or the waterfront, this is your place. They have singles with air-con but common shower for S$25. Singles/doubles with air-con and shower are S$37.

The *YWCA Hostel* (tel 336 1212) at 6-8 Fort Canning Rd is behind the Supreme House, quite close to the Orchard Rd

YMCA. A double room with air-con and shower costs S$45. Nice dorm rooms are available for S$15; they only take women or couples. This place has been recommended by solo women travellers as a safe and secure place.

Camping

You can camp out at Sentosa Island where there are pre-erected four-person tents for S$12 per night.

There's also the good *East Coast Campsite* on East Coast Parkway, at the five-km marker.

Places to Stay – middle

The problem with Singapore is the lack of good middle-range accommodation. Like Singapore's bottom-end accommodation, there are no new places being built to fill the demand, and some have also fallen prey to redevelopment. But the main reason for the decline of hotels in this range is the number of hotels charging what can only be classed as top-end prices.

There were some good three-star hotels that charged discount rates and were very reasonably priced, but all that has changed and even some hotels scraping to garner two stars charge top-end prices. The hotels listed here are mostly second-string, relatively modern places with air-con, phone and TV, but most could do with a face-lift.

Some of the bottom-end hotels listed, like the excellent Orchard Rd YMCA, are really good quality middle-range hotels. Others like the Majestic in Chinatown or the South-East Asia Hotel in Waterloo St are comparable to the cheaper places listed here.

The *New 7th Storey Hotel* at 228-229 Rochor Rd is an up-market cheapie; Rochor Rd runs from Beach Rd to Bencoolen St, parallel to Middle Rd.

At the railway station, the *Station Hotel* has seen better days and is a little inconveniently located for most things in modern Singapore. It may be ideal, however, if you've just arrived after a long train trip and can't face heading straight into the city.

Smaller modern hotels with air-con and bathrooms include the *Hotel Bencoolen* on Bencoolen St, situated amongst the rock-bottom Chinese hotels. It's cheaply put together and no bargain. Better is the rather new *Strand Hotel* practically next door to the Hotel Bencoolen, but it's way overpriced at $110/125.

The *Metropole Hotel* is on Seah St behind the Raffles. It is a fairly new, eight-storey hotel and one of the better mid-range places.

The *Broadway Hotel* on Serangoon Rd is one of the few hotels in Little India. The rooms need a little maintenance but have TV and are comfortable. There's a good, cheap Indian restaurant downstairs and all-in-all it's good value in this price range.

You can find a few reasonably priced hotels around Orchard Rd. On Kramat Rd, one block north from Orchard Rd, the *Supreme Hotel* is central but nothing special for the price.

In the quiet residential area to the north of Orchard and Tanglin roads are some good hotels. The *Sloane Court* on Balmoral Rd is a small Tudor-style hotel in a garden setting with an English pub. A few hundred metres away in Balmoral Crescent is the *Hotel VIP*, which has a swimming pool. Also in this area, the *RELC International House* (RELC stands for Regional English Language Centre) has a hotel in its complex next to the Shangri-La Hotel on Orange Grove Rd. There is no service charge or government tax at these three hotels.

To the south of Orchard Rd, just off River Valley Rd, is the *Tanglin Court Hotel*. It is away from the action but is a small, homy hotel and reasonably priced.

Lloyd's Inn is a pleasant, small but modern hotel on Lloyd Rd, less than a 10-minute walk from Orchard Rd. The location is quiet and the rooms are competitively priced.

There are other mid-range places around Singapore, but they are not so conveniently located. These include the *Lion City Hotel* on Tanjong Katong Rd in the Geylang area; the *Duke Hotel* and *Sea View Hotel*, both off the East Coast Parkway; the *Great Eastern*, seven km to the north-east of the city on Macpherson Rd; and the *Mount Emily Hotel* on Upper Wilkie Rd, between Little India and Orchard Rd.

Most of the mid-range hotels in the listings that follow have air-conditioning. Those hotels with an asterisk (*) show net prices (service charge and tax is included in the price); add a 10% service charge and 3% government tax to the others. The rates shown are for singles/doubles, and the price ranges are for standard and deluxe rooms. Deluxe normally means a slightly larger room with a better view. When accommodation is tight, expect to pay deluxe prices.

Hotel Bencoolen (tel 336 0822), 47 Bencoolen St, singles S$85 to S$110, doubles S$90 to S$125

Broadway Hotel (tel 292 4661), 195 Serangoon Rd, singles S$80 to S$90, doubles S$90 to S$100

Duke Hotel (tel 345 3311), 42-46 Meyer Rd, singles S$90 to S$190, doubles S$120 to S$220

Great Eastern Hotel (tel 284 8244), 401 MacPherson Rd, singles S$80 to S$85, doubles S$85 to S$95

Lion City Hotel (tel 744 8111), 15 Tanjong Katong Rd, singles or doubles S$78 to S$90

Lloyd's Inn (tel 7377309), 2 Lloyd Rd (off Killiney Rd), singles S$70, doubles S$80

Metropole Hotel (tel 336 3611), 41 Seah St, singles S$70 to S$95, doubles S$80 to S$95

Mount Emily Hotel (tel 338 9151), 10a Upper Wilkie Rd, singles S$110 to S$120, doubles S$120 to S$130

New 7th Storey Hotel (tel 337 0251), 229 Rochor Rd, singles or doubles S$59 to S$75

RELC International House (tel 737 9044), 30 Orange Grove Rd, singles or doubles S$102 to S$120

Sea View Hotel (tel 345 2222), Amber Close, singles S$120 to S$170, doubles S$140 to S$190

*Sloane Court Hotel** (tel 235 3311), 17 Balmoral Rd, singles or doubles S$88

Station Hotel (tel 222 1551), Railway Station, Keppel Rd, singles S$45, doubles S$50

Strand Hotel (tel 338 1866), 25 Bencoolen St, singles S$110, doubles S$120

Supreme Hotel (tel 737 8333), 15 Kramat Rd, singles or doubles S$85

*Tanglin Court Hotel** (tel 737 3581), 2/4 Kim Yam Rd, singles S$78, doubles S$88

*Hotel VIP** (tel 235 4277), 5 Balmoral Crescent, singles or doubles S$100

Places to Stay – top end

Singapore has a huge number of 'international standard' hotels, many of them built in the mid-80s. As a result, the number of rooms available increased dramatically just as the number of visitors had levelled out! Recently, however, all of that has changed as the number of hotel rooms has levelled out while the number of visitors has increased dramatically.

Occupancy rates have been hovering around 90%, and Singapore's hoteliers have been rubbing their hands with glee. Prices are finally levelling off but it's unlikely that they will drop to the level of the late '80s, when there were real hotel bargains to be found in Singapore. Only a few new hotels are planned, and the hotel industry is not going to repeat the building glut of the '80s.

New projects and extensions to existing hotels that will open over the next couple of years include the Beaufort, Chinese Inn, Orchard, Pacific, Four Seasons, Cairnhill and Regent hotels. And, of course, the grand old Raffles, sorely missed for a couple of years, is ready to re-open after extensive renovations and extensions. These projects should add another 2000 rooms to Singapore's hotel scene but it is only a rise of about 10%, so you can expect prices to stay high.

The top-end hotels have a number of characteristics in common. For a start, a great many of them are strung along Singapore's 'hotel alley', Orchard Rd (see the Orchard Rd map). This is very much the tourist centre of Singapore with hotels, airline offices and shopping centres in profusion. Many other hotels are in roads off Orchard Rd – like Scotts Rd, Tanglin Rd, Somerset Rd or Orange Grove Rd.

Orchard Rd is easily reached by bus from Changi Airport – bus No 390 runs along Penang Rd and Orchard Blvd, parallel to Orchard Rd, and then loops back along Tanglin Rd and Orchard Rd itself. Orchard Rd is also well-serviced by the MRT, with Somerset and Orchard stations on Orchard Rd, and Newton station at the top (north-eastern) end of Scotts Rd.

As a rough demarcation line, 'top end' refers to hotels where a double costs over S$140 a night. Singapore's best hotels will generally cost over S$200 a night for a double, and many were designed to cater for expense account travellers. Naturally, all these hotels will be air-conditioned, all rooms will have bathrooms and in almost all cases there will be a swimming pool and a variety of restaurants, coffee shops and bars. Top-end hotels can be subdivided into 'super-luxury', 'other big hotels' and 'old fashioned' categories.

Super-Luxury Singapore has a number of hotels that in price and standards rise a cut above the mere international-standard hotels. They include the twin-towered *Mandarin Singapore* on Orchard Rd at the corner of Orchard Link – with 1200 rooms it is also (currently) the largest hotel in Singapore and is topped by a revolving restaurant. The *Shangri-La* is set in five hectares of garden on Orange Grove Rd, just a few minutes' walk from the north-western end of Orchard Rd. The rooms in the Garden Wing each have their own balcony overflowing with plants. The *Omni Marco Polo* at the Grange and Tanglin roads intersection is also surrounded by landscaped gardens.

The international chains are well represented in this group. The *Hyatt Regency Singapore* on Scotts Rd is currently one of the most expensive hotels in Singapore, as is the *Sheraton Towers* also on Scotts Rd. The smaller *Hilton Singapore* on Orchard Rd is another hotel edging towards the upper-notch bracket.

The massive Marina Square complex is a testament to rampant capitalism and rises from the wasteland of reclamation across the bay from the city centre. Here you'll find the *Marina Mandarin*, *Oriental* and *Pan Pacific*, with competing lobbies that owe their inspiration to Hollywood special effects movies. The Oriental's towering, curved lobby and the Marina Mandarin (complete with 21-storey Hanging Gardens of Babylon atrium) get the mega-starship awards.

Other Big Hotels The greatest concentra-

tion of luxury hotels is at the top (north-western) end of Orchard Rd and the streets that run of it, such as Tanglin, Orange Grove and Scotts roads. The Orchard and Newtown MRT stations are within walking distance of most of these hotels.

At the intersection of Tanglin, Orange Grove and Orchard roads is the *Orchard Parade Hotel*, and opposite, on the corner of Orange Grove and Orchard roads, is the *Orchard Hotel*. If you continue north-west up Orange Grove Rd to Lady Hill Rd, you'll find the *Ladyhill Hotel*, a smaller place with a particularly attractive garden setting.

On Claymore Drive, which runs parallel with Orchard Rd, the *Hotel Negara* was one of the first international hotels in Singapore, but it is now a relatively small hotel compared to the huge new hotels. It's a 'bracket creeper', jumping from the mid-range to the top end with the hotel market upturn.

Nearby is the *Regent Hotel* at 1 Cuscaden Rd. It's in the impressive-lobby category and edging into the super-luxury category. Just off Tanglin Rd on Nassim Hill, the *ANA* is of a similar standard and has gone for the old-world look. Also on Nassim Hill, the *Hotel Premier* is a small hotel that is used as a training centre for hotel and catering staff. The standards of service are therefore usually better than the small size might indicate.

On the corner of Scotts and Orchard roads, the *Dynasty Hotel* is a strange skyscraper-topped-by-a-pagoda building. Opposite the Hyatt Regency along Scotts Rd is another of the international chain hotels, the *Royal Holiday Inn*. Nearby is the *York Hotel* on Mount Elizabeth.

At the end of Scotts Rd near the Newton MRT and the Sheraton Towers is the pretentiously named *Melia at Scotts*. Nearby is the smaller *Hotel Asia* but it's not in the same league as its more expensive neighbours.

Heading back (south-east) down Orchard Rd is the luxurious *Crown Prince Hotel* at the corner of Bideford St, and the newly restored *Mandarin* at the corner of Orchard Link. Further down Orchard Rd, the *Phoenix Hotel* sits on top of the Somerset MRT station. The *Hotel Grand Central* is centrally located but not particularly grand; it's on Kramat Lane, one block north of Orchard Rd. The French-run *Meridien* is nearby; the same operators also run the *Meridien Changi* at the airport. On Penang Rd, which runs parallel to Orchard Rd, the *Cockpit Hotel* was much used by airline crew at one time – hence the name. The *Imperial Hotel* on Jalan Rumbia enjoys a hilltop location near River Valley Rd.

Over on Havelock Rd, south of Orchard Rd, is another hotel enclave, including the *Apollo*, *King's*, *Miramar*, *River View* and *Glass* hotels. It's not far from Chinatown and you can walk to Orchard Rd, but they are basically in the middle of nowhere. Because of this they tend to be slightly cheaper than the Orchard Rd hotels.

If you want to experience the atmosphere of Chinatown, the futuristic *Furama Hotel* on Eu Tong Sen St is right in the centre of things. The *Amara Hotel* on Tanjong Pagar Rd is on the edge of Chinatown not far from the railway station, and nearby is the *Harbour View Dai-Ichi*. Both are near the Tanjong Pagar MRT station.

Then there's the tallest hotel in the world, the 73-storey *Westin Stamford*, and its sister hotel the *Westin Plaza*, with countless restaurants and lounges, and two rooftop swimming pools. These hotels are on top of the Raffles City shopping centre and the City Hall MRT station.

The *Carlton* is a relatively new and very expensive hotel on Bras Basah Rd near Victoria St. On Coleman St, over towards the business centre of Singapore, is the *Peninsula Hotel* and its sister hotel the *Excelsior*, while *Allson's Hotel* is on Victoria St northeast of Bras Basah Rd. The *Bayview Inn* in Bencoolen St is a good three-star hotel with a rooftop swimming pool. It's at lower end of this range but its once bargain rates have sky-rocketted.

The *New Park Hotel* is on Kitchener Rd in Little India and has recently undergone extensive renovations. The *Golden Landmark*, on the corner of Victoria and Arab streets right next to the Bugis MRT station,

has middle-eastern inspired architecture to match its location. At the end of Arab St on Beach Rd, the *Plaza* is well-appointed but looks like an overgrown motel with a highrise plonked on top.

Other hotels include the *Cairnhill* on Cairnhill Circle; the *Equatorial* on Bukit Timah Rd, further out from Orchard Rd; the *Novotel Orchid Inn* on Dunearn Rd; the smaller *Garden Hotel* on Balmoral Rd; and the *Paramount Hotel* on Marine Parade.

Old Fashioned Singapore also has a couple of hotels with definite old Eastern flavour and style.

Close to the waterfront at the junction of Bras Basah Rd and Beach Rd, the venerable *Raffles* is as much a superb tourist attraction as it is a fine old hotel. The hotel has been through massive renovations to restore its grandeur and it is now ringed by new extensions. To the purist it ain't the old Raffles, but the restorations are faithful to the original and the extensions are in keeping with the style. When it reopens (before the end of 1991), Raffles will be all suites and very expensive.

The bars and restaurants still conjure up all the mysteries of the Orient and what other hotel can claim that a tiger was once shot in the billiards room? The Raffles is built around a beautiful central courtyard complete with fan-shaped travellers' palms – the only two-dimensional tree.

On Scotts Rd is the larger *Goodwood Park Hotel*, designed by the same architect that designed Raffles. Its architecture is more ornate and, if anything, even more delightful than the Raffles. It began life as the Teutonia Club for the German community in Singapore, but was used by the Australian army after WW II when they investigated Japanese war crimes. It is set on six hectares, and is Singapore's most expensive hotel.

Allson's Hotel (tel 336 0811), 101 Victoria St, singles S$200 to S$300, doubles S$230 to S$350

Amara Hotel Singapore (tel 733 2666), Tanjong Pagar Rd, singles S$190 to S$220, doubles S$200 to S$230

ANA (tel 732 1222), Nassim Hill, singles S$300, doubles S$330

Apollo Singapore (tel 733 2081), Havelock & Outram roads, singles S$160 to S$250, doubles S$250 to S$260

Hotel Asia (tel 737 8388), 37 Scotts Rd, 146 rooms, singles S$120 to S$150, doubles S$140 to S$170

Bayview Inn (tel 337 2882), 30 Bencoolen St, singles S$150 to S$170, doubles S$160 to S$180

Boulevard Hotel Singapore (tel 737 2911), Cuscaden Rd, singles S$225 to S$305, doubles S$305 to S$335

Cairnhill Hotel (tel 734 6622), 19 Cairnhill Circle, singles or doubles S$125 to S$145

Carlton Hotel (tel 338 8333), 76 Bras Basah Rd, singles S$220 to S$240, doubles S$240 to S$260

Cockpit Hotel (tel 737 9111), 6/7 Oxley Rise & Penang Rd, singles S$140 to S$220, doubles S$160 to S$240

Crown Prince Hotel (tel 732 1111), 270 Orchard Rd, singles S$260 to S$290, doubles S$290 to S$320

Dynasty Hotel (tel 734 9900), 320 Orchard Rd, singles S$210 to S$230, doubles S$230 to S$250

Hotel Equatorial (tel 732 0431), 429 Bukit Timah Rd, singles S$160 to S$180, doubles S$180 to S$200

Excelsior (tel 338 9644), Coleman St, singles S$170 to S$185, doubles S$185 to S$200

Furama Singapore (tel 533 2177), Eu Tong Sen St, singles S$200 to S$220, doubles S$220 to S$240

Garden Hotel (tel 235 3344), 14 Balmoral Rd, 216 rooms, singles S$140 to S$160, doubles S$170 to S$190

Glass Hotel (tel 733 0188), 317 Outram Rd, singles or doubles S$170 to S$200

Golden Landmark Hotel (tel 297 2828), 390 Victoria St, singles S$180 to S$200, doubles S$200 to S$220

Goodwood Park Hotel (tel 737 7411), 22 Scotts Rd, singles or doubles S$335 to S$400

Hotel Grand Central (tel 737 9944), Kramat Lane & Cavanagh Rd, singles S$105 to S$120, doubles S$120 to S$135

Harbour View Dai Ichi (tel 222 1133), 81 Anson Rd, singles S$180 to S$200, doubles S$200 to S$240

Hilton International Singapore (tel 737 2233), 581 Orchard Rd, singles S$280 to S$300, doubles S$300 to S$320

Holiday Inn Park View (tel 733 8333), 11 Cavenagh Rd, singles S$220 to S$240, doubles S$240 to S$270

Hyatt Regency Singapore (tel 733 1188), 10-12 Scotts Rd, singles or doubles S$330 to S$380

Imperial Hotel (tel 737 1666), 1 Jalan Rumbia, singles S$175 to S$210, doubles S$195 to S$230

King's Hotel (tel 733 0011), Havelock Rd, singles S$180 to S$220, doubles S$200 to S$240

Ladyhill Hotel (tel 737 2111), Lady Hill Rd, singles S$140 to S$180, doubles S$160 to S$200

Mandarin Singapore (tel 737 4411), 333 Orchard Rd, singles S$280 to S$300, doubles S$320 to S$340

Marina Mandarin Singapore (tel 338 3388), 6 Raffles Blvd, singles S$250 to S$300, doubles S$290 to S$340

Melia At Scotts (tel 732 5885), 45 Scotts Rd, singles S$230 to S$290, doubles S$260 to S$320

Hotel Meridien Singapore (tel 733 8855), 100 Orchard Rd, singles S$230 to S$290, doubles S$260 to S$320

Hotel Meridien Changi (tel 734 3863), 2 Netheravon Rd, singles S$185 to S$205, doubles S$205 to S$225

Hotel Miramar (tel 733 0222), 401 Havelock Rd, singles S$140 to S$160, doubles S$170 to S$190

Hotel Negara (tel 737 0811), 15 Claymore Drive, singles S$105 to S$135, doubles S$125 to S$155

Hotel New Otani Singapore (tel 339 2941), 177A River Valley Rd, singles S$260 to S$300, doubles S$280 to S$320

New Park Hotel (tel 295 0122), 181 Kitchener Rd, singles S$180 to S$230, doubles S$200 to S$270

Novotel Orchid Inn (tel 250 3322), 214 Dunearn Rd, singles S$190 to S$210, doubles S$210 to S$230

Omni Marco Polo (tel 474 7141), Tanglin Rd, singles or doubles S$300 to S$350

Orchard Hotel (tel 734 7766), 442 Orchard Rd, singles S$190 to S$240, doubles S$230 to S$260

Orchard Parade Hotel (tel 737 1133), Tanglin Rd, singles S$210 to S$240, doubles S$230 to S$260

Oriental (tel 338 0066), Marina Square, 5 Raffles Ave, singles S$295 to S$350, or doubles S$330 to S$390

Pan Pacific (tel 336 8111), Marina Square, 7 Raffles Blvd, singles or doubles S$320 to S$360

Paramount Hotel (tel 344 5577), 25 Marine Parade Rd, singles S$150 to S$165, doubles S$150 to S$180

Peninsula Hotel (tel 337 8091), Coleman St, singles S$160 to S$175, doubles S$175 to S$190

Hotel Phoenix Singapore (tel 737 8666), Orchard & Somerset roads, singles S$180 to S$220, doubles S$200 to S$240

Plaza Hotel (tel 298 0011), Beach Rd, singles S$180 to S$270, doubles S$200 to S$300

Hotel Premier (tel 733 9811), 22 Nasim Hill, singles S$120 and doubles from S$150

Raffles Hotel (tel 337 8041), 1-3 Beach Rd

Regent (tel 733 8888), 1 Cuscaden Rd, singles or doubles S$275 to S$325

River View Hotel (tel 732 9922), 382 Havelock Rd, singles S$140 to S$180, doubles S$160 to S$200

Hotel Royal (tel 253 4411), 36 Newton Rd, singles S$120 to S$130, doubles S$150 to S$160

Royal Holiday Inn (tel 737 7966), 25 Scotts Rd, singles S$260 to S$300, doubles S$300 to S$340

Shangri-La Hotel (tel 737 3644), 22 Orange Grove Rd, singles S$300 to S$425, doubles S$315 to S$455

Sheraton Towers (tel 737 6888), 39 Scotts Rd, singles or doubles S$350

Westin Plaza (tel 338 8585), 2 Stamford Rd, singles S$290 to S$320, doubles S$330 to S$360

Westin Stamford (tel 338 8585), 2 Stamford Rd, singles S$250 to S$300, doubles S$290 to S$340

The York Hotel (tel 737 0511), 21 Mount Elizabeth, singles S$230 to S$250, doubles S$255 to S$265

PLACES TO EAT

Singapore is far and away the food capital of Asia. When it comes to superb Chinese food, Hong Kong may actually be a step ahead but it's Singapore's sheer variety and low prices which make it so good. Equally important, Singapore's food is so accessible – you haven't got to search out obscure places, you don't face communication problems and you don't need a lot of money.

Alternatively, if you want to make gastronomic discoveries, there are lots of out-of-the-way little places where you'll find marvellous food that few visitors know about. The Singaporean enthusiasm for food (and economical food at that) is amply illustrated by the competitions newspapers run every so often to find the best hawker's stall in the city. To get to grips with food in Singapore, you firstly have to know what types of food are available, and then where to find them.

There are some good guides to finding the best eating places. Pick up a copy of the free *Singapore 101 Meals* booklet from the tourist office which lists 101 interesting dining-out possibilities. The recommendations are excellent and range all the way from hawkers' centres to flashy international hotel restaurants. The *Singapore Official Guide*, another free booklet, also has an excellent food section with numerous restaurant recommendations. *The Guide to Singapore Hawker Food* by James Hooi, available in most bookstores, has good descriptions of hawkers' food and lists average prices.

For descriptions of some of the culinary delights you are likely to encounter, see the Food section in the Malaysia Facts for the Visitor chapter.

Hawkers' Food

Traditionally, hawkers had mobile food stalls (pushcarts), set up their tables and stools around them and sold their food right on the streets. Real, mobile, on-the-street hawkers have now been replaced by hawkers' centres where a large number of stationary hawkers can be found under the one roof. These centres are the baseline for Singapore food, where the prices are lowest and the eating is possibly the most interesting.

Scattered amongst the hawkers are tables and stools, and you can sit and eat in any area you choose – none of them belong to a specific stall. A group of you can sit at one table and all eat from different stalls and purchase drinks from another.

One of the wonders of food-centre eating is how the various operators keep track of their plates and utensils – and how they manage to chase you up with the bill. The real joy of these food centres is the sheer variety; while you're having Chinese food, your companion can be eating a biryani and across the table somebody else can be trying the satay. As a rough guide, most one-dish meals cost from S$1.50 to S$3, the price is higher for more elaborate dishes.

There are hundreds of hawkers' centres all over Singapore, and many new shopping complexes and housing blocks set aside areas for the hawkers. There's even a pretty good food centre in the basement of Changi Airport! All centres are government licensed and subject to health department regulations, so there are no problems as all are perfectly safe and healthy.

City Centre In the business centre, *Empress Place* beside the Singapore River and *Boat Quay* directly across from it on the other bank are pleasant places to sit beside the river and have a meal. They are both very busy at lunchtime; Boat Quay closes in the evening.

On the waterfront is *Telok Ayer Market* on

Robinson Rd at the corner of Boon Tat St. The building itself is a wonderful example of intricate Victorian cast-iron architecture in the railway-station mould. It was dismantled during the building of the MRT but is now back on the original site and lovingly restored. It will reopen late 1991 and is destined to house tourist shops as well as food stalls.

North of the river on Hill St, the *Hill St Food Centre* is popular, and across the road the *Funan Centre* has a more up-market air-conditioned food-stall area on the 7th floor.

The famous *Satay Club*, by the waterfront at the foot of Stamford Rd near Raffles, is a colourful place to dine. The satay here is the best in Singapore, just make sure you specify how many sticks (30c a time) you want or they'll assume your appetite is much larger than you will. It's only open in the evening, when the waterfront is also a popular strolling area. There are Chinese food stalls in the circular building next to the Satay Club – this is a good place for steamboat.

Orchard Rd *Newton Circus Hawker Centre* is at the top (north-eastern) end of Scotts Rd, right near the Newton MRT station. It is very popular with tourists and therefore tends to be a little more expensive, but it is lively and open until the early hours of the morning. For a minor extravagance, try the huge prawns.

South-east down Orchard Rd is another popular food centre upstairs in the *Cuppage Centre*. The downstairs section is a vegetable and produce market with a wonderful selection of fruit. It is mainly a daytime centre and closes around 8 pm. The open court from the centre to Orchard Rd is very popular for an evening beer or an outdoor meal.

The *Scotts Picnic Food Court* in the Scotts Shopping Centre on Scotts Rd, just off Orchard Rd by the Hyatt Hotel, is quite a different sort of food centre. It's glossier and more restaurant- like than the general run of food centres, and the stalls around the dining area are international – as well as a variety of Chinese possibilities there is also Indian, Western and vegetarian food available. In the same vein are the food stalls downstairs in *Orchard Towers* on the corner of Orchard and Claymore roads.

Bencoolen St In the Bencoolen St area, there are a number of good food centres near Rochor Canal Rd. The *Albert Centre* on Albert Rd between Waterloo and Queen streets is an extremely good, busy and very popular centre which has all types of food at low prices. The *Albert St Complex* on the corner of Bencoolen and Albert streets now contains the famous Fatty's Chinese restaurant; *Wing Siong Fatty's Restaurant* is at No 01-33 of the complex, and a number of food stalls are around the corner. Across the street in the basement of the Sim Lim Square complex is the *Tenco Food Centre*, a relatively new and very clean establishment. One of the stalls is called *Excellent Duck*.

The Fortune Centre at the corner of Middle Rd and Bencoolen St also has a few food stalls on the 1st floor in an air-conditioned setting. The *ABC Eating House* is a cheap cafeteria-style restaurant with a number of hawkers' dishes.

On the corner of Bukit Timah and Serangoon roads at the start of Little India, the large *Zhujiao Centre* is a market with a number of food stalls upstairs. As you would expect, Indian food dominates.

Jalan Besar Jalan Besar has two food centres, one halfway down Jalan Besar on the corner of Jalan Berseh and the lively *Bugis Square Centre* at the end of Jalan Besar near Lavender St.

Chinatown There are a number of excellent food centres in the Chinatown area. The *People's Park Complex* has a good, large food centre, and the *Maxwell Food Centre* is an old-fashioned centre on the corner of South Bridge and Maxwell roads. While you wander around Chinatown you can find some of the best Chinese food stalls in town at the *Chinatown Complex* on the corner of Sago and Trengganu streets, where there is also a market. There's also a hawkers' centre alongside the *Tanjong Market*, not far from the railway station, and at the *Amoy St Food Centre*, where Amoy St meets Telok Ayer St.

Other Areas The *Rasa Singapura Food Court* is a collection of hawkers selected in a special competition to find the best stalls for each dish. It used to be on Tanglin Rd (the site is now being redeveloped) and was more up-market to cater for the Orchard Rd crowds. Most of the hawkers have moved to the Bukit Turf Club on Turf Club Rd and they have taken the name with them. During the week, it's open for lunch and dinner until 11 pm. On weekends, it's open all day until midnight but you have to pay entry to the races until 6 pm.

The *Taman Serasi Food Centre* has one of the best settings – it is next to the Botanical Gardens north-west of the city centre on Cluny Rd, just off Napier Rd.

For Malay food during the day, go to the *Geylang Serai Market* on Changi Rd in Katong. This is the predominately Malay area in Singapore, and it's worth a visit just to see the market, which is more traditional than the new complexes. To get there, take the MRT to Paya Lebar station and walk east along Sims Ave to Geylang Serai.

The Hawkers' Variety Some typical hawkers' food you may find includes carrot cake, or *chye tow kway*, (S$1.50 to S$3) – also known as radish cake, it's a vegetable and egg dish, tasting something like potato omelette, and totally unlike our Western health-food idea of carrot cake.

Indian biryanis cost from S$2 to S$4 or you can have a murtabak for around S$2. Naturally, chicken rice and *char siew*, or roast pork, will always be available in food centres (S$1.80 to S$3). All the usual Cantonese dishes like fried rice (S$1.50 to S$3), fried vegetables (S$3), beef & vegetables (S$5), and sweet & sour pork (S$3 to S$5) are available, plus other dishes like fish heads with black beans & chilli from S$3 to S$5.

There will often be Malay or Indonesian stalls with satay from 25c to 35c a stick, *mee rebus* from S$1 to S$1.20, and *gado gado* or *mee soto* at similar prices. *Won ton mee*, a substantial soup dish with shredded chicken or braised beef, costs from S$2 to S$3. You could try a *chee chong fun*, a type of stuffed noodle dish, which costs from S$1.50, depending on whether you want the noodles with prawns, mushrooms, chicken or pork. *Hokkien fried prawn mee* costs from S$1.50 to S$3, *prawn mee soup* from S$1 to S$2, *popiah* (spring rolls) $1 and *laksa* from S$1.50 to S$2. There's also a whole variety of other dishes and soups.

Or, you can even opt for Western food like sausage, egg & chips for S$3.40, burgers for S$3 or fish & chips for S$3. Drinks include beer for S$3, soft drinks from 60c, ais kacang for 80c or sugar-cane juice from 50c to 80c depending on the size. Fruit juices such as melon, papaya, pineapple, apple, orange or starfruit range from 80c to S$1.50. To finish up you might try a fruit salad for S$2 or a *pisang goreng* (fried banana) for 50c.

Chinese Food

Singapore has plenty of restaurants serving everything from a south Indian rice plate to an all-American hamburger, but naturally it's Chinese restaurants that predominate. They range from streetside hawkers' stalls to fancy five-star hotel restaurants with a whole gamut of possibilities in between.

Cantonese The *Manhill* (tel 474 6635) at 99 Pasir Panjang Rd and its companion the *Hillman* (tel 221 5073) at 159 Cantonment Rd are two traditional Cantonese restaurants with excellent food and moderate prices in straightforward surroundings. At the opposite end of the scale in size and setting are the *Peking Mayflower* (tel 737 1224) at the International Building at 360 Orchard Rd and the *Mayflower* (tel 220 3133) at the DBS Building on Shenton Way. They're both huge Hong Kong-style dim-sum specialists, but surprisingly reasonable considering all the carpeting and air-conditioning there. Dim sum starts from around S$1 per plate. The Shenton Way area has many other good Chinese eating places.

Another dim-sum place is the luxurious

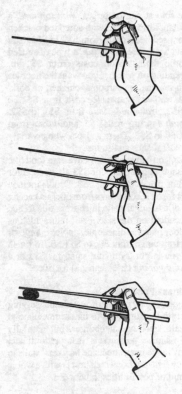

How to use Chopsticks

Shang Palace (tel 737 3644) in the Shangri-La Hotel on Orange Grove Rd. Remember that dim sum is a lunchtime or Sunday breakfast dish – in the evening these restaurants revert to other menus.

Other more expensive Cantonese restaurants include the old-fashioned *Majestic* (tel 223 5111) on Bukit Pasoh Rd near Chinatown. The *Xiang Man Lou* (tel 338 7651) has good food in a glittering, gaudy setting. It is on the 1st floor of the Bras Basah Complex on the corner of Bain St and North Bridge Rd near the Raffles Hotel. It is moderately priced and recommended.

Wing Siong Fatty's Restaurant (tel 338 1087), at 01-33 Albert Complex on Albert St near the corner of Bencoolen St, is one of the cheapest and most popular places to eat in town. Fatty's used to be further up Albert St near Serangoon Rd and has been a Singapore institution for decades.

Beijing Although Cantonese is the most readily available Chinese cuisine in Singapore, you can also find most of the regional variations. However, they tend to be more expensive than the common, everyday Cantonese restaurants.

If you've got a yen to try Peking duck, then the *Eastern Palace* (tel 337 8224) on the 5th floor of Supreme House, 9 Penang Rd, is one of the best Beijing restaurants. The *Imperial Herbal Restaurant* (tel 337 0491) in the Metropole Hotel, 41 Seah St near Raffles Hotel, has an extensive range of good Beijing-style food and you can order dishes recommended by the resident herbalist. Lu Bian (the whip) provides extra potency for men.

Szechuan Szechuan, or Sichuan, restaurants are common; this spicy food is popular with Singaporeans. Restaurants include the reasonably priced *Omei* (tel 737 2735) in the Grand Central Hotel at the cheaper end of the scale and the decidedly expensive *Golden Phoenix* (tel 732 0431) in the Hotel Equatorial at the other. *Long Jiang* (tel 732 1111) in the Crown Prince Hotel, 270 Orchard Rd, is moderately priced and recommended. The *Red Lantern* (tel 535 0577) is an up-market revolving restaurant at Clifford Pier with views across the harbour. It serves Cantonese as well as Szechuan food for around S$20 per dish. There is a reasonably priced beer garden downstairs for lunch.

The *Cherry Garden* (tel 338 0066) in the Oriental Hotel, Marina Square, is another top-quality Szechuan restaurant which also features other cuisines.

Hokkien Hokkien food is not all that popular despite the large number of Hokkiens in Singapore, but *Beng Hiang* (tel 221 6684) at Food Alley, 20 Murray St, is renowned for its Hokkien food. In fact Food Alley is a great place to try all of Singapore's various cuisines. It features around 10 mid-range restaurants representing most Chinese cuisines and Indian food.

Beng Thin Hoon Kee (tel 553 7708) is on the 5th floor of the OCBC Centre on Chulia St; it is a short walk from Raffles Place MRT station and has moderately priced Hokkien seafood. The *Prince Room Restaurant* (tel 337 7021) on the 3rd floor of the Selegie Complex, 285 Selegie Rd, has good steamboats for S$10 per person.

Teochew Teochew (also called Chiu Chao and Chao Zhou) food is a widely available cuisine. You can try it at the traditional *Chui Wah Lin* (tel 221 3305) at 49 Mosque St where a request for suggestions and prices will be readily answered. The Ellenborough St market is noted for its Teochew food stalls.

In the DBS Building on Shenton Way is the *Swatow Teochow* (tel 221 7936) – try the roast goose or shark's fin soup. There is also a branch at Centrepoint on Orchard Rd.

Hainanese Chicken rice is a common and popular dish all over town. Originally from Hainan in China, chicken rice is a dish of elegant simplicity and in Singapore they do it better than anywhere. *Swee Kee* (tel 337 0314) at 51 Middle Rd, close to the Raffles Hotel, is a long-running specialist with a very high reputation. Chicken and rice served with chilli, ginger and thick soya sauce is S$3.30. They also do steamboats; a S$20 version has a stock enriched by various Chinese herbs and Mao Tai wine.

A stone's throw from Swee Kee you'll find *Yet Con* (tel 337 6819) at 25 Purvis St which some claim is the best of all Singapore's chicken-rice places. This area north-west of Beach Rd is something of a Hainanese stronghold.

Vegetarian Chinatown has some good-value vegetarian restaurants, including the *Happy Realm* (tel 222 6141) on the 3rd floor of Pearl's Centre on Eu Tong St and the *Kingsland Vegetarian Restaurant* (tel 534

1846) on the 3rd floor of the People's Park Complex.

Near Bencoolen St, *Kwan Yim* (tel 338 2394) is another traditional and long running vegetarian restaurant. It's at 190 Waterloo St in the South-East Asia Hotel.

At 143 and 153 Kitchener Rd, between Jalan Besar and Serangoon Rd, the *Fut Sai Kai* (which translates as 'monk's world') is another spartan old coffee shop where the speciality is vegetarian cooking. Prices are not cheap but it offers a good chance to sample a slightly unusual variation of Chinese cuisine.

Seafood Singapore has another local variation on Chinese food which is worth making the effort to try. Seafood in Singapore is simply superb, whether it's prawns or abalone, fish-head curry or chilli crabs. Most of the better seafood specialists are some distance out from the city centre but the trip is worthwhile.

The UDMC Seafood Centre, at the beach on East Coast Parkway, is very popular in the evenings. It is more a collection of restaurants than a hawkers' centre but the prices are moderate for seafood. Here you will find the *Chin Wah Heng* with the usual glass tanks containing crabs, eels, prawns and fish all ready for the wok. The *Red House Seafood Restaurant* is good value and the *Bedok Sea View* is also very popular.

At 610 Bedok Rd, the *Long Beach Seafood Restaurant* (tel 344 7722), one of Singapore's best known seafood restaurants, is famous for its black pepper crabs and 'live drunken prawns' (soaked in brandy). It is casual and you can dine outside or in the air-conditioned section.

Ng Tiong Choon Sembawang Fish Pond (tel 754 1991) is a different style of restaurant built on stilts over an old fish pond. It is two km off the Mandai Rd out past the zoo in a beautiful rural setting. The seafood is excellent and expensive. Ring for details of the minibus service.

Other seafood restaurants include the *Choon Seng* (tel 288 3472) at 892 Ponggol Rd, Ponggol Point, at the north end of the

Indian Muslim food is something of a hybrid. It is the simpler south Indian version of what is basically north Indian food. Typical dishes are biryani, served with chicken or mutton curry, roti and murtabak. It can be found all over Singapore but the main centre is in North Bridge Rd opposite the Sultan Mosque. Indian Muslim food is also well represented in the hawkers' centres; you can have a superb chicken biryani from just S$2.50 to S$3.50.

For the rich north Indian curries and tandoori food, you have to go to more expensive restaurants. They can be found all around Singapore, but once again Little India has a concentrated selection.

To sample eat-with-your-fingers south Indian vegetarian food, the place to go is the Little India district off Serangoon Rd. The famous and very popular *Komala Vilas* (tel 293 6980) at 76 Serangoon Rd was established soon after the war and has an open downstairs area where you can have masala dosa (S$1.50) and other snacks. The upstairs section is air-conditioned and you can have their all-you-can-eat rice meal for S$4. Remember to wash your hands before you start, use your right hand and ask for eating utensils only if you really have to! On your way out, try an Indian sweet from the showcase at the back of the downstairs section.

Two other rice-plate specialists are *Sri Krishna Vilas* at 229 Selegie Rd and *Ananda Bhavan* at 219-221 Selegie Rd. There are several other Indian eateries on and off Serangoon Rd and a main contender in the local competition for the best south Indian food is the *Madras New Woodlands Cafe* (tel 297 1594) at 14 Upper Dickson Rd off Serangoon Rd, around the corner from Komala Vilas. A branch of the well-known Woodlands chain in India, New Woodlands serves freshly prepared vegetarian food in very clean air-conditioned rooms. The yoghurt is particularly good. Prices are about the same as at Komala Vilas.

island, or the *Jurong Seafood Restaurant* (tel 265 3525) at 35 Jurong Pier Rd on the southwest coast near the Jurong Bird Park. The trip out to Ponggol Point on bus No 82 or 83 is quite an experience in itself; you pass miles of cemeteries and then chicken and pig farms – surprisingly rural for Singapore.

Indian Food

There are three types of Indian food in Singapore: south Indian, Indian Muslim and north Indian.

South Indian food is mostly vegetarian and Little India is the main centre for it. You can get a thali, an all-you-can-eat rice plate with a mixture of vegetable curries, for less than S$5.

Race Course Rd, a block north-west from Serangoon Rd, is also a good area for curry. Try the *Banana Leaf Apolo* (tel 293 8682) at 56 Race Course Rd for superb nonvegetarian

Indian food, including Singapore's classic fish-head curry for around S$4. The very popular *Muthu's Curry Restaurant* (tel 293 7029) at 78 Race Course Rd also specialises in fish-head curry and other seafood dishes. In between these two are a couple of good north Indian restaurants with typically dark decor. The *Delhi Restaurant* (tel 296 4585) at 60 Race Course Rd has Mughlai and Kahmiri food, with curries from S$6 to S$10. Expect to pay around S$20 per person with bread, side dishes and drinks. *Nur Jehan* (tel 292 8033) at 66 Race Course Rd is slightly cheaper and also has tandoori and other north Indian food.

For cheap north Indian food in Little India, the small *Bombay Coffee House*, in the Broadway Hotel at 195 Serangoon Rd, has good curries and kormas from S$3 to S$6 and breads such as naan for S$1. The *Ranu Mahal*, 13 Upper Dickson Rd opposite the New Woodlands, also has cheap north Indian food as well as south Indian dishes.

For Indian Muslim food (chicken biryani for S$3.50, as well as murtabak and fish-head curry), there are a string of venerable establishments on North Bridge Rd, near the corner of Arab St, opposite the Sultan Mosque. Each of them has the year of founding proudly displayed on their signs out the front, and they are great places for biryani and other Indian dishes at very low prices. The *Victory* (established 1910) is at 701 North Bridge Rd, the *Zam Zam* (established 1908) is at 699 and the *Singapore* (established 1911) is at 697 North Bridge Rd. Further along is the *Jubilee* at 771 North Bridge Rd and at 791-797 the *Islamic* is very similar.

There's a small, basic Indian Muslim place called *Sahib Restaurant* at 129 Bencoolen St near Middle Rd, across from the Fortune Centre. They have very good food and specialise in fish dishes, including fish-head curry, but have chicken and vegetable items too. Meals are around S$4 and they are open 24 hours.

The *Moti Mahal Restaurant* (tel 221 4338), another up-market north Indian place, proudly proclaims it is 'one of the best Indian restaurants anywhere *(Far Eastern Economic Review)*' on the sign out the front. It doesn't quite live up to the review but the food is good and costs around S$20 per person. It's in Food Alley at 18 Murray Terrace, near the corner of Maxwell and Neil roads.

Malay & Nonya Food

You can find Malay and Nonya food in the central business and Orchard Rd districts of Singapore, and there is the occasional stall or two at some of the food centres. *Bibi's Restoran* on the 2nd floor of Peranakan Place at 180 Orchard Rd has a selection of Nonya snacks. Nearby at 36 Emerald Hill Rd is the excellent *Azizas Restaurant* (tel 235 1130), serving authentic Malay meals for around S$20 per person.

Bintang Timur (tel 235 3539) also has good Malay food and is similarly priced. It is on the 2nd floor of the Far East Plaza, 14 Scotts Rd, and there is a branch in the UIC building at 5 Shenton Way in the city centre. *Satay Anika* has satay and other dishes in sanitised surroundings on Orchard Rd. There are two restaurants – in the Scotts Picnic Food Court in the Scotts Shopping Centre and on the 1st floor of Centrepoint at 176 Orchard Rd.

Reasonably priced Nonya food can be found at the *Nonya & Baba Restaurant* (tel 734 1382), 262-264 River Valley Rd, not far from the corner of Tank Rd. There are Nonya buffets at the King's and Apollo hotels in Havelock Rd, and the Bayview Inn in Bencoolen St has a good lunchtime buffet for S$12 on Wednesdays, Saturdays and Sundays. In Holland Village, the *Baba Cafe* (tel 468 9859) at 25B Lorong Liput has good-value food in an attractive setting.

One of the best places to go for Malay and Nonya food is east of the city in the Geylang and Katong districts. Along (and just off) Joo Chiat Rd between East Coast and Geylang roads in particular are good hunting grounds for all kinds of Asian foods – Indian, Malay, Nonya, nasi padang, various kinds of Chinese, Thai and Middle Eastern. This area probably has the liveliest local night scene in the city.

There is a place on East Coast Rd just past Siglap Rd called *East Peranakan Inn* that has good Nonya and Malay food. Another branch is the *Peranakan Inn* (tel 440 6194) at 210 East Coast Rd. Slightly pricier Nonya food (S$4 to S$10 per dish) is served in an air-conditioned room at *Guan Hoe Soon* (tel 440 5650), 214 Joo Chiat Rd; it is open from 11 am to 10 pm.

Other Asian Food

If you like the fiery food of north Sumatra, there are a number of nasi padang specialists, one of the best known being *Rendezvouz* at 4-5 Bras Basah Rd, at the junction with Prinsep St. It's open lunchtimes only from 11 am to 3 pm and closed on Wednesdays. They also have a second branch at 02-19 in the Raffles City Shopping Centre on Bras Basah Rd which is open daily until 9.15 pm, but closed on Wednesdays. *Salero Bagindo* is a nasi padang chain with restaurants in the Tanglin Shopping Centre, 19 Tanglin Rd, and the Far East Plaza, 14 Scotts Rd.

There are several Thai restaurants along Joo Chiat Rd in the Katong district – *Chiangmai* at 328 Joo Chiat Rd, *Pattaya Eating House* at 402 Joo Chiat Rd, and *Haadyai Beefball Restaurant* at 467 Joo Chiat Rd. Closer to town, *Parkway Thai* (tel 737 8080) in Centrepoint, 176 Orchard Rd, has an extensive menu and is moderately priced. *Paregu* (tel 733 4211) in Orchard Plaza, 150 Orchard Rd, has excellent food and also features Vietnamese dishes.

There is no shortage of good Japanese restaurants in Singapore where the food is, of course, expensive. Try the elegant *Ginga* (tel 732 9922) in the River View Hotel, or *Nadaman* (tel 737 3644), a branch of the Japanese chain in the Shangri-La Hotel in Orange Grove Rd.

Finally, there's Taiwanese food – try the *May Garden* in Orchard Towers or the reasonably priced *Goldleaf* at 160 Orchard Rd.

Western Food

Fast Food Yes, you can get Western food in Singapore too – there's even a couple of dozen *McDonald's*. You'll find them along Orchard Rd near Scotts Rd, round the corner on Scotts Rd itself, in front of the Plaza Singapura and at the Orchard Rd YMCA. There are lots more all over town including one at People's Park and Changi Airport.

There are also *A&W Root Beer, Kentucky Fried Chicken* (nearly 40 of them), *Burger King, Dunkin' Donuts, Dennys, Pizza Hut, Baskin Robbins* and *Swensen's Ice Cream* outlets, so there's no shortage of Western fast food.

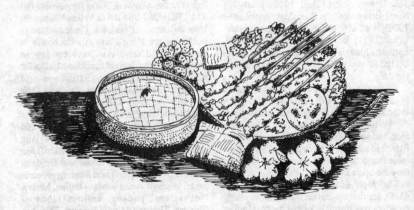

Italian If you want good Italian food in Singapore, steer clear of the chain stores run by youths suffering from corporate brainwashing and serving soggy pizza and pasta with insipid sauces.

Pete's Place (tel 733 1188) in the Hyatt Regency Singapore is the best value for good Italian food in a rustic setting with a good salad bar. *Pasta* (tel 467 0917), 23 Lorong Mambong, Holland Village, has home-made pasta and is reasonably priced. *Grand Italia* (tel 733 0188) in the Glass Hotel is more upmarket, but is also good value considering the quality and variety of the dishes. *Prego Ristorante Italiano* (tel 338 8585) in the Westin Stamford Hotel and *Ristorante Bologna* (tel 338 3388) in the Pan Pacific Hotel are the two top Italian places to eat in town.

French A number of restaurants do a pretty good job of convincing you that you're in France, even though you're almost on the equator. *Le Restaurant de France* (tel 733 8855) in the Meridien Singapore Hotel is one of the best French restaurants in Singapore and has an eight-course set meal for S$80, or take your credit card to *Maxim's de Paris* in the Regent Singapore. *L'Escargot* (tel 737 1666) in the Imperial Hotel has an executive lunch for S$18 but otherwise expect to pay around S$80 per person.

Other Cheaper Western-style restaurants can be found at places like the *Ponderosa* (tel 336 0139) in the Plaza Singapura, where you can get a steak and serve yourself from a salad bar.

For up-market Western food at bargain prices, the Singapore Hotel Association's Training & Educational Centre (tel 235 9533) at 24 Nassim Hill has two restaurants, *Bouganville* and *Rosette*. Now open to the public, the place is really a training centre for hotel dining room food preparation and presentation. They offer set, five-course meals at lunch and dinner as well as an à la carte menu in a fairly elegant setting with items such as escargot, Scottish salmon and duck

à l'orange. Lunch is S$13.20 and dinner is S$16.50.

Many other cuisines are represented in Singapore. For German food, there is the *Brauhaus Restaurant & Pub* (tel 250 3116), United Square, 101 Thomson Rd. *Movenpick* (tel 235 8700) in the Scotts Shopping Centre is a Swiss restaurant well- patronised by yuppies. The food is good but expensive.

Eurasian Settlement (tel 440 9892), 83B East Coast Rd, is a well-known Portuguese restaurant popular with expats. *El Felipes Cantina* (tel 733 3551), B1-01 Orchard Towers at the corner of Orchard and Claymore roads, is the best place for Mexican food; it has huge serves and moderate prices.

If you want music while you dine, try *Nutmegs* (tel 733 1188) at the Hyatt Regency Singapore where you can eat American nouvelle cuisine and listen to jazz. *Saxophone Bar & Grill* (tell 235 8385), 23 Cuppage Terrace just off Orchard Rd, is a pleasant place to dine alfresco and listen to the music coming from inside. The food is continental.

Breakfast

The big international hotels have their large international breakfast buffets of course (around S$18 to S$20) but there are also lots of little places for breakfast around the Bencoolen St cheap-hotel area. Most of them will rustle you up toast and jam without too much difficulty – try the coffee bar right next to Airmaster Travel on Prinsep St.

There are a number of small Indian coffee shops which do cheap Chinese and Indian breakfasts – take your pick of dosa and curry or you-tiao and hot soy milk. Roti chanai with a mild curry dip is a delicious and economical breakfast available at *Meng Tong* at 74 Bencoolen St or *Tong Hoe* at 84 Bencoolen St – two places that look ripe for development, so they may not be there long.

There are many places which do a fixed-price breakfast – continental or American. Try the *Silver Spoon Coffee House* in Supreme House on Penang Rd off Orchard Rd for a S$4.50 breakfast. Another good breakfast place is *Mr Cucumber* in the

Clifford Centre off Raffles Place – a continental breakfast is S$2.90.

McDonalds and *A&W* do fast-food breakfasts, you can have a McDonald's 'big breakfast' for S$3.50 or hotcakes and syrup for S$1.50.

Odds & Ends

Naturally, Singapore has a lot of places to eat in the obscure odds and ends category. If you want a light snack at any time of the day, there are quite a few Chinese coffee bars selling interesting cakes which go nicely with a cup of coffee or tea.

For Western-style pastries, head for the *Café d'Orient de Delifrance* at Peranakan Place on Orchard Rd – the croissants and coffee are hard to beat for breakfast. Other branches are in Shenton House, 3 Shenton Way; 02-19 Clifford Centre, 24 Raffles Place; at 02-136 Marine Centre; and in the Dynasty Hotel, 320 Orchard Rd.

The small *L E Cafe* at 264 Middle Rd, under the Sun Sun Hotel almost at Selegie Rd, is an interesting place with European and oriental cakes and pastries. It is a good place for breakfast or a snack. Or, try cakes, cookies, yoghurt and muesli in *Steeple's Deli* at 02-25 Tanglin Shopping Centre on Tanglin Rd. They also do great deli-style sandwiches from S$6 to S$8.

Long John Silver is a fish & chip food chain that does good seafood meals, including fish, chips and corn on the cob for S$5.50. There's one near Scotts Food Centre and one next to Centrepoint shopping complex on Orchard Rd.

There are plenty of supermarkets in Singapore with everything from French wine and Australian beer to yoghurt, muesli, cheese and ice cream. A pot of tea on the lawn at the Raffles Hotel is a fine investment and a chance to relive the Singapore of an earlier era. You can get a beer (S$3 to S$3.50) at almost any coffee shop but there are also plenty of bars as well as the big hotels.

ENTERTAINMENT & SPORTS
Entertainment
After Dark Singapore has plenty of night life, although it's certainly not of the Bangkok or Manila sex and sin variety. Even Bugis St, Singapore's raucous transvestite parade ground, has totally disappeared in the construction of the MRT subway system.

Bugis St was never, officially, more than simply another food-stall centre but, in practice, at the witching hour certain young men turned into something much more exotic than pumpkins. A new (no doubt highly sanitised) Bugis St will soon open at the end of Albert St near the old site. The transvestite scene is now around the Johore Rd and Desker Rd areas.

Still, if you're worried that Singapore is simply too squeaky clean for belief, you may be relieved to hear that there's a real locals-only, low-class, red-light district stretching along a narrow alley from Jalan Besar to Serangoon Rd. It's a depressing sight – rows of blockhouse rooms with women standing in doorways while a constant stream of men walk through inspecting the wares. Outside, hawkers sell condoms and potency pills, and makeshift tables are set up with card games to gamble on.

The predominantly Malay district of Geylang is full of houses and bars operated by organised Chinese gangs who employ women of all nationalities, including Indonesians, Indians and the occasional Caucasian. Of course, Singapore caters to business needs, and there is no shortage of 'health centres' and escort services.

The Tropicana, Singapore's most famous strip club, has gone and all the action is now across the Causeway in Johore Bahru. It is ironic that Singaporeans have to venture to Islamic Malaysia for risqué nightlife. *Mechinta* at 1 Jalan Skudai, Johore Bahru, is the best known of these clubs.

Live Music Singapore does have a music scene, but if you are looking for an interesting, sweaty, low-life rock 'n roll pub with lots of action – forget it. Singapore's music scene is definitely 'smart casual'.

While there are a few local bands, most are imports – Western musicians picking up work in Asia, and Filipino bands – playing jazz, pop covers, old favourites or even something more risqué like the blues. In Singapore, punks are disobedient youngsters who won't do their homework.

Some venues don't have a cover charge, but drinks are expensive and you can expect to pay at least S$8 for a glass of beer. Most have happy hours until 8 pm but the music doesn't start until later.

Some of the tourist magazines such as *The Singapore Visitor* have reasonable gig guides, or look in the local newspapers. The *Straits Times* has a good gig guide on Thursdays in the 'Times Zone Central' section.

The Orchard Rd area is the main centre for live music, and Orchard Towers at 400 Orchard Rd has a concentration of venues. *Top Ten* on the 4th floor is Singapore's most popular nightspot and caters for the more affluent. It mostly has local pop groups, although sometimes it gets top-name acts. Open from 9 pm to 3 am daily, it's S$25 for the first drink on Fridays and Saturdays and S$15 for the rest of the week; you can expect to pay more for top bands.

Caesar's on the 2nd floor of Orchard Towers features many imported bands. The cover charge is S$20 on Fridays and Saturdays and S$12 during the rest of the week. *Ginivy*, also on the 2nd floor of Orchard Towers, has two types of music – country and western. This is the place for macho Singapore cowboys. On the 1st floor is *Club 392* which has local and imported bands. Happy hours are from 4 to 9 pm and midnight to 2 am.

Brannigans in the Hyatt Regency, 10-12 Scotts Rd, is still one of the most popular venues in Singapore and has live bands every night until 1 pm, except Sunday.

Anywhere on the 4th floor of the Tanglin Shopping Centre, 19 Tanglin Rd, is a longrunning rock 'n roll place with a good atmosphere. It's not as up-market as most and there is no cover charge.

Bibi's, upstairs at Peranakan Place on Orchard Rd, is usually lively, features local bands and is popular with visitors and expats. It is open from 11 am to 1 am, and until 2 am on Fridays and Saturdays. Nearby, the *Saxo-phone Bar & Restaurant*, 3 Cuppage Terrace near the corner of Orchard Rd, is a small place with blues and jazz music. It's so small that the band has to play on a platform behind the bar, but it's unpretentious and a good place to strike up a conversation. You can also dine outside and listen to the music. There is no cover charge.

Another jazz venue is *Somerset's* at the Westin Stamford, Raffles City, 2 Stamford Rd. It's a very popular venue, especially during the Sunday jam sessions.

Cheers, in the Novotel Orchid Inn at 214 Dunearn Rd, has bands, performing staff and high bar prices.

Singapore has a number of quieter lounges with resident middle-of-the road entertainers and piano bars. In the Orchard Rd hotel area, you can find *Jimm's Pub* in the Hotel Negara, the *Manhattan Grill* at the Boulevard Hotel and the *Piano Lounge* in Melia at Scotts.

Discos Singapore has no shortage of discos. They often have a first drink charge of around S$15 to S$20 on weekdays and S$20 to S$30 on weekends. Women usually pay less.

The Warehouse, 332 Havelock Rd, is near the Havelock Rd hotels and features a Bugis St facade inside in an attempt to recall the atmosphere of the old sin centre. It doesn't succeed but the place is lively and popular with under 25s. *The Library* in the Mandarin Hotel on Orchard Rd is a subterranean club where nonmembers can dance after 9 pm. *Scandals* in the Westin Plaza Hotel is one of the most sophisticated discos and has impressive sound and light effects. It is open until 3 am and has a cover charge.

Singapore's latest 'in' spot is the *Hard Rock Cafe*, Orchard Place, Cuscaden Rd, with the usual rock memorabilia and crowds queuing to get in. It has nonstop music and high prices.

Chinoiserie in the Hyatt Regency and *Xanadu* in the Shangri-La Hotel are up-market places that attract an older clientele.

TGIF (Thank God Its Friday) is on the 4th floor of the Far East Plaza on Scotts Rd. It is more of a laid-back restaurant and bar with a small dance floor and video screens.

For a disco with a difference, the *Equator Dream* (tel 533 2733) is a floating disco that leaves from Clifford Pier. The cost is S$20 on weekdays and S$30 on weekends; you have to book.

Karaoke The Karaoke craze is rampant throughout South-East Asia, and Singapore is no exception. You can sing along to your old favourites and impress or amuse your friends, though it is most unlikely you will be laughed at. It's great fun and you can watch if you prefer not to sing, but expect to be asked.

There are at least a couple of dozen Karaoke lounges in Singapore including: *Hoshi Karaoke Lounge*, 6th floor, Lucky Plaza, 304 Orchard Rd; *Meisho Karaoke Lounge* on the 3rd floor of Lucky Plaza; and *Kin Kawa Karaoke Lounge* in the Cuppage Plaza.

Cinema There are plenty of cinemas in Singapore, although the Singaporean taste in Western films runs very much to the action-packed spectaculars – despairing Singaporean movie fans occasionally pen letters to the *Straits Times* asking why one acclaimed film or another has never (and may never) be shown in Singapore. Or, you can catch a Chinese kung-fu film or see an all-singing, all-dancing Indian movie.

Singapore has an annual film festival and the various expatriate clubs also show movies. The Alliance Française often has movies open to the public, some with English subtitles.

Theatre Singapore's theatre scene is not exactly thriving, though more local plays are being produced. The Annual Drama Festival is held around August and the Singapore Festival of Arts, which features many free performances, is held every two years (the next is in 1992). Performances are listed in newspapers and the two main venues are the *Drama Centre* (tel 336 0005) on Fort Canning Rd and the *Victoria Theatre* (tel 336

2151), Empress Place. *Bibi's Theatre Pub & Restaurant* (tel 737 4411), Peranakan Place, also has interesting local plays.

Chinese Opera In Chinatown or in the older streets around Serangoon Rd and Jalan Besar, you may chance upon a *wayang* – the brilliantly costumed Chinese street operas. In these noisy and colourful extravaganzas, overacting is very important; there's nothing subtle about it at all. The best time of year to see one is around September during the festival of hungry ghosts. They are often listed in the 'What's On' section of the *Straits Times*.

Cultural Shows At the Mandarin Hotel on Orchard Rd there is *ASEAN Night* from Tuesday to Sunday at 7.45 pm. It features dancing and music from all over the region. The show costs S$18 for adults and S$14 for children; including dinner it is S$36 for adults and S$23 for children.

The *Instant Asia* show has local dances and a snake charmer at S$5 for adults and S$2 for children. It is at the Cockpit Hotel on Penang Rd at 11.45 am and at the Singa Inn Seafood Restaurant (tel 345 1111), East Coast Parkway, in the evenings.

The Cockpit Hotel also puts on the *Lion City Revue*, which includes the acrobatic lion dance. The cost is S$30 for adults and S$20 for children, including dinner.

The Hyatt Regency has Chinese, Malay and Indian performances in their *Malam Singapura* show. With dinner, the cost is S$38 for adults and S$22 for children.

Other The big hotels have cocktail lounges and there are some Chinese nightclubs. The *Neptune Theatre Restaurant*, Collyer Quay, has a cabaret and Cantonese food. *Lido Palace* in the Glass Hotel on Outram Rd also has a Chinese cabaret and dance hostesses. In the same vein is *Golden Million Nite-Club* in the Peninsula Hotel on Coleman St.

Decidedly more high-brow entertainment can be found at the *Victoria Concert Hall* (tel 338 1230), the home of the Singapore Symphony Orchestra. Concerts of classical

Chinese music are also performed by the Singapore Broadcasting Corporation's Chinese Orchestra (tel 256 0401 ext 2732).

Sports

Singapore's private clubs and country clubs have excellent sporting facilities but there are also fine public facilities, such as those at Farrer Park near Little India, and a host of commercial ventures.

Archery Contact the Archery Club of Singapore (tel 258 1140) at 5 Bintang Walk.

Badminton Badminton is popular in South-East Asia and the region has produced world champions in this sport. Courts at the Singapore Badminton Hall (tel 344 1773) on Guillemard Rd are open from 8 am to 11 pm; bookings are essential.

Bowling Tenpin bowling is very popular in Singapore. The cost per game is around S$2 to S$3; shoe hire is around 50c. Some alleys include:

Jackie's Bowl
    542B East Coast Rd (tel 241 6519)
Marina Bowl
    7 Marina Grove, Marina South (tel 221 0707)
Orchard Bowl
    8 Grange Rd (tel 737 4744)
Superbowl
    15 Marina Grove, Marina South (tel 221 1010)

Cricket The Singapore Cricket Club holds matches every weekend on the Padang from March to October. The club is for members only but spectators are welcome.

Golf Singapore has plenty of golf courses, though some are for members only or do not allow visitors to play on weekends. A game of golf costs around S$50 on weekdays, and from S$80 to S$100 on weekends. Club hire is expensive. The following courses have 18 holes, except for Changi, Seletar and Warren, which are nine-hole courses.

Changi Golf Club
    Netheravon Rd (tel 545 1298)

Jurong County Club
    Jurong Town Hall Rd (tel 560 5655)
Keppel Club
    Bukit Chermin (tel 273 5522)
Raffles Country Club
    Jalan Ahmad Ibrahim (tel 861 7655)
Seletar Country Club
    Seletar Airbase (tel 481 4745)
Sembawang Country Club
    Sembawang Rd (tel 257 0642)
Sentosa Golf Course
    Sentosa Island (tel 275 0022)
Singapore Island Country Club
    Upper Thomson Rd (tel 459 2222)
Warren Golf Course
    Folkstone Rd (tel 777 6533)

Singapore has driving ranges at the Parkland Golf Driving Range (tel 440 6726), 920 East Coast Parkway, and the Marina Bay Golf & Country Club (tel 221 2811), Marina South, which also has putting greens.

Horse Racing The beautifully landscaped Bukit Turf Club is on Bukit Timah Rd. The racing calendar is part of the Malaysian circuit and races are held in Singapore once a month. At other times, races are broadcast on the huge video screen. The races are usually held on weekends and admission is S$5 – ring 469 3611 for information. Betting is government controlled, though it is said that the secret societies still control most of the off-course gambling. There is also an excellent hawkers' centre at the turf club.

Horse Riding You can hire horses from the Singapore Polo Club (tel 256 4530), Thomson Rd, at S$30 for 45 minutes. You can also watch polo matches on Tuesdays, Thursdays and weekends at 5.30 pm.

Squash Most of the country clubs have squash courts. Some of the public courts include:

East Coast Recreation Centre
    East Coast Parkway (tel 449 0541)
Farrer Park
    Rutland Rd (tel 251 4166)
National Stadium
    Kallang (tel 348 1258)

Swimming Singapore has a number of beaches for swimming – try East Coast Park, Changi Village, Sentosa or the other islands (see Islands, Beaches & Water Sports in the Things to See section in this chapter). On East Coast Parkway is the Big Splash complex which has a number of pools including a wave pool and a gigantic water slide. Admission is S$3 for adults and S$2 for children. There is a similar complex at the CN West Leisure Park, 9 Japanese Garden Rd, Jurong.

Singapore has plenty of public swimming pools; admission is 60c. The Farrer Park Swimming Complex in Dorset Rd is the closest to the Bencoolen St and Orchard Rd areas.

Tennis Tennis courts cost from S$3 to S$6 per hour. Courts available for hire include:

Clementi Recreation Centre
    12 West Coast Walk (tel 778 8966)
Farrer Park Tennis Courts
    Rutland Rd (tel 251 4166)
Singapore Tennis Centre
    East Coast Parkway (tel 442 5966)
Tanglin Tennis Centre
    Sherwood Rd (tel 473 7236)

Water Sports The East Coast Sailing Centre (tel 449 5118), 1210 East Coast Parkway, is the place to go for windsurfing and sailing. Sailboards cost S$10 per hour with a minimum of two hours hire; lessons are available. They also rent Laser-class boats for $20 per hour. Windsurfers and aquabikes are also available for hire on Sentosa Island.

For water-skiing, Ponggol Boatel (tel 282 6879), at Ponggol Point in the north of the island, rents boats, a driver and gear for S$50 per hour.

THINGS TO BUY
One of Singapore's major attractions is, of course, shopping. There are plenty of bargains to be had on all sorts of goods, but there are also a number of guidelines to follow if you want to be certain to get your money's worth. First of all, don't buy anything unless you really want it and don't buy anything

where the hassle of getting it back home will cost you more than the savings you make. Remember that 'duty free' and 'free port' are somewhat throwaway terms. Firstly, not everything is loaded down with import duty in your own country, and secondly, Singapore also has some local industries to protect.

Singapore, however, is one of the best places in South-East Asia for shopping; Hong Kong is cheaper for clothes but Singapore is competitive for electrical goods.

Price
Before you leap on anything as a great bargain, find out what the price really is. If you're going to Singapore with the intention of buying a camera or a tape recorder for example, check what they would cost you back home first. Then, when you reach Singapore, first find out what the 'real' price is. It's no triumph to knock a starting price of S$200 down to S$150 if the real price was S$150 to start with.

To find out what something should cost, you can check prices out with the main agent or showroom in Singapore, or you can check a big fixed-price department store where the price is unlikely to be rock bottom, but is most likely to be in the ball park. Most importantly, ask around. Never buy in the first shop you come to; always check a few places to see what is being asked.

If you arrive by air, pick up a copy of *Shopping & Eating* by the Civil Aviation Authority of Singapore. This excellent guide to Changi Airport lists the prices of goods

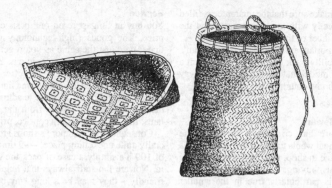

available at the duty-free shops. Use it to compare the prices of electronic goods, watches, clothing etc, at the shops around town. Except for truly duty-free items like cigarettes and alcohol, you can expect prices in the shops around Singapore to be 10% to 20% less than at the airport. However, quite often you'll find that the prices at the airport compare very favourably, especially for cheaper items, and after hours of trudging around town trying to get the best price, you may only have saved yourself a few dollars off the airport price. You can buy duty-free goods at the airport on arrival before you go through customs.

Bargaining

In Singapore, bargaining is the rule but there is no guide as to the bargaining technique used: you may be quoted double the right price, 50% more or a good price first up with little or no reduction, no matter how hard you bargain.

If you have no idea of the right price, your only alternative is to shop around and offer well under the starting price. You can gradually keep raising your price; after a while you should know what is a good price. This can be a frustrating and time-consuming process, for you and the shopkeepers. The secret of successful bargaining is to keep it good humoured and try to make them move

rather than you. Your first gambit can be 'is that your best price', for their opening offer almost certainly won't be. Then when you have to make an offer go lower than you are willing to spend but not so low that you seem totally uninterested.

You have to try and give the impression that if the price isn't right you can quite happily do without the goods, or that if the price isn't right the shop next door's price probably will be. Also remember that when you've made an offer, you've committed yourself. If you really don't want something don't offer anything or you might just end up buying it with a totally ludicrous offer.

Except in the department stores, don't assume that because an item has a price tag that you cannot bargain. This is particularly true in the craft and souvenir stores that cater mainly to tourists. Remember that it is possible to bargain too hard, and be wary of prices that are too low.

Guarantees

Guarantees are an important consideration if you're buying electronic gear, watches, cameras or the like. You must be sure that the guarantee is an international one – usually this is no problem but check it out before you start haggling. A national guarantee is next to useless – are you going to bring your calculator back to Singapore to be fixed?

Finally, make sure that the guarantee is filled out correctly with the shop's name and the serial number of the item written down.

As important as the guarantee is the item's compatibility back home. You don't want a brand or model that has never found its way to your home country.

Buyer Beware

Singapore has consumer laws and the government wants to promote the island as a good place to shop, however, you should be wary when buying.

This is particularly true in the smaller stores and when you try to get too good a deal. A shopkeeper may match your low price but short-change you by not giving you an international guarantee or the usual accessories. For example, you may be offered a very low price for a camera, only to find that the guarantee is only good for Singapore, the batteries and case are extra and the price quoted is for a brand-name body with a no-name lens.

Make sure you get exactly what you want before you leave the store. Check your receipts and guarantees – make sure they are dated and include serial numbers and the shop's stamp.

Check for the right voltage and cycle when you buy electrical goods. Singapore, Australia, New Zealand, Hong Kong and the UK use 220 to 240 volts at 50 cycles while the US, Canada and Japan use 110 to 120 volts at 60 cycles. Check the plug – most shops will fit the correct plug for your country.

Singapore enforces international copyright laws so being palmed off with pirated goods is not such a problem these days. You should be wary but the only real instances of this are the watch sellers who sidle up to you along Orchard Rd and offer you a 'Rolex' for ridiculously low prices.

If you have any problems take your purchases back to the store or contact the Consumers' Association of Singapore (tel 222 4165) or the Singapore Tourist Promotion Board (tel 339 6622).

Service

You buy in Singapore on one basis only – price. The goods (high-technology goods that is) are just the same as you'd get back home, so quality doesn't enter into it. You're not going to come back for after-sales service, so service doesn't come into the picture either. You're not there to admire the display or get good advice from the assistants. In Singapore it's price, price, price.

Consequently, Singapore's shops are generally quite unexciting places – 99 times out of 100 it's simply a case of pack the goods in. Nor are the staff always that helpful or friendly – they may be a long way behind Hong Kong shop assistants when it comes to out-and-out rudeness, but a few shopping trips in Singapore will soon indicate why the government runs 'be polite' campaigns so often!

Where to Shop

Singapore is almost wall-to-wall with shops but there are certain places worth heading to for certain items. The major shopping complexes on and around Orchard Rd all have a very wide variety of shops and goods. Complexes in this area include Plaza Singapura, Specialists' Centre, Lucky Plaza, Orchard Towers, the Shaw Centre and Far East Plaza on Scotts Rd and the Tanglin Centre on Tanglin Rd.

Some of the bigger shopping complexes in Singapore include the Liang Court Centre on River Valley Rd, opposite the National Theatre, and the huge Marina Square, which is modestly called the 'Shop on the Bay'. East of the city is Parkway Parade on Marine Parade Rd, and in Chinatown, the People's Park Complex and the People's Park Centre are good places to shop. The Geylang Serai and Katong districts are interesting, everyday shopping areas, and there are air-conditioned shopping complexes such as the City Plaza and the Tanjong Katong Complex.

Singapore has a number of Chinese emporiums, if you're after something from the People's Republic. Try Overseas in the People's Park Complex in Chinatown or

Chinese in the International Building on Orchard Rd.

There are also a wide variety of department stores offering both their own brand goods and other items, generally at fixed prices – ideal if you've had enough of bargaining. They include shops like C K Tang, Isetan, Metro or Yaohan, all with branches along Orchard Rd. For a limited, but very cheap, selection of electrical and household goods, try the Indian department stores in the Serangoon Shopping Plaza.

For oddities, you could try Chinatown or the shops along Arab St. High St and North Bridge Rd also provide more traditional shopping possibilities. The famous Change Alley, a narrow tunnel running between Collyer Quay and Raffles Place, is still hanging on in the face of redevelopment but is now supplemented by a modern, overhead shopping arcade.

Shopping Complexes Some of the shopping centres in Singapore include:

Albert Complex
  60 Albert St
Blanco Court
  585 North Bridge Rd
Centrepoint
  176-184 Orchard Rd
Cuppage Centre
  55 Cuppage Rd
Far East Plaza
  14 Scotts Rd
Forum Galleria
  583 Orchard Rd
Funan Centre
  109 North Bridge Rd
High Street Centre
  1 North Bridge Rd
International Building
  300 Orchard Rd
Liang Court Complex
  177 River Valley Rd
Liat Towers
  541 Orchard Rd
Marina Square
  6 Raffles Blvd
Meridien Shopping Centre
  100 Orchard Rd
Orchard Plaza
  150 Orchard Rd

Orchard Point
  160 Orchard Rd
Paragon
  290 Orchard Rd
Parkway Parade
  80 Marine Parade Rd
Peninsula Plaza
  111 North Bridge Rd
People's Park Centre
  101 Upper Cross St
People's Park Complex
  Eu Tong Sen St
Plaza Singapura
  68 Orchard Rd
Promenade
  300 Orchard Rd
Raffles City
  250 North Bridge Rd
Scotts
  6 Scotts Rd
Serangoon
  320 Serangoon Rd
Shaw Centre
  1 Scotts Rd
Sim Lim Tower
  10 Jalan Besar
South Bridge Centre
  95 South Bridge Rd
Specialists' Centre
  277 Orchard Rd
Tanglin
  19 Tanglin Rd
Wisma Atria
  435 Orchard Rd

Department Stores Some of the department stores in Singapore include:

C K Tang
  320 Orchard Rd
Daimaru
  177 River Valley Rd
Galleries Lafayette
  Liat Towers, 541 Orchard Rd
Isetan
  Wisma Atria, 435 Orchard Rd
John Little
  Specialists' Centre, 277 Orchard Rd
Le Classique
  2 Tanglin Rd
Metro
  Lucky Plaza, 304 Orchard Rd
  Royal Holiday Inn, 25 Scotts Rd
  Marina Square, Raffles Blvd
Robinsons
  Centrepoint, Orchard Rd

St Michael of Marks & Spencer
    Centrepoint, Orchard Rd
Tokyu
    Marina Square, Raffles Blvd
Yaohan
    Plaza Singapura, Orchard Rd
    80 Marine Parade Rd

What to Buy

From clothes irons to luggage and from oriental rugs to model aeroplanes, Singapore's shops have whatever you want. Singapore is even a good place to shop for medical needs – spectacles are cheap, and for that matter so is dental work. Lefties can try the Left-Handed Shop in the Far East Shopping Plaza on Orchard Rd. The following information, only a sample of Singapore's shopping possibilities, suggests places to start looking.

Arts, Crafts & Antiques Singapore has no shortage of arts and antiques, mostly Chinese but also from all over Asia. When buying antiques, ask for a certificate of antiquity, which is required in many countries to avoid paying customs duty. A good guide is *Antiques, Arts & Crafts in Singapore* by Ann Jones (Times Books International, Singapore, 1988).

Tanglin Shopping Centre is one of the easiest places to find arts and antiques. Check out Antiques of the Orient which has a fascinating collection of antiquarian books, maps and prints. Marina Square also has a number of expensive shops specialising in oriental arts. In the Holland Road Shopping Centre in Holland Village, dozens of shops sell everything from cloisonné ware to Korean chests.

Also good for antiques and furniture is the Watten Rise district where you'll find large shops like Tomlinson Antique at 32-34 Watten Rise and Shang Gift & Decor at 24 Watten Rise. Upper Paya Lebar Rd, northeast of the city centre, has a number of antique shops including Mansion Antique House at No 107 and Just Anthony at No 379.

Other good areas for antiques, and slightly less grandiose second-hand goods, are Chinatown and River Valley Rd. In Chinatown, try the area around Smith St and Temple St. There is a whole host of shops selling goods ranging from trinkets and souvenirs, basketware, fans and silk dressing gowns to more expensive curios and antique pottery. For antiques, try Soon Thye Cheang at 31 Temple St and Chan Pui Kee on the edge of Chinatown at 86 Neil Rd. On River Valley Rd, near Tank Rd, is another cluster of antique shops.

Kelantan Lane, off Jalan Besar near Little India, has interesting second-hand shops. Arab St is a good place for South-East Asian crafts such as caneware, batik and leather goods.

Cameras & Film Cameras are available throughout the city, but Peninsula Plaza on North Bridge Rd has one of the greatest concentrations of camera dealers. Camera equipment is not such a bargain these days as camera prices are often as heavily discounted in the West as in Singapore or Hong Kong. Australians and New Zealanders will find the prices attractive, but most Europeans and North Americans can buy camera equipment as cheap, if not cheaper, at home.

When buying film, bargain for lower prices if you're buying in bulk – 10 films cost less than 10 times one film. Developing is cheap all over Singapore, eg a roll of print film costs about S$2 for developing and 20c to 40c per print. Developing and mounting for a 36 slide film costs as little as S$12. Kodachrome slide film has to be sent to Australia for developing and can take up to a week, but other slide film takes about a day, or there are one-hour express services. Fuji has a laboratory in Singapore.

Clothes & Shoes Clothes and shoes – imported, locally made and made to measure – are widely available but Singapore is not as cheap as most other Asian countries; Hong Kong for example is cheaper. The cost of clothes in Malaysia is about the same. Some of the best buys in Singapore include brandname jeans (Levis, Wranglers, etc) and sneakers (Reeboks, Adidas).

Many of the department stores have reasonably priced clothes. Lucky Plaza on

Orchard Rd is a good centre for cheap clothes and shoes, but bargain hard for everything. The Fu Lou Shou Complex on the corner of Rochor Rd and Waterloo St also has a number of cheap clothing and shoe stores.

Wisma Atria, Orchard C&E and OG Department Store are good places on Orchard Rd for clothes. There are plenty of expensive boutiques selling designer labels: try the Promenade Shopping Centre and Paragon Shopping Centre.

Computers In the computer realm, software and software manuals were once very cheap, but now that Singapore is enforcing international copyright laws, all the cheap software is across the Causeway in Malaysia at Johore and Kuala Lumpur. However, blank diskettes, accessories and 'cloned' hardware are still bargains. For American-made or Japanese-made name-brand hardware, prices are good but not necessarily as low as in the countries of origin. The best place to shop for computer gear is the Funan Centre on North Bridge Rd. Pro Data computers is in the Peninsula Plaza, also on North Bridge Rd.

Electronic Goods TVs, CDs, VCRs, CBs – you name it, all the latest hi-tech audio-visual equipment is available all over Singapore at very competitive prices. With such a range to choose from, it's difficult to know what to buy; it pays to do a little research into makes and models before you arrive in Singapore. Make sure your guarantees are world-wide, your receipts are properly dated and stamped, and your goods are compatible with electricity supplies and systems (there are two main types of TV system used, PAL in Australia and much of Europe, and NTSC in the USA and Japan – video recorders must be compatible to the system you use) in your country of origin.

Sim Lim Tower on Jalan Besar is dedicated to electronic goods – you can buy everything from cassette players to capacitors – and is particularly good for stereo gear. Plaza Singapura on Orchard Rd also has a number of shops selling electronic goods, but really you can buy electronic goods everywhere in Singapore.

Jewellery Gold shops abound in Singapore. Gold jewellery is sold according to weight, and quite often the design and work is thrown in for next to nothing. Gold is often 22 to 24 carat and you should always retain a receipt showing weight and carat. Gold shops are all over town, but you'll find a concentration in Little India, the South Bridge Centre on South Bridge Rd and People's Park Complex in Chinatown.

Singapore is a good place to buy pearls and gemstones but you really need to know the market. Jade is a Chinese favourite and expensive. In general, the lighter in colour the more expensive it is. Beware of imitation jade and don't pay too much for cheap jade, such as the dark Indian jade. Examine solid jade pieces for flaws, as these may be potential crack lines.

Musical Instruments Guitars, keyboards, flutes, drums, electronic instruments, recording equipment, etc are all good buys, though not necessarily as cheap as the country of origin. Good shops to try include: Swee Lee Company, No 03-09 Plaza Singapura, 68 Orchard Rd and City Music, No 02-12 Peace Centre, 1 Sophia Rd on the corner of Selegie Rd. Yamaha have a number of showrooms, including one on the 7th floor of Plaza Singapura in Orchard Rd. If you want to lug around a piano, Singapore Piano Company is also in the Plaza Singapura.

The cheap pirated tapes are things of the past but legitimate tapes, records and CDs are reasonably priced.

Sporting Goods Almost every shopping centre in Singapore has a sports store offering brand-name equipment and sportswear at good prices. Most of the department stores also have well-stocked sports sections. For general sports stores, Bras Basah Complex and Peninsula Plaza on North Bridge Rd have a good selection. Lucky Plaza on Orchard Rd has a number of sports shops including Dive Asia and Sea-Land Sports for scuba equipment.

For golf supplies, the Far East Plaza on Orchard Rd has the greatest number of shops. For brand name bicycles and components, try Soon Watt & Co, 418 Changi Rd, or Kian Hong, 313 Tanjong Katong Rd. For equestrian gear go to Connoisseurs in the Shaw Centre on Scotts Rd.

Around Singapore

Singapore is only a stone's throw from its two larger neighbours, Malaysia and Indonesia. Both can be visited in less than an hour from Singapore, and on weekends and holidays Singaporeans flee the lion city in search of fun and sun. The beach resorts and towns of southern Malaysia are just across the Causeway, while Indonesia's Riau Archipelago has a number of islands, particularly Batam and Bintan islands, which have well-developed tourist facilities.

INDONESIA – RIAU ARCHIPELAGO

Indonesia is a fascinating collection of islands and cultures. If you have a few days to spare and the money for airfares, you can make a number of short tours from Singapore. You can arrange a trip independently or there are dozens of packages available from Singaporean travel agents.

Some easily reached highlights of Indonesia are: Lake Toba and Bukittinggi in Sumatra; Jakarta, Yogyakarta and Borobudur in Java; and, of course, Bali. For day trips, there are the islands of the Riau Archipelago.

Scattered across the South China Sea like confetti, the 3000 islands of the Riau Archipelago, which cover an area over 170,000 sq km, curve south-east from Sumatra to Kalimantan and north to Malaysia.

Tanjung Pinang on Bintan Island is the main centre in the archipelago, and Batam Island is a major resort only half an hour from Singapore. Both islands can be visited as a day trip from Singapore, and there is a

wide variety of accommodation for longer stays.

Singapore investors are pouring millions of dollars into the islands, and the Indonesian and Singaporean governments are developing the area as a special economic zone that will support a variety of industries. Singapore is also seeking to build a dam on Batam to supply its water, and thus reduce its dependence on Malaysia for this essential commodity. This caused consternation in Malaysia, ever suspicious of Singapore, but the Malaysians are also responding to Singaporean overtures to join a tri-national economic zone backed by Singaporean capital.

Most nationalities – including citizens of the USA, Canada, Australia, New Zealand, UK, Ireland, Netherlands and most other European countries – do not require a visa to Indonesia for a visit of up to two months. The Indonesian monetary unit is the rupiah (rp). Indonesian exchange rates are: S$1 = 1103 rp, US$1 = 1947 rp.

For more information, contact the Indonesia Tourist Promotion Office (tel 534 2837), 12-03 Ocean Building, 10 Collyer Quay, Singapore.

Batam Island

Squashed between Singapore and Bintan Island is Batam Island. Almost as big as Singapore itself, Batam is rapidly being developed as a resort for Singaporeans. Land prices have skyrocketed as Singaporeans buy land for holiday houses and investment. With the efficient ferry service, it is possible to live on Batam and commute to Singapore. Batam is a duty-free port with a number of new shopping centres built more to attract Indonesian tourists than Singaporeans.

Nagoya (or Lubuk Baja) Nagoya, the main town, is a new collection of huge hotels, shopping edifices, restaurants and discos. Sekupang is the immigration entry point and has accommodation and a shopping centre. Batu Ampar is the centre for the oil-support industry, and the Batam Centre on Tering

Bay is to become a huge business and tourist development.

For beaches, the best are around Nongsa on the island's north coast. It is also possible to hire boats to other small islands near Batam.

There is a taxi counter and a moneychanger in the Sekupang Ferry Terminal. The large hotels also have taxi counters, or you can hail a taxi on the street.

Places to Stay & Eat Nagoya has several large hotels including the *Batam Jaya Hotel* (tel 58707, or 292 2222 in Singapore) on Jalan Raja Ali Haji and the *Holiday Hotel* (tel 58616) on Jalan Imam Bonjol. Both are in the centre of town and rooms start from around US$15. The *Gita Wisata Hotel* (tel 58104), Baloi Indah, and the *Hotel Halmaya* on Jalan Pelita are cheaper alternatives.

The *Batam Island Country Club* (tel 22825, or 225 6819 in Singapore), on a beach facing Singapore at Sekupang, is one of the largest hotels on Batam. At Nongsa are two big resort hotels: *Batam View Hotel* (tel 22281, or 235 4366 in Singapore) with singles for US$65, doubles US$75 and suites from US$90 to US$180; and the *Turi Beach Resort* (tel 21543, or 235 5544 in Singapore) with singles for US$75, doubles US$85, family rooms US$95 and suites from US$140 to US$200.

Nagoya has plenty of restaurants, and a hawkers' centre opens in the evening. It also has some good seafood places; a few km away the *Rejeki Restaurant* at Pantai Batu Besar is a good seafood restaurant built on stilts over the water.

Getting There & Away See the Singapore Getting There & Away chapter for details on ferries from Singapore to Batam. From Sekupang to Singapore the fare is 17,500 rp.

From Kabil, on the eastern side of the island, there are regular ferries to Tanjung Uban on Bintan Island, but it is much easier to catch the ferry from Sekupang to Tanjung Pinang on Bintan.

Merpati flies from Batam Island to Bandung and Palembang, and from Tanjung Pinang to Jakarta and Pekanbaru. Garuda has daily flights from Batam to Jakarta, Pekanbaru, Medan, Pontianak and Balikpapan.

Bintan Island

Bintan Island is the main centre of the Riau Archipelago. It is a stopover point to other parts of Indonesia and has some fine beaches with opportunities for diving and snorkelling. The best of the beaches are at Berakit, Teluk Dalam and Pasir Panjang in the north, and Pantai Trikora on the east coast.

Tanjung Pinang Tanjung Pinang is the main town on Bintan Island and a good base for exploring other islands. There is an old section of the town built on stilts over the sea, yet in its own way it is a rather cosmopolitan town with an aura of prosperity and growth.

The **Riau Kandil Museum** has a mishmash treasure trove of artefacts from the days of the sultanates and the Dutch, including old guns, ceramics, charts, antique brassware and other memorabilia.

Other sights include the old harbour of **Pejantan II** and some Chinese temples, one in town and another across the harbour by sampan in the stilt village of Senggarang. Or, you could charter a sampan up the **Snake River** (Sunggai Umar) and through the mangroves to see the Chinese temple with its gory murals of the trials and tortures of hell. Nearby, you can see the ruins of old **Sea Dayak villages**.

Pantai Trikora This resort beach is a narrow strip of white sand around a little half-moon bay, with the Pantai Trikora Country Club overlooking it. The hotel is made up of timber bungalows on stilts. Trikora can get quite crowded, especially on weekends.

Charter a taxi or an *ojek* (motorcycle) to get to Pantai Trikora, about 20 km from Tanjung Pinang. The trip takes 45 minutes.

Gunung Bintan Besar You can climb Gunung Bintan Besar (348 metres) in about two hours. It's a fair way out of Tanjung Pinang by road or boat.

Pantai Dwi Kora About a 20-minute drive from Tanjung Uban, on the west coast of Bintan, is a beach called Pantai Dwi Kora which faces Batam Island. It's a long strip of white, palm-fringed sand with a clear, calm sea; a fine place for a swim. It can also get very crowded on weekends.

Nearby Islands Just off Tanjung Pinang is a lump of rock called **Pulau Bayan**. Once a dry dock and repair yard, it has now been cleared of scrap metal to make way for the construction of a massive boat marina with a hotel, swimming pool, helipad and other facilities for wealthy Singaporeans (all within sight of the Indonesian shanties).

Also close to Tanjung Pinang is tiny **Pulau Penyenget**. Once home to the Riau kings, it has ruins, graveyards and other reminders of the past dotted all over the island. Out past Penyenget on **Pulau Terkulai**, the lighthouse keeper lives in solitary splendour. There are beautiful beaches but to get there you have to charter a boat.

Places to Stay Tanjung Pinang has budget accommodation at the *Hotel Surya* on Jalan Bintan, the *Tanjung Pinang Hotel* (tel 21236) on Jalan Pos and the *Sampurna Inn* on Jalan Yusuf Kahar for around US$5. The *Wisma Riau* (tel 21023) on Jalan Yusuf Kahar has rooms for around US$10 with

private bathroom. It's very clean and comfortable.

The top-end places to stay are the *Hotel Sampurna Jaya* (tel 21555) at Jalan Yusuf Kahar 15 with rooms from US$50 and the *Riau Holidays Indah* (tel 21812) built on pylons over the water near a long pier. Prices start from US$40/50. The *Pantai Trikora Country Club* has rooms from US$40.

Places to Eat Eat at the night markets (Pasar Malam Ria), which are great for people watching and for the variety of delicious food available – particularly Indonesian, Chinese and seafood dishes. Stalls outside the coffee shops have good-value food during the day.

Getting There & Away See the Singapore Getting There & Away chapter for details of the ferries from Singapore to Bintan Island.

Motorboats to Penyenget depart from halfway along the main pier at Tanjung Pinang and cost 300 rp per person each way. You can also charter a boat.

From Tanjung Pinang, there are flights to Batam, Jakarta, Pekanbaru, Palembang, Padang, Medan, Pontianak and Balikpapan.

Getting Around The only bus services in Tanjung Pinang operate to Tanjung Uban. The main method of transport is the ojek (public motorcycle).

MALAYSIA

Facts about the Country

HISTORY

It is only since WW II that Malaysia, Singapore and Brunei have emerged as three separate independent countries. Prior to that they were all loosely amalgamated as a British colony, Sarawak excepted, and earlier still they might have been independent Malay kingdoms, or part of the greater Majapahit or Srivijaya empires of what is now Indonesia. In the dim mists of time it's possible that Malaysia was actually the home of the earliest Homo sapiens in Asia. Discoveries have been made in the gigantic Niah Caves of Sarawak which indicate that the Stone Age human was present there, and in other caves of north Borneo and the Malay peninsula, as long as 40,000 years ago.

Early Trade & Empires

Little is known about these Stone Age Malaysians, but around 10,000 years ago the aboriginal Malays – the Orang Asli – began to move down the peninsula from a probable starting point in south-west China. Remote settlements of Orang Asli can still be found in parts of Malaysia, but 4000 years ago they were already being supplanted by the Proto-Malays, ancestors of today's Malays, who at first settled the coastal regions, then moved inland. In the early centuries of the Christian era Malaya was known as far away as Europe. Ptolemy showed it on his early map with the label 'Golden Chersonese'. It spelt gold not only to the Romans for it wasn't long before Indian and Chinese traders also arrived in search of that most valuable metal and Hindu mini-states sprung up along the great Malay rivers.

The Malay people were basically similar ethnically to the people of Sumatra, Java and even the Philippines and from time to time various South-East Asian empires extended their control over all or part of the Malay peninsula. Funan, a kingdom based in modern-day Kampuchea, at one time controlled the northern part of the peninsula.

From the 7th century the great Sumatran-based Srivijaya empire, with its capital in Palembang, held the whole area and even extended its rule into Thailand.

In turn Srivijaya fell to the Java-based Majapahit empire, then in 1403 Parameswara, a Sumatran prince, established himself at Melaka which soon became the most powerful city-state in the region. At this time the spice trade from the Moluccas was beginning to develop and Melaka, with its strategic position on the straits which separate Sumatra from the Malay peninsula, was a familiar port for ships from the East and West.

In 1405 the Chinese admiral Cheng Ho arrived in Melaka with greetings from the 'Son of Heaven' and, more importantly, the promise of protection from the encroaching Siamese to the north. With this support from China the power of Melaka extended to include most of the Malay peninsula. At about the same time, Islam arrived in Melaka and soon spread through Malaya.

The Portuguese Period

For the next century Melaka's power and wealth expanded to such an extent that the city became one of the wealthiest in the East. So wealthy in fact that the Portuguese began to take an overactive interest in the place and after a preliminary skirmish in 1509 Alfonso de Albuquerque arrived in 1511 with a fleet of 18 ships and overpowered Melaka's 20,000 defenders and their war elephants. The Sultan of Melaka fled south with his court to Johore where the Portuguese were unable to dislodge him. Thus Melaka came to be the centre of European power in the region while Johore grew to be the main Malay city-state, along with other Malay centres at Brunei in north Borneo and Acheh in the north of Sumatra.

The Portuguese were to hold Melaka for over 100 years although they were never able to capitalise on the city's fabulous wealth and superb position. Portuguese trading power and strength was never great enough to take full advantage of the volume of trade that used to flow through Melaka but, more importantly, the Portuguese did not develop the complex pattern of influence and patronage upon which Melaka had based its power and control. Worse, the Portuguese reputation for narrow-mindedness and cruelty had preceded them and they gained few converts to Christianity and little support for their rule.

Thus the other Malay states were able to grow into the vacuum created by the Portuguese takeover of Melaka and while they squabbled and fought between themselves they also had the strength to make attacks on Melaka. Gradually Portuguese power declined and after long skirmishes with the Dutch, who supported the rulers of Johore, Melaka eventually fell to them, after a long and bitter siege, in 1641.

The Dutch Period

Like the Portuguese, the Dutch were to rule Melaka for over a century but, also like the Portuguese, the Dutch failed to recognise that Melaka's greatest importance was as a centre for entrepôt trade. To an even greater extent than their predecessors the Dutch tried to keep Melaka's trade totally to themselves and as a result Melaka continued to decline. Also the greatest Dutch interest was reserved for Batavia, modern-day Jakarta, so Melaka was always the poor sister to the more important Javan port.

The British Arrive

Meanwhile the British were casting eyes at Malaya again. They had shown an interest in the area then decided to concentrate on their Indian possessions, but in 1786 Captain Francis Light arrived at Penang and this time British intentions were firm ones. Light followed a free trade policy at Penang, a clear contrast to the monopolistic intentions of the Portuguese and then the Dutch in Melaka. As a result Penang soon became a thriving port and by 1800 the population of the island,

virtually uninhabited when Light took over, had reached 10,000.

While Penang was a success story locally it did not meet the high expectations of the British East India Company and in 1795 the company also found itself controlling Melaka due to events in Europe. When Napoleon overran the Netherlands the British temporarily took control of Melaka and later on the other Dutch possessions in the region. In 1814, with Napoleon defeated, an agreement was reached on the return of these possessions and by 1818 Melaka and Java had been returned to Dutch control.

During the years of British rule, however, there had been a number of advocates for greater British power in the region – one of the most outspoken being Thomas Stamford Raffles. He had decided that Britain, not the Netherlands, should be the major power in the region, but was unable to convince his superiors in London that this was a wise plan. In 1818, however, the re-establishment of Dutch power had caused sufficient worry to the company officials in Calcutta that Raffles was told to go ahead and establish a second British base further south than Penang. In early 1819 Raffles arrived in Singapore and decided this should be the place. By 1826 Singapore became part of the British Straits Settlement, governed from Bengal in India along with Melaka and Penang, and had a population already approaching 100,000.

The British Period

Despite British rule the straits continued to be a fairly frontier-like area. Piracy, long a popular activity, still thrived although the British eventually got around to cracking down on it. Curiously piracy has had a revival in the 1980s and a number of ships have been boarded and the ship's safes ransacked or the crew robbed as they approached the Indonesian islands around Singapore!

The developments through the balance of the 19th century were chiefly economic ones, but in their wake they brought enormous changes to the racial make-up of the region. There had been Chinese settlers in

Malaya from the time of Cheng Ho's visit to Melaka in the early 1400s, but in the 1800s they began to arrive in much greater numbers. The main attraction was tin and at mining towns around Kuala Lumpur and Perak fortunes were quickly won and lost. In 1877 rubber plantations began to spring up all over the peninsula. Since the indigenous supply of labour was not sufficient, labourers were imported from the British plantations in India. Thus by the turn of the century Malaya had a burgeoning economy, but also a vastly different racial mix than a century before. Whereas Malaya had been predominantly populated by Malays now it also had large groups of Indians and Chinese. Furthermore, with the arrival of women settlers the labourers who had come there only to work now began to think of settling down and staying on.

As in India the British managed to bring more and more of the country under their control without having to fight for it or even totally govern it. Internal government was left up to the local sultans while the British provided 'advisers' and managed external affairs. In 1867 the Straits Settlements became a crown colony and was no longer governed from India. In 1895 Perak, Selangor, Negri Sembilan and Pahang became the Federated Malay States. Johore refused to join the federation while Kelantan, Terengganu, Perlis and Kedah were still controlled by the Thais until 1909.

Meanwhile in Borneo

Across in North Borneo events sometimes read more like Victorian melodrama than hard fact. In 1838 James Brooke, a British adventurer, arrived in Borneo with his armed sloop to find the Brunei aristocracy facing rebellion from the dissatisfied inland tribes. He quelled the rebellion and in gratitude was given power over part of what is today Sarawak. Appointing himself 'Rajah Brooke' he successfully cooled down the fractious tribes, suppressed head-hunting, eliminated the dreaded Borneo pirates and founded a personal dynasty that was to last

for over 100 years. The Brooke family of 'White Rajahs' gradually brought more and more of Borneo under their power until the Japanese arrived during WW II.

The development of British power in Sabah was much more prosaic. Once part of the great Brunei empire, Sabah came under the influence of the British North Borneo Company after centuries of being avoided due to its unpleasant pirates. At one time Kota Kinabalu was known as Api Api, 'Fire, Fire', from the pirates' tiresome habit of repeatedly burning it down. Eventually in 1888 the whole north Borneo coast was brought under British protection although Mat Salleh, a Sabah rebel, held out against British power until his death in 1900.

The WW II Period

From the turn of the century until WW II Malaya became steadily more prosperous although the peninsula continued to forge ahead of the north Borneo states. The various peninsula states came more under British influence, whilst more and more Chinese and Indian immigrants flooded into the country eventually outnumbering the indigenous Malays. By the time WW II broke out in Europe, Malaya supplied nearly 40% of the world's rubber and 60% of its tin.

When the war arrived in Malaya its impact was sudden and devastating. A few hours before the first Japanese aircraft was sighted over Pearl Harbor the Japanese landed at Kota Bharu in the north of Malaya and started their lightning dash down the peninsula. British confidence that they were more than a match for the Japanese soon proved to be sadly misplaced and it took the Japanese little over a month to take Kuala Lumpur and a month after that they were at the doors of Singapore. North Borneo had fallen to the Japanese with even greater speed.

The Japanese were unable to form a cohesive policy in Malaya since there was not a well organised Malay independence movement which they could harness to their goals. Furthermore many Chinese were bitterly opposed to the Japanese who had invaded

China in the 1930s. Remnants of the British forces continued a guerrilla struggle against the Japanese throughout the war and the predominantly Chinese Communist Malayan People's Anti-Japanese Army also continued the struggle against the Japanese.

Postwar & the Emergency

Following the sudden end of WW II, Britain was faced with reorganising its position in Malaya. There had not been the same concerted push towards independence which India had been through in the inter-war years so while independence and the end of colonial rule was clearly a long-term programme, in the short term British rule was likely to continue.

At first the plan was to take over the rule of Sabah, Sarawak and Brunei, to form the Malay states into a Malay Union and to rule Singapore as a crown colony. This plan faced one major obstacle – all prior British plans for Malaya had been based on the premise that the country was Malayan despite the increased population of people from either Chinese or Indian descent. With their increase this premise became less and less realistic. Through WW II the population of Indians and Chinese had become much more settled than before and now there was even less likelihood of them returning to their 'homelands'. British acceptance of this fact of life naturally provoked strong Malay opposition.

Faced with these difficulties the British soon had an even greater problem to grapple with – the Emergency. In 1948 the Malayan Communist Party, which had fought against the Japanese throughout the war, decided the time had come to end British colonial rule and launched a guerrilla struggle which was to continue for 12 years. The Communist threat was eventually declared over in 1960 although there were sporadic outbreaks of violence until 1989. In part this was because the Communists were never able to gain a broad spectrum of support. They were always predominantly a Chinese grouping and while the Malays might have wanted independence from Britain they certainly did not want rule by the Chinese. Nor were all Chinese in favour of the party; it was mainly an uprising of the peasantry and lower classes.

Despite the diminished threat of Communist takeover, guerrillas were still resident in the jungle around the Thai border until the last remaining faithful accepted the government's long-standing amnesty in 1989.

Independence

In 1955 Britain agreed that Malaya would become fully independent within two years. Malaya duly achieved *merdeka* (independence) in 1957 despite unsuccessful meetings with Chin Peng, leader of the Communist forces, in an attempt to end the now merely smouldering Emergency. Tunku Abdul Rahman was the leader of the new nation which came into existence with remarkably few problems.

In Singapore things went nowhere near as smoothly and politics became increasingly more radical. The election in 1959 swept Lee Kuan Yew's People's Action Party (PAP) into power, but they faced a whole series of major problems. When the Federation of Malaya was formed in 1948 the Malay leaders were strongly opposed to including Singapore because this would have tipped the racial balance from a Malay majority to a Chinese one. Furthermore while politics in Malaya were orderly, upper class and gentlemanly, in Singapore they were anything but.

Nevertheless, to Singapore, merger with Malaya seemed to be the only answer to high unemployment, a soaring birth rate and the loss of its traditional trading role with the growth of independent South-East Asian nations. Malaya was none too keen to inherit this little parcel of problems, but when it seemed possible that the moderate PAP party might be toppled by its own left wing the thought of a moderate Singapore within Malaysia became less off-putting than the thought of a communist Singapore outside it. Accordingly in 1961 Tunku Abdul Rahman agreed to work towards the creation of Malaysia which would include Singapore. To balance the addition of Singapore, discussion also commenced on adding Sarawak, Sabah and Brunei to the union. This proposal was welcomed by Britain which had been facing the problem of exactly what to do with its North Borneo possessions.

Confrontation

Accordingly in 1963 Malaysia came into existence although at the last moment Brunei, afraid of losing its oil wealth, refused to join. No sooner had Malaysia been created than problems arose. First of all the Philippines laid claim to Sabah, which had been known as North Borneo prior to the union. More seriously Indonesia laid claim to the whole place and Sukarno, now in the final phase of his megalomania, commenced his ill-starred 'Confrontation'. Indonesian guerrilla forces crossed the borders from Kalimantan (Indonesian Borneo) into Sabah and Sarawak and landings were made in Peninsular Malaysia and even in Singapore. British troops, having finally quelled the Emergency only four years earlier, now found themselves back in the jungle once again.

Singapore Departs

At the same time relations between Malaya and Singapore soured almost as soon as Malaysia was formed. The spectre of Chinese domination appeared and Singapore refused to extend the privileged position held by Malays in Malaya to Malays in Singapore. In August 1965, exactly two years after Malaysia was created, Singapore was kicked out.

Racial Problems

Despite the fact that the Malaysian economy was very stable, things were not so smooth politically. One of the cornerstones of the government's policy had been to right the imbalance between the various elements of Malaysia's population.

In 1969 only 1.5% of company assets in Malaysia were owned by Malays and per capita income amongst Malays was less than 50% of that of non-Malays. Attempts to unify Malaysia by making Bahasa Malaysia the one national language also created resentment amongst the non-Malays as did the privileges Malays had in land ownership, business licences, educational opportunities and government positions. In 1969 violent intercommunal riots broke out, particularly in Kuala Lumpur, and hundreds of people were killed.

Following these riots the government moved to improve the position of Malays in Malaysia with much greater speed. The title *bumiputra* or 'sons of the soil' was created to define the indigenous Malay people; this meant not only Malays, but also the aboriginal inhabitants and the indigenous peoples of Sarawak and Sabah. New guidelines were instituted stipulating how much of a company's share must be held by *bumiputras* and in other ways enforcing a Malay share in the nation's wealth.

Although many Chinese realised that Malaysia could never attain real stability without an equitable distribution of the country's wealth there was also much resentment and many talented people either left the country or simply withdrew their abilities and capital. Fortunately Malaysia's natural wealth enabled it to absorb these inefficiencies, but the problems of bringing the Malays to an equal position in the nation, economically as well as politically, is one that is still not fully resolved.

After 1969 Malaysia made dramatic changes in economic as well as social policy. Tunku Abdul Rahman retired in 1970 and was succeeded by his deputy, Tun Abdul Razak, as prime minister and head of the ruling party, the United Malay National Organisation (UMNO).

Malaysia Today

In the last two decades Malaysia has emerged as a responsible and stable regional power. It has prospered economically although in the recent past it was almost totally dependent on world commodity prices (rubber, palm oil, tin and timber).

These days it is diversifying its economic base and is one of the fastest growing economies in Asia.

The country is also under intense pressure from international bodies to stop exporting tropical timber from its rapidly diminishing rainforest areas – an issue it has paid little more than lip service to up until now.

Regionally it is an important member of the Association of South-East Asian Nations (ASEAN) and has a defence agreement with Australia, New Zealand, Singapore and the UK.

Politically, UMNO continues to dominate the government and Prime Minister Datuk Seri Mahathir Mohamad remains unthreatened in his leadership. As has been the case since 1957, UMNO is the dominant Malay party in the National Front, a coalition of UMNO, the Malaysian Chinese Association (MCA) and the Malaysian Indian Congress (MIC). Nonetheless, the opposition has grown in strength with the strongly Chinese DAP taking much of the vote from the more moderate MCA, and the emergence of Semangat '46, a breakaway group from within UMNO led by Tunku Razaleigh Hamzah. However, despite a spirited election campaign in 1990, the government was again returned with a large majority.

Dr Mahathir, the most controversial of Malaysia's four prime ministers, presides over a growing and prosperous Malaysia but he is known for his confrontationalist politics. Noted for his Malay chauvinism, since coming to power in 1981 he has presided over a split in his own party, detained 107 people without trial in 1987 and he dismissed six judges in 1988. Unlike his political opponent, Razaleigh, Mahathir is one of the few Malay political leaders who has not come from the royal families of Malaysia.

GEOGRAPHY

Malaysia consists of two distinct parts. Peninsular Malaysia is the long finger of land extending down from Asia as if pointing towards Indonesia and Australia. Much of the peninsula is covered by dense jungle, particularly in its northern half where there are also high mountains, and the central area is very lightly populated. While on the western side of the peninsula there is a long fertile plain running down to the sea, the mountains descend more steeply on the eastern side where there are also many more beaches.

The other part of the region, making up more than 50% by area, is East Malaysia – the northern part of the island of Borneo. The larger, southern part is the Indonesian state of Kalimantan. East Malaysia is divided between Sarawak and Sabah with Brunei a small enclave between them. Both parts are covered by dense jungle with many large river systems, particularly in Sarawak. Mt Kinabalu in Sabah is the highest mountain in South-East Asia between the Himalaya and New Guinea at 4101 metres.

CLIMATE

Malaysia has a typically tropical climate – it's hot and humid year round. Once you've got used to the tropics it never strikes you as too uncomfortable though, it's simply almost always warm and sunny. The temperature rarely drops below 20°C even at night and usually climbs to 30°C or more during the day.

Rain, when it comes, tends to be short and sharp and is soon replaced by more of that everpresent sunshine. At certain times of the year it may rain every day but it's rare that it rains all day. Although the region is

Malays, Malaya & Malaysia

Malays are the indigenous people of Malaysia although they are not the original inhabitants. Malaya is the old name for the country which, prior to 1963, consisted only of Peninsular Malaya. With the amalgamation of Malaya, Sarawak and Sabah the title Malaysia was coined for the new nation and the peninsula is now referred to as Peninsular Malaysia while Sarawak and Sabah are referred to as East Malaysia.

monsoonal it's only on the east coast of Peninsular Malaysia that you have a real rainy season – elsewhere it's just a time of year when the average rainfall is heavier than at other times of year.

West coast Malaysia gets heavier rainfall from September to December. On the east coast, and also in Sarawak and Sabah, October to February is the wet season. Throughout the region the humidity tends to hover around the 90% mark, but on the peninsula you can always escape from heat and humidity by retreating to the delightfully cool hill stations.

FLORA & FAUNA

Malaysia is part of the region possessing the most ancient rainforests in the world, having remained virtually unchanged for many millions of years. In just one country it's possible to see the entire spectrum – from the extensive, lowland rainforest tracts, to the summits of several mountainous areas. West Malaysia sits at the centre of what has evolved into the most complex, diverse animal and plant communities ever known. Situated along the north of the great island of Borneo, East Malaysia is more on the periphery of this tropical lushness, but still has much of this diversity.

It is the remarkable climatic stability of this region which has made its forests such a major focal point of scientific interest for many years. Within these vast jungles nature has run rampant for so long that just about every type of bizarre animal or plant known today has survived somewhere there. In fact, scientists are still far from knowing even a significant percentage of the mysteries concealed in these forests. Regrettably, the focal point has shifted to one of concern to understand this living laboratory before it is irretrievably consumed by uncontrolled development and inadequate conservation measures.

In Peninsular Malaysia alone there are over 8000 species of flowering plants, including 2000 trees, 800 orchids and 200 palms. Here is found the world's tallest tropical tree species, the *tualang*, reaching a height of 80 metres, with a base diameter of over three metres. The *rafflesia* is the world's largest flower measuring up to one-metre across and weighing up to nine kg.

There are over 200 species of mammals, 450 of birds, 250 of reptiles (including 100 snakes, 14 tortoises and turtles and three crocodiles), 90 frogs and 150,000 insects (including the giant birdwing butterflies and the Atlas moth). There are snakes, lizards and frogs which can 'fly', spiders that eat birds, giant (as well as flying) squirrels, and many smaller creatures which have 'giant' versions. Even the leeches can seem huge after a day on some of the jungle trails!

Mammals include elephants, rhinos (very rare now), tapirs, tigers, leopards, honey bears, several kinds of deer, tempadau (forest cattle), various gibbons and monkeys (including in Borneo the orang-utan and the bizarre proboscis monkey in which the male has a huge, pendulous nose), scaly anteaters (pangolins) and porcupines, to name a few.

The bird life features spectacular pheasants, hornbills (including the rare helmeted hornbill, prized for its 'ivory' – actually the base of its 'horn' or casque) and many groups of colourful birds, such as kingfishers, sunbirds, pittas, woodpeckers, trogons and barbets. Snakes include cobras, notably the spitting cobra, which shoots venom into the eyes of its prey, vipers (the kind seen in snake temples), pythons (including the reticulated python, the world's longest snake, with some growing over 10 metres) and colourful tree snakes (most are harmless to humans).

National Parks

The British established the first national park in Malaysia in 1938 and it is now included in Taman Negara, Malaysia's major (and Peninsular Malaysia's only) national park. Its future is still not secured as sections are threatened by various development plans. East Malaysia has several national parks, forming a valuable, but still inadequate network.

The greatest concern today is to see more areas protected in Peninsular Malaysia, because the diversity of the flora & fauna is the richest, containing much that does not extend to Borneo. Many areas have been proposed for protection, with the most important area being the lowland forests of Endau-Rompin (perhaps the last refuge for the Sumatran rhinoceros, photographed in the wild only in December 1983), straddling the borders of Pahang and Johore. Today we can see an increase in public awareness of these and other environmental problems. In the 1970s the region of Gunung Mulu, in east Sarawak, was the centre of what became the most intensively studied tropical forest area in the world, leading to the establishment of a major national park there.

For those who wish to experience the primeval world of the ancient rainforests, Taman Negara offers a spectacular introduction, but there are other places which can be visited in Peninsular Malaysia, and a visit to East Malaysia is recommended, if only to see (and perhaps climb) Mt Kinabalu. Details are provided here for the main national parks and several other places.

Accommodation is not a problem when visiting most national parks, and various categories, from hostel to chalet, are available. Transport and accommodation operations are increasingly being handled by private tour companies, and you have to book in advance and pay a deposit. Best times: June to September (east coast, including Taman Negara); October through March (west coast). For Taman Negara contact Pernas (tel 03-2434929, fax 03-2420416) 73 Jalan Raja Chulan, 50200, Kuala Lumpur.

In Sabah contact the Sabah Parks office (tel 088-211585), Box 10626, Kota Kinabalu. It's in Block K of the Sinsuran Kompleks on Jalan Tun Fuad Stephens, opposite the waterfront. In Sarawak, contact the National Parks & Wildlife office (tel 082-248088), on the 7th floor of the Satok building on Jalan Satok, about a km west of the centre of Kuching. It is always advisable to settle all arrangements and fees in advance. Best time is April to the end of October. Basic information is available in all areas, and may be found in tourist offices also.

Taman Negara National Park A scenic region of forested plateau, hills and mountains covering 4343 sq km, the national park ranges from 120 to 2150 metres (the summit of Gunung Tahan, the highest mountain in Peninsular Malaysia). It is traversed by several rivers, and of these, the Tembeling provides access to the park headquarters. From Kuala Lumpur take a bus or taxi to Kuala Tembeling via Jerantut. Here you meet the park boat for the 60-km trip into the park, taking three to four hours. Around the headquarters are several trails, and a number of observation hides can be visited. For the adventurous, it's a nine-day return trip to Gunung Tahan; otherwise there is much to do walking the trails, watching at the hides, or arranging a river trip. The park's popularity has grown dramatically in recent years and new gateways to the park are being planned.

Templar Park This park of 12 sq km was originally established as a botanical reserve in 1955, but is now a fully protected area, about 30 minutes from Kuala Lumpur. Signs of former tin-mining operations can be seen but today it is a popular place for a day trip. The dominant feature of the area is the 305-metre limestone hill Bukit Takun. The main trail to the summit is the centre of activity for many visitors and offers good views. There are many caves there, too, with little known about them – a good place to go if you're contemplating Mt Kinabalu. It is reached on the Rawang road, turning off at the 21-km peg. The road forks ahead, with a right turn indicating the main Templar Park area, while Bukit Takun is straight ahead. Also near there are the Kancing Falls and Serendah Forest Reserve.

Bukit Lagong Forest Reserve This 607-hectare reserve, close to Kuala Lumpur, includes a Forest Research Institute. There are several attractions for visitors, including a picnic area near a waterfall, a small museum and an arboretum. The 300-metre peak of Bukit Lagong can be climbed on a good trail through undisturbed forest (about two hours up). A visit may be arranged by contacting the Director, Forest Research Institute, Kepong, Selangor. A guide is needed for Bukit Lagong.

Endau-Rompin Park This wildlife reserve is the last refuge in Malaysia of the Sumatran rhinoceros. It is on the east coast of the peninsula on the border between Johore and Pahang. The park is accessible by car along a rough road from Kahang on the Keluang-Mersing road. It is also possible to reach the park by boat along the Endau River. There is a camping ground but the park is not well developed for visitors.

Entry permits can be obtained from the State Security Council, 2nd floor, Bangunan Sultan Ibrahim, Bukit Timbalan, Johore Bahru.

Gunung Mulu National Park This is Sarawak's largest national park, covering an area of 544 sq km. The park contains Sarawak's second highest peak, Gunung Mulu, 2376 metres of sandstone and Gunung Api, 1750 metres of limestone. The surrounding vegetation varies from peat swamp to limestone and forest terrain.

This national park contains about 1500 species of flowering plants, including 10 species of the famous pitcher plant. The pitcher plants attract many scientists and students of botany to Gunung Mulu. Removing these plants from the national park, or from the country, is strictly prohibited – there is a smuggling network.

Another feature of Gunung Mulu National Park is the underground cave system, apparently the most extensive cave network in the world. At present you can only visit the Deer Cave and part of the Clearwater Cave. The Deer Cave runs through an entire mountain and is the largest cave passage known. Clearwater Cave, the longest cave in South-East Asia, has a length of 51½ km. There are many other caves in the park but authorities are still in the process of 'preparing' them for the public.

Gunung Mulu is a popular destination in Sarawak, though it is an expensive place to visit.

Bako National Park A small park of 26 sq km in west Sarawak, the Bako National Park is on the peninsula at the mouth of the Bako River. It features sandstone cliffs and sandy bays, with a range of forest types, including mangroves. Access is only by boat, about 30 minutes from Kuching to Kampung Bako, from where you take another boat into the park. The park has beach areas and a network of paths. There is a variety of hostel accommodation and food supplies are available but expensive. It's a pleasant place to spend a few days in.

Niah National Park This 31-sq km park was originally established to protect the valuable Niah Caves, made famous by the discoveries of traces of early humans dating back 35,000 years. The caves are also remarkable for the millions of bats and swiftlets which roost there. The swiftlets are famous, as their nests made of saliva are collected for bird's nest soup. The mass movements of these bats and swiftlets through the mouth of the Great Cave are a spectacular sight at dawn and dusk. Other examples of cave life can be seen, and if you are lucky you may see the black-and-white bat hawk at the entrance waiting to pounce on a bat or swiftlet.

The park, in east Sarawak, is easily accessible from Bintulu or Miri via nearby Batu Niah. Cheap hostel space or more expensive resthouses are readily available. The walk from the park headquarters to the caves includes the famous three-km plank trail, which takes 45 minutes to one hour. There are other trails in the park and a longhouse nearby. It's one of the most popular destinations in Sarawak.

Tunku Abdul Rahman National Park This park covers five islands off Kota Kinabalu, Sabah, and has an area of about 49 sq km. The feature attractions are coral reefs and beaches that can only be visited by making arrangements with private boat operators, which is good if you can organise a small group. Park headquarters are on Pulau Manukan, the second largest island. There are visitor facilities on this island (chalets), and on Pulau Sapi (day-use facilities, walking trails, good beaches), Pulau Gaya (walking trails) and Pulau Mamutik (rest-house).

This park partly developed from the notion that protecting offshore islands also protected the flora & fauna of Sabah until it was demonstrated that most of it is not found off the mainland. Fortunately, it led to the establishment of the first valuable marine park, with the hope that Malaysia will protect more of its marine resources.

Kinabalu National Park

This magnificent park of about 750 sq km was established in 1964 to protect the massif of Mt Kinabalu and its environs. The region has been a focal point of exploration and scientific investigation in Borneo for over a century. Today the focus has shifted more towards tourism as the climb to the summit offers an exciting enticement to the visitor.

The park headquarters (1560 metres) is about 85 km from Kota Kinabalu at Simpangan. Getting there takes about two hours and buses stop there on the way to Ranau or Sandakan. It is advisable to book ahead for accommodation at the headquarters and the mountain huts in case large groups of summit seekers may be arriving.

There is plenty of information available at park headquarters for planning your ascent. Plan to spend at least two nights on the mountain in case fickle weather conditions force you to wait for a clear morning to reach the top. The best time to be there is at or near sunrise. On a clear morning the vista is incredible and exhilarating and worth all the time spent getting there.

The trail, starting on a road, is well marked all the way up, with steeper sections graded and other aids provided nearer the top. The Panar Laban huts and those just below it (around 3340 metres) are the main stop for climbers and a good base for exploring the upper terrain, but Sayat Sayat Hut (3800 metres), although smaller, can give you more time to reach the summit and await the sunrise. You'll need to carry some good cold-weather gear as it gets bloody cold up at the huts at night. Guides are compulsory for all visitors. At least a week is needed at the park. Around the headquarters there are several shorter trails, and a day or overnight trip can be made to the Poring Hot Springs, about 20 km by road on the other side of Ranau.

Kinabalu offers one of the best opportunities to see the changes in the forests, which become very stunted near the top. The famous pitcher plants can be seen along the trail, with the largest ones capable of holding two litres of water. There are many fascinating animals found in the upper levels of Kinabalu, with the most obvious being squirrels and birds, notably the mountain blackbird and the Kinabalu friendly warbler. A native rat species has found the huts to be a good food source and some have learned to lift the lid on rice pots and steal leftovers.

Sepilok Orang-Utan Rehabilitation Centre

If you go to Sandakan, it is worth visiting this centre. This centre was originally designed for looking after orang-utans before releasing them back into the wild, but it has become a little touristy and the animals are the main attraction. Some other animals are also kept there, and there is a very good visitor centre. Through the compound there are some forest trails which offer good walking in lowland forest. The forest on the seaward side of the reserve contains proboscis monkeys and it is possible to organise a boat to try and see them. Check with the centre or at the Sabah Parks office in Sandakan.

Danum Valley Field Centre

This field centre west of Lahad Datu in eastern Sabah has been set up by the Sabah Foundation and a few timber companies to study the affects of logging on the forest.

There are numerous jungle trails along which you can spot a wide variety of birds and animals. Hostel and resthouse accommodation is available and you can either cater for yourself or take meals in the rest-house. There are usually a few expatriate scientists doing research here. It's an excellent place to find out a bit more about the forests and wildlife of Sabah, although accommodation and transport are not that cheap.

Semenggoh Wildlife Rehabilitation Centre
This is the Sarawak equivalent of the Sepilok centre in Sabah. It is, however, a much less interesting place to visit, simply because there are very few animals here, and it's hard to find anyone who speaks English. It's still worth visiting if you can't make it to Sepilok.

GOVERNMENT
Malaysia is a confederation of 13 states and a capital district of Kuala Lumpur. Nine of the peninsular states have sultans and every five years an election is held to determine which one will become the *Yang di-Pertuan Agong* or 'King' of Malaysia.

The states of Sabah and Sarawak in East Malaysia are rather different from the Peninsular Malaysian states since they were separate colonies, not parts of Malaya, prior to independence. They still retain a greater degree of local administration than the peninsular states.

ECONOMY
Malaysia is a prosperous and progressive country and one of the world's major suppliers of tin, natural rubber and palm oil. Indeed, rubber plantations, interspersed with oil palm plantations, seem to cover a large part of the peninsula. In East Malaysia the economy is based on timber and in Sarawak oil and pepper are major exports.

In recent years Malaysia's GNP has been growing at around 8% and its light industrial base has been expanding rapidly to provide real export income. Oil has also helped to boost the economy and oil income is transforming the face of east coast Malaysia. Malaysia is seen as one of the next generation of 'tigers' (the booming Asian economies of Korea, Taiwan, Hong Kong and Singapore). This healthy economic base

contributes to Malaysia's position as one of the best-off countries in Asia.

POPULATION
Malaysia's population is currently around 17.5 million but at the 'Happy Family Movement' exhibition in Kuala Lumpur in May 1990 the Information Minister urged couples to have more children, otherwise the population target of 70 million by 2100 would not be achieved!

PEOPLE
The people of Malaysia come from a number of different ethnic groups – Malays, Chinese, Indian, indigenous Orang Asli and the various tribes of Sarawak and Sabah.

It's reasonable to say that the Malays control the government while the Chinese have their fingers on the economic pulse. Approximately 85% of the population lives in Peninsular Malaysia and the remaining 15% in the much more lightly populated states of Sabah and Sarawak.

Peninsular Malaysia
Malays The Malays are the majority indigenous people of the region although they were preceded by aboriginal people, small pockets of whom still survive. The Malays are Muslim and despite major changes in the last decades are still to some extent 'country' rather than 'city' people.

Despite the fact that they only account for around 50% of the population of Peninsular Malaysia (much less in Borneo) they are largely responsible for the political fortunes of the country.

Chinese The Chinese are later arrivals. Although some have been there since the time of Admiral Cheng Ho's visit to Melaka in 1403, the vast majority of the region's Chinese settlers have arrived since the beginning of the 19th century.

The majority arrived here from southern provinces of China but belong to different dialect groups, the major ones being Hakkas, Hokkiens, Teochews, Cantonese and

Hainanese. Although all Chinese use a similar script the dialects are not necessarily mutually comprehensible and a Hokkien and a Hakka speaker may well have to resort to English or Malay to communicate!

The Baba Chinese of Melaka speak a regional Malay dialect but are still culturally Chinese.

The Chinese comprise about 35% of the population in Peninsular Malaysia, 30% in Sarawak and around 20% in Sabah. They are generally traders and merchants.

Indians The region's Indian population arrived later still and in a more organised fashion. Whereas the Chinese flooded in of their own volition the Indians were mainly brought in to provide plantation labour for the British colonists. The majority of the Indian population are Tamils while the rest are mainly Malayalis from the other southern state of Kerala, with a smattering of Kashmiris, Punjabis and Bengalis. They account for around 12% of the population on the peninsula, and are mainly concentrated in the larger towns of the west coast.

Orang Asli There are still small scattered groups of Orang Asli, 'original people', in Peninsular Malaysia. These Proto-Malay people number around 50,000 and are the descendants of the people who inhabited the peninsula before the Malays arrived. Although most have given up their nomadic or shifting-agriculture techniques and have been absorbed into modern Malay society, there are still a few groups of Orang Asli living in the forests.

East Malaysia
The population make-up of the east Malaysian states of Sabah and Sarawak is far more complex than in Peninsular Malaysia, with around 25 ethnic groups in the two states.

Malays The indigenous Malays, who make up around 20% of the population, are descended from local people who converted to Islam, and adopted Malay customs around 400 years ago.

The Melanie, who number around 100,000 in Sarawak, are also native Malays but are ethnically different from the Malays in that they have different physical characteristics and speak different dialects. Most Melanaus are followers of Islam, while the rest have been converted to Christianity.

Chinese The Chinese minority in the east Malaysian states is less significant than on the mainland but is no less important as they are basically the merchants and have a large influence on the economy.

Dayaks Dayak is the term used to cover the non-Muslim people of Borneo. These people migrated to Borneo at times and along routes which are not clearly defined. It is estimated that there are more than 200 Dayak tribes in Borneo.

Sarawak The most important ethnic group in Sarawak are the Iban who number around 450,000. The early Europeans in the area named them Sea Dayaks, as they used to make forays down the rivers and out to sea. They were fierce headhunters and gave the Europeans a bad time along the coasts. Today the Iban are largely longhouse dwellers who live along the Rejang and Baram rivers in Sarawak.

The Land Dayaks (Bidayuh), who number around 130,000 in Sarawak, are another important grouping, who live along the rivers in Sarawak's First Division, the area around Kuching including the Skrang River.

The other much smaller tribes, including the Kenyah, Kayan, Kelabit, Lun Bawang, Kajang, Kedayan, Bisaya and Punan constitute around 5% of Sarawak's total population. It's these small tribal communities of Sarawak who are worst hit by the logging which is currently destroying the rainforests at an incredible rate. The Penan (Punan) are particularly hard hit as they lead a purely hunter-gatherer existence relying totally on the forest for food and shelter. The other communities practise the much maligned (by the government) slash-and-burn agriculture and so while they are less devastated by the loss of forest, still find their land, lifestyle and customs under seige from the disruption.

Sabah The people of Sabah are different again and while there are significant minorities of Chinese (20%) and Bajaus (10%), the major ethnic group is the Kadazans, who account for around 25%. Other smaller groups include the Murut (5%), Malays, Orang Sungai ('river people'), Sulu, Tidong and Bisaya. There are also significant numbers of refugees/immigrants from both the Philippines and Indonesia, and they reside mostly in the eastern towns of Sandakan, Lahad Datu and Tawau.

The Kadazans are traditionally agriculturalists and longhouse dwellers who live mainly in the west of the state. These days there have been large scale conversions to Christianity and Islam and many Kadazans have moved to the cities.

The Bajau live mainly in the north-west of the state, and around Semporna in the south-east. They were originally Sulu Sea pirates but these days pursue the much more prosaic practices of agriculture and animal husbandry.

The only other group of any size is the Murut, who number around 40,000 and live in the south-west in the Tenom area. They are agriculturalists who used to occupy a much larger area of Sabah but were pushed south by the migrating Kadazans.

ARTS & CULTURE

It's along the east coast of Peninsular Malaysia, the predominantly Malay part of Malaysia, that you'll find Malay arts and crafts, culture and games at their liveliest and most widely practised.

Silat

Also known as *bersilat* this is the Malay martial art which originated in Melaka in the 15th century. Today it is a highly refined and stylised activity, demonstrations of which

are often performed at ceremonies and weddings, accompanied by music from drums and gongs.

Wayang Kulit – Shadow Play

Similar to the shadow puppet performances of other South-East Asian countries, in particular Java in Indonesia, the *wayang kulit* retells tales from the Hindu epic the *Ramayana*.

The *To'Dalang* or 'Father of the Mysteries' sits behind the semi-transparent screen and manipulates the buffalo-hide puppets whose images are thrown onto the screen. Characters include heroes, demons, kings, animals and, ever favourites, clowns.

Performances can last for many hours and throughout that time the puppeteer has to move the figures, sing all the voice parts and conduct the orchestra – it's a feat of some endurance. There are two forms of Wayang Kulit – the *wayang siam* and *wayang*

Shadow Puppet

melayu. Performances often take place at weddings or after the harvest.

Dances & Other Activities

There are a variety of dances and dance dramas performed in Malaysia. *Menora* is a dance drama of Thai origin performed by an all-male cast dressed in grotesque masks.

Ma'yong is a similar traditional form of theatre but the participants are of both sexes. These performances are often made at Puja Keteks, Buddhist festivals held at temples in Kelantan, near the Thai border.

The *ronggeng* is one of the oldest and most traditional Malay dance forms. *Rebana kercing* is a dance performed by young men to the accompaniment of tambourines. Other dances, not all of which are from the east coast, include the *tari piring*, *hadrah* and *zapin*.

Berdikir Barat is a comparatively recent activity – a sort of poetic debating contest where two teams have to ridicule and argue with each other in instantaneously composed verse!

Musical Instruments

As in other parts of the region Malay music is principally percussion. The large, hollowed-out log drum known as a *rebana* is one of the most important Malay instruments. Drum-beating contests are sometimes held. The *kertok* is a small drum which takes its name from the distinctive sound it makes.

Crafts

Batik Although originally an Indonesian craft, batik has made itself equally at home in Malaysia. You'll find it in Penang on the west coast but Kelantan is its true home.

Batik cloth is produced by drawing out a pattern with wax and then dyeing the material. The wax is then melted away by boiling the cloth, and a second wax design is drawn in. By repeating waxing, dyeing and boiling processes an intricate and beautifully coloured design is produced.

Batik can be found as clothes, cushion covers, tablecloths, placemats or simply as works of art. Malay designs are usually less traditional than those found in neighbouring Indonesia. The wax designs can either be drawn out on a one-off basis or printed on with a stencil.

Kain Songket & Other Weaving A speciality of Kelantan, *kain songket* is a handwoven fabric with gold and silver threads woven into the material. Clothes made from this beautiful fabric are usually reserved for the most important festivals and occasions. *Mengkuang* is a far more prosaic form of weaving using pandanus leaves and strips of bamboo to make baskets, bags and mats.

Silver & Brasswork Kelantan is famed for its silversmiths who work in a variety of ways and specialise in filigree and repousse work. In the latter, designs are hammered through the silver from the underside. Kampung Sireh at Kota Bharu is a centre for silverwork. Brasswork is an equally traditional skill in Kuala Terengganu.

Avoiding Offence

Like many Muslim countries Malaysia has been going through a period of increasing concentration on religion and religious activity in the past 10 years or so. It's wise to be appropriately discreet in dress and behaviour, particularly on the more strictly Muslim east coast of the peninsula.

For women, topless bathing is definitely not acceptable and away from the beaches you should cover as much as possible. Don't take your cue from fellow travellers but from Malaysian women. For men, shorts are considered odd attire for adults but are not necessarily offensive. Bare torsos are not considered acceptable in the villages and towns.

Unfortunately women may encounter unwanted attention from Malaysian men who consider Western women to be of loose morals. Dressing conservatively will help to alleviate any problems.

Events

Top-Spinning (Main Gasing) Spinning tops hardly seems to be an activity for grown-ups to engage in but *gasing*, Malaysian tops, are not child's play. A top can weigh up to seven kg and it takes a good deal of strength to whip the five-metre cord back and spin them competitively.

Main gasing contests are held in east coast villages during the slack time of year while the rice is ripening. Contests are usually between teams of fighting tops, where the attackers attempt to dislodge the defenders from a prearranged pattern, or there are contests for length of spin. The record spinning time approaches two hours!

Kite-Flying Flying kites is another child's game that takes on adult-size proportions on the east coast. Kite-flying contests include events for greatest height reached and also competitions between fighting kites.

The kites, which can be up to 2½ metres wide, are real works of art. There are cat kites, bird kites and, most popular, the *wau balun* or moon kite. An attachment to the front of the kite makes a humming noise and in favourable conditions a kite may be left flying, humming pleasantly, all night. Kites are popular souvenirs of Malaysia and a stylised Kelantan kite is the symbol of Malaysian Airlines System (MAS).

Sepak Raga One of the most popular kampung games, the equipment needed to play *sepak raga* is simplicity itself – a lightweight ball made of strips of rotan. Drawn up in a circle the opposing teams must keep the ball continuously in the air, using legs, head and shoulders. Points are scored for each time a team member hits the ball.

Sepak takraw is a version of the same game where the players hit the ball back and forth over a net just like in volleyball – but again without using hands. It's a popular sport in a number of South-East Asian countries and the Thais are the champions.

RELIGION

The variety of religions found in Malaysia is a direct reflection of the diversity of races living there. Although Islam is the state religion of Malaysia, freedom of religion is guaranteed. The Malays are almost all Muslims and there are also some Indian Muslims. The Chinese are predominantly followers of Taoism and Buddhism, though some are Christians. The majority of the region's Indian population come from south India and are Hindu. Although Christianity has made no great inroads into Peninsular Malaysia it has had a much greater impact upon East Malaysia where many of the indigenous people have converted to Christianity, although others still follow their animist traditions.

Islam

In the early 7th century in Mecca, Mohammed received the word of Allah (God) and called on the people to turn away from pagan worship and submit to the one true God. His teachings appealed to the poorer levels of society and angered the wealthy merchant class. By 622 life had become sufficiently unpleasant to force Mohammed and his followers to migrate to Medina, an oasis town some 300 km to the north. This migration – the *hijrah* – marks the beginning of the Islamic calendar, year 1 AH or 622 AD. By 630 Mohammed had gained a sufficient following to return and take Mecca.

With boundless zeal the followers of Mohammed spread the word, using force where necessary, and by 644 the Islamic state covered Syria, Persia, Mesopotamia, Egypt and North Africa; in following decades its influence would extend from the Atlantic to the Indian Ocean.

Islam is the Arabic word for submission, and the duty of every Muslim is to submit themselves to Allah. This profession of faith (the *Shahada*) is the first of the Five Pillars of Islam, the five tenets in the Koran which guide Muslims in their daily life:

Shahada 'There is no God but Allah and Mohammed is his prophet' – this profession of faith is the fundamental tenet of Islam. It is to Islam what The Lord's Prayer is to Christianity, and it is often quoted (eg to greet the newborn and farewell the dead).

Salah The call to prayer. Five times a day – at dawn, midday, mid-afternoon, sunset and nightfall – Muslims must face Mecca and recite the prescribed prayer.

Zakat It was originally the act of giving alms to the poor and needy and the amount was fixed at 5% of one's income. It has been developed by some modern states into an obligatory land tax which goes to help the poor.

Ramadan This is the ninth month of the Muslim calendar when all Muslims must abstain from eating, drinking, smoking and sex from dawn to dusk. It commemorates the month when Mohammed had the Koran revealed to him; the purpose of the physical deprivation is to strengthen the will and forfeit the body to the spirit.

Hajj The pilgrimage to Mecca, the holiest place in Islam. It is the duty of every Muslim who is fit and can afford it to make the pilgrimage at least once in their life. On the pilgrimage, the pilgrim (*hajji*) wears two plain white sheets and walks around the *kabbah*, the black stone in the centre of the mosque, seven times. Other ceremonies such as sacrificing an animal and shaving the pilgrim's head also take place.

According to Muslim belief, Allah is the same as the God worshipped by Christians and Jews. Adam, Abraham, Noah, Moses, David, Jacob, Joseph, Job and Jesus are all recognised as prophets by Islam. Jesus is not, however, recognised as the son of God. According to Islam, all these prophets partly received the word of God but only Mohammed received the complete revelation.

In its early days Islam suffered a major schism that divided the faith into two streams: the Sunnis (or Sunnites) and the Shi'ites. The prophet's son-in-law, Ali, became the fourth caliph following the murder of Mohammed's third successor, and he in turn was assassinated in 661 by the governor of Syria, who set himself up as caliph. The Sunnis, who comprise the majority of Muslims today, are followers of the succession from this caliph, while the Shi'ites follow the descendants of Ali.

Chinese Religion

The Chinese religion is a mix of Taoism, Confucianism and Buddhism. Taoism combines with old animistic beliefs to teach people how to maintain harmony with the universe. Confucianism takes care of the political and moral aspects of life. Buddhism takes care of the afterlife. But to say that the Chinese have three religions – Taoism, Buddhism and Confucianism – is too simple a view of their traditional religious life. At the first level Chinese religion is animistic, with a belief in the innate vital energy in rocks, trees, rivers and springs. At the second level people from the distant past, both real and mythological, are worshipped as gods. Overlaid on these beliefs are popular Taoism, Mahayana Buddhism and Confucianism.

On a day-to-day level the Chinese are much less concerned with the high-minded philosophies and asceticism of Buddha, Confucius or Lao Zi than they are with the pursuit of worldly success, the appeasement of the dead and the spirits, and the seeking of hidden knowledge about the future. Chinese religion incorporates what the West regards as superstition; if you want your fortune told, for instance, you go to a temple. The other important thing to remember is that Chinese religion is polytheistic. Apart from Buddha, Lao Zi and Confucius there are many divinities such as house gods and gods and goddesses for particular professions.

The most important word in the Chinese popular religious vocabulary is *joss* (luck), and the Chinese are too astute not to utilise it. Gods have to be appeased, bad spirits blown away and sleeping dragons soothed to keep joss on one's side. *Fung-shui* (literally wind-water) is the Chinese technique of manipulating or judging the environment. Fung-shui uses unseen currents that swirl around the surface of the earth and are caused by dragons which sleep beneath the ground. In Hong Kong, if you want to build a house or find a suitable site for a grave then you call in a fung-shui expert; the wrath of a dragon which woke to find a house on his tail can easily be imagined! In Hong Kong some villages even have groves of trees planted for good spirits to live in.

Integral parts of Chinese religion are death, the afterlife and ancestor-worship. At least as far back as China's Shang Dynasty there were lavish funeral ceremonies involving the internment of horses, carriages, wives and slaves. The more important the person the more possessions and people had to be buried with him since he would require them in the next world. The deceased had to be kept happy because his powers to inflict punishments or to grant favours greatly increased after his death. Even today a traditional Chinese funeral can still be a lavish event.

Hinduism

On first appearances Hinduism is a complex religion, but basically it postulates that we all go through a series of rebirths and reincarnations that eventually lead to *moksha*, the spiritual salvation which frees one from the cycle of rebirths. With each rebirth you can move closer to or further from eventual moksha; the deciding factor is your karma, which is literally a law of cause and effect. Bad actions during your life result in bad karma, which ends in lower reincarnation. Conversely, if your deeds and actions have been good you will reincarnate on a higher level and be a step closer to eventual freedom from rebirth. Dharma, or the natural law, defines the total social, ethical and spiritual harmony of your life.

Hinduism has three basic practices: *puja*, or worship; the cremation of the dead; and the rules and regulations of the caste system. Although still very strong in India the caste system was never significant in Malaysia, mainly because the labourers who were brought here from India were mainly from the lower classes.

Westerners often have trouble understanding Hinduism, principally because of its vast pantheon of gods. In fact you can look upon all these different gods simply as pictorial representations of the many attributes of a god. The one omnipresent god usually has three physical representations: Brahma, the creator; Vishnu, the preserver; and Shiva, the destroyer or reproducer. All three gods are usually shown with four arms, but Brahma has the added advantage of four heads to represent his all-seeing presence. The four

Vedas, the books of 'divine knowledge' which are the foundation of Hindu philosophy, are supposed to have emanated from his mouths.

Hinduism is not a proselytising religion since you cannot be converted. You're either born a Hindu or you are not; you can never become one.

FESTIVALS & HOLIDAYS

With so many cultures and religions there is quite an amazing number of occasions to celebrate in Malaysia. Although some of them have a fixed date each year, the Hindus, Muslims and Chinese all follow a lunar calendar which results in the dates for many events varying each year. Each year, the Tourist Development Corporation (TDC) puts out a *Calendar of Events* booklet with specific dates and venues of various festivals and parades.

The major Muslim events each year are connected with Ramadan, the 30 days during which Muslims cannot eat or drink from sunrise to sunset.

Fifteen days before the commencement of Ramadan the souls of the dead are supposed to visit their homes on Nisfu Night. During Ramadan Lailatul Qadar, the 'Night of Grandeur', celebrates the arrival of the Koran on earth from heaven before its revelation by Mohammed. A Koran-reading competition is held in Kuala Lumpur (and extensively televised) during Ramadan.

Hari Raya Puasa marks the end of the month-long fast with three days of joyful celebration. This is the major holiday of the Muslim calendar and it can be difficult to find accommodation in Malaysia, particularly on the east coast. Hari Raya Haji marks the day when pilgrims in Mecca touch the Black Stone. Other festivals include:

14 January

Thai Pongal A Hindu harvest festival marking the beginning of the Hindu month of Thai, considered the luckiest month of the year.

January-February

Chinese New Year Dragon dances and pedestrian parades mark the start of the new year. Families hold open house, unmarried relatives (especially children) receive *ang pows* (money in red packets), businesses traditionally clear their debts and everybody wishes you a Kong Hee Fatt Choy (a happy & prosperous new year).

Birthday of Chor Soo Kong Six days after the new year the number of snakes at Penang's snake temple, dedicated to Chor Soo Kong, is supposed to be the greatest.

Birthday of the Jade Emperor Nine days after the new year a Chinese festival honours Yu Huang, the Supreme Ruler of Heaven, with offerings at temples.

Ban Hood Huat Hoay A 12-day celebration for the Day of Ten Thousand Buddhas is held at the Kek Lok Si Temple in Penang.

Chap Goh Meh On the 15th day after Chinese New Year the celebrations officially end.

Chingay In Johore Bahru processions of Chinese flag bearers, balancing bamboo flag poles six to 12 metres long, can be seen on the 22nd day after the new year.

Thaipusam One of the most dramatic Hindu festivals in which devotees honour Lord Subramaniam with acts of amazing masochism. In Kuala Lumpur, they march in a procession to the Batu Caves carrying *kavadis*, heavy metal frames decorated with peacock feathers, fruit and flowers. The kavadis are hung from their bodies with metal hooks and spikes driven into the flesh. Other devotees pierce their cheeks and tongues with metal skewers or walk on sandals of nails. Along the procession route the kavadi carriers dance to the drum beat while spectators urge them on with shouts of 'Vel, Vel'. In the evening the procession continues with an image of Subramaniam in a temple car.

In Penang, Thaipusam is celebrated at the Waterfall Temple. This festival is now officially banned in India.

Late February

Kwong Teck Sun Ong's Birthday Celebration of the birthday of a child deity at the Chinese temple in Kuching.

March-April

Tua Peck Kong Paper money and paper models of useful things to have with you in the afterlife are burnt at the Sia Sen Temple in Kuching.

Easter On Palm Sunday a candlelight procession is held at St Peter's in Melaka. Good Friday and Easter Monday also witness colourful celebrations at St Peter's and other Melaka churches.

Panguni Uttiram On the full moon day of the Tamil month of Panguni, the marriage of Shiva to Shakti and of Lord Subramaniam to Theivani is celebrated.

Birthday of the Goddess of Mercy Offerings are made to the very popular Kuan Yin at her temples in Penang and Kuala Lumpur.

Cheng Beng On Cheng Beng (All Soul's Day) Chinese traditionally visit the tombs of their ancestors to clean and repair them and make offerings.

Sri Rama Navami A nine-day festival held by the Brahman caste to honour the Hindu hero of the Ramayana, Sri Rama.

Birthday of the Monkey God The birthday of T'se Tien Tai Seng Yeh is celebrated twice a year. Mediums pierce their cheeks and tongues with skewers and go into a trance during which they write special charms in blood.

April-May

Songkran Festival A traditional Thai Buddhist New Year in which Buddha images are bathed.

Chithirai Vishu Start of the Hindu New Year.

Puja Pantai A large three-day beach festival held five km south of Kuala Terengganu.

Birthday of the Queen of Heaven Ma Cho Po, the Queen of Heaven and Goddess of the Sea, is honoured at her temples.

Wesak Day Buddha's birth, enlightenment and death are celebrated by various events including the release of caged birds to symbolise the setting free of captive souls.

Early May
Sipitang Tamu Besar Annual market celebration at Sipitang near Beaufort in Sabah. Blowpipe competitions feature among the events.

May
Start of the turtle season; from then, through to September giant turtles come ashore along the beach at Rantau Abang on the east coast of the peninsula each night to lay their eggs.

10-11 May
Kadazan Harvest Festival A thanksgiving harvest festival by the Kadazan farmers of Sabah, marked by the sumazau Kadazan dance.

30-31 May
Kota Belud Tamu Besar Bajau horsemen feature in this annual market festival at Kota Belud, near Kota Kinabalu in Sabah.

1-2 June
Gawai Dayak Annual Sarawak festival of the Dayaks to mark the end of the rice season. War dances, cockfights and blowpipe events all take place.

4 June
Birthday of the Yang di-Pertuan Agong Celebration of the official birthday of Malaysia's Supreme Head of State.

29 June
Festa de San Pedro Christian celebration in

honour of the patron saint of the fishing community, particularly celebrated by the Eurasian-Portuguese community of Melaka.

June
Birthday of the God of War Kuan Ti, who has the ability to avert war and protect people during a war, is honoured on his birthday.

June-August
Dragon Boat Festival Commemorating the death of a Chinese saint who drowned himself. In an attempt to save him the local fishing community paddled out to sea, beating drums to scare away any fish that might attack him. To mark the anniversary today, this festival is celebrated with boat races in Penang.

June-September
Muul Hijrah A Muslim holiday commemorating the flight, or *hijrah* of the Prophet Mohammed from Medina to Mecca in 622.

1 July
Keningau Tamu Besar Market festival at Keningau in Sabah with buffalo races, blowpipe competitions and other events.

29 July
Tuaran Tamu Besar Tuaran, only 35 km from Kota Kinabalu, celebrates its annual market festival with boat races as well as Bajau horseriders and other events.

Late July
Lumut Sea Carnival At Lumut, the port for Pangkor Island, boat races, swimming races and many other events are held.

July
Birthday of Kuan Yin The Goddess of Mercy has another birthday!

Hari Raya Haji Muslim holiday.

Feast of St Anne A Roman Catholic festival celebrated at St Anne's Church in Penang.

July-August

Sri Krishna Jayanti A 10-day Hindu festival celebrating popular events in Krishna's life is highlighted on day eight by celebrations of his birthday. The Laxmi Narayan Temple in Kuala Lumpur is a particular focus.

31 August

National Day Hari Kebangsaan Malaysia celebrates Malaysia's independence with events all over the country, but particularly in Kuala Lumpur where there are parades and a variety of performances in the Lake Gardens.

31 August

Beaufort Tamu Besar Another annual market festival in Sabah.

August

Festival of the Seven Sisters Chinese girls pray to the Weaving Maid for good husbands.

Festival of the Hungry Ghosts The souls of the dead are released for one day of feasting and entertainment on earth. Chinese operas and other events are laid on for them and food is put out, which the ghosts eat the spirit of but thoughtfully leave the substance for mortal celebrants.

August-September

Vinayagar Chathuri During the Tamil month of Avani prayers are offered to Vinayagar, another name for the extremely popular elephant-headed god Ganesh.

1-22 September

Feast of Santa Cruz A month-long pilgrimage season at the Church of Santa Cruz at Malim, Melaka.

15-20 September

Papar Tamu Besar Annual market festival in an area of Sabah renowned for its beautiful Kadazan girls.

September

Moon Cake Festival The overthrow of the Mongol warlords in ancient China is celebrated by eating moon cakes and lighting colourful paper lanterns. Moon cakes are made with bean paste, lotus seeds and sometimes a duck egg.

September-October

Thimithi – Fire Walking Ceremony Hindu devotees prove their belief by walking across glowing coals at the Gajah Berang Temple in Melaka.

Navarathri In the Tamil month of Purattasi the Hindu festival of 'Nine Nights' is dedicated to the wives of Shiva, Vishnu and Brahma. Young girls are dressed as the goddess Kali.

Festival of the Nine Emperor Gods Nine days of Chinese operas, processions and other events honour the nine emperor gods. At the Kau Ong Yah Temples in Kuala Lumpur and Penang fire-walking ceremonies are held on the evening of the ninth day.

Prophet Mohammed's Birthday Muslims pray and religious leaders recite verses from the Koran.

1-31 October

Puja Ketek Offerings are brought to Buddhist shrines or keteks in the state of Kelantan. Traditional dances are often performed.

Menggatal Tamu Besar Another Sabah market festival.

7 October

Universal Children's Day A rally for children in Kuala Lumpur.

Mid-October

Kudat Tamu Besar Another Sabah market festival.

October-November

Kantha Shashithi Subramaniam, a great fighter against the forces of evil, is honoured during the Hindu month of Aipasi.

Deepavali Later in the same month Rama's victory over the demon King Ravana is celebrated with the 'Festival of Lights' where tiny oil lamps are lit outside Hindu homes.

Birthday of Kuan Yin The birthday of the popular Goddess of Mercy is celebrated yet again.

Kartikai Deepam Huge bonfires are lit to commemorate Shiva's appearance as a pillar of fire following an argument with Vishnu and Brahma. The Thandayuthapani Temple in Muar is a major site for this festival.

22 November
Guru Nanak's Birthday The birthday of Guru Nanak, founder of the Sikh religion, is celebrated on this day.

December
Pesta Pulau Penang Month-long carnival on Penang Island featuring many water events including dragon boat races towards the end of the festival.

Winter Solstice Festival Chinese festival to offer thanks for a good harvest.

25 December
Christmas Day

LANGUAGE
The official language is Bahasa Malaysia or 'Bahasa'. You can get along quite happily with English throughout Malaysia and, although it is not the official language, it is often still the linking language between the various ethnic groups, especially for the middle classes. When a Tamil wants to speak to a Chinese or a Chinese to a Malay it's likely they'll speak in English. English was once the main language of instruction at higher levels of education but Bahasa Malaysia is now being introduced as the sole language of instruction at all levels. As a consequence there has been a decline in the proficiency of English amongst younger Malaysians.

Other everyday languages include the Chinese dialects like Hakka or Hokkien. Th majority of the region's Indians speak Tam although there are also groups who spe Malayalam, Hindi or another Indian la guage.

Bahasa is virtually the same as Indonesi but there are a number of different word Many of the differences are in the loan wor – English based for Malaysian and Dut based for Indonesian. If you are coming fro Indonesia and have developed a proficien in the language, you may be initially co fused by the pronunciation. Because Baha is a second language for most people Indonesia, its pronunciation is taught schools and is fairly standard. In Malaysia is subject to many regional variances in pr nunciation and slang – so much so that Malaysian from Negri Sembilan may ha difficulty understanding someone fro Kelantan.

Bahasa is, at least in its most basic for very simple. There are no tense changes f example; you indicate the tense by usir words such as yesterday or tomorrow or y just add *sudah* (already) to make anythir past tense. Many nouns are pluralised simp by saying them twice – thus *buku* is 'book *buku-buku* is 'books'. Or *anak* is 'child *anak-anak* is 'children'.

The everyday street language is oft referred to as *bahasa pasar* or market la guage. Other language simplification include the omission of the articles 'the', ' or 'an'. Thus you just say *buku baik* rath than 'a good book' or 'the good book'. Th verb 'to be' is also omitted so again it woul be *buku baik* rather than 'the book is good Bahasa is also a very musical and evocati language – 'the sun', for example, is *ma hari* or 'the eye of the day'!

Just as many Hindi words have found the way into Indian-English so many Mala terms are used in everyday English. You often read in the papers or see ads with th word *bumiputra*, which literally means 'so of the soil' but is used to specify that the jo or whatever is open only to Malay-Malay sians not Indian-Malaysians Chinese-Malaysians. Papers occasional

Top Left: Old Man, Malaysia (PS)
Top Right: Malaysia (PS)
Bottom Left: School Children, Kampung Ayer, Brunei (HF)
Bottom Right: Children on boat, Malaysia (PS)

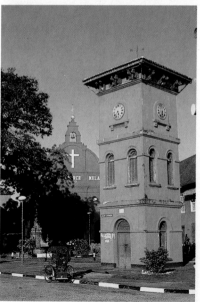

Top Left: Temple, Melaka (TW)
Top Right: NR, Melaka (TW)
Bottom Left: Clocktower & Christ Church, Melaka (TW)
Bottom Right: Porta de Santiago, Melaka (TW)

complain about *jaga keretas* – they're people who operate car parking rackets – pay them to 'protect' your car while it's parked or you'll wish you had. Or you may hear of a couple being accused of *khalwat* – literally 'close proximity' and something unmarried Muslims should not be suspected of!

Lonely Planet also publishes *Indonesia Phrasebook* which is a handy pocket-sized introduction to Bahasa.

New Spelling The new spelling system in Bahasa Malaysia brings it into line with Indonesian. However, many of the old spellings are still in use for place names and people's names. The main changes are that 'c' is used instead of 'ch' and is pronounced as in the English word 'church', and 'o' often becomes 'u' when it is the final syllable, eg kampung not kampong, Teluk not Telok.

Civilities

thank you (very much)
  terima kasih (banyak)
please
  silakan
good morning
  selamat pagi
good day (around midday)
  selamat tengah hari
good afternoon
  selamat petang
good night
  selamat malam
goodbye (to person staying)
  selamat tinggal
goodbye (to person going)
  selamat jalan
sorry
  maaf
excuse me
  permisi

Questions

How are you?
  Apa khabar?
What is this?
  Apa ini?
What is your name?
  Siapa nama kamu?

My name is...
  Nama saya...
How many km?
  Berapa kilometer?
Where is/Which way?
  Di mana/Ke mana?
How much?
  Berapa?

Getting Around

ticket	*tikit*
ticket window	*tempat tikit*
bus	*bas*
train	*keretapi*
ship	*kapal*
boat	*bot*
bicycle	*basikal*
rickshaw/trishaw	*beca*
town	*bandar*
small town	*pekan*

Numbers

1	*satu*
2	*dua*
3	*tiga*
4	*empat*
5	*lima*
6	*enam*
7	*tujuh*
8	*delapan/lapan*
9	*sembilan*
10	*sepuluh*
11	*sebelas*
12	*dua belas*
20	*dua puluh*
21	*dua puluh satu*
30	*tiga puluh*
53	*lima puluh tiga*
100	*seratus*
1000	*seribu*
½	*setengah*

Time

when?	*bila?*
tomorrow	*besok*
yesterday	*kelmarin*
hour	*jam*
week	*minggu*
year	*tahun*
what is the time?	*pukul berapa?*

how long?	*berapa lama?*
7 o'clock	*pukul tujuh*

Days of the Week

Monday	*hari Isnin*
Tuesday	*hari Selasa*
Wednesday	*hari Rabu*
Thursday	*hari Kamis*
Friday	*hari Jumaat*
Saturday	*hari Sabtu*
Sunday	*hari Minggu*

Some Useful Phrases

I want to go to...	*Saya mau ke...*
bank	*bank*
street	*jalan*
post office	*pejabat pos*
immigration	*imigresen*

How much for...?	*Berapa harga...?*
one night	*satu malam*
one person	*satu orang*

I don't understand.
Saya tidak mengerti.

Some Useful Words

sleep	*tidur*
bed	*tempat tidur*
room	*bilik*
bathroom	*bilik mandi*
toilet	*tandas, bilik air*
soap	*sabun*
shop	*kedai*
this/that	*ini/itu*
big/small	*besar/kecil*
here/there	*di sini/di sana*
stop	*berhenti*
another	*satu lagi*
no, not, negative	*tidak*
open/closed	*buka/tutup*
see	*lihat*
good, very nice	*bagus*
no good	*tidak baik*
all right, good, fine	*baik*
finished	*habis*
dirty	*kotor*
expensive	*mahal*

Food *(Makanan)*

plain rice	*nasi kosong*
fried rice	*nasi goreng*
boiled rice	*nasi putih*
rice with odds & ends	*nasi campur*
fried noodles	*mee goreng*
noodle soup	*mee kuah*
soup	*sup*
fried vegetables	*cap cai*
with crispy noodles	*tami*
sweet & sour omelette	*fu yung hai*
fish	*ikan*
chicken	*ayam*
egg	*telur*
pork	*babi*
frog	*kodok*
crab	*kepiting/ ketam*
beef	*daging lembu*
prawns	*udang*
potatoes	*kentang*
vegetables	*sayur-sayuran*

Drinks *(Minum-Minuman)*

drinking water	*air minum*
orange juice	*air jeruk/oren*
coffee	*kopi*
tea (with milk and sugar)	*teh*
tea (with sugar but no milk)	*teh-o*
tea (without sugar and milk)	*teh kosong*
milk	*susu*

Extras

butter	*mentega*
sugar	*gula*
salt	*garam*
ice	*ais* or *ais batu*

Description

sweet	*manis*
steaming hot	*panas*
spicy hot	*pedas*
cold	*sejuk*
delicious	*enak*
special	*istimewa*

Finally for vegetarians *Saya tidak mau ikan, ayam atau daging* means 'I do not want fish, chicken or meat'.

Facts for the Visitor

VISAS

Commonwealth citizens, citizens of the Republic of Ireland, Switzerland, the Netherlands and Liechtenstein do not require a visa to visit Malaysia. Citizens of the USA, Germany, France, Italy, Norway, Sweden, Denmark, Belgium, Finland, Luxembourg and Iceland do not require a visa for a visit not exceeding three months. Seven-day visas are granted to citizens of Czechoslovakia, Hungary, Poland, Russian, Yugoslavia, Rumania and Bulgaria.

Normally you get a 30-day or 60-day stay permit on arrival, depending on your expected length of stay. This is extendable up to three months. It's a straightforward procedure which can be done in major cities.

Note that Sabah and Sarawak are treated in some ways like separate countries. Your passport will be checked again on arrival in each state and a new stay permit issued. You are usually issued with a 60-day permit on arrival in Sarawak, 30-day permit when arriving in Sabah. Travelling directly from either Sabah or Sarawak back to Peninsular Malaysia, however, there are no formalities and you do not start a new entry period, so your 60 or 30-day permit from Sabah or Sarawak remains valid.

Thai Visas

You can get Thai visas from the embassies in Singapore or Kuala Lumpur or the consulates in Penang or Kota Bharu. The consulates are quick and convenient.

There are three types of Thai visa: if you have an onward air ticket and will not be staying in Thailand for more than 14 days then you do not need to prearrange a visa and can get a free entry permit on arrival by air or land; for M$15 you can get a one-month transit visa; or for M$30 a two-month tourist visa. Three photos are required.

Indonesian Visas

For most Western nationalities no visa is required on arrival in Indonesia as long as you have a ticket out (not always rigidly enforced) and do not intend to stay for more than two months. The only catch is that the 'no visa' entry only applies if you both enter and leave Indonesia through certain recognised gateways. These entry and exit points include all the usual airports and seaports, but there are some places like Jayapura in Irian Jaya, not on the list. If you intend to arrive or leave Indonesia through one of the oddball places then you have to get a visa in advance.

When the new regulations were first introduced some travellers discovered to their expense that Indonesian diplomatic offices did not know the full story on the new plan and happily told them that entering without a visa at Jakarta was fine, failing to add if you tried to leave from Jayapura you would be told no. These days the regulations are well understood.

EMBASSIES
Malaysian Embassies

Visas can be obtained at Malaysian diplomatic missions overseas including:

Australia
    7 Perth Ave, Yarralumla, Canberra ACT 2600 (tel (062) 731543)
Brunei
    Lot 12, 6th Floor, Darussalam Complex, Bandar Seri Begawan (tel (02) 28401)
Canada
    60 Boteler St, Ottawa, Ontario K1N 8Y7 (tel (613) 237-5182)
France
    2 Bis Rue Benouville, Paris 75116, France (tel 45531185)
Germany
    Mittelstrasse 43, 5300 Bonn 2 (tel (0228) 376803)
Hong Kong
    24th Floor, Malaysia Building, 50 Gloucester Rd, Wanchai (tel (5) 270921)

India
  50M Satya Marg, Chanakyapuri, New Delhi
  110021 (tel 601291)
  287 TTK Rd, Madras 600018 (tel 453580)
Indonesia
  17 Jalan Imam Bonjol, Jakarta (tel 336438)
  11 Jalan Diponegoro, Medan, Sumatra (tel 25315)
  42 Jalan A Yani, Pontianak, Kalimantan (tel 2986)
Japan
  20-16 Nanpeidai-machi, Shibuya-ku, Tokyo 150 (tel (03) 770-9331)
Myanmar
  82 Diplomatic Quarters, Pyidaundsu Yeikhta Rd, Rangoon (tel 20248)
Netherlands
  Rustenburgweg- 2, 2517 KE, The Hague (tel (070) 506506)
New Zealand
  10 Washington Ave, Brooklyn, Wellington (tel 852439)
Pakistan
  224 Nazimuddin Rd, F-7/4, Islamabad (tel 820147)
Papua New Guinea
  Unit 1, 2nd Floor, Pacific View Apartments, Pruth St, Korobosea, Port Moresby (tel 252076)
Philippines
  107 Tordesillas St, Salcedo Village, Makati (tel 817-4581)
Singapore
  301 Jervois Rd, Singapore 1024 (tel 2350111)
Sri Lanka
  87 Horton Place, Colombo 7 (tel 94837)
Thailand
  35 South Sathorn Rd, Bangkok 10500 (tel 286-1390)
  1 Sukhum Rd, Songkhla (tel 311062)
UK
  45 Belgrave Square, London SW1X 8QT (tel (071) 235-8033)
USA
  2401 Massachusetts Ave NW, Washington DC 20008 (tel (202) 328-7700)

Foreign Embassies in Malaysia

Countries with diplomatic representation in Malaysia include:

Australia
  6 Jalan Yap Kwan Sweng, Kuala Lumpur (tel 03-2423122)
Brunei
  MBF Plaza, Jalan Ampang, Kuala Lumpur (tel 03-4574149)
Canada
  Plaza MBS, Jalan Ampang, Kuala Lumpur (tel 03-2612000)

Denmark
  Angkasa Raya Building, Jalan Ampang, Kuala Lumpur (tel 03-2416088)
France
  196 Jalan Ampang, Kuala Lumpur (tel 03-2484122)
  Wisma Rajab, 82 Bishop St, Penang (tel 04-629707)
Germany
  3 Jalan U Thant, Kuala Lumpur (tel 03-2429666)
India
  Wisma Selangor Dredging, Kuala Lumpur (tel 03-2617000)
Indonesia
  233 Jalan Tun Razak, Kuala Lumpur (tel 03-9842011)
  467 Jalan Burma, Penang (tel 04-25162)
  5A Pisang Rd, Kuching, Sarawak
  Jalan Karamunsing, Kota Kinabalu, Sabah (tel 088-54100)
  Jalan Kuharsa, Tawau, Sabah
Japan
  Wisma AIA, Jalan Ampang, Kuala Lumpur (tel 03-2320270)
  2 Jalan Biggs, Penang (tel 04-368222)
Myanmar
  7 Jalan Taman U Thant, Kuala Lumpur (tel 03-2424085)
Netherlands
  4 Jalan Megra, Kuala Lumpur (tel 03-2431143)
New Zealand
  193 Jalan Tun Razak, Kuala Lumpur (tel 03-2486422)
Philippines
  1 Changkat Kia Peng, Kuala Lumpur (tel 03-2484233)
Singapore
  209 Jalan Tun Razak, Kuala Lumpur (tel 03-2616277)
Sri Lanka
  29 Jalan Yap Kwan Seng, Kuala Lumpur (tel 03-2423094)
Sweden
  6th Floor, Angkasa Raya Building, Jalan Ampang, Kuala Lumpur (tel 03-2485981)
Switzerland
  16 Persiaran Madge, Kuala Lumpur (tel 03-2480622)
Thailand
  206 Jalan Ampang, Kuala Lumpur (tel 03-2488222)
  1 Jalan Ayer Rajah, Penang (tel 04-23352)
UK
  13th Floor, Wisma Damansara, Jalan Semantan, Kuala Lumpur (tel 03-2541533)
  c/o Price Waterhouse, UMBC Building, Lebuh Pantai, Penang (tel 04-621700)

USA
376 Jalan Tun Razak, Kuala Lumpur (tel 03-2489011)

MONEY
Exchange Rates

The following table shows the exchange rates:

A$1	=	M$2.15
C$1	=	M$2.38
DM1	=	M$1.65
HK$1	=	M$0.35
NZ$1	=	M$1.65
SIN$1	=	M$1.55
UK£1	=	M$4.80
US$1	=	M$2.79

Currency

The Malaysian dollar is known as the ringgit, and although it used to be on a par, and was interchangeable, with the Singapore dollar, these days it is worth much less than the Singapore dollar.

Notes in circulation are M$1, M$5, M$10, M$20, M$50, M$100, M$500 and M$1000; the coins in use are 1, 5, 10, 20 and 50 sen, and a new M$1.

All major credit cards are widely accepted at major hotels, restaurants and craft shops.

Banks are efficient and there are also plenty of moneychangers. Banks usually charge commission, typically around M$3 per transaction, whereas the moneychangers have no charges but their rates vary more, so know what the current rate is before dealing with moneychangers. For cash you'll generally get a better rate at a moneychanger than in a bank – it's usually quicker too.

Costs

Malaysia can pretty much cost you what you want. If you're travelling on a shoestring budget then there are lots of hotels where a couple can get a quite decent room for around US$5 but if you want to spend US$100 a night that's no problem either in a lot of places.

Food is a delight, and an economical delight at that. There's an incredible variety of restaurants, offering excellent food at amazingly cheap prices. You'll wonder if anyone ever eats at home when you can get an excellent meal in a small restaurant for not much over US$1 – chicken rice with soup, a soft drink, a cup of coffee and a couple of varieties of tropical fruit to finish up with will set you back less than US$3 in any food centre. Meanwhile at the other end of the scale the fancy hotels and restaurants in the main cities offer French cuisine at Parisian prices.

It's the same story when it comes to getting around. If you want to travel by

chauffeur-driven air-conditioned car you can, but there are lots of cheaper and quite comfortable means of getting around. There are plenty of reasonably priced and reasonably honest taxis for local travel – there's no need to get into the frantic bargaining sessions or fear the subsequent arguments that taxi travel in some Asian countries entails. For long distance, Malaysia has excellent buses, trains and surprisingly economical taxis, all at very reasonable prices.

On top of these travel essentials – accommodation, food and transport – you'll also find non-essentials and luxuries are moderately priced, even downright cheap.

Tipping
Tipping is not normally done in Malaysia. The more expensive hotels and restaurants have a 10% service charge, while at the cheaper places tipping is not expected. Taxi and rickshaw drivers will naturally not knock back a tip should you decide to give one but, again, it's not expected as a matter of course.

WHAT TO BRING
There's really very little you need to worry about forgetting when you come to Malaysia or Singapore. There are none of those problems of finding your favourite brand of toothpaste or even common medicines. If you want a film for your camera it will be cheaper here than at home.

Clothes are readily available and very reasonably priced. The best advice is to bring as little with you as possible; travelling light is the only way to travel. In any case you don't need too much to start with as the weather is perpetually of the short sleeve variety. Although if you're planning to head up to the hill stations you may appreciate a sweater or light jacket in the evenings.

Dress is casual throughout the region – budget travellers may find a set of 'dress up' gear sensible for dealing with officialdom but you're highly unlikely to need a coat and tie or equivalent too often.

Sensible accessories include sunglasses, a hat, a water bottle/canteen, pocket knife, a day pack, a basic first-aid kit and a money belt or pouch.

TOURIST INFORMATION
Malaysia has an efficient national tourist body, the Malaysian Tourist Development Corporation (TDC). It produces a massive amount of glossy brochures and other literature, most of it fairly useful. Because 1990 was Visit Malaysia Year a huge effort went into bringing out up-to-date brochures and hopefully this information will be kept current.

There are also a number of local tourist promotion organisations, such as the Penang Tourist Association, who back up the TDC's activities.

Local Tourist Offices
The TDC maintains the following offices in Malaysia:

Johore Bahru
   Ground Floor, Komtar Building (tel 07-223590)
Kota Kinabalu
   Ground Floor, Wing Onn Life Building, Jalan Sagunting (tel 088-211698)
Kuala Lumpur
   Level 2, Putra World Trade Centre, Jalan Tun Ismail (tel 03-2746063)
   KL Visitors Centre, 3 Jalan Sultan Hishamuddin (tel 03-2301369)
   Malaysia Tourism Information Centre, Jalan Ampang (tel 03-2434929)
Kuala Terengganu
   2243 Ground Floor, Wisma MCIS, Jalan Sultan Zainal Abidin (tel 09-621893)
Kuching
   2nd Floor, AIA Building, Jalan Song Thian Cheok (tel 082-246575)
Penang
   10 Jalan Tun Syed Sheh Barakbah, Georgetown (tel 04-620066)

Overseas Reps
The TDC also maintains the following offices overseas and they are good places for information before you leave:

Australia
   Ground Floor, 65 York St, Sydney (tel (02) 294441)
France
   2 Bis Rue Benouville, 75116 Paris

Germany
> Rossmarkt 11, Frankfurt am-Main (tel (069) 283782)

Hong Kong
> Ground Floor, Malaysia Building, 50 Gloucester Rd (tel (5) 285810)

Japan
> 2nd Floor, Nichiginmae Kyodo Building, 3-4 Nihombashi-Hongokucho, Chuo-ku, Tokyo 103 (tel (03) 279-3081)

Singapore
> 10 Collyer Quay, 01-03 Ocean Building (tel (02) 532-6351)

Thailand
> 315 Silom Rd, Bangkok 10500 (tel (02) 234-0313)

Taiwan
> 147 Chu Ann Din How Building, Fu-Hsin South Rd, Section 1, Taipei

UK
> 57 Trafalgar Square, London WC2N 5DU (tel (071) 930-7932)

USA
> 818 West 7th St, Suite 804, Los Angeles (tel (213) 689-9702)

BUSINESS HOURS

Government offices are usually open Monday to Friday from around 8.30 am to 12.15 pm, and then again from 1 to 5 pm. On Friday the lunch break usually lasts from 11.15 am to 2.15 pm. On Saturday mornings the offices are open from 8.30 am to 1 pm. These hours vary slightly from state to state; on the east coast of the peninsula most offices are closed on Friday afternoons.

Shop hours are also somewhat variable although Monday to Saturday from 9 am to 6 pm is a good rule of thumb. Major department stores, Chinese emporiums and some stores catering particularly to tourists are open until 9 pm seven days a week.

POST

Malaysia has an efficient postal system with good poste restantes at the major post offices. Post offices are open from 8 am to 5 pm from Monday to Friday and 8 am to 12 noon on Saturdays.

Aerogrammes and postcards cost M$0.40 to any destination.

Posting Parcels

It's easy to send parcels from any major post office although the rates are fairly high. The surface mail rates are as follows:

Destination	1 kg	5 kg	10 kg
Australia	M$17.90	M$25.00	M$34.70
UK	M$21.70	M$35.00	M$46.00
USA	M$11.60	M$42.30	M$80.10

TELEPHONE
Local Calls

There are good telephone communications throughout the country. You can direct dial long-distance calls between all major towns in Malaysia. Local calls cost 10 sen for unlimited time.

All over the country you'll come across card phones (*Kadfon*) and these take plastic cards and are convenient. Cards can be bought from post offices in denominations of M$3, M$5, M$10, M$30 and M$50. It's not possible to make international calls from a Kadfon.

Calls to Singapore are STD rather than

international calls. Dialling codes for Malaysia include:

Town	Area Code
Cameron Highlands	05
Ipoh	05
Johore Bahru	07
Kota Bharu	09
Kota Kinabalu	088
Kuala Lumpur	03
Kuala Terengganu	09
Kuantan	09
Kuching	082
Labuan	087
Langkawi	04
Melaka	06
Miri	085
Penang	04
Sandakan	089
Singapore	02

International Calls

International calls can be direct dialled from Kuala Lumpur, Penang and Kota Kinabalu. The service is fast and efficient and reasonably priced.

In the major centres there are reverse charge (collect) direct phones which get you through directly to the international operator in a specific country, from where you can make a reverse charge or credit card call. The countries hooked into this service are UK, USA, Australia, Japan and the Netherlands.

TIME

Malaysian time is eight hours ahead of GMT (UTC), two hours behind Australian eastern standard time (Sydney and Melbourne), 13 hours ahead of American eastern standard time (New York) and 16 hours ahead of American western standard time (San Francisco and Los Angeles). Thus 12 noon in Malaysia is 2 pm in Sydney, 4 am in London, 11 pm in New York and 8 pm the previous day in Los Angeles.

ELECTRICITY

Electricity supplies are dependable throughout Malaysia. Supply is 220-240 volts, 50 cycles.

BOOKS & BOOKSHOPS

There are a wide variety of books available in Malaysia and a number of good bookshops in which to find them. The main chains are MPH and Berita.

In Kuala Lumpur the best bookshops are on Jalan Bukit Bintang. The Bukit Bintang Plaza has MPH and Berita bookstores. The Central Market also has a Berita bookshop. In the Weld Supermarket building on Jalan Raja Chulan there's a big branch of Times bookshops.

In Penang there are several good bookshops along Beach Rd (Jalan Pantai) and the E&O Hotel also has a good bookshop. Major hotels also often have book stalls, but on the east coast the selection of bookshops is not as good as elsewhere.

People & Society

Kampong Boy, and the more recently published *Town Boy*, by Lat (Straits Times Publishing) provide a delightful introduction to Malay life. They're a humorous autobiographical cartoon series on growing up in a village (kampung) and then moving to the town of Ipoh.

Culture Shock, by JoAnn Craig, is an attempt to explain the customs, cultures and lifestyles of Malaysia and Singapore's polyglot population to expatriates working there.

History

There are quite a few books on the history of Malaysia. *A Short History of Malaysia, Singapore & Brunei*, C Mary Turnbull (Cassell Australia, 1980), may fit the bill if you simply want a straightforward and not overlong history from early civilisation to modern politics. *A History of Malaya* by R Winstedt (Porcupine Press, 1979) is another standard history.

There has been a great deal of interest in the fall of Malaysia and Singapore and the subsequent Japanese occupation and the internal and external struggles of the '50s and '60s. These include: *The Jungle is Neutral*, F Spencer Chapman (originally published 1949; now available in a Mayflower paperback), recounts the hardships and adventures of a British guerrilla force that fought on in the jungles of Malaya for the rest of the war.

The War of the Running Dogs – Malaya 1948-1960, Noel Barber (first published 1971; now a Fontana paperback) recounts the events of the long running Communist insurrection.

The Undeclared War – The Story of the Indonesian Confrontation, Harold James and Denis Sheil-Small (originally published 1971; now a paperback from the University of Malaya Co-Operative Bookshop). No sooner had the Communist struggle ended than the confrontation with Indonesia commenced. This book tells the story of that strange and disorganised argument.

The Malay Dilemma, written in 1970 by Mahathir Mohamed who became Prime Minister in 1981. It is interesting both for its not altogether optimistic analysis of the problems facing Malaysia and the fact that it was banned for a number of years. It has now been republished in a Federal Publications paperback.

Fiction

Singapore and Malaysia have always provided a fertile setting for novelists and Joseph Conrad's *The Shadow Line* and *Lord Jim* both use the region as a setting. Somerset Maugham also set many of his classic short stories in Malaya – look for the *Borneo Stories*.

The Malayan Trilogy, Anthony Burgess (Penguin paperback) is a classic series of long stories of life in Malaya during the declining years of Britain's colonial management.

The Consul's File, by Paul Theroux, is a very readable collection of short stories set in, of all places, Ayer Hitam near Kuala Lumpur. Theroux's *Saint Jack* is set in Singapore.

Turtle Beach, Blanche d'Alpuget (Penguin, 1981), is an Australian award-winning novel which gives an insight into the Vietnamese boat people, the impact of their arrival in Malaysia and the racial tension those events engendered – with flashbacks to the horrors of 1969.

North Borneo

Nineteenth Century Borneo – A Study in Diplomatic Rivalry, Graham Irwin (Donald Moore Books, Singapore), is the best book on the fascinating history of Sarawak, Sabah and Brunei.

Rajah Charles Brooke – Monarch of all he Surveyed, Colin N Criswell (Oxford University Press, 1978), tells you more about the White rajahs.

Vanishing World, the Ibans of Borneo, Leigh Wright (Weatherhill, 1972), has some beautiful colour photographs.

A Stroll Through Borneo, James Barclay (Hodder & Stoughton, 1980), is a delightful tale of a long walk and river trip through Sarawak, Sabah and Indonesian Kalimantan. The contrasts between Malaysian bureaucracy and the Indonesian variety are enlightening, with the Malaysians coming off distinctly second best.

Into the Heart of Borneo, Redmond O'Hanlon (Random House, New York 1984), is the amusing story of two foreigners as they journey by foot and boat into Borneo.

Travel Guides

Insight Malaysia, part of the Apa guide series, features their usual collection of text and photographs.

Jalan Jalan (also from the Singapore-based Apa company) is a coffee-table book on Malaysia. It's as much a photographic book as a travel book since it covers Malaysia with a series of photographs taken with a 8 x 10 large format studio camera. The description of how the photographs were taken and the travels around Malaysia (by motorcycle) to take them is as interesting as the pictures themselves.

South-East Asia on a shoestring (Lonely Planet), is our overall guidebook to the region. If you're travelling further afield there are other LP guides to most South-East and North-East Asian countries. Lonely Planet's *Singapore - City Guide* is available for travellers just going to Singapore

Time Travel in the Malay Crescent by Wayne Stier is an unusual guidebook, written in the second person, present tense. There are some maps and travel information at the back of the book, but most of the text consists of tales gathered and events which occurred while the author was in Malaysia. Some of the stories about the more remote areas of Sarawak and Sabah are very interesting.

MAPS

It's not possible to get the detailed maps of Malaysia which were available during the colonial period because of fears that they will fall into communist hands. You can, however, get good road maps from petrol stations. Probably the best is the Shell one which is larger scale since it is two-sided. On the other hand the Mobil map also shows relief.

The *Malaysia* map produced by Nelles Verlag for APA Maps is excellent for the peninsula and East Malaysia, it also has a number of city maps. It has a scale of 1:1.5 million and is widely available in Malaysia.

A very good map, particularly for roads, is the *Asian Highway Route Map – Singapore, Malaysia, Thailand, Laos* which is published by the United Nations, Escap,

LP's *Singapore - City Guide*

Transport & Communications Division. It's available from the Singapore Automobile Association headquarters for just S$1.

MEDIA
Newspapers & Magazines

Malaysia has newspapers in English, Malay, Chinese and Tamil. The *New Straits Times* is the main offering in English. It is a broadsheet paper with good coverage of local and overseas events. Other English-language papers tend to be more regional and include the *Star* and the *Malay Mail*, and in East Malaysia you have locals such as the *Borneo Post* and the *Sarawak Tribune*.

In Bahasa Malaysia the main paper, and the one with highest circulation of any paper, is the *Berita Harian*, while a second string paper is the *Utusan Malaysia*.

Asian and Western magazines are readily available throughout the region.

Radio & TV

Radio and TV are equally cosmopolitan in their languages and programming. Malaysia has two government TV channels (RTM 1 and 2) and a commercial station, TV3. Programmes range from local productions in the various languages to imports from the USA and UK.

FILM & PHOTOGRAPHY

Malaysia is, of course, a delightful area to photograph. There's a lot of natural colour and activity and the people have no antipathy to being photographed. It is, of course, polite to ask permission before photographing people or taking pictures in mosques or temples. There is usually no objection to taking photographs in places of worship, in Chinese temples virtually anything goes.

The usual rules for tropical photography apply: try to take photographs early in the morning or late in the afternoon. By 10 am the sun will already be high in the sky and colours are easily washed out. A polarising filter can help to keep down the tropical haze. Try to keep your camera and film in a happy environment – don't leave it out in direct sunlight, try to keep film as cool as possible after use. Colour film can be developed quickly, cheaply and competently, but Kodachrome colour slides are usually sent to Australia for developing. Ektachrome, however, can be developed in Singapore.

Film is cheap and readily available in Malaysia, though slide film is not so cheap and the range is often limited. Processing is also reasonably priced.

HEALTH

Malaysia enjoys good standards of health and cleanliness. The usual rules for healthy living in a tropical environment apply. Ensure that you do not become dehydrated, particularly before you have acquired some acclimatisation, by keeping your liquid intake up. Wear cool, lightweight clothes and avoid prolonged exposure to the sun. Treat cuts and scratches with care since they can easily become infected.

Travel health depends on your pre-departure preparations, your day-to-day health care while travelling and how you handle any medical problem or emergency that does develop. While the list of potential dangers can seem quite frightening, with a little luck, some basic precautions and adequate information, few travellers experience more than upset stomachs.

Dr Ann Faraday and Professor John Wren-Lewis recommend that:

If you are in need of medical services in any of the smaller towns, we strongly recommend the government hospitals, which are either completely free or make a nominal M$1 charge and go out of their way to be helpful to travellers. Medical staff and most of the senior nursing staff speak good English and there is rarely any need to wait for long. We especially commend the staff at the government hospitals in Tapah, Tanah Rata (Cameron Highlands) and Kuala Lipis.

In major cities the queue situation is likely to be a very different story, though staff are in our experience no less helpful and may help a helpless-looking foreigner to jump the huge lines. However, it may be simpler (especially in Kuala Lumpur) to resort to a private clinic, in which case the minimum charge for a visit is about M$20. If you are contemplating visits to jungle areas you should certainly go to a hospital for anti-malarials.

Travel Health Guides

There are a number of books on travel health:

Staying Healthy in Asia, Africa & Latin America, Volunteers in Asia. Probably the best all-round guide to carry, as it's compact but very detailed and well organised.

Travellers' Health, Dr Richard Dawood, Oxford University Press. Comprehensive, easy to read, authoritative and also highly recommended, although it's rather large to lug around.

Where There is No Doctor, David Werner, Hesperian Foundation. A very detailed guide intended for someone, like a Peace Corps worker, going to work in an undeveloped country, rather than for the average traveller.

Travel with Children, Maureen Wheeler, Lonely Planet Publications. Includes basic advice on travel health for younger children.

Pre-Departure Preparations

Health Insurance A travel insurance policy to cover theft, loss and medical problems is a wise idea. There are a wide variety of policies and your travel agent will have recommendations. The international student travel policies handled by STA or other student travel organisations are usually good value. Some policies offer lower and higher medical expenses options but the higher one is chiefly for countries like the USA which have extremely high medical costs. Check the small print:

- Some policies specifically exclude 'dangerous activities' which can include scuba diving, motorcycling, even trekking. If such activities are on your agenda you don't want that sort of policy.
- You may prefer a policy which pays doctors or hospitals direct rather than you having to pay on the spot and claim later. If you have to claim later make sure you keep all documentation. Some policies ask you to call back (reverse charges) to a centre in your home country where an immediate assessment is made.
- Check if the policy covers ambulances or an emergency flight home. If you have to stretch out you will need two seats and somebody has to pay for them!

Medical Kit A small, straightforward medical kit is a wise thing to carry. A possible kit list includes:

* Aspirin or Panadol – for pain or fever
* Antihistamine (such as Benadryl) – useful as a decongestant for colds, allergies, to ease the itch from insect bites or stings or to help prevent motion sickness
* Antibiotics – useful if you're travelling well off the beaten track, but they must be prescribed and you should carry the prescription with you
* Kaolin preparation (Pepto-Bismol), Imodium or Lomotil – for stomach upsets
* Rehydration mixture – for treatment of severe diarrhoea, this is particularly important if travelling with children
* Antiseptic, mercurochrome and antibiotic powder or similar 'dry' spray – for cuts and grazes
* Calamine lotion – to ease irritation from bites or stings
* Bandages and Band-aids – for minor injuries
* Scissors, tweezers and a thermometer (note that mercury thermometers are prohibited by airlines)
* Insect repellent, sunscreen, suntan lotion, chap stick and water purification tablets

Ideally antibiotics should be administered only under medical supervision and should never be taken indiscriminately. Overuse of antibiotics can weaken your body's ability to deal with infections naturally and can reduce the drug's efficacy on a future occasion. Take only the recommended dose at the prescribed intervals and continue using the antibiotic for the prescribed period, even if the illness seems to be cured earlier. Antibiotics are quite specific to the infections they can treat, stop immediately if there are any serious reactions and don't use it at all if you are unsure if you have the correct one.

In many countries if a medicine is available at all it will generally be available over the counter and the price will be much cheaper than in the West. However, be careful of buying drugs in developing countries, particularly where the expiry date may have passed or correct storage conditions may not have been followed. It's possible that drugs which are no longer recommended, or have even been banned, in the West are still being dispensed in many Third World countries.

Health Preparations Make sure you're healthy before you start travelling. If you are embarking on a long trip make sure your teeth are OK; there are lots of places where a visit to the dentist would be the last thing you'd want to do.

If you wear glasses take a spare pair and your prescription. Losing your glasses can be a real problem, although in Malaysia it is not a problem to get new spectacles made up quickly and cheaply.

If you require a particular medication take an adequate supply, as it may not be available locally. Take the prescription, with the generic rather than the brand name (which may not be locally available), as it will make getting replacements easier. It's a wise idea to have the prescription with you to show you legally use the medication – it's surprising how often over-the-counter drugs from one place are illegal without a prescription or even banned in another.

Immunisations Vaccinations provide protection against diseases you might meet along the way. For some countries no immunisations are necessary, but the further off the beaten track you go the more necessary it is to take precautions. In Malaysia, vaccinations against cholera and yellow fever are only required if you've recently come from an infected area – there are no other health requirements on arrival. Although Peninsular Malaysia is not malarial you should take precautions if you're visiting Sarawak or Sabah, particularly if you will be travelling upriver. Your doctor will prescribe a daily or weekly anti-malarial drug.

All vaccinations should be recorded on an International Health Certificate, which is available from your physician or government health department.

Plan ahead for getting your vaccinations: some of them require an initial shot followed by a booster, while some vaccinations should not be given together. Most travellers from

Western countries will have been immunised against various diseases during childhood but your doctor may still recommend booster shots against measles or polio, diseases still prevalent in many developing countries. The period of protection offered by vaccinations differs widely and some are contraindicated if you are pregnant.

In some countries immunisations are available from airport or government health centres. Travel agents or airline offices will tell you where. The possible list of vaccinations includes:

Smallpox Smallpox has now been wiped out worldwide, so immunisation is no longer necessary.

Cholera Some countries may require cholera vaccination if you are coming from an infected area, but protection is not very effective; only lasts six months and is contraindicated for pregnancy.

Tetanus & Diptheria Boosters are necessary every 10 years and protection is highly recommended.

Typhoid Protection lasts for three years and is useful if you are travelling for long in rural, tropical areas. You may get some side effects such as pain at the injection site, fever, headache and a general unwell feeling.

Infectious Hepatitis Gamma globulin is not a vaccination but a ready-made antibody which has proven very successful in reducing the chances of hepatitis infection. Because it may interfere with the development of immunity, it should not be given until at least 10 days after administration of the last vaccine needed; it should also be given as close as possible to departure because of its relatively short-lived protection period of six months.

Yellow Fever Protection lasts 10 years and vaccination is required in Malaysia if you have come from an area where the disease is endemic, chiefly in Africa and South America. Vaccination is contraindicated during pregnancy but if you must travel to a high-risk area it is probably advisable.

Basic Rules

Care in what you eat and drink is the most important health rule; stomach upsets are the most likely travel health problem but the majority of these upsets will be relatively minor. Don't become paranoid, trying the local food is part of the experience of travel after all.

Water In the major towns and cities in Malaysia you can drink tap water but it is still wise to ensure that water has been boiled in kampungs or off the beaten track. If you don't know for certain that the water is safe always assume the worst.

Water Purification The simplest way of purifying water is to boil it thoroughly. Technically this means boiling for 10 minutes, something which happens very rarely! Remember that at high altitude water boils at lower temperature, so germs are less likely to be killed.

Simple filtering will not remove all dangerous organisms, so if you cannot boil water it should be treated chemically. Chlorine tablets (Puritabs, Steritabs or other brand names) will kill many but not all pathogens. Iodine is very effective in purifying water and is available in tablet form (such as Potable Aqua), but follow the directions carefully and remember that too much iodine can be harmful.

If you can't find tablets, tincture of iodine (2%) or iodine crystals can be used. Two drops of tincture of iodine per litre or quart of clear water is the recommended dosage; the treated water should be left to stand for 30 minutes before drinking. Iodine crystals can also be used to purify water but this is a more complicated process, as you have to first prepare a saturated iodine solution. Iodine loses its effectiveness if exposed to air or dampness so keep it in a tightly sealed container. Flavoured powder will disguise the taste of treated water and is a good idea if you are travelling with children.

Food Salads and fruit should be washed with purified water or peeled where possible. Ice cream is usually OK if it is a reputable brand name. Thoroughly cooked food is safest but not if it has been left to cool or if it has been reheated. Take great care with shellfish or fish and avoid undercooked meat. If a place looks clean and well run and if the vendor also looks clean and healthy, then the food is probably safe. In general, places that are packed with travellers or locals will be fine, while empty restaurants are questionable.

Nutrition If your food is poor or limited in availability, if you're travelling hard and fast and therefore missing meals, or if you simply lose your appetite, you can soon start to lose weight and place your health at risk.

Make sure your diet is well balanced. Eggs, tofu, beans, lentils and nuts are all safe ways to get protein. Fruit you can peel (bananas, oranges or mandarins for example) is always safe and a good source of vitamins. Try to eat plenty of grains (rice) and bread. Remember that although food is generally safer if it is cooked well, overcooked food loses much of its nutritional value. If your diet isn't well balanced or if your food intake is insufficient, it's a good idea to take vitamin and iron pills.

Make sure you drink enough – don't rely on feeling thirsty to indicate when you should drink. Not needing to urinate or very dark yellow urine is a danger sign. Always carry a water bottle with you on long trips. Excessive sweating can lead to loss of salt and therefore muscle cramping. Salt tablets are not a good idea as a preventative, but in places where salt is not used much adding salt to food can help.

Everyday Health A normal body temperature is 98.6°F or 37°C; more than 2°C higher is a 'high' fever. A normal adult pulse rate is 60 to 80 per minute (children 80 to 100, babies 100 to 140). You should know how to take a temperature and a pulse rate. As a general rule the pulse increases about 20 beats per minute for each °C rise in fever.

Respiration (breathing) rate is also an indicator of illness. Count the number of breaths per minute: between 12 and 20 is normal for adults and older children (up to 30 for younger children, 40 for babies). People with a high fever or serious respiratory illness (like pneumonia) breathe more quickly than normal. More than 40 shallow breaths a minute usually means pneumonia.

Many health problems can be avoided by taking care of yourself. Wash your hands frequently – it's quite easy to contaminate your own food. Clean your teeth with purified water rather than straight from the tap. Avoid climatic extremes: keep out of the sun when it's hot, dress warmly when it's cold. Avoid potential diseases by dressing sensibly. You can get worm infections through walking barefoot or dangerous coral cuts by walking over coral without shoes. You can avoid insect bites by covering bare skin when insects are around, by screening windows or beds or by using insect repellents. Seek local advice: if you're told the water is unsafe due to jellyfish, crocodiles or bilharzia, don't go in. In situations where there is no information, discretion is the better part of valour.

Medical Problems & Treatment

Potential medical problems can be broken down into several areas. First there are the climatic and geographical considerations – problems caused by extremes of temperature, altitude or motion. Then there are diseases and illnesses caused by insanitation, insect bites or stings, and animal or human contact. Simple cuts, bites or scratches can also cause problems.

Self-diagnosis and treatment can be risky, so wherever possible seek qualified help. Although we do give treatment dosages in this section, they are for emergency use only. Medical advice should be sought before administering any drugs.

An embassy or consulate can usually recommend a good place to go for such advice. So can five-star hotels, although they often recommend doctors with five-star prices. (This is when that medical insurance really comes in useful!)

Climatic & Geographical Considerations

Sunburn In Malaysia you can get sunburnt so use a sunscreen and take extra care to cover areas which don't normally see sun – eg your feet. A hat provides added protection, and you should also use zinc cream or some other barrier cream for your nose and lips. Calamine lotion is good for mild sunburn.

Prickly Heat Prickly heat is an itchy rash caused by excessive perspiration trapped under the skin. It usually strikes people who have just arrived in a hot climate and whose pores have not yet opened sufficiently to cope with greater sweating. Keeping cool by bathing often, using a mild talcum powder or even resorting to air-conditioning may help until you acclimatise.

Heat Exhaustion Dehydration or salt deficiency can cause heat exhaustion. Take time to acclimatise to high temperatures and make sure you get sufficient liquids. Salt deficiency is characterised by fatigue, lethargy, headaches, giddiness and muscle cramps and in this case salt tablets may help. Vomiting or diarrhoea can deplete your liquid and salt levels. Anhydrotic heat exhaustion, caused by an inability to sweat, is quite rare. Unlike the other forms of heat exhaustion it is likely to strike people who have been in a hot climate for some time, rather than newcomers.

Heat Stroke This serious, sometimes fatal, condition can occur if the body's heat-regulating mechanism breaks down and the body temperature rises to dangerous levels. Long, continuous periods of exposure to high temperatures can leave you vulnerable to heat stroke. You should avoid excessive alcohol or strenuous activity when you first arrive in a hot climate.

The symptoms are feeling unwell, not sweating very much or at all and a high body temperature (39°C to 41°C). Where sweating has ceased the skin becomes flushed and red. Severe, throbbing headaches and lack of coordination will also occur, and the sufferer may be confused or aggressive. Eventually the victim will become delirious or convulse. Hospitalisation is essential, but meanwhile get patients out of the sun, remove their clothing, cover them with a wet sheet or towel and then fan continually.

Fungal Infections Hot weather fungal infections are most likely to occur on the scalp, between the toes or fingers (athlete's foot), in the groin (jock itch or crotch rot) and on the body (ringworm). You get ringworm (which is a fungal infection, not a worm) from infected animals or by walking on damp areas, like shower floors.

To prevent fungal infections wear loose, comfortable clothes, avoid artificial fibres, wash frequently and dry carefully. If you do get an infection, wash the infected area daily with a disinfectant or medicated soap and water, and rinse and dry well. Apply an anti-fungal powder like the widely available Tinaderm. Try to expose the infected area to air or sunlight as much as possible and wash all towels and underwear in hot water as well as changing them often.

Cold Too much cold is just as dangerous as too much heat, particularly if it leads to hypothermia. If you are trekking at high altitudes or simply taking a long bus trip over mountains, particularly at night, be prepared.

Hypothermia occurs when the body loses heat faster than it can produce it and the core temperature of the body falls. It is surprisingly easy to progress from very cold to dangerously cold due to a combination of wind, wet clothing, fatigue and hunger, even if the air temperature is above freezing. It is best to dress in layers; silk, wool and some of the new artificial fibres are all good insulating materials. A hat is important, as a lot of heat is lost through the head. A strong, waterproof outer layer is essential, as keeping dry is vital. Carry basic supplies, including food containing simple sugars to generate heat quickly and lots of fluid to drink.

Symptoms of hypothermia are exhaustion, numb skin (particularly toes and fingers), shivering, slurred speech, irrational or violent behaviour, lethargy, stumbling, dizzy spells, muscle cramps and violent bursts of energy. Irrationality may take the form of sufferers claiming they are warm and trying to take off their clothes.

To treat hypothermia, first get the patient out of the wind and/or rain, remove their clothing if it's wet and replace it with dry, warm clothing. Give them hot liquids – not alcohol – and some high-kilojoule, easily digestible food. This should be enough for the early stages of hypothermia, but if it has gone further it may be necessary to place victims in warm sleeping bags and get in with them. Do not rub patients, place them near a fire or remove their wet clothes in the wind. If possible, place a sufferer in a warm (not hot) bath.

Altitude Sickness Acute Mountain Sickness or AMS occurs at high altitude and can be fatal. The lack of oxygen at high altitudes affects most people to some extent. Take it easy at first, increase your liquid intake and eat well. Even with acclimatisation you may still have trouble adjusting – headaches, nausea, dizziness, a dry cough, insomnia, breathlessness and loss of appetite are all signs to heed. If you reach a high altitude by trekking, acclimatisation takes place gradually and you are less likely to be affected than if you fly straight there.

Mild altitude problems will generally abate after a day or so but if the symptoms persist or become worse the only treatment is to descend – even 500 metres can help. Breathlessness, a dry, irritative cough (which may progress to the production of pink, frothy sputum), severe headache, loss of appetite, nausea and sometimes vomiting are all danger signs. Increasing tiredness, confusion and lack of coordination and balance are real danger signs. Any of these symptoms individually, even just a persistent headache, can be a warning.

There is no hard and fast rule as to how high is too high: AMS has been fatal at altitudes of 3000 metres, although 3500 to 4500 metres is the usual range. It is always wise to sleep at a lower altitude than the greatest height reached during the day.

Motion Sickness Eating lightly before and during a trip will reduce the chances of motion sickness. If you are prone to motion sickness try to find a place that minimises disturbance – near the wing on aircraft, close to midships on boats, near the centre on buses. Fresh air usually helps, reading or cigarette smoke doesn't. Commercial anti-motion-sickness preparations, which can cause drowsiness, have to be taken before the trip commences; when you're feeling sick it's too late. Ginger is a natural preventative and is available in capsule form.

Diseases of Insanitation
Diarrhoea A change of water, food or climate can all cause the runs; diarrhoea caused by contaminated food or water is more serious. Despite all your precautions you may still have a bout of mild travellers' diarrhoea but a few rushed toilet trips with no other symptoms is not indicative of a serious problem. Moderate diarrhoea, involving half a dozen loose movements in a day, is more of a nuisance. Dehydration is the main danger with any diarrhoea, particularly for children, so fluid replenishment is the number one treatment. Weak black tea with a little sugar, soda water, or soft drinks allowed to go flat and diluted 50% with water are all good. With severe diarrhoea a rehydrating solution is necessary to replace minerals and salts. You should stick to a bland diet as you recover.

Lomotil or Imodium can be used to bring relief from the symptoms, although they do not actually cure the problem. Only use these drugs if absolutely necessary – eg if you *must* travel. For children Imodium is preferable, but do not use these drugs if the patient has a high fever or is severely dehydrated.

Antibiotics can be very useful in treating severe diarrhoea especially if it is accompanied by nausea, vomiting, stomach cramps or mild fever. Ampicillin, a broad spectrum penicillin, is usually recommended. Two capsules of 250 mg each taken four times a day is the recommended dose for an adult. Children aged between eight and 12 years should have half the adult dose; younger children should have half a capsule four times a day. Note that if the patient is allergic to penicillin ampicillin should not be administered.

Three days of treatment should be sufficient and an improvement should occur within 24 hours.

Giardia This intestinal parasite is present in contaminated water. The symptoms are stomach cramps, nausea, a bloated stomach, watery, foul-smelling diarrhoea and frequent gas. Giardia can appear several weeks after you have been exposed to the parasite. The symptoms may disappear for a few days and then return; this can go on for several weeks. Metronidazole known as Flagyl is the recommended drug, but it should only be taken under medical supervision. Antibiotics are of no use.

Dysentery This serious illness is caused by contaminated food or water and is characterised by severe diarrhoea, often with blood or mucus in the stool. There are two kinds of dysentery. Bacillary dysentery is characterised by a high fever and rapid development; headache, vomiting and stomach pains are also symptoms. It generally does not last longer than a week, but it is highly contagious.

Amoebic dysentery is more gradual in developing, has no fever or vomiting but is a more serious illness. It is not a self-limiting disease: it will persist until treated and can recur and cause long-term damage.

A stool test is necessary to diagnose which kind of dysentery you have, so you should seek medical help urgently. In case of an emergency, note that tetracycline is the prescribed treatment for bacillary dysentery, metronidazole for amoebic dysentery.

With tetracycline, the recommended adult dosage is one 250 mg capsule four times a day. Children aged between eight and 12 years should have half the adult dose; the dosage for younger children is a third of the adult dose. It's important to remember that tetracycline should be given to young children only if it's absolutely necessary and only for a short period; pregnant women

should not take it after the fourth month of pregnancy.

With metronidazole, the recommended adult dosage is one 750 mg to 800 mg capsule three times daily for five days. Children aged between eight and 12 years should have half the adult dose; the dosage for younger children is a third of the adult dose.

Cholera Cholera vaccination is not very effective. However, outbreaks of cholera are generally widely reported, so you can avoid such problem areas. The disease is characterised by a sudden onset of acute diarrhoea with 'rice water' stools, vomiting, muscular cramps, and extreme weakness. You need medical help – but treat for dehydration, which can be extreme, and if there is an appreciable delay in getting to hospital then begin taking tetracycline. See the Dysentery section for dosages and warnings.

Viral Gastroenteritis This is caused not by bacteria but, as the name suggests, by a virus. It is characterised by stomach cramps, diarrhoea and sometimes by vomiting and/or a slight fever. All you can do is rest and drink lots of fluids.

Hepatitis Hepatitis A is the more common form of this disease and is spread by contaminated food or water. The first symptoms are fever, chills, headache, fatigue, feelings of weakness and aches and pains. This is followed by loss of appetite, nausea, vomiting, abdominal pain, dark urine, light-coloured faeces and jaundiced skin; the whites of the eyes may also turn yellow. In some cases there may just be a feeling of being unwell or tired, accompanied by loss of appetite, aches and pains and the jaundiced effect. You should seek medical advice, but in general there is not much you can do apart from resting, drinking lots of fluids, eating lightly and avoiding fatty foods. People who have had hepatitis must forego alcohol for six months after the illness, as hepatitis attacks the liver and it needs that amount of time to recover.

Hepatitis B, which used to be called serum

hepatitis, is spread through sexual contact or through skin penetration – it could be transmitted via dirty needles or blood transfusions, for instance. Avoid having your ears pierced, tattoos done or injections where you have doubts about the sanitary conditions. The symptoms and treatment of type B are much the same as for type A, but gamma globulin as a prophylactic is effective against type A only.

Typhoid Typhoid fever is another gut infection that travels the faecal-oral route – ie contaminated water and food are responsible. Vaccination against typhoid is not totally effective and it is one of the most dangerous infections, so medical help must be sought.

In its early stages typhoid resembles many other illnesses: sufferers may feel like they have a bad cold or flu on the way, as early symptoms are a headache, a sore throat, and a fever which rises a little each day until it is around 40°C or more. The victim's pulse is often slow relative to the degree of fever present and gets slower as the fever rises – unlike a normal fever where the pulse increases. There may also be vomiting, diarrhoea or constipation.

In the second week the high fever and slow pulse continue and a few pink spots may appear on the body; trembling, delirium, weakness, weight loss and dehydration are other symptoms. If there are no further complications, the fever and other symptoms will slowly go during the third week. However you must get medical help before this because pneumonia (acute infection of the lungs) or peritonitis (burst appendix) are common complications, and because typhoid is very infectious.

The fever should be treated by keeping the victim cool and dehydration should also be watched for. Chloramphenicol is the recommended antibiotic but there are fewer side effects with ampicillin. The adult dosage is two 250 mg capsules, four times a day. Children aged between eight and 12 years should have half the adult dose; younger children should have a third of the adult dose.

Patients who are allergic to penicillin should not be given ampicillin.

Worms These parasites are most common in rural, tropical areas and a stool test when you return home is not a bad idea. They can be present on unwashed vegetables or in undercooked meat and you can pick them up through your skin by walking in bare feet. Infestations may not show up for some time, and although they are generally not serious, if left untreated they can cause severe health problems. A stool test is necessary to pinpoint the problem and medication is often available over the counter.

Diseases Spread by People & Animals
Tetanus This potentially fatal disease is found in undeveloped tropical areas. It is difficult to treat but is preventable with immunisation. Tetanus occurs when a wound becomes infected by a germ which lives in the faeces of animals or people, so clean all cuts, punctures or animal bites. Tetanus is known as lockjaw, and the first symptom may be discomfort in swallowing, or stiffening of the jaw and neck; this is followed by painful convulsions of the jaw and whole body.

Rabies Rabies is found in many countries and is caused by a bite or scratch by an infected animal. Dogs are a noted carrier. Any bite, scratch or even lick from a mammal should be cleaned immediately and thoroughly. Scrub with soap and running water, and then clean with an alcohol solution. If there is any possibility that the animal is infected medical help should be sought immediately. Even if the animal is not rabid, all bites should be treated seriously as they can become infected or can result in tetanus. A rabies vaccination is now available and should be considered if you are in a high-risk category – eg, if you intend to explore caves (bat bites could be dangerous) or work with animals.

Tuberculosis Although this disease is widespread in many developing countries, it is not a serious risk to travellers. Young children are more susceptible than adults and vaccination is a sensible precaution for children under 12 travelling in endemic areas. Tuberculosis (TB) is commonly spread by coughing or by unpasteurised dairy products from infected cows. Milk that has been boiled is safe to drink; the souring of milk to make yoghurt or cheese also kills the bacilli.

Diptheria Diptheria can be a skin infection or a more dangerous throat infection. It is spread by contaminated dust contacting the skin or by the inhalation of infected cough or sneeze droplets. Frequent washing and keeping the skin dry will help prevent skin infection. A vaccination is available to prevent the throat infection.

Sexually Transmitted Diseases Sexual contact with an infected sexual partner spreads these diseases. While abstinence is the only 100% preventative, using condoms is also effective. Gonorrhoea and syphilis are the most common of these diseases; sores, blisters or rashes around the genitals, discharges or pain when urinating are common symptoms. Symptoms may be less marked or not observed at all in women. Syphilis symptoms eventually disappear completely but the disease continues and can cause severe problems in later years. The treatment of gonorrhoea and syphilis is by antibiotics.

There are numerous other sexually transmitted diseases, for most of which effective treatment is available. However, there is no cure for herpes and there is also currently no cure for AIDS. The latter is common in parts of Africa and is becoming more widespread in Thailand and the Philippines. Using condoms is the most effective preventative.

AIDS can be spread through infected blood transfusions; most developing countries cannot afford to screen blood for transfusions. It can also be spread by dirty needles – vaccinations, acupuncture and tattooing can potentially be as dangerous as intravenous drug use if the equipment is not clean. If you do need an injection it may be a good idea to buy a new syringe from a pharmacy and ask the doctor to use it.

Insect-Borne Diseases
Malaria This serious disease is spread by mosquito bites. If you are travelling in endemic areas it is extremely important to take malarial prophylactics. Symptoms include headaches, fever, chills and sweating which may subside and recur. Without treatment malaria can develop more serious, potentially fatal effects.

Antimalarial drugs do not actually prevent the disease but suppress its symptoms. Chloroquine is the usual malarial prophylactic; a tablet is taken once a week for two weeks prior to arrival in the infected area and six weeks after you leave it. Unfortunately there is now a strain of malaria which is resistant to Chloroquine and if you are travelling in an area infected with this strain an alternative drug is necessary. East and Central Africa, Papua New Guinea, Irian Jaya, the Solomons and Vanuatu are the most dangerous areas, but note that other places are not necessarily 100% safe: only in Central America, the Middle East and West Africa is Chloroquine completely effective. Where resistance is reported you should continue to take Chloroquine but supplement it with a weekly dose of Maloprim or a daily dose of Proguanil.

Chloroquine is quite safe for general use, side effects are minimal and it can be taken by pregnant women. Maloprim can have rare but serious side effects if the weekly dose is exceeded and some doctors recommend a check-up after six months continuous use. Fansidar, once used as a Chloroquine alternative, is no longer recommended as a prophylactic, as it can have dangerous side effects, but it may still be recommended as a treatment for malaria. Chloroquine is also used for malaria treatment but in larger doses than for prophylaxis. Doxycycline is another antimalarial for use where Chloroquine resistance is reported; it causes hypersensitivity to sunlight, so sunburn can be a problem.

Mosquitoes appear after dusk. Avoiding

bites by covering bare skin and using an insect repellent will further reduce the risk of catching malaria. Insect screens on windows and mosquito nets on beds offer protection, as does burning a mosquito coil. Mosquitoes may be attracted by perfume, aftershave or certain colours. The risk of infection is higher in rural areas and during the wet season.

Dengue Fever There is no prophylactic available for this mosquito-spread disease; the main preventative measure is to avoid mosquito bites. A sudden onset of fever, headaches and severe joint and muscle pains are the first signs before a rash starts on the trunk of the body and spreads to the limbs and face. After a further few days, the fever will subside and recovery will begin. Serious complications are not common.

Typhus Typhus is spread by ticks, mites or lice. It begins as a bad cold, followed by a fever, chills, headache, muscle pains and a body rash. There is often a large painful sore at the site of the bite and nearby lymph nodes are swollen and painful.

Tick typhus is spread by ticks. Trekkers in southern Africa may be at risk from cattle or wild animal ticks. Scrub typhus is spread by mites that feed on infected rodents and exists mainly in Asia and the Pacific islands. You should take precautions if walking in rural areas in South-East Asia. Seek local advice on areas where ticks pose a danger and always check yourself carefully for ticks after walking in a danger area. A strong insect repellent can help, and serious walkers in tick areas should consider having their boots and trousers impregnated with benzyl benzoate and dibutylphthalate.

Cuts & Scratches

Skin punctures can easily become infected in hot climates and may be difficult to heal. Treat any cut with an antiseptic solution and mercurochrome. Where possible avoid bandages and Band-aids, which can keep wounds wet. Coral cuts are notoriously slow to heal, as the coral injects a weak venom into the wound. Avoid coral cuts by wearing shoes when walking on reefs, and clean any cut thoroughly.

Bites & Stings

Snakes To minimise your chances of being bitten always wear boots, socks and long trousers when walking through undergrowth where snakes may be present. Don't put your hands into holes and crevices, and be careful when collecting firewood.

Snake bites do not cause instantaneous death and antivenenes are usually available. Keep the victim calm and still, wrap the bitten limb tightly, as you would for a sprained ankle, and then attach a splint to immobilise it. Then seek medical help, if possible with the dead snake for identification. Don't attempt to catch the snake if there is even a remote possibility of being bitten again. Tourniquets and sucking out the poison are now comprehensively discredited.

Bees & Wasps Bee and wasp stings are usually painful rather than dangerous. Calamine lotion will give relief or ice packs will reduce the pain and swelling.

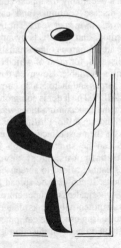

Spiders & Scorpions There are some spiders with dangerous bites but antivenenes are usually available. Scorpion stings are notoriously painful and in Mexico can actually be fatal. Scorpions often shelter in shoes or clothing.

Sea Creatures Certain cone shells found in Australia and the Pacific can sting dangerously or even fatally. There are various fish and other sea creatures which can sting or bite dangerously or which are dangerous to eat. Again, local advice is the best suggestion.

Leeches & Ticks Leeches are normally present in damp rainforest conditions; they attach themselves to your skin to suck your blood. Trekkers often get them on their legs or in their boots. Salt or a lighted cigarette end will make them fall off. Do not pull them off, as the bite is then more likely to become infected. An insect repellent may keep them away. Vaseline, alcohol or oil will persuade a tick to let go. You should always check your body if you have been walking through a tick-infested area, as they can spread typhus.

Bedbugs & Lice Bedbugs live in various places, but particularly in dirty mattresses and bedding. Spots of blood on bedclothes or on the wall around the bed can be read as a suggestion to find another hotel. Bedbugs leave itchy bites in neat rows. Calamine lotion may help.

All lice cause itching and discomfort. They make themselves at home in your hair (head lice), your clothing (body lice) or in your pubic hair (crabs). You catch lice through direct contact with infected people or by sharing combs, clothing and the like. Powder or shampoo treatment will kill the lice and infected clothing should then be washed in very hot water.

Women's Health
Gynaecological Problems Poor diet, lowered resistance due to the use of antibiotics for stomach upsets and even contraceptive pills can lead to vaginal infections when travelling in hot climates. Keeping the genital area clean, and wearing skirts or loose-fitting trousers and cotton underwear will help to prevent infections.

Yeast infections, characterised by a rash, itch and discharge, can be treated with a vinegar or even lemon-juice douche or with yoghurt. Nystatin suppositories are the usual medical prescription. Trichomonas is a more serious infection; symptoms are a discharge and a burning sensation when urinating.

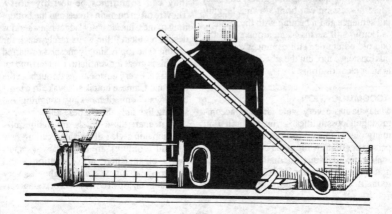

Male sexual partners must also be treated, and if a vinegar-water douche is not effective medical attention should be sought. Flagyl is the prescribed drug.

Pregnancy Most miscarriages occur during the first three months of pregnancy, so this is the most risky time to travel. The last three months should also be spent within reasonable distance of good medical care, as quite serious problems can develop at this time. Pregnant women should avoid all unnecessary medication, but vaccinations and malarial prophylactics should still be taken where possible. Additional care should be taken to prevent illness and particular attention should be paid to diet and nutrition.

DRUGS
In Malaysia the answer is simple – don't. Drug trafficking carries a mandatory death penalty. In almost every village in Malaysia you will see anti-'dadah' (drugs) signs portraying a skull and cross-bones and a noose. No one can say they haven't been warned!

Under Malaysian law all drug offenders are considered equal and being a foreigner will not save you from the gallows, as the 1987 execution of two Australians found guilty of charges relating to heroin possession proved.

The penalties are severe and the authorities seem to catch a steady stream of unsuccessful peddlers, smugglers and users. Mere possession can bring down a lengthy jail sentence and a beating with the rotan.

Heroin still seems to be around, and the odd old opium den still continues a precarious existence too, but the advice in Malaysia is steer clear of drugs.

ACCOMMODATION
Malaysia has a very wide range of accommodation possibilities – you can still find many places to stay for less than US$5 per person per night while at the other end of the scale more luxurious 'international standard' hotels can be well over US$100 a night for a room. Accommodation possibilities include:

International Hotels
There are modern, multistorey, air-con, swimming pool, all mod-cons hotels of the major international chains (Hyatts, Holiday Inns, Hiltons) and of many local chains such as the Merlin hotels found all over Malaysia. In these hotels nightly costs are generally from M$100 and up for a double. Malaysia has not suffered the price hikes of neighbouring Singapore, but Kuala Lumpur or Penang have seen climbing occupancy rate and higher prices.

Traditional Chinese Hotels
At the other end of the price scale are the traditional Chinese hotels found in great numbers all over Malaysia. They're the mainstay of the budget travellers and backpackers and in Malaysia you can generally find a good room for M$10 to M$16. Chinese hotels are generally fairly spartan – bare floors, just a bed, a couple of chairs and a table, a wardrobe and a sink. The showers and toilets (which will almost inevitably be Asian squat style) will generally be down the corridor. A couple of catches and points to watch for: couples can sometimes economise by asking for a single since in Chinese hotel language single means one double bed, double means two beds. Don't think this is being tight, in Chinese hotels you can pack as many into one room as you wish.

The main catch with these hotels is that they can sometimes be terribly noisy. They're often on main streets and the bottom rung of the Chinese hotel ladder has a serious design problem – the walls rarely reach the ceiling. The top is simply meshed or barred in. This is great for ventilation but terrible for acoustics. Every noise carries throughout the hotel and Chinese hotels all awake to a terrible dawn chorus of hawking, coughing and spitting like only the Chinese know how.

That apart these hotels are delightfully traditional in style (all swishing ceiling fans and old furniture), are almost always spotlessly clean (there are exceptions) and they're great fun to stay in. They're very often built on top of coffee bars or restaurants so food is never more than a few steps away. And they're cheap.

There are also many older-style Chinese places a notch up from the most basic places, where M$10 to M$20 will get you a fan-cooled room with common facilities. For M$20 to M$30 you can often find air-conditioned rooms with attached bathroom – but still basically Chinese in their spartan style.

Other Possibilities

There are also a number of alternatives to the cheap hotels in Malaysia. For a start some of the old British-developed resthouses are still in operation. During the colonial era these were set up to provide accommodation for travelling officials and later provided excellent shelter for all types of tourists and travellers. Many of the resthouses are still government owned but are now privately operated. They have been turned into mid-range resorts, but there are still resthouses for officials where foreign visitors can stay in traditional style and often at pleasantly low prices.

There are a number of YMCAs and YWCAs around Malaysia and at one time there were also a string of youth hostels. Unfortunately some of them were inconveniently situated and almost all of them suffered from extremely indifferent operators. Combined with the competition from cheap hotels most of the hostels have now closed; a shame since some of them were very pleasant.

Malaysia also has a number of cheap local accommodation possibilities, usually at beach centres. These may be huts on the beach or guest houses – private homes or rented houses divided by partition walls into a number of rooms. Dormitory accommodation is usually available. Rooms are usually spartan but this is the cheapest accommodation around and often the nicest as they can have a real family atmosphere. They often cater only to foreign travellers and offer lots of extras to outdo the competition, such as free tea and coffee, bicycles, transport and even haircuts. A dorm bed will

cost M$5 to M$8, and rooms from M$8 to M$20.

Finally there's the Malaysian Village Homestay programme, which organises for foreigners to stay with Malaysian families in villages within a 50-km radius of Kuala Lumpur. The cost is M$25 per person per day, and this includes all meals. Contact the office at 178 Jalan Tuanku Abdul Rahman in KL for more details (tel 03-2920319).

Taxes & Service Charges

In Malaysia there's a 5% government tax that applies to all hotel rooms. On top of this there's a 10% service in the more expensive places. You are not expected to tip in addition to this. Expensive places almost always quote prices exclusive of tax and service charge – this is represented as ++, eg $120++ for a double. Nett means that tax and service charges are included. Tax and service charges are also applied to food, drinks and services in the more expensive hotels and restaurants.

Cheap Malaysian hotels, however, generally quote a price inclusive of the 5% government tax.

FOOD

While travelling around some parts of Asia is as good as a session with Weight Watchers, Singapore and Malaysia are quite the opposite. The food is simply terrific, the variety unbeatable and the costs pleasantly low. Whether you're looking for Chinese food, Malay food, Indian food, Indonesian food or even a Big Mac (巨無霸) you'll find happiness!

Chinese Food

You'll find the full range of Chinese cuisines in Singapore and Malaysia although if you're kicking round the backwoods of Sabah or Sarawak Chinese food is likely to consist of little more than noodles and vegetables.

Cantonese When people in the West speak of Chinese food they probably mean Cantonese food. It's the best known and most popular variety of Chinese cooking even in Singapore where the majority of Chinese are not Cantonese, as they are in Hong Kong. Cantonese food is noted for the variety and freshness of its ingredients. The food is usually stir-fried with just a touch of oil to ensure that the result is crisp and fresh. All those best known 'Western Chinese' dishes fit into this category – sweet & sour dishes, won ton soup, chow mein, spring rolls.

With Cantonese food the more people you can muster for the meal the better because dishes are traditionally shared so that everyone manages to sample the greatest variety. A corollary of this is that Cantonese food should be balanced – traditionally all foods are said to be ying – 'cooling' – like vegetables, most fruits, and clear soups or yang – 'heaty' – starchy foods and meat. A cooling dish should be balanced by a heaty dish, too much of one or the other is not good for you.

Another Cantonese speciality is dim sum or 'little heart'. Dim sum is usually eaten at lunch time or as a Sunday brunch. Dim sum restaurants are usually large, noisy affairs and the dim sum, little snacks that come in small bowls, are whisked around the tables on individual trolleys or carts. As they come by you simply ask for a plate of this or a bowl of that. At the end of the meal your bill is toted up from the number of empty containers on your table. Eating dim sum is generally fun as well as tasty.

Cantonese cuisine can also offer real

extremes – shark's fin soup or bird's nest soup are expensive delicacies from one end of the scale; mee (noodles) or congee (rice porridge) are cheap basics from the other end.

North & West China Far less familiar than the dishes of Canton are the cuisines from the north and west of China – Sichuan, Shanghai and Beijing. Sichuan (or Szechuan) food is the fiery food of China, the food where the peppers really get into the act. Whereas the tastes of Cantonese food are delicate and understated, in Sichuan food the flavours are strong and dramatic – garlic and chillies play their part in dishes like diced chicken or sour & hot soup.

Beijing food is, of course, best known for the famous Peking duck where the specially fattened ducks are basted in syrup and roasted on a revolving spit. The duck skin is served as a separate first course. Like the other northern cuisines Beijing food is less subtle, more direct than Cantonese food. Although Beijing food is usually eaten with noodles or steamed buns in China, because rice does not grow in the cold northern Beijing region, in Singapore it's equally likely to come with rice.

Food from Shanghai is to some extent a cross between northern and Cantonese cuisines – combining the strong flavours of the north with the ingredients of Canton. It is not easy to find, however, in Singapore.

South China Cantonese is, of course, the best known southern Chinese cuisine but it is quite easy to find a number of other regional styles – particularly since so many of the region's Chinese are Hokkiens or Hakkas. One of the best known of these southern dishes comes from the island of Hainan. Throughout Malaysia one of the most widespread and also most economical meals you can find is Hainanese chicken rice. It's one of those dishes the very simplicity of which ensures its quality. Chicken rice is simply steamed chicken, rice boiled or steamed in the chicken stock, a clear soup and slices of cucumber. Flavour this delicate dish with soy or chilli sauce and you've got a delicious meal for $2.50 to $3.50. The Hainanese also produce steamboat, a sort of oriental variation on a Swiss fondue where you have a boiling stockpot in the middle of the table into which you dip pieces of meat, seafood or vegetables.

The Hokkiens come from the Fukien province in China and make up the largest dialect group in Singapore. Although Hokkien food is rated way down the Chinese gastronomic scale they have provided the unofficial national dish of Singapore – Hokkien fried mee. It's made of thick egg noodles cooked with pork, seafood and vegetables and a rich sauce. Hokkien popiah spring rolls are also delicious.

Teochew food, from the area around Swatow in China, is another style noted for its delicacy and natural flavour. Teochew food is also famous for seafood and a popular food-centre dish is *char kway teow* – broad noodles, clams and eggs fried in chilli and black bean sauce. Hakka food is noted for its simple ingredients and the best known Hakka dish, again easily found in food centres, is *yong tau foo* – bean curd stuffed with minced meat.

Taiwanese food includes rice porridge, a healthy and economical meal, often with small side dishes of oysters, mussels or pork stewed in a rich sauce.

Indian Food

Indian food is one of the region's greatest delights, indeed it's easier to find really good Indian food in Singapore or Malaysia than in India! Very approximately you can divide Indian food into southern, Muslim and northern – food from southern India tends to be hotter with the emphasis more on vegetarian food, while Muslim food tends to be more subtle in its spicing and uses more meat. Muslim food is a mixture of south and north Indian influences and has developed a distinctly Malaysian style. The rich Moghul dishes of northern India are not so common and are generally only found in more expensive restaurants. Common to all Indian food

are the spices or masala, the lentil soup known as *dhal*, the yoghurt and water drink known as *lassi* and the sauces or condiments known as chutneys.

The typical south Indian dish is a rice plate. If you ask for one in a vegetarian restaurant you won't get a plate at all, instead a large *daun pisang* (banana leaf) is placed in front of you and on this a large mound of rice is placed then scoops of a variety of vegetable curries are added around the rice and a couple of papadums tossed in for good measure. With your right hand, for south Indian vegetarian food is never eaten with utensils, you then knead the curries into the rice and eat away. When your banana leaf starts to get emptier you'll suddenly find it refilled – for the rice plate is always an 'as much as you can eat' meal. When you've finished fold the banana leaf in two, with the fold towards you, to indicate that you've had enough.

Other vegetarian dishes include the popular *masala dosai*. A masala dosai is a thin pancake which, when rolled around the masala (spiced vegetables) with some *rasam* (spicy soup) on the side, provides about the cheapest light meal you could ask for. An equivalent snack meal in Indian Muslim restaurants is *murtabak*, made from paper thin dough which is then folded with egg and minced mutton filling and lightly grilled with oil. Or a *roti chanai* – made from murtabak dough – which you dip into a bowl of dhal or curry. This is a very popular and filling breakfast throughout the region. Or perhaps a samosa – roughly an Indian equivalent of a Chinese spring roll.

A favourite Indian Muslim dish, and one which is cheap, easy to find and of excellent standard, is biryani. Served with a chicken or mutton curry the dish takes its name from the saffron-coloured rice it is served with.

A particular favourite is the north Indian tandoori food which takes its name from the clay tandoor oven in which meat is cooked after an overnight marinade in a complex yoghurt and spice mixture. Tandoori chicken is the best known tandoori dish. Although rice is also eaten in north India it is not so much the ever present staple it is in the south. North Indian food makes wide use of the delicious Indian breads like chapatis, parathas or rotis.

Malay, Indonesian & Nyonya Food

Surprisingly Malay food is not as easily found in Malaysia as Chinese or Indian food although many Malay dishes, like satay, are everywhere. Satay is delicious tiny kebabs of chicken, mutton or beef dipped in a spicy peanut sauce. Some Malay dishes you may have a chance to try include *tahu goreng* – fried soy bean curd and bean sprouts in a peanut sauce; *ikan bilis* (anchovies) – tiny fish fried whole; *ikan assam* – fried fish in a sour tamarind curry; *sambal udang* – fiery curry prawns. *Ayam goreng* is fried chicken and *rendang* is a sort of spiced curried meat in coconut marinade. *Nasi goreng* (or fried rice – 'nasi' is rice and 'goreng' is fried) is widely available but it is as much a Chinese and Indian dish as Malay, and each style has its own flavours. *Nasi lemak* is coconut rice served with fried ikan bilis, peanuts and a curry.

Malay food is very similar to Indonesian and you'll find a few Indonesian restaurants in Malaysia and Indonesian dishes on the menu in larger restaurants. *Gado gado* is an Indonesian salad dressed with a peanut sauce. In Sumatra the Indonesian food bends much more towards curries and chillies. The popular Sumatran dish is *nasi padang* – rice from the town of Padang. In a nasi padang restaurant all the different dishes are on display in the window and you select as many as you want to share amongst your group.

Nyonya cooking is a local variation on Chinese and Malay food – it uses Chinese ingredients, but with local spices like chillies and coconut cream. Nyonya cooking is essentially a home skill, rather than a restaurant one – there are few places where you can find Nyonya food. *Laksa lemak*, a spicy coconut-based noodle soup, is a classic Nyonya dish that has been adopted by all Malaysians.

Other Cuisine

Western fast-food addicts will find Ronald McDonald, the Colonel from Kentucky and A&W have all made inroads into the regional eating scene. At big hotels you can find all the usual Western dishes. In Singapore you will also find Japanese, Korean and other regional restaurants. There are modern air-conditioned supermarkets where you can find anything from yoghurt to packaged muesli.

Desserts

Although desserts are not a really big deal in the region you can find some interesting after dinner snacks like *pisang goreng* (banana fritters) or even *bo-bo cha-cha*, which is similar to *ais kacang* and *cendol* (refer to the section on drinks). Ice-cream addicts will be relieved to hear they can find good ice cream all over the region including soft-serve, multiflavour gelati-style, or packaged ice cream on a stick.

Tropical Fruit

Once you've tried rambutans, mangosteens, jackfruit and durians how can you ever go back to boring old apples and oranges? If you're already addicted to tropical fruit, Singapore and Malaysia are great places to indulge the passion. If you've not yet been initiated then there could hardly be a better place in the world to develop a taste for exotic flavours. The places to head for an easy introduction are the fruit stalls which you'll find in food centres or even just on the streets. Slices of a whole variety of fruits (including those dull old apples and oranges) are laid out on ice in a colourful and mouth-watering display which you can make a selection from for just 30 sen and up. You can also have a fruit salad made up on the spot from as many fruits as you care to choose. Some tastes to sample include:

Rambutan The Malay name means 'spiny' and that's just what they are. Rambutans are the size of a large walnut or small tangerine and they're covered in soft red spines. You peel the skin away to reveal a very close cousin to the lychee with cool and mouth-watering flesh around a central stone.

Pineapple Probably the most popular tropical fruit, a slice of pineapple is always a delicious thirst quencher. You've not really tasted pineapple until you're handed a whole one, skin sliced away and with the central stem to hold it by while the juice runs down your arm!

Mangosteen One of the finest tropical fruits, the mangosteen is about the size of a small orange or apple. The dark purple outer skin breaks open to reveal pure white segments shaped like orange segments – but with a sweet-sour flavour which has been compared to a combination of strawberries and grapes. Queen Victoria, so the story goes, offered a considerable prize to anybody able to bring a mangosteen back intact from the East for her to try.

Durian The region's most infamous fruit, the durian is a large oval fruit about 20 to 25 cm long although it may often grow much larger. The durian is renowned for its phenomenal smell, a stink so powerful that first timers are often forced to hold their noses while they taste. In fact durians emanate a stench so redolent of open sewers that in season you'll see signs in hotels all over Malaysia warning that durians are expressly forbidden entry. It's definitely an aquired taste – the nearest approximation I can make is onion-flavoured ice cream.

When the hardy, spiny shell is cracked open pale white-green segments are revealed with a taste as distinctive as their smell. Durians are so highly esteemed that great care is taken over their selection and you'll see gourmets feeling them carefully, sniffing them reverently and finally demanding a preliminary taste before purchasing. Durians are also expensive and unlike other fruits which are generally ying (or cooling) durians are yang (or heaty). So much so that the durian is said to be a powerful aphrodisiac. It's no wonder that durians are reputed to be the only fruit which a tiger craves!

Jackfruit or Nangka This enormous watermelon-size fruit hangs from trees and when opened breaks up into a large number of bright orange-yellow segments with a slightly rubbery texture. Externally the nangka is covered by a green pimply skin, but it's too big and too messy to clean to make buying a whole one worthwhile. From street fruit stalls you can often buy several nangka segments skewered on a stick.

Papaya The papaya or paw paw originated in Central America but is now quite common throughout South-East Asia and is very popular at breakfast time when, served with a dash of lemon juice, a slice of papaya is the perfect way to start the day. The papaya

Mangosteen

Durian

Jackfruit or Nangka

Rambutan

is about 30 cm or so in length and the bright orange flesh is somewhat similar in texture and appearance to pumpkin but related in taste to a melon. The numerous black seeds in the centre of a papaya are said to have a contraceptive effect if eaten by women.

Starfruit The starfruit takes its name from the fruit's cross-sectional star shape. A translucent green-yellow in colour, starfruit has a crisp, cool, watery taste.

Custard Apple or Zirzat Sometimes known as soursop or white mango, the custard apple has a warty green outer covering and is ripe and ready to eat when it begins to look slightly off – the fresh green skin begins to look blackish and the feel becomes slightly squishy. Inside the creamy white flesh has a deliciously thirst-quenching flavour with a hint of lemon in it. This is another fruit you can often find at fruit stalls.

Other Fruit Then there are coconuts, mangoes, lychees, bananas (26 varieties!), jambus (guavas), dukus, chikus, jeruks, even strawberries up in the Cameron Highlands. Plus all the temperate climate fruits which are imported from Australia, New Zealand and further afield.

DRINKS
Nonalcoholic Drinks

Life can be thirsty in Malaysia so you'll be relieved to hear that drinks are excellent, economical and readily available. For a start, water can be drunk straight from the taps in most larger Malaysian cities (which is a far cry from many Asian countries where drinking water without elaborate sterilising preparations is foolhardy).

Secondly there are a wide variety of soft drinks from Coca-Cola, Pepsi, 7-Up and Fanta to a variety of F&N flavours including sarsaparilla (for root beer fans). Soft drinks generally cost around $1.

You can also find those fruit juice-in-a-box drinks all over the region with both normal fruit flavours and also oddities like chrysanthemum tea.

Sipping a coffee or tea in a Chinese coffee shop or restaurant is a time-honoured pursuit at any time of day or night. If you want your tea, which the Chinese and Malays make very well, without the added thickening of condensed milk, then ask for *teh-o*. Shout out – as it's another one of those words which

Zirzat or Custard Apple

Starfruit

Chiku

cannot be said quietly. If you don't want sugar either you have to ask for *teh kosong*, but you're unlikely to get it, they simply cannot believe anyone would drink tea that way!

Fruit juices are very popular and very good. With the aid of a blender and crushed ice, delicious concoctions like watermelon juice can be whipped up in seconds. Old-fashioned sugar-cane crushers, which look like grandma's old washing mangle, can still be seen in operation.

Halfway between a drink and a dessert are

cendol and ais kacang. An ais (ice) kacang is rather like an old-fashioned sno-cone but the shaved ice is topped with syrups and condensed milk, and it's all piled on top of a foundation of beans and jellies! It sounds gross and looks lurid but tastes terrific! Cendol consists of coconut milk with brown sugar syrup and greenish noodle-like things topped with shaved ice (also tastes terrific).

Other oddities? Well, the milky white drink in clear plastic bins at street drink sellers is soybean milk which is also sold in a yoghurty form. Soybean milk is also available in soft drink bottles. Medicinal teas are a big deal with the health-minded Chinese.

Alcohol
Beer drinkers will probably find Anchor Beer or Tiger Beer to their taste although the minimum price for a bottle of beer is at least M$2.50. Irish travellers may be surprised to find that Guinness has a considerable following – in part because the Chinese believe it has a strong medicinal value. ABC Stout is a cheaper local equivalent of the dark black brew.

Take the Children
Researching the first edition of this book was familiar in one respect and totally unfamiliar in another. It was familiar in that we'd pretty well covered Malaysia in the past. We'd made one trip all over the country on a motorcycle and in subsequent years had returned to Malaysia on a number of occasions, travelling by air, train, bus, long-distance taxi and even by thumb. So we felt pretty well at home in Malaysia and knew our way round fairly well. The trip was totally unfamiliar in that it was the first time out with our daughter, who was seven months old when we arrived in Singapore at the start of our travels.

The end verdict? Harder work than we might have expected but quite possible and in many ways great fun. For starters Malaysia is a very civilised country for travelling with kids. It's clean and hygienic by Asian standards and travel is relatively easy. Equally important the people of Singapore and Malaysia love kids, especially blond blue-eyed ones, so Tashi was thoroughly spoilt. The pleasant surprises were how well equipped many places were to deal with children. Even the tiniest little coffee-shop restaurants seemed to have a high chair ready to be whisked out when we appeared. And, of course, Chinese food is designed to be messed with – you're bound to end up with prawn shells and fish bones littered all around you, so any additional mess a baby can make hardly seems to matter.

As far as the Western necessities of dealing with babies went everything was pretty simple. Milk is, of course, hard to obtain, as in most of Asia, but we did find plenty of fruit juice, soy milk drinks and often did find milk too. Our initial intention to wash nappies (diapers) as we went along soon went out the window. Perhaps if you're travelling slowly you could manage that, but when you're covering a lot of ground (as you have to when researching a guidebook) it simply wasn't possible to get them dried in time to move on. But finding disposable nappies was no trouble as they are available in even the smallest towns, and prices were not much more than in the West. They were usually American (higher stick failure) or Japanese (pretty, but not always effective).

As for Tashi, she had a great time, loved Chinese food (especially baby sweet corn), delighted in the water (beach or pool) and generally enjoyed herself. The biggest problem, and this would have been a problem anywhere, not just in Asia, was that she was too big to take along after she'd reached her bedtime but too small to keep up late. At times we had to miss meals or rush out for take-aways because she was asleep and could not be stirred. Plus the constant moving, every second night a new hotel room, did unsettle her a bit and we had rather too many middle-of-the-night wake-ups for comfort. But then Tashi has never been a great sleeper. We've subsequently made several more trips in Asia with Tashi and, when he came along, her younger brother Kieran. For more information on taking the kids see Maureen's book *Travel with Children*.

Tony Wheeler

Getting There & Away

AIR

Airline Tickets – A Warning

Malaysia has a reputation as a good place for buying discounted airline tickets. As in many other places in the world ticket discounting can be a slightly shady activity – it may be under the counter, quietly tolerated or even openly tolerated but it's never totally free and open. Additionally the official attitudes towards it can blow hot and cold – one year it's OK (happy days, the prices drop); the next year it's a no-no (disaster, the prices soar). It can also go in and out of official favour depending on where you want to fly to – one year tickets to Europe may be a bargain, tickets around Asia very expensive. The next year the opposite may apply.

So don't expect anything when it comes to cheap tickets – what applies this week may not apply next. Nevertheless Kuala Lumpur and Penang are certainly two of the best places around to find bargains on airline tickets. Beware, however, of unscrupulous people in this field. There are many fly-by-night operators and the agent everybody speaks highly of one year can all too easily do a midnight flit next. As did a ticket agent we recommended in the previous edition of this book. Many travellers have written to us recommending particular agents and where appropriate we've mentioned agents who have been highly and frequently recommended. Curiously enough, however, some agents, in Penang in particular, seem to simultaneously get 'great guy, very reliable' recommendations and 'danger, avoid at all costs' warnings!

For flights within the Singapore and Malaysia region, Singapore Airlines and MAS charge a cancellation penalty (25% of the fare) if you do not notify them 72 hours before the flight.

To/From Europe

Tickets are available from travel agents in London to Kuala Lumpur from around UK£270 to UK£300 or return from around UK£500 to UK£550. It's possible to get flights from London to Australia with stopovers in Singapore or Kuala Lumpur from around UK£900 return. To Auckland with a Singapore stopover costs around UK£520 one way. For more information check the travel ad pages in *Time Out* or the *Australasian Express*. Two good agents for cheap airline tickets are Trailfinders at 46 Earls Court Rd, London, UK or STA at 74 Old Brompton Rd, London, UK.

To/From Australia

MAS flights between Melbourne/Sydney to Singapore via Kuala Lumpur are A$1020 return in the low season and A$1200 return in the high season. The one-way economy fare on the same route is A$550 in the low season and A$800 in the high season.

To/From New Zealand

MAS flies between Auckland and Kuala Lumpur. The fare is M$1430 from Kuala Lumpur one way, or NZ$1400 return from Auckland.

To/From the USA

There is now a lot of ticket discounting with Asian airlines from the US west coast to Asia. Whereas this used to be basically a closed shop operation for Asians only it's now fairly wide open. It's possible to find fares from the US west coast to Malaysia for around US$550 one way or US$900 return. Scan the Sunday travel section of west coast newspapers like the *LA Times* or the *San Francisco Chronicle-Examiner* for agents handling discounted tickets. Some cheap fares include a stopover in Hong Kong. There are also budget and super Apex fares available out of the west coast. Similar deals from the east coast can be found in the Sunday papers there.

To/From Thailand

You can fly from Kuala Lumpur to Bangkok for about M$220. Or from Penang to Hat Yai for M$120 or to Phuket for slightly more. Add on a Phuket to Bangkok flight and it works out no more expensive than flying to Bangkok directly. Flying from Penang to Hat Yai or Phuket can save a lot of time wasted in crossing the border by land.

To/From Indonesia

There are several interesting variations from Indonesia to Malaysia. The short hop from Medan in Sumatra to Penang costs around US$80. There are also weekly flights between Kuching in Sarawak and Pontianak in Kalimantan, the Indonesian part of the island of Borneo, for M$160. Similarly at the eastern end of Borneo there is also a weekly connection between Tawau in Sabah and Tarakan in Kalimantan.

To/From India & Other Places in Asia

Although Indonesia and Thailand are the two 'normal' places to travel to or from there are plenty of other possibilities including India, Sri Lanka, Myanmar, Hong Kong or the Philippines. For details on cheap air fares check the relevant sections in Singapore and Penang – these are the two airline ticket centres.

LAND

To/From Thailand

You can cross the border by land at Padang Besar (road or rail), Changlun-Sadao (road) or Keroh-Betong (road) in the west or at Rantau Panjang-Sungai Golok in the east. For information on Thai visas, refer to the Visas section in the Malaysia – Facts for the Visitor chapter.

Road – West Coast Although there are border points at Padang Besar and Keroh the majority of travellers cross by road between Changlun and Sadao for Hat Yai. There's a long stretch of neutral territory between these two points so although you can easily get a bus or taxi up to Changlun on the Malaysian side and on from Sadao to Hat Yai

on the Thai side, crossing the actual border is difficult. There are two easy alternatives – one is a Thai taxi from Georgetown (see Penang) for around M$25 to Hat Yai. The other is to cross at Padang Besar, where the railway also crosses and where the border is an easy walk across. Note that the Sadao-Changlun border is only open to 6 pm. From Hat Yai there are plenty of buses and trains to Phuket, Bangkok or other places.

Road – East Coast From Kota Bharu you can take a No 29 bus to Rantau Panjang – the 45-km trip takes 1½ hours and costs about M$2. Once there you've got a half-km walk to the Thai railway station at Sungai Golok. An express train departs Sungai Golok for Bangkok every day at 10.55 am and arrives in Bangkok at 7.05 am the next day. There's a 'rapid' train everyday at 10.05 am which arrives at 6.35 am. These trains go through Hat Yai. A number of travellers have pointed out in the past that the Malay immigration post at Rantau Panjang is very slack and it's quite easy to miss them, but it seems to be more efficient now. Local buses would zip straight by, since locals did not need special clearance to go to Sungai Golok. It's your responsibility to make sure your passport is stamped on entry. Failure to do so can mean a stiff fine for 'illegal entry'.

Train The rail route into Thailand is on the Butterworth-Alor Setar-Hat Yai route which crosses into Thailand at Padang Besar. You can take the International Express from Butterworth all the way to Bangkok with connections from Singapore and Kuala Lumpur. On Sunday nights there is a special 1st class coach attached to the night express from Kuala Lumpur which is then attached to the Monday International Express from Butterworth. Once in Hat Yai there are frequent train and bus connections to other parts of Thailand . See table below.

To/From Indonesia

Road It is possible, although difficult, to cross the land border between Malaysia and Indonesia between Pontianak in Kalimantan and Kuching in Sarawak. For information on Indonesian visas, refer to the Visas section in the Malaysia – Facts for the Visitor chapter.

From Pontianak you catch a bus to the Indonesian border town of Entikong (5500 rp). The trip takes eight to nine hours, is very dusty and there are four buses daily. The border closes at 5 pm so if you arrive too late to cross, you may have to catch a bus 15 km back to the town of Balikarangan (500 rp), where there is accommodation (3000 rp single).

From Entikong to the border is six km, so take a motorcycle for 500 rp. The border opens at 8 am Indonesian time, 9 am Malaysian time. You can change money at the border or in the town of Batas on the Malaysian side. From the border catch a bus into Batas, and from there another bus to Serian, and another to Kuching.

SEA

To/From Thailand

Boat – West Coast There are a number of yachts operating between Penang and Phuket in Thailand. Typical trips sail Penang, Langkawi, Ko Phi Phi, Krabi and Phuket taking four or five days at a cost of US$180 per perosn. Look for advertisements in the cheap hotels and restaurants in Georgetown.

Cheaper and more frequent are the small boats that skip across the border from Kuala Perlis in the north-west corner of Malaysia to Setul in Thailand. There are customs and immigration posts here so you can cross quite legally although it's an unusual and rarely used entry/exit point. The boats will be those open long boats, unique to Thailand, with a car engine mounted on gimbels on the back and a long, solid shaft from the end of the engine driving the prop. The whole engine is swivelled to steer the boat. Fare for the short trip is around M$4 and from Setul you can bus to Hat Yai. Make sure you get your passport stamped on entry.

To/From Indonesia

Boat There are four regular services between Malaysia and Indonesia – Penang-Medan and Melaka-Dumai connecting Peninsular Malaysia with Sumatra, and Tawau-Tarakan connecting Sabah with Kalimantan in Borneo.

The Penang-Medan ferry service is now operated by the high-speed catamaran *Selesa Express*. It operates on Tuesdays and Fridays, leaving Penang at 8 am and on the

		Singapore	Kuala Lumpur	Butterworth
Hat Yai	1st class	S$116.50	M$ 69.10	M$ 24.20
	2nd class	S$ 52.80	M$ 31.50	M$ 11.20
Bangkok	1st class	S$175.60	M$128.20	M$ 83.30
	2nd class	S$ 80.30	M$ 59.00	M$ 38.70

Schedule:

48			49
13.40	Butterworth		12.25
15.10	Alor Setar		10.51
16.40*	Hat Yai		07.05*
08.35*	Bangkok		15.15*

* Thai time is one hour behind Malaysian time.

Train No 48   International Express from Butterworth runs daily
Train No 49   International Express from Bangkok runs daily

In addition there is a small express surcharge on the International Express. Additional cost for berth ranges from around M$6 to M$25 depending on whether you want a 2nd class upper, 2nd class lower, 1st class ordinary or 1st class air-con.

Top: Masjid Jame, Kuala Lumpur (PT)
Left: Railway Station, Kuala Lumpur (PT)
Right: Dayabumi Complex, Kuala Lumpur (PT)

Top: Panglima Mosque, Ipoh (JC)
Left: Turtle Pond, Sam Poh Tong Temple (HF)
Right: Sam Poh Tong Temple, Ipoh (HF)

return trip leaving Medan at 1.30 pm. The fare is M$100 one way (M$180 return) in 1st class, M$90 (M$160) in economy class.

There are two ferry services operating between Melaka and Dumai. One of them operates once a week, leaving Dumai on Saturdays at 10 am reaching Melaka at 2 pm and from Melaka back to Dumai at the same hour on Thursdays. The fare is M$80 one way or M$150 return. The other ferry service is operated by Tunar Rupat Express company and their boat takes just 2½ hours at the same price of $80 (see the Melaka Getting There & Away section in the Peninsular Malaysia chapter).

In Borneo the MV *Sasaran Muhibbah Express* operates between Tawau and Nunukan and Tarakan in Kalimantan. It leaves from the customs wharf around the back of the large supermarket. The schedule is a bit complicated. On Monday, Wednesday and Friday it leaves Tawau at 9 am and heads for Nunukan (45 minutes, M$25, or 15,000 rp in the opposite direction) and Tarakan (M$60) and back to Nunukan the same day, leaving Tarakan at 3 pm. The following day it departs Nunukan at 1 pm and returns to Tawau. On Sunday it leaves Nunukan at 5.30 am instead of 1 pm so it can then leave Tawau for Sipadan at 7 am. On Saturday the boat sails just from Tawau to Nunukan and return.

If travelling to Nunukan or Tarakan, it's worth noting that visas cannot be issued on arrival; you must get one before crossing into Indonesia.

To/From India
Boat After five years out of operation the shipping service between Madras (India) and Penang finally recommenced in late 1990. It's operated by the 800-passenger MV *Vignesswara*.

LEAVING MALAYSIA
Departure Tax
Malaysia levies airport taxes on all its flights. It's M$3 on domestic flights, M$5 to Singapore or Brunei and M$15 on other international flights. If you buy your tickets in Malaysia the departure tax is included in the price.

Getting Around

AIR

The Malaysian Airline System (MAS) is the country's main domestic operator. The Air Fares chart details some of the main regional routes and their fares in Malaysian dollars. MAS has many other regional routes in Sarawak and Sabah. It operates Airbuses, Boeing 737s and Fokker F50 on its domestic routes plus 12- seater Twin Otters on most of the more remote Sarawak and Sabah routes.

You can save quite a few dollars if flying to Sarawak or Sabah by flying from Johore Bahru rather than Singapore. The regular economy fare is M$147 from Johore Bahru to Kuching against S$170 from Singapore. To Kota Kinabalu, the respective fares are M$301 against S$346. To persuade travellers to take advantage of these lower fares MAS offers a bus service directly from its Singapore downtown office to the Johore Bahru airport.

MAS also has a number of special night flights and advance purchase fares. The 14-day advance purchase tickets are available for one-way/return flights from:

Destination	Fare
JB to Kuching	M$125/250
JB to Kota Kinabalu	M$256/512
KL to Kuching	M$197/394
KL to Kota Kinabalu	M$323/646

There are also a few economy night flights between Kuala Lumpur and Kota Kinabalu (M$266/532), Kuching (M$162/324) and Penang (M$61/112).

If you are travelling with two other people, you can save 50% on regular MAS economy air fares between West and East Malaysia by booking and paying as a group (group must comprise three people) at least seven days in advance. For flights within West Malaysia or within East Malaysia (but not between the two), groups of three people can travel for 75% of the regular economy fare if they book and pay together, at least seven days in advance. Families (couples with or without kids) can get a 25% reduction on one of the adult fares if they are buying a return ticket to any destination within Malaysia.

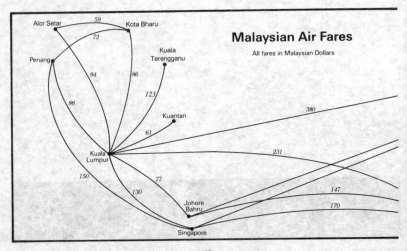

Malaysian Air Fares

All fares in Malaysian Dollars

In East Malaysia, where air transport is much more important than on the peninsula, there are many local flights and often this is the only quick way in or out. These flights are very much dependent on the vagaries of the weather. In the wet season places like Bareo can be isolated for days at a time, so don't venture into this area if you have a very tight schedule. During school holidays these flights are completely booked up and there's very little chance of getting a seat, even if you go to the airport and hope for a cancellation. At other times it's relatively easy to get a seat on a few days' notice.

Warning

Fares on flights between Singapore and Malaysia cost the same dollar figure whether bought in Malaysia or Singapore. Thus a Penang-Singapore ticket costs M$150 in Malaysia, while a Singapore-Penang ticket costs S$150 in Singapore. You can't, however, buy a Singapore-Penang ticket in Malaysia for the regular Malaysian ringgit rate; the conversion is done so you pay the equivalent of the fare in Singapore dollars.

BUS

Malaysia has an excellent bus system. There are public buses on local runs and a variety of privately operated buses on the longer trips as well as the big fleet of Expres Nasional express buses. In larger towns there may be a number of bus stops – a main station or two plus some of the private companies may operate directly from their own offices.

Buses are fast, economical, reasonably comfortable and seats can be reserved. On many routes there are also air-conditioned buses which usually cost just a few ringgit more than the regular buses. They make mid-day travel a sweat-free activity, but beware – as one traveller put it, 'Malaysian air-conditioned buses are really meat lockers on wheels with just two settings: cold and suspended animation'.

TRAIN

Malaysia has a modern, comfortable and economical railway service although there are basically only two railway lines. One runs from Singapore to Kuala Lumpur, Butterworth and on into Thailand. The other branches off from this line at Gemas and

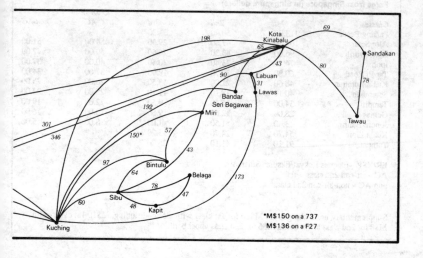

*M$150 on a 737
M$136 on a F27

Fares from Butterworth

Classes	1st	2nd	3rd	ER/XSP AC	non-AC
Padang Besar	20.70	9.30	5.80		
Alor Setar			3.50	12.00	9.00
Taiping	11.70	5.30	3.30	12.00	9.00
Ipoh	22.50	10.20	6.30	17.00	14.00
Tapah Road	29.20	13.20	8.10	20.00	17.00
Kuala Lumpur	47.40	21.40	13.20	28.00	25.00
Seremban	57.10	25.80	15.80	32.00	29.00
Tampin	62.00	27.90	17.20	34.00	31.00
Gemas	69.20	31.20	19.20	38.00	35.00
Johore Bahru	92.30	41.60	25.60	48.00	45.00
Singapore	96.00	43.30	26.60	50.00	47.00
Kuala Lipis	96.00	43.30	26.60		
Tumpat	132.40	59.70	36.70		

Fares from Kuala Lumpur

Classes	1st	2nd	3rd	ER/XSP AC	non-AC
Padang Besar	65.60	29.60	18.20		
Alor Setar	57.10	25.80	15.80	32.00	29.00
Butterworth	47.40	21.40	13.20	28.00	25.00
Ipoh	25.50	11.50	7.10	18.00	15.00
Tapah Road	18.90	8.50	5.30	15.00	12.00
Seremban	9.00	4.10	2.50	11.00	8.00
Tampin	15.20	6.90	4.20	13.00	10.00
Gemas	21.90	9.90	6.10	16.00	13.00
Johore Bahru	45.00	20.30	12.50	27.00	24.00
Singapore	48.60	21.90	13.50	28.00	25.00
Kuala Lipis	49.80	22.50	13.80		
Tumpat	86.20	38.90	23.90		

Fares from Singapore (in Singapore dollars)

Classes	1st	2nd	3rd	ER/XSP AC	non-AC
Padang Besar	113.00	50.90	31.30		
Alor Setar	105.70	47.60	29.30	54.00	51.00
Butterworth	96.00	43.30	26.60	50.00	47.00
Ipoh	74.10	33.40	20.50	40.00	37.00
Tapah Road	60.80	30.70	18.90	37.00	34.00
Kuala Lumpur	48.60	21.90	13.50	28.00	25.00
Seremban	40.10	18.10	11.10	25.00	22.00
Tampin	34.00	15.40	9.50	22.00	19.00
Gemas	28.00	12.60	9.50	19.00	16.00
Johore Bahru	3.40	1.50	1.00	8.00	5.00
Kuala Lipis	54.70	24.70	15.20		
Tumpat	91.10	41.10	25.20		

ER/XSP – Ekspres Rakyat/Ekspres Sinaran
AC – air-con 2nd class
non-AC – non-air-con 2nd class

Supplementary berth charges are M$20 for 1st class with air-conditioning, M$10 1st class ordinary, M$8 for 2nd class lower berth, M$6 for 2nd class upper berth.

Timetables for the main express train services are as follows:

Train No	ER 1	ORD 51	XSP 3	ORD 55
Classes	*1,2,3*	*2,3*	*1,2*	*1,2*
Butterworth	07.45	08.30	14.15	22.00
Ipoh	10.36	12.35	17.09	01.56
Kuala Lumpur	13.45	17.50	20.15	06.40

Train No	XSP 4	ORD 52	ER 2	ORD 56
Classes	*1,2*	*2,3*	*1,2,3*	*1,2*
Kuala Lumpur	07.30	08.15	15.00	22.00
Ipoh	10.29	12.40	18.07	02.15
Butterworth	13.35	17.50	21.10	06.40

Train No	XSP 5	ORD 57	ER 1	ORD 61
Classes	*1,2*	*2,3*	*1,2,3*	*1,2*
Kuala Lumpur	07.30	08.30	14.00	22.00
Tampin	09.24	10.51	15.56	00.25
Johore Bahru	13.23	17.05	19.49	06.00
Singapore	14.05	18.00	20.30	06.55

Train No	ER 2	ORD 58	XSP 6	ORD 62
Classes	*1,2,3*	*2,3*	*1,2*	*1,2*
Singapore	07.45	08.30	14.45	22.00
Johore Bahru	08.13	09.03	15.13	22.33
Tampin	12.14	14.43	19.20	04.31
Kuala Lumpur	14.30	17.50	21.25	07.00

Train No	ORD 91	ORD 81	ORD 97
Classes	*2,3*	*1,2,3*	*2,3*
Tumpat	06.15	10.30	-
Wakaf Bahru	06.45	10.58	-
Kuala Lipis	16.03	18.33	14.05
Jerantut	-	20.25	15.26
Gemas	-	23.55	-

Train No	ORD 82	ORD 98	ORD 92
Classes	*1,2,3*	*2,3*	*2,3*
Gemas	02.30	-	-
Jerantut	05.52	17.57	-
Kuala Lipis	07.00	19.17	08.30
Wakaf Bahru	15.12	-	18.11
Tumpat	15.50	-	18.50

ER – Ekspres Rakyat, XSP – Ekspres Sinaran, ORD – Ordinary
There are a number of other *biasa* (ordinary) train services, particularly on the central route to the east coast where there are numerous local trains. For details on the train fares and schedules to Hat Yai and Bangkok in Thailand see the Malaysia – Getting There & Away chapter.

runs through Kuala Lipis up to the north-east corner of the country near Kota Bharu. Other lines are just minor branches off these two routes and are not much used. Malaysia's first railway line was a 13-km route from Taiping to Port Weld which was laid in 1884, but is no longer in use. By 1903 you could travel all the way from Johore Bahru to near Butterworth and the extension of the line to the Thai border in 1918 and across the causeway to Singapore in 1923 meant you could travel by train from Singapore right into Thailand. In 1931 the east coast line was completed, effectively bringing the railway system to its present state.

The KTM, Keretapi Tanah Melayu, offers a number of concessions to travellers including a Railpass entitling the holder to unlimited travel for 30 days for M$175 or 10 days for M$85. The pass entitles you to travel on any class of train, but does not include sleeping berth charges. Railpasses are only available to foreign tourists and can be purchased at a number of main railway stations.

Malaysia has two types of rail services. There are the conventional 1st, 2nd and 3rd class trains with both express and slower ordinary services. On these trains you can reserve seats on 1st and 2nd class up to 90 days in advance and there are day and overnight trains. On the overnight trains sleeping berths are available in 1st and 2nd class. The other trains are known as the Ekspres Rakyat (People's Express) and the Ekspres Sinaran. These trains only have air-con or non-air-con carriages, and only stop at main stations. Consequently they are faster than the regular express trains. In fact in most respects these services are definitely the ones to take. Fares on the Ekspres Rakyat and Ekspres Sinaran are very reasonable, not much more than 3rd class for the non-air-con carriages, and not much more than 2nd class for air-con. Ekspres Rakyat and Ekspres Sinaran services only operated between Singapore and KL or KL and Butterworth.

In Sabah there's also a small narrow-gauge line which can take you through the Pegas River gorge from Tenom to Beaufort. It's a great trip and is well worth doing.

TAXI
Long-Distance Taxis
Malaysia's real travel bargain is the long-distance taxis. They make Malaysian travel, already easy and convenient even by the best Asian standards, a real breeze. A long-distance taxi is usually a diesel Mercedes, Peugeot or, more recently, Japanese car. In almost every town there will be a 'teksi' stand where the cars are lined up and ready to go to their various destinations. As soon as a full complement of four passengers turns up off you go. Between major towns the wait will rarely be long.

You can often get the taxis to pick you up or drop you off at your hotel or for four times the single fare you can 'charter' the whole taxi. You can also take a taxi to other destinations at charter rates. Taxi fares generally work out at about twice the comparable bus fares. Thus from KL to Butterworth it's M$30, KL to Melaka is M$13.

Of course there has to be a drawback to all this and that is the frightening driving which the taxi drivers often indulge in. They don't have as many head-on collisions as you might expect, but closing your eyes at times of high stress certainly helps.

CAR RENTAL & DRIVING
Rent-a-car operations are well established in Malaysia. In many Asian countries driving is either a fraught experience (ever seen the rush hour in Bangkok or Jakarta?), full of local dangers (I'd hate to think what would happen if you collided with a cow in India), or the roads are terrible, cars unavailable or for some other reason driving yourself is not really possible. None of these drawbacks apply in Malaysia. The roads are generally of a high standard, there are plenty of new cars available and driving standards are not too hair raising.

Basically driving in Malaysia follows much the same rules as in Britain or Australia – cars are right-hand drive, you drive on the left side of the road. The only additional precaution one needs to take is to remain constantly aware of the possible additional road hazards of stray animals, the large number of cyclists and the occasional suicidal motorcyclist.

Although most drivers in Malaysia are relatively sane, safe and slow there are also a fair few who specialise in overtaking on blind corners and otherwise trusting in divine intervention. Long-distance taxi drivers are particular specialists in these activities. Malaysian drivers also operate a curious signalling system where a left flashing indicator means 'you are safe to overtake'... or 'I'm about to turn off'... or 'I've forgotten to turn my indicator off'... or something.

Petrol is more expensive than in the USA, more comparable with the price in Australia, and a bit cheaper than in Europe at around M$0.95 a litre. Remember that wearing safety belts *is* compulsory, although these are fitted to the front seats only. Parking regulations are a little curious – they have a strange human parking meter system where your car collects a stack of little tickets under its wiper and you then have to find somebody to pay for them at so many cents per ticket.

Major rental operators in Malaysia include Avis, Budget, Hertz, National and Thrifty although there are numerous others including many local operators only found in one city. Rates are quoted both for unlimited distance and with an additional mileage charge, cheaper rates are available by the week. Unlimited distance rates are typically around M$800 per week including insurance and collision damage waiver. This is for a Proton Saga, the most popular car in Malaysia. It is basically a Mitsubishi assembled under licence in Malaysia. Charges for a Toyota Corolla are around M$1150, and for a Nissan Bluebird M$1400.

The Automobile Association of Malaysia (tel 03-417137) is at Lot 20/24 Hotel Equatorial, Jalan Sultan Ismail, Kuala Lumpur. They will let you join their organisation if you have a letter of introduction from your own automobile association.

HITCHING

Malaysia has long had a reputation for being an excellent place for hitchhiking and it's generally still true. You'll get picked up both by expats and by Malaysians and Singaporeans, but it's strictly an activity for foreigners – a hitchhiking Malaysian would probably just get left by the roadside! So the first rule of thumb in Malaysia is to look foreign. Look neat and tidy too, a worldwide rule for successful hitching, but make sure your backpack is in view and you look like someone on their way around the country.

Apart from the basic point of hitching, getting from A to B cheaply, hitching in Malaysia has the additional benefit that it's a fine way to meet the local people. Foreign hitchhikers are also looked upon as a neutral ear – you're likely to find out much more about the *bumiputra* situation from disgruntled Chinese when you're in their car. Or hear much more about the Chinese from disgruntled Malays!

On the west coast of Malaysia, particularly on the busy Johore Bahru-Kuala Lumpur-Butterworth route, hitching is generally quite easy. Much of the traffic is business people, the sort of people interested in conversation and likely to pick up hitch-

AWAS

KAWASAN KEMALANGAN

Danger Sign for Drivers

hikers. On the east coast traffic can often be quite light and there may be long waits between rides. Hitching in East Malaysia also depends on the traffic although it's quite possible.

BOAT

There are no services connecting the peninsula with East Malaysia. On a local level there are boats between the peninsula and offshore islands, and along the rivers of Sabah and Sarawak – see the relevant sections for full details.

LOCAL TRANSPORT

Local transport varies widely from place to place. Almost everywhere there are taxis and in most cases these are metered. In major cities there are buses – in Kuala Lumpur the government buses are backed up by private operators.

In many towns there are also bicycle rickshaws – while they are dying out in Kuala Lumpur and have become principally a tourist gimmick in many Malaysian cities they are still a viable form of transport. Indeed in places like Georgetown, with its convoluted and narrow streets, a bicycle rickshaw is probably the best way of getting around. See the relevant city sections for more details on local transport.

Peninsular Malaysia – West Coast

The east and west coasts of Peninsular Malaysia are surprisingly different both in population and in geography. The west coast is more heavily populated and connected by more roads and railways. To a large extent this is a factor of geography – the west coast is lower lying and has a larger coastal plain area before the land rises up into the central mountain range. Therefore cities on the west coast were established earlier than on the east coast and roads and communications were also built and developed. It was on the west coast that tin was initially discovered and where the rubber plantations were first developed – the two mainstays of the economy. Since more of the cities are on this side of the peninsula this is also much more the 'Chinese' half of the peninsula.

South of Kuala Lumpur

JOHORE BAHRU

Capital of the state of Johore, which comprises the entire southern tip of the peninsula, Johore Bahru is the southern gateway to Peninsular Malaysia. Connected to Singapore by the 1038-metre-long causeway, JB (as it is known throughout the country) inevitably suffers as a poor relation to its more glamourous neighbour. Despite its historical significance and the various points of interest in the city few travellers pause in JB; it's just the place where you get your passport stamped on arrival or departure in Malaysia.

With the devaluing of the Malaysian ringgit against the Singapore dollar, JB has become a popular place with Singaporeans looking for shopping bargains and cheap fuel, although it is an offence for them to leave Singapore Island with less than half a tank of fuel!

History
Johore has had a long and colourful history.

When Melaka fell to the Portuguese the sultans fled to the Johore River and re-established their capital there at Johore Lama. In 1536 a Portuguese fleet attacked and sacked the town, but Johore was soon rebuilt another 30 km upriver. Further attempts also failed to destroy the Johore sultanate, but in 1866 Sultan Abu Bakar, who had been educated by the British in Singapore, moved his capital to its present location and renamed it Johore Bahru (New Johore). Abu Bakar was a modern and progressive ruler and to this day Johore is one of Malaysia's most prosperous states.

Orientation
The road and railway across the causeway run straight into the middle of JB through the modern shopping centre of the town. The taxi and bus stations are to the left, the railway station to the right. The main hotel and restaurant area is in the Jalan Meldrum area, which runs parallel to Jalan Tun Abdu Razak, between it and Jalan Wong Ah Fook.

A little beyond the station you turn off to the right towards the east coast, a congested trip as far as Kota Tinggi. If you're heading towards Kuala Lumpur (KL) or Melaka on the west coast then you turn off to the left almost as soon as you cross the causeway and for the first few km the road runs right along the waterfront with good views across to Singapore Island.

The airport is 30 km from the city centre.

Information
There's a TDC tourist office (tel 07-223590) on the ground floor of the Komtar building, a high-rise city landmark on Jalan Tun Abdu Razak, a couple of hundred metres north of the railway station. It is open Monday to Friday from 8 am to 4.15 pm and Saturday from 8 am to 12.45 pm.

The taxi station is a two-storey building on Jalan Wong Ah Fook, while the bus station is a few minutes' walk from the city

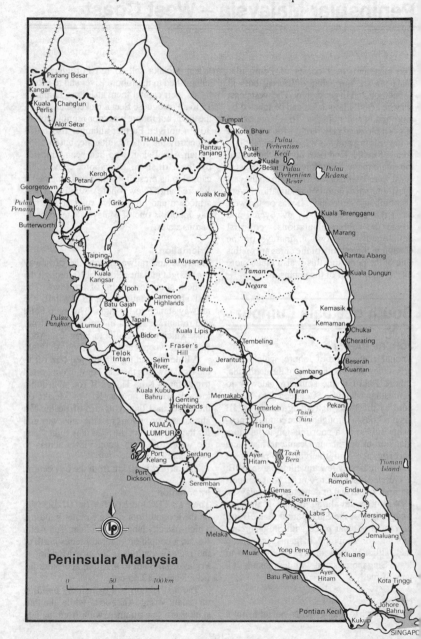

Peninsular Malaysia

0   50   100 km

centre (see map). The railway station is right in the centre of town. The booking office is open from 9 am to 6 pm daily.

Istana Besar (Royal Museum)

Overlooking the Straits of Johore, the Istana Besar is the main palace of the Johore royal family. It was built in Victorian style by anglophile Sultan Abu Bakar in 1866.

The palace has undergone recent renovation and is now open to the public as a Royal Museum. It is full of the Sultan's possessions, furniture and hunting trophies and is set out much as it was when in use as the palace. There are some superb pieces – Chinese, Japanese, Indian and local carved wooden pieces, an amazing full size crystal-glass table and chairs from France, while the hunting room has some bizarre exhibits including elephant's-foot umbrella stands and antelope-leg ashtrays! A guide accompanies you around the palace, pointing out items of interest and answering questions.

The palace is open daily from 9 am to 6 pm, although there's no entry after 5 pm. Entrance for foreigners is a hefty US$7 per person, payable in ringgit; Malaysians and students pay M$5. Despite the price, it's well worth a visit.

The 53-hectare palace grounds are beautifully manicured and are a great breathing space for this fairly cramped city. There are good views across the Straits of Johore, although Singapore's industrial backside is not terribly picturesque.

Other Buildings

The Abu Bakar Mosque is on Jalan Abu Bakar and was built from 1892 to 1900. The large mosque can accommodate 2000 people and overlooks the Straits of Johore.

With a 32-metre-high tower that serves as a city landmark, Bukit Serene is the actual

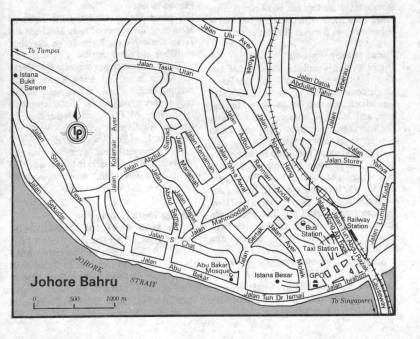

Johore Bahru

residence of the Sultan of Johore. The Istana Bukit Serene was built in 1932 but is not open to the public.

Another city landmark is the 64-metre-high square tower of the imposing State Secretariat building on Bukit Timbalan, overlooking the city centre. It was built in the 1940s. On the seafront opposite the courthouse the ugly Sultan Abu Bakar Monument was erected in 1955.

Places to Stay – bottom end

Few visitors stay in JB; it's too close to the greater attractions of Singapore. On the other hand Johore is an important business centre, in part due to the volume of trade carried on between Malaysia and Singapore, so there are plenty of hotels, although prices are generally high for Peninsular Malaysia.

At the bottom of the price scale there are a couple of Chinese cheapies on Jalan Meldrum right in the centre of town. The *Hotel Chean Seng* is a very basic Chinese cheapie with typical partitioned rooms with mesh around the top, fan and bath. It costs M$15 for a room with one large bed and is as basic as you'd expect for that price.

Places to Stay – middle

The best value is probably the *Hotel JB* (tel 07-224788) at 80A Jalan Wong Ah Fook. Single/double rooms go for M$29/30 with fan and common bath, M$38/42 with fan and bath, and M$44/50 with air-con and bath. The rooms here are fairly clean and not as box-like as some other places.

Also good value is the *Top Hotel* (tel 07-244755) at 12 Jalan Meldrum. All rooms have air-con and attached bath. The charges are M$36/42 for a single/double. Just around the corner at 2 Jalan Siew Niam is the *Hotel Le Tian* (tel 07-248151). The rooms are shabby, a bit on the small side, but have air-con and attached bath, and go for M$38/48.

Another reasonable place is the *Fortuna Hotel* (tel 07-238671) at 29A Jalan Meldrum. Rooms in this clean and well-kept place go for M$50 for air-con doubles with attached bath (no singles).

More expensive still is the new *Causeway Inn* (tel 07-248811) at 6A Jalan Meldrum. All rooms have air-con, TV and attached bath. Some also have good views across the Straits of Johore. Singles cost from M$44 to M$80, doubles from M$51 to M$87.

Places to Stay – top end

There's no shortage of top-end places in JB. The *Tropical Inn* (tel 07-247888) at 15 Jalan Gereja has 160 rooms from M$92/105. The hotel has a restaurant and coffee house as well as a bar and health centre, but no swimming pool.

The *Merlin Tower Inn* (tel 07-225811) on Jalan Meldrum charges M$100/130.

The *Holiday Inn* (tel 07-323800) is a couple of km north of the centre in Century Gardens on Jalan Dato Sulaiman. Rooms cost from M$180/200. There is a swimming pool, health club, restaurant and 24-hour coffee lounge.

Places to Eat

For good Malay food try the *Restoran Medina* on the corner of Jalan Meldrum and Jalan Siew Niam. They serve excellent murtabak and other curries.

There's a food centre opposite the railway station on Jalan Tun Abdu Razak. In the evening there's a fairly active *pasar malam* (night market) outside the Hindu temple on Jalan Wong Ah Fook, and another near the Komtar building between Jalan Wong Ah Fook and Jalan Tun Abdu Razak.

All the major hotels have their own restaurants. The coffee shop in the *Holiday Inn* is open 24 hours and serves reasonably priced local and Western dishes.

Getting There & Away

Air The MAS office (tel 07-220888) is on the ground floor of the Orchid Plaza on Jalan Wong Ah Fook. JB is well served by MAS flights, and, as an incentive to fly from JB rather than Singapore, fares from here to other places in Malaysia are much cheaper than from Singapore. There are flights from JB to: Kota Kinabalu (daily, M$301), KL (six daily, M$77), Kuching (daily, M$147) and Penang (three weekly, M$148).

Bus With Singapore so close travel connections are important. Due to the hassles of crossing the causeway – customs, immigration and so on – there's a much wider selection of buses and long-distance taxis to other towns in Peninsular Malaysia from JB than there are in Singapore.

The regular bus No 170 operates every 15 minutes between JB and Queen St in Singapore; it costs 90 sen. The Johore Bahru Express costs M$1 and its Singapore terminus is at Rochor Rd, only a stone's throw from the No 170 bus terminus.

There are regular buses to Melaka (M$10), KL (M$15), Ipoh (M$26) and Butterworth (M$30). To the east coast there are departures to Kota Tinggi, Kuantan (M$15) and Mersing.

Train There are daily trains from JB to KL and Butterworth, and these can be used to get to most places on the west coast. The line passes through Tampin (for Melaka), Seremban, KL, Tapah road (for Cameron Highlands), Ipoh and Taiping. There are also trains to Singapore but it's more convenient to take a bus or taxi. See the Malaysia Getting Around chapter for full schedule and fare information.

Taxi You can make the trip across the causeway to Queen St in Singapore by taxi for M$7 per person if you want to wait for one to fill up, or M$35 for the whole vehicle. From Singapore the fares are the same, but in Singapore dollars.

From the JB taxi station there are regular taxis to Kota Tinggi (M$3.30), Kuantan (M$10), Melaka (M$17.40) and KL (M-$32.35); add M$2 for air-con.

Car Rental The main car rental companies have offices in JB, and include:

Avis
    Tropical Inn Hotel, 15 Jalan Gereja (tel 07-244824)

Budget
    2nd Floor, Orchid Plaza, Jalan Wong Ah Fook (tel 07-243951)
Hertz
    1 Jalan Trus, (tel 07-237520)
National
    195G Tingkat Bawah, Km 7 Jalan Skudai (tel 07-370088)
Thrifty
    Holiday Plaza, Jalan Dato Sulaiman (tel 07-332313)

Getting Around
To/From the Airport JB's airport is 30 km out of JB on the road to Melaka and KL – take a taxi.

Taxi Taxis around town are plentiful, unmetered and cheap. Agree on a fare before you set off.

AROUND JOHORE BAHRU
Kukup
About 40 km south-west of JB on the Straits of Melaka, across from Sumatra, is the fishing village of Kukup. The village is famous throughout Malaysia and Singapore for its seafood, especially prawns, and for its open-air restaurants, most of which are built on stilts over the water.

Next to Kukup is Kampung Air Masin (Salt Water Village), renowned for its top quality *belacan* (shrimp paste).

Both villages are largely inhabited by Hokkien Chinese. Nowadays Kukup is a favourite stop for package tours from Singapore and abroad, although it should be avoided on weekends as it is full of day-trippers from Singapore.

JOHORE BAHRU TO MELAKA
The main road north from JB runs to KL and Melaka. It's a productive region of oil palm, rubber and pineapple plantations.

At Ayer Hitam, an important crossroads, you can turn left to go to Batu Pahat, Muar and Melaka; continue straight on for Segamat, Seremban and KL or alternatively for Segamat and Temerloh; or you can turn right for Kluang and Mersing on the east coast.

Ayer Hitam is a popular rest stop for buses, taxis and motorists so there are lots of small restaurants. Kampung Macap, south of Ayer Hitam, is well known for its Aw Pottery works.

Batu Pahat is a riverine town famed for its Chinese cuisine although it also has a minor reputation as a 'sin city' for jaded Singaporeans. Accommodation can be hard to find on weekends. Muar, the second largest town in Johore, is another riverside town. It is a centre of traditional Malay culture, including ghazal music and the Kuda Kepang, 'prancing horse', dances. It's a typical Malaysian town with plenty of Chinese restaurants and hotels but no tourists. Between Muar and Melaka there are a number of kampungs with traditional-style Melaka houses.

Mt Ophir (Gunung Ledang) has a series of waterfalls and pools for swimming on one side. There's also a trail that goes a long way up. 'The falls are a lot nicer than those at Kota Tinggi and they stretch along the mountainside for a longer way', reported a visitor. Local kids camp there and leave a lot of rubbish. To get there take a Muar-Segamat bus and get out at the 40-km marker or ask the conductor. It's then a km-plus walk through the plantation to the bottom of the falls.

Places to Stay

Batu Pahat The *Batu Pahat Rest House* (tel 07-441181) at 80 Jalan Tasek has air-con doubles for M$32 or at the *Fairyland Hotel* (tel 07-441777) on Jalan Rahmat you can get a good large double room with fan for less than M$20. For something a bit more salubrious try the *De Mandarin Inn* (tel 07-444011) at 7 Jalan Zabedah where air-con rooms cost M$39, or the *Hotel Carnival* (tel 07-415122) at 2 Jalan Fatimah which has rooms for M$80 and up.

Kluang In Kluang there's the *Kluang Rest House* (tel 07-721567) on Jalan Pejabat Kerajaan with rooms from M$32, or for something cheaper there's the basic *Ria*

Hotel (tel 07-719320) at 57 Jalan Dato Captain Ahmad which costs M$20.

Muar In Muar you can stay at the very good *Muar Rest House* (tel 07-922306) at 2222 Jalan Sultanah where air-con doubles cost M$27 to M$30; it has a restaurant overlooking the river . There're plenty of other hotels including the *Mido Hotel* (tel 07-922724) at 127F Jalan Abdullah with rooms for M$18, and the *Lee Wa Hotel* (tel 07-921604) at 44 Jalan Ali which costs M$18.

Segamat The *Silver Inn* (tel 07-912213) at 11 Jalan Ros has rooms for M$20. At 26 Jalan Ros there's the more expensive *Silver Merlin Inn* (tel 07-919913) with singles from M$30 and doubles from M$40. The *Segamat Rest House* (tel 07-917199) on Jalan Buloh Kasap has rooms for M$29.

MELAKA

Malaysia's most historically interesting city, Melaka (Malacca), has been through some dramatic events over the years. The complete series of European incursions in Malaysia – Portuguese, Dutch and British – were played out here. Yet this was an important trading port long before the first Portuguese adventurers set foot in the city.

Today it's a sleepy backwater town and no longer of any major commercial influence.

It's a place of intriguing Chinese streets and antique shops, old Chinese temples and cemeteries and nostalgic reminders of the now-departed European colonial powers. The traditional Malay kampung house in the Melaka area is distinctive for its colourful arched entrance steps, examples of which can be seen along the river in east Melaka or in the Tanjung Kling district north of the city.

History

Under the Melaka sultanates the city was a wealthy centre of trade with China, India, Siam and Indonesia due to its strategic position on the Straits of Melaka. The Melaka sultanates were the beginning of what is today Malaysia, and some Malaysians say this city is where you find the soul of Malaysia.

In 1405 Admiral Cheng Ho, the 'three-jewelled eunuch prince', arrived in Melaka bearing gifts from the Ming Emperor, the promise of protection from archenemies (the Siamese) and, surprisingly, the Muslim religion. Chinese settlers from this earliest contact came to be known as the Babas or Straits Chinese; they are the longest-settled Chinese people in Malaysia. Despite internal squabbles and intrigues Melaka grew to be a powerful trading state and successfully repulsed Siamese attacks.

In 1509 the Portuguese, seeking trading opportunities in the East, arrived at Melaka but after an initially friendly reception, the Melakans attacked the Portuguese fleet and took a number of prisoners.

This action was the pretext for an outright assault by the Portuguese and in 1511 Alfonso d'Albuquerque took the city and the Sultan fled to Johore where he re-established his kingdom. Under the Portuguese, Melaka continued to thrive as a trading post, the fortress of A'Famosa was constructed and missionaries like the famous Francis Xavier strove to implant Christianity.

The period of Portuguese strength in the East was a short one. As Dutch influence in Indonesia grew and Batavia (modern-day Jakarta) developed as the principal European port of the region, Melaka declined. Finally the Dutch attacked the city and in 1641 it passed into their hands after a siege lasting eight months.

The Dutch built fine public buildings and churches, which today are the most solid reminders of the European presence in the city, but like their Portuguese predecessors they stayed in power only about 150 years.

In 1795 the French occupied Holland so the British, allies of the Dutch, temporarily took over administration of the Dutch colonies.

The British administrators, essentially traders who were opposed to the Dutch policy of trade monopoly, clearly saw that the Dutch and British would be bitter rivals in Malaysia, when and if Melaka was returned. Accordingly in 1807 they commenced to demolish the fortress to ensure that if Melaka was restored to the Dutch it would be no rival to the British Malayan centres.

Fortunately Stamford Raffles, the far-sighted founder of Singapore, stepped in before these destructive policies could go too far and in 1824 Melaka was permanently ceded to the British in exchange for the Sumatran port of Bencoolen (Bengkulu today).

From that time until independence, all of Peninsular Malaysia was under British influence or control except for the period of Japanese occupation during WW II. Under the British, Melaka once more flourished as a trading centre although it was soon superseded by the growing commercial importance of Singapore.

Orientation

Melaka is a small town – easy to find your way around and compact enough to explore on foot, bicycle or trishaw. Jalan Munshi Abdullah is the main road through Melaka and travelling on this road you could zip through Melaka thinking it was simply another noisy small Malaysian town.

The interesting and older parts of Melaka are mainly closer to the waterfront, particularly around the old Dutch-built Stadthuys (town hall) where you'll also find the tourist office, Christ Church, St Paul's Church, Porta de Santiago and the museum.

Information

The local tourist office (tel 06-236538) is right in the heart of the city, opposite the Christ Church. It is staffed by very helpful people, and they conduct river tours daily. The office is open Monday to Friday from 8 am to 5 pm (closed Friday lunch time), Saturday 8.45 am to 1.30 pm, and Sunday from 9 am to 12.30 pm.

The GPO is three km north of central Melaka. To get there, take a bus No 19 from the bus terminal.

Melaka has a local bus station, and express

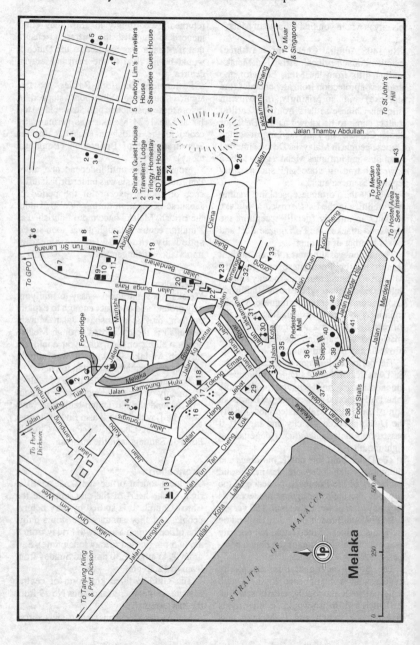

5 Cowboy Lim's Travellers House
6 Sawasdee Guest House

1 Shirah's Guest House
2 Triology Homestay
3 Travellers' Lodge
4 SD Rest House

Melaka

STRAITS OF MALACCA

■ PLACES TO STAY

4   Plaza Inn
5   May Chiang Hotel
7   Majestic Hotel
8   City Bayview Hotel
9   Hong Kong Hotel
10 Ng Fook Hotel
11 Ramada Renaissance Hotel
12 Wisma Hotel
13 Paradise Hostel
18 Chong Hoe Hotel
20 Valiant Hotel
21 Central Hotel
24 Palace Hotel
27 Kane's Tours & Hostel
43 Kancil Guest House

▼ PLACES TO EAT

19 New Tai Tee Bakery
22 Tai Chong Hygienic Ice Cafe
23 Sri Lakshmi Vilas Restaurant
29 Jonkers Melaka Restoran
32 Restoran Veni
33 UE Tea House
37 A&W Restoran Keluarga

OTHER

1   Local Bus Stand
2   Taxi Station
3   Express Bus Terminal
6   Church of St Peter
14 Kampung Hulu Mosque
15 Buddhist Temple
16 Cheng Hoon Teng Temple
17 Kampung Kling Mosque, Sri
    Pogyatha Vinoyagar Temple
25 Bukit China
26 Hang Li Poh Well, Po San Teng
28 Baba-Nyonya Heritage
    Museum
30 Christ Church
31 Church of St Francis
34 Tourist Office
35 Stadthuys
36 St Paul's Church
38 Dumai Ferry Office
39 Porta de Santiago
40 Cultural Museum (Muzium
    Budaya)
41 Sound & Light Show
42 Proclamation of Independence
    Hall

bus terminal and a taxi station, all in the same area beside Jalan Hang Tuah.

If you are driving your own vehicle Melaka's one-way traffic system will probably frustrate you at every turn.

Stadthuys

The most imposing relic of the Dutch period is the massive pink town hall which was built between 1641 and 1660. It is believed to be the oldest Dutch building in the East and is used today for government offices. It displays all the typical features of Dutch colonial architecture, including substantial solid doors and louvred windows. At the time of writing it was under renovation but may be open by now. The other buildings around the main square, including the old clock tower, also follow the same pink theme.

Christ Church

Nearby, facing one end of the main square, is the bright red Christ Church. The pink bricks were brought out from Zeeland in Holland and faced with local red laterite when the church was constructed in 1753. Under the British the church was converted for Anglican use, but it still has its old Dutch tombstones laid in the floor and its massive 15-metre-long ceiling beams, each cut from a single tree.

St Paul's Church

Bukit St Paul (St Paul's Hill) rises up above the Stadthuys and on top stand the ruins of St Paul's Church. Originally built by the Portuguese in 1571 as the small 'Our Lady of the Hill' chapel, it was regularly visited by Francis Xavier. Following his death in China the saint's body was brought here and buried for nine months before being transferred to Goa in India where it remains today.

In 1556 the church was enlarged to two storeys and a tower was added to the front in

1590. The church was renamed following the Dutch takeover, but with the completion of their own Christ Church at the base of the hill it fell into disuse. Under the British it lost its tower, although a lighthouse was built in front of it, and it eventually ended up as a powder magazine. The church has been in ruins now for 150 years, but the setting is beautiful, the walls imposing and fine old Dutch tombstones stand around the interior.

Church of St Peter

This unexceptional church was built in 1710 by descendants of the early Portuguese settlers and has some interesting stained-glass windows and old tombstones. It does not get much use for most of the year but it comes alive on Good Friday when Melakans flock here. Many of them make the occasion an excuse for an annual trip home from other parts of the country. The church is still associated with the Portuguese church in Macau.

Porta de Santiago

Raffles may have stepped in before the complete destruction of the old Portuguese fortress, but it was a near thing. All that was left was the main gate to A'Famosa, the Porta de Santiago. Curiously this sole surviving relic of the old fort originally constructed by Alfonso d'Albuquerque bears the Dutch East India Company's coat of arms. This was part of the fort which the Dutch reconstructed in 1670 following their takeover. The gate stands at the base of St Paul's Hill and a path leads up behind it to St Paul's Church.

This is also the site of the sound and light show each evening at 8.15 in Malay and at 10 pm in English. During Ramadan there are English shows only, at 8.30 pm. Entry is M\$5 and it's worth the money, even though the commentary is shamefully political.

Medan Portuguese

A few km beyond the fort is the area known as the Medan Portuguese, or Portuguese Square. In this small kampung there are about 500 descendants of marriages which took place between the colonial Portuguese

and Malays 400 years ago. There's little of interest for the visitor there except for the restaurants and cultural shows on Saturday nights at 8 pm when Chinese, Portuguese, Indian and Malay cultural ensembles perform for M\$2.

St John

Although the British demolished most of Porta de Santiago they left the small Dutch fort of St John untouched. It stands on a hilltop a little to the east of town, but there's not much to be seen.

Museums

Proclamation of Independence Hall

Housed in a typical Dutch house dating from 1660, this small museum has historical displays on the events leading up to independence in 1957. It is a bit dry but good for people with a keen interest in the political history of Malaysia.

Entrance to the museum is free and it is open Tuesday to Sunday from 9 am to 6 pm but closed on Friday from 12 noon to 3 pm and all day Monday.

Cultural Museum On the other side of St Paul's Hill is a wooden replica of a Melaka sultan's palace which contains the Muzium Budaya or Cultural Museum. Although the exhibits concentrate on traditional Melakan culture, there are also exhibits from other parts of Malaysia. Included are apparel, games, weaponry, musical instruments, stone inscriptions, photographic exhibits, and a diorama of the sultan's court, with costumed mannequins representing the various positions held within the hierarchy. Admission to this interesting building costs M\$1.50.

Baba-Nyonya Heritage Museum At 48-50 Jalan Tun Tan Cheng Lock in the old part of the city is a traditional *peranakan* (Straits-born Chinese) townhouse which has been made into a small museum of sorts. The architecture of this type of house, of which many survive in Melaka today, has been described as 'Chinese Palladian' and

'Chinese Baroque'. The interiors of these houses contain open courtyards which admit sun and rain. The interior of the house is arranged so that it looks like a typical 19th century Nyonya-Baba residence.

It is owned by a Baba family who conduct tours of the house. Furniture consists of Chinese hardwoods fashioned in a mixture of Chinese, Victorian and Dutch designs with mother-of-pearl inlay. 'Nyonya Ware', multicoloured designs from Jiangxi and Guangzhou provinces in China made specifically for Straits Chinese, is also on display. Nyonya ceramics and tilework are usually a blend of pinks, yellows, dark blues and greens.

The museum (tel 06-231273) is open from 10 am to 12.30 pm and 2 to 4.30 pm. Admission is a steep M$7, which includes a good 45-minute tour of the house – well worth it if you have an interest in peranakan culture.

A *kris* (traditional Malay knife)

Masjid Tengkera

This 150-year-old mosque, two km along the road towards Port Dickson, is of typical Sumatran design, featuring a square, cake-layered look. In its graveyard is the tomb of Sultan Hussain of Johore who, in 1819, signed over the island of Singapore to Stamford Raffles. The Sultan later retired to Melaka where he died in 1853. Get there on bus No 18 from Jalan Kubu.

Cheng Hoon Teng Temple

This fascinating temple on Jalan Tokong in the old part of the city is the oldest Chinese temple in Malaysia and has an inscription commemorating Cheng Ho's epochal visit to Melaka. The brightly coloured roof bears the usual assortment of mythical Chinese creatures. Entered through massive hardwood doors, the interior is equally colourful and ornate. The temple's ceremonial mast rises above the old houses in this part of Melaka.

The name literally means 'Temple of the Evergreen Clouds' and was founded in 1646 by Kapitan China Lee Wei King, a native of Amoy in China. All materials used in building the original temple were imported from China, as were the artisans who designed and built it in the southern Chinese style to pay respect to the San Y Chiao, or Three Teachings of Buddhism, Taoism and Confucianism.

Sam Po Kong Temple & Hang Li Poh Well

Apart from his real-life role as an admiral and ambassador, Cheng Ho is also religiously venerated and this temple is dedicated to him. Built in 1795, it's at the foot of Bukit China and nearby is the Hang Li Poh Well, named after the Princess Hang Li Poh. Also known as the Sultan's Well, it is said to date back to the founding of Melaka in the 14th century by Raja Iskander Shah. Cheng Ho drank from the well, legends relate, after which its water became incredibly pure and taking a drink would ensure a visitor's return to the city. Today the water is visibly impure and tossing a coin into the well is the recommended way of ensuring a return trip.

Bukit China

In the mid-1400s the Sultan of Melaka's ambassador to China returned with the Ming Emperor's daughter to wed the Sultan and thus seal relations between the two countries. She brought with her a vast retinue, including 500 handmaidens, and Bukit China (China Hill) was established as their residence. It has been a Chinese area ever since and, together with two adjoining hills, forms a Chinese graveyard covering over 25 hectares. With over 12,000 graves it is said to be the largest in the world outside China itself. Some of the ornate graves date back to the Ming dynasty, but unhappily most of them are now in a sorry state.

Chinese graveyards are often built on hillsides because the bulk of the hill shields the graves from evil winds while at the same time the spirits get a good view of what their descendants are up to down below. In our more space-conscious modern world Chinese graves are gradually losing their spacious and expansive traditional design.

Old Melaka

The old part of Melaka is a fascinating area to wander around in. Although Melaka has long lost its importance as a port, ancient-looking junks still sail up the river and moor at the banks. Today, however, their cargo is not the varied treasures of the East, but simply mundane charcoal for the cooking fires of the city. There's a good view of the river and boats from the bridge beside the tourist office.

You may still find some of the treasures of the East in the antique shops scattered along Jalan Hang Jebat, formerly known as Jonkers St. You'll find a whole assortment of interesting shops and the odd Chinese or Hindu temple or mosque squeezed into this intriguing old street. Melaka is famed for its antique shops and there are several along the street which are worth a leisurely browse.

The Sri Pogyatha Vinoyagar Moorthi Temple, dating from 1781, and the Suma-tran-style Kampung Kling Mosque are both in this area. Jalan Tun Tan Cheng Lock, running parallel to Jalan Hang Jebat, is also worth a stroll.

Minangkabau Houses

There are many fine old Minangkabau-style houses around Melaka. Note the characteristic 'buffalo horn' roof shape, the verandah and lower-level *anjong* (pre-verandah). The steps which lead up to the sometimes intricately carved wooden houses are often decorated with beautiful tiles.

Beaches

Melaka's beaches offer little attraction. Tanjung Kling and, a little further out, Pantai Kundor, are the main beaches but the Straits of Melaka have become increasingly polluted over the years and it's worst around Melaka itself. There are also occasional plagues of jellyfish.

Organised Tours

Boat Trips The tourist office runs daily riverboat tours of Melaka which leave from the quay behind the tourist office. The trip takes 45 minutes, costs M$5, and passes through the downtown area, a few small riverside fish markets and a Malay kampung with traditional Melaka-style houses. Departures are at 10 and 11 am, 12 noon, 2, 3 and 4.30 pm. There has to be at least four passengers before the tour will operate, or you can pay M$20. They're not very exciting trips but most people seem to enjoy them.

The small island of Pulau Besar, a little south of Melaka, is a popular weekend joy ride – there are boats operating across from Umbai near Melaka. On a clear day you can see Sumatra from Tanjung Kling – it's only about 50 km away.

Festivals

Major festivals in Melaka include the Good Friday and Easter Sunday processions at St Peter's and the feast in June in honour of the patron saint of the fishing community at the same church.

The nationwide bathing festival known as

Mandi Safar is exuberantly celebrated at Tanjung Kling during the Muslim month of Safar.

Places to Stay − bottom end

Hostels Melaka has quite a number of traveller-oriented hostels. The *Paradise Hostel* (tel 06- 230821) at 4 Jalan Tengkera is just after the Jalan Kubu intersection on the way north. Rates in this clean and friendly place start at M$5 for dorm accommodation, M$8 for singles or M$12 with private bath, and doubles for M$10 or M$15 with bath. There's a washing machine and fridge for use by guests. The hostel's card claims that the hostel is 8½ minutes and 947 metres from the bus terminal.

Another good place is the *Kancil Guest House* at 177 Jalan Bandar Hilir. It's very clean, quiet and secure although it is a bit of a walk from the centre with your pack. There are cooking facilities and a small garden out the back. The notice board at this hostel is an excellent source of information. Accommodation costs are M$5 for dorm beds, or M$8/10 for single/double rooms. They rent bicycles for M$3 per day and these are an ideal way of seeing the town's somewhat scattered sights. To get there catch bus Nos 17 or 25 (fare 30 sen) from the local bus station and get off at the Chinese temple on Jalan Bandar Hilir, from where it's just a short walk. A taxi or trishaw should cost about M$5.

The *Trilogy Homestay* (tel 06-245319), a short walk from Jalan Bandar Hilir, is run by a friendly couple; dorm beds cost M$5 and doubles from M$14 to M$18. They also have mountain bikes to rent for M$5 per day. The hostel is in a complex of characterless new buildings built on reclaimed land. The official address is 223B Taman Melaka Raya.

Confusingly all the streets in this area of reclaimed land are collectively known as Jalan Taman Melaka Raya. The comfortable *Travellers' Lodge* at 214B Jalan Taman Melaka Raya, near the Trilogy, has dorm beds for M$5, singles from M$9 to M$12 and doubles for M$15.

Cowboy Lim's Travellers House at 269 Jalan Melaka Jaya is run by a real character.

Dorm beds cost M$7 and single/double rooms go for M$12/16. A frugal breakfast is included in the price.

Across the road from Cowboy Lim's is the comfortable and well kept *SD Rest House* where all the rooms are air-con. Others in the same area are the *Shirah's Guest House* at 229-230B, the *Sawasdee Guest House* at 217B and the *Holiday Home Stay* at 305A.

Lastly there's *Kane's Tours & Hostel* (tel 06-235124) at 136A/1 Jalan Laksamana Cheng Hoe (also called Jalan Panjang). Rates are much the same as the other hostels but it is a bit cramped and gloomy compared with the other places.

Hotels Melaka is also well endowed with hotels in all price ranges.

Of the cheapies, one of the better ones is the *Ng Fook* (tel 06-228055) at 154 Jalan Bunga Raya, just north of Jalan Munshi Abdullah. It's basic but OK with double rooms for M$13.80, or M$18.40 with bath and M$25.30 with air-con and bath. A few doors away is the *Hong Kong Hotel* which is very similar.

Cheaper still is the *Central Hotel* (tel 06-222984) in a very good location at 31 Jalan Bendahara. Rooms cost M$10/12 for singles/doubles with fan, and M$12/14 with fan and bath. It's a bit shabby but at these prices is hard to beat. The *Valiant Hotel* (tel 06-222799) almost next door is a step up the scale and has rooms for M$16/18 with fan, M$18/20 with fan and bath, and M$25/28 with air-con and bath.

For a little bit more the rambling old *Majestic Hotel* (tel 06-222367) at 188 Jalan Bunga Raya is a good deal and is reminiscent of the Cathay Hotel in Penang. The high ceilings and swishing fans add to the cool lazy atmosphere and there's a bar, restaurant and car park. Rooms cost M$20/25 with fan, or M$38/40 with bath and air-con.

At 100 Jalan Munshi Abdullah the *Cathay Hotel* (tel 06-223337) has seen better days but is not bad value. The front rooms should be avoided as the road is noisy as hell. Rooms cost M$14/18 with fan, M$28/30 with bath and air-con.

In the old part of town the *Chong Hoe Hotel* (tel 06- 226102) at 26 Jalan Tukung Emas is well located and good value at M$14/17 with fan and common bath, and M$20/25 with air-con and attached bath.

A few km out of the centre on the Port Dickson road is the rambling old *Westernhay Hotel* in the same mould as the Majestic Hotel in town. It's run by a friendly Chinese family and is good value at M$22 for a double with fan, or M$28 with air-con and bath. Breakfast and other meals are available.

Places to Stay – middle

A good place in this range is the *May Chiang Hotel* (tel 06-222101) at 52 Jalan Munshi Abdullah, just a few minutes' walk from the bus and taxi stations. Rooms in this very friendly and immaculately clean place cost M$26/30 with fan and bath, and M$30/35 with air-con and bath.

The *Wisma Hotel* (tel 06-239800) is close by near the corner of Jalan Bendahara. It's a bit drab and characterless and overpriced at M$29/40 with air-con and bath.

Other places in this price range include the *Plaza Inn* (tel 06-24088) at 2 Jalan Munshi Abdullah with rooms at M$45 to M$80, and the *Palace Hotel* (tel 06-225115) at 201 Jalan Munshi Abdullah which charges M$50 to M$75 for rooms with air-con and bath.

Places to Stay – top end

The 240-room *Merlin Inn Malacca* (tel 06-24077) on Jalan Munshi Abdullah has rooms with air-con, bath and TV which range from M$70 to M$300. The hotel also has a swimming pool.

On Jalan Bendahara, the *Ramada Renaissance Hotel* (tel 06-248888) charges from M$300 upwards for its rooms. Facilities here include swimming pool, tennis and squash courts and disco.

Another top-end place is the *City Bayview Hotel* (tel 06-239888), also on Jalan Bendahara. It has single/double rooms from M$160 to M$170.

Places to Eat

Melaka's real eating centre is along Jalan Taman, on what used to be the waterfront. The permanent stalls along here serve all the usual food centre specialities. It's just a pity that with the land reclamation the view is now of a wooden fence with seascapes painted on it, rather than the sea itself. Just walk along and see what attracts you, but one very good place is the *Bunga Raya Restaurant* at No 40 which has excellent steamed crabs.

Right in the centre of town, on Jalan Laksamana, there is only one very good restaurant which caters to travellers' tastes. The *Restaurant Kim Swee Huat* at No 38 has an impressive menu; for breakfast you can get muesli, porridge or toast.

Another good place for breakfast is the *Melaka Pandan Restoran* behind the tourist office, although at M$7 it's not that cheap. It's an outdoor place with umbrellas and is a popular watering hole with locals and visitors alike.

In the heart of the old town on Jalan Hang Jebat the *Jonkers Melaka Restoran* is in a traditional peranakan house and serves both Western and Nyonya dishes. The set-menu of four Nyonya dishes for M$12 is a good deal. The restaurant is open daily from 10 am to 7 pm.

Amongst Melaka's many other restaurants and cafes two worth trying out are the *Tai Chong Hygienic Ice Cafe* at 39/72 Jalan Bunga Raya where a wide variety of ice-cream treats and snacks are available, and the *UE Tea House*, 20 Lorong Bukit China, which is a great place for a dim sum breakfast with prices from 50 sen per plate.

Near the intersection of Jalan Temenggong and Jalan Bendahara in the city centre are a few south Indian daun pisang restaurants. The *Sri Lakshmi Vilas* is typical and has cheap roti chanai and murtabak. The *Sri Krishna Bavan* is right next door and is very similar. Around the corner at 34 Jalan Temenggong the *Restoran Veni* is an Indian cafe, a good place for a roti chanai breakfast.

Burger freaks should head for the *A & W Restoran Keluarga* down off Jalan Kota. It's one of the A&W chain and has all the usual fast-food stuff.

For cakes, buns and other sweet sticky things the *New Tai Tee Bakery* on Jalan Bendahara has a good selection.

All the larger hotels (Wisma, Regal, Palace) have air-con restaurants or coffee lounges with a predilection for fixed-price lunches or dinners in 'English style' for around M$10. Just the thing if you want soup, chicken & chips and dessert.

If you're staying in the area of new buildings on reclaimed land where many of the new backpackers' hotels are located, you'll have no trouble finding somewhere to eat. This is becoming the Melaka restaurant centre with numerous restaurants, bars and small cafes.

Finally there's Medan Portugis, Portuguese Square, where you can sample Malay-Portuguese cuisine at tables facing the sea. They serve excellent seafood here and for around M$15 per person you can eat very well. Take bus No 17 from the local bus station. Just outside the square is a Malay-Portuguese restaurant, the *San Pedro*. The food is similar to what you find in the square but the atmosphere is more intimate and the prices higher.

On the road between Melaka and Tanjung Kling are a few large outdoor Chinese seafood restaurants, including the *Seaview* and *Lucky*. They are all right on the waterfront and are not that cheap.

Things to Buy

It's worth strolling through the antique shops along Jalan Hang Jebat (Jonkers St) in the old part of town. Although you won't find any bargains, there's an incredible array of old things.

For more modern tourist-oriented stuff, try the row of stalls which stand back-to-back with the food stalls on Jalan Merdeka.

Getting There & Away

Melaka is 149 km from KL, 216 km from JB and just 90 km from Port Dickson.

Air You can fly to Melaka from KL or JB. The MAS office (tel 06-575761) is at 238 Taman Melaka Raya, Bandar Hilir.

Bus There are plenty of buses and long-distance taxis. To or from KL there are 10 daily Jebat Express buses from the express bus terminal for M$6.50 with air-con. If for any reason you can't get a direct KL-Melaka bus it's easy enough to go to Seremban and change there.

Melaka-Singapore Express buses leave hourly from 8 am to 6 pm from the local bus stand and the fare is M$11. The trip takes around 5½ hours and you should book in advance at the office at the bus station.

From the express bus terminal, the Murni Express company runs buses to Lumut at 9 am, 12 noon and 9.30 pm for M$17. There are also regular buses for Butterworth (M$21.40) and Kuantan (M$11).

Train There is no railway station in Melaka but the main north-south line passes within 20 km, so travelling by train and then taxi or bus is an option. The nearest railway station is at Tampin and taxis run between the two places frequently, or there are buses for M$3.

Taxi Taxis leave from the taxi station just opposite the local bus station and operate to Port Dickson (M$8), Muar (M$4), Kluang (M$4) and KL (M$13).

Boat There're now two ferry services to Dumai in northern Sumatra. One of them operates once a week; from Dumai each Saturday at 10 am, reaching Melaka at 2 pm and from Melaka back to Dumai at the same hour on Thursdays. Fare is M$80 one way or M$150 return. You can book tickets at Atlas Travel Service (tel 06-220777) on Jalan Hang Jebat in Melaka.

The other ferry service, operated by the Tunar Rupat Utama Express company (tel 06-232505), is at 17A Jalan Merdeka. Their boat takes just 2½ hours at the same price of M$80. Unfortunately you need a visa to enter or leave Indonesia through Dumai and you have to visit the Indonesian Embassy in KL to get one.

Getting Around

You can easily walk around the central sights or rent a bike from one of the hostels for M$3 a day.

To get out to Tanjung Kling take Patt Hup bus No 51 from the local bus station; the fare is 60 sen.

A bicycle rickshaw is the ideal way of getting around compact and slow-moving Melaka. By the hour they should cost about M$7, or M$2 for any one-way trip within the town, but you'll have to bargain.

AROUND MELAKA

Tanjung Kling/Pantai Kundor

This area about 10 km north of Melaka used to be the travellers' centre in this area but these days with the heavily polluted beaches and limited budget accommodation, few travellers make it out here. Tanjung Kling is actually a suburb of Melaka and is on the main road to Port Dickson, while Pantai Kundor is right on the water and is a couple of km further from town.

Places to Stay & Eat In Tanjung Kling the *Melaka Beach Bungalow & Youth Hostel* (tel 06-512395) is about the best out of town accommodation. It is in a modern house in a new residential area at 739C Spring Gardens, just off the main Port Dickson road about nine km north of town. Dorm beds cost M$5, doubles M$28 with bath and fan, and M$35 with air-con and bath. To get there take any Patt Hup bus from the local bus stand. If you call ahead the friendly proprietor will keep an eye out for you on the main road.

Sandwiched between the main road and the beach, a little further from town, is the very pleasant *Shah's Beach Resort* (tel 06-511120). It's certainly not a budget place but is well set out, has a swimming pool, bar and restaurant. Accommodation is in chalet-type rooms which cost M$98 by the pool, M$90 by the beach and M$80 near the road. All rooms have air-con and bath. If things are slack it should be possible to get a discount of 10% or so. If you're not staying here but would like to use the pool it costs M$6 per day, M$10 on weekends.

Out at Pantai Kundor itself there're a few options. The first place you come to is the *Motel Tanjung Kling* (tel 06-511652), a run-down hotel with a very pleasant location right by the water. The gloomy rooms are poor value at M$22 with fan and bath, and M$32 with air-con.

A bit further along is the *Yashica Restaurant & Travellers' Hostel*, which is just a glorified tin shed with very basic, but undeniably cheap, rooms at M$7/10 for a single/double. For that you get a mattress and fan in a small room. Meals are available.

If you want to stay at Pantai Kundor the best bet is the *Straitsview Lodge* (tel 06-514627), a km or so past Yashica. Set in an old holiday house, it's a very pleasant place with polished wooden floors and plenty of space. Run by a friendly Malaysian guy, Kamal, the lodge rooms are good value at M$18/20 for a single/double with fan, and M$35 with air-con and bath. Meals are available or there're a couple of basic warungs close by. He also has bikes, canoes and boats for hire.

Getting There & Away Catch a Patt Hup bus No 51 from the local bus stand. They go every half hour or so. A share-taxi costs around M$1 per person, or M$6 to M$8 for the whole vehicle.

Tanjung Bidara

About 20 km north-west of Melaka on the way to Port Dickson is Tanjung Bidara, one of the west coast's better beach areas, but as with all the beaches on this coast pollution is a problem. There is a large public beach with toilet and shower facilities, as well as numerous food stalls.

Places to Stay The only accommodation is the rather exclusive *Tanjung Bidara Beach Resort* (tel 06-531201) with its modern chalets and motel, lounge and swimming pool. There are 80 rooms here which cost from M$70, although discounts should be available if things are slow.

Pengkalan Kempas

About 50 km north of Melaka is the small town of Pengkalan Kempas. Just a short distance on the Lubok China or Melaka side of town a sign indicates the grave of Sheikh Ahmad Majnun, about 100 metres off the road. This local hero died in 1467 and beside his grave, which is sheltered by a structure in the final stages of complete collapse, are three two-metre-high stones standing upright in the ground.

These mysterious stones, known as the sword, the spoon and the rudder, are thought to be older than the grave itself. Immediately in front of the grave is another stone with a hole through it. The circular opening is said to tighten up on the arm of any liar foolish enough to thrust it through.

PORT DICKSON

There's nothing of great interest in Port Dickson (PD) itself although it's a pleasant enough small port town. South of the town, however, there is a stretch of beach extending for 16 km to Cape Rachado and it's almost clean enough to swim in. There are a number of places to stay along the beach and it's an interesting walk along the coast to the cape.

Originally built by the Portuguese in the 16th century the lighthouse offers fine views along the coast – on a clear day you can see Sumatra, 38 km away across the Straits of Melaka. The turn-off to the lighthouse is near Km 13, or it's just a short stroll along the beach from the Pantai Motel. Officially you need permission from the Marine Department in Melaka if you want to ascend the lighthouse.

Places to Stay

There's no reason to stay in Port Dickson unless you stay on the beach, so the hotels in and close to the town itself can be discounted. The beach stretches south of Port Dickson for 16 km to Cape Rachado, but the best beach starts from around the eight-km peg. Many of the resort places along here are definitely a bit rough around the edges these days. Despite this they are very popular, especially on weekends when all the cheaper places (apart from the youth hostel) seem to be fully booked.

The *Port Dickson Youth Hostel* is above the road at 6½ km. It attracts few visitors although it costs just M$7 per night in freshly painted dormitories. Although there are no meals or cooking facilities there are plenty of shops and warungs in front of the hostel on the main road.

At Km 7 the *Coastal Inn* (tel 06-473343) is a shabby old place which dates back to pre-independence days. All rooms have air-con and attached bath and cost M$38.50 – not a good deal. A little further on is the large *Tanjung Tuan Beach Resort* (tel 06-473013), a fairly modern place with swimming pool and tennis and squash courts. On weekdays single/double rooms cost M$60, while on weekends it costs M$94.

Next up is the *Si-Rusa Beach Resort* (tel 06-405233) at Km 12. All rooms have air-con and cost M$69 with bath, M$92 with fridge and TV or M$110 with sea view. Close by is the very upmarket *Ming Court Hotel* (tel 06-405244) with rooms for M$150 to M$1150 and all the facilities you'd expect to find in a place like this. Just a short distance further on there're a couple of places at Km 13. The Chinese *Kong Ming Hotel* (tel 06-405683) is right by the beach. It's nothing special but is reasonably priced at M$23 for a double. Also here is the *Lido Hotel* (tel 06-405273) which is also right on the beach and is set in spacious grounds. Rooms cost M$30 for a double, M$38 with air-con and M$45 for a triple.

The last area with accommodation is at Km 15 but these places are set a km or so off the main road. The *Pantai Motel* (tel 06-405130) has a variety of rooms and prices, ranging from M$29/40 to M$65/80. This place is set right on the beach but has definitely seen better days. The *Halcyon Guest House* is an unattractive brick place set back from the beach. Rooms cost M$30 with bath, M$45 with bath and air-con.

Getting There & Away

Port Dickson is 94 km south of KL, only 34

km south of Seremban and 90 km north of Melaka. You can get there by taxi or bus from any of these places. By bus it's M$3.30 from Melaka, M$3.70 from KL. A taxi is about M$6.50 from either town.

From Port Dickson town there are buses which will drop you off anywhere along the beach.

SEREMBAN

South of KL, Seremban is the capital of Negri Sembilan or 'Nine States' – a group of small Malay lands united by the British. This is the centre of the Minangkabau area of Malaysia. Originating in Sumatra, the Minangkabau people have a matrilineal system whereby inheritance passes through the female rather than the male line. They take their name from the unique architecture of their buildings where the roof sweeps up at each end like buffalo horns or 'minangkabau'.

State Museum

The small state museum is a good example of Minangkabau architecture. Originally the home of a Malay prince, it was brought to its present location and reassembled in the lake area which overlooks the commercial part of town. Traditionally Minangkabau houses were built entirely without nails.

The museum is open from 9.30 am to 12 noon and 2 to 5.30 pm daily (9.30 am to 1 pm on Wednesdays, 9.30 am to 6 pm on holidays) and houses a small collection of ceremonial weapons and other regalia.

State Mosque

Lower down towards the town is the new state mosque with its nine pillars symbolising the nine states of Negri Sembilan.

Places to Stay – bottom end

The bustling streets of Seremban have the usual varied assortment of cheap Chinese hotels. The cheapest place in town is the *Wang Seng Hotel* (tel 06-725669) on Jalan Birch which has rooms for M$8/10, but don't expect too much. The *Tong Fong* (tel 06-

723022), also on Jalan Birch is a similar place with similar prices.

Places to Stay – middle

Up the scale a bit there's the *Carlton Hotel* (tel 06-725336) at 47 Jalan Tuan Sheikh which has rooms for M$20 to M$50. The *Century Hotel* (tel 06-726261) at 25 Jalan Tuanku Munawair is similarly priced.

Places to Stay – top end

At the top of the range there's the *Tasik Hotel* (tel 06-730994) on Jalan Tetamu with rooms for M$85 to M$95.

Places to Eat

There are all sorts of restaurants, including a drive-in *A&W* restaurant, just to prove Seremban has made it into the 20th century!

Getting There & Away

Seremban is 62 km south of KL, connected by the same modern highway that now extends to Melaka. From KL there are frequent buses (M$2.50) and taxis (M$5). It's a further 34 km south to Port Dickson or 82 km to Melaka.

AROUND SEREMBAN
Kajang

This town, about 20 km south of KL on the Seremban-KL route is said to have the best satay in all of Malaysia. If your meal time is approaching it's worth stopping.

Minangkabau Houses

If you want to study more Minangkabau architecture take a bus from Seremban east towards Kuala Pilah. Get off eight to 10 km out where there are many traditional houses on both sides of the road. Pantai and Nilai, a short distance north-east of Seremban, also have Minangkabau houses.

Kuala Pilah

Kuala Pilah, 40 km east of Seremban, has an interesting old Chinese temple on Jalan Lister near the bus station. Seri Menanti, 16 km from Kuala Pilah, has a palace or istana in Minangkabau style and also a royal mosque. The central pillars of the istana are impressively carved.

Kuala Lumpur

Malaysia's capital city is a curious blend of the old and new. On one hand it's a modern and fast moving city although the traffic never takes on the nightmare proportions of Bangkok. It has gleaming high-rise office blocks beside multilane highways, but the old colonial architecture still manages to stand out proudly. It's also a blend of cultures – the Malay capital with a vibrant Chinatown, an Indian quarter and a playing field in the middle of the city where the crack of cricket bat on ball can still be heard.

History

Kuala Lumpur, or KL, as it's almost always called, came into being in the 1860s when a band of prospectors in search of tin landed at the meeting point of the Klang and Gombak rivers, and named the place Kuala Lumpur – 'Muddy Estuary'. More than half of those first arrivals were to die of malaria and other tropical diseases, but the tin they discovered in Ampang attracted more miners and KL quickly became a brawling, noisy, violent boom town.

As in other parts of Malaysia the local sultan appointed a 'Kapitan China' to bring the unruly Chinese fortune seekers into line – a problem which Yap Ah Loy jumped at with such ruthless relish that he became known as the founder of KL.

In the 1880s successful miners and merchants began to build fine homes along Jalan Ampang, the British resident Frank Swettenham pushed through a far-reaching new town plan and in 1886 a railway line linked KL to Port Klang.

The town has never looked back and now it's not only the business and commercial capital of Malaysia, but also the political capital. Today with a population of one million it is also the largest city in Malaysia.

Although not a fascinating city to visit, KL does have enough attractions to make it a pleasant place to spend a few days.

Orientation

The real heart of KL is Merdeka Square, not far from the confluence of the two muddy rivers from which KL takes its name. Easily spotted because of its 95-metre-high flagpole, here parades and ceremonies are held on festive occasions. Just to the south-east of this square is the modern business centre of KL and the older Chinatown – they simply merge into each other. Across the Klang River is the railway station and the modern national mosque.

Heading east from Merdeka Square area is Jalan Tun Perak, a major trunk road which leads to the transport hub of the country, the Pudu Raya bus and taxi station on the eastern edge of the central district.

Running north from Merdeka Square is Jalan Tuanku Abdul Rahman (henceforth known as Jalan TAR). It runs one way north-south and there are a number of KL's popular cheaper hotels and more modern buildings along there. The student travel office is in the Asia Hotel at the northern end of the road. Jalan Raja Laut runs parallel to Jalan TAR and takes the northbound traffic. Both roads are horrendously noisy.

The GPO is just to the south of that central Merdeka Square and a little further on is the national mosque and the KL railway station, and beyond them is KL's green belt where you can find the Lake Gardens, National Museum and Monument and the Malaysian Parliament.

KL is a relatively easy city to find your way around, although getting from place to place on foot around the city can be frustrating as the new six-lane traffic roads and flyovers divide the area up into sections which are not connected by footpaths.

Information

Tourist Information KL is perhaps a little overendowed with tourist offices. The TDC tourist information counter (tel 03-2746063) is on level two of the Putra World Trade Centre on Jalan Tun Ismail in the north-east

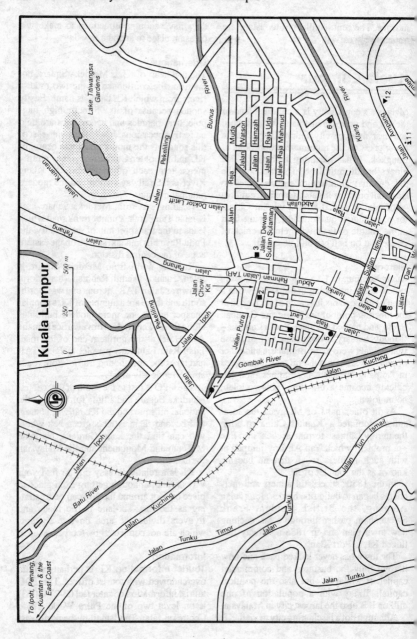

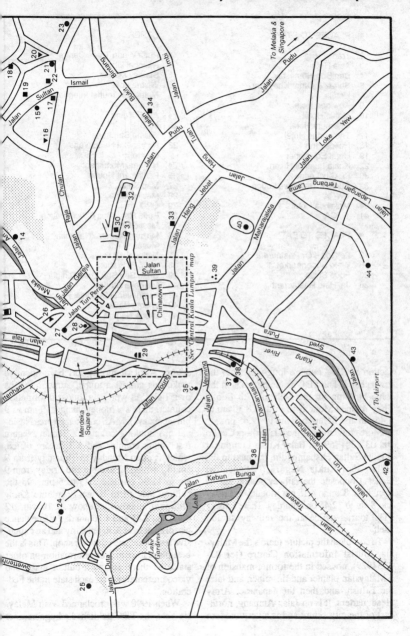

■ PLACES TO STAY

2	Transit Villa
3	Asia Hotel
4	Ben Soo Homestay
8	Shiraz & Omar Khayyam Hotels
9	Kowloon Hotel
10	Merlin Hotel
13	Coliseum Hotel
17	The Lodge Hotel
18	Holiday Inn
19	Hotel Equatorial
22	Kuala Lumpur Hilton
30	KL City Lodge
32	Sunrise Travellers Lodge
33	YWCA
34	Malaysia Hotel
41	YMCA

▼ PLACES TO EAT

12	Le Coq d'Or Restaurant
16	Weld Supermarket
20	Food Stalls
26	Jai Hind Restaurant

OTHER

1	Putra World Trade Centre
5	National Library
6	Sunday Market
7	Wisma Loke
11	Malaysian Tourist Information Centre
14	AIA Building
15	MAS
21	Wisma Stephens
23	Karyaneka Handicrafts Centre
24	National Monument
25	Parliament House
27	Map Sales
28	Masjid Jame
29	GPO
31	Pudu Raya Bus & Taxi Station
35	Masjid Negara
36	Muzium Negara (National Museum)
37	National Art Gallery
38	Railway Station
39	Chan See Shu Yuen Temple
40	Merdeka Stadium
42	International Buddhist Pagoda
43	Wisma Belia
44	Istana Negara

section of KL – rather a long way from the town centre. The TDC headquarters is in the same building on the 24th to 27th floors. They're open Monday to Friday, 8.30 am to 4.45 pm and Saturday 8 am to 12.45 pm.

More convenient is the KL Visitors Centre (tel 03-2301369) in Balai Kuala Lumpur at 3 Jalan Sultan Hishamuddin. It's next to the Balai Seni Lukis Negara (National Art Gallery) opposite the railway station and is open from 8 am to 4.15 pm Monday to Friday and 8 am to 12.45 on Saturday. There's also a TDC tourist office at the railway station itself.

To complete the picture there's the Malaysia Tourist Information Centre (tel 03-2434929), housed in the former mansion of a Malaysian planter and tin-miner, and later the British, and then the Japanese, Army Headquarters. It is on Jalan Ampang, northeast of the city centre and is a very modern set-up. A lot of money has been spent to make this almost a tourist attraction in its own right. As well as a tourist information counter, there's a moneychanger (9 am to 9 pm weekdays), MAS counter, Expres Nasional bus booking counter, a Taman Negara reservation counter and a Telekom office, which is open Monday to Thursday from 9 am to 1 pm and 2 to 5 pm and Friday from 9 am to 12.30 pm and 2.45 to 5 pm. On the cultural side there is the 10-minute *Know Malaysia* audiovisual show at 10 am, 12 noon and 2.45 and 4.30 pm daily, free dance performances at 3.30 pm daily and an expensive restaurant and souvenir shop. This is the best place to come for information on other states as there are push-button maps and video presentations on each state in the Federation.

When 1990 was proclaimed Visit Malaysia Year, the TDC published a huge number of brochures on cities, states and national parks. These are available from any of the tourist offices and hopefully they will be kept up to date.

Money There are plenty of banks throughout the central area of KL. For moneychangers try Jalan Sultan near the Kelang bus station or Jalan Ampang.

Post & Telecommunications The huge GPO building is across the Klang River from the central district. It is open Monday to Saturday from 9 am to 6 pm. The poste restante mail is held at the information desk.

For international calls in business hours the best place to head for is the previously mentioned Malaysia Tourist Information Centre. At other times the Telekom office on Jalan Gereja in the centre is open 24 hours a day.

Cultural Centres & Libraries The following libraries are maintained in KL:

Alliance Francaise
    15 Lorong Gurney (tel 03-2925929)
Australian Information Library
    Jalan Yap Kwan Seng (tel 03-2423122)
British Council
    Jalan Bukit Aman (tel 03-2987555)
Dewan Bahasa & Pustaka
    Jalan Wisma Putra (tel 03-2481011)
Goethe Institute
    1 Langgak Golf (tel 03-2422011)
Indonesian Library
    Jalan Tun Razak (tel 03-9845532)
Japan Information Library
    Persiaran Stoner (tel 03-2438044)
National Library
    Jalan Raja Laut (tel 03-2923144)
New Zealand Library
    Jalan Tun Razak (tel 03-2486422)

Travel Agencies MSL (tel 03-2984132) in the Asia Hotel is the Student Travel Australia agent and usually has some interesting fares on offer. They also handle student cards.

Bookstores There's a branch of Times bookstores in the Weld Supermarket complex on the corner of Jalan P Ramlee and Jalan Raja Chulan, east of the city centre.

Map Sales The National Map Sales office is on Jalan Tun Perak, but they won't sell you larger scale maps since they're all 'restricted' – due to fear of Communists getting hold of them and finding out where KL is. Visiting scholars may find the library at the University of Malaya useful; buses run there from the Kelang bus station.

Merdeka Square

Across the road from the Sultan Abdul Samad building is Merdeka Square, which was part of the open field formerly known as the Padang. It was there during the colonial days that Malaysia's administrators engaged in that curious British rite known as cricket. Malaysia's independence was proclaimed there in 1957, but despite this, the cricket games still go on.

Beside Merdeka Square is the Royal Selangor Club which became a social centre for KL's high society in the tin-rush days of the 1890s. It's still a gathering place for KL VIPs.

Chinatown

Just south of the Masjid Jame are the teeming streets of KL's Chinatown. Bounded by Jalan Sultan, Jalan Cheng Lock and Jalan Sultan Mohammed, this crowded, colourful area is the usual melange of signs, shops, activity and noise. At night the central section of Jalan Petaling is closed to traffic to become a brightly lit and frantically busy pasar malam.

There are many historic Chinese shops still standing in KL's Chinatown and local conservation groups are making efforts to protect them from city development and to restore them to their former glory.

The section of Jalan Hang Kasturi between Jalan Cheng Lock and Lebuh Pudu is a pedestrian mall and, along with the redeveloped Central Market which is now a handicraft market, is the new focal point of Chinatown.

Historic Buildings
Sultan Abdul Samad Building Designed by the British architect Norman and built between 1894 and 1897, the Sultan Abdul

Samad building, formerly known as the Secretariat building, and the adjoining old GPO and City Hall are in a Moorish style similar to that of the railway station. The Sultan Abdul Samad building is topped by a 43-metre-high clock tower.

Norman was also responsible for several other buildings in this area, including the building opposite the old GPO. It now houses Infokraf, the information centre on Malaysian handicrafts.

Railway Station KL's magnificent railway station, close to the the national mosque, is a building full of Eastern promise. Built in 1911, this delightful example of British colonial humour is a Moorish fantasy of spires, minarets, towers, cupolas and arches. It couldn't look any better if it had been built as a set for some whimsical Hollywood extravaganza.

Across from this superb railway station is the equally wonderful Malayan Railway Administration building. Almost directly across the station stands the shell of the once-gracious colonial Majestic Hotel. It has been taken over by the government and now contains a national art gallery.

Museums & Galleries

Muzium Negara At the southern end of the Lake Gardens and less than a km along Jalan Damansara from the railway station, the national museum was built on the site of the old Selangor Museum, which was destroyed during WW II. Opened in 1963, its design and construction is a mixture of Malay architecture styles and crafts. It houses a varied collection on Malaysia's history, arts, crafts, cultures and people.

There are interesting sections on the history of KL, Chinese traditions, the Orang Asli and the country's economy. An unusual exhibit is the elephant's skull which derailed a train. It's doubtful that the elephant actually charged the ironclad monster which was invading its jungle domain.

Another strange sight is an 'amok catcher', an ugly barbed device used to catch and hold a man who has run amok. There are frequent art exhibitions held at the museum and outside there are railway engines, an aircraft and other larger items.

Admission to the museum is free and it is open daily from 9 am to 6 pm except on Fridays when it closes between 12 noon and 2.45 pm. Minibus Nos 17, 20, 24, 25, 34 or 37 as well as most S J Kenderaan buses will take you to the museum.

Numismatic Museum This small museum houses an interesting collection of coins and notes in the Maybank building on Jalan Tun Perak.

Armed Forces Museum This museum has a collection of weapons, paintings, uniforms and other military paraphernalia on the inside, and large weapons such as cannons and tanks on the outside.

The museum is well to the south of the city centre and can be reached by minibus No 19 from Jalan Tun HS Lee in Chinatown. It is open Saturday to Thursday from 10 am to 6 pm.

National Art Gallery The exhibits change regularly and include art from around the world, often quite modern. The art gallery is housed in the former Majestic Hotel, opposite the railway station. It's not worth a special trip, but if you're in the vicinity (say waiting for a train), you could while away half an hour or so there.

Admission is free and the hours are 10 am to 6 pm seven days a week except for prayer closing 12.15 to 2.45 pm on Fridays and all day on Hari Raya Haji.

Mosques, Temples, Pagodas & Churches

Masjid Jame The 'Friday Mosque' is built at the confluence of the Klang and Gombak rivers and overlooks Merdeka Square. This was the place where KL's founders first set foot in the town and where supplies were landed for the tin mines.

In a grove of palm trees the mosque is a picturesque structure with onion domes and minarets striped in red and white. It was built

Top: Kapitan Kling Mosque, Penang (TW)
Left: Kuan Yin Teng, Georgetown (TW)
Right: Wat Chayamangkaleram, Penang (HF)

Top: Pantai Kok (HF)
Left: Langkawi (PS)
Right: Terrace farming, Cameron Highlands (HF)

in 1907 and is at its best when viewed at sunset and early evening from the Jalan Benteng market across the river. There is a new mirror-glass office building which gives excellent reflections of the mosque.

Masjid Negara Sited in seven hectares of landscaped gardens the modernistic national mosque is one of the largest in South-East Asia. A 73-metre-high minaret stands in the centre of a pool and the main dome of the mosque is in the form of an 18-pointed star which represents the 13 states of Malaysia and the five pillars of Islam. Forty-eight smaller domes cover the courtyard; their design is said to be inspired by the Grand Mosque in Mecca. The mosque, which is close to the railway station, can accommodate 8000 people.

Visitors must remove their shoes upon entry and be 'properly' attired – they'll lend you a robe should your own clothing not be suitable. It's open for non-Muslims from 8 am to 6 pm daily except on Fridays when the hours are 2 to 6 pm. Women must use a separate entrance.

Chan See Shu Yuen Temple The typically ornate Chan See Shu Yuen Temple stands at the end of Jalan Petaling. Built in 1906, this fine Chinese temple marks the boundary of Chinatown.

Sze Yah Temple This small temple hidden behind some shops on Lebuh Pudu near Central Market is one of the oldest in KL. 'Kapitan China' (Yap Ah Loy) himself organised its construction and there's a photograph of him on an altar in the back of the temple.

Sri Mahamariamman Temple Dating from 1873, the Sri Mahamariamman Temple is a large and ornate south Indian Hindu temple. It's also in Chinatown on Jalan Tun HS Lee.

The temple was refurbished in 1985 and houses a large silver chariot dedicated to Lord Murga. During the Thaipusam festival this chariot is a central part of a long procession to Batu Caves.

International Buddhist Pagoda This modern pagoda is in the south of KL, off Jalan Tun Sambanthan. On the same site is a Bodhi tree and a Buddhist shrine dating back to late last century built by Sinhalese Buddhists.

St Mary's Church Close to the Royal Selangor Club and dating back to 1894, St Mary's Church was designed by the same man who was responsible for the Sultan Abdul Samad building, and houses a fine pipe organ.

Lake Gardens

The 60-hectare gardens form the green belt of KL. They were originally founded in 1888 and you can rent boats on Tasik Perdana, the 'Premier Lake', which was once known as Sydney Lake. They cost M$4 per hour and are available only on Saturdays from 2 to 5.30 pm and Sundays from 8 am to 5.30 pm.

A minibus No 10 will take you to the gardens.

National Monument This massive monument overlooks the Lake Gardens from a hillside at their northern end. Sculptured in bronze in 1966 by the creator of the Iwo Jima monument in Washington DC, the monument commemorates the successful defeat of the communist terrorists during the Emergency.

Parliament House Overlooking the Lake Gardens, Malaysia's Parliament House is dominated by an 18-storey office block. There are dress regulations for visitors – no shorts and for women dresses must be below the knee.

Jalan Ampang

Lined with impressive mansions, Jalan Ampang was built up by the early tin millionaires. Today many of the fine buildings have become embassies and consulates so that the street is KL's 'Ambassador's Row'. One of these fine 'stately homes' has been converted into a luxurious restaurant, Le Coq d'Or, while another has become the previously mentioned Malaysia Tourism Information Centre.

Markets

KL has a number of markets which are worth investigating. The Central Market in China-town was previously the city's produce market but has now been refurbished to become the focus for handicraft and art sales. There are shops on two levels and a poorly patronised hawkers' centre on the top floor. The centre also has a variety of other food outlets, most of them fast-food places.

At night Jalan Petaling in Chinatown becomes an incredibly busy pasar malam and is an excellent place to have a Chinese *al fresco* meal or snack, or pick up some cheap clothes or a kg of lychees or mangoes – well worth a visit.

In the Kampung Bahru area north-east of the city centre is the site, each Saturday night, for KL's Sunday Market – possibly because it continues through into Sunday morning. It's a food and produce market, a handicrafts market and a place to sample a wide variety of Malay foods.

Activities

There's a swimming pool in a private sports club just off Jalan Hang Jebat in the south-eastern corner of Chinatown. It is open daily from 10 am to 12.30 pm and 3 to 8 pm; entry is M$2 all day.

Organised Tours

MSL Travel in the Asia Hotel have day tours for M$27 or morning tours for M$16.

Amshield (tel 03-2383319) has half-day city tours at 9 am and 2 pm for M$22. They visit the Karyaneka Handicrafts Emporium, Masjid Jame, National Museum and the Masjid Negara. The same company also operates Cultural Night Tours of the city for M$55 including dinner. The tour goes to the Sri Mahamariamman Temple, Chinatown and a Malay restaurant featuring traditional dancing.

Places to Stay – bottom end

Bottom-end accommodation in KL consists of a variety of Chinese hotels and a choice of hostels. Many of the cheap hotels in town are brothels. Some will rent rooms but others don't want straight business at all. None of them seem to be particularly rough and tough, but women should certainly be aware of the situation. Hotels with signs written only in Malay, 'Rumah Tumpangan', as a general rule, offer more than just rooms. Nearly all the ones listed here are straight.

There are a couple of good hunting areas for cheap hotels. The Jalan Tuanku Abdul Rahman area, with a number of hotels along the street, is a good place to look. There are a number of good places around Chinatown, including some traditional old Chinese places. The hostels are scattered mainly south of the centre.

Hostels KL has a number of good hostels which cater almost exclusively to the budget traveller. Most travellers doing it all on the cheap find these places ideal. They all offer similar services: dorm beds as well as rooms, cooking and washing facilities, a fridge and a notice board.

A very popular place right on the edge of Chinatown and only a few minutes' walk from the Pudu Raya bus and taxi station is the *Travellers' Moon Lodge* (tel 03-2306601) at 36 Jalan Silang. Run by a very amenable guy named Fred, the hostel offers dorm beds for M$8.50, and there are a few rooms for M$20 with fan, and this price includes a breakfast of bread, butter, jam and tea or coffee. A good place.

Another popular place is the *Sunrise Travellers Lodge* (tel 03-2308878) at 89-B Jalan Pudu Lama, a small street which loops off Jalan Pudu right near the Pudu Raya bus and taxi station. It is very similar to the Moon Lodge and is almost as popular. Dorm beds cost M$9, or there are rooms from M$23 to M$25 with fan. A light breakfast is also included in the price.

The *KL City Lodge* (tel 03-2305275), at 16A Jalan Pudu, is right opposite the bus station. This is much more a regular hotel but is still popular among travellers. Dorm beds cost M$8.50 or M$10 with air-con, while

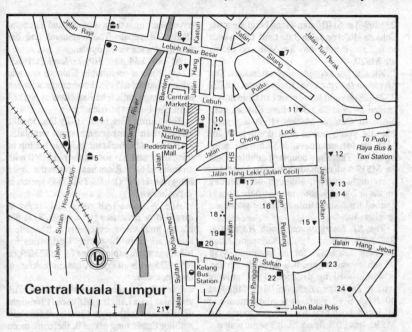

Central Kuala Lumpur

- ■ PLACES TO STAY

  7   Traveller's Moon Lodge
  9   Meridian International Youth Hostel
  14   Furama Hotel
  17   Malaya Hotel
  19   Leng Nam Hotel
  20   Starlight Hotel
  22   Hotel Lok Ann
  23   Colonial Hotel

- ▼ PLACES TO EAT

  6   Vatican Bar
  8   Shakey's Pizza & White Castle
  11   McDonald's

  12   Kentucky Fried Chicken
  13   Angel Cake House
  15   Nam Heong Restaurant
  16   Gourmet Food Centre
  21   Food Stalls

  OTHER

  1   Old GPO
  2   Infokraf
  3   British Council Library
  4   Dayabumi Complex
  5   GPO
  10   Sze Yah Temple
  18   Sri Mahamariamman Temple
  24   Swimming Pool

rooms are M$25 for a double or M$20/30 with air-con.

Up between Jalan Raja Laut and Jalan TAR is another good place, the *Transit Villa* (tel 03-4410443) at 36-2 Jalan Chow Kit, a small road near the 7-Eleven store at the northern end of Jalan Raja Laut. Dorm beds in this friendly place cost M$9, while double/triple rooms cost M$24/29. Also in this area is the *Ben Soo Homestay* (tel 03-

2718096) at 61-B Jalan Tiong Nam, near the Sentosa Hotel on Jalan Raja Laut. Dorm beds in this small homestay are M$8 and rooms are M$20.

KL also has a couple of youth hostels. The *Meridian International Youth Hostel* (tel 03-2321428) is right in the centre of Chinatown, tucked away at 36 Jalan Hang Kasturi, very close to Central Market. It is a typical friendly youth hostel with dorm beds for M$6.50 for members, M$7.50 for non-members. There're a couple of double rooms for M$19 with common bath. The hostel has a midnight curfew, although on Saturday nights at 2 am (Sunday morning) the door is opened for a short time to let the late-night revellers in.

The *KL International Youth Hostel* (tel 03-2306870) is at 21 Jalan Kampung Attap and beds cost M$12 for the first night, M$8 on subsequent nights. It is fully air-con and is within walking distance of the railway station. The *Wisma Belia* (tel 03-2744833) at 40 Jalan Syed Putra is a government-run affiliated hostel. It has air-con rooms for M$30, less 20% discount. It's some way out of the town centre but bus No 52 takes you there.

Finally there are the Ys. The *YMCA* (tel 03-2741439) is at 95 Jalan Padang Belia, south of the centre off Jalan Tun Sambanthan. Its distance from the centre makes it an unattractive option unless you have your own transport. Dorm beds go for M$20, or there're rooms from M$18/25. Take a minibus No 12 and ask for the Lido Cinema.

The *YWCA* (tel 03-283225) is much more central at 12 Jalan Hang Jebat and has rooms at M$15/25 for singles/doubles for women, and takes couples for M$35 and has family rooms for M$50 – a good deal.

Hotels – Jalan TAR Moving up Jalan TAR from its junction with Jalan Tun Perak there's the *Coliseum Hotel* (tel 03-2926270) at No 100 with its famous old-planter's restaurant. All rooms share common bath facilities and are M$19 with fan and M$26 for a double with air-con. Recently, there

have been some reports of rats and a general state of disrepair. The restaurant and bar downstairs are very popular.

At No 134 the *Tivoli Hotel* (tel 03-2924108) is a reasonable Chinese cheapie which charges M$17/21 for rooms with fan and common bath. The *Rex Hotel* at No 134 is similar but not as friendly.

The *Shiraz Hotel* (tel 03-2922625) at 1 Jalan Medan Tuanku on the corner with Jalan TAR is an unremarkable place at the top of this range, and has rooms for M$35/40 with air-con and bath. Right next door is the *Omar Khayyam Hotel* (tel 03-2988744) which is very similar.

At 319-1 Jalan TAR you'll find the *Paradise Bed & Breakfast* (tel 03-2922872) but it's not great value, especially as it's quite a long walk from the centre. Dorm beds for M$10, single/double rooms for M$23/29, or M$29/35 with air-con. A basic breakfast is also included.

Further north the area between Jalan TAR and Jalan Raja Laut is a fairly seedy red-light district and although there's absolutely nothing threatening about it, there are more pleasant places to stay elsewhere.

Hotels – Chinatown Cheapest of the Chinese cheapies is the *Leng Nam Hotel* (tel 03-2301489) at 165 Jalan Tun HS Lee. Basic rooms with fan cost M$17. Another place which seems to get a steady trickle of travellers is the well-camouflaged *Wan Kow Hotel* at 16 Jalan Sultan. Rooms with fan and common bath cost M$19 for one or two people.

Also good value in Chinatown is the *Colonial Hotel* (tel 03-2380336) at 39 Jalan Sultan, where single/double rooms go for M$18/23, or with air-con for M$26. There are many more cheap hotels in Chinatown, most of them short-time places.

At the top of the range there's the comfortable *Hotel Lok Ann* (tel 03-2389544) at 113A Jalan Petaling. Here you'll pay M$54 for a double with air-con. The *Starlight Hotel* (tel 03-2389811) at 90 Jalan Hang Kasturi has doubles with bath and air-con for M$41 and is recommended by many travellers.

Places to Stay – middle

Jalan TAR The *Kowloon Hotel* (tel 03-2926455) at 142 Jalan TAR is a very modern and clean hotel which is an incredible bargain. The decor is definitely over-the-top tacky but the rooms are large and have air-con, bath and TV. Single/double rooms cost M$65/80 and the beds are big enough for two.

At the top end of Jalan TAR is the *Asia Hotel* (tel 03-2926077) at 69 Jalan Haji Hussein. Formerly the South-East Asia, this long-running place has recently been tarted up and now charges M$105 for its standard rooms, from M$135 for deluxe rooms; there are no singles.

Chinatown On Jalan Tun HS Lee the *Hotel Malaya* (tel 03-2327722) has good rooms for M$80/90 with air-con and attached bath.

Also worth trying is the *Hotel Furama* (tel 03-2301777) in the Kompleks Selangor on Jalan Sultan. Rooms in this relatively modern place cost M$86/98 with air-con and bath. Also on Jalan Sultan is the *Mandarin Hotel* (tel 03-2303000) with rooms from M$55.

The relatively new *Hotel Pudu Raya* (tel 03-2321000), atop the Pudu Raya bus & taxi station, deserves a special mention. Clean, modern, quiet air-con rooms are M$87/M$98 for single/double and you couldn't ask for a more convenient location. The hotel can book plane tickets as well as bus travel, and there is a health club with sauna, massage rooms and a small gym.

The wonderfully situated, but extremely run down, *Station Hotel* in the KL railway station has been closed for some time while undergoing what is supposed to be a major renovation. It's supposed to be open again in 1992.

Elsewhere There are plenty of other medium-range hotels around town. One good one, worth a mention because it has a swimming pool, is *The Lodge Hotel* (tel 03-2420122) on the corner of Jalan Raja Chulan and Jalan Sultan Ismail, east of the centre. Rooms at this friendly older-style place,

dwarfed by the high-rise places around it, cost M$88 for a comfortable air-con double with bath.

Places to Stay – top end

Kuala Lumpur also has a number of very expensive hotels, starting at the very top with the 580-room *Kuala Lumpur Hilton* (tel 03-2422222) on Jalan Sultan Ismail, with rooms from M$150 and up. Also on this road is the *Regent of Kuala Lumpur* (tel 03-2425588) which has prices ranging from M$160 to M$1700.

The Holiday Inn chain have two hotels in KL. The *Holiday Inn City Centre* (tel 03-2939232) is indeed in the city centre on Jalan Raja Laut. Room rates are from M$120 to M$500. The *Holiday Inn on the Park* (tel 03-2481066) is on Jalan Pinang and costs from M$230.

Other city centre top-end hotels include the *Ming Court Kuala Lumpur* (tel 03-2619066) on Jalan Ampang with rooms from M$160, the *Pan Pacific Hotel* (tel 03-4425555) on Jalan Chow Kit with rooms from M$140, and the *Equatorial Hotel* (tel 03-2617777) on Jalan Sultan Ismail where rooms start from M$240/260.

Places to Eat

Food Markets KL has some very good night-time eating places. At dusk Jalan Petaling is closed to traffic between Jalan Cheng Lock and Jalan Sultan and the tables are set up outside the Chinese restaurants, which are on Jalan Hang Lekir between Jalan Petaling and Jalan Sultan. These places are fairly touristy and the prices reflect this, but it's still the best place to eat in the evenings. There are also stalls in this area selling peanut pancakes, sweets, drinks and fruit.

Other night markets with good food include the Sunday market out at Kampung Bahru, and a street off Jalan Tuanku Abdul Rahman close to the Asia Hotel. Both are good places for Malay food.

There's another food stall area wedged between Jalan Sultan Mohammed and the river, just south of the Kelang bus station, close to the flyover across the river. Atop

Central Market, there is a hawkers' centre called *Taman Selera* with all the usual Malaysian food but, unlike the market itself, the hawkers' centre lacks atmosphere and is not at all popular.

The Gourmet Food Centre right in the centre on Jalan Petaling is a handy modern little food centre with a variety of food on offer.

If you're out along Jalan Raja Chulan east of the centre there's another hawkers' centre just past Wisma Stephens on the left-hand side. The food here is mainly Indian and Malay.

Indian Food At 15 Jalan Melayu, near the corner of Jalan TAR and Jalan Tun Perak, there's the *Jai Hind*. It's a good place for Indian snacks and light meals.

Upstairs at 60A Jalan TAR *Bangles* is an Indian restaurant with a good reputation. Further along, the *Shiraz* on the corner of Jalan TAR and Jalan Medan Tuanku is a good Pakistani restaurant. Some prefer the similar *Omar Khayyam* next door. There are several north Indian restaurants in the area around Wisma Loke.

The *Bilal* restaurants – there are branches at 40 Jalan Ipoh, 33 Jalan Ampang and 37 Jalan TAR – are other good Indian restaurants. They do good roti chanai and murtabaks.

For south Indian food, head to the Brickfields area where there are four or five daun pisang (banana leaf) restaurants serving rice with vegetarian, fish, chicken, and mutton curries. One of the best is *Devi's*.

In Bangsar on Lorong Maarof is the renowned *Devi Annapoorna*, which is staffed by volunteers from the Indian arts community and is entirely vegetarian. Food is served on a *thali*, the traditional stainless steel plate. It is one of the best Indian restaurants in KL.

Chinese Food Chinese restaurants can be found all over the place, but particularly around Chinatown and along Jalan Bukit Bintang, which is off Jalan Pudu past the Pudu Raya bus and taxi station. There are

excellent lunchtime dim sums at the expensive *Merlin Hotel* and also at the *Overseas* in Central Market.

A local speciality in KL is *bah kut teh*, supposed to have originated in Klang. It's pork ribs with white rice and Chinese tea and is a very popular breakfast meal.

Malay Food There are Malay *warungs* (small eating stalls) and *kedai kopis* here and there throughout KL, but especially along Jalan TAR. Several of those in the vicinity of the Coliseum Hotel are excellent and cheap; look for the nasi lemak in the early mornings. The *Restoran Imaf* is a good bet just down from Minerva Bookshop. The area around Stadium Merdeka is also renowned for its Malay warungs.

The *Yazmin Restaurant* (tel 03-241 5655), behind the KL Hilton on Jalan Kia Peng, is a top-end Malay restaurant where a feed costs about M$30 per person à la carte or M$45 if you do the buffet and cultural performance.

In the Bukit Bintang Plaza on Jalan Bukit Bintang there're a couple of more upmarket Malay restaurants – the *Rasa Utara* (tel 03-2438234) and the *Satay Anika* (tel 03-2483113). In the Hotel Nanyang building on Jalan Sultan the *Simcili Vegetarian Restoran* has decent food for around M$2.50 to M$8. It is open from 10 am to 9.30 pm.

The *Nelayan Floating Restaurant* (tel 03-4228600) at Lake Titiwangsa Gardens off Jalan Kuantan in north KL is an amazing place. Huts are built over the lake and the daily-changing menu features six cuisines. It's one of the best 'splurge' restaurants for Malay food.

Thai Food KL has a couple of expensive Thai restaurants, namely the *Restoran Seri Changmai* at 14 Jalan Perak, and the *Sawasdee Thai Restaurant* in the Holiday Inn on the Park.

A cheaper place is the *Restoran Thai Kitchen* (tel 03-2744303) in Central Market on Jalan Hang Kasturi.

Japanese Food For Japanese food the

choices are limited, and expensive. Try the *Edogin* at 207A Jalan Tun Razak or the *Munakata* in the Menara Promet on Jalan Sultan Ismail.

Western Food KL has a surprising variety of Western restaurants including, at the bottom of Jalan TAR, *Kentucky Fried Chicken* and *A&W* take-aways. There are several American-style hamburger joints around the bus station including *Wendy's*, *McDonald's* and *White Castle*.

Not to be missed is the restaurant in the *Coliseum Hotel* on Jalan TAR where they have excellent steaks. When they say it's served on a sizzle plate they really mean it; the waiters zip up behind you and whip a bib around your neck to protect your clothes from the sizzle. For around M$20 you can get a great steak and salad, they also do roast chicken and grilled fillet of sole with chips. The place is quite a colonial experi-ence which has scarcely changed over the years.

There are lots of restaurants along Jalan Bukit Bintang including a *McDonald's* at the junction with Jalan Ismail, a *Dunkin' Donuts*, a 24-hour *Kentucky Fried Chicken* outlet, *Texas Chicken* and various bakeries, Indian and Chinese restaurants. At No 81 the *Castell Grill* is a more upmarket place.

In Chinatown don't miss the *Angel Cake House* on Jalan Sultan. They offer all kinds of buns and rolls stuffed with chicken curry or cheeses and fresh from the oven. Also available are pizza, macaroni, fruit tarts and chocolate cakes.

The KL airport is well equipped with res-taurants including an *A&W Hamburger* stand.

Finally, *Le Coq d'Or* (tel 03-2429732), a restaurant in a fine turn-of-the-century mansion on Jalan Ampang, is expensive but not quite as expensive as the elegant sur-

---

Hash House Harriers

The internationally known Hash House Harriers was first established in KL in 1938 by a group of British colonials who found themselves drinking too much and needing exercise. Hash house was the nickname for the dining room of the Selangor Club Chambers, a social centre of the times. The harrier idea of a group of runners chasing papers along trails set by an appointed member ('the hare') was not altogether new – previous groups had existed in KL, Ipoh, JB and Melaka in colonial Malaya. In Shanghai and Kuching the sport was carried out on horseback. However, it was the original Hash House Harriers (HHHs) that institutionalised harrying to such a degree that it became an expat tradition all over Asia.

Until 1961 there was only the KL Hash but in the following year a second chapter opened in Singapore, followed by Brunei, Kuching, Kota Kinabalu, Ipoh and Penang. Eventually the first group outside of Singapore/Malaysia was opened in Perth in 1967. There are around 500 HHHs in 70 countries and there are annual interhash meetings at a different place each year.

A hash run: the hare goes to the run site – which changes with each run – a few hours in advance and lays an irregular trail (sometimes including false trails) using paper markers. The point is to allow faster runners to scout for the next bit of trail while slower harriers catch up. The run begins with a call of 'on, on' – the slogan of all HHHs – and when looking for paper markers runners shout out 'are you?' to which runners ahead reply 'checking' to help in trail finding. The typical run lasts one to 1½ hours and is followed by beer drinking at the end of the trail and a meal at a local restaurant. In KL the meals are usually at a Chinese restaurant and each runner contributes about US$3 to cover costs.

There are several branches in the KL area, including one for men only (the original tradition), one for women only (the Hash House Harriettes), the rest mixed. Most of the larger Malaysian towns have their own branches. All of the Malaysian hash clubs have locals amongst their membership.

The hash welcomes guest participants and for those so inclined, a hash run would be an interesting way to meet both locals and expats while seeing a bit of the Malaysian countryside since runs tend to be held in secondary jungle areas, or on rubber or oil palm estates. For information write to the Kuala Lumpur Hash House Harriers, PO Box 10182, Kuala Lumpur.

roundings might indicate; expect to pay around M$50 for two. The food is actually about the standard of a reasonable Australian pub counter meal! It's open daily from 12 noon to 2.30 pm and 7 to 10 pm.

Entertainment

KL has plenty of discos, bars and the dreaded karaoke lounges. The following nightclubs are all open (and licensed) until 7 am: *Phases 2; Spuds; Betelnut; Mirrors,* Wisma Stephens; *11 LA,* Lorong Ampang; *October Cherry,* 145 Jalan Ampang; *Club Oz* (in the Hotel Shangri-La) and the *Tin Mine* (in the Hilton).

Karaoke enthusiasts can head for the *Tapagayo* on Jalan Bukit Bintang or *Hearts* in the Ampang Park Shopping Complex on Jalan Ampang.

For a quiet drink in a bar, the *Coliseum Hotel* at 100 Jalan TAR is a great escape, or the *Vatican* on Lebuh Pasar Besar, a place popular with local expatriates.

Free dance performances are held at the *Malaysia Tourist Information Centre* (tel 03-2434929) at 3.30 pm daily.

Things to Buy

Karyaneka Handicraft Centre out past the Hilton on Jalan Raja Chulan displays a wide variety of local craftwork in quasi-traditional settings. Hours are 9 am to 6 pm except Friday when they close at 6.30 pm.

The night market along Jalan Petaling is a good place to shop for cheap clothes. 'Genuine' Lacoste shirts sell for around M$10, while copy jeans and designer T-shirts are also very cheap and virtually indistinguishable from the real McCoy.

Jalan TAR has a variety of shops including local crafts along the arcade known as Aked Ibu Kota. Jalan Melayu has Indonesian religious goods and also local batik and other art. Pewterware, made from high-quality Malaysian tin, is an important local craft. You can see batik and silver or copperwork being done near the Batu Caves. Purchases can also be made there. Jalan Petaling is, of course, one of the most colourful shopping streets in KL, particularly at night.

The large Weld Supermarket with a number of other shops in the same complex, is on Jalan Raja Chulan. Two other modern shopping centres are the Bukit Bintang Plaza and the Sungai Wang Plaza, both on Jalan Bukit Bintang. Plaza Imbi, around the corner on Jalan Imbi, is a small complex that contains several computer hardware/software dealers.

The Central Market complex, housed in a cavernous art deco building (formerly a wet market) between the GPO and Chinatown, offers an ever-changing selection of Malaysian art, clothes, souvenirs and more. It's not particularly cheap but is a good place to shop for gifts if you're on your way home. Occasionally there are free cultural performances as well featuring Malaysian dance, gamelan or silat.

Getting There & Away

Kuala Lumpur is Malaysia's principal international arrival gateway and a central travel crossroads for bus, train or taxi travel.

Air Kuala Lumpur is well served by international airlines and there are flights to and from Australia, Singapore, Indonesia, Thailand, India, Philippines, Hong Kong and various destinations in Europe.

Some of the airline offices in KL include:

Aeroflot
    Wisma Tong Ah, 1 Jalan Perak (tel 03-2613331)
Air Lanka
    Perangsang Segumal Building, Jalan Kampung Attap (tel 03-2740893)
British Airways
    Hotel Merlin, Jalan Sultan Ismail (tel 03-2426177)
Cathay Pacific
    UBN Tower, 10 Jalan P Ramlee (tel 03-2383377)
China Airlines
    Amoda Building, 22 Jalan Imbi (tel 03-2427344)
Garuda
    1st Floor, Angkasa Raya Building, Jalan Ampang (tel 03-2483542)

KLM
  Regent of KL Hotel, Jalan Sultan Ismail (tel 03-2427011)
MAS
  UMBC Building, Jalan Sulaiman (tel 03-2308844)
  MAS Building, Jalan Sultan Ismail (tel 03-2610555)
  24-hour reservation (tel 03-7747000)
Philippine Airlines
  Wisma Stephens, Jalan Raja Chulan (tel 03-2429040)
Qantas
  UBN Tower, 10 Jalan P Ramlee (tel 03-2389133)
Royal Brunei
  Blue Moon Travel, Merlin Hotel, Jalan Sultan Ismail (tel 03-2426550)
Singapore Airlines
  Wisma SIA, Jalan Dang Wangi (tel 03-2987033)
Thai International
  Kuwasa Building, 5 Jalan Raja Laut (tel 03-2937100)

On the domestic network, KL is the hub of MAS services and there are flights to:

Destination	Frequency	Fare
Alor Setar	four daily	M$94*
Ipoh	seven daily	M$55
JB	six daily	M$77
Kota Bharu	four daily	M$86*
Kota Kinabalu	five daily	M$380*
Kuala Terengganu	three daily	M$86
Kuantan	five daily	M$61
Kuching	five daily	M$231*
Labuan	three weekly	M$380
Langkawi	daily	M$112
Miri	three daily	M$367
Penang	10 daily	M$86*
Singapore	eight daily	M$130

* Cheaper night fares and advance purchase fares are applicable on some flights on these routes.

Bus There is a wide variety of bus services, the majority of which operate from the busy Pudu Raya bus and taxi station on Jalan Pudu, just east of Chinatown. Inside the station there are a couple of dozen bus company ticket windows, so it's just a matter of checking them out and finding one with a departure time that suits you. There are departures to most places throughout the day, and at night to main towns. Outside the station on Jalan Pudu there's at least another

dozen companies, so it's worth checking these as well.

There's a left luggage office in the Pudu Raya bus and taxi station. It is open daily from 8 am to 10 pm and the charge is M$1 per item per day. There's also a left luggage office at the Kelang bus station which charges the same rate.

Typical fares from KL are:

Destination	Fare
Singapore	M$16
JB	M$15
Melaka	M$6.25
Lumut	M$12
Ipoh	M$8.50
Cameron Highlands	M$9.25
Butterworth	M$14.70
AlorSetar	M$32

Buses to Kelang (No 58 Express), Port Kelang (No 225 Express) and Shah Alam (No 222) leave from the Kelang bus station at the end of Jalan Hang Kasturi in Chinatown.

Train Kuala Lumpur is also the hub of the railway system and there are daily departures for Butterworth, Wakaf Baru (for Kota Bharu), JB and Singapore. See the Malaysia Getting Around chapter for full fare and schedule information.

Taxi While the buses depart from downstairs the taxis are upstairs in the Pudu Raya bus and taxi station although there are also long-distance taxi offices along Pudu Rd near the bus station. There are lots of taxis, and fares include Seremban M$6, Melaka M$13, JB M$31, Ipoh M$17, Taiping M$22, Butterworth M$30, Genting Highlands M$8, Kuantan M$22, Kuala Terengganu M$36, Kota Bharu M$40 and Singapore M$36.

Air-con taxis also run on these routes and cost a couple of ringgit more.

Getting Around
To/From the Airport Taxis from KL's international airport operate on a coupon system.

You purchase a coupon from a booth at the airport and use it to pay the driver. The system has been designed to eliminate fare cheating from the airport. Going to the airport is not so simple because the taxi drivers are uncertain about whether they will get a return trip – count on about M$20. Beware of taxi touts at the airport – they'll cost you more.

You can also go by bus – the No 47 operates every hour or so from the Kelang bus station on Jalan Sultan Mohamed and costs M$1.50. The trip takes 45 minutes though it's a good idea to leave more time since traffic can be bad. The first departure is at 6 am.

Bus There are two bus systems operating in KL. City bus companies include Sri Jaya, Len Seng, Len, Ampang, Kee Hup and Toong Foong. The fares on most of these buses starts from 20 sen for the first km and go up five sen each two km. The faster minibuses operate on a fixed fare of 50 sen anywhere along their route. Whenever possible have correct change ready when boarding the buses, particularly during rush hours. There are a number of bus stands around the city including the huge Pudu Raya bus and taxi station on Jalan Pudu and the Kelang bus station on Jalan Sultan Mohamed.

The bus system is fairly baffling and unless you're going to be in KL for sometime there's little point in trying to come to grips with it, especially as the taxi fares are so cheap. The central area is pretty compact and the only times you really need public transport is for trips out of the city and to the airport.

Taxi Trishaws have virtually disappeared from KL's heavily trafficked streets but there are plenty of taxis and fares are quite reasonable. They start from 70 sen for the first 1.6 km, then an additional 30 sen for each 0.8 km. Air-conditioned taxis start from M$1 and the air-con charge is made irrespective of whether the air-con is in operation or not. From midnight to 6 am there's an additional

50% supplement on top of the meter fare and extra passengers (more than two) are charged 10 sen each.

Kuala Lumpur's taxi drivers are not keen on going to the airport or from the railway station on the meter – in those cases you'll have to bargain your fare. It shouldn't be more than a couple of dollars from the railway station to most places in KL.

The other difficulty that you may come across is that Chinese taxi drivers who don't speak English are often unwilling to take foreigners, so don't be surprised if you have to flag down two or three cabs before one stops.

Car Rental All the major companies have offices at the airport as well as the following city offices:

Avis
    40 Jalan Sultan Ismail (tel 03-2423500)
Budget
    Wisma MCA, 163 Jalan Ampang (tel 03-2611122)
Hertz
    214A Kompleks Antarabangsa, Jalan Sultan Ismail (tel 03-2433014)
National
    Wisma HLA, Jalan Raja Chulan (tel 03-2480522)
Thrifty
    LPPKN Building, Holiday Inn City Centre Annex, 12-B Jalan Raja Laut (tel 03-2932388)

AROUND KUALA LUMPUR
Batu Caves

The huge Batu Caves are the best-known attraction in the vicinity of KL. They are just 13 km north of the capital, a short distance off the Ipoh road. The caves are in a towering limestone formation and were little known until about 100 years ago. Later a small Hindu shrine was built in the major cave and it became a pilgrimage centre during the annual Thaipusam festival.

The major cave, a vast open space known as the Cathedral Cave, is reached by a straight flight of 272 steps. Also reached by the same flight of steps is the long and winding Dark Cave, but this has been closed for some time because quarrying in the limestone outcrop has made the caves unsafe. There are a number of other caves in the same formation, including a small cave, at the base of the outcrop which has been made into a museum with figures of the various Hindu gods; admission is 50 sen.

There's good Indian vegetarian food at the restaurant closest to the caves themselves.

Getting There & Away To reach the caves take minibus No 11 (60 sen) from Jalan Pudu or Jalan Semarang or Len Seng bus No 69 or 70 from Jalan Raja Laut/Jalan Ampang. The bus trip takes about 45 minutes and it's wise to tell the driver you're going all the way to the caves; if there aren't many people it sometimes stops earlier. Minibus No 11 is more frequent and more convenient.

During the Thaipusam festival you can take a train to the caves – No 140 leaves the KL railway station at 9 am and No 141 leaves Batu Caves at 11.30 am. The trip takes 35 minutes and costs M$2 one way.

National Zoo & Aquarium
East of KL on the road to Ulu Kelang, about 13 km out, is the 62-hectare site of the National Zoo and Aquarium. Laid out around a central lake, the zoo collection emphasises the wildlife found in Malaysia. There are elephant rides and other amusements for children.

The zoo is open daily from 9 am to 6 pm and admission is M$4, plus M$1 if you want to use your camera. To get there take a Len Seng bus No 177 or a Lenchee bus No 180 from Lebuh Ampang, or you can take minibus Nos 17 or 23 also from Lebuh Ampang.

Mimaland
On the road to the Genting Highlands, 18 km from KL, Mimaland is a 120-hectare amusement park – mainly intended for children. It's intended to be a 'Malaysia in Miniature' and amongst the attractions are a fishing and boating lake, a huge natural swimming pool, a small zoo and a collection of full-size dinosaur models.

The park is open daily from 9 am to 6 pm and admission is M$6 (M$8 on Sunday).

Places to Stay You can stay at Mimaland in the lodge (M$10) or in Malaysian cottages known as *bagans* (M$120); phone 03-2434117 for details.

Getting There & Away You can get there on a Len Seng bus No 168, marked 'Mimaland', from Jalan Ampang.

Orang Asli Museum
One km past Mimaland is this very informative museum which gives some good insights into the life and culture of Peninsular Malaysia's 70,000 indigenous inhabitants. It's well worth a look.

It is open from Saturday to Thursday from 9.30 am to 5.30 pm; admission is free.

Templar Park
Beside the Ipoh road, 22 km north of KL, Templar Park was established during the colonial period by the British High Commissioner Sir Gerald Templar. The 1200-hectare park is intended to be a tract of jungle, preserved within easy reach of the city. There are a number of marked jungle paths, swimming lagoons and several waterfalls within the park boundaries.

Just north of the park is a 350-metre-high limestone formation known as Bukit Takun and close by the smaller Anak Takun which has many caves.

Getting There & Away To get to Templer Park, take bus Nos 66, 72, 78 or 83 from the Pudu Raya bus and taxi station. The bus fare is 95 sen and the trip takes 35 minutes.

Batik Factory Selayang
On the Ipoh road, just north of the turn-off to the Batu Caves, is the Batik Factory Selayang where you can see batik-making demonstrations from 8.30 am to 1 pm and 2 to 5 pm Monday to Sunday.

Selangor Pewter Factory
On the north-eastern outskirts of the city, on

Jalan Pahang, you can visit the Selangor Pewter Factory between 8.30 am and 4.45 pm daily and see Malaysia's famous pewter products being made.

Petaling Jaya

Petaling Jaya (PJ) is a modern suburb of KL. Originally developed as a dormitory town to the capital, it has grown so rapidly and successfully that it has become a major industrial centre in its own right. PJ has a population approaching 250,000. The University of Malaya is en route to PJ.

In recent years, PJ has become a centre of good nightlife and gourmet restaurants, partly because the per capita income is higher than in KL and also because many of the higher-salaried expats working in the KL area live there.

Places to Stay Accommodation in PJ is expensive. The best bet is to just come here for a day trip from KL, but remember that taxis have a 50% surcharge after midnight.

The cheapest place is the *South Pacific Hotel* (tel 03-7569922) at 7 Jalan 52/16, which is off Jalan Yong Shook Lin. It has rooms from M$30. Next up the scale is *Shah's Village Hotel* (tel 03-7569322), owned by the same people who have the Shah's Beach Resort in Melaka. It's at 3 Lorong Sultan and rooms start at M$65.

Other places here include the *Petaling Jaya Hilton* (tel 03-7559122) at 2 Jalan Barat, the *Merlin Subang* (tel 03-7335211) at Jalan 12/1 Subang Jaya and the *Hyatt Saujana Hotel & Country Club* (tel 03-7461188) on the Subang Airport Highway.

Places to Eat Petaling Jaya's countless restaurants include Nyonya-Baba cuisine, banana-leaf Indian, Malay, Chinese and Thai. The food at *Thai Kitchen* in PJ's SS2 district (sections are numbered; SS – 'subsection') may be the best Thai food in the KL area and the menu is in Thai, Malay and English.

One of the only two Sinhalese restaurants in the KL area is in PJ, too, the *Sri Asoka* at 27 Jalan 20/16 in the Paramount Gardens

area. Food is tasty and cheap – specialities are kiri buth, a Sinhalese version of nasi lemak (breakfast only), spicy duck hot fry, seeni sambol, sweet and salty lassis, and appam in the evenings. Opening hours are 7 am to 9 pm.

Asha's Home-Cooked Curries in 'New Town' is often recommended by locals for a good daun pisang lunch. Also in the same shop is a good Chinese claypot rice vendor. *Devi's* on Jalan Gasing is another good banana-leaf place.

Sheikh Hassan and *Syed*, both opposite the PJ Hilton, do good Indian Muslim and Malay food.

Entertainment Two clubs featuring good live jazz are *All That Jazz* (tel 03-7553152) at 14 Jalan 19/36 and *Jazz Boulevard* (tel 03-7199018), 65 Jalan SS21/1A.

If your tastes are country & western your best bet is *Texas Bar & Dallas Grill* (tel 03-7193848), on Jalan SS22/25. They serve Texas-style food as well as having live country & western music which is most likely played by Portuguese-Malay musicians from Melaka.

Some of Malaysia's top pop music bands perform at *Piccadilly* in the Kimisawa complex in PJ's Damansara Utama district. This is also the closest KL or PJ comes to a Western-style singles scene. There's a M$20 cover charge here. A more low-key music stop is *Treffpunkt*, on the next lane over from Piccadilly.

Getting There & Away Buses between PJ run regularly from the Kelang bus station on Jalan Sultan Mohamed in KL.

Port Kelang

Thirty km south-west of the capital, Port Kelang is the major seaport for KL. Port Kelang is famous for its excellent seafood, particularly chilli crabs. There are good seafood places only a couple of minutes' walk from the bus terminus. Public ferries leave for offshore islands and passengers are taken out in curious-looking rowing boats.

Only eight km before Port Kelang you

pass through Kelang, the royal capital of Selangor with a royal mosque and istana. Morib, south of Port Kelang and 64 km from KL, is a popular weekend escape and beach resort.

Places to Stay The *Embassy Hotel* (tel 03-386901) at 2 Jalan Kem has rooms from M$36. Cheaper places include the *Hotel Deluxe* (tel 03-766288) at 41 Jalan Watson and the *Hotel International* (tel 03-3688746) at 147 Jalan Watson, both with rooms from around M$20.

Getting There & Away The No 225 express bus from the Kelang bus station in KL to Port Kelang costs M$1.50.

Shah Alam

The newly established capital of Selangor State is undergoing a major construction and development plan with the intention of making it a worthy state centre. A new museum, cultural centre, theatre and huge library are being built on a hill overlooking the city's artificial lakes and close to the new state mosque. The sparkling silver and blue mosque, which looks like a lunar station, is worth a look if you have time. The city of Shah Alam itself is almost deserted except for the bustling campus of the Institut Teknologi MARA.

Kuala Lumpur to Penang

GENTING HIGHLANDS

Where the style of other Malaysian hill stations is old English, in the Genting Highlands it's modern skyscrapers; where the entertainment at the older stations is jungle walks here it's a casino; instead of waterfalls and mountain views Genting has an artificial lake and a cable car. If that does not sound to your taste then drive straight by, for the Genting Highlands is a thoroughly modern hill station designed to cater for the affluent citizens of KL, just an hour to the south.

The first stage of the Genting Highlands was opened in the early '70s and there are now three hotels and associated developments. These include Malaysia's only casino in the 18-storey Genting Hotel, with all the usual Western games of chance and Eastern favourites like keno and tai sai. Patrons must be 21 years old and Malaysian citizens have to pay M$200 to get in. Men must wear a tie to enter the casino – or pay M$3 to hire 'Malaysian national dress'. There is a sign denying Muslims entrance by decree of the Sultan of Selangor.

Then there's the four-hectare artificial lake with boating facilities which is encircled by a miniature railway for children. Naturally there's a golf course 700 metres down from the hotels, reached by a cable car. Forgetting nothing, the resort also has a bowling alley and a cave temple, the Chin Swee Temple, on the road up to the resort. Of course Genting has cooler weather like any other hill station; the main part of the resort is at a little over 1700 metres altitude.

Places to Stay & Eat

The emphasis is on international standards but there is one place offering if not cheap at least economy accommodation. The *Palangi Hotel* (tel 03-2113813) has rooms from M$60 and during the week you may be able to get this down to as low as M$40. At the top there's the 700-room *Genting Hotel* (tel 03-2112345) with rooms from M$125 and every mod con imaginable from saunas and swimming pool to tennis courts and a 'revolving disco restaurant'! The *Highland Hotel* (tel 03-2112812), has 240 rooms from around M$80.

There are often two-day and three-day packages offered at the Genting Highlands, including accommodation and some meals.

Getting There & Away

Air The jet-set way to the Genting Highlands is by helicopter. A service operates between KL's Subang Airport or the Segambut Helipad in KL to the highlands.

Bus There is also a regular M$4.50 bus service between the Pudu Raya bus and taxi station in KL and the Genting Hotel in Genting. There are about nine services daily on weekdays, more on weekends. The Genting Highlands Tours & Promotion Board (tel 03-2613833), on the 9th floor of Wisma Genting on Jalan Sultan Ismail in KL runs day tours to the highlands – M$40 gets you transport there and back, a KL city tour, and M$9 of gambling chips. Buses leave major hotels between 9 and 9.30 am, returning at 3.30 and 8 pm.

Taxi You can also get there by share-taxi for M$8 in around an hour; it's about 50 km from KL.

FRASER'S HILL

Fraser's Hill takes its name from Louis James Fraser, a reclusive ore-trader who lived there around the turn of the century. It's said he ran a remote and illegal gambling and opium den, but he was long gone when the area's potential as a hill station was recognised in 1910. The station, set at a cool 1524 metres altitude, is quiet and relatively undeveloped – possibly because it's not the easiest hill station to get to.

Information

The information office (tel 09-382201) is between the golf club and the Merlin Hotel, near the post office. They can supply maps and information brochures and they will also book accommodation in Fraser's Hill – but not at the resthouse which is in Selangor rather than Pahang (the state boundary runs through the town). It is open daily from 9 am to 7 pm daily.

There are films on Saturdays and Sundays at the Merlin Hotel which also has a bank branch which is open Monday to Friday from 10 am to 3 pm, and Saturday from 9.30 to 11.30 am. Outside these hours change money at the Merlin itself.

Nightlife on Fraser's consists of hanging out at the outdoor tables in front of the Puncak Inn or sitting before the fire in the Merlin lounge listening to schmaltzy organ music. By 10 pm everyone's in bed.

Things to See & Do

As in the Cameron Highlands there are many beautiful gardens around the town and also many wild flowers carpeting the hills. The jungle walks are much more jungle strolls than real walks. The golf course forms the real 'centre' of Fraser's Hill and there are other sporting facilities which include tennis and squash courts. A round of golf costs M$15 for green fees, M$10 for club hire and M$15 for three balls.

About five km from the information office is the Jeriau Waterfall with a swimming pool fed from the falls. Unfortunately the path leading to the falls is closed.

Places to Stay – bottom end

If you're in need of something really reasonably priced try the *Corona Nursery Youth Hostel* (tel 09-382225), the flower nursery about a 40-minute walk from the information office. It's run by a friendly Indian family. Basic rooms are M$7 per person and you can use a gas stove. This place is very isolated at the end of the road and unless you have transport is a hassle to get to.

The best place to stay is the relaxed *Gap Rest House* right at the Gap turn-off on the main road, eight km below Fraser's itself. It has capacious rooms for M$21 with bath and these are big enough for three people with room to spare. In fact this wonderfully old-fashioned place is so much better value than anything up the hill that it's worth staying down there and just visiting Fraser's Hill for the day. It's in a pretty setting, has a comfortable lounge, a good restaurant serving cheap and excellent Chinese and Western food and bathtubs with real hot water (if the generator is up to it!). The electricity goes off at midnight. To get up to Fraser's just wait at the barrier and hitch or take a bus.

Places to Stay – middle

Most of the accommodation in this range is run by the Fraser's Hill Development Corporation (FHDC), a government-contracted *bumiputra* organisation.

Rates at FHDC lodgings are slightly lower during the designated off-seasons, from 15 January to 9 March, 25 June to 14 July and 15 September to 14 November. All rates given are for the off-season – but just add M$5 for peak periods. All FHDC accommodation must be booked at the helpful and informative information centre. On weekends during the peak season you should call ahead to ensure there's space.

The *Pekan Bungalow* is right by the golf course and costs M$35/40 for singles/doubles. The *Temerloh Bungalow* is within walking distance of the centre and has good views; M$30/35 for singles/doubles. The *Raub Bungalow* is not far past the Pekan Bungalow and is still not far from the centre; rooms cost M$45.

The other two bungalows, *Rompin* and *Jelai* are further from the centre – a long walk. Both cost M$40/45.

In some of these bungalows you often get excellent, old-fashioned service although the facilities may have seen better days – it rains a lot in Fraser's and rooms tend to be a bit musty. The *Selangor Rest House* has rooms from M$30 and, as it's across the state line, is handled by the Selangor state government. Make reservations with the District Office in Kuala Kubu Bahru on the main KL to Ipoh road.

The *Puncak Inn* is right above the shops

1 Ye Olde Smokehouse	9 Information Office
2 Rompin Bungalow	10 Post Office
3 Nursery	11 Selangor Rest House
4 Temerloh Bungalow	12 Fraser's Hill Merlin Hotel
5 Ye Olde Tavern	13 Raub Bungalow
6 Puncak Inn	14 Pine Resort Condominiums
7 Sports & Golf Complex	15 Corona Nursery Youth Hostel
8 Pekan Bungalow	

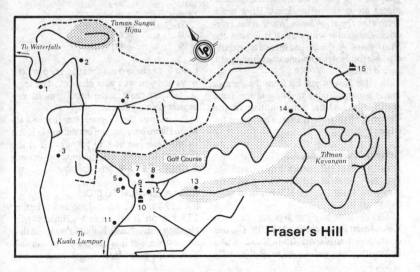

Fraser's Hill

in the little shopping centre and charges M$55 for double rooms, which rises to M$75 in season.

Places to Stay – top end

At the top end of the scale there's the *Fraser's Hill Merlin Hotel* (tel 09-382300) with 109 rooms from M$130 – during the week if things are slack they may be offering rooms for M$100. It's overlooking the golf course. There are many other bungalows and a set of condominiums on Fraser's that are privately owned by corporations for employee use or by time-share owners in KL.

Places to Eat

There's a reasonable selection of places to eat, all near the Puncak Inn. At one end of the inn is the Chinese *Hill View Restaurant* which has quite good food and snacks, while at the other end is the friendly Malay *Arzed Restaurant*. Between the two is the Malay *Restoran Puncak*, which serves roti chanai any time of day.

There's a snack bar in the Sports Club and the straightforward (the name says it all) *Kheng Yuen Lee Eating Shop* right near the gate for 'the gap'. Neither of the Chinese places are open for breakfast. Up a notch there's the *Temerloh Steak House* at the Temerloh Bungalow with steaks at around the M$10 mark. At the top end there's the expensive Merlin Hotel with one restaurant and a coffee house.

Ye Olde Tavern just up from the Puncak Inn is a mock-Tudor building in the same style as the Olde Smokehouse in the Cameron Highlands. It's not a bad place for a beer.

Getting There & Away

Fraser's Hill is 103 km north of KL and 240 km from Kuantan on the east coast. By public transport Fraser's Hill is a little difficult to get to.

There's a twice-daily bus service from Kuala Kubu Bahru costing M$1.95. The bus is supposed to depart from Kuala Kubu Bahru at 8 am and 12 noon (but usually

leaves about 30 minutes late), and from Fraser's Hill at 10 am and 2 pm.

A taxi from Kuala Kubu Bahru is M$30 for the whole taxi. A bus from KL's Pudu Raya bus and taxi station to Kuala Kubu Bahru is M$3; a share-taxi is M$6. Kuala Kubu Bahru is 62 km north of KL, just off the KL-Butterworth road and the KL-Butterworth railway line.

If you're driving be warned that there's no fuel station in Fraser's; the nearest places with fuel are Raub and Kuala Kubu Bahru.

The last eight km up to Fraser's Hill is on a steep, winding, one-way section. At the Gap you leave the Kuala Kubu Bahru to Raub road to make this final ascent. Traffic is permitted uphill and down at the following times:

Up to Fraser's Hill from the Gap

7.00	to	7.40 am
9.00	to	9.40 am
11.00	to	11.40 am
1.00	to	1.40 pm
3.00	to	3.40 pm
5.00	to	5.40 pm
7.00	to	7.40 pm

Down from Fraser's Hill

8.00	to	8.40 am
10.00	to	10.40 am
12 noon	to	12.40 pm
2.00	to	2.40 pm
4.00	to	4.40 pm
6.00	to	6.40 pm

From 7.40 pm to 6 am the road is open both ways and you take your chances! The logic is that you can see the headlights of any vehicle coming the other way.

If you miss the 12 noon bus from Kuala Kubu Bahru bus, you can get the Kuala Kubu Bahru-Raub bus at 2.30 pm, get off at the Gap and try your luck hitching up the hill during the 3 to 3.40 pm 'up' period.

KUALA LUMPUR TO IPOH

It's 219 km from KL to Ipoh and a further 173 km on from there to Butterworth. Heading north, Kuala Kubu Bahru is the first larger town, but it is just off the main road. This is the place from where buses run to

Fraser's Hill. Continuing north you pass through Tanjung Malim and Selim River. During WW II the British forces made a last-ditch attempt to halt the Japanese advance at Selim River, but failed.

Continuing north you reach Bidor, from where you can turn off for Teluk Intan, then Tapah, the gateway to the Cameron Highlands. At Kampar you can, if you have your own transport, turn off for Lumut and Pangkor Island, but there are a number of routes to this port. Finally you reach Ipoh, heralded by a number of dramatic limestone outcrops and a devastated landscape – a legacy of the tin mines which operated in the area earlier this century.

Places to Stay & Eat
If you get stuck in Kuala Kubu Bahru, there are two cheap hotel/restaurants, one Chinese and one Muslim, at the town's main crossroads (Jalan Merdeka and Jalan Sultan Hamid). There is a small coffee shop at the bus stand where you can get cheap refreshments.

There are resthouses in Tapah, Teluk Intan and Selim River. The *Selim River Rest House (Rumah Rehat)* is, according to one traveller, 'fantastic value'. There's also the *Hotel Bunga Raya* which has basic rooms for M$12. In addition to the resthouse's popular restaurant, there are many stalls with good cheap food, including Indian food, in the vicinity.

CAMERON HIGHLANDS
Malaysia's most extensive hill station, about 60 km off the main KL-Ipoh-Butterworth road at Tapah, is at an altitude of 1500 to 1800 metres. It's a little difficult to pinpoint exactly where the Cameron Highlands are and at what altitude because they consist of a series of villages strung along the main road.

The Highlands take their name from William Cameron, the surveyor who mapped the area in 1885. He was soon followed by tea planters, Chinese vegetable farmers and finally by those seeking a cool escape from the heat of the lowlands.

The temperature rarely drops below 8°C or climbs above 24°C and the area is fairly fertile. Vegetables grow in profusion, flowers are cultivated for sale all over Malaysia, it's the centre of Malaysian tea production and wild flowers bloom everywhere.

The cool weather tempts visitors to exertions normally forgotten at sea level – there's an excellent golf course, a network of jungle trails, waterfalls and mountains and less taxing points of interest such as a colourful Buddhist temple and a number of tea plantations where visitors are welcome.

Orientation
From the turn-off at Tapah it's 46 km up to Ringlet, the first village of the Highlands. Ringlet is not particularly interesting and although there are a number of places to stay most visitors press on higher up. Soon after Ringlet you skirt the lake created by the Sultan Abu Bakar Dam.

About 14 km past Ringlet you reach Tanah Rata, the main town of the Highlands. Only a few km further brings you up to the golf course around which you'll find most of the Highlands' more expensive accommodation.

Continue on beyond the golf course and at around the 65-km peg you reach the other main Highland town, Brinchang, where there are more restaurants and cheap hotels.

The road continues up beyond Brinchang to smaller villages and the Blue Valley Tea Estate at 90 km, off to the north-east, or to the top of Gunung Brinchang at 80 km, to the north-west.

Information
The main town of Tanah Rata has a variety of mainly lower-priced hotels and a wide choice of restaurants. The post office, banks and taxi station are also there and some buses terminate at Tanah Rata.

There's a reasonable colour sketch map of the Highlands available for M$2 from some of the shops in the main street.

Things to See
The **Sam Poh Temple**, just below Brinchang

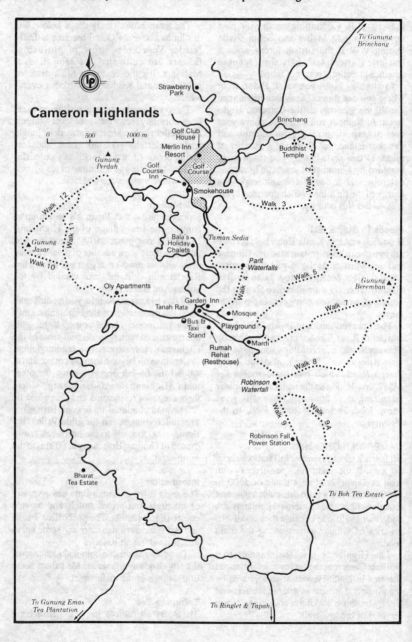

Cameron Highlands

0   500   1000 m

To Gunung Brinchang

Strawberry Park

Golf Club House

Merlin Inn Resort

Golf Course Inn

Golf Course

Smokehouse

Brinchang

Buddhist Temple

Walk 2

Walk 3

Gunung Perdah

Walk 12

Walk 11

Gunung Jasar

Walk 10

Taman Sedia

Bala's Holiday Chalets

Parit Waterfalls

Walk 4

Walk 5

Gunung Beremban

Oly Apartments

Garden Inn

Tanah Rata

Bus & Taxi Stand

Mosque

Playground

Mardi

Walk 7

Rumah Rehat (Resthouse)

Walk 8

Robinson Waterfall

Walk 9

Walk 9A

Robinson Fall Power Station

Bharat Tea Estate

To Boh Tea Estate

To Gunung Emas Tea Plantation

To Ringlet & Tapah

and about one km off the road, is a typically Chinese kaleidoscope of colours with Buddha statues, stone lions and incense burners. **Mardi** is an agricultural research station in Tanah Rata – visits must be arranged in advance.

There are a number of **flower nurseries**, **vegetable** and **strawberry farms** in the Highlands. There is an **Orang Asli settlement** near Brinchang but there's little reason to visit it.

About 10 km beyond Brinchang is the **Butterfly Garden** where there are over 300 varieties fluttering around. It's worth a visit if you can hitch there or have your own vehicle.

Tea Plantations

A visit to a tea plantation is a popular Highlands activity. The first tea was planted in 1926. The main plantation is the Boh Tea Estate.

There are free guided tours roughly every hour between 9 am and 4.30 pm. The tea is still cured with wood fires as the wood apparently imparts some flavour to the finished product. Perhaps the most amazing part of the operation is the packing. This is all done by hand and as payment is made according to quantity, the speed at which these women work has to be seen to be believed. They can pack a minimum of 1000 of the smallest packs per day, for which they get paid M$20 per 1000.

The turn-off is about nine km down from Tanah Rata, and the estate is about six km off the main road. It's a pleasant walk, or there

are daily buses from Ringlet at 6.30 and 11.30 am and 3.15 and 5.15 pm.

The Sungai Palas Tea Estate is on the Gunung Brinchang road and is also open to the public, although it is a lot less accessible.

Walks

There are a variety of walks around the Highlands, leading from place to place or to waterfalls, mountain peaks and other scenic spots. The walks are not all well kept and sometimes can be difficult to follow. In addition there are no high-quality maps available. Those supplied by the information centre or available from hotels are generally only sketch maps.

You should take care not to get lost and to bring some emergency supplies on the longer or more difficult walks. Walks 4, 9,

---

Tea Processing

Tea bushes are plucked every seven to eight days. A plucker can gather about 40 kg in a day and it takes five kg of leaves to make one kg of tea. The collected leaves are weighed and 'withered' – a drying process in which air is blown across troughs by fans in order to reduce the moisture content by about 50%. The dried leaves are then rolled to twist, break and rupture the leaf cells and release the juices for fermentation. The finer leaves are then separated out and the larger ones are rolled once again.

Fermentation, which is really oxidisation of the leaf enzymes, has to be critically controlled to develop the characteristic flavour and aroma of the tea. The fermented leaves are then 'fired', a process in which excess moisture is driven off in a drying machine. It is at this time that the leaves become black. Finally the tea is sorted into grades and stalks and fibres are removed before it is stored in bins to mature.

11 and 12 (as far as Robinson Falls) are recommended as family strolls taking only about an hour. Walks 3, 5 and 10 are longer walks taking two or more hours; while Walks 1, 2, 7 and 8 are 'tough going'.

The walks are generally interesting as they pass through relatively unspoiled jungle and the cool weather makes walking a pleasure. Walk 12 is particularly good for wild flowers – the Highlands are famed for their orchids. The deviation from Walk 12 up to the summit of 1576-metre Gunung Perdah is a good short walk.

Although the walks around the Highlands are all relatively short there is obviously great potential for longer walks from there. A glance at the map will indicate what a short, straight-line distance it is from the Highlands down to Ipoh or the main road. Any walk outside the immediate area has to be announced to the local authorities, however, and once again there are no good maps available.

Waterfalls Walk 4 from Tanah Rata leads to the Parit Waterfalls, but unfortunately these are more like a 'sewerage fall' as all the garbage from the village close by finds its way here. The falls can also be reached from the road around the golf course. Either walk is less than a km. You can make an interesting longer walk by taking Walk 9 to the Robinson Falls, then the steep and 'mildly' challenging Walk 8 to the top of Beremban, then Walk 3 to the golf course or Walks 3 and 2 to the Buddhist temple, finally returning to Tanah Rata on Walk 4 past the Smokehouse and the Parit Waterfalls. That makes an interesting round-trip walk taking three or so hours. Another round trip is Walk 10 to Gunung Jasar and back via Walk 12.

Mountains Gunung Brinchang at 2032 metres is the highest point reached by surfaced road on the peninsula. It's a long slog on foot but if you are driving it's a must. The road is narrow and incredibly steep in places but the views from the top are superb.

The two-km Walk 7 from the Mardi station will take you to the top of 1841-metre Gunung Beremban. You can also reach the summit by the three-km Walk 3 from Hopetown near the golf course.

Gunung Jasar is 1696 metres high and is reached on Walk 10 which runs between the golf course and Tanah Rata. From Tanah Rata there are directional signs from near Highland Villa at the far end of town. It's two km from there or coming down from the Hilltop Bungalow at the golf course it's about 2½ km along Walk 12 and then Walk 10.

Golf & Tennis

If you want a game of golf you'll need to be suitably dressed as regulations ban singlets and 'revealing' shorts. You also need proper golf shoes (rent for M$5). The other expenses are M$40 green fees for a whole day, or M$20 for nine holes or an afternoon, M$10 club hire and M$3 per ball. The course is open from 7 am to 7 pm but the hire shop only from 9 am to 6 pm.

Across the road from the golf shop there's a couple of tennis courts for hire. The cost is M$4 per hour, M$8 per hour for two racquets, and M$13.50 for a tube of three balls. Inquire at the golf shop.

Places to Stay

The Highlands can be very busy in April, August and December during the school holidays when many families go there for vacations. At these times it is a good idea to book accommodation. Prices in the cheaper places can be variable with demand – if it's a peak time and few rooms are available you can expect prices to soar. If it's quiet then prices are definitely open to negotiation. Don't accept the first price you're given. Even in the low season prices are definitely high compared with other towns. Finding a room for less than M$20 can be a problem.

Most of the cheap hotels are in Tanah Rata. There is a couple of places in Ringlet but there's little reason to stay here as it's 14 km from Tanah Rata. The other place with hotels is Brinchang, the secondary highland town a few km beyond Tanah Rata. Although prices are a bit cheaper than Tanah Rata, like

Ringlet there is little reason to stay here, especially if you are dependent on public transport.

The middle and top-end hotels are scattered around the Highlands, mostly between Tanah Rata and Brinchang.

Places to Stay – bottom end

Tanah Rata The most popular place with travellers is *Bala's Holiday Chalets* (tel 05-941660), about two km from town along the road to Brinchang. Beds in basic share rooms go for M$5 or there's a variety of rooms up to M$50, although they'll ask M$80 if they think you're mug enough to pay that much. They have recently added some upstairs rooms and these may be more expensive. The views from the lawn are very good and the place is in a quiet area. Probably the most attractive thing about this place is the fact that Bala runs daily tours at 10 am and 2 pm for M$6 per person, and these give you the opportunity to see things that would otherwise be inaccessible. Reasonable meals are available and there's a decent notice board.

Another popular place which has been recommended is *Father's Guest House*, up a flight of around 100 steps opposite the Oly Apartments at the Ringlet end of Tanah Rata.

Of the regular hotels in Tanah Rata the best value is the *Seah Meng Hotel* (tel 05-941618) at 39 Main Rd. It's a clean Chinese cheapie with doubles for M$26, or M$45 with bath. The *Woh Nam Hotel* is also cheap at M$25 but the rooms only have double beds.

Right at the end of the strip is the *Highlands Lodge* (tel 05-941922) at 4 Main Rd.

It's a bit seedy but cheap at M$15 for singles/doubles with common bath, and there are dorm beds for M$7.

The *Federal Hotel* (tel 05-941777) at 44 Main Rd has singles (double bed) with common bath for M$20, or doubles with bath for M$45. On the wall at reception there's a good survey map of the area. The *Town House Hotel* (tel 05-941666) at 41 Main Rd has single/double rooms for M$28/38, or M$48 with bath attached. This place is also the agent for the Expres Nasional bus company.

Brinchang All Brinchang's hotels are around the central square. The *Golden Star Hotel* (tel 05-941247) is about the best value with large rooms for M$20 with attached bath.

The *Hotel Sentosa* (tel 05-941907) is about the cheapest habitable place with rooms for M$15 for a single/double with common bath. Right next door is the *Sastro Hotel* which charges M$20/30 for good sized rooms with attached bath.

The *Silverstar Hotel* (tel 05-941387) is another cheap place with rooms for M$15/25 with attached bath.

The *Wong Villa* (tel 05-941145) is just north of the central square and has dorm beds for M$5, and beds for M$6 per person in share rooms.

Places to Stay – middle

The *Government Rest House (Rumah Rehat)* is a great place to stay, *if* you can get in. Double rooms with sitting room and bathroom go for just M$40, but because it is such

---

Jim Thompson

The Cameron Highlands' most famous jungle walker was the man who never came back from his walk. American Jim Thompson is credited with founding the Thai silk industry after WW II. He made a personal fortune and his beautiful, antique-packed house beside a *khlong* (canal) in Bangkok is a major tourist attraction today. On 26 March 1967 he was holidaying in the Highlands and left his villa for a pre-dinner stroll – never to be seen again. Despite extensive searches the mystery of Jim Thompson's disappearance has never been explained. Kidnapped? Taken by a tiger? Or simply a planned disappearance or suicide? Nobody knows.

a good deal is often booked out, especially on weekends and school holidays.

The *Garden Inn* (tel 05-941911) is just the other side of the kids' playground in Tanah Rata. Officially the rates are M$69 for a standard double, but unless things are heavily booked you shouldn't have to pay more than M$50. The rooms are fairly large and have polished wooden floors, attached bath and hot water. They also have more expensive deluxe rooms.

Between Tanah Rata and Brinchang, the *Golf Course Inn* (tel 05-941411) not surprisingly overlooks the golf course. Standard rooms cost M$88/98, and suites are available for M$190.

In Brinchang the *Parklands Hotel* (tel 05-941299) is a new place with small but well-appointed rooms for M$58, rising to M$78 in the high season.

Places to Stay – top end

The 'olde worlde' style *Lakehouse* (tel 05-996152) overlooks the lake near Ringlet and is very upmarket. Rooms cost M$225/270 with breakfast, and there are also three-room cottages for M$950.

Back by the golf course on the other side of Tanah Rata there's a couple of very good top-end places. *Ye Olde Smokehouse* (tel 05-941214) is a copy of an old English pub and looks the part from the outside, although it's a bit tacky inside. Rooms here cost from M$115/140 for singles/doubles. Overlooking the northern end of the golf course is the *Merlin Inn Resort* (tel 05-941205) which has double rooms for M$180.

A km or so past the golf course, and at the top of a windy side road, is the new *Strawberry Park Resort* (tel 05-941166). It's a huge new apartment type set-up and is popular among Singaporeans on package holidays. The room rates are M$185 for a single/double, or M$220 to M$360 for an apartment.

Places to Eat

Tanah Rata The cheapest food in Tanah Rata is to be found at the row of Malay foodstalls along the main street. One stall, called the *Excellent Food Centre* has an extensive menu and good food. On Saturday nights it becomes a 'sizzler' restaurant and is a cheap place to have a steak. Adjoining this stall is the *Fresh Milk Corner*, which, as you may have guessed, sells fresh pasteurised milk,

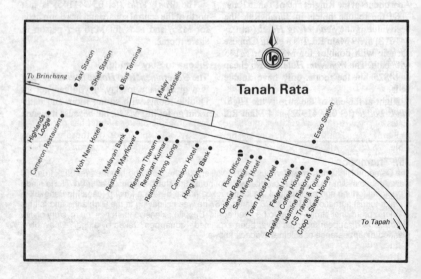

Ye Olde Smokehouse

yoghurt and lassis. Other stalls have Chinese food, satay and all the usual Malay dishes – just wander along until you see something attractive.

On the other side of the road there are a number of restaurants in the row of shops. The *Restaurant Kumar* and adjacent *Restoran Thanam* both serve good Malay and Indian food including rotis, murtabak and biryani.

For something a bit more sophisticated, try the set lunch or dinner at the *Oriental Restaurant*, also in the main street. It's a traditional 'steamboat' meal and is very good value at M$10 per person. Steamboat is the Highlands' real taste treat. It's that Chinese equivalent of a Swiss fondue where you get plates of meat, shrimp, vegetables and eggs and brew your soup over a burner on the table. You need at least two people, but the more the better.

Further along Main Rd is the *Jasmine Restaurant* which has a set four-course Chinese meal for M$10 – also good value. At the *Roselane Coffee House* they serve good breakfasts for M$5, and at lunch and dinner have a set meal of soup, main course and ice cream for M$6.30.

If you're staying at *Bala's* then it's easiest

to eat there as well. They have an extensive menu with all the old travellers' favourites, and excellent scones, jam and cream. In the evening they have a set menu banquet which is good value, although it gets the thumbs down from quite a number of travellers.

In addition to these places, all the middle and top-end hotels have their own expensive restaurants. *Ye Olde Smokehouse* is 'ideal for homesick Brits' where you can get expensive tea and scones, sandwiches with the crusts cut off and fairly pricey meals.

Brinchang Brinchang has a small night market which sets up in the main square in the late afternoon so you can eat for just a couple of ringgit then. Otherwise the restaurant in the *Sentosa Hotel* has reasonable Malay Muslim food, or there're a few Chinese places like the *Restoran Sakaya* and the *Restoran You Ho*.

Up the scale a bit is the restaurant on the ground floor of the *Parkland Hotel*. The focus is on Western food with steaks for M$15 to M$18, and other Chinese and Malay dishes, including steamboat for M$12 per person.

Ringlet There are a number of Chinese kedai

kopis in Ringlet, or you can have a banana-leaf meal at the *Sri Melor Restoran*.

Getting There & Away

Bus It's a long and gradual climb from Tapah to the Highlands with plenty of corners on the way. From the Golf Course Inn down to the main road junction one visitor reported counting 653! Bus No 153 runs approximately every hour from 8 am to 5 pm from Tapah to Tanah Rata; the trip takes about two hours. The fare is M$3 or M$3.30 to Brinchang. All the bus drivers on this route seem to be frustrated racing drivers and the way they drive can be fairly hair-raising.

Long-distance buses can be booked at Bala's, or at CS Travel & Tours on the main street in Tanah Rata. Departures include Singapore (M$28), Melaka (M$17.50), Butterworth (M$9), Kuantan (M$22), KL (M$7.50), Kuala Terengganu (M$25), Lumut (M$7.50) and Alor Setar (M$14).

Taxi There are regular taxis from the taxi stand (tel 05-941555) on the main street. Things are much busier in the mornings. The fares are M$6 to Tapah, M$11 to Ipoh and M$20 to KL.

Getting Around

Bus Most of the buses coming up from Tapah to Tanah Rata continue on to Brinchang, so getting between those two places is no problem between 7.30 am and 7 pm.

From Tanah Rata to Kampung Raja, 25 km away across the Highlands, there are eight buses daily from 7.30 am to 6 pm. It's quite a scenic trip, and you can use these buses to get to the butterfly farm past Brinchang.

Taxi For touring around, a cab costs M$12 per hour, or up to Gunung Brinchang and back is M$40.

The trip from Tanah Rata to Ringlet costs M$8, or M$12 to Boh Tea Estates.

IPOH

The 'city of millionaires' made its fortune from the rich tin mines of the Kinta Valley. The elegant mansions of Ipoh testify to the many successful Chinese miners. It's an ongoing process since many of the mines around Ipoh are still producing today.

For the visitor Ipoh's mainly a transit town, a place where you change buses if you're heading for Pangkor Island, or where you pause to sample what is reputed to be some of the finest Chinese food in Malaysia. It's worth a longer visit to explore the Buddhist temples cut into the limestone outcrops north and south of the town.

'Old Town' Ipoh is centred along the Kinta River between Jalan Sultan Idris Shah and Jalan Sultan Iskandar Shah and is worth a wander for the old Chinese and British architecture. The grand civic buildings close to and including the railway station give some idea just how prosperous this city must have once been.

To local visitors Ipoh has another side, as this is Malaysia's sin city renowned for its massage parlours and strip clubs and a frequent target of ribald comments and jokes.

Information

There are branches of both the Hong Kong & Shanghai and the Standard Chartered banks on Jalan Station near the clock tower. On Jalan Lahat opposite the Krishna Bhavan Restaurant there's a moneychanger which is open slightly longer hours.

Temples

There are cave temples both south and north of the town – the most important being the Perak Tong Temple about six km north of town, and the Sam Poh Temple a few km south of town. Both are right on the main road and so easy to get to.

Perak Tong Temple The main feature of this large and impressive complex of caverns and grottoes is the paintings on the interior walls, done by artists from all over South-East Asia. There're various figures of the Buddha, and a huge bell in the main chamber which is rung every time someone makes a donation.

A winding series of 300 odd steps leads up

through a hole on the cave wall to a painting of the Goddess of Mercy, and from here there are good views of the surrounding countryside – it's just a pity that Ipoh's factories clutter the immediate area.

Sam Poh Tong Temple This temple to the south of town is very popular with people passing by, and the main attraction seems to be the tortoise pond in a small natural courtyard created ages ago when the roof of a cave collapsed. There are literally dozens of tortoises here swimming in the thick green water. The tortoises are 'released' into the pond by locals as it is apparently good luck to do so. As you enter the temple you'll be accosted by kids trying to sell you bunches of greenery to feed the tortoises.

Inside the temple itself there's a huge cavern with a small reclining Buddha, and various other smaller caverns. There's a vegetarian restaurant to the right of the temple entrance. All the dishes sold are soya bean based, despite tags such as roast duck, etc.

The ornamental garden in front of the temple is quite scenic and is a popular spot to have your photo taken.

The temple is open daily from 7.30 am to 5 pm and can be reached by a Kampar bus No 66, or a M$2 taxi ride.

Mekprasit Temple The Mekprasit Temple is a Thai Buddhist temple about three km north of town at 102-A Kuala Kangsar Rd, the main Taiping road. The main feature of the temple is the 24-metre-long reclining Buddha, one of the largest in Malaysia.

Places to Stay – bottom end

There are plenty of hotels in all price categories in Ipoh. At the bottom end of the price scale, the *New South Eastern Hotel* (tel 05-548709) at 48 Jalan Lahat is a Chinese cheapie of the most basic variety. The rooms are noisy as it's right on a busy intersection but it is very handy for transport connections. Rooms with fan cost M$13.50.

The main hotel area, however, is around the Jalan Chamberlain area, south of the main drag, Jalan Sultan Iskandar. As the roads around here are busy most rooms which overlook the street are badly affected by traffic noise, so ask for a room at the back. The *Beauty Hotel* on Jalan Yang Kalsom is reasonably clean, and is cheap at M$14 for rooms with fan and common bath. A better bet is the *Cathay Hotel* (tel 05-513322) nearby which charges M$14/19 for singles/doubles with fan, and M$18/25 with air-con and bath.

Of a slightly better standard is the *Embassy Hotel* (tel 05-549496) at 35 Jalan Chamberlain where rooms with fan and bath cost M$17/21, or M$27 for an air-con double with attached bath.

Places to Stay – middle

The best bet in this price range is the *Win Wah (Winner) Hotel* (tel 05-515177) on Jalan Ali Pitchay. This spotless Chinese hotel has rooms for M$32 for a large room with air-con, attached bath and hot water – good value.

Back on Jalan Chamberlain the *Hollywood Hotel* (tel 05-515404) at No 74 has small rooms with air-con and bath for M$27/35. This is not such a great deal but the hotel does have a good restaurant on the ground floor.

Places to Stay – top end

If you feel like lashing out the *Station Hotel* (tel 05-512588) on the 3rd floor of the amazing railway station building is a nostalgia trip par excellence. The atmosphere is straight out of the colonial days – high ceilings, wide verandahs with potted plants and swishing ceiling fans. It's tatty around the edges these days but is still a wonderful relic of Ipoh's former glory days. All rooms are air-con and feature a huge sitting room complete with fridge and TV, a small bedroom and a bathroom. The rates are quoted at M$70/100 but this is definitely bargainable – the place was empty when we visited. It's hard to see how this place can survive much longer. To get to the reception desk take the ancient lift to the 3rd floor.

Much more modern and with less atmosphere is the *Ritz Garden Hotel* (tel 05-547777)

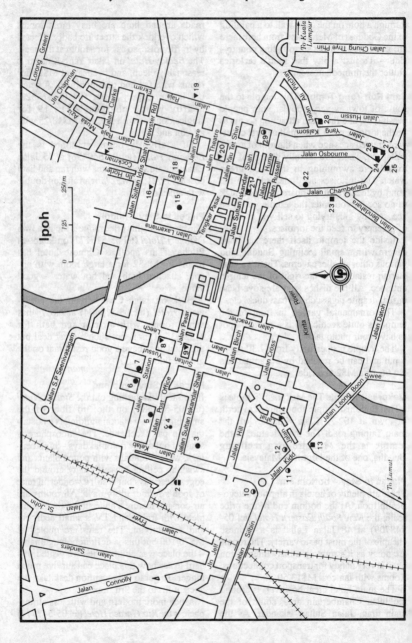

Ipoh

0   125   250/m

■ PLACES TO STAY

13 New South Eastern Hotel
23 Embassy Hotel
24 Hollywood Hotel
25 Ritz Garden Hotel
26 Beauty Hotel
27 Cathay Hotel
28 Win Wah (Winner) Hotel

▼ PLACES TO EAT

8 Kong Heng Coffee Shop, Food Centre
9 Restoran Chui Kah
14 Krishna Bhavan Restaurant
16 Lido Cake & Hot Bread Shop
17 Kentucky Fried Chicken
18 McDonald's
19 French & Noor Jahan Bakeries
20 Food Centre
21 Food Centre
24 Rahman Restaurant

OTHER

1 Railway Station
2 GPO
3 Police
4 Mosque
5 Clock Tower
6 Hong Kong & Shanghai Bank
7 Standard Chartered Bank
10 City Buses
11 Long-Distance Bus Station
12 Lumut Buses
15 Central Market
22 Rex Theatre
29 Hosni Express Buses

at 79 Jalan Chamberlain where rooms cost M$75 for an air-con double.

Another top-end place is the *Excelsior Hotel* (tel 05-536666) on Clarke St with rooms from M$110, and there's the *Royal Casuarina* (tel 05-505555) on Jalan Gopeng with rooms from M$145.

Places to Eat

Ipoh has plenty of restaurants and the rice noodle dish known as kway teow is reputed to be better in Ipoh than anywhere else in Malaysia. The city's most well-known place for kway teow is *Kedai Kopi Kong Heng* on Jalan Leech between Jalan Pasar (Market) and Jalan Station. The kway teow soup there is M$2.50 and has tender strips of chicken and prawns. They also have good roast chicken and popiah. Kong Heng is one of the oldest Chinese restaurants in the city, but it is only open at lunch time. There are several others like it on and off Jalan Leech.

In the same area the *Restoran Chui Kah* on the corner of Jalan Leech and Jalan Pasar is an upmarket Chinese restaurant which specialises in steamboat.

Right next door to the Kong Heng on Jalan Leech is a new hawkers' centre with plenty of variety – the laksa and popiah are worth trying, and the ais kacang is excellent. Beer drinkers may not find this place to their liking as alcohol isn't served.

There's another good food centre on Jalan Raja Musa Aziz just south of Jalan Sultan Iskandar. The stalls are arranged round a small square, and it's a popular place with locals in the evening – you'll often see local lads playing the traditional *sepak takraw* ball game. The food stalls have all the usual stuff – rice, noodles, curries, seafood, satay, popiah – but again, no alcohol is served here.

For Malay food the *Rahman Restaurant* on Jalan Chamberlain is very clean and has a wide range of dishes. They also have an air-con room upstairs but that's closed on Sundays. Near the bus station you have the *Krishna Bhavan Restaurant* on Jalan Lahat which also serves Malay curries.

The Central Market is huge and has a wide range of fruit and vegies if you are putting your own meals together. On the street which runs along the northern edge of the market the *Lido Cake & Hot Bread Shop* has good breads and pastries. Jalan Raja Ekram has a couple of similar bakeries (*French* and *Noor Jahan*) although they're inferior to the Lido.

Finally for something more familiar there's a *McDonald's* outlet on Jalan Clare near Central Market.

Getting There & Away
Bus Ipoh is on the main KL-Butterworth

road; 219 km north of KL, 173 km south of Butterworth. The bus station is in the southeast corner of the city centre, a taxi ride from the main hotel area. There are numerous companies here with departures at varying times. The touts are fairly vigorous so there's no danger of not being able to find a bus. All the air-con departures, and most of the non-air-conditioned ones, to places outside the immediate Ipoh area leave at night. Hosni Express, one of the bigger and more reliable operators, has an office on Jalan Raja Ekram which is handy if you're staying in that area.

Lumut buses leave from across Jalan Kidd from the bus station.

Destinations and fares include Butterworth (M$6.50), KL (M$8.20), Lumut (M$3.50), Port Dickson (M$13), Alor Setar (M$25), Kuantan (M$19.50), Melaka (M$13) and Singapore (M$25). Tickets should be booked in advance.

Taxi Long-distance taxis leave from beside the bus station. Destinations include Taiping (M$6), Butterworth (M$12), Lumut (M$6) and KL (M$17).

AROUND IPOH
Kellie's Castle
This amazing leftover from the colonial times is set by a small river about 30 km south-west of Ipoh. Unfortunately the only access is by taxi or your own vehicle.

The castle referred to is in fact an old unfinished mansion. It was to be one in the mould of great colonial houses, complete with Moorish style windows and even a lift. A wealthy British plantation owner, William Kellie Smith, who lived in a splendid mansion in this area early this century, commissioned the building of the 'castle' which was to be the home of his (as yet unborn) son. Hindu artisans were brought in from India to work on the mansion.

The house was completed but never occupied and these days the jungle is slowly taking over.

Close by is a Hindu temple, built for the artisans by Smith, and to show their gratitude they placed a statue of him, complete with white suit and topee, among the Hindu deities on the temple roof! The temple is a little hard to locate, so you'll have to ask directions.

LUMUT
The Malaysian Navy has its principal base in this town – a replacement for the old base in Singapore. In spite of the navy presence, this small river port of 33,000 is little more than a departure point for nearby Pangkor Island.

The resthouse, a stone's throw from the ferry pier, used to have a small museum, but its contents were transferred to the museum in Taiping some years ago. All that's left now is a group of cannons from the Dutch fort on Pangkor and a group of Malay cannons cast in Aceh in north Sumatra about 200 years ago. Lumut is the site for the Pesta Lumut sea carnival in July-August each year.

At Teluk Rubiah, not far from Lumut, there's a Marine Farmhouse. Sam Khoo, of Pangkor Island's 'mini camp' fame, also established this place, where he raises tiger prawns, crabs and other seafood creatures. Visitors are welcome to come and have a look at how he's doing.

Information
If you're driving and on your way to Pangkor, there's a 24-hour long-term car park behind the Shell petrol station. Cars are kept undercover and are guarded, and the charge is M$2 per day.

Places to Stay & Eat
If you get marooned in Lumut because you missed the last ferry to Pangkor, there is a reasonable choice of Chinese hotels and plenty of restaurants.

The *Hotel Lumut* (tel 05-935771) with rooms around M$12 is typical. There's good Indian food next door. The *Phin Lum Hooi Hotel* (tel 05-935641), about half a km from the bus stand, charges M$12 for a single and is very good, clean and friendly. The restaurant downstairs is decorated with a collection of shark fins! The fine old waterfront *Government Rest House* (tel 05-935938) has rooms from M$15 to M$35 a double.

Out of town the *Lumut Country Resort* (tel 05-935009) has rooms from M$90 and an excellent restaurant.

Getting There & Away

Bus Lumut is 206 km south of Butterworth or 101 km from Ipoh, the usual place for Lumut buses if you're travelling north on the KL-Butterworth road. There are daily buses Butterworth-Lumut for M$8.50 or you can get a bus to Taiping about every half hour and another bus on from there.

Probably the best way to go is Ipoh-Lumut. There are buses hourly from Lumut for M$3. There are also direct buses from KL to Lumut several times per day. The trip takes about six hours and costs M$12 by an air-con bus.

There's also a daily bus from Tapah in the Cameron Highlands to Lumut for M$8.

Taxi Long-distance taxis are M$15 per person for Butterworth-Lumut or M$6 for Ipoh-Lumut.

PULAU PANGKOR

The island of Pangkor is close to the coast off Lumut – easily accessible via Ipoh. It's a popular resort island for its fine and often quite isolated beaches, many of which can be walked to along an interesting 'around the island' track.

Taking the regular ferry service from Lumut you go out the Dindings River by the Malaysian Navy base. On the mainland coast the huge, almost Singapore-like, apartment complex has been built as naval quarters. Although the base is nearly in full operation it doesn't seem to have made a big difference to Pangkor life. The sailors have their own beach near Lumut, Teluk Batik, and about the only time they make it over to Pangkor is for Sunday picnics.

A visit to the island is principally a 'laze on the beach' operation, but there are also a number of interesting things to do.

Pangkor is a fairly conservative place – it's wise to behave and dress discreetly. It's also a very friendly place and travellers have written of being invited to weddings, festi-vals and other events even during short visits to the island.

Pangkor's only drawback is that it can get very crowded on weekends and, to a much greater extent, during school holidays. It's a popular local resort, only a short ferry ride from the mainland and close to large population centres so crowds are inevitable. During the week, however, the beaches are fairly empty.

Litter on the beaches used to be a big problem but fortunately the local authorities took it upon themselves to get the place cleaned up. To a large extent they have succeeded and while you'll still see some stuff lying around, it is a huge improvement. The day-trippers picnicking on the beach seem to be the main offenders. Signs line the beach at Pasir Bogak warning of the fines applicable to litterers.

Orientation

Finding things on Pangkor is very simple. On the east coast of the island, facing the mainland, there's a continuous village strip comprising Sungai Pinang Kecil (SPK), Sungai Pinang Besar (SPB) and Pangkor village.

The ferry from Lumut stops at SPK before Pangkor village which is where you'll find the restaurants and shops. The road which runs along the coast on this side turns west at Pangkor village and runs directly across the island, only a km or two wide at this point, to Pasir Bogak where you find almost all the accommodation. From there it runs to the northern end of the island, reaching Pangkor's other hotel at Teluk Belanga in the north-west. The road from there back to the eastern side of the island is really only suitable for motorcycles – cars go via Pasir Bogak.

Information

There's a bank in Pangkor village which is open the usual hours, and a moneychanger on the road to Pasir Bogak which is open longer hours.

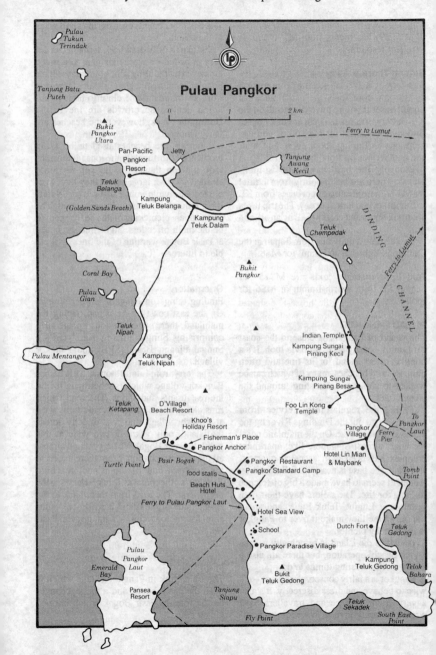

Pulau Tukun Terindak

Tanjung Batu Puteh

Pulau Pangkor

0   1   2 km

Ferry to Lumut

Bukit Pangkor Utara

Pan-Pacific Pangkor Resort

Jetty

Tanjung Awang Kecil

Teluk Belanga

(Golden Sands Beach)

Kampung Teluk Belanga

Kampung Teluk Dalam

Teluk Chempedak

DINDING

Coral Bay

Bukit Pangkor

Pulau Gian

Teluk Nipah

CHANNEL

Pulau Mentangor

Kampung Teluk Nipah

Indian Temple

Kampung Sungai Pinang Kecil

Kampung Sungai Pinang Besar

Teluk Ketapang

D'Village Beach Resort

Khoo's Holiday Resort

Fisherman's Place

Pangkor Anchor

Foo Lin Kong Temple

Pangkor Village

To Pangkor Laut

Turtle Point

Pasir Bogak

Pangkor Restaurant

Pangkor Standard Camp

Ferry Pier

Hotel Lin Mian & Maybank

Tomb Point

food stalls

Beach Huts Hotel

Ferry to Pulau Pangkor Laut

Hotel Sea View

School

Dutch Fort

Teluk Gedong

Pangkor Paradise Village

Kampung Teluk Gedong

Telok Bahara

Pulau Pangkor Laut

Emerald Bay

Bukit Teluk Gedong

Pansea Resort

Tanjung Siapu

Teluk Sekadek

Fly Point

South East Point

Beaches

Pasir Bogak is OK for swimming but during holidays it's crowded, at least by Malaysia's 'empty beach' standards. Golden Sands Beach (Teluk Belanga) at the other end of the island is pleasant, although access is restricted to hotel guests, and in between them are a number of virtually deserted beaches which you can reach by boat, on foot or on motorcycles.

The best beach on this side is at Coral Bay, about a 20-minute bicycle ride from Pasir Bogak. The water is a clear emerald-green due to the presence of limestone and usually the beach is quite clean and pretty.

Turtles come in to lay their eggs at night on Teluk Ketapang beach, only a short walk north of Pasir Bogak. May, June and July are the main months and June is usually best of all if you want to go midnight turtle spotting. Sightings are becoming increasingly rare these days.

Emerald Bay on nearby Pulau Pangkor Laut is a beautiful little horseshoe-shaped bay with clear water, fine coral and a gently sloping beach. However, the entire island of Pangkor Laut has been taken over by a French hotel-restaurant conglomerate and as soon as you step off the ferry from Pasir Bogak you'll be hit for a use fee of M$30 per person. The fee includes a M$15 lunch and the use of Pansea facilities, including the swimming pool, beaches, and beach cabanas. The Pan-Pacific Resort at Teluk Belanga is similarly restrictive.

Exploring the Island

The island lends itself well to exploration by motorcycle, bicycle or on foot. Spend a day doing a loop of the island – there are a few deserted beaches on the western side to stop off at. It takes about an hour by motorcycle to do the loop, or about six hours on foot.

On the eastern side, from Sungai Pinang Kecil it's a continuous village strip on to Pangkor village – messy but full of interest. There's boat building, fish being dried or frozen, a colourful south Indian temple – lots to look at.

In Sungai Pinang Besar the Foo Lin Kong Temple is worth a quick look. Located on the side of the hill, the main 'attraction' is a mini Great Wall of China! It also has some tacky rock paintings and other features of dubious artistic merit. The animal cages are downright depressing. The temple is signposted 'Pangkor Great Wall' from the main road.

Dutch Fort

Pangkor's one bit of history is three km south of Pangkor village at Teluk Gedong. There the Dutch built a wooden fort in 1670 – after they had been given the boot from Lower Perak. In 1690 they rebuilt the fort in brick, but lost it soon afterwards. The Dutch retook the fort in 1693 but despite frequent visits did not reoccupy it until 1745 and only three years later they abandoned it for good. The old fort was totally swallowed by the jungle in 1973 when it was rebuilt as far as the remaining bricks would allow.

On the waterfront a little beyond the fort is a huge stone on which the coat of arms of the Dutch East India Company (VOC) has been inscribed along with a carving which supposedly depicts a tiger stealing a child. This is said to relate to an incident when a child of a local European dignitary disappeared while playing near the rock. The Dutch liked the idea of the tiger story; the more likely explanation is that the boy was abducted by some of the disenchanted locals.

The road ends at Teluk Gedong and the footpath continues a little further. Note how well kept most of the houses are in this Malay kampung. Drums and tubs of flowers border the houses and more hang from the roof edges.

Places to Stay

Almost all Pangkor's accommodation possibilities are grouped at each end of the very pleasant beach at Pasir Bogak, on the opposite side of the island from Pangkor village. As Pangkor is primarily a tourist resort, accommodation is generally more expensive than elsewhere.

Starting at the eastern end there's the new *D'Village Beach Resort* which is mainly tented accommodation ranging from little two-person jobs up to 10-person tents. The cost is M$7 per person, the drawbacks being a lack of shade and exposure to some fairly stiff breezes in the afternoons. They also have a few basic chalets along the beach front, and these are not bad value at M$70 for a double with dinner and breakfast.

Next up is *Khoo's Holiday Resort* (tel 05-951164). This used to be Sam Khoo's Mini Camp and was a popular travellers' hangout. These days unfortunately it has been redeveloped and an ugly concrete building has replaced the attap huts. It seems the local authority gave them the choice of replacing the huts or closing the whole place down. The new rooms are all concrete and very cell-like and not very pleasant. Dorm beds cost M$7, rooms with fan and bath are M$50, or with air-con and bath M$75.

With the demise of Sam Khoo's the best place to stay at any reasonable price is the *Pangkor Anchor*, a short distance along from Khoo's. Run by the very down-to-earth Mrs Wong, this place is kept spotlessly clean and is well managed. Small mosquito-proof A-frame huts rent for M$12/18 and for this you get a mattress on the floor. It's a good place, although children are not made especially welcome and there's a bit of the 'lights out' mentality of a youth hostel.

At the other end of the beach, where the road from Pangkor village crosses the island, are the other hotels. The *Hotel Sea View* has air-con rooms for M$85 with bath, pleasant chalets for M$100, family rooms for M$109, all including breakfast. There's also a 15% off-season discount. The hotel's restaurant is about the best place to eat at this end of the beach as it is right on the edge of the water – very pleasant at sunset.

The *Beach Huts Hotel* (tel 05-951359) has rooms at similar prices but these do not include breakfast. It is also right on the beach although there are a few hawkers' stalls and warungs cluttering the beach at this point. When the resort currently under construction next to the Beach Huts is finished it seems likely that these stalls will be moved along.

On the other side of the road behind the beach is the *Standard Pangkor Camp* (tel 05-951878) which has cramped A-frame huts for M$10/12 or small rooms with fan and common bath for M$27. Unfortunately this place is on the wrong side of the road and you have to walk around the other resorts to get to the beach.

Right at the southern end of Pasir Bogak, past the Hotel Sea View and the school, is the *Pangkor Paradise Village* (tel 05-951496). It is set well apart from the other places and so is much quieter, but it also lacks atmosphere and the accommodation is basic. The very small A-frame huts cost M$8/12 with just a thin mattress on the floor. They also have a row of new chalets for M$45 with bath but these are real hot-boxes.

Apart from Pasir Bogak there is also the Japanese-managed *Pan-Pacific Pangkor Resort* (tel 05-951091) at Teluk Belanga (Golden Sands Beach) at the other end of the island. The Pan-Pacific has rooms starting at M$240 but off-season discounts are available. There are also package deals from KL which include transport to Pangkor and two or three-night accommodation. There is a variety of sporting and recreational facilities, including a nine-hole golf course, and the hotel is on a very pleasant stretch of beach, nicely isolated from the local development which mars Pasir Bogak. The beach here is restricted to hotel guests only but if you want to pay M$30 you can use the pool and beach (not the golf course) and get a M$15 lunch included.

Pulau Pangkor Laut, the island opposite Pasir Bogak, is totally in the grasp of *Pansea on the Island* (tel 05-951320, in KL 03-2421589), which is managed by a French multinational hotel corporation. Any traveller boarding a ferry for Pangkor Laut from Pasir Bogak or Pangkor village will be interrogated as to the purpose of the trip – are you putting up at the resort or paying for day use (M$30). Since the French took over from local management, they have been promoting the place through international yacht races and tennis tournaments. There is a small swimming pool, six tennis courts, two restaurants, a disco, and three or four private beaches around the island, including the pic-

Top: Marang (VB)
Bottom: Merang (PT)

Top: Typical House, Kuala Terengganu (PT)
Left: Tioman Island Golf Course Club House (PT)
Right: Gua Charas Caves (PT)

turesque Emerald Bay on the side facing away from Pangkor. Posted rates are M$77 per person double occupancy or M$98 for a single. During the week there are usually discounts available to around M$60 per person.

Pangkor Village In the village of Pangkor there are a couple of cheap Chinese hotels, including the *Hotel Lin Mian* right near the Maybank. It has relatively cheap rooms but also has the inconvenience of being a couple of km from the beach.

Places to Eat

Pasir Bogak All the hotels have restaurants and there are a few other places as well. Up near the Pangkor Anchor, the *Fisherman's Place* serves fresh and tasty seafood and Chinese dishes, and they have a good breakfast menu. It's a popular place both with locals and travellers.

In the area of Khoo's there are a number of hawkers' stalls selling snack food, and you also find these in front of the Beach Huts Hotel. Close by here are a number of fairly shabby warungs serving cheap and basic meals.

Tucked away along a small dirt road which runs alongside the Pangkor Standard Camp is the *Pangkor Restaurant*, a cheap seafood and Chinese food restaurant which is popular with the locals.

The restaurant in the *Hotel Sea View* is outdoors right by the beach and while the food is only mediocre it's an excellent place to watch the sunset from. The restaurant in the *Beach Huts Hotel* suffers from somewhat inept management but the food is not bad.

Pangkor Village In Pangkor village there's a proliferation of kedai kopis serving the usual Chinese food, while the *Restoran Kasim Selamat* does good roti chanai and murtabak.

Getting There & Away

Boat The two ferry companies, Min Lian and Feri Expres, between them run ferries between Lumut and Pangkor village every 20 minutes from 6.45 am to 7.30 pm from Lumut, and from 6.45 am to 6.40 pm from Pangkor.

The fare is M$1 each way but you can only buy M$2 return tickets. On the return journey you can use the boats of either company, regardless of which one you used to get to the island.

From Lumut there are four ferries daily to the northern end of the island across the isthmus from the Pan Pacific Resort, the first at 8.45 am, the last at 6.30 pm.

The other ferry service connects Lumut with the Pansea Resort on Pulau Pangkor Laut. It operates five times daily from 8 am to 6.30 pm. There are also old boats operated by the Pansea Resort which shuttle between the resort and Pasir Bogak, mainly taking staff to or from the island. There are 10 daily from Pasir Bogak from 7.30 am to 10.45 pm. The fare is M$3 but if you are day-tripping you'll be up for M$30 for day-use of the resort's facilities and lunch.

Getting Around

Bus There are buses every half hour or so which run from Pangkor village across the island to the far end of the beach at Pasir Bogak and back again.

Taxi Pangkor has plenty of taxis, which seem to be old retired long-distance Mercedes from the mainland or brand new minibuses. The standard fare is M$3 from Pangkor to Pasir Bogak.

Bicycle & Motorcycle The ideal way to see the island is by bicycle or motorcycle. There are a number of places at Pasir Bogak which rent them out and the prices are very reasonable: M$4 per hour or M$25 per day for a motorcycle, and M$4 per day for a bicycle.

KUALA KANGSAR

The royal town of Perak state is beside the highway, north of Ipoh. A couple of km out of town is the Ubadiah Mosque with its fine golden onion-dome. It's probably the finest mosque in Malaysia although it looks almost as if it's viewed through a distorting mirror since its four minarets are squeezed up tightly against the dome.

Overlooking the river is the palace or Istana Iskandariah, but it's not open to visitors. There is also an earlier istana and an intricately carved ceremonial hall.

Kuala Kangsar was the birthplace of Malaysia's great rubber industry. A number of rubber trees had been planted at the agricultural station there, from seed stock smuggled from Brazil, but it was not until the invention of the pneumatic tyre in 1888 that rubber suddenly came into demand and rubber plantations sprang up across the country.

All of the trees for the new plantations are descended from the original rubber trees in Kuala Kangsar. You can still see one of those first trees in the district office compound and another near the agriculture department office.

Places to Stay

The *Double Lion Hotel* (tel 05-862020) at 74 Jalan Kangsar is cheap at just M$10 but also extremely basic. A better bet is the *Mei Lai Hotel* (tel 05-861729) at 7F Jalan Raja Chulan which has rooms with attached bath from M$16, and more expensive air-con rooms.

Getting There & Away

Kuala Kangsar is 50 km north of Ipoh, just off the main KL-Butterworth road. It's 123 km south of Butterworth, 269 km north of KL. A bus from Butterworth takes 2½ hours and costs M$6.

TAIPING

The 'town of everlasting peace' hardly started out that way. A century ago, when it was known as Larut, the town was a raucous, rough-and-tumble tin mining centre – the oldest one in Malaysia.

Bitter feuds broke out three times between rival Chinese secret societies with injury, torture and death taking place on both sides. When colonial administrators finally brought the bloody mayhem under control in 1874 they took the prudent step of renaming the town.

Apart from misty, Chinese-looking views Taiping also has quite a number of well-preserved old Anglo-Malay buildings. Along with Penang, this is a favourite spot for wealthy Malaysians to retire to.

Taiping is a low-key town; there's good food in the night market, a great museum and no tourists.

Lake Gardens

Taiping is renowned for its beautiful Lake Gardens, built on the site of an abandoned tin mine right beside the town in 1890. The well-kept gardens owe some of their lush greenery to the fact that Taiping has the highest annual rainfall in Peninsular Malaysia. There's also a small zoo in the Lake Gardens while in the hills which rise above the gardens is Maxwell Hill, the oldest hill station in Malaysia.

The Prison

At the far end of the gardens is a prison used by the Japanese during the war and later as a rehabilitation centre for captured Communists during the Emergency. Today it houses political detainees under the ISA (Internal Security Act) ruling.

Taiping State Museum

Just beyond the prison is the Taiping State Museum which is open from 9 am to 5 pm daily, but closed from 12 noon to 2.30 pm on Fridays. It's the oldest museum in Malaysia and its contents include interesting exhibits on the aboriginal people of this area although its fairy-tale architecture is probably its most interesting aspect.

Things to See

Taiping was also the starting point for Malaysia's first railway line; opened in 1885 it ran 13½ km to Port Weld, but is now closed.

Taiping has an **Allied war cemetery** beside the Lake Garden and in the town itself there are some **interesting old buildings** from the colonial period, including the old town office.

The **Ling Nam Temple** is the oldest Chinese temple in Perak and has a boat figure dedicated to the Chinese emperor who built the first canal in China. On Station St there's an interesting south Indian **Hindu temple**.

Places to Stay & Eat

Taiping has plenty of cheap Chinese hotels. The *Wah Bee Hotel* is a old wooden place on the main street which has cheap and basic rooms for M$15. Another cheapie is the *Hotel Peace* (tel 05-823379) at 32 Jalan Iskandar which charges around M$12 for a double room with common bath.

Up the scale a notch is the *Hotel Nanyang* (tel 05-824488) at 129 Jalan Pasar where rooms with fan and bath go for M$18.

Better still is the *New Rest House (Rumah Rehat Baru)* (tel 05-822044) in Taman Tasik, which is a curious mixture of Sumatran and classical Roman styles. Overlooking the Lake Gardens, it's clean, secure and very good value at M$28 for large doubles with fan, or M$39 with air-con. Rooms either have a view out over the prison or the golf course. Unfortunately minimal maintenance is carried out and there're signs of decay everywhere. The airy restaurant here serves decent meals. It's about a km from the centre so you'll need a taxi to get there.

Taiping's large night market has many open-air eating stalls and satay is one of the city's specialities.

Getting There & Away

Bus Taiping is several km off the main KL-Butterworth road. It's 88 km south of Butterworth and 304 km north of KL. If you're heading south from Butterworth to Lumut for Pangkor Island and miss the direct bus it's straightforward to take a Butterworth-Taiping bus and another bus on from Taiping to Lumut.

MAXWELL HILL

Also known as Bukit Larut, the oldest hill station in Malaysia is 12 km from Taiping at an altitude of 1019 metres. It was formerly a tea estate but has now been closed and the quiet little station is simply a cool and peaceful place to be. There are no golf courses, fancy restaurants or other hill station trappings – let alone casinos.

Getting up to Maxwell Hill is half the fun and once there you've got fine views down over Taiping and the Lake Gardens far below. From Cottage, the summit you can walk to from Maxwell Hill, you can see the coast all the way from Penang to Pangkor on a clear day.

Few people visit Maxwell Hill and in fact the eight bungalows there will only accommodate a total of 53 visitors. During the school holidays of April, August and December all eight are full. The electricity is off from 7.30 am to 6.30 pm and again from midnight to 6 am.

Places to Stay

You can book space in one of the eight bungalows by ringing 05-827241 or by writing to the Superintendent, Tempat Per-anginan, Taiping. If you've not booked earlier you can ring from the Land Rover station at the bottom of the hill.

There are two resthouse bungalows – *Bukit Larut* (also known as the Maxwell) and *Gunung Hijau* (or Speedy), with rooms from M$18. Other bungalows are *Cendana* (Hut) and *Tempinis* (Treacher). They're all between Km 10 and Km 12 pegs from the base of the hill.

Getting There & Away

Prior to WW II you had a choice of walking, pony-back or being carried up in a sedan chair for there was no road to the station. Japanese POWs were put to work building a road at the close of the war and it was opened in 1948.

Private cars are not allowed on the road so if you want to go it has to be in the government Land Rovers that run a regular service from the station at the foot of the hill, just above the Taiping Lake Gardens. They operate every hour on the hour from 8 am to 6 pm and the trip takes about 40 minutes.

The winding road negotiates 72 hairpin

bends on the steep ascent and traffic is strictly one way. You can glimpse superb views through the trees on the way up. The up and down Land Rovers meet at Tea Gardens, the midway point. Fares from the bottom vary from about M$1 to the Tea Gardens to M$3 all the way to Cottage. Alternatively you can walk to the top in about three hours.

To book a seat on a Land Rover (advisable) ring the station at the bottom of the hill on 05-827243.

BUTTERWORTH

There's no reason to pause in Butterworth; it's just a port for ferries to Penang Island and the site of a large Australian air force base.

Most of the land transport (buses, trains, taxis) between Penang and other places on the peninsula and Thailand actually leaves from Butterworth, right next to the ferry terminal for ferries to and from Georgetown.

Places to Stay

If for some reason you want to stop in Butterworth, there are a number of hotels. The cheap *Capital Hotel* (tel 04-344822) has basic rooms for M$10, and the *Ambassadress Hotel* (tel 04-342788) at 4425 Jalan Bagan Luar, has air-con rooms from M$22.

At the other end of the scale there's the *Travel Lodge* (tel 04-348889) at 1 Lorong Bagan Luar which has singles/doubles for M$60 to M$120.

Getting There & Away

See the Penang section for details of transport to and from Butterworth.

Penang

The oldest British settlement in Malaysia, predating both Singapore and Melaka, is also one of Malaysia's major tourist attractions. This is hardly surprising, for the 285 sq km island of Penang has popular beach resorts and an intriguing and historically interesting town which is also noted for its superb food.

Penang's major town, Georgetown, is often referred to as 'Penang' although correctly that is the name of the island (the actual Malay spelling is Pinang). It's a real Chinatown with far more Chinese flavour than Singapore or Hong Kong. Those larger cities have had their Chinese flavour submerged under a gleaming concrete, glass and chrome confusion, but in the older parts of Georgetown the clock seems to have stopped 50 years ago. It's an easy going, colourful city where the bicycle rickshaw is still the most sensible means of transport.

Penang's beaches are touted as a big drawcard for visitors, but they really are somewhat overrated. They're not as beautiful, as clean or as spectacular as the tourist literature would make out. Beaches close to the city also suffer to some extent from pollution. The beaches along the north coast are the most visited and the most accessible. There are other beaches around the south of the island, but these are not easily accessible without your own transport.

History

In 1786 Captain Francis Light, on behalf of the East India Company, acquired possession of Penang (Betelnut) Island from the local sultan in return for protection. He renamed the island Prince of Wales Island, and it's said that Light loaded his ship's cannons with silver dollars and fired them into the jungle to encourage his labourers to hack back the undergrowth. Whatever the truth of the tale, he soon established the small town of Georgetown, named after the Prince of Wales, who later became King George IV, with Lebuh Light, Chulia, Pitt and Bishop as its boundaries. Founding towns must have been a Light family tradition because his son is credited with the founding of Adelaide in Australia; which is today a sister city to Georgetown. Light also negotiated with the sultan for a strip of land on the mainland adjacent to the island, and this became known as Province Wellesley.

To encourage settlers, Light permitted new arrivals to claim as much land as they could clear, and this, coupled with the duty-free port which Light had declared, quickly attracted settlers from all over Asia. Although virtually uninhabited in 1786, by the turn of the century Penang was home to over 10,000 people.

The local economy was slow to develop, as mainly European planters set up pepper and spice plantations, all of which were slow growing crops and required a high initial outlay, and they were hindered by a limited labour force.

Up until 1805 Light remained the sole administrator of the settlement, but in that year Penang became a presidency government, on a par with the cities of Madras and Bombay in India, and so gained a much more sophisticated administrative structure.

Penang has always been a cosmopolitan place and has attracted dreamers, artists, intellectuals and dissidents. Three of the five social action organisations singled out by Malaysian Prime Minister Mahathir as 'thorns in the flesh of the nation' are based in Penang. In 1816 the first English-language school in South-East Asia was opened in Georgetown.

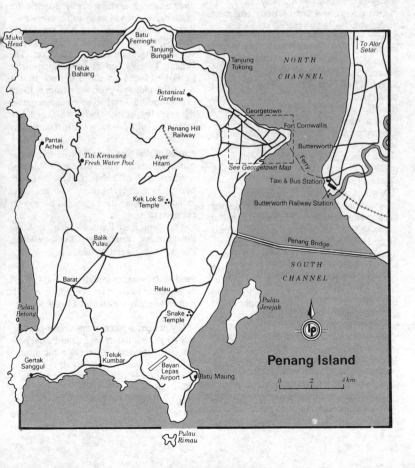

Penang Island

GEORGETOWN
Orientation

Georgetown has a population of about 400,000 while that of the whole island is around half a million. Georgetown is in the north-east of the island, where the straits between the island and the mainland are at their narrowest.

A vehicle and passenger ferry service operates 24 hours a day across the three-km-wide channel between Georgetown and Butterworth on the mainland. South of the ferry crossing is the Penang Bridge – the longest in Asia – which links the island with Malaysia's north-south highway.

Georgetown is a compact city and most places can easily be reached on foot or by bicycle rickshaw. Two important streets to remember are Lebuh Chulia and Lebuh Campbell. Both run away from the ferry waterfront and terminate on Jalan Penang.

You'll find most of Georgetown's popular cheap hotels along Lebuh Chulia or close to it, while Lebuh Campbell is one of the town's main shopping streets. Jalan Penang is another popular shopping street and in this area you'll find a number of the more expensive hotels including, at the waterfront end of Jalan Penang, the venerable Eastern & Oriental (E&O) Hotel.

If you follow Jalan Penang south you'll pass the modern multistorey blot on the skyline known as the Kompleks Tun Abdul Razak (KOMTAR), where the MAS office is located, and eventually leave town and continue towards the Bayan Lepas Airport. If you turn west at the waterfront end of Jalan Penang you follow the coastline and eventually come to the northern beaches, including Batu Ferringhi. This road runs right round the island and eventually brings you back into town, via the airport.

Finding your way around Georgetown is slightly complicated by the street names. Jalan Penang may also be referred to as Jalan Pinang or as Penang Rd – but there's also a Penang St, which may also be referred to as Lebuh Pinang! Similarly Pitt St is sometimes called Lebuh Pitt, but Lebuh Chulia is always Lebuh Chulia, never Chulia St. The old spelling for Lebuh is Leboh and some of the street signs still use this spelling.

Information

Tourist Information The Penang Tourist Association (tel 04-366665) is on Jalan Tun Syed Sheh Barakbah, close to Fort Cornwallis in the centre of Georgetown. They are a useful source of information and the office is open from 8 am to 4.15 pm Monday to Friday and 8 am to 12.45 pm on Saturdays.

The TDC tourist office also has an office (tel 04-620066) just a few doors along in the same building with all the usual TDC literature, although nothing really specific for Penang. It is open Monday to Thursday from 8 am to 12.45 pm and 2 to 4.15 pm, Friday from 8 am to 12.15 pm and 2.45 to 4.15 pm, and Saturday from 8 am to 12.45 pm. The Penang Tourists Guides Association office (tel 04-614461) on the 3rd floor of the Komtar building is open daily from 9.30 am to 6.30 pm and is staffed by volunteer guides who really know their stuff and are extremely helpful with specific inquiries.

Money There are branches of the major banks on Lebuh Pantai near the GPO. At the northern end of Lebuh Chulia there are numerous moneychangers who are open longer hours than the banks and have competitive rates.

The American Express agent is Mayflower Acme Tours, Tan Cheng building, Pengkalan Weld (tel 04-623724).

Post & Telecommunications The GPO is in the centre of town on Lebuh Downing. It is open Monday to Saturday from 8.30 am to 4.30 pm.

If you need a parcel wrapped for posting, MS Ally, a stationers on Lebuh Pantai near the GPO provides the service for around M$3.

The Telekom office is on Jalan Burma, a 15-minute walk from Lebuh Chulia. It is open 24 hours a day and calls can be made quickly and easily. There is also a phone here which you can use to get through instantly to the operator in your home country and make reverse charge (collect) or credit card calls.

Immigration The immigration office (tel 04-615122) is on Lebuh Pantai in the centre of town.

Consulates Medan, the entry point from Penang to the Indonesian island of Sumatra, is counted as one of the 'usual' entry points where visitors can be issued a visa on arrival. Which is just as well, because the Indonesian Consulate in Penang has long had a reputation for being much less than helpful. The Thai Consulate, on the other hand, is a good place for obtaining Thai visas. Thai visas cost M$31; lots of places up and down Lebuh Chulia will obtain the visa for you for an additonal M$8.

France
    Wisma Rajab, 82 Lebuh Bishop (tel 04-629707)
Indonesia
    467 Jalan Burma (tel 04-25162)
Japan
    2 Jalan Biggs (tel 04-368222)
Thailand
    1 Jalan Ayer Rajah (tel 04-23352)
UK
    c/o Price Waterhouse, UMBC Building, Lebuh Pantai (tel 04-621700)

Travel Agencies Penang has many travel agents, mostly at the northern end of Lebuh Chulia, offering excellent bargains in discounted airline tickets. Although most of them are fine there are some who are not totally trustworthy.

Silver-Econ Travel (tel 04-629882) at 436 Lebuh Chulia and MSL (tel 04-24748) at 340 Lebuh Chulia (affiliated with Student Travel Australia) are both reliable operations. Another good, reliable agency which many travellers deal with is Happy Holidays (tel 04-629222) at 442 Lebuh Chulia. See the Getting There & Away section for more on airline ticket discounters.

Libraries & Bookshops The Penang Library is on the 1st floor of the Dewan Sri Pinang on Lebuh Duke. It has a large collection of books of local interest and is open from 9 am to 5 pm, Mondays to Fridays and from 9.30 am to 1 pm on Saturdays.

The British Council Library (tel 04-370330) is at 43 Green Hall and is open Tuesday and Wednesday from 10 am to 8 pm, Thursday and Friday from 10 am to 6pm and Saturday from 10 am to 4 pm.

The Alliance Francaise (tel 04-366008) is at 32 Jalan Kelawai and has library which is open from 9.30 am to 12 noon and 3.30 to 7.30 pm on weekdays only. The Malaysian German Society Library (tel 04-366853) is at 250B Jalan Air Itam and is open 9.30 am to 1 pm and 2.30 to 6 pm on weekdays. There are several fairly good bookshops along Lebuh Pantai and a good one in the E&O Hotel.

Emergency Outpatient medical care is generally inexpensive in Malaysia. The following hospitals are recommended for travellers. Dial 999 for ambulance service.

General Hospital
    Jalan Residensi (tel 04-373333)
Penang Adventist Hospital
    465 Jalan Burma (tel 04-373344)

Vice There are traces of Georgetown's seamier past and intrepid travellers can still find opium dens in operation. There are still a lot of drugs in Georgetown, but Malaysia's penalties for drug use are very severe (death for possession of more than 15 grams of any contraband) so beware of those trishaw riders offering a supermarket variety of illegal drugs. Prostitution is also big in Penang and trishaw drivers will try to push girls as much as drugs to unaccompanied male travellers.

Fort Cornwallis
The timeworn walls of Fort Cornwallis in the centre of town are one of Penang's oldest sites. It was there that Light first set foot on the virtually uninhabited island and established the free port where trade would, he hoped, be attracted from Britain's Dutch rivals. At first a wooden fort was built but

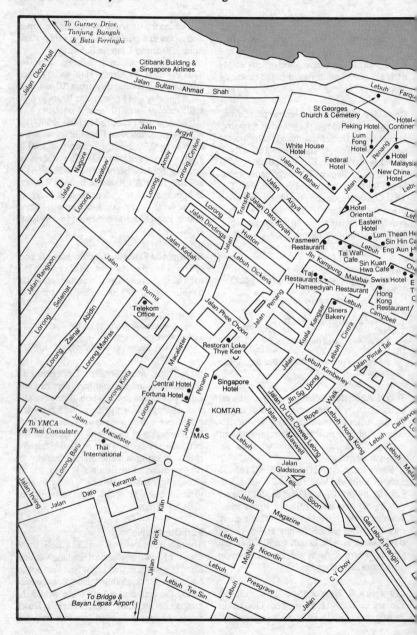

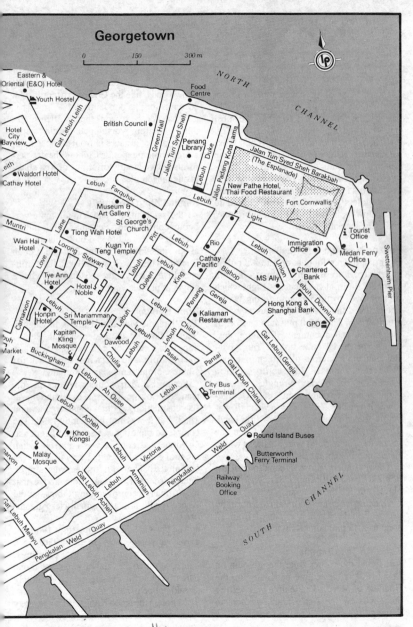

Georgetown

0   150   300 m

Eastern &
Oriental (E&O) Hotel

Youth Hostel

NORTH

Hotel
City
Bayview

Food
Centre

CHANNEL

British Council

Green Hall

Penang
Library

Waldorf Hotel
Cathay Hotel

Lebuh Farquhar

Museum &
Art Gallery

St George's
Church

Tiong Wah Hotel

Jalan Tun Syed Sheh Barakbah
(The Esplanade)

New Pathe Hotel,
Thai Food Restaurant

Fort Cornwallis

Muntri
Lane

Wan Hai
Hotel

Lorong
Stewart

Kuan Yin
Teng Temple

Love

Tye Ann
Hotel

Hotel
Noble

Honpin
Hotel

Sri Mariamman
Temple

Kapitan
Kling
Mosque

Dawood

Carnavon

Market

Buckingham

Khoo
Kongsi

Malay
Mosque

Ah Quee

Acheh

Victoria

Armenian

Gat Lebuh Acheh

Gat Lebuh Melayu

Pengkalan Weld Quay

Rio

Cathay
Pacific

Kaliaman
Restaurant

City Bus
Terminal

Round Island Buses

Butterworth
Ferry Terminal

Railway
Booking
Office

SOUTH

CHANNEL

Light

Immigration
Office

MS Ally

Hong Kong &
Shanghai Bank

GPO

Tourist
Office

Medan Ferry
Office

Chartered
Bank

Swettenham Pier

Chartered
Bank

Holoman
L43 Jln. Anson

between 1808 and 1810 convict labour was used to replace it with the present stone structure.

Today only the outer walls of the fort stand. The area within has been made into a park, but it's liberally studded with old cannons. Many of these were retrieved from local pirates although they were originally cast by the Dutch. Seri Rambai, the most important and largest cannon, faces the north coast and dates back to the early 1600s. It has a chequered history of being passed from the Dutch to the Sultan of Johore to the Portuguese and then to pirates before ending up at the fort. It's famed for its procreative powers and childless women are recommended to place flowers in the barrel of 'the big one' and offer special prayers.

Penang Museum & Art Gallery

From the town's foundation site it's only a short stroll to the museum on Lebuh Farquhar. In front is a statue of Light which was removed by the Japanese during WW II but retrieved and re-erected, minus its sword, after the war. The small museum has lots of old photos and documents, furniture, costumes, the medal collection of Tun Abdul Rahman and numerous other memorabilia.

There's a small, interesting section recounting the bloody wrangles between Chinese secret societies in 1867. Georgetown, it appears, suffered a near civil war before the administrators took a firm hand. The societies were heavily fined and the proceeds used to build police stations which subsequently kept the peace.

The art gallery is upstairs and one of the original Penang Hill funicular railcars is displayed outside the museum.

Opening hours are from 9 am to 5 pm daily except Fridays when it is closed from 12 noon to 2.45 pm; admission is free.

Kuan Yin Teng Temple

Just round the corner from the museum on Lebuh Pitt is the temple of Kuan Yin, the Goddess of Mercy. The temple was built in the 1800s by the first Chinese settlers in Penang. It's not a terribly impressive or interesting temple, but it's right in the centre of the old part of Georgetown and is the most popular Chinese temple in the city. Perhaps it's Kuan Yin's own reputation as a goddess on the lookout for everyone's well-being or possibly it's the presence of other well-known gods, like the God of Prosperity, that accounts for this popularity.

Whatever the reasons there's often something going on; worshippers burning paper money at the furnaces in front of the temple, a night-time puppet or Chinese theatre performance, or simply offerings of joss sticks inside the temple.

Kapitan Kling Mosque

At the same time Kuan Yin's temple was being constructed, Penang's first Indian Muslim settlers set to and built this mosque at the junction of Lebuh Pitt and Lebuh Buckingham. In a typically Indian-influenced Islamic style the mosque which has a single minaret is yellow.

Khoo Kongsi

The 'Dragon Mountain Hall' is in Cannon Square close to the end of Lebuh Pitt. A kongsi is a clan house, a building which is part-temple and part-meeting hall for Chinese of the same clan or surname.

Penang has many kongsis, but this one, the clan house of the Khoos, is easily the finest. Its construction was first considered around 1853, but it was not built until 1898. The completed building was so magnificent and elaborate that nobody was surprised when the roof caught fire on the very night it was completed! That misfortune was simply interpreted as a message from above that they'd really been overdoing things, so the Khoos rebuilt it in a marginally less grandiose style.

The present kongsi, dating from 1906 and extensively renovated in the 1950s, is a rainbow of dragons, statues, paintings, lamps, coloured tiles and carvings, and is one part of colourful Penang which definitely should not be missed.

Although the Khoo Kongsi is far and away the most well-known kongsi in Georgetown, there are a number of others, including the modern Lee Kongsi on Jalan Burma, the combined kongsi of the Chuah, Sin and Quah clans at the corner of Jalan Burma and Codrington Ave, the Khaw Kongsi on Jalan Burma and the Yap Kongsi on Lebuh Armenian.

Sri Mariamman Temple

Lebuh Queen runs parallel to Lebuh Pitt, and about midway between the Kuan Yin Temple and the Kapitan Kling Mosque you'll find another example of Penang's religious diversity.

The Sri Mariamman Temple is a typical south Indian temple with its elaborately sculptured and painted gopuram towering over the entrance. Built in 1883, it's the oldest Hindu temple in Georgetown and testifies to the strong Indian influence you'll also find in this most Chinese of towns.

Wat Chayamangkalaram

At Lorong Burma just off the road to Batu Ferringhi is a major Thai temple – 'Temple of the Reclining Buddha'. This brightly painted temple houses a 32-metre-long reclining Buddha, loudly proclaimed in Penang as the third longest in the world – you can take that claim with a pinch of salt since there's at least one other in Malaysia that is larger, plus one in Thailand (at least) and two in Burma. Nevertheless, it's a colourful and picturesque temple and there's a Burmese Buddhist temple directly across the road from it, with two large stone elephants flanking the gates.

Penang Buddhist Association

Completed in 1929 this is a most unusual Chinese Buddhist temple. Instead of the usual gaudy and colourful design of most Chinese temples it is quiet, tasteful and refined. The Buddha statues are carved from Italian marble, and glass chandeliers, made in Penang, hang from above. It's on Jalan Anson.

Other Mosques, Churches & Temples

Close to the Kapitan Kling Mosque, the Malay mosque on Lebuh Aceh is unusual for its Egyptian-style minaret – most Malay mosques have Moorish minarets.

Also in the centre, St George's Church on Lebuh Farquhar was built in 1818 and is the oldest Anglican church in South-East Asia. The gracefully proportioned building with its marble floor and towering spire was built by convict labour. Also on Lebuh Farquhar is the double-spired Cathedral of the Assumption. The cemetery nearby tells the usual wistful story of the early deaths of English administrators and their families.

The Shiva temple on Jalan Dato Keramat is hidden behind a high wall, but the Nattukotai Temple on Waterfall Rd is the largest Hindu temple in Penang and is dedicated to Bala Subramaniam.

On Jalan Perak, Wat Buppharam is the oldest Thai temple in Penang and has a pagoda and two 30-metre-long dragons. Out at Tanjung Tokong the Tua Pek Kong Temple is dedicated to the God of Prosperity and dates from 1837. Finally the Penang State Mosque at Ayer Itam is glossy and new and there are good views from the 50-metre-high minaret.

Around Town

Georgetown is a delight to simply wander around at any time of day. Set off in any direction and you're certain to find and see plenty of interesting things, whether it's the beautiful old Chinese houses, an early morning vegetable market, a temple ceremony, the crowded shops or a late pasar malam.

Jalan Penang and Jalan Campbell are the main shopping streets with modern air-conditioned shops, but it's along the more old-fashioned streets like Lebuh Chulia or Rope Walk that you'll find the unusual bargains – like a 'Beware of the Dog' sign that adds the warning in Malay (*Awas – Ada Anjing*) and in Chinese ideograms. At the Lebuh Farquhar end of Jalan Penang there are a string of handicraft and antique shops.

Trishaws are the ideal way of getting around Georgetown, particularly at night when trishaw travel takes on an almost magical quality.

All the usual Chinese events are likely to be taking place at any time – a funeral procession with what looks like a run-down Dixieland jazz band leading the mourners, colourful parades at festival times, trishaws wobbling by with whole families aboard, ancient grandmas pushing out their stalls to set up for a day's business. All around you'll hear those distinctively Chinese noises: the clatter of mahjong tiles from inside houses, the trilling of caged songbirds, and everywhere loud arguments and conversations – for Chinese is not a quiet language.

Nor can you miss Georgetown's other inhabitants. Tamils from the south of India cool boiled milk by nonchalantly hurling it through the air from one cup to another. Money changing is almost exclusively an Indian enterprise and a stocky Sikh with an antique-looking gun can be seen guarding many banks or jewellery shops. Altogether Georgetown is a place where there's always something of interest.

Organised Tours

Many companies offer local tours – you'll see sandwich boards along the sidewalks. MSL Travel on Lebuh Chulia is reliable and has a 3½-hour tour for M$20. A Penang Hill trip, including the train up, takes four hours and costs M$30. They also have an office on Lebuh Chulia. The tourist office also has official guides for personal tours.

Festivals

All the usual festivals are celebrated in Penang, but some with special energy. In December the annual Pesta Pulau Penang or Penang Islands Festival is highlighted by colourful dragon boat races. There are also parades, carnivals and all the fun of the fair.

The masochistic Hindu festival of Thaipusam is celebrated in Penang with a fervour to rival Singapore and KL but without quite the same crowds. The Nattukotai Temple on Waterfall Rd is the main centre in Penang for the activities.

At Chinese New Year a wayang or Chinese opera takes place at the snake temple near Bayan Lepas. The number of snakes in residence is also said to be highest at that time of year.

The tourist office can tell you what festivals are approaching, where events occur and can also offer information about their origins and significance.

Places to Stay – bottom end

Hostels Penang has a well situated, but extremely anonymous, *Youth Hostel* (Asrama Belia) right next door to the gracious old E&O Hotel on Lebuh Farquhar. It takes in only YHA members and dorm beds cost M$5. There are shared facilities and the front door closes at midnight. The reception office is on the 2nd floor at the back of the building, and there are discounts for longterm stays.

The *YMCA* (tel 04-362211), at 211 Jalan Macalister, is close to the Thai Consulate which is an important Penang address for many travellers. Singles/doubles cost M$30/32 or M$35/37 with air-con. All rooms have attached showers. There's a M$2 temporary membership charge for nonmembers of the YMCA, but this can be waived if you're a YHA member or have a student card. The YMCA also has a TV lounge and cafeteria.To get there take a bus No 7.

Finally the *YWCA* is much further out at 8A Green Lane and, unlike the YMCA, it's single sex only.

Hotels There are a great number of cheap hotels around Georgetown, some of them very pleasant. Stroll down Lebuh Chulia, Lebuh Leith or Love Lane and you'll come across them.

The *New China Hotel* (tel 04-631601) at 22 Lebuh Leith, under new management, is not as good as it used to be according to recent reports from travellers. Singles/doubles with fan cost M$18/27, and doubles with attached bath are M$40. There's also a somewhat airless dorm at M$5.50. It has a restaurant serving Western food and breakfasts and there's a bar at the back which can be noisy at times.

Two popular places, of a better standard than the New China, are the *Swiss Hotel* (tel 04-620133) at 431-F Lebuh Chulia and the *Eng Aun* (tel 04-612333) directly across the road at 380 Lebuh Chulia are good value. The Swiss Hotel has rooms with fan and common bath at M$13.20/21 single/double. The Eng Aun charges M$14.30/18.70 for large single/double rooms with common facilities. They also have a travel agency downstairs. Both of these spacious hotels attract a steady stream of travellers and have large car parks in front – which also insulates them from street noise.

At 282 Lebuh Chulia the *Tye Ann Hotel* (tel 04-614875) is very popular, particularly for its breakfasts downstairs in the restaurant section. Rooms cost M$16 single or double and there are also M$6 dorm beds.

In the streets just off Lebuh Chulia there are a number of popular places. At 35 Love Lane the *Wan Hai Hotel* (tel 04-616853) is a good Chinese cheapie with dorm beds for M$6 and rooms for M$16 with common bath. It's a quiet place with reasonable rooms and a small roof terrace. Nearby are small, interesting light-industrial-type shops,

including a place which makes mahjong tiles.

The *Tiong Wah Hotel* (tel 04-622057), at 23 Love Lane, is a typical older style Chinese place in a very quiet area. Rooms with common bath go for M$16/18.

At 36 Lorong Pasar, just one small block in from Lebuh Chulia, the *Hotel Noble* (tel 04-612372) is a quiet place with rooms for M$14/18 with common bath.

Back on Lebuh Chulia near the junction with Jalan Penang there're a few more places if none of the above appeal. The *Eastern Hotel* (tel 04-614597) at 509 Lebuh Chulia has rates which vary with the season, from M$14/22 for singles/doubles up to M$16/26. Next door at 511 Lebuh Chulia is the *Hang Chow Hotel* (tel 04-610810) which has typical basic rooms for M$14/16. There's a restaurant and moneychanger on the ground floor.

The *Lum Thean Hotel* (tel 04-614117) at 422 Lebuh Chulia is not too promising with its modern facade but behind it you'll find a typical Chinese hotel. It's also about the cheapest air-con place and doubles with bath cost M$33. Cheaper rooms with fan and bath go for M$17/26.

At 64-1 Lebuh Bishop the *Hotel Rio* (tel 04-650010) has rooms for M$22/28 with common bath, and is in a quiet street.

If you avoid the noisy front rooms, the *Singapore Hotel* (tel 04-620323) at 495-H Jalan Penang is not a bad deal. Rooms with fan and bath cost M$19, or M$22/29 with air-con and bath.

During peak travel times it can sometimes be difficult to find a room, but there are many more cheap Chinese hotels on Lebuh Chulia, Lebuh Campbell and the small connecting streets – a quick wander around will turn up any number of them.

Places to Stay – middle
For a bit of a splurge you can stay at the wonderful-looking and very friendly *Cathay Hotel* (tel 04-626271), halfway between the Oriental and the Merlin near the New China Hotel at 22 Lebuh Leith. The cavernous lobby nearly equals the exterior. Prices for

the huge spotless rooms are M$40/46 for singles/doubles with fan and bath, M$50/58 with air-con and attached bath.

Right next door to the Cathay at 13 Lebuh Leith, the *Waldorf Hotel* (tel 04-626140) is new and characterless but has reasonable rooms (all air-con) for M$41/58 with bath attached. It's a bit overpriced considering what else is available.

At 273-B Lebuh Chulia, opposite the Tye Ann, the *Honpin Hotel* (tel 04-625243) is a relatively new place with reasonable rooms from M$25 to M$30 with bath, M$40 with air-con and bath.

On Lebuh Light there's the *New Pathe Hotel* (tel 04-620195), an older place right by a park. It has good-sized rooms for M$44 with air-con and bath. It's just a pity that all the rooms have frosted glass so you can't take advantage of the view.

Jalan Penang also has a few middle-priced places, but avoid the rooms which overlook the noisy street. The *Hotel Central* (tel 04-366411) is at 404 Jalan Penang although the main entrance is on Lorong Macalister. Single/double rooms with air-con and attached bath go for M$46/55. Next door the *Hotel Fortuna* (tel 04-24301) is marginally cheaper at M$40/48.

On top of Penang Hill there's the small *Bellevue Hotel* (tel 04-892256), formerly known as the Penang Hill Hotel, which is not only small and quiet with a delightful garden but also very tastefully decorated – its owner is one of Malaysia's foremost architects. The rooms are also reasonably priced at M$60 to M$80.

Places to Stay – top end

Penang's biggest hotels, of the resort variety, are out at Batu Ferringhi. In Georgetown itself you mainly find the older hotels or the second-string places.

Grandest (and oldest) is the fine old *Eastern & Oriental* (E&O) Hotel (tel 04-638322), one of those superb old establishments in the Raffles manner – indeed it was built by the Sarkies Brothers who also constructed the Raffles in Singapore, and the Strand in Rangoon. The E&O

hotel was built in 1885, is right on the waterfront and has beautiful gardens right down to the water. It has featured in several Somerset Maugham stories. Single/double rooms cost from M$105/115 to M$230/250.

While Lebuh Chulia is the main street in Georgetown for cheap hotels, Jalan Penang is where you find most of the more expensive places. Virtually across the road from the E&O and at the top of Jalan Penang is the much more modern *City Bayview Hotel* (tel 04-633161), topped by a revolving restaurant with great views over Georgetown. Rooms here go for M$155/165 up to M$200/210. In the basement is the Penny Lane disco which plays all '60s music.

Another very central place is the *Oriental Hotel* (tel 04-24211) on the corner of Jalan Penang and Lebuh Chulia. It has good-sized rooms for M$85. The *Federal Hotel* (tel 04-24101) at 55 Jalan Penang has 80 rooms from M$65 to M$180.

The *Merlin Inn* (tel 04-376166) on Jalan Burma is another of Penang's top-class places, and has prices to match; M$125 to M$300 for well-appointed single/double rooms.

Places to Eat

Penang is another of the region's delightful food trips with a wide variety of restaurants and many local specialities to tempt you.

For a start, there are two types of soup, or laksa, that are particularly associated with Penang. Laksa assam is a fish soup with a sour taste from the tamarind or assam paste; it is served with special white laksa noodles. Originally a Thai dish, laksa lemak has been adopted by Penang. It's basically similar to laksa assam except coconut milk is substituted for the tamarind.

Seafood is, of course, very popular in Penang and there are many restaurants that specialise in fresh fish, crabs and prawns – particularly along the northern beach fringe.

Despite its Chinese character Penang also has a strong Indian presence and there are some popular specialities to savour. Curry kapitan is a Penang chicken curry which supposedly takes its name from a Dutch sea captain asking his Indonesian mess boy what was on that night. The answer was 'curry kapitan' and it's been on the menu ever since.

Murtabak, a thin roti chanai pastry stuffed with egg, vegetables and meat, while not actually a Penang speciality, is done with particular flair on the island.

Indian Food Amongst the more popular Indian restaurants is *Dawood* at 63 Lebuh Queen, opposite the Sri Mariamman Temple. Curry kapitan is just one of the many curry dishes at this reasonably priced restaurant. Beer is not available (since it's run by Indian Muslims), but the lime juice is excellent and so is the ice cream.

On Lebuh Campbell the *Taj Restaurant* at 166 and the *Hameediyah Restaurant* at 164A both have good curries and delicious murtabak.

The *Yasmeen Restaurant* at 177 Jalan Penang, near the corner of Lebuh Chulia, is another place for murtabak, but this is also an excellent place for a quick snack of roti chanai with dhall dip – a cheap meal at any time of the day. They also serve excellent chicken and mutton biryani on Fridays and Sundays.

Penang has a 'little India' along Lebuh Pasar between Lebuh Penang and Lebuh Pitt and along the side streets between. Several small restaurants and stalls in this area offer cheap north (Muslim) and south Indian food. Between Lebuh Queen and Lebuh King on Lebuh Pasar is the easy-to-miss *Krishna Vilas*, good for south Indian breakfasts – idli (steamed rice flour cakes) and dosai – and very cheap. On the corner of Lebuh King and Lebuh Bishop you can get a whole selection of curry dishes plus rice and chapatis at *Rio*.

For something a bit more upmarket try the *Kaliaman Restaurant* on Lebuh Penang. This air-con place has south Indian banana-leaf meals at lunch time for M$3, or M$4 for non-vegetarian, and does excellent north Indian food in the evenings.

Chinese Food There are so many Chinese restaurants in Penang that making any spe-

cific recommendations is really rather redundant.

At 29 Lebuh Cintra the *Hong Kong Restaurant* is good, cheap and varied and has a menu in English. One of Georgetown's 'excellent Hainanese chicken rice' purveyors is the *Sin Kuan Hwa Cafe*, on the corner of Lebuh Chulia and Lebuh Cintra.

More good Chinese food can be found at the fancier *Dragon King* on the corner of Lebuh Bishop and Lebuh Pitt which specialises in traditional Nyonya wedding cuisine and is definitely worth a try. Expect to pay around M$20 for two.

One of the most popular outdoor Chinese places is *Hsiang Yang Cafe* across the street from the Tye Ann Hotel on Lebuh Chulia. It's really a hawkers' centre, with a cheap and good Chinese buffet (rice with three or four side dishes for M$2.50), plus noodles, satay and popiah vendors.

The *Tzechu-lin* at 229-C Burmah Rd is a Buddhist vegetarian restaurant which has excellent food. Expect to spend around M$20 for two.

Breakfasts & Western Food At breakfast time the popular travellers' hangout is the *Tye Ann Hotel* on Lebuh Chulia. People visit this friendly little establishment for its excellent porridge, toast and marmalade and other breakfast favourites. Western breakfasts are also available at the *New China, Eng Aun, Swiss, Cathay* and opposite the Wan Hai. Another morning hang-out is the tiny *Eng Thai Cafe* at 417B Lebuh Chulia, not far from the Eng Aun and Swiss hotels. There are other small Chinese cafes with Western breakfast menus like the popular little *Sin Hin Cafe* at 402 Lebuh Chulia. At 487 Lebuh Chulia the very popular *Tai Wah Coffee Shop* buzzes with activity all day long and until late at night.

For a splurge the four-course set lunch at the *E&O Hotel* is good value, although you have to sit inside. To eat on the terrace outside you have to order à la carte.

At the supermarket in the Komtar building you can find all the usual supermarket goodies. The Komtar is also a happy hunting ground if you're after fast food. On floors 1 to 3 you'll find *Kentucky Fried Chicken, McDonald's, Shakey's, White Castle, Pizza Hut, A&W* and *Satay Ria*. On the 5th floor there's a pleasant hawkers' centre with all the usual Chinese and local dishes.

Diner's Bakery, opposite the Meerah Restaurant on Lebuh Campbell, has great baked goodies ranging from cheesecake to wholemeal bread although there are cheaper bakeries around. Another good bakery is the *Maxim Bakery* on Jalan Penang near the Central Hotel.

Night Markets Georgetown has a wide selection of street stalls with nightly gatherings at places like Gurney Drive or along the Esplanade. The latter is particularly good for trying local Penang specialities.

The big pasar malam changes venue every two weeks, so check at the tourist office for its current location. It's mainly for clothes and other household goods but there are a few hawkers' stalls. It doesn't really get going until around 8 pm.

Medicated tea is a popular item and one Georgetown tea stall has a sign announcing that it will cure everything from 'headache, stomachache and kidney trouble' to 'malaria, cholera and' (wait for it) 'fartulence'.

AROUND GEORGETOWN
Penang Hill
Rising 830 metres above Georgetown, the top of Penang Hill provides a cool retreat from the sticky heat below – it's generally about 5°C cooler than at sea level. From the summit you've got a spectacular view over the island and across to the mainland. There are pleasant gardens, a small cafe and a hotel as well as a Hindu temple or a Muslim mosque on the top. Penang Hill is particularly pleasant at dusk as Georgetown, far below, starts to light up.

The idea of a hill resort was first mooted towards the end of the last century, but the first attempt at a mountain railway was a dismal failure. In 1923 a Swiss-built funicular railway system was completed and the tiny cable-pulled cars have trundled up and

down ever since. The trip takes half an hour with a change of train at the halfway point. A few years ago the original funicular cars were changed for more modern ones, but the queues on weekends and public holidays can still be as long as ever.

Getting There & Away Take bus No 1 from Pengkalan Weld to Ayer Itam (every five minutes, 55 sen), then bus No 8 to the funicular station (30 sen). The ascent of the hill costs M$3 for the round trip. There are departures every 30 minutes from 6.30 am to 9.30 pm from the bottom, 9.15 pm from the top. There are later departures until midnight on Wednesdays and Saturdays. The queues here are often horrendous – waits of half an hour and more are not uncommon.

The energetic can get to the top by an interesting eight-km hike starting from the Moon Gate at the Botanical Gardens. The hike takes nearly three hours so be sure to bring along a water bottle.

Kek Lok Si Temple
On a hilltop at Ayer Itam, close to the funicular station for Penang Hill, stands the largest Buddhist temple in Malaysia. The construction commenced in 1890 and took more than 20 years to complete.

The entrance is reached through arcades of souvenir stalls, past a tightly packed turtle pond and murky fish ponds until you reach the Ban Po Thar or 'Ten Thousand Buddhas' Pagoda.

A 'voluntary' contribution is the price to climb to the top of the seven-tier, 30-metre-high tower which is said to be Burmese at the top, Chinese at the bottom and Thai in between. In the other three-storey shrine there is a large Thai Buddha image that was donated by King Bhumibol of Thailand. Standing high above all the temple structures is a striking white figure of Kuan Yin, the Goddess of Mercy.

To get there from Georgetown, take a MPPP bus No 1 from Maxwell Rd or a green bus.

Ayer Itam

Ayer Itam Dam, three km from Kek Lok Si, has an 18-hectare lake. It's one of several reservoirs on the island. Penang's largest Hindu temple, the Nattukotai Chettiar, is on top of a hill beyond the dam. There's a good view from the top, 233 metres above sea level. This is the most important site in Penang for ceremonies during the Thaipusam festival.

Botanical Gardens

Penang's 30-hectare botanical gardens are off Waterfall Rd and are also known as the Waterfall Gardens after the stream that cascades through them down from Penang Hill. They've also been dubbed the Monkey Gardens due to the many monkeys that appear on the lawn for a feed early each morning and late each afternoon. The gardens also have a small zoo and from them a path leads up Penang Hill.

Take a bus No 7 from Lebuh Chulia.

AROUND THE ISLAND

You can make an interesting circuit of the island either in your own car, on a motorcycle or (at a push) bicycle, on a tour, or by public transport. On a motorcycle or by car, figure on about five hours with plenty of sightseeing and refreshment stops. If you are on a bicycle allow all day. It's 70 km all the way round, but it's only along the north coast that the road runs right on the coast so you're not beside the beaches all the way. The following takes you from Georgetown in a clockwise direction around the island.

Snake Temple

At Km 15, a couple of km before the airport, you reach Penang's famous snake temple, the 'Temple of the Azure Cloud'. The temple was built in 1850 and is dedicated to Chor Soo Kong.

If you fancy it live snakes are draped over you. The snakes are venomous Wagler's Pit Vipers and are said to be slightly 'doped' by the incense smoke which drifts around the temple. There is no admission fee to the temple although 'donations' are requested.

The number of snakes tends to vary through the year.

Batu Maung

After the snake temple you soon reach a turn-off to the small Chinese fishing village of Batu Maung, about three km away. There's an expensive seafood restaurant built on stilts over the water. It's an excellent place for a meal at sunset. There is a also small children's playground with concrete animal figures.

Bayan Lepas

Next up is the village of Bayan Lepas and Penang's international airport. Just beyond Bayan Lepas a small shrine dedicated to the legendary Admiral Cheng Ho (see Melaka) marks a huge 'footprint' on the rock which is said to belong to the famous eunuch.

Teluk Kumbar

Back on the main road you climb up, then drop down to Teluk Kumbar, from where you can detour to the fishing village of Gertak Sanggul. You'll pass some beaches, including Pantai Asam, on the way. Although very scenic these beaches are not all that good for swimming.

Balik Pulau

A little further on you reach Balik Pulau, the main town you pass through on the island circuit. There are a number of restaurants and cafes but no accommodation – going round the island has to be a one-day operation, unless you bring camping gear. Balik Pulau is a good place to have lunch though, and a must is the local speciality *laksa balik pulau*. It's a tasty rice-noodle concoction with a thick fish broth, mint leaves, pineapple slivers, onions and fresh chillies.

Between Balik Pulau and Sungai Pinang you pass through an area of Malay kampungs – if you're on a bicycle or motorcycle (the side roads aren't quite wide enough for cars), turn off at Jalan P Pasir and tour the picture-perfect village there, with neatly kept traditional Malay houses, flower gardens

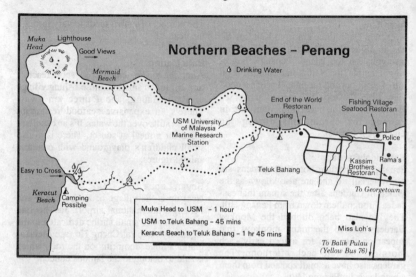

(Map) Northern Beaches – Penang

Muka Head — Lighthouse — Good Views — Mermaid Beach — Easy to Cross — Keracut Beach — Camping Possible — USM University of Malaysia Marine Research Station — Drinking Water — End of the World Restoran — Camping — Fishing Village Seafood Restoran — Police — Kassim Brothers Restoran — Rama's — Teluk Bahang — To Georgetown — Miss Loh's — To Balik Pulau (Yellow Bus 76)

Muka Head to USM – 1 hour
USM to Teluk Bahang – 45 mins
Keracut Beach to Teluk Bahang – 1 hr 45 mins

and coconut groves that look like they've been swept.

Sungai Pinang & Pantai Acheh

Next is Sungai Pinang, a busy Chinese village built along a stagnant river – the antithesis of the preceding Malay village, but worth a peek nonetheless. Further on another road turns off to Pantai Acheh, another small fishing village with very little of interest.

Titi Kerawang

From the turn-off to Pantai Acheh the road starts to climb and twist, offering glimpses of the coast and the sea far below. The jungle becomes denser and before long you reach Titi Kerawang, a waterfall just off the road with a natural swimming pool. During durian season, there are stalls set up along the road selling the spiky orbs and you can also see the trees themselves, with durians suspended over waiting nets.

Forest Recreation Park

After the descent down towards the north coast you come to the Forest Recreation Park not far from Teluk Bahang. It's a nice spot

and there are freshwater pools and trails covering 100 hectares.

Butterfly Farm

A short distance closer to the coast is the Butterfly Farm. It has 3000 live butterflies representing over 50 species, and also has a mounted insect display, and a huge (and expensive) souvenir shop. It's open from 9 am to 5 pm daily, 6 pm on weekends; admission is M$3.

Teluk Bahang

Finally you get back to the coast at Teluk Bahang, the village which marks the western end of the northern beach strip. There is little development here and it's still principally a small fishing village.

There are a couple of batik factories where you're welcome to drop in and see the processes involved in making batik. They also have showrooms where you can buy a wide variety of batik articles – the prices marked are on the high side but you may be able to bargain.

From Teluk Bahang you can also trek down the beach to Muka Head, the isolated rocky promontory marked by a lighthouse at

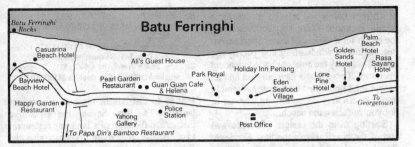

Batu Ferringhi

the extreme north-western corner of the island. South of Muka Head is Keracut Beach, also called Monkey Beach, where there are shelters, pit toilets, and lots of bird and monkey life – camping is possible. Refer to the map for hiking routes.

Places to Stay Take the beachward road from the roundabout, follow it round to just before the Balai Polis and on the right at No 365, Mk 2, is *Rama's* (tel 04-811179) with beds for M$5, or single/double rooms for M$12 with discounts for longer stays. It's run by a Hindu family and is well kept.

Miss Loh has a guest house off the main road towards the butterfly farm. She can be contacted at the shop at 59 Kwong Tuck Hing. There's a sign saying 'Guesthouse Information'. Dorm beds are M$5, doubles are M$10 and M$12.

Places to Eat Food in the shopping area of Teluk Bahang is good and you can get excellent murtabaks at the *Kassim Brothers Restoran* at 48 Main Rd. They also do many other dishes, including banana pancakes (actually banana murtabaks), steamed crab, south Indian dishes like dosai, and milk shakes.

The *End of the World* restaurant at the other end of the village has no menu but serves excellent fresh seafood dishes.

Batu Ferringhi
A little further along the coast Batu Ferringhi (Foreigner's Rock) is the resort strip with a number of large hotels. The beach itself is

somewhat of a disappointment compared to other beaches in Malaysia and the water is not of the tropically clear variety you might expect. At the western end, just past the Bayview Hotel, is the most popular swimming area but the litter on and behind the beach here is a disgrace. There are better swimming beaches a few km further on towards Teluk Bahang.

As this is the resort hotel strip, the main road is lined with expensive tourist-oriented shops, restaurants and car and motorcycle rental places. There are also plenty of moneychangers to welcome you.

Places to Stay – bottom end Few travellers seem to stay out at Batu Ferringhi these days, and so only two places in this range seem to be taking travellers on a regular basis; *Ali's Guest House* (tel 04-811316), right on the beach, and the *Beng Keat Guest House* (tel 04-811987).

Ali's is the better, with rooms from M$15, clean bathrooms, a restaurant and a garden in front. The Beng Keat is behind the Batik Fashion House on the main road, and has small rooms with a double bed for M$12, or much better double rooms with attached bath for M$20.

Places to Stay – top end Batu Ferringhi's 'international standard' hotels, all right on the beach, are strung out along more than a km of coastline. Although Batu Ferringhi is far from the best beach in Malaysia these beachfront hotels are relaxed places for a family vacation. There are facilities along the beach for a variety of water sport activities, including windsurfing and paraflying, offered either by the hotels or by independent operators. These hotels have air-con and all except the Lone Pine Hotel have swimming pools. Prices vary depending on whether or not you're facing the beach.

Starting from the eastern (Georgetown) end of the beach there's the new *Ferringhi Beach Hotel* which has perhaps the best sea view of all the Batu Ferringhi biggies – it's right on a jutting point just before Batu Ferringhi proper.

Next comes *Rasa Sayang Hotel* – the largest and most expensive of them all. Its design is an exotic interpretation of traditional Malay styles and it's the one place at Batu Ferringhi with real local character.

Right beside it is the smaller, older and quite reasonably priced *Palm Beach Hotel*. The large and new *Golden Sands Hotel* is next to that and next again is the older and much lower-key *Lone Pine Hotel*. This is the cheapest of these hotels. The Palm Beach, Rasa Sayang, and Golden Sands are all under the same management and if you stay at one you can use the facilities of all three.

There's quite a gap before the *Holiday Inn Penang*, another gap before the *Casuarina Beach Hotel* (both newer places), and finally there's the newly renovated and extended *Bayview Beach Hotel* at the far end of the beach. The beach slopes into the water a little more gradually there, so the swimming is better at this end.

Ferringhi Beach Hotel (tel 04-805999), 136 rooms, singles M$170, doubles M$200

Rasa Sayang Hotel (tel 04-811811), 320 rooms, singles M$130 to M$170, doubles M$155 to M$200

Palm Beach Hotel (tel 04-811621), 145 rooms, singles M$90 to M$110, doubles M$100 to M$140

Golden Sands Hotel (tel 04-811911), 310 rooms, singles from M$190, doubles from M$220

Lone Pine Hotel (tel 04-811511), 54 rooms, singles M$60 to M$70, doubles M$75 to M$80

Holiday Inn Penang (tel 04-811601), 159 rooms, singles from M$150 to M$260, doubles M$170 to M$260

Casuarina Beach Hotel (tel 04-811711), 175 rooms, singles from M$150, doubles from M$200

Bayview Beach Hotel (tel 04-811311), 74 rooms, singles M$80 to M$90, doubles M$90 to M$170

Places to Eat All the big hotels have restaurants. The Rasa Sayang has a positive plethora of them, from a Japanese restaurant to a 'British grill room'. There's also the *Eden Seafood Village* on the main road, which has typical Chinese food with the accent on seafood, and night-time entertainment.

Further along the road in the main group of shops is a couple of cheap restaurants – the *Helena* and the *Guan Guan Cafe*. You can get a good meal at either of these places for just a couple of dollars.

Also here is the more upmarket *Pearl Garden Restaurant* serving Chinese food.

A short distance towards Teluk Bahang brings you to the *Happy Garden Restaurant*, a pleasant outdoor place serving Western and Chinese meals. Alongside the Happy Garden there's a side road which leads to *Papa Din's Bamboo Restaurant* which is run by an interesting and friendly old gentleman and has excellent, economically priced Malaysian food.

Tanjung Bungah

When heading west from Georgetown, Tanjung Bungah (Cape of Flowers) is the first real beach, but it's not attractive for swimming.

Places to Stay & Eat There are a number of small Chinese hotels and restaurants along the coast from Georgetown. At the Georgetown end of the beach there is the *Orchid Hotel* (tel 04-891111) which has 323 rooms. Singles cost from M$125 to M$175, and doubles from M$170 to M$300 (peak season rates).

The *Motel Sri Pantai* (tel 04-895556) has 21 rooms ranging from M$60 to M$80.

Places to Eat On the hillside above the road

is the *Sri Batik* restaurant which serves Malay food and has good views out over the water, or on the main road there's the *Hollywood* with a variety of dishes including European and Chinese.

GETTING THERE & AWAY

Air
Airline offices in Penang include:

Cathay Pacific
    28 Jalan Penang
MAS
    Kompleks Tun Abdul Razak, Jalan Penang (tel 04-620011)
Singapore Airlines
    Wisma Penang Gardens, Jalan Sultan Ahmad Shah (tel 04-363201)
Thai Airways International
    Wisma Central, 202 Jalan Macalister (tel 04-366233)

The MAS office in the Komtar building is open from 8.30 am to 6 pm Monday to Saturday, 8.30 am to 1 pm on Sunday.

International MAS flies to Medan in Sumatra – a very popular route for travellers. MAS and SIA have regular flights to Singapore. MAS and Thai Airways or Thai International fly between Penang and Hat Yai, Phuket and Bangkok. Other international connections include direct flights to Hong Kong with Cathay Pacific or to Madras in India with MAS. See the introductory Malaysia Getting There & Away chapter for fare details.

Penang is a major centre for cheap airline tickets, but there have also been numerous cut-and-run merchants at work. You'll hear lots of stories of rip-offs. The Western agents operating in Georgetown seem to be as much to blame as anybody else so relying on your own is no insurance. Ask around and be careful although Penang is, overall, a good place for buying tickets.

Fares tend to vary with the airline; the cheapest tickets to London, for example, are with Aeroflot or Bangladesh Biman, but some typical one-way tickets on offer in Penang include:

Destination	Fare
Medan	M$220
Madras	M$680
Hat Yai	M$120
Phuket	M$125
Bangkok	M$312
Hong Kong	M$720
London	M$850 to M$1000 from KL
USA (West)	M$1000 to M$1200 from KL
Australia (East)	M$800 to M$1000 from Singapore

Other quoted fares include: Singapore to Jakarta (M$220 one way), Bangkok-Rangoon-Kathmandu (M$480), KL to Perth (M$700). Interesting multistop or return fares can also be found.

You could take the southern Pacific route Singapore, Jakarta, Noumea, Sydney, Noumea, Auckland, Papeete and Los Angeles for M$1450 to M$1600.

Multistop fares to Europe or through Asia are not so easy, but you could do Penang-Bangkok-Delhi for M$700 with extensions on to Europe.

Domestic Penang is well served on the MAS domestic network:

Destination	Frequency	Fare
JB	thrice weekly	M$148
Kota Bharu	twice daily	M$72
KL	10 daily	M$86
Langkawi	daily	M$42
Singapore	twice daily	M$150

Bus
The bus terminal is beside the ferry terminal in Butterworth. Some travel agents in Georgetown (several are near the Eng Aun and Swiss hotels for example) offer good bargains on bus tickets. The long-distance buses which these places deal with often leave from somewhere in Georgetown rather than Butterworth. As this is more convenient than having to get yourself across to the bus station on the ferry it's worth taking one which does leave from Georgetown.

To Kuala Perlis, for the Langkawi ferry, the bus is M$6 by Ebban Express from the Butterworth terminal. The trip takes around five hours along the very congested main road. There are departures at 6, 8, 11 am and

12 noon only. To Lumut, for Pangkor Island, it is M$8.50.

There are also bus services out of Malaysia to Hat Yai for M$20, Phuket (M$40), Surat Thani (M$40) and Bangkok (M$60).

Typical fares (and departures times from Butterworth) to other places are:

Destination	Frequency	Fare
Alor Setar	every 15 minutes	M$3.20
Kota Bharu	9.30 pm	M$18.00
Kuala Terengganu		M$22.00
Kuantan		M$25.00
Taiping		M$3.00
Ipoh	hourly	M$6.50
Tapah		M$12.00
KL	hourly	M$15.00
Melaka	9 pm	M$26.00
JB	6.30 pm	M$28.00
Singapore	5.30 pm	M$30.00

Train

The railway station is, like the bus and taxi stations, right by the ferry terminal at Butterworth.

The introductory Malaysia Getting There & Away and Getting Around chapters have full details on fares and schedules for the Butterworth, KL, Singapore services and the international train services to Hat Yai and Bangkok in Thailand.

You can make reservations at the station (tel 04-347962) or at the Railway Booking Station (tel 04-610290) at the ferry terminal, Pengkalan Weld, Georgetown. There's a good left-luggage facility at the station; the charge is 50 sen per item per day and it's open 5.30 am to 9 pm daily.

Taxi

Yes, the long-distance taxis also operate from a depot beside the Butterworth ferry terminal. It's also possible to book them at some of the hot spot backpacker hotels or directly with drivers. Typical fares include:

Destination	Fare
Alor Setar	M$7.80
Ipoh	M$13.50
KL	M$30.00

Kota Bharu	M$31.00
Lumut	M$15.25
Taiping	M$7.25
Tapah	M$18.00
JB	M$61.00

There are Thai taxis operating to Hat Yai – a convenient way of getting across the border. They're usually big old Chevies and you'll find them at the popular cheap hotels in Georgetown – the fare is around M$25.

Car

Penang Bridge, completed in 1985, is the longest bridge in Asia and said to be the third longest in the world. If you drive across you'll have to pay a M$7 toll at the toll plaza at Prai on the mainland.

Boat

The ferry service to Medan is operated by the high-speed catamaran *Selesa Express*. It operates on Tuesdays and Fridays, leaving Penang at 8 am and on the return trip leaving Medan at 1.30 pm. The fare is M$100 one way (M$180 return) in 1st class, M$90 (M$160) in economy class.

The other five days a week it operates to Langkawi, leaving Penang at 9 am and on the return trip leaving Langkawi at 6 pm. The fare is M$40 one way (M$70 return) in 1st class, M$35 (M$60) in economy class. The operator is Kuala Perlis-Langkawi Ferry Service (tel 04-625630) and there's a booking office almost beside the tourist office across from Fort Cornwallis.

There are a number of yachts operating between Penang and Phuket. Typical trips sail Penang, Langkawi, Ko Phi Phi, Krabi and Phuket taking four or five days at US$180 per person.

After five years out of operation the shipping service between Penang and Madras in India finally recommenced in late 1990. It's operated by the 800-passenger MV *Vignesswara*.

GETTING AROUND
To/From the Airport

Penang's Bayan Lepas Airport with its Minangkabau-style terminal is 18 km south of Georgetown. A coupon system operates for taxis from the airport. The fare to Georgetown is M$15, or M$18 for an air-con taxi.

You can get a yellow bus No 83 to the airport from Pengkalan Weld for M$1.25 – they operate on this route from 6 am to 10 pm. Taxis take about 30 minutes from the centre of town, the bus an hour.

Around the Island

Getting around the island by road is easiest with your own transport, particularly since the road does not actually run along the coast except on the northern side and you have to leave the main road to get out to the small fishing villages and isolated beaches.

For around M$3 to M$4, depending on where and when you stop, you can make the circuit by public transport. Start with a yellow bus No 66 and hop off at the snake temple. Bus No 83 will take you all the way to Balik Pulau from where you have to change to another yellow bus, a No 76 for Teluk Bahang.

There are only half a dozen of these each day and the last one leaves around mid-afternoon so it's wise to leave Georgetown early and check the departure times when you reach Balik Pulau. At Teluk Bahang you're on the northern beach strip and you simply take a blue Hin bus No 93 to Georgetown.

Bus There are three main bus departure points in Georgetown and five types of buses. The city buses (MPPP Buses) all depart from the terminal at Lebuh Victoria which is directly in front of the ferry terminal. Fares range from 25 sen to 55 sen and the main routes are:

Destination	Frequency	Fare
Ayer Itam	every five minutes	55 sen
Bagan Jermal	every 10 minutes	45 sen
Jelutong	every five minutes	45 sen
Jalan Yeap Chor Ee via Jalan Perak	every 10 minutes	55 sen
Green Lane via Dhoby Ghaut	every one hour & five minutes	55 sen
Green Lane via Jalan Patani	every 16 minutes	55 sen
Botanical Gardens	every 30 minutes	45 sen
Penang Hill Railway from Ayer Itam	every 20 minutes	30 sen
Green Lane via Caunter Hall Rd	every 16 minutes	55 sen
Kampung Melayu	every 16 minutes	55 sen
Bukit Glogor	every one hour & 10 minutes	55 sen
Ayer Itam from Jelutong	every 20 minutes	45 sen
Bagan Jermal from Jelutong	every 30 minutes	55 sen

The other main stand is at Pengkalan Weld where you can take green, blue or yellow buses. These are the buses to take if you want to do a circuit of the island or get out to Batu Ferringhi and the other northern beaches. Take a blue Hin bus No 93 to Batu Ferringhi or Teluk Bahang.

The green buses run to Ayer Itam like the MPPP bus No 1. Blue buses run to the northern beaches. Yellow buses go to the south and west of the island including the aquarium, snake temple, airport and right round to Teluk Bahang.

Bicycle Trishaw

Taxi Penang's taxis are all metered but getting the drivers to use the meters is virtually impossible, so it's a matter of negotiating the fare before you set off. Some sample fares from Georgetown are Batu Ferringhi M$15, Botanical Gardens M$10, Penang Hill/Kek Lok Si M$10, Snake Temple M$15, and the airport M$15.

Car Rental The addresses of some car rental companies include:

Avis
    E&O Hotel, 10 Lebuh Farquhar (tel 04-631685)
Budget
    Town House Hotel, 70 Jalan Penang (tel 04-631240)
Hertz
    38 Lebuh Farquhar (tel 04-635914)
National
    17 Lebuh Leith (tel 04-629404)
Thrifty
    Ming Court Inn, 202A Jalan Macalister (tel 04-363688)

Trishaw Bicycle rickshaws are ideal on Georgetown's relatively uncrowded streets and cost around M$1 per km, but as with the taxis, agree on the fare before departure.

If you come across from Butterworth on the ferry, grab a trishaw to the Lebuh Chulia cheap hotels area for M$3 although you can walk there in five or 10 minutes. The riders will know plenty of other hotels if your selected one is full. For touring, the rate is around M$10 an hour.

Bicycle & Motorcycle If you want to pedal yourself you can hire bicycles from various places. The Eng Aun Hotel in Georgetown has them for M$5 per day or there are various places at Batu Ferringhi where you can hire them at more expensive rates.

Motorcycles can also be hired for around M$25 per day. Most of the places renting motorcycles are in Batu Ferringhi, but on Lebuh Chulia Yasin, a bookstore/money-changer next to the Eng Thai Cafe has a few well-maintained 70 to 125cc bikes for rent, as well as bicycles.

Boat There's a 24-hour ferry service between Georgetown and Butterworth on the mainland. Passenger ferries and ferries for cars and trucks operate from adjacent terminals. Ferries operate every 20 minutes from 6 am to midnight and then every hour after midnight. The vehicular ferries operate only slightly less frequently, but do not operate at all between 10 pm (10.20 pm from Penang) and 6.30 am, except on Saturdays, Sundays and public holidays when they continue to 1.30 am.

Fares are only charged from Butterworth to Penang; the other direction is free. The adult fare is 40 sen, and cars with driver cost from M$4 to M$6 depending on the engine capacity.

North of Penang

On the north-western corner of the peninsula the states of Kedah and Perlis are the rice bowls of Malaysia. A green sea of rice paddies stretches away from the road for much of the distance through the state. Perlis is also the smallest state in Malaysia and both states are important gateways into Thailand.

For travellers the most important towns in the state are likely to be the large town of Alor Setar and the small fishing ports of Kuala Perlis and Kuala Kedah, from where ferries operate to Langkawi.

GUNUNG JERAI

At 1206 metres, Kedah Peak or Gunung Jerai is the highest peak in north-west Peninsular Malaysia. It's between the main road and the coast west of Gurun, 60 km north of Butterworth, and is topped by a 6th-century Hindu shrine.

The area around the Bujang River which flows off the mountain is the location of important archaeological sites where statues, inscriptions and ancient tombs left by a Pallava cultural outpost of south India have been discovered.

There is a museum at Bukit Batu Pahat where the Candi Bukit Batu Pahat Temple has been reconstructed. Other finds are displayed in the Alor Setar State Museum.

ALOR SETAR

The capital of Kedah state is on the mainland north of Penang on the main road to the Thai border and it's also the turnoff point for Kuala Perlis, from where ferries run to Langkawi Island. Few people stay very long in Alor Setar although it does have a few places of interest.

The Padang

The large open town square has a number of interesting buildings around its perimeter. The Balai Besar or 'Big Hall' was built in 1898 and is still used by the Sultan of Kedah for ceremonial functions. On the other side of the square is the Zahir Mosque; it's the state mosque and one of the largest in Malaysia, and was completed in 1912.

The Balai Nobat, an octagonal building topped by an onion-shaped dome, houses the nobat, or royal orchestra. A nobat is principally composed of percussion instruments and the drums in this orchestra are said to have been a gift from the Sultan of Melaka in the 15th century.

On the main road north is the State Museum, built in a style similar to that of the Balai Besar. The museum has a good collection of early Chinese porcelain and artefacts from the archaeological excavations made at the Bujang Valley. Next to the museum is the royal boathouse where royal barges and boats are housed.

Places to Stay

There are a number of cheap hotels around the bus and taxi stations in the centre of town.

The *Station Hotel* (tel 04-723855) at 74 Jalan Langgar is one of the cheapest in town with rooms from M$14. The *Regent Hotel* (tel 04-721291) at 1536 Jalan Sultan

Badlishah is a step up the scale with air-con rooms for M$26. The *Hotel Mahawangsa* (tel 04-721835) at 449 Jalan Raja, diagonally opposite the GPO, has similar rooms at similar rates, though the Regent is slightly better value. The *Hotel Samilla* (tel 04-722344) at 27 Jalan Kanchut is one of Alor Setar's better hotels and has singles/doubles for M$58/66. Right at the top there's the *Kedah Merlin Inn* (tel 04-735917) at 134 Jalan Sultan Badlishah with singles/doubles from M$105.

Places to Eat

Alor Setar has some surprisingly good and economical restaurants. On Jalan Tunku Ibrahim is the *Restoran Empire*. It's a hawkers' centre in a restored wet market, where there's a good selection of fruit juices, chicken rice, rojak (similar to gado-gado), appam balik, curry sambal rice, and a local speciality called mee jawa, spicy noodles in a sauce of bean curd, potatoes, squid, peanuts, bean sprouts and appam chips – very tasty.

On Jalan Sultan Badlishah south of the Merlin is a popular Thai Muslim place, *Hajjah Restoran*.

Along Jalan Langgar near the local bus terminal are several coffee shops serving inexpensive Malay and Chinese food.

Getting There & Away

Alor Setar is 91 km north of Butterworth and is served by MAS. The road between Butterworth and Alor Setar carries a surprising amount of traffic. By bus it's M$3.20 to Butterworth, M$12 to Ipoh, M$18 to KL and M$33 to Singapore. A taxi costs M$3 per person to Kuala Perlis, M$7.80 to Butterworth.

There are also buses to Hat Yai in Thailand for M$10 – go to the Tunjang Ekspres office at the bus station. Although you can easily get to Changlun, the Malay border post for Thailand, by bus or taxi, it is then very difficult to cross the long strip of neutral territory to Sadao, the Thai border post, as there is no regular transport that just goes across the border.

If, however, you go to Padang Besar,

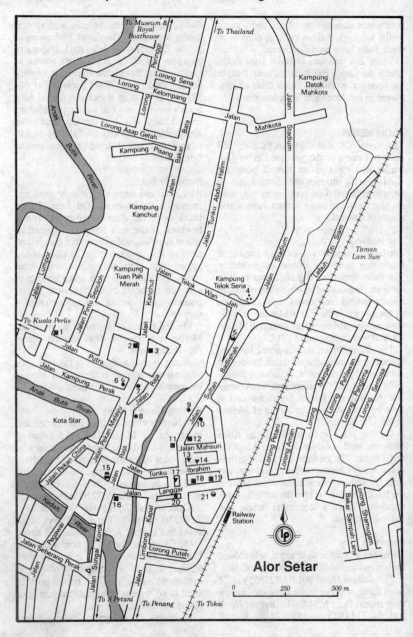

To Museum & Royal Boathouse

To Thailand

Anak Butik River

Lorong Peninggi

Lorong Sena

Lorong Kelompang

Lorong Bata

Jalan Mahkota

Kampung Datok Mahkota

Stadium

Lorong Asap Getah

Kampung Pisang

Jalan Bakar

Kampung Kanchut

Jalan Tunku Abdul Halim

Taman Lam Sun

Lebuh Titi Siam

Kampung Tuan Pah Merah

Jalan Kanchut

Jalan Telok Wan

Kampung Telok Sena

Jalan Stadium

Jalan Telok Jah

To Kuala Perlis

Jalan Lumpur

Jalan Pintu Sepuloh

Jalan Raja

Jalan Putra

Jalan Kampung Perak

Anak Butik River

Kota Star

Jalan Pekan Melayu

Jalan Sultan Badlishah

Merpati

Lorong Panglima

Lorong Pahlawan

Lorong Sentosa

Jalan Pekan China

Jalan Raja

Jalan Tunku Ibrahim

Jalan Mahsuri

Lorong Petani

Lorong Aman

Kedah River

Jalan Langgar

Jalan Kapal

Lorong Shamugam

L. Bakar Sampah Lana

Railway Station

Jalan Pegawai

Jalan Sungai Korok

Limbing

Lorong Puteh

Jalan Seberang Perak

Alor Setar

0   250   500 m

To S Petani

To Penang

To Tokai

1
2 3
5
4
6
7
8
9
10
11 12
13 14
15
16
17
18 19
20
21

■ PLACES TO STAY

1	Hotel Miramar
2	Federal Hotel
3	Hotel Samilla
11	Kedah Merlin Inn
12	Regent Hotel
16	Hotel Mahawangsa
18	Yuan Fang Hotel
19	Kuan Siang Hotel

▼ PLACES TO EAT

13	Rose Restoran
14	Hajjah Restoran
17	Restoran Empire

OTHER

4	Thai Temple
5	Express Bus Station
6	Zahir Mosque
7	Balai Nobat
8	Balai Besar
9	National Bank
10	MAS Office
15	GPO
20	Taxis
21	Local Buses

where the railway line crosses the border, you can simply walk across and take a bus from there into Hat Yai. Padang Besar can be reached by road, although the main road to Thailand crosses the border at Changlunadao.

This is a prime smuggling route with both Malaysians and Thais. Malaysia's green-uniformed Anti-Smuggling Unit occasionally makes an arrest, but the overall trade is hardly affected. If the smuggling were somehow halted, Pekan Siam and Padang Besar would become ghost towns virtually overnight.

There is no through train from Alor Setar to Hat Yai, except for the International Express from Singapore, which doesn't take passengers at Alor Setar.

The port of Kuala Kedah is just 12 km away on the coast, and from here ferries run

to Langkawi; see the Langkawi section for details.

KANGAR

Kangar, 56 km north-west of Alor Setar, is the main settlement in the state of Perlis. It's a low-lying town surrounded by rice paddies.

North of Kangar is Padang Besar, a border town to Thailand. It's a popular place to visit because of the duty-free market that operates there, in the neutral territory between the two countries.

Arau, near Kangar, is the royal capital of Perlis and has an istana and a royal mosque. Kaki Bukit in the extreme north-west corner of the state has some interesting limestone caverns from which tin is mined.

Places to Stay

Kangar has a number of hotels including the *Hotel Malaysia* (tel 04-761366) at 65 Jalan Jubli Perak where rooms begin at M$20. The more expensive *Federal Hotel* (tel 04-766288) at 104 Jalan Kangar has air-con rooms from M$35, as well as cheaper fan-cooled rooms.

The cheapest in town is the *Hotel Ban Cheong* (tel 04-761184) at Jalan Kangar and rooms start as low as M$12.

Top of the pile is the *Sri Perlis Inn* (tel 04-767266) also on Jalan Kangar where air-con rooms with bath cost from M$40 to M$90.

KUALA PERLIS

This small port town in the extreme north-west of the peninsula is visited mainly as the departure point for Langkawi. You can also use Kuala Perlis as an unusual gateway into Thailand.

The main part of Kuala Perlis is just a couple of streets with plenty of restaurants and shops, one hotel and no banks. Kangar is only 10 km away if you need more facilities.

If you've got some time to kill waiting for a boat there's plenty to see. Beside the dock there's an ice works and fish are packed into ice-filled crates on the quay. You can cross the river by a footbridge to the other part of town where the houses and mosques are built on stilts over the water around the mangrove swamps.

Places to Stay
Kuala Perlis' one and only hotel is the *Soon Hin* opposite the taxi stand where a room will cost you M$10.

Getting There & Away
There are direct buses from Butterworth at 6, 8, 11 am and 12 noon for M$6. They connect, more or less, with ferry departures. A taxi between Butterworth and Kuala Perlis costs M$10, although departures are infrequent.

From Alor Setar there are buses at regular intervals for M$2.60 or taxis at M$3 per person (M$12 for an entire taxi). Buses also depart from Kuala Perlis to Padang Besar (for Thailand) for M$1.90 (taxi M$3.30) and to KL for M$20. The short taxi ride into Kangar costs 60 sen.

LANGKAWI
The 99 islands of the Langkawi group are 30 km off the coast from Kuala Perlis, at the northern end of Peninsular Malaysia. They're accessible by boat from Kuala Perlis, Kuala Kedah and Georgetown (Penang); or by air from Penang, 112 km south, and KL.

The islands, strategically situated where the Indian Ocean narrows down into the Straits of Melaka, were once a haven for pirates and could easily have become the site for the first British foothold in Malaya instead of Penang. Earlier they were charted by Admiral Cheng Ho on his visit to Melaka in 1405.

Today they're a quiet and relatively unspoiled place with a population of around 30,000. In the last few years Langkawi has seen a lot of tourist development as it has become the government's main target for tourist promotion. This doesn't mean that the island has been ruined, however. Fortunately

the development has been coordinated so that any construction work is low-key and in keeping with the surroundings. What it does mean is that you now have a choice of everything from a basic locally run beach hut to a megabuck resort with every conceivable facility, and there's a casino under construction. The infrastructure has also been improved with an immaculate and well-signposted bitumen road right around the island, a new airport and increased ferry services. Although during school holidays and at the peak time of November to February Langkawi gets very crowded, at other times of the year supply far outstrips demand and the prices come down considerably.

Although quite a pleasant place to visit, Langkawi doesn't have the atmosphere (or the beaches) of the islands on the east coast, or even Pangkor further south on the west coast, perhaps because it is relatively isolated.

Orientation
Kuah, in the south-west corner of the island and with a population of about 2000, is the main town and the arrival point for the ferries from Kuala Perlis and Kuala Kedah. There are a few places to stay but the beaches are elsewhere on the island.

Pantai Cenang and Pantai Kok are on the south-western coast of the island and are the best places to stay. Pantai Cenang is the more developed and popular of the two, although the water here is constantly fairly murky and not that great for swimming. The beach at Pantai Kok is much better but there are fewer facilities there.

Along the north coast of the island the only accommodation is in resorts at Datai in the west and Pantai Rhu in the east. The latter probably has the best beach on the island. In between the two is the island's main jetty at Teluk Ewa, and it's here that the ferry from Penang berths. It is also the site of a huge and ugly concrete factory so if you are arriving from Penang by boat it's not a terribly encouraging first impression.

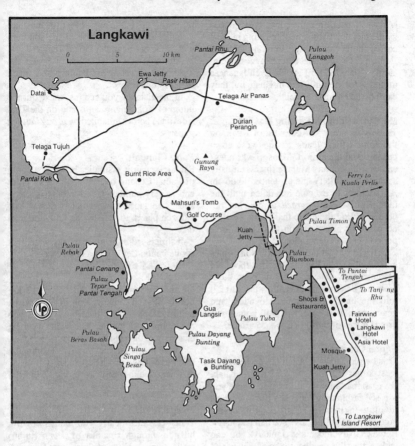

Information

The TDC has a tourist office (tel 04-789789) in the customs building at the main wharf in Kuah. It is open daily from 9 am to 6 pm.

Langkawi is part of Kedah state and so banks and government offices are closed on Fridays. Saturdays are half-days and Sundays are normal business days.

For international reverse charge (collect) calls to Australia, UK, Japan and the USA there's a phone in the Langkawi Island Resort which gets you through direct to the operator in your home country.

Kuah

The island's main town is a one-street affair along the waterfront. The bay is dotted with sunken fishing boats – the remains of confiscated Thai poachers or unlicensed local boats, which have sunk while the government slowly got around to prosecuting the fishing community.

Kuah's only 'sight' is the picturesque waterside mosque with its golden dome and Moorish arches and minarets rising above the palm trees.

There are also many small duty-free shops in Kuah. Cigarettes and liquor, including

Malaysian beer, are quite cheap as evidenced by the fact that fishing people sitting in local coffee shops can be seen smoking Dunhill, Benson & Hedges, and Peter Stuyvesant cigarettes – only M$1.50 a pack. Even Japanese motorcycles are duty-free in Kuah, but they can't be taken off the island.

Mahsuri's Tomb & Padang Masirat

These sites are a few km west of Kuah, on the road which leads to the west coast beaches and the airport. Mahsuri was a legendary 10th-century Malay princess unjustly accused of adultery and sentenced to death. All attempts to execute her failed until the indignant Mahsuri *agreed* to die, but not before issuing the curse that 'there shall be no peace or prosperity on this island for a period of seven generations'.

A result of that curse can still sometimes be seen at nearby Padang Masirat, the 'field of burnt rice'. There, villagers once burnt their rice fields rather than allow them to fall into the hands of Siamese invaders and heavy rain, it is said, this still sometimes brings traces of burnt rice to the surface.

Pantai Cenang

This two-km strip of beach lies at the south-west corner of Langkawi, 25 km from Kuah.

A sandbar appears at low tide where you can see fascinating local sea life – conches inching their way along, hermit crabs, urchins, sand dollars, live starfish and more. Between November and January, you can walk across this sandbar to the nearby island of Rebak – but make sure you walk back before the sandbar disappears as you only have about two hours. Another nearby island is Pulau Tepor which can be reached by a hired boat from Cenang Beach.

Pantai Cenang is where most of the local beach chalet development is happening and it seems everyone wants a piece of the action. There are new chalets going up all the way along this beach. Unfortunately, because the blocks of land are long and narrow, the beach frontage is minimal and so most of the chalets only have a view of the chalet in front. During the season it seems all these places fill up, but at any other time most are virtually empty, especially at the southern end of the beach and at Pantai Tengah.

Although it's quite a pretty beach the water is never very clear. Pantai Kok is much better in this respect.

In the distance you can just make out the hump of Koh Adang, an island on the Thai side of the border inhabited by *orang laut* sea gypsies.

Pantai Tengah

Pantai Tengah is a smaller beach just south of Pantai Cenang over a small rocky point and is very similar. Development is going ahead here too so there should be at least half a dozen places to stay by the time you read this.

It suffers from the same murky water that spoils Pantai Cenang to a large extent.

Pantai Kok

On the western part of the island, 12 km north of Pantai Cenang, Kok Beach fronts a beautiful bay surrounded by limestone mountains and jungle. The water is a bit clearer here than at any of the other beaches.

There is one large expensive resort and a number of low-key chalet places.

Telaga Tujuh is only a 2½-km walk from Pantai Kok.

Telaga Tujuh

Water cascades nearly 100 metres down a hillside through a series of seven (tujuh) wells (telaga). You can slide down from one of these shallow pools to another near the top of the falls – the stone channels are very smooth.

To get there you'll have to take a taxi to Pantai Kok and then walk 2½ km, or go by motorcycle, in which case you drive to the end of the road about one km past Pantai Kok, and turn along the gravel road to the right, away from the new resort, owned by the same people who run the Pelangi Resort at Pantai Cenang.

Datai

Datai is some distance off the main road

round the island. It is the site for a new mega-resort complete with casino – it may be finished by now.

Pasir Hitam

A couple of km west of Pantai Rhu, this beach is noted for its black sand although it's not a real black sand beach – simply streaks of black through the sand. It's really a very contrived attraction as the beach is only a couple of metres wide and is at the foot of a five-metre drop, so you can't even walk along it. There are the inevitable souvenir stalls and drink stands.

The waters off Pasir Hitam are dotted with huge boulders.

Pantai Rhu

Just beyond Pantai Hitam there's a roundabout, with a turn-off to the north to Pantai Rhu, while the main road continues on back to Kuah.

Pantai Rhu is one of Langkawi's better beaches. The water is shallow and at low tide you can walk across the sand bank to the neighbouring island, except during monsoon season. The water swirls across the bank as the tide comes in.

Around the promontory, accessible by boat, is the Gua Cherita cave. Along the coast for a couple of km before the beach the tiny fish known as ikan bilis (anchovies) are spread out on mats to dry in the sun.

This is the best isolated beach and the resort here is very pleasant. It's just a pity that someone was allowed to build an ugly condominium right next door.

Telaga Air Panas

These hot springs are towards the north of the island, not far from the turn-off to Pantai Rhu. Like so many places in Malaysia there's an intriguing legend to go with them.

The island's two most powerful families, so the story goes, became involved in a bitter argument over a marriage proposal. A fight broke out and all the kitchen utensils were used as missiles. The gravy (kuah) was spilt at (yes!) Kuah and seeped into the ground at Kisap (seep). A pot landed at Belanga Perak

(broken pot) and finally the saucepan of hot water (air panas) came to land here.

The fathers of these two families got their come-uppance for causing all this mayhem – they are now the island's two major mountain peaks. The hot springs themselves are no tourist attraction – just an ugly little clump of green buildings by the roadside.

Durian Perangin

Fifteen km north of Kuah is the turn-off to this waterfall. There's a small sign by the shop there and a larger sign by a second turn-off a bit further on.

The falls are three km off the road – the first part of the path is passable by motorcycle. The falls are best seen at the end of the monsoon season, late September, early October.

Other Islands

Pulau Dayang Bunting The 'Lake of the Pregnant Maiden', on the island of the same name south of Langkawi itself, is a freshwater lake with good swimming.

A legend states that a childless couple, after 19 years of unsuccessful efforts, had a baby girl after drinking from this lake. Since then it has been a popular pilgrimage centre for those in search of children! Legend also says that the lake is inhabited by a large white crocodile.

Nearby on the same island is Gua Langsir, the 'Cave of the Banshee', which is inhabited by thousands of bats. Marble is quarried on the island and shipped to the mainland for processing. To get to this island you must hire a boat from the Kuah jetty or Pantai Cenang.

Boat trips to Pulau Dayang Bunting usually add in a stop at Pulau Singa Besar, where there is reasonable snorkelling. During the monsoon season, July to mid-September, the seas are usually too rough and unpredictable for boat trips to Dayang Bunting. From Cenang boats can be hired for about M$10 per person, eight to a boat.

Pulau Bumbon Only 10 minutes from the Kuah jetty, this island has five bungalows and some longhouse rooms which you can rent for M$10. There's a pleasant beach nearby and another about 15 minutes' walk over the hill. You should be able to find someone else to shuttle you across for around M$5 to M$8.

Places to Stay – Kuah

A short ride by share-taxi will take you from the pier to any of Kuah's cheaper accommodation, all of which is strung out along the waterfront around the bay. Kuah is practically a one-street town and that street follows the bay all the way.

On past the mosque, about a km from the pier, you'll come to Kuah's first two hotels. The *Asia Hotel* (tel 04-788216) has only air-con rooms with TV, and these cost M$40. A few doors down at the *Langkawi Hotel* (tel 04-788248), rooms start at M$33 for a double with fan, M$40 with air-con TV and bath.

The *Fairwind Hotel* (tel 04-788287) is also here and has doubles with fan for M$22, with air-con for M$30. Right next door is an unofficial hotel, *Langkawi Holidays* which charges M$30/35 for double rooms with air-con and common bath.

Further away from the jetty, about a km past the hospital is the *Malaysia Hotel & Restaurant* (tel 04-788298), a travellers' favourite run by Mr Vellu and his family. Rooms start at M$10 for a small single with common bath and go up to M$30 for a double with air-con. There's an Indian restaurant downstairs, and they also hire taxis, boats, motorcycles and bicycles at lower rates than just about anyone else on the island. At the jetty, look for a taxi with the licence plate KV259 for free transport to the hotel and discounted transport elsewhere.

In the top end bracket is the *Langkawi Island Resort* (tel 04-788209), which you pass just before docking as you arrive at Langkawi. The TDC-operated hotel has all the facilities you'd expect of a resort hotel – swimming pool, health centre, squash courts, disco and restaurant. The room rates are M$143/165 up to M$165/187. The hotel

is closed for two months in the off-season – 15 September to 15 November.

Places to Stay – the beaches

Pantai Cenang There's a whole range of accommodation at Pantai Cenang from basic chalet places to the international standard Pelangi Beach Resort. They are all ranged along the two km of beach here between the turn-off to Kuah at the northern end and Pantai Tengah to the south.

At the budget places you pay around M$20 to M$30 for a chalet with bath attached, or there are a few cheaper ones available with common bath.

The cheapest place is the *Delta Motel* (tel 04-911307) which is the last place before the headland which separates Pantai Cenang from Pantai Tengah. It's one of the older places along here and has A-frame chalets for M$30 with bath, or M$15 without.

Back towards the north is the *Sura* (tel 04-911232) and *Samila*, two basic and cramped places with fairly unattractive chalets for M$25 with bath. Right across the road is the new and racy *Sri Inai* (tel 04-911269) with a restaurant, souvenir shop and cars and motorcycles for hire. The rooms cost M$25.

The *AB Motel* (tel 04-911300) is next and is one of the older established places on Pantai Cenang. It is also about the best value here, with big chalets around a lawn for M$20 to M$30, all with bath, and there's a decent restaurant.

Next door to the AB is the *Sandy Beach Motel* (tel 04-911308), probably the most popular place but one which suffers from inept management, overcrowding and a horrendously smelly drain by the road. The A-frame chalets near the beach are quite good but towards the road they are packed a bit too tightly together. They cost M$25 for a double with fan, M$35 with fan and bath. The ugly block of air-con rooms should also be completed by now.

Right across the road is the *Beach View Motel* which has a view of nothing at all. Small chalets with fan and attached bath go for M$25. There's a small shop here which

Top: Stove front, Kuantan (PT)
Left: Market, Kuala Terengganu (TW)
Right: Rice paddies near Kota Bharu (TW)

Top: Sampan Bar, Teluk Chempedak (PT)
Left: Kota Bharu Market (PT)
Right: Sultan's Palace, Kota Bharu (PT)

sells basic items, and they have motorcycles for rent.

Next door to the Sandy Beach is a mid-range place, the *Semarak Beach Resort* (tel 04-911377) which has pleasant chalets and lawns, and an excellent, if slightly expensive, restaurant. The spacious chalets go for M\$55 with fan and bath, or there are large family chalets for M\$230 with fridge, TV and bathrooms.

After a gap of a couple of hundred metres there's another group of new places, including the very pleasant *Beach Garden & Bistro* (tel 04-911363), run by a German couple. It has a swimming pool and just a dozen rooms which cost M\$150 with air-con and bath. The restaurant here is excellent.

The most northerly place on this beach, and so the first you come to when coming from Kuah or the airport, is the very flash Singapore-owned *Pelangi Beach Resort* (tel 04-911001) with every luxury including island swimming pool, sports facilities, restaurant and even electric buggies to take you to your room! No expense has been spared on this place, and the prices are remarkably reasonable at M\$80/110 up to M\$120/150.

Pantai Tengah There is a lot less development here, and all of it (so far) is very low-key chalet places. Just after the headland which separates the two beaches is a group of three new places – *Green Hill Beach Motel* (tel 04-911282), the *Sugar Sands* (tel 04-911317) and the *Tanjung Malie*. They seem to merge together and there's only one restaurant between the three of them. Until the palm trees grow and give some shade these places will remain fairly stark and hot.

After a gap of undeveloped land (probably built on by now) is a couple more places right at the end of the beach. *Charlie Motel* (tel 04-911200) is right on the beach and has been around for some years. It's also cheap at M\$15 with fan, M\$25 with fan and bath, and there are a couple of two-room bungalows for M\$36, and a restaurant.

Back from the beach a bit is the new *Harmony Chalets* with small chalets for M\$25. As with all places along the beaches

here, prices are definitely negotiable, especially in the off-season.

Pantai Kok There are a few places to choose from here, and they are spread out along about 500 metres of beach. The best place is probably *The Last Resort* (tel 04-740545) run by an expatriate English man and his Malay wife. Although incomplete at the time of writing, they should have 20 chalets by now, some with air-con (M\$50), the others with fan (M\$35), all with bath attached. They also have a restaurant.

The *Country Beach Motel* (tel 04-411447) next door is in a pleasant spot and the front chalets are well located. Overall it's good value at M\$15 for rooms with common bath, M\$20 for double chalets with fan and bath, and M\$60 with bath and air-con. The restaurant here serves good food and they have motorcycles and bikes for rent.

The other places here are not as good. The *Mila Beach Motel* (tel 04-911253) is very exposed as there're no trees. They only have three chalets and these are quite good value at M\$30 with bath. There's also the scruffy *Dayang Beach Resort* (tel 04-788590) and the *Pantai Kok Motel*.

Right at the far end of the beach is the new *Burau Bay Beach Resort*, another expensive place in the mould of the Pelangi.

Pantai Rhu The only place here is the low-key *Mutiara Beach Hotel* (tel 04-788488) with swimming pool and restaurant. Room rates from M\$99 to M\$145.

Places to Eat

Kuah Chinese food is available in the restaurants at the *Asia Hotel* and *Langkawi Hotel*.

There are a number of other Chinese and Indian restaurants and stalls along the road through Kuah. You can buy excellent roti chanai in the various Indian places, also dosai and other south Indian foods in the restaurant in the *Malaysia Hotel* at 66 Pokok Assam. The Chinese restaurant across the road has excellent food. As in so many other Malaysian towns Kuah has a far greater number and variety of eating places than its size would indicate.

There are fruit stalls lining the main road, and the main market has the usual array of fruit and vegies.

Pantai Cenang Many of the hotels at Pantai Cenang have restaurants. The one at the *Sandy Beach* is probably the most popular and indeed the food is quite good, although it does take some time to arrive. The *Semarak* next door serves very good food although it is somewhat pricey. The *AB* serves cheap seafood.

If you feel like a splurge there're a couple of places to try. The *Beach Garden & Bistro* has a restaurant right on the beach and serves excellent Western food at around M$12 to M$15 per dish.

The *Pelangi* resort has a sumptuous dining room with M$30 buffet meals including dances, or there're poolside barbecue buffets for M$28, and breakfast buffet for M$17.

Pantai Kok The *Country Beach* and *The Last Resort* both have restaurants serving seafood and other local dishes.

Getting There & Away
Air MAS have daily flights between Langkawi and KL (M$112), Penang (M$42) and Singapore (M$180). The MAS office (tel 04-788209) is in the Langkawi Island Resort, about a km out of Kuah, past the main jetty.

Taxi Between the jetty and Kuah town itself a share-taxi costs 60 sen.

Boat The ferry service operating between Penang and Langkawi is the high-speed catamaran, *Selesa Express*. It operates on Mondays, Wednesdays, Thursdays, Saturdays and Sundays leaving Penang at 9 am and Langkawi on the return trip at 6 pm. The fare is M$40 one way (M$70 return) in 1st class, M$35 (M$60) in economy class. The

operator is Kuala Perlis-Langkawi Ferry Service (tel 04-625630) and there's a booking office (in Penang) almost beside the tourist office from Port Cornwallis. During the monsoon season (July to September) sailings may be cancelled due to rough weather – August is usually the worst month.

Ferries between Kuala Perlis and Langkawi leave hourly in either direction between 8 am and 6 pm and the trip takes around one hour. Fares depend on demand; if there're plenty of passengers you pay the full fare (M$10 to M$12), but if things are slack they discount to M$5. When leaving Langkawi touts will besiege you at the main jetty, so just take your time and check out which boat is going at what time.

There are also regular ferries between Langkawi and the small port town of Kuala Kedah, not far from Alor Setar. The fare is M$12.

There are a number of yachts operating between Penang and Phuket in Thailand which stop at Langkawi (see Getting There & Away in the Penang section).

There are rumours of various new services starting up, including a daily service to Penang, and a resumption of the service to Satun in Thailand – check with the tourist office for the latest developments.

Getting Around
To/From the Airport The only means of transport to or from the airport is by taxi. The fares are fixed (and high) and you buy a coupon at the desk before leaving the airport terminal. The charges are M$12 to Pantai Kok, Teluk Ewa, Pantai Rhu or the Langkawi Island Resort, M$10 to Pantai Cenang or Kuah.

Bus You've got to get out and about on Langkawi since there's little of interest in Kuah itself. The bus station is opposite the hospital, in the centre of town. The problem with the buses is that services are not that frequent and are limited in scope – the only places served from Kuah are Pantai Cenang and Tanjung Ewa.

To both places there are 13 buses daily

from 6.20 am to 6.15 pm. On Fridays there are only six buses to each place.

Motorcycle The easiest way to get around is to hire a motorcycle (usually Honda 70 step-thrus) for the day. You can do a very leisurely circuit of the island (70 km) in a day and as the roads are excellent and virtually devoid of other traffic, it's very pleasant and easy riding even for the inexperienced.

There are many places in Pantai Cenang which rent motorcycles, and none seem too fussed about whether you have a licence or not. There are also places in Kuah and Pantai Kok where it's possible to rent them. The charge is usually M$20 to M$30 per day plus fuel.

Bicycle Most of the places with motorcycles also have bikes for rent. Mountain bikes cost M$12 per day.

Peninsular Malaysia – East Coast

Whereas the western side of the peninsula is the more crowded, enterprising, strongly Chinese-influenced part of the country, the east coast is open, relaxed and very Malay in character. It's a long series of gleaming beaches, backed by dense jungle and interspersed with colourful and easygoing fishing villages.

Along this coast you also have the opportunity to see some traditional Malay handicrafts and culture or even stay in a small kampung and watch the scarcely changing rituals of village life.

To some extent, the east coast's slower development is a result of its relative isolation. There were few roads along the coast until WW II and it was well into the '70s before the last of the ferries across the many east coast rivers was replaced by a bridge. Today you can follow an excellent 730-km road all the way from Johore Bahru (JB), across the causeway from Singapore in the south, to Kota Bharu, close to the Thai border in the north.

The east-west road, running across the top of the peninsula, has also brought about an increase of visitors to the east coast. With the completion of the central highway, which runs parallel to the old railway line through the dense jungle, it's possible to get to Kota Bharu from Kuala Lipis in five or six hours – the jungle train takes a lot longer but, with all the locals and their produce on board, it's a more interesting and colourful trip. There is some spectacular scenery along this route.

The east coast is affected by the monsoon – November to January (particularly December) – and the heavy rainfall sometimes floods rivers and makes road travel a difficult proposition. From May to the end of August is the main tourist season, when accommodation can get tight in the more popular places such as Tioman Island, but visitor numbers are relatively low compared to other parts of South-East Asia.

Remember that the east coast is predominantly Malay and Muslim, therefore, Friday will be the day of rest. Solo women travellers should exercise a little caution. Dressing conservatively will help to avoid unwanted attention from the 'hello, my darling' brigades, and topless bathing is a no-no.

Johore Bahru to Kuantan

KOTA TINGGI

The small town of Kota Tinggi is 42 km from JB on the road to Mersing. The town itself is of little interest but the waterfalls at Lumbong, 15 km north-west of the town, are a very popular weekend retreat.

The falls, at the base of 624-metre-high Gunung Muntahak, leap down 36 metres and then flow through a series of pools which are ideal for a cooling dip. The smaller pools are shallow enough for safe use by children. Entry to the falls is M$1.

A couple of km from Kota Tinggi town is Kampung Kelantan, where the sultans of Johore have their mausoleums.

Places to Stay & Eat

At the falls you can stay at the *Waterfall Chalet* (tel 07-241957) where rooms cost from M$30 to M$45 per night, complete with cooking facilities and fridges. Weekend bookings are heavy. There is a restaurant on the hillside facing the falls, and also a camping area.

If you're desperate for somewhere cheaper to stay, you could try the basic, noisy *Hotel Koko*, which has rooms from M$11. Similar hotels include the *Hotel Kolee* and *Hotel Kota*. The *Hotel Bunga Raya*, opposite the bus station, is the best of the cheap hotels and a double with bath costs M$21.

Getting There & Away

Bus Regular buses (No 41, M$2) and taxis (M$3) go from JB to Kota Tinggi. From Kota Tinggi to the waterfalls take bus No 43 (80 sen).

JOHORE LAMA

Following the fall of Melaka to the Portuguese the Malay kingdom was transferred to Johore Lama, about 30 km down the Johore River from Kota Tinggi. The town was built as a fortified capital between 1547 and 1587 but later abandoned as JB rose in prominence. There were a number of skirmishes between Malay and Portuguese fleets along the Johore River and on two occasions the town was sacked and burnt.

Today the old fort of Kota Batu, overlooking the river, has been restored but getting to Johore Lama entails arranging a boat for the downriver trip.

JASON'S BAY (Teluk Mahkota)

A turn-off 13 km north of Kota Tinggi leads down 24 km of rather rough road to the sheltered waters of Jason's Bay. There are 10 km of sandy beach but few facilities at this relatively isolated spot.

DESARU

On a 20-km stretch of beach at Tanjung Penawar, 88 km north-east of JB and also reached via Kota Tinggi, this beach resort area is a popular weekend escape for Singaporeans. The beach is quite good but it's not particularly interesting for international visitors to Malaysia.

Places to Stay & Eat

Accommodation is mostly top-end resorts, but there is a camping site where you can stay for M$5 per person in tents, or M$26 in chalets. The only problem is that the only place to eat is at the big hotels.

There are three large resorts right on the beach. The *Desaru Golf Hotel* (tel 07-821101), has 100 rooms priced between M$115 and M$280; the *Desaru View Hotel* (tel 07-821221), has 134 rooms from M$190 to M$750; and the *Desaru Holiday Resort* (tel 07-821240) has chalets from M$80 to M$200.

Getting There & Away

Buses (M$3.20) and taxis operate from Kota Tinggi. A popular way for Singaporeans to reach Desaru is to take the ferry to Penengerang from Changi Point for S$4, and from there a taxi to Desaru costs M$30.

MERSING

Mersing is a small fishing village on the east coast of Peninsular Malaysia. It's the departure point for the boats which travel between the mainland and the beautiful islands lying just off the coast in the South China Sea. The river bustles with fishing boats and there's plenty to see. Mersing has an impressive-looking mosque on a hill above the town and some good beaches such as Sri Pantai and Sekakap – six and 13 km south; and Ayer Papan and Panyabong – 10 and 50 km to the north.

As you enter town and cross over the bridge to the roundabout, Jalan Abu Bakar is the main street leading to the boat dock. Jalan Ismail also meets the roundabout and runs roughly parallel to Jalan Abu Bakar. Travellers' cheques can be changed at the Bank Bumiputra Malaysia Berhad, on Jalan Ismail, or at the licensed moneychanger in the goldsmith shop on Jalan Abu Bakar.

Places to Stay

Sheikh Tourist Agency (tel 07-793767), 1B Jalan Abu Bakar, is the travellers' place with dorm beds for M$5, and the travel agency downstairs provides good information. It's opposite the post office a few hundred metres before the boat dock.

The *Traveller's Hotel*, at the far end of Jalan Ismail, is the cheapest and most basic hotel in town with rooms for M$8 if you bargain. Better value is the *East Coast Hotel* (tel 07-791337), at 43A Jalan Abu Bakar, which has clean, large rooms from M$10. Next door at 44A is the *Syuan Koong Hotel* (tel 07-791498) with rooms from M$12.

The *Mandarin Hotel*, opposite the local bus and taxi station, is popular with travellers and the Tioman boat touts will take you there. The best thing about this place is the friendly owner and his sharp sense of humour, but unfortunately his rooms aren't as sparkling as his wit. Basic rooms start at M$12, most cost M$15 to M$20.

Much better is the popular *Hotel Embassy* (tel 07-791301), on Jalan Ismail near the roundabout, where clean comfortable rooms with attached bath and fan cost M$15 to M$25.

Three hotels have air-con rooms with attached bath, but the standards are no better than the Embassy. The *Cathay Hotel*, in a small street off Jalan Ismail, has rooms from M$21, and the *Golden City* on Jalan Abu Bakar charges around M$25. The *Mersing Hotel* on Jalan Dato Mohammed Ali has carpeted rooms and occasional hot water for M$30.

The *Mersing Rest House* (tel 07-791101), 490 Jalan Ismail, is a fair hike from town. Rooms cost M$35, but are often fully booked.

The top hotel is the *Mersing Merlin Inn* (tel 07-791312), two km from town on the Endau Rd. It's not exactly international standard, but is fully air-conditioned and has a swimming pool. Singles/doubles are M$90/100.

Places to Eat

For breakfast, Chinese restaurants do the usual toast, coffee and eggs or the *E&W Bakery* on Jalan Ismail is OK, but for a better selection of fresh cakes and bread, try the *Sri Mersing Cafe* on Jalan Sulaiman.

For cheap Chinese food, there are lots of cafes on Jalan Sulaiman or Jalan Abu Bakar. For cheap, tasty Indian food, try the *Taj Mahal Restoran* on Jalan Abu Bakar and the *Sri Laxmi Restoran* at 30 Jalan Dato Mohammed Ali. For Padang food, try the restaurant next to the moneychanger on Jalan Abu Bakar.

You can get good seafood in Mersing. The restaurant in the *Hotel Embassy* is good, and there are some more expensive places on the Endau Rd.

Getting There & Away

Mersing is 133 km north of JB and 189 km south of Kuantan. The local bus and taxi station is opposite the Mandarin Hotel on Jalan Sulaiman near the river. Long-distance buses stop at the Restoran Malaysia opposite the roundabout. You can buy tickets at the restaurant, but as the buses only pass through Mersing on their way to/from Kuantan or Singapore, it can be difficult to get a seat, especially on weekends. A taxi to JB costs M$11.

Getting a seat on a bus to Singapore is also difficult, but express and regular buses to JB are fairly frequent and leave from the local bus station. It costs around M$11 to Singapore, M$6 to JB.

When arriving from Tioman, most of the boats reach Mersing in the early afternoon. There is an express bus to Kuantan at 1.30 pm (M$10), but during the week the next bus is at 10.30 pm. The alternative is to take one of the regular share-taxis (M$15), or local buses via Endau and Pekan.

TIOMAN ISLAND

The largest and most spectacular of the east coast islands, Tioman is 39 km long and 12 km wide. Tioman has beautiful beaches, clear water and coral for snorkelling or diving enthusiasts, but its major attraction has to be the contrasts and diversity it offers – high mountains and dense jungle are only a short walk away from the coast. As evidence of the island's abundant natural beauty, it's generally quoted that this was the setting for the mythical Bali Hai in the film *South Pacific*. Two thousand years ago, Arab traders noted Tioman on their charts as a place with good anchorages and fresh water. It's an island that would be hard to miss with spectacular peaks like Batu Sirau and Nenek Semukut at the southern end of the island. To this day the streams run rapid and clear from the high peaks of the island.

Tioman has also been blessed with some delightful names. The highest peak, Gunung Kajang is 'Palm-Frond Hill'. Gunung Chula Naga is 'Dragon-Horn Hill' and the villages are equally imaginatively named. There's

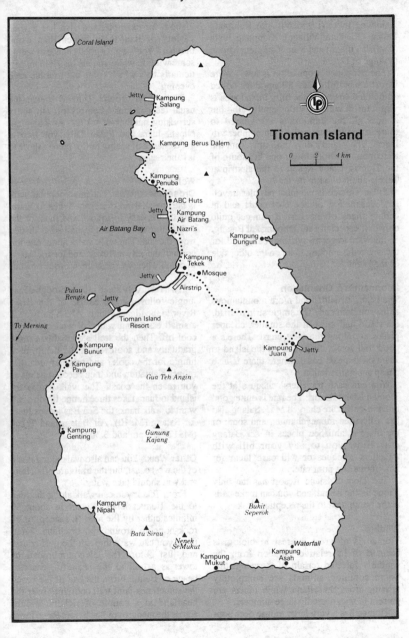

Coral Island

Jetty
Kampung Salang

Kampung Berus Dalem

Tioman Island

0   2   4 km

Kampung Penuba

ABC Huts

Jetty
Kampung Air Batang

Nazri's

Air Batang Bay

Kampung Dungun

Kampung Tekek

Mosque

Jetty

Airstrip

Pulau Rengis

Jetty

To Mersing

Tioman Island Resort

Kampung Bunut

Kampung Paya

Kampung Juara   Jetty

Gua Teh Angin

Kampung Genting

Gunung Kajang

Kampung Nipah

Bukit Seperok

Batu Sirau

Nenek SeMukut

Waterfall
Kampung Asah

Kampung Mukut

Kampung Tekek (Lizard Village), Kampung Lalang (Elephant Village), Kampung Juara (Catfish Village) and even Kampung Mukut (Village of Doubt).

The permanent population is low – there is just a handful of small kampungs dotted around the coast and the hilly inland area is virgin forest with no settlements at all – but almost all the kampungs are geared to tourism and visitors usually outnumber villagers. The island's only road runs from the telecommunications tower one km south of the Tioman Island Resort to the airstrip at Tekek, about two km north.

Pulau Tioman is the most popular travellers' destination on the east coast and at certain times of the year it can get quite crowded, especially at Kampung Air Batang. If you want to get away from it all, head for the isolated Kampung Juara on the other side of the island.

Information & Orientation

The island is wilder and more mountainous at the southern end. The single strip of road, the resort and most of the smaller, cheaper places are along the west coast. There's a good trail across the 'waist' of the island to Juara on the east coast, where there is also cheap accommodation.

You can cash travellers' cheques at the Tioman Island Resort. The rate is quite good but non-guests are charged M$5. Salang also has a licensed moneychanger, and some of the more established places in Air Batang will allow you to pay your bill with travellers' cheques or will cash them for non-guests at a poor rate.

The Tioman Island Resort has the only phone on the island, and you can make calls at the booth next to the reception desk.

Wildlife

Tioman is of great interest to biologists because of its relative isolation from the similarly forested terrain of the peninsula. Some common animals are completely missing from the island while others are present in unexpectedly large numbers.

Tioman has a very large mouse deer pop-

ulation, for example, and also has a wide variety of lizards in larger than usual numbers. You've got a good chance of seeing some wildlife while you are on Tioman, particularly bats which come out in force each evening.

The waters around Tioman shelter the usual technicolour assembly of fish and a surprising number of turtles. At Kampung Nipah, Juara and Pulau Tulai you have a good chance of seeing turtles come ashore to lay their eggs.

Walks

Cross-Island Walk The most popular walk is the cross-island trek from Tekek to Juara. The trail is easy to follow, and most of the way is through the jungle, and so is shaded from the sun. The walk starts about one km north of the jetty in Tekek, and the trail starts to climb when you pass the mosque on your left.

It's a relatively steep climb through dense jungle following the course of the Besar River to the highest point. About halfway is a small cascading waterfall where you can cool off. Then the trail slopes down more gradually and soon leaves the damp, dark jungle for the cooler and brighter area of a rubber plantation and then coconut palms as you reach the coast. The walk across the island to Juara takes three hours. If you don't want to walk back, the Sea Bus leaves Juara for Salang (M$10), Air Batang and Tekek (M$12) at 2 pm and 3.30 pm.

Other Walks You can also walk along much of the west coast, but the trails are often faint and you should take water.

From Tekek you can walk along the road to the Tioman Island Resort in about 30 minutes either by the road (it's steep) or by rock-hopping around the headland. From there you can walk through the golf course and just before the telecommunications tower is a trail to the beautiful, deserted beach of Bunut. From the end of the beach the sometimes faint trail continues over the headland to a couple of rickety bridges across the mangroves just before Paya. From

Paya you can walk south to Genting – the trail is easy to follow and there are houses along the way to ask directions.

Heading north from Tekek, you cross the small headland to Air Batang and from ABC Huts at the other end of the bay it's a steep 10-minute climb over the headland to Penuba Bay and Monkey Beach. The trail then goes through the rainforest to a deserted yellow-sand beach, where the trail continues at the other end over the next headland to a white-sand beach. At the end of this is a rotten, washed-out bridge where the trail starts the long, steep climb over the headland to Salang. The trail is faint here but the undergrowth is not thick if you lose the trail. It takes about three hours from Air Batang to Salang.

Places to Stay & Eat

Accommodation can become tight from June to August, but during the heavy November to January monsoon the island is almost deserted.

Apart from the international standard Tioman Island Resort, accommodation is mostly in the form of budget huts and long-house rooms, or more expensive chalets. A lot of the places quote rates of M$4 or M$5 per person, but single travellers will have difficulty finding an individual hut or room for those rates. It's worth bargaining, especially for longer stays.

The huts, usually with *atap* (thatched) roofs, are simple with two or three beds or even mattresses on the floor. Some have electricity from 6 pm to 6 am but most don't. Expect to pay M$10.

Rooms are usually in longhouse blocks. Mostly they are cheap plywood constructions but can be comfortable motel-style rooms. The cheap rooms aren't as attractive as the huts but often have electricity and sometimes attached bathrooms. Prices range from M$8 to M$15, up to M$30 for a good room with bath, fan and mosquito net.

Chalets are wooden bungalows, usually detached with atap roofs, verandahs, attached bath, electricity, etc. They offer attractive mid-range accommodation for

M$25 to M$30. Almost all the new places being built on Tioman are chalets.

The popular beaches for foreign backpackers are Air Batang, Salang, Juara and Tekek, while the southern beaches – Genting, Paya and also Tekek – are popular with Malaysian and Singaporean visitors during holiday periods.

Resort The *Tioman Island Resort* (tel 09-445445), is the only international class hotel on the island. It has 185 rooms, and big extensions due to open, from around M$125 to M$285, with discounts of up to 25% from November to February. Most rooms are chalet-style with air-con but are relatively simple, which is OK since the hotel's number one attraction is the delightful beach. The hotel has a very impressive range of facilities – a beautiful nine-hole golf course, tennis, horse-riding, jet-skis, scuba diving, etc.

This hotel can be heavily booked, particularly during school holidays. The restaurant is very good, though by no means cheap.

Kampung Tekek Tekek is the largest village on the island and the administrative centre. The airport is here and there are a few well-stocked shops. Tekek's beach is good, though the string of cheap places to stay north of the jetty are something of a blight on the landscape. A little overpriced, but by far the best part of Tekek, is to the south of the jetty where it's less crowded and there's a beautiful stretch of sandy beach.

From the boat jetty there are a whole string of anonymous places to the north that provide cheap rooms for M$6 to M$15, depending on the number of people. Just ask for a room at a likely looking place. They fill up quickly during school holidays and long weekends, when unfortunately the beach becomes a littered mess. They don't have their own restaurants, but meals are available at the small eating places clustered together next to the jetty. Some of the operators in Tekek (and elsewhere) have been known to charge outrageous prices at peak times – just keep walking, you're bound to find a reasonably priced room.

There are about half a dozen places to stay between the jetty and the track to Juara. One of the better places and one of the few with a sign is *Rahim's* where older rooms with bath and fan cost from M$10, and newer rooms are M$15. Further along, just before the track to Juara, is *Railey's Villa*. A lot of travellers stay here, mostly because the owner is one of the most persistent touts when the boats arrive. The accommodation is OK, but don't pay any more than M$10 for a hut or M$5 for a dorm bed.

Spaced out along the track past Railey's is another half a dozen places to stay. The well-run *Tioman Enterprise* has good rooms from M$10. For cheap huts (M$8) ask at the small eating place advertising 'pure island food'.

Towards the northern end of Tekek Bay are a few good places with attractive settings in amongst the greenery. They are quiet, mostly because few people can be bothered walking this far. *Ramli's* has huts for M$10 and chalets for M$25. They have their own restaurant, but it's more popular for the drinks than the food. They also have a small dive business here. Next along is *Azura's* with only two chalets for M$25. At the end of the bay is *Mango Grove*, which has a restaurant and a batik shop. Huts cost M$8 to M$10. It's a good quiet place but the beach out the front is rocky.

To get to the southern places you can walk along the beach and ford the shallow river, or it's a five-minute walk along the airport road. The first place you come to is *Tekek Inn*, which has rooms and huts for M$15 to M$20, and chalets for M$25. Like all the places on this part of the beach, it has its own restaurant.

Next door is the friendly *Sri Tioman* where small huts with mattresses on the floor and mosquito nets cost M$10 to M$15. Chalets cost M$25. The *Coral Reef* is the cheapest place here with basic rooms from M$10, and a few chalets that are usually full. They rent bicycles for M$2 per hour.

Towards the end of the beach, and right next to each other, are two more upmarket places. *Babura* has a block of very good rooms with bath, mosquito nets and fans for M$30. *Swiss Cottages* seems to prefer tour groups and charges accordingly. Its chalets on the beach are the nicest in Tekek, but are way overpriced at M$68. Other chalet rooms cost M$45, and they have the gall to charge M$35 for grotty three-bed rooms that cost M$15 elsewhere.

On the airport road behind Coral Reef is *Liza Restaurant*, Tekek's most expensive eating place. They have good seafood and Western dishes such as spaghetti, but the servings are small and not very good value.

Kampung Air Batang This village is north of Tekek. It's the main travellers' centre with a whole host of cheap accommodation and chalets. Huts cost M$8 to M$10 and most of the places have their own restaurants and serve good, cheap food.

The pretty bay has more greenery than Tekek but, while the beach is good for sunbathing, most of it is far too rocky for swimming. The exception is the beautiful stretch of beach in front of Nazri's with good snorkelling off the point.

ABC is so popular that Air Batang itself is often known as ABC. This is the place to meet other travellers, not to get away from it all. Accommodation ranges from M$10 huts to M$30 chalets. The guys that run the place are friendly and jovial, and the restaurant is one of the best in Air Batang.

Nazri's, at the southern end of the bay, is the other long-established place. It doesn't have ABC's atmosphere, but it does have the best beach. It has a wide variety of huts, rooms and chalets from M$8 to M$30. The restaurant is lively and pumps out the music in the evenings.

If you head north from the jetty, one of the first places you come to is *South Pacific*. A dorm bed is M$4, rooms are M$8 to M$12 with attached bath and small chalets on the beach with attached bath are M$15. This is one of the best buys and consequently fills up quickly.

Further along is *Johan's House* with huts, *CT's Cottages* chalets, and then *Tioman House* with solid wooden huts from M$10. Then there's *Coconut Cafe* with rooms behind, and a laundry service next door, followed by *Double Ace*. *Rinda House*, next to ABC, has some roomy huts with upstairs sleeping platform for M$12.

Heading south from the jetty is *Zinza's Cafe*, *Nordin House*, *Lugam House*, *Mawar*, *Warisan Tioman Heritage*, *Idris*, *Mahawar Restaurant* and *Seri Bungur* just before Nazri's. These places are spaced out and fairly quiet with huts and rooms for around M$10, but chalets are popping up all over the place.

As for the 'top end', ABC's chalet rooms are reasonable but Nazri's are better. There's a new place right at the jetty with good chalets for M$30. *Warisan Tioman Heritage* is a big place with plenty of chalets crammed together for M$25. The nicest place is *CT's Cottages* with just four attractive chalets with tiled bathrooms in a manicured garden setting. The cost is M$30.

Penuba Bay Over the headland from ABC, the *Penuba Bay Cafe* has a few huts for M$10 and a couple of chalets on the hill. It's certainly peaceful, but accommodation is limited so it's worth checking to see if there's room before lugging your gear over the headland.

Kampung Salang The small bay at Salang is one of the most beautiful on Tioman. The only problem is that accommodation is limited and often full. Salang is popular with divers and Ben's Diving Centre, run by a Malay guy who lived in Germany for several years, offers one dive, boat and equipment for M$70 per person or M$80 for two dives.

Indah Salang has a big restaurant and bar and is pressing for resort status, but accommodation is still fairly basic and the service is very slow.

At the other end of the beach, *Salang Sayang* is popular with tour groups. Small huts cost M$12 or larger ones are M$15. They have a big restaurant and also cash travellers' cheques.

One of the best buys is the *Salang Damai Restaurant*. It has good, cheap food and a few rooms for M$10. *Nora Chalets*, back

from the beach, costs M$15 to M$20, and *Salang Baru Chalet* has rooms for M$12.

Kampung Juara Accommodation is plentiful and slightly cheaper than the other beaches, but because of its isolation, Juara doesn't get as crowded. The beach is excellent, though the sea is very rough in the monsoon season. You can also arrange river trips and excursions to the nearby rubber plantation. Two boats a day go from the west of the island, or some of the small boats from Mersing will continue on to Juara for an extra M$15. If enough people want to go direct to Mersing from Juara, a boat costs M$20 per person.

There are at least half a dozen places to stay, and many will provide share rooms for M$4 per person. *Happy Cafe*, right by the jetty, is a clean and tidy little establishment where one small room with a double bed and mosquito net costs M$8. The cafe is good and there is a library for guests.

Atan's has a number of thatched huts for M$8, and chalets for M$14. *Door Ray Me* and *Rainbow Cafe* have huts and rooms for M$8. *Mutiara's* has huts for M$8 and the chalets are particularly good value, with attached bathrooms, and electricity in the evenings, for M$12.

Kampung Paya Paya is a few km south of the Tioman Island Resort. The beach is OK but nothing special. The only thing of note is the *White Sand Beach Resort* (tel 07-792253) that caters to package groups from Singapore. It has a big atap-roof restaurant and bar, and comfortable but simple chalets from M$60/70 for singles/doubles. You can certainly get better value elsewhere. There are a few other decrepit places to stay, the pick of which is the *Norlida Cafe* with rooms for M$10.

Kampung Genting Genting is the second largest village on the island and more traditional than the other beaches. Very few Westerners ever come here. This is the place to practise your Bahasa Malaysia, and outside of weekends and holiday periods you'll have the place to yourself. The beach is rocky around the jetty, but good at the southern end. Genting is easily reached from Mersing, but there are no regular boats to other parts of the island.

There's a whole string of cheap places to stay with rooms for M$8 to M$10. *Shmaimunah House* is on the best part of the beach. Huts, rooms and chalets range from M$8 to M$20. *Genting Damai* is the top place, with a good restaurant and comfortable chalets for M$25. Next door, the *Genting Village Resort*, is good value for groups with big four-bed rooms for M$15 and chalets for M$20.

Kampung Nipah This is the place if you really want to get away from it all. The beach is superb with good snorkelling and, apart from a couple of longhouse blocks that are only open during the holiday periods, there's only one place to stay.

Desa Nipah has delightful, traditional-style chalets with attached bathrooms, but there is no electricity. They range from M$25 to M$70 for a two-storey chalet that sleeps 10 people. Dormitory accommodation is available for M$8 to M$10, and the restaurant is reasonably priced.

Only the boats to and from Mersing stop here, by arrangement, and there are no trails to Nipah. Zamri, the owner, says he can arrange transport to the other beaches if his place is full.

Getting There & Away
Air Tradewinds and Pelangi Air have daily

flights to/from Singapore for M$100. Pelangi also flies daily to KL (M$103), and to Kuantan (M$63) on Tuesdays, Fridays and Sundays. You can book tickets at Bukharie Services in Tekek. The office is a five-minute walk from the airport, past the school and over the bridge on the airport/resort road.

Boat A whole flotilla of boats make the 50-km trip from Mersing to Tioman. Boats are advertised as fast, moderate and slow, though some of the fast boats are really moderate ones and some of the moderate ones are just larger slow boats with comfortable seats.

The true fast boats, such the *Pantas Express*, are air-conditioned, take about 1½ hours and cost M$25 one way. They normally only stop at Paya, the resort and Tekek. You can then take the Sea Bus (see Getting Around in this section) to the other beaches. The Tioman Island Resort's boat, which costs M$30, usually only goes to the resort. It's well worth taking a fast boat during the monsoon season – battling the swells for five hours in a small fishing boat is no fun.

Moderate boats take about three to four hours and cost M$20. The slow fishing boats which take about four to five hours cost M$15. These boats will usually drop you off at any of the beaches on the west coast, but check when you buy your ticket. Some will continue to Juara for an extra M$15. The boats go on demand, but there are usually plenty of boats throughout the day.

The Mersing jetty is five minutes' walk from the town centre and you'll find the offices for boats to all the islands in this area. The major operator is the Tourist Boats Association (tel 07-792501), 1 Jalan Abu Bakar, which is a co-operative of the Tioman-based boat owners. You can also arrange trips to the other islands.

Because of silting at the mouth of the Mersing River, the large fast boats can only leave and arrive at high tide, which varies but is usually around 1 pm. When leaving Tioman, be suspicious of fast boats that leave early in the morning; ask what time they arrive, not how long the trip takes. You may find that your fast boat goes around to all the jetties, picking up passengers while it waits for the tide to rise. You may even be stranded, waiting outside Mersing, while the small slow boats sail on in.

Getting Around

Boat The excellent Sea Bus service operates regular boats between the resort, Tekek, Air Batang and Salang. About eight boats per day go in both directions, eg boats leave Air Batang for Tekek and the resort at 8, 9 and 10.30 am and 1.30, 3.30, 4.15, 5.30 and 6 pm. Services are less frequent during the monsoon season. Tekek to Air Batang (or ABC as it appears on the schedules) or the resort is M$3, to Salang is M$6. Air Batang to Salang is M$4. They run like clockwork, and you can buy tickets from agents at the jetties, or in restaurants. You can also pay on the boat, but don't expect them to change a M$50 note.

The Sea Bus also has two boats per day to Juara for M$15, a round-island trip for M$30, and a Coral Island trip for M$16 to M$20. The round-island trip leaves around 9 am and stops at most of the beaches and Kampung Asah from where it is a 10-minute walk to the waterfall. The Coral Island boat drops you off in the morning and picks you up in the afternoon – bring your own snorkelling gear.

If you want to get to the southern beaches, ask the captain of the round-island boat to drop you off. But if you want to return you'll have to wait for one of the boats from Mersing, which may well mean an overnight stay, or longer.

It's also possible to charter boats for M$180 to M$200 per day.

OTHER ISLANDS

Although Tioman is the largest and best-known of the islands off Mersing, there are many others, most of them uninhabited and often too rocky and precipitous to land on. Many islands off the coast of Mersing have beautiful white sandy beaches and are surrounded by crystal-clear waters. They aren't as spectacular as Tioman, though they are

less crowded. Accommodation is mostly mid-range chalets, and the prices tend to be higher than Tioman.

Pulau Rawa

This tiny island is 16 km from Mersing. The beach is superb and you can snorkel or dive in the crystal-clear waters, though much of the coral is dead around the island itself.

Places to Stay The *Rawa Safaris Island Resort* (tel 07-791204) is the only place to stay. Simple but comfortable thatched bungalows cost M$50 and rooms cost M$55 to M$80. The restaurant has a bar, and facilities include windsurfing, canoeing, scuba diving and snorkelling. The resort has its own boat, and the booking office is in Mersing. Round-trip fare is M$16.

Pulau Sibu

Sibu is one of the largest and most popular islands. The beaches are beautiful and good for snorkelling, and there are jungle treks across the island. Windsurfers and canoes can be hired.

O & H Kampung Huts has budget chalets for M$12 to M$15. The restaurant is good and reasonably priced. *Sea Gypsy Village Resort* has traditional-style chalets with attached bathroom for M$30 and M$35. The more upmarket places are the *Sibu Island Resort* (tel 07-316201), and *Sibu Island Cabanas* (tel 07-317216), which has rooms from M$50 and deluxe bungalows for M$90.

Bookings for O & H and Sea Gypsy Village can be made at the Sibu office (tel 07-793125), 9 Jalan Abu Bakar, near the jetty in Mersing. The two-hour trip costs M$20 return. Sibu can also be reached from Tanjong Sedili (M$2.70 per person by taxi from Kota Tinggi). From Sedili, boats leave at 10 am and 4.30 pm and cost M$22 return for the 2½ hour trip.

Pulau Babi Besar

This island is one of the closest to the peninsula. Boats take about an hour to reach the island from Mersing and cost M$18 return.

Accommodation is mostly more expensive chalets.

One of the cheapest is *Radhin Chalets* (tel 07-793124) at M$25 for an A-frame chalet. Others include *Besar Beach Club* (tel 07-792589), *Whitsand Beach Resort* (tel 07-314511) and *Pulau Besar Village Resort* (tel 07-791205). *Hill Side Chalet* (tel 07-236603) is the top place and costs M$60 to M$95 for bungalows.

Pulau Tengah

Near Pulau Babi Besar, Tengah is 16 km off the coast and takes an hour by boat (M$8 one way). Once a Vietnamese refugee camp, it is now gazetted as a marine park and leather-back turtles come here to lay their eggs in July.

Pirate Bay (tel 07-241911) is the only resort, and chalets cost from M$50/75 for singles/doubles. The resort is run by an Italian, Signor Pino, and his Malaysian wife, so the food in the restaurant is varied, and good.

Pulau Hujung & Pulau Aur

These remote islands have no facilities to offer but there are huts on the beach. Hujung is closer to the mainland and boats to the other islands may be able to drop you off. Pulau Aur is the most remote island and the boat trip takes at least four hours. If you want to stay on these islands, you can either camp or find someone to open one of the huts for you – the Mersing boat operators might be able to help you.

ENDAU

There's little of interest in Endau itself, but you can hire boats to make trips up the remote Endau River to the Endau-Rompin Park and Orang Asli settlements in the interior.

You can get about 110 km upriver in fair size boats, almost to Kampung Patah which is the last village up the river. From there smaller boats are required to negotiate the rapids into Orang Asli country. Smaller boats can be hired at Kampung Punan, about 100 km from Endau.

ENDAU-ROMPIN PARK

This wildlife reserve is one of the largest on the peninsula and is the last refuge in Malaysia of the Sumatran rhinoceros. The park is not developed for visitors, but the adventurous can make the river trip past mangrove swamps and mud flats to the headwaters of the Endau River.

Entry permits are necessary and can be obtained from the State Security Council, 2nd floor, Bangunan Sultan Ibrahim, Bukit Timbalan, JB.

The tourist office in JB can put you in touch with agencies that can arrange treks in the park.

There is a camping ground near Gunung Janing.

Boats can be hired in Endau for around M$150 to make the all-day trip up the Endau River to the park. The park can also be reached by a rough road from Kahang on the Keluang-Mersing road.

KUALA ROMPIN & NENASI

Again there is nothing to see or do in the town, but with a 4WD vehicle you can go inland to Iban, 10 km, and a further 25 km to Kampung Aur where there are Orang Asli settlements.

At Nenasi boats can be hired and you can go upriver to the Orang Asli village of Kampung Ulu Serai.

Places to Stay

Near Kuala Rompin at the 122½ milestone the small *Government Rest House* (tel 09-565245), has rooms at M$14 to M$25.

PEKAN

The royal town of Pahang state has a couple of well-built white-marble mosques and the Sultan's palace, the modern Istana Abu Bakar. The istana is on the Kuantan edge of town.

The Museum Sultan Abu Bakar is the state museum and features exhibits on Pahang's royal heritage. It is closed on Fridays.

The Pahang River, crossed at this town by a lengthy bridge, is the longest river in Malaysia and was the last east coast river to be bridged. At the river mouth on the other side is the small fishing village of Kuala Pahang.

A road follows the Pahang River to Chini from where you can reach Tasik Chini (see the Around Kuantan section). Buses run along this road.

Silk-weaving can be seen at Kampung Pulau Keladi, only about five km out of Pekan.

Places to Stay

The *Pekan Hotel* (tel 09-571378) at 60 Jalan Clifford and the *Ching Hiang Hotel* (tel 09-571378) have rooms for around M$10. There's also the equally cheap *Pekan Rest House* (tel 09-571240).

Kuantan

About midway up the east coast from Singapore to Kota Bharu, Kuantan is the capital of the state of Pahang and the start of the east coast beach strip which extends all the way to Kota Bharu.

Kuantan is a well organised, bustling city and is a major stopover point when you are travelling north, south or across the peninsula. Kuantan itself has little to offer the visitor, but there are a number of interesting places nearby.

Information

The tourist information stand is at the rear of the Kompleks Terantum, Kuantan's biggest shopping complex and 22-storey office block.

The post office and most of the banks are up the far end of Jalan Mahkota, which changes name to Jalan Haji Abdul Aziz. Hamid Bros, a bookshop at 23 Jalan Mahkota, is a licensed moneychanger and also has some English-language books.

Mr Dobi is a laundromat at 128 Jalan Telok Sisek, near the Hotel New Meriah, and charges M$5 for a full-load wash and dry (they do the work).

Things to See

Take a stroll along the riverbank and watch the activity on the wide Kuantan River. From the jetty at the end of Jalan Masjid you can get a ferry across the river for about 50 sen to the small fishing village of Kampung Tanjung Lumpur.

The Kuantan area produces some good handicrafts, and there is a batik factory a few km from the town centre on the road to the airport. On Jalan Besar near the Samudra River View Hotel are a number of shops selling local trinkets and craftwork. Bargain hard. For antiquities from China and South-East Asia, take your credit card to Golden Light Antiques, E-1486 Jalan Dato Wong Ah Jang.

The main market is held on Saturdays, on the main road to the airport near the turn-off to Mersing, about four km from town.

Teluk Chempedak

Kuantan's major attraction is Teluk Chempedak Beach, about four km from the town. The beach, bounded by rocky headlands at each end, is quite pleasant but there are better beaches on the peninsula. There are a number of walking tracks in the park area on the promontory.

Teluk Chempedak, which was a quiet little place until the early '70s, now has two international hotels and a row of bars, clubs and restaurants. The foreshore is paved and lined with shops, restaurants and food stalls. It's a popular promenade and meeting place in the evenings, and has the feel of a built-up European resort. On the Hyatt's beachfront is a small wooden junk which carried 162 Vietnamese boat people on their hazardous voyage to the West – it's now the 'Sampan Bar' where you can pay over the odds for a beer or coke.

Places to Stay

Kuantan Kuantan has dozens of cheap Chinese hotels and a few upmarket places, but the big international hotels are a few km out of town at Teluk Chempedak.

On Jalan Mahkota near the taxi station, the *Min Heng Hotel* (tel 09-524885) is the cheapest in town at M$9/10 for singles/doubles. It's a classic Chinese cheapie – bare floorboards, wire-topped walls, *pintu pagar* (saloon doors) on the outside of the rooms, and very basic.

The *Tong Nam Ah Hotel* (tel 09-521204) on Jalan Besar near the bus station is a good, cheap hotel with rooms for around M$13. The *Hotel Raya Baru* (tel 09-522344), in between the taxi and bus stations, is better but overpriced at M$24 for a room. However, it is open 24 hours if you arrive on a night bus.

On Jalan Telok Sisek, between Jalan Merdeka and Jalan Bank, are a number of cheap hotels. *Hotel New Embassy* (tel 09-524277), 52-54 Jalan Telok Sisek, has good rooms with balcony for M$12 and more expensive rooms with bath and air-con. A few doors along, the *Mei Lai Hotel* is noisy but clean and a good buy at M$10/12 for singles/doubles. On the corner of Jalan Merdeka is the *Hotel Embassy*, which costs M$20 for a room with bath. The *Sin Nam Fong* (tel 09-521561) at 44 Jalan Telok Sisek

has cheap rooms for M$13 but other hotels have more appeal. Around the corner on Jalan Mahkota, the *Hotel Malaysia* (tel 09-521587) is very clean but a little expensive at M$15.

For a room with attached bath, the *New Capitol Hotel* (tel 09-507276), 55 Jalan Bukit Ubi, has spotless rooms for M$18. *Hotel New Meriah* (tel 09-525433), 142 Jalan Telok Sisek, is a good mid-range place with carpeted rooms with attached bath and occasional hot water. Internal-facing rooms cost M$25 or larger street-facing rooms are M$28.

Near the local bus station are two new Indian-run hotels. They are cheaply put together by partitioning off the floors above shops, but their newness means they are spotlessly clean and well appointed. *Hotel Sri Intan* (tel 512000), 13-15 Jalan Stadium, has rooms with air-con (that works) and attached bath for M$24 to M$32. Next door, the *Hotel Makmur* has air-con rooms without bath for M$20 to M$24.

Hotel Beserah (tel 09-526144) was once a top hotel but has seen better days. Large singles/doubles with attached bath and hot

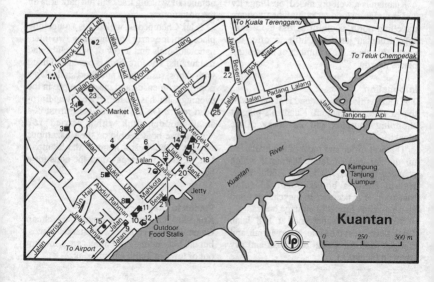

water cost M$40/50 to 65. The government-run *Annexe Rest House* is on Jalan Telok Sisek about 1½ km before Teluk Chempedak. It's a good value mid-range place and fan-cooled rooms cost M$19/25. Bus No 39 will get you there – get off where it rejoins the main road.

For three-star, fully air-con Western-style hotels, in ascending order of quality are: *Suraya Hotel* (tel 09-524266) with rooms for M$75 and M$85, *Hotel Pacific* (tel 09-511981) at M$70 and M$90, and *Samudra River View Hotel* (tel 09-522707) which costs M$92.

Teluk Chempedak The alternative to staying in Kuantan itself is out at Teluk Chempedak Beach where there's a wide variety of accommodation.

The *Asrama Bendahara* (tel 09-525930) is the lowest-priced place with dorm beds at M$7 and rooms for M$15 and M$18. It's a little overpriced, but has a certain run-down charm. It has a cheap open-air restaurant and is a friendly place, popular with travellers.

There's a group of 'motels' in the street behind Hotel Hillview. Some are very seedy and ill-cared-for but the *Sri Pantai Bungalows* (tel 09-524749) at No 19 has good, clean, carpeted rooms with fan for M$20. There are plenty of other places in this street charging M$17 to M$20 for a room – just ask at a 'room to let' sign.

Near the Bendahara is the *Kuantan Hotel* (tel 09-524755) with good fan rooms for M$38 and air-con rooms for M$52. Round on the main road there's the musty *Hill View Hotel* (tel 09-521555) with rooms for M$46. The *Samudra Beach Resort* (tel 09-505933) is a long walk around the promontory from the main beach and at low tide the beach out the front is very shallow and sometimes dirty. Nonetheless the motel rooms are very well appointed and it's the best mid-range accommodation in Teluk Chempedak. Rooms cost M$46 and there's a restaurant.

The two top places are the *Hyatt Kuantan* (tel 09-525211) and the adjoining *Hotel Merlin* (tel 09-522388), which together take up most of the beach front. The Hyatt is suffering from a dose of concrete fade but it has a far more impressive list of facilities than the Merlin. Most Hyatt rooms cost from M$130 to M$200, the Merlin costs from M$100 to M$170.

Places to Eat
Kuantan Kuantan has a good selection of eating places. The food stalls on Jalan Mahkota serve excellent Chinese food and cold beer, as well as satay, Muslim and Indian food. The small Muslim food stalls dotted along the riverbank, behind the long-distance bus station, are a great place to sit and watch the boats pass by. The seafood is particularly good and the prawns are huge. In the evenings food stalls set up near the

■ PLACES TO STAY

3	Hotel Pacific
5	New Capitol Hotel
8	Min Heng Hotel
10	Hotel Raya Baru
11	Hotel Tong Nam Ah
17	Suraya Hotel
18	Hotel New Embassy
21	Samudra River View Hotel
22	Hotel Beserah
24	Hotel Makmur
25	Hotel New Meriah

▼ PLACES TO EAT

13	Food Stalls
20	Tiki's Restoran

OTHER

1	Hindu Temple
2	Stadium
4	MAS
6	Immigration
7	Local Bus Stand
9	Taxi Station
12	Bus Station
14	Malayan Banking
15	Tourist Office
16	Post Office
19	Chartered Bank
23	Local Bus Station

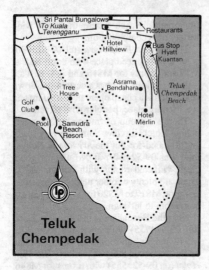

Teluk Chempedak

local bus station and there are a few interesting serve-yourself nasi padang places, and good Chinese seafood satay – select what you want and cook them in the vats of boiling water.

For breakfast, try *Tiki's Restoran* up the far end of Jalan Mahkota. It's only open during the day and the two ever-busy brothers who run this place really welcome travellers. Western-style breakfasts, including a newspaper to read, and excellent local dishes are available for around M$2.

There are plenty of good bakeries around, including the one under the Min Heng Hotel, the *Terantum Bakery & Cafe* in the Kompleks Terantum, and several along Jalan Bukit Ubi.

Not far from Tiki's Restoran is the popular *Restoran Cheun Kee* which serves good Chinese food for around M$3. There's some good Indian restaurants on Jalan Bukit Ubi, past Jalan Gambut.

For something more upmarket, *The Ark* is a floating restaurant serving Western and local dishes, and is moored on the river near the end of Jalan Penjara.

Teluk Chempedak Food is one of Teluk Chempedak's main attractions. Apart from the food stalls at the end of the beach, and the restaurant at the Asrama Bendahara, there's not much in the way of cheap eats. However, the flash restaurants are not as expensive as they look and are moderately priced for the excellent food they serve.

On the foreshore, *Pattaya* and *Restoran Din* are pleasant, open-air places specialising in seafood, though the air-con places on the main road are generally better value. The air-con restaurants serve mostly Chinese seafood and Malay specialities. Dishes start from M$5 and go up to M$25 for a whole lobster. *Nisha's*, a north Indian restaurant, has good tandoori food and breads.

The big hotels have the usual selection of restaurants, and the M$24 banquet at the Hyatt is an all-you-can-eat affair.

Getting There & Away
Air MAS (tel 09-521218) has direct flights to Singapore (M$120) and KL (M$61), and handles bookings for Pelangi Air flights to Kerteh and Tioman.

Bus All the bus company offices are at the bus station, and many operate the same routes, so just choose one that goes at a time that suits you.

Buses to KL leave from 7.30 am until 1 am in the morning and cost M$11. Buses to Mersing (M$11), JB ($M15) and Singapore (M$16) leave between 9 am and 1 pm, and then 11 pm. There is also an extra bus to Mersing at 5.30 pm. For Cherating, take the 'Kemaman' bus No 27 from the main bus station for M$2.20. The trip takes about one hour. Buses go throughout the day to Kuala Terengannu (M$8) and Kota Bharu (M$15), and there are a couple of late night buses. For Taman Negara, direct buses to Jerantut (M$7.70) leave between 9 am and 3 pm. Buses to Melaka (M$13) leave around 8 am and 2 pm. For Penang (M$24.50) buses leave in the evening, or you can take the 9.30 am bus to Ipoh (M$19.50) and get a connection there.

Taxi Taxis cost M$4 to Pekan, M$15 to

Mersing. Heading north it's M$5 to Kemaman and you'll have to pay the same to Cherating. To Kuala Terengganu is M$17 or M$25 to Kota Bharu. Across the peninsula it's M$9 to Temerloh, M$13 to Jerantut, M$18 to Raub and M$20 to KL.

Getting Around
Bus Bus No 39 will take you to Teluk Chempedak for 50 sen. You can catch it at the local bus station or, more conveniently, at the M3 bus stand on the corner of Jalan Mahkota and Jalan Masjid. In theory the buses are supposed to pull in to the stand facing Jalan Masjid but in practice you have to stand on Jalan Mahkota and hail them down, 20 metres past the M2 bus stand.

AROUND KUANTAN
Beserah
The small, interesting fishing village of Beserah is only 10 km north of Kuantan and is a centre for local handicrafts including batik, carvings and shell items from the village of Sungai Karang, a little further north. Kite-flying, top-spinning and other east coast activities occasionally can be seen there. Batu Hitam is a good beach just north of Beserah.

Places to Stay & Eat The popular shoe-string travellers' place in Beserah is known as *Jaafar's Place*. It's a kampung house about a half km off the road on the inland side. A sign points it out and bus drivers know it. Accommodation costs M$9 a night

including a light breakfast and other meals are available. Facilities are very basic.

Reactions to this place are varied – some travellers feel it's restful, easy-going and friendly while others claim it's a 'pack-them-in rip-off' with 'bad food and zero facilities'. There's no denying that the places at Cherating, 40 km north, offer a lot more for little more.

Getting There & Away Buses to Kemaman (No 27), Balok (No 30) or Sungai Karang (No 28), all pass through Beserah. They leave from the main bus station and the fare is 50 sen.

Berkelah Falls
The Berkelah Falls are about 50 km from Kuantan – the final six km involve a jungle trek from the main road. The falls come down a hillside in a series of eight cascades. The Marathandhavar Temple is the site for a major Hindu festival in March or April each year.

Getting There & Away Catch a bus to Maran from the main bus station for M$3.35. At Maran, you'll see a bridge by the river. This is where the walk to the falls begins (there is a sign indicating the direction). The jungle

track is overgrown due to the lack of use and maintenance. The walk takes about three hours.

Gua Charas (Charas Caves)

Twenty-six km north of Kuantan at Panching, the limestone outcrop containing the Charas (also spelt Charah) caves rises sheer from the surrounding palm plantations. The caves owe their fame to a Thai buddhist monk who came to meditate here about 50 years ago. There's a monk in residence and the caretaker's wife can tell you about the caves.

It's a steep climb up an external stairway to the caves' entrance. In the more enclosed cave there's a nine-metre-long reclining Buddha carved from solid rock, and other Buddhist statuary. Once a year in July, sunlight penetrates the cave and illuminates the head of the reclining Buddha.

Admission is M$1. The caves are lit but bring a torch to explore the side caverns, or you can hire one for M$2.

Three km before Panching is a turn-off that leads to the airport and the Pandan waterfalls, five km from the main road.

Getting There & Away Take the Sungai Lembing bus (No 48) from the main bus station in Kuantan and get off at the small village of Panching. From the bus stop in town it's a hot four-km walk each way, but there's usually someone visiting the caves who will stop and offer you a lift. Traffic is heaviest on Sundays. The alternative is to hire someone in Panching to give you a lift on the back of their motorcycles for around M$2.

Sungai Lembing

This old tin mining town boasted the world's longest underground tin mine, until it went unto receivership after the collapse of tin prices in the late '80s. There's talk of opening the mine as a tourist attraction but at the moment it is still closed. There are a few old colonial buildings, but otherwise there's not much to see. Sungai Lembing is about 25 km past Panching and can be reached by bus No 48.

Gunung Tapis Park If you have your own 4WD vehicle, you can make a 16-km side trip from Sungai Lembing to Gunung Tapis Park. This park is noted for its rapids, hot springs and fishing. The park is not developed but there are plenty of good spots for camping. Arrangements can be made through the tourist information office in Kuantan.

Tasik Chini

Turn south from the Temerloh road 56 km west of Kuantan, and 12 km from the turn-off is Kampung Belimbing, the main access point for Tasik Chini. From there you can hire a boat to cross the Pahang River and go through the jungle up the Chini River to the lotus-covered expanse of Tasik Chini.

The lake is in fact a series of 12 lakes, and around its shores live the Jakun people, an Orang Asli tribe of Melayu Asli origin. The Jakun believe that the spirit of the lake is the serpent Naga Seri Gumum, which translates in the tourist literature as Loch Ness monster.

It's a beautiful area and you can walk for miles in jungle territory. There is a resort which organises jungle treks to Gunung Chini and the Orang Asli village of Kampumg Gumum, as well as boating, fishing and canoeing trips. Tasik Chini is a popular day trip for tour groups, which take the boats from Belimbing.

Places to Stay & Eat The *Lake Cini Resort* (tel 03-2433890), on the shores of the lake, has good cabins with attached bathroom for M$55/65 for singles/doubles. Some cabins are also set aside for dormitory accommodation and a bed in a six-bed cabin costs M$15. Outside of school holidays you may well have a dormitory to yourself. Camping facilities are also available for M$2 per person per site and a three-person tent costs M$5.

The restaurant at the resort serves simple food for M$4 to M$6 per dish. All accommodation, food and equipment rental is subject to a 10% service charge.

Getting There & Away Tasik Chini can be reached by boat from Belimbing or by road from Pekan, but both ways are difficult by public transport.

The tourist information stand in Kuantan can arrange day trips to Tasik Chini for M$50 per person but the cheapest tours are from Cherating at M$35 per person.

From Kuantan you can catch a bus to Maran and get off at the Tasik Chini turn-off, from where it's 12 km to Kampung Belimbing.

Buses from Maran go via the turn-off to Belimbing every two hours or so, but there's no fixed schedule and you may be in for a long wait. Traffic to Belimbing is light.

From Belimbing you can hire a boat to Tasik Chini. The cost is M$40 per boat for a day trip, including a tour of the lakes and a visit to an Orang Asli village, or M$70 for a drop off and pick up if you stay at the resort. A boat can take four people.

The alternative is to take a bus to Kampung Chini from Kuantan or Pekan. The Mara bus No 121 marked 'Cini' leaves Kuantan's main bus station around 10 am, 1 and 3 pm, but check at the Mara Holdings office. The bus takes two hours and costs M$4.30. It's eight km from Kampung Chini to the resort on an unmade road. Without a car, the only way to get to the resort is by hiring someone with a motorcycle to take you there for about M$5. If you stay at the resort, they can drop you at Kampung Chini when you leave.

Kuantan to Kuala Terengganu

The 218 km between Kuantan and Kuala Terengganu is probably the most interesting stretch of road along the east coast although it now embraces miles of new petro-chemical developments. The road runs close to the coast most of the way, and there are many good beaches and a number of interesting offshore islands.

There are many places to stay along the coast, as well as several interesting small towns and fishing villages.

BESERAH TO CHERATING
There are small resorts along this stretch of coast offering good mid to upper range accommodation. The sheltered beaches are quite good but the water is very shallow when the tide is out.

North of Beserah, the small island of Ular, 'Snake Island', is only a short distance offshore and easily reached by a local fishing boat. It's then only a couple of km north of there to the kampung of Cherating, a very popular backpackers' centre.

Places to Stay
Gloria Maris (tel 09-587788) is 9½ km from Kuantan, one km past Beserah. Chalets on the beach cost M$40. Further along is the village of Balok and *Le Village*, a new, small resort. Good chalets with bath and air-con cost M$85 plus tax and service charge. There is a pool and a good restaurant, and they rent bicycles.

Tanjong Geylang Beach Resort (tel 09-587254), just off the main road one km past Le Village, is an older motel-style place. The rooms are musty, but large and comfortable, and cost M$55. Further down the same road is the large *Coral Beach Resort* (tel 09-587544). It is approaching international standard and costs M$130/150 for internal facing rooms and M$190/210 for rooms facing the beach.

CHERATING
This is one of the most popular travellers' centres on the east coast, and there's a host of good, cheap accommodation and restaurants. Cherating, meaning sand crab, is actually divided into two parts – the main village and, two km further north, Pantai Cherating, which is the travellers' centre.

Many people visiting Cherating settle down and stay for weeks. Cherating has a long stretch of beach, which is not exactly pristine but it is good for swimming. There are also the secluded bays just to the north, and at certain times of the year turtles come ashore to lay their eggs at Chendor Beach, right by Club Mediterranée. You cannot walk along the beach to Chendor due to the rocky headland, but word spreads quickly if the turtles come ashore and you may be able to arrange a lift.

Cherating is promoted as a cultural village and most of the places to stay have a family atmosphere and try to involve their guests in aspects of traditional kampung life. Cherating is not a traditional kampung, but it's a good place to learn Malaysian board games and sports and, sometimes, shadow-puppet shows are arranged. You can also do batik courses – the one at the souvenir centre has been recommended as the best.

Cherating is also a good base to explore the surrounding area. You can arrange minitreks and river trips, and most of the places to stay can arrange tours to Tasik Chini (M$35); Gua Charas, Sungai Lembing and Pandan Falls (M$30); and Pulau Ular.

A few km along the beach towards Kuantan, beyond the Cherating River, there is still a Kampuchean refugee camp.

Places to Stay & Eat

Accommodation ranges from basic A-frame huts, each with a double mattress and light, but without a fan, to more comfortable 'chalets' with a bathroom. Most of the A-frame huts cost around M$10 and sleep two people; the chalets range from M$15 to M$30. Most of the places have their own restaurants and you can easily spend a few days in Cherating and not sample them all.

On the main road are two of the longest running homestays – *Mak Long Teh's* and *Mak De's*. Both places charge M$12 for accommodation, breakfast and dinner, or M$17 including lunch. All-you-can-eat meals at both places are excellent. Mak Long Teh's is affiliated with the Malaysian Youth Hostel Association.

Closer to the beach, *Maznah Guest House* is one of the cheapest around at M$8. *Cherating Indah* has good chalets for M$12 and M$20 with bath. The *Riverside* is popular, with some basic huts for M$8, but most are M$10 to M$12 or M$18 with attached bath and worth the extra few ringgit. *Hussaien's Bungalows* has rundown-looking places for M$10, but they are roomy and

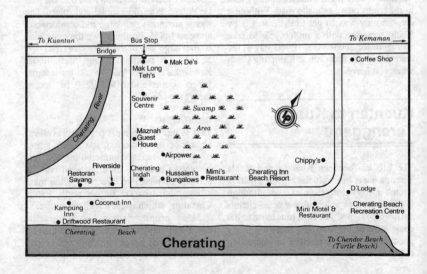

better than they look. The restaurants at the Riverside and Hussaien's are both very good.

Further south is the *Restoran Sayang*, which has a few rooms and huts for M$15, but the best thing here is the Indian set meals for M$6. The *Coconut Inn* is a friendly, well-kept place with small A-frame huts from M$10, larger ones for M$12 to M$14 and chalets with attached bath for M$18. Next door is the *Kampung Inn* with a number of chalets for M$15 to M$25 and they can also provide dormitory accommodation for M$5 per person. Nearby is the *Driftwood Restaurant*, which has a good bar but the food is overpriced.

At the other end of the beach is the *Cherating Beach Recreation Centre*, where rooms and huts cost M$10 to M$15 and chalets with bath are M$25. The big restaurant and bar blasts music out in the evening. *D'Lodge*, next door, has a few huts for M$10.

Mini Motel is more upmarket than most and has a good restaurant. Rooms cost M$10 to M$35 (with air-con) and chalets are M$25. Across the road, *Chippy's* has one of the best, and most crowded, restaurants in Cherating. Rooms cost M$10 to M$12 but avoid the ones next to the restaurant, which can rock-on until the early hours of the morning.

Cherating Inn Beach Resort caters mostly for Singaporean package groups and has overpriced chalets for M$40. *Airpower*, behind Hussaien's, is run by the same people who have the travellers' centre in Singapore. Chalets with attached bath cost M$30. Perhaps it will be worth it when they build their planned swimming pool. Last, but not least, is *Mimi's Restaurant* with a varied menu and some of the cheapest and best food in Cherating.

The other alternatives are the big resorts such as *Cherating Holiday Villa* (tel 09-2434693). This resort has a swimming pool and is two km south of the main accommodation centre near Cherating village. Rooms cost M$90/110 for singles/doubles.

To the north of Cherating is the large (325 room) and securely guarded *Club*

Méditerranée (tel 09-591131). This was the first Club Med holiday resort in Asia and the majority of people who stay there come to Malaysia from Europe or Australia on all-inclusive package deals. However, if you've always wanted to try a Club Med there are often short-stay packages offered in Malaysia. Regular cost? Over M$1000 a week!

Getting There & Away

To get to Cherating, catch a bus marked 'Kemaman' from the main bus station in Kuantan. Buses leave every hour, the fare is M$2.20 and the journey takes one hour. From Cherating to Kuantan, wave down a bus to Kuantan from the bus stop outside Mak Long Teh's.

KEMAMAN

About 25 km north of Chendor, Kemaman is the first town of any size north of Kuantan and also the first town you reach in Terengganu. It merges with Chukai, the adjoining town.

Places to Stay

The bus station is in Chukai, and if you go out of the bus station and turn right you'll come to the *Hotel Kim Thye* and then the *Hotel Kemaman*, two basic cheapies. Further along this road around the bend are two mid-range places: the *Rest House*, next to the taxi station, and the *Riverview*.

Getting There & Away

Buses to Cherating cost 80 sen. To Marang is M$5.50 by express bus or you can catch a local bus to Dungun and then another bus from there. Taxis cost M$12 to Kuala Terengganu, M$5.40 to Kuantan, and M$6 to Dungun.

KERTEH

Kerteh is a modern town, grown up with the wealth of Kuala Terengganu's offshore oil. Esso and Petronas have their oil refineries here, and Kerteh's airport services this satellite town, but public transport connections are not good.

There are some beautiful beaches along

the stretch of coast near Kerteh, but there is no accommodation. Kemasik's palm-fringed beach has some of the clearest water on the east coast, and Kijal and Paka are picturesque fishing villages.

KUALA DUNGUN

From Kemaman there are more stretches of beach, more small kampungs and fishing villages at river mouths, before you reach Kuala Dungun which is actually a couple of km off the main road.

The beaches where the giant leatherbacks come in to lay their eggs stretch north of there. From Kuala Dungun you can make a 1½-hour boat trip to Kuala Sungai Ceralak near Kampung Jagung, and then walk through the forest to the Ceralak Falls. The main reason to come to Kuala Dungun is to catch a bus or taxi out again, but there are plenty of hotels if you need to spend the night.

Buses run every hour to Kuantan (M$8)

and Kuala Terengganu (M$4). Buses to Mersing (M$16) and Singapore (M$23) leave at 9.30 am and 9.30 pm and buses to KL (M$16.50) leave at 10.30 am and 10 pm.

RANTAU ABANG

This is the principal turtle beach and the prime area for spotting the great leatherback turtles during the laying season. The long, sandy beach is good for long, lonely walks. Swimming is possible but the undertow can be savage. The Turtle Information Centre, run by the Department of Fisheries, is right near the main budget accommodation centre. They have good displays and show films six times a day. The centre is open every day during the turtle-watching season but otherwise closed on Fridays and public holidays. Note that the nearest bank is at Kuala Dungun, 22 km south.

August is the peak egg-laying season, when you have an excellent chance of seeing turtles, but you may also be lucky in June and

Turtles

Turtle-watching is one of the big attractions of the east coast. There are seven species of turtles and all seven pay annual visits to the coast from 35 to 150 km north of Kuantan.

The villagers believe that the giant leatherback turtles are attracted to Rantau Abang every year because of a large black stone resembling a turtle in the river. A more mundane explanation is that the sharp drop-off at the beach means that the turtles' laborious climb onto land is made considerably easier. At other times of the year the leatherbacks can wander as far away as the Atlantic Ocean, but each year between June and September they return to this one Malaysian beach to lay their eggs.

The egg-laying process is an awesome one, for the female leatherbacks can weigh up to 750 kg (three-quarters of a ton!) and reach over three metres in length. They crawl laboriously up the beach and, well above the high-tide line, dig a deep hole in the sand for their eggs. Usually they dig a false decoy hole first and fill it in again before digging the real hole.

Into this cavity the turtle lays, with much huffing and puffing, about 100 eggs which look rather like large ping pong balls. Having covered the eggs she then heads back towards the water, leaving tracks as if a tank had just driven down the beach. It all takes an enormous effort and several times the turtle will pause to catch her breath as 'tears', to keep sand out of her eyes, trickle down.

Finally the giant turtle reaches the water and an amazing transformation takes place. The heavy, ungainly, cumbersome creature is suddenly back in its element and glides off silently into the night.

The whole process can take two or more hours from start to finish and in each laying season an individual turtle may make several trips to the beach before disappearing until the next year.

The eggs take about 55 days to hatch. It's a fraught process, for many eggs are taken by crabs and other predators. Newly-hatched young turtles are seized by birds on their perilous crawl to the sea and those that reach the water are easy prey for fish and other creatures. It's a long time before they rival their parents in size.

July. Full moon and high-tide nights are said to be best. The villagers know the season is about to end when the smaller green turtles come to lay their eggs – a week later the leatherbacks are gone until next year.

Unfortunately, the east coast's primary tourist attraction has resulted in a decline in turtle numbers, but the government is making a concerted effort to preserve the turtles and their egg-laying habitat. The gross behaviour of the past – pulling the turtles' flippers, shining lights in their eyes, taking the eggs and even riding on the turtles' backs – is punishable with heavy fines. Flash photography and shining torches on the turtles is prohibited, and you must keep a reasonable distance.

The beach is now divided into three sections during the season – prohibited, semi-public (where you have to buy tickets) and free access – in an attempt to control the 'hang gang, the turtles are up' mentality.

Places to Stay & Eat

Right on the beach near the Turtle Information Centre are two travellers' places. *Awang's* (tel 09-842236) advertises from Tioman to Kota Bharu and hence gets most of the travellers. Don't believe their advertised rates of M$3 per person; if you press hard you may be able to get a bed for M$4 but the rooms are mostly M$10 to M$12. They've grown complacent here and the rooms could do with some maintenance, but it has a good restaurant and it is right on the beach.

Ismael's, next door, has similar rooms for M$10 to M$12. It's well kept and friendly, and tends to be less crowded than Awang's.

Probably the top budget place, recommended by many travellers, is *Dahimah's*, about one km south towards Dungun. Dorm beds cost M$5 and most rooms cost M$10. They have a good restaurant and arrange trips, including to Pulau Tenggol.

The *Merantau Inn* (tel 09-841131) is a mid-range motel-style place at Kuala Abang, roughly midway between Dungun and Rantau Abang. Chalets cost from M$40 to M$70.

Thirteen km north of Kuala Dungun, the elegant *Tanjung Jara Beach Hotel* (tel 09-841801) is a 100-room beach resort set on a beautiful beach. It may not have the international facilities of some of the other resorts on the east coast, but its superb layout, modelled after a Malay palace, makes it the most beautiful. There's a pool, bar and restaurant and singles/doubles cost M$150/180, or bungalow suites are M$400.

The resort also operates the *Rantau Abang Visitor Centre*, one km north of the Turtle Information Centre. Very comfortable chalets with four beds cost from M$60 to M$90 depending on the season, making them good value for groups and families.

Getting There & Away

Rantau Abang is only about 22 km north of Kuala Dungun, which in turn is 80 km south of Kuala Terengganu and 138 km north of Kuantan. The nearest airport is at Kerteh, where there are flights to Kuantan, Kuala Terengganu and KL.

Dungun-Kuala Terengganu buses run in both directions every hour and there's a bus stop right near the Turtle Information Centre. Rantau Abang to Terengganu costs M$3 and to Dungun costs M$1. Heading south you can try to hail down a long-distance bus, or take the bus to Dungun from where hourly buses go to Kuantan, as well as buses to Mersing, Singapore and KL.

MARANG

Marang, a large fishing village on the mouth of the Marang River, is very picturesque. The river is dotted with brightly painted boats, the water is crystal clear and thick with fish, and over on the beach kampung huts are interspersed with swaying coconut palms. Marang is a popular travellers' centre and it's a beautiful place to relax. It is also the departure point for Kapas Island. Marang is a conservative village however, especially across the river from the main town, and reserve in dress and behaviour is recommended.

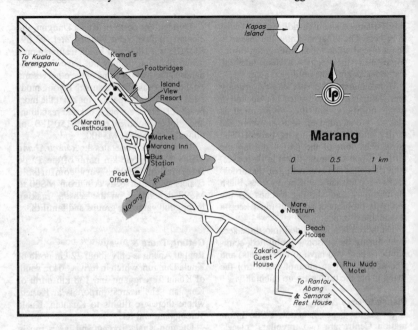

Places to Stay & Eat

A number of travellers' places have sprung up, and more are being built. The budget guest houses are mostly on the northern side of the river or close to town, and the mid-range places stretch south of Marang around Rhu Muda.

Marang Inn (tel 09-681878), on the main street near the bus station, costs M$4 for a dorm and M$10 for a room. It's very popular, good value and has the best food in town.

Most of the guest houses close to town are on the lagoon, a stone's throw from the beach. *Kamal's* is the longest running and one of the best. It's a friendly place with a nice garden setting. Dorm beds are M$4, rooms are M$10 and chalets are M$12. The *Island View Resort* (tel 09-682006) is also good, has free bicycles for guests and charges the same as Kamal's. On the hill behind Kamal's is the *Marang Guesthouse*. It's a notch up from the other guest houses and has its own restaurant, but it's a bit dull.

A dorm bed is M$5, rooms are M$12 and M$15 with bath and mosquito nets. A new place is due to open on the beach, opposite the Island View.

Apart from the restaurants at the Marang Inn and Marang Guesthouse, there are good food stalls near the market and some grotty restaurants on the main street.

Two km south of the river around the 20-km marker is the *Zakaria Guest House*. It's cheap at M$5 in the dorm or M$10 a room, but it's a fair way from the beach and lacks atmosphere. Nearby, the *Beach House* (tel 09-682403) is very welcoming and the most attractive place in Marang. It's right on a beautiful stretch of beach in a lovely garden setting, but it's overpriced at M$25 for a basic chalet up to M$120 for a six-bed, two-storey chalet. Most are M$40 to M$50. The restaurant is dull and a rip-off. Bargain for the room and eat elsewhere.

The *Mare Nostrum* (tel 09-681433), around the corner from the Beach House, is also a little overpriced but better value. Simple A-frame chalets are M$10/16 for singles/doubles, and more luxurious chalets with bath are M$45. The restaurant is good and reasonably priced.

Further south are more places to stay, but they are a long way from anywhere. The *Rhu Muda Motel*, sandwiched between the the main road and the beach, is well kept and costs M$16 for A-frames and M$26 for good rooms with bath. The restaurant is good.

The *Kapas Island Transit & Beach Park*, at the 22-km marker, charges M$5 in a dorm, or M$10 to M$12 for a room with fan. They arrange Kapas Island and scuba diving trips. The *Semarak Rest House*, near the 23-km marker, has large chalets on the beach. Each has four rooms and a central dining/living area. Good rooms with bath cost M$25, or a whole chalet costs M$120. At Kampung Pulau Kerengga, about 10 km from Marang, is *Liza Inn Marang* (tel 09-632989), which has dorm beds for M$10 and chalets for M$30/40.

Getting There & Away
Marang is 45 minutes south of Kuala Terengganu and regular buses run to and from Dungun and Kuala Terengganu. Hail down any bus as the express buses also stop sometimes. The fare is M$1 to Kuala Terengganu.

PULAU KAPAS
Six km offshore from Marang is the beautiful, small island of Kapas, with clear water and powdery white sand beaches. All the accommodation is clustered together on one small beach in the centre of the island, but you can walk around the headlands to quieter beaches, and there is also a rough track across the island. Kapas is best avoided during holidays and long weekends when it is overrun with day trippers.

Kapas is billed as a snorkellers' paradise, though coral is scarce on the most accessible beaches facing the coast. Pulau Raja, the tiny island just off Kapas, has good snorkelling and you can arrange with the boat operators to visit Raja on the way to Kapas.

Places to Stay & Eat
Most people visit Kapas on a day trip, but there are three places to stay, and each has its own restaurant. *Kapas Island Beach Resort* (tel 09-632989) has a few A-frame huts for M$15 and rooms for M$20 to M$28 with bath. As with all the places you can get a single for M$10. *Mak Cik Gemuk Chalets* (tel 09-681221) has the most rooms and charges M$15 or M$20 with bath. *Zaki Beach Chalet* (tel 09-811475) is the top place, with rooms for M$15, M$20 with bath, or M$25 for chalets with bath, fan and mosquito nets (a definite bonus at night). It is also possible to camp on the beach to the south, but bring your own food and water.

Getting There & Away
There's no problem getting a boat to Kapas – most of the places to stay in Marang can arrange it for you, or there are booking offices on the main street. Most boats leave around 9 am and the cost is M$7.50 one way.

Kuala Terengganu

Standing on a promontory formed by the South China Sea on one side and the wide Terengganu River on the other, Kuala Terengganu is the capital of Terengganu state and the seat of the sultan. Oil revenue is changing the face of Kuala Terengganu, from a sprawling oversized fishing village of stilt houses to a bustling modern city. The most obvious example of this new wealth is the huge new bridge that spans the river, avoiding the previous detour on the highway to Kota Bharu.

Kuala Terengganu still has a quiet backwater feel once you get away from the main streets and there's enough to keep you amused during a short stay.

Information
Jalan Sultan Ismail is the modern, wide main street where you will find most of the banks. The state tourist office is near the post office and is usually the best for information on

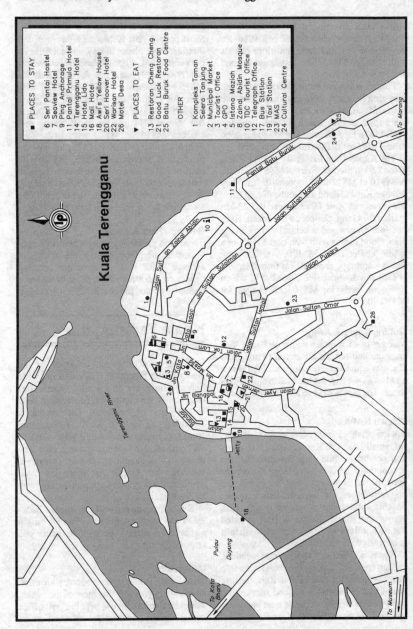

Kuala Terengganu

■ PLACES TO STAY

6 Seri Pantai Hostel
7 Seaview Hotel
9 Ping Anchorage
11 Pantai Primula Hotel
14 Terengganu Hotel
15 Hotel Lido
16 Mali Hotel
18 Awi's Yellow House
20 Seri Hoover Hotel
22 Warisan Hotel
26 Motel Desa

▼ PLACES TO EAT

13 Restoran Cheng Cheng
21 Good Luck Restoran
25 Batu Buruk Food Centre

OTHER

1 Kompleks Taman
   Selera Tanjung
2 Municipal Market
3 Tourist Office
4 GPO
5 Istana Maziah
8 Zainal Abidin Mosque
10 TDC Tourist Office
12 Telegraph Office
17 Bus Station
19 Taxi Station
23 MAS
24 Cultural Centre

attractions in and around Kuala Terengganu. The tourist police post at the bus station is also very helpful and can point you in the right direction. The TDC tourist office can give you a full range of brochures for other parts of Malaysia. Dobi Ria is a laundromat at 9 Jalan Kampung Dalam.

Things to See & Do

Most of Kuala Terengganu's colourful atmosphere can be appreciated along **Jalan Bandar**, Kuala Terengganu's Chinatown. Wander along the street from the taxi station end and you'll find interesting little Chinese shops, a bustling Chinese temple and narrow alleys leading to jetties on the waterfront.

The municipal **market** is colourful and active, with fruit and foods of all types on sale. When they say the fish is fresh, they really mean it – the fishing boats dock right outside! The floor above the fish section has a fabulous collection of batik and songket.

Continuing past the market, you come to the **Istana Maziah** on your right. The sultan's palace is closed to the public, except for some ceremonial occasions. Behind the istana is the gleaming new **Zainal Abidin Mosque**.

Pantai Batu Buruk is the city beach and a popular place to stroll in the evening when the food stalls open up. It is a pleasant stretch of sand but swimming can be dangerous here. Across the road, the **Cultural Centre** sometimes stages pencak silat and wayang shows on Fridays between 5 and 6.30 pm. Check with the tourist office.

The **Istana Tengku Long Museum** is housed in the old sultan's palace at Losong, a few km from town on the bank of the river. The wooden palace buildings are set in attractive gardens and there's a boat museum. Apart from the occasional exhibition, it's not really worth visiting until the state museum moves there from Bukit Kecil.

The jetty behind the taxi station is the place for a 40-sen ferry ride to **Pulau Duyung**, the largest island in the estuary. Fishing boats are built there using age-old techniques and tools; it's always worth a wander around.

A boat from beside the market will take you across to Kampung Seberang Takir, a fishing village on the other side of the river mouth. Five km upriver is **Kampung Pulau Rusa** which has a number of interesting old traditional houses. Ferries and buses go there. You can also hire a boat on an hourly or daily basis to explore further upriver.

Places to Stay – bottom end

Ping Anchorage (tel 09-620851), upstairs at 77A Jalan Dato Isaac, is the No 1 travellers' place. It has an excellent rooftop restaurant and bar and also organises tours to Kapas, Sekayu Falls, Kenyir Lake, etc. It's under the same management as the Marang Inn and will drop you in Marang for free. Dorm beds are M$5, rooms are M$10 to M$12, and M$15 with attached bath. The rooms are good, but most have wire-topped walls and can be noisy.

Awi's Yellow House is a unique guest house built on stilts over the river. It's in the boat-building village on Pulau Duyung, a 15-minute ferry ride across the river. A bed with mosquito net costs M$5 per night in the open dorm or in thatched bungalows. Tea and coffee is free and most people cook their own food, but there is a small restaurant next door. It's a beautiful, relaxed place and highly recommended.

The *Rex Hotel*, right opposite the bus station on Jalan Masjid, has good clean rooms with bath from M$14. A few doors down the street, the *Hotel Evergreen* (tel 09-622505) has rooms without bath for M$12.

There are some more cheap hotels on Jalan Banggol, behind the bus station, but avoid the *Bunga Raya* and *Golden City*, which have noisy bars upstairs and are of doubtful repute. The *Mali Hotel* (tel 09-623278) is the best on Jalan Banggol and good value at M$13/17 for singles/doubles with bath and fan.

The *Terengganu Hotel* (tel 09-622900), opposite the taxi station on Jalan Sultan Ismail, is reasonable value with rooms at M$14 with fan or M$23 with air-con and attached bath. Other cheap hotels on Jalan

Sultan Ismail include the *Hotel Lido* (tel 09-621752) and the *Tong Nam* (tel 09-621540).

Over near the istana are two good cheapies. The *Seaview Hotel* (tel 09-621911) has big rooms with fan for M$14. The *Seri Pantai Hostel* (tel 09-635766), 35 Jalan Sultan Zainal Abidin, costs M$7 in large dorms or M$13.50 for double rooms overlooking the sea. It's usually quiet unless a school group arrives.

Places to Stay – middle

The *Meriah Hotel* (tel 09-627983), 67 Jalan Sultan Ismail, has fan rooms for M$18/24 with bath, and large air-con rooms for M$24/32. Next door, the *Warisan Hotel* (tel 09-622688) was once a top hotel but has seen better days. It is fully air-con and singles/doubles cost M$38/55. The restaurant downstairs is cheap, but nasty.

Similar to the Warisan is the *Seri Hoover* (tel 09-633833), at 49 Jalan Sultan Ismail, with rooms from M$44 to M$78 with TV and hot water.

Places to Stay – top end

The *Motel Desa* (tel 09-623033) has well-appointed rooms with fridge, TV and hot water. It's in a beautiful garden setting on the top of Bukit Pak Api, but to stay there you really need your own transport. Singles/

doubles cost M$88/99, and there's a restaurant.

The *Pantai Primula Hotel* (tel 09-622110) is the only international-class hotel in Kuala Terengganu. This concrete high-rise on Pantai Batu Buruk has a swimming pool, three restaurants and all the services you could want, but with so many top hotels on much better beaches, the Pantai Primula has trouble filling its rooms. Consequently you can expect to get a discount on the quoted rates, which are: M$110/130 for standard rooms, $M170/190 for deluxe rooms (ie overlooking the sea) and M$350 to M$1500 for suites.

Places to Eat

You can find food stalls on Jalan Tok Lam near the telegraph office and at the Batu Buruk Food Centre on the beach front. The 2nd floor of the new Kompleks Taman Selera Tanjung is devoted to food stalls, and you can get good satay and other Malay food.

For Indian food, the *Sri Shanmuga*, 59B

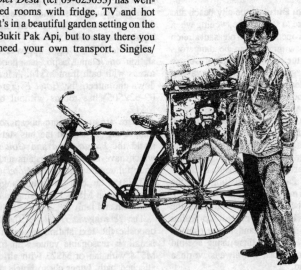

Jalan Tok Lam, is cheap and one of the best in town.

If you have trouble deciphering Chinese menus then the *Restoran Cheng Cheng* at 224 Jalan Bandar is a good place to head for. It's very popular, always crowded at meal times and very reasonably priced. It's buffet style – you get a plate of rice or noodles and help yourself to the display of vegetable and meat dishes. The staff will price your meal using their colour-coded peg system – when you've finished eating take the plate with peg to the counter and pay.

One of the best areas for Chinese food is at the southern end of Jalan Banggol around the Plaza Perdana. Among the restaurants here are the *Chuan Kee* on Jalan Banggol, which has good chicken rice and fruit juices, and the *Good Luck Restoran* around the corner on Jalan Engku Sar. The Good Luck is a bit more expensive but it has an extensive menu, and you can sit at tables on the pavement and watch life roll by. This area is quite lively in the evenings and you can sing at a nearby Karaoke bar after your meal.

If you feel like a minor extravagance the *Pantai Primula Hotel* sometimes puts on an excellent smorgasbord of Malay food. There are also some upmarket seafood restaurants at Batu Buruk.

Things to Buy
Kuala Terengganu is a good place to buy batik and songket, the intricate weaving using gold and silver threads. You can see silk-weaving at the Suterasemai Centre, a few km from town on the road to Marang. The handicraft centre is 10 km from town at Rhusila, not far from Marang, but the best place to buy handicrafts is upstairs at the central market.

Getting There & Away
Air MAS (tel 09-621415), 13 Jalan Sultan Omar and Pelangi Air service Kuala Terengganu. There are direct flights to/from KL (M$123), Penang (M$80) and Kerteh (M$80). A taxi to the airport costs around M$15.

Bus The bus station is on Jalan Masjid, about 100 metres from Jalan Sultan Ismail, but it will eventually shift a few hundred metres further down Jalan Masjid on the opposite side of the street.

Heading south, there are regular buses to Marang (M$1), Rantau Abang (M$3) and Kuantan (M$8). For Mersing (M$14), JB (M$22) and Singapore (M$23), buses leave around 9 am and 9 pm.

Buses to Kota Bharu (M$6.80) leave every 1½ to two hours from 8.30 am to 7 pm. There are also buses to KL (M$20) and a 9 am bus to Butterworth (M$23).

Taxi The main taxi stand is at the bottom of Jalan Sultan Ismail, right at the waterfront. It costs M$2 to Marang, M$10 to Jerteh (for Kuala Besut), M$6 to Rantau Abang, M$12 to Kota Bharu, M$15 to Kuantan, M$60 to Penang, and M$35 to KL.

Getting Around
Bus There are regular regional buses from the bus station. For the museum take a Losong bus; for the handicraft and silk-weaving centres take a Marang or Medan Jaya bus.

Taxi You can get a taxi around town from the small long-distance taxi stand on Jalan Banggol, behind the bus station. Expect to pay a minimum of M$5.

Trishaw Kuala Terengganu was once the trishaw capital of Malaysia, and while their numbers have dropped, they are still the main form of intra-city transport and cost roughly M$1 per km.

AROUND KUALA TERENGGANU
Sekayu Waterfalls
The Sekayu Waterfalls are 56 km south-west of Kuala Terengganu. You can catch a bus or taxi to Kuala Berang, and from there it is about 15 km to the falls where there are

pleasant natural swimming pools. There is a resthouse and chalets, costing M$30 to M$36 per night. Phone the District Office in Kuala Berang (tel 09-811259) for bookings.

Lake Kenyir

Lake Kenyir was formed by the construction of the Kenyir Dam, finished in 1985. The dam is 15 km from Kuala Berang and can be combined with a trip to the Sekayu Waterfalls. There is a visitors' centre at the dam extolling the virtues of hydro-electric power and explaining the engineering marvels that produced the project, but the real attraction of the lake lies in the surrounding jungle that hasn't been flooded.

There are two waterfalls, the Batu Biwa limestone caves, and the lake borders on Taman Negara National Park. At present you can stay at the resthouse in Kuala Berang or house boats on the lake, but there are plans to build chalets and develop the area as a new gateway to Taman Negara.

Getting There & Away You can reach Kuala Berang by bus or taxi from Kuala Terengganu, but from Kuala Berang to the lake you'll have to hire a taxi or private car for around M$20. You can arrange day trips or accommodation at the state tourist office in Kuala Terengganu, or the Ping Anchorage has two-day trekking tours for M$88.

Kuala Terengganu to Kota Bharu

At Kuala Terengganu the main road leaves the coast and runs inland to Kota Bharu, 165 km north, via Jerteh. The quiet coastal backroad from Kuala Terengganu to Penarik runs along a beautiful stretch of coast and there are other turn-offs from the main road to fishing villages and quiet beaches. For cyclists there is also a back road along the coast from Penarik to Kuala Besut.

The final stretch into Kota Bharu runs through fertile rice-growing areas, mirroring the similar area in Kedah and Perlis at the northern end of the peninsula on the western side.

BATU RAKIT

Twenty-four km north of Kuala Terengganu is the small village of Batu Rakit. The beach is quite good, though not as good as those further north. You can stay at the *Pantai Batu Rakit Guest House* for M$24 a night. Take the Batu Rakit bus from Kuala Terengganu for $1.20 and from the bus station walk down to the beach and turn left to get to the guest house.

MERANG

The sleepy little fishing village of Merang (not to be confused with Marang) is 14 km north of Batu Rakit. There's nothing to do here, but the beautiful beach is lined with coconut palms and lapped by clear water. Merang is also the place to get boats to Pulau Redang and other nearby islands.

Further north are more beautiful beaches, at Bari and Penarik, but there is no accommodation.

Places to Stay & Eat

From the moment you take your shoes off at the door, you are treated to traditional hospitality at *Man's Homestay*. Man speaks excellent English and can show you around the village and arrange fishing trips. Facilities are basic – you sleep on camp beds in the family house and wash from the well, but huts are being built. The cost is M$10 per night including all meals. Man's is half a km from the T-intersection in the village, on the Penarik road.

The other place to stay is the *Merang Beach Resort*. Comfortable but plain A-frame chalets cost M$25 or rooms with bath and fan cost M$40. Breakfast and lunch are available for an extra M$10. It's overpriced, but right on a great stretch of beach. The resort's beach is the place to swim, as the villagers are not used to the sight of semi-naked foreigners.

Apart from Man's and the resort, a few kedai kopis have basic rice and curry meals.

Sarawak River, Kuching (DR)

Top Left: Bintulu, Sarawak (DR)
Top Right: Iban Man, Lemanok River, Sarawak (DR)
Bottom Left: Bako National Park, Sarawak (DR)
Bottom Right: Niah Caves National Park, Sarawak (HF)

Getting There & Away

Don't go to Merang if you're in a hurry. Buses are infrequent and hitching is slow. From Kuala Terengganu take one of the three or four daily Penarik buses, or one of the Econovans. The Econovan service is a local enterprise operating out of the vacant lot, destined to be the new bus station, on Jalan Masjid.

Coming from the north, get off at Permaisuri on the main highway and then take one of the hourly buses to Penarik. From Penarik there are occasional buses to Merang, but don't bother waiting – take a share-taxi (M$2), Econovan, or hitch.

PULAU REDANG

One of the largest and most inaccessible of the east coast islands, Pulau Redang has long been the secret of divers. Like most of the islands it is a protected marine park, and offers excellent diving and snorkelling. There is an interesting fishing village on stilts, and to the south of the island are the beautiful bays of Teluk Dalam, Teluk Kalong and Pasir Panjang.

Nearby Islands

Pulau Lang Tengah is an uninhabited island about 10 km from Redang and has excellent snorkelling. Pulau Pinang is the small island opposite the fishing village, and other nearby islands include Pulau Tenggol, Pulau Ekor Tebu and Pulau Ling. Pulau Bidong, halfway between Redang and Kuala Terengganu, is a Vietnamese refugee camp. Pulau Lima, a group of five islands two hours by boat from Redang, also has good snorkelling.

Places to Stay

Diving companies and tour groups offer camping trips, however, you can stay at *Dahlan Beach Chalet* at Pasir Panjang for M$20 per night or M$10 in large tents. Facilities are primitive, with bush toilets and basic washing facilities, but a shower block is planned. You must ring Dahlan in Kuala Terengganu (tel 09-627050) and make advance arrangements.

Getting There & Away

For individual travellers the only feasible way to get there is with a tour group. Dahlan arranges trips for divers and you may be able to join one of his groups. If so, the return fare on his speedboat is M$30. Otherwise you'll have to hire a boat from Merang for around M$200 return, or from Kuala Terengganu for around M$250. Man, from Man's Homestay in Merang, can arrange a boat and camping equipment for a trip to Redang or Lang Tengah, but it's only economical for groups of six or more. It is very difficult to get a boat to Redang in the monsoon.

KUALA BESUT

Kuala Besut, on the coast south of Kota Bharu, has a reasonably pleasant beach and is an interesting, though grubby, fishing village. A visit to this town is usually just a preliminary to a trip to Perhentian Island.

A few km south of Kuala Besut is Bukit Keluang, an attractive beach with small caves reached by a wooden walkway. A resort is being built here. Bukit Belatan waterfall, in the Gunung Tebu Forest Reserve, is 11 km from Jerteh.

Places to Stay

Like most resthouses, Kuala Besut's has been sold off to private enterprise. It's a pity because the old run-down resthouse was cheap, right on the beach and almost always empty. The new resort is a big, white concrete block costing M$60 and up for a room. It's a km south of town over the bridge at Pantai Air Tawar – take any southbound bus or a trishaw. If you want budget accommodation, ask around in the shops on the main street next to the river.

Getting There & Away

From the south, take a bus to Jerteh on the main highway, from where buses (M$1) go every 40 minutes to Kuala Besut. From Kota Bharu it's easier to get off at Pasir Puteh, and take a bus from there. A share-taxi from Jerteh or Pasir Puteh to Kuala Besut costs M$1.50. Taxis from Kuala Terengganu cost M$10; from Kota Bharu M$5.

PERHENTIAN ISLANDS

A two-hour boat trip from Kuala Besut will take you to the beautiful islands of Perhentian Besar and Perhentian Kecil, just 21 km off the coast.

A narrow strait separates the 'besar', or big island, from the 'kecil', or small island. Pulau Perhentian Besar has most of the accommodation; Pulau Perhentian Kecil is the administrative centre and has a fair-sized village with a few kedai kopis and shops.

As far as things to 'see and do' go, it's simply a case of lazing around and watching the coconuts fall. There are beautiful beaches and excellent snorkelling. Bring plenty of books and suntan lotion.

Tourist development has been slow to reach these quiet islands, but expect things to change. There are plans for a hydrofoil service from the Kuala Besut resort, and Pelangi Air is thinking of operating flights to Perhentian Besar. Bye bye paradise.

Walks

Well-marked walking trails cross Perhentian Besar through the jungle to isolated bays. Over the headland past the resthouse and the new jetty are some private chalets – the trail starts behind the furthest chalet from the beach. It's uphill and then down to a long sweeping bay. Halfway along this bay is an arrow pointing inland – this trail leads to the resort and takes 45 minutes. If you continue along the bay the trail over the island starts at the other end of the beach. The cross-island walk takes about 2½ hours.

Places to Stay & Eat

Pulau Perhentian Besar There are two basic choices: the resort or the 'budget accommodation beach'.

The *Perhentian Island Resort* (tel 01-333910) is 'Where reality becomes a fan-tasy'. The slogan is probably inspired by the superb beach and its beautiful coral, and has nothing to do with drugs. The resort is comfortable and attractive but not of international standard. A-frame chalets on the hill are M$32, roomy bungalows are M$52 and a bed in the large, often empty, dorms is

M$12. The only problem is the food, which is ordinary and expensive for what you get. Everything is subject to 10% service charge and 5% government tax.

The budget accommodation beach faces the mainland and is just across the strait from the village on Kecil. It's a 20-minute clamber over two headlands from the resort. Accommodation is basic – there is no electricity and washing is from wells. Food can sometimes be in short supply, and snacks, bottled water and cigarettes are expensive so bring your own.

To the left of the beach as you arrive is *Coco Hut*, which has thatched A-frame huts for M$8. Next door is *Hamid's* with rooms for M$10. *Rosli Chalet* caters mostly for divers, and a bed in a large tent costs M$3 per person or a dorm bed costs M$5. Rooms are M$15. They also serve breakfast and dinner.

Further along the beach around the bend is the *Coral Cave Cafe*, the most popular place to eat. A marvel of architectural simplicity and beauty, it is just a thatched roof strung between the large boulders on the beach with table and chairs beneath. Don't expect it to be there in the monsoon though!

Past the Coral Cave is *Abdul's Chalets* the quietest and one of the best places to stay. Rooms with big verandahs cost M$10.

Over the headland, next to the resthouse, is *Isabella Coffee Shop* which has good food and great squid. The large resthouse lies vacant most of the time, and since the opening of the resort it is only for government officials.

You can also find yourself a quiet place to camp beyond the resthouse, and there are a couple of bungalows for long-term rent between the resort and the budget accommodation beach.

Pulau Perhentian Kecil It is possible to rent a room in the village for about M$5 per night, or if you really want to get away from it all there is a small, basic resort at Pasir Petani with bungalows for M$10. The boats from the mainland will drop you at Pasir Petani, or it's a 30-minute walk from the village.

Getting There & Away

The one-way trip from Kuala Besut to Perhentian costs M$15. Most boats leave Perhentian early in the morning and return late morning and throughout the afternoon. The boats will drop you off at any of the beaches. If you stay at the resort or Pasir Petani, it's a good idea to arrange the return journey with the boat captain.

Small boats ply between the two islands for M$1 per person.

Kota Bharu

In the north-east corner of the peninsula, Kota Bharu is the capital of the state of Kelantan, the termination of the east coast road and a gateway to Thailand.

At first glance Kota Bharu is much like the other east coast cities – a bustling town set on the banks of a wide river, with plenty of modern architecture (some inspiring, most not) and a hint of the colonial. But if you scratch the surface, Kota Bharu has a number of attractions and is a good base for exploring the surrounding region. Many travellers stop there overnight on their way to or from Thailand, but end up staying much longer.

Kota Bharu is Malaysia at its most Malayan – a centre for Malay culture, crafts and religion. It's the place to see kite-flying contests, watch batik being made, admire traditional woodcarving, photograph the colourful marketplace and marvel at the skills of songket weavers and silversmiths.

Kota Bharu is a good place to sample traditional Malay culture, but the true Malay spirit is in the villages of Kelantan and Kota Bharu is a good base to explore the surrounding countryside. Much of Kelantan's character can be attributed to the fact that Kelantan was one of the last states to come under British rule. For centuries Siam held loose claims on Kelantan, and it was not until 1910 that the British installed an adviser. Even then power remained largely with traditional leaders, and the state never received the direct control or development as did the western states.

Orientation & Information

Kota Bharu is initially a difficult town to find your way around. With the exception of the Hotel Perdana's town map, the tourist maps are hopelessly out of scale and the good government map is classified as restricted. On top of this, streets change names – such as Jalan Tok Hakim/Padang Garong/Pengkalan Chepa – and the numbering system for buildings would keep a team of cryptographers gainfully employed for years.

The centre of town is a busy area, north of the clock tower, bounded by Jalan Pintu Pong, Jalan Kebun Sultan/Jalan Mahmud, Jalan Hospital and Jalan Temenggong.

The Kota Bharu tourist information centre (tel 09-785534) is open Saturday to Wednesday from 8 to 12.45 am and 2 to 4.30 pm, Thursday from 8 am to 1.15 pm; it's closed on Fridays. It's on Jalan Sultan Ibrahim, just south of the clock tower. The tourist centre has good handouts, and if you want detailed information ask for Roselan Hanafiah, Kota Bharu's very knowledgeable tour guide.

In Kelantan, state public offices and banks are closed Thursday afternoons and Fridays, but open on Saturdays and Sundays.

The Royal Thai Consulate (tel 09-722545) is on Jalan Pengkalan Chepa and is open from 9 am to 4 pm from Sundays to Thursdays, but is usually closed for lunch between 12.30 and 2.30 pm. Banks are open between 10 am and 3 pm Saturdays to Wednesdays, 9.30 to 11.30 am Thursdays and closed on Fridays. You'll find a number of banks on Jalan Tok Hakim/Padang Garong.

Things to See

If your time is limited, you can take a pleasant one or two-hour stroll around the Padang Merdeka area, preferably in the morning when it's cool. The markets and the performances at the Gelanggang Seni should also not be missed.

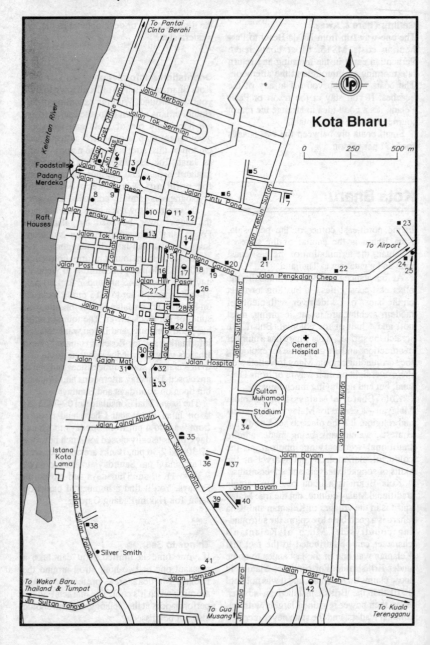

Padang Merdeka

The central Padang Merdeka (Independence Square) was built as a memorial following WW I. It is best known as the place where the British exhibited the body of Tok Janggut, 'Father Beard', a respected elder who was killed at Pasir Puteh in 1915 after leading a 2000-strong uprising against increasing British dominance and their land tax system. The square itself is just fenced-off grass, but there are several points of interest nearby.

At the end of the square is the **Istana Balai Besar** or 'Palace of the Large Audience Hall', constructed largely of timber in 1844. It is only used for ceremonial occasions, but it is symbolically the cultural heart of Kota Bharu.

The adjacent **Royal Museum** is housed in the Istana Jahar, which dates from 1887 and is a wonderful mixture of traditional architecture and Victoriana. Next along is the **State Mosque,** which looks more like a Portuguese church, and then the **Religious Council Building,** another fine piece of local architecture in the same vein as the Istana Jahar.

Further along is the **Karyaneka Handicraft Centre,** which is the oldest brick building in town. Constructed in 1913, it was used by the Japanese army as their headquarters during WW II. The handicrafts and prices are not that stunning, but the small art gallery upstairs has interesting exhibitions of traditional arts.

At the other end of the square on the riverbank are a number of good food stalls, and if you go south along the river you'll see the **raft houses** that still exist in defiance of modern amenities.

Around the corner in Jalan Post Office Lama is the interesting CK Lam's **antique shop,** crammed with everything from hand-carved bird cages to old musical instruments.

While you're here, wander along **Jalan Pasar Lama,** a neglected but picturesque street that once thrived with river commerce.

Markets

The central market is one of the most colourful

and active in Malaysia. It is in a modern octagonal building with traders selling fresh produce on the ground floor, and on the floors above are stalls selling spices, basketware and other goods. Near the market is the Bazaar Buluh Kubu, a good place to buy handicrafts.

The old central market consists of a complete block of food stalls on the ground floor, and the stalls on the 1st floor have a good selection of batik, songket and clothes.

Cultural Centre (Gelanggang Seni)

One of the best things about Kota Bharu is the chance to see performances of top-spinning, traditional dance dramas, wayang kulit, and other traditional activities. They're at Gelanggang Seni, across the road from the Hotel Perdana on Jalan Sultan Mahmud, from February to October, except during Ramadan. Free afternoon and evening sessions are held on Saturdays, Sundays, Mondays and Wednesdays. Check with the tourist information centre for more details.

State Museum

The State Museum is opposite the clock tower, next to the tourist information centre.

Events

Each year around August, Kota Bharu has a bird-singing contest when you can see the prized Merbok or Ketitir birds perform. There are also contests every Friday morning in a village about seven km downriver from Kota Bharu. The spectacular kite festival is usually held in May, the drum festival in July, and the top-spinning contest in September. The sultan's birthday celebrations involves a week of cultural events. The dates vary so check with the tourist information centre or get a hold of the TDC's 'Calender of Events' brochure.

Organised Tours

The tourist information centre has expensive but rewarding tours: a morning craft tour (M$35), a river safari and jungle-trekking tour (M$60), and a three-day 'kampung experience' tour (M$160) where you stay with a family and get the opportunity to learn local crafts.

Places to Stay – bottom end

Guest Houses Kota Bharu is overrun with good cheap guest houses. Competition is fierce and, unless otherwise stated, all charge M$4 for a dorm bed, M$8/10 for singles/doubles. Accommodation is usually simple, but they provide free tea and coffee, lots of interesting travellers' information and a relaxed atmosphere. Most have bicycles and cooking facilities.

There are two basic categories of guest houses. The first is those close to the centre of town, which are usually rented floors above shops divided into plywood-walled rooms. They all have a good atmosphere and are the most conveniently located, but tend to be noisy. The second category is those in private houses, which are quieter and more comfortable but are often a long walk from the main attractions.

Of the places close to the centre, the *KB Inn* (tel 09-741786) and *Yee Guest House* (tel 09-741944) are a couple of doors from each other on Jalan Padang Garong, not far from the bus station. Both are friendly places but the Yee is better – it has a good common room and the ever-fussing Nasron to look after you. Upstairs at 35 Jalan Pintu Pong, next to Kentucky Fried Chicken, is the *City Guest House*, a spotlessly clean well-run place and quieter than most. Further out on Jalan Pengkalan Chepa is the ever-popular *Town Guest House* (tel 09-785192). The big plus is the roof-top restaurant with good cheap food. If you ring they will pick you up from the bus station.

Probably the best in town is the *Ideal Travellers' Guest House* (tel 09-7442246), in a private house down an alley off Jalan Pintu Pong. It's quiet, central and has a pleasant garden, but is often full. Apart from the standard rates, they have rooms with attached bath for M$12. They also run the *Friendly Guest House*, a few hundred metres away, just off Jalan Kebun Sultan. It's not as attractive, but is also quiet and has good rooms, most with attached bath for M$10/12.

On Jalan Pengkalan Chepa near the Royal Thai Consulate is the *Rainbow Inn Guest House*. This house has a pleasant garden and some great artwork on the walls, courtesy of inspired travellers. Across the road and up an alley is the popular *Mummy's Hitec Hostel* in an old house with a large garden. Mummy is a real character and enjoys a night out with the boys. Extras include free haircuts. A trishaw to the Rainbow Inn or Mummy's Hitec costs about M$1, or take bus Nos 4, 8A or 9 for 40 sen.

The best value in town has to be *De 999 Guest House* at M$3/6 for good singles/ doubles including breakfast and free bicycles. It's not far from the long-distance bus station in the small street directly behind the Irama Hotel, at number 3188-G. The house is hard to find – there's only a tiny sign on the gate. The *Rebana Hostel*, up an alleyway off Jalan Sultan Zainab, is a long way from the town centre but worth the effort. It's a lovely house, decorated Malay-style with lots of artwork around. There's a variety of rooms, ranging from the M$4 dorm and pokey M$6 singles, to some beautiful old rooms and chalets in the garden for M$10 to M$15.

The *Kampung Lodge* (tel 09-741955), on the corner of Jalan Pasar Lama and Jalan Tengku Besar, is right opposite Padang Merdeka, but the owner seems unaware of what the other guest houses are charging. Rates are M$6 for a dorm bed, M$16/21 for singles/doubles, but it's easy to bargain.

Apart from the guest houses, which cater almost exclusively to Westerners, are the *asramas*, which are guest houses catering almost exclusively to Malaysians. They generally charge M$5 in large dorms and M$10 for rooms. There are a number on and around Jalan Tok Hakim, or there's the *Hitect Hostel* (tel 09-740961), a YHA affiliate, near the old central market.

Hotels Of course there are also plenty of cheap Chinese hotels. A basic but interesting old hotel is the *Thye Ann Hotel* (tel 09-785907), on Jalan Hilir Pasar opposite the old central market, with huge doubles for

M$15. Other possibilities, where you can get a room for around M$12, are on Jalan Padang Garong/Jalan Tok Hakim. At the bus station is the noisy *Hotel Kelantan*. Further along towards the river are the *Ah Chew* (bless you) and the *Mee Chin*. Right near the river are the *Hotel North Malaya* and the *New Bali*.

Places to Stay – middle

Opposite the central bus station, the *Hotel Suria* (tel 09-743310) has large rooms with bath and air-con for the 'discount' rate of M$22/32. It's very good value and they even throw in 'free breakfast for foreigner'. The *Hotel Tokio Baru* (tel 09-749488), on Jalan Tok Hakim near the Temenggong Hotel, is a better class of cheap hotel with fan rooms from M$26 and air-con rooms from M$32.

The *Hostel Pantai* is not a hostel and is more like a cheap motel. Large rooms with attached bath and air-con cost M$32. It's down a small street off Jalan Kebun Sultan.

The *Hotel Irama* (tel 09-78971), Jalan Sultan Ibrahim, has faded rooms with bath and air-con for M$35 up to M$60 for a suite. It also owns the *Hotel Apollo* next door where rooms cost M$25. Better appointed and better value is the large *Indah Hotel* (tel 09-781277), opposite Padang Merdeka on Jalan Tengku Besar. It scrapes into the two-star category and singles/doubles cost from M$38/46.

The *Kencana Inn* (tel 09-747994), Jalan Padang Garong, is fully air-con and at the top of this range with rooms for M$60/70 to M$80/90. They also have a cheaper place on Jalan Doctor, the *Kencana Inn City Centre* (tel 09-740944), which is a few steps down in quality and charges M$45/50.

The *Temenggong Hotel* (tel 09-783844), on Jalan Tok Hakim, is on a par with the Kencana Inn but better value with discount rates of M$55/65 to M$75/85.

Places to Stay – top end

Right in the centre on Jalan Datuk Pati, the architecturally eccentric *Hotel Murni* (tel 09-782399) is a notch above the best mid-range places and is popular with business people.

Singles/doubles cost M$92/104 to M$167/184.

The top hotel is undoubtedly the *Hotel Perdana* (tel 09-785000) on Jalan Sultan Mahmud. Superior rooms cost M$130/160 and deluxe rooms are M$150/185. It's the biggest hotel in Kota Bharu, is fully air-con with swimming pool, bowling alley, squash and tennis courts, and has a wonderful camp bell boy.

Places to Eat

The best and cheapest Malay food in Kota Bharu is found at the night market, opposite the central bus station. The food stalls are set up in the evenings and there's a wide variety of delicious, cheap Malay food. You can buy a snack or main meal, and then buy rice wrapped in banana leaf from one of the rice stalls (the adventurous can try the blue rice). You can sit at any of the tables, eat your meal and order a drink. Traditionally you eat with the right hand – each table has a jug of water and a roll of tissue paper to clean your fingers – or there are forks and spoons. Local specialities include: *ayam percik* (marinated chicken enclosed between bamboo skewers)

Wau Bulan – Malaysian Kite

and *nasi kerabu* (rice with coconut, fish and spices).

More good food stalls are next to the river opposite the Padang Merdeka, and at the stadium, which has a number of stalls selling ABC (ais batu kacang – the shaved ice dessert).

There are plenty of Chinese restaurants around town, including good chicken rice places on Jalan Padang Garong near the Kencana Inn. The *Restoran Vegetarian*, on Jalan Post Office Lama opposite the antique shop, has good Chinese vegetarian food.

The *Razak Restoran*, corner Jalan Datok Pati and Jalan Padang Garong, is cheap and has excellent Indian Muslim food.

The *A&N Restaurant* is a mid-range restaurant serving Chinese and Malay food. The best thing is that you can dine in the pleasant garden behind the restaurant. It's opposite Padang Merdeka on Jalan Tengku Besar, 150 metres from the Indah Hotel.

For top range restaurants, try the Murni and Perdana hotels.

Things to Buy

Kota Bharu is a centre for Malay crafts. Batik, songket, silverware, woodcarving and kite-making factories and shops are dotted around town.

One of the best places to see handicrafts is on the road to Pantai Cinta Berahi. There are a number of workshops representing most crafts, stretched out along the road all the way to the beach. Just out of town the road turns to the right, at Kampung Penambang, and close to each other you'll find a batik and songket centre, a kite-maker and a woodcarver. Past the nine-km marker at Kampung Badang is a good silversmith and a handicraft centre. Further on at Kampung Kemumin is the workshop of master kite-maker, Yasok Haji Umat. There are plenty of other craft places, open every day except Friday. You can take bus No 10 to get to them, but the best way is by car or bicycle as they are spread out over a six-km stretch.

There are also silversmiths on Jalan Sultanah Zainab, and the Semasa Batik Factory is on the road to Gua Musang, down the road besides Lee's garage, which you reach on bus No 5. The markets are as good a place as any to buy handicrafts if you know the prices and bargain hard. For batik, you can also try Wisma Batik, on Jalan Che Su, just around the corner from the Hotel Murni.

Getting There & Away

Air The MAS office (tel 09-747000) is opposite the clock tower on Jalan Gajah Mati. Direct flights go to Penang (M$72), Alor Setar (M$59) and KL (M$86). The airport is eight km from town – take bus No 9 from the old central market. A taxi costs around M$10.

Bus The state-run SKMK is the largest bus company, and runs all the city and regional buses, as well as most of the long-distance buses. It operates from the central bus station (city and regional buses) and the Langgar bus station (long-distance buses). All the other long-distance bus companies operate from the Jalan Hamzah external bus station. On arrival in Kota Bharu some of the buses will drop you at the central bus station, but they don't depart from there.

SKMK are the easiest to deal with as they have ticket offices at all the bus stations. Long-distance departures are from the Langgar bus station but, just to make things confusing, a few evening buses also go from the central bus station. Ask which station your bus departs from when you buy your ticket, and book as far ahead as possible, especially for the Butterworth (Penang) buses.

SKMK has regular buses to Kuala Terengganu (M$6.80) and Kuantan (M$16). Buses to Johore Bharu (M$24), Singapore (M$25) and KL (M$25) leave at 8 pm (also 9 pm to KL). The bus to Butterworth (M$18) departs at 10 am and takes about seven hours. There is a bus to Jerantut (M$18) at 8.30 am. Other destinations are Alor Setar, Kuala Lipis, Temerloh, Dungun and Grik.

The other companies cover many of the same routes (but not Butterworth as yet) and are worth trying if the SKMK buses are full. Buy your tickets at the Jalan Hamzah external bus station, or some of the companies have agents at the Bazaar Buluh Kubu. Bumi Express is the only company with buses to Malacca.

All regional buses go from the central bus station to: Wakaf Baru (Nos 19, 27, 27a, 43), Rantau Panjang (Nos 29, 29a, 36), Tumpat (No 19), Bachok (Nos 2, 23, 29), Pasir Puteh (Nos 3, 3a), Jerteh (No 3a), Kuala Krai (Nos 5, 57) and Gua Musang (No 57).

Train The jungle railway starts at Tumpat and goes through Kuala Krai, Gua Musang, Kuala Lipis, Jerantut (for Taman Negara National Park) and eventually meets the Singapore-KL line at Gemas. Travel is slow but the scenery is certainly worth it. The nearest station to Kota Bharu is at Wakaf Baru, a 50 sen trip on bus Nos 19 or 27.

The 'express train' leaves at 10.50 am. Both 2nd and 3rd class are comfortable – the only difference between the two is that 3rd class gets more crowded, but you'll usually have no problems getting a seat at Wakaf Baru. There are also ordinary trains, which have limited seats, stop at every station, and are usually crammed with agricultural produce as well as people. Refer to the introductory Getting Around chapter for the train timetable and fare details.

Taxi The taxi station is on the southern side of the bus station, and there is an overflow station during the day at the site of the night market.

Main taxi destinations and costs are: Kuala Terengganu (M$12), Kuantan (M$25), KL (M$35), Butterworth (M$30) and JB (M$52).

To Thailand The Thai border is at Rantau Panjang (Sungai Golok on the Thai side), 1½ hours by bus from Kota Bharu. Bus No 29 departs on the hour from the central bus station and costs M$2. From Rantau Panjang walk across the border, and then it's about one km to the station or a trishaw costs M$3. Malaysian currency is accepted in Sungai Golok. Share-taxis from Kota Bharu to Rantau Panjang cost M$4.

From Sungai Golok there is a train to

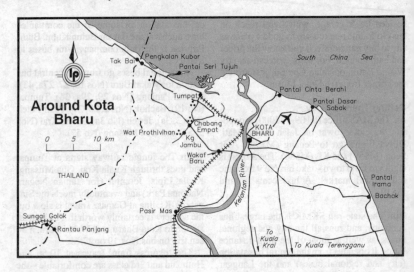

Surathani at 6 am, one to Bangkok at 10.05 am and an express train to Bangkok at 10.55 am. All stop at Hat Yai and Surathani. Buses to Hat Yai leave from the Valentine Hotel in Sungai Golok until 3 pm, and there are taxis to Yala and Narathiwat town.

An alternative route into Thailand is via Pengkalan Kubor on the coast. It's more time-consuming and very few travellers go this way. See Around Kota Bharu for more details.

Getting Around
Bus Most of the city buses leave from the middle of the old central market, on the Jalan Hilir Pasar side, or from opposite the Bazaar Buluh Kubu. To Pantai Cinta Berahi (PCB), the Beach of Passionate Love, take bus No 10 for 90 sen. It leaves from the Bazaar Buluh Kubu or you can catch it at the bus stand in front of the Kencana Inn.

Trishaw Trishaws are still the most common transport around town. A short journey up to a km costs M$1.

AROUND KOTA BHARU
Masjid Kampung Laut
Reputed to be the oldest mosque in Penin-

sular Malaysia, this mosque was built about 300 years ago by Javanese Muslims as thanks for a narrow escape from pirates.

It originally stood at Kampung Laut, just across the river from Kota Bharu, but each year the monsoon floods (November to January) caused considerable damage to the wooden mosque and in 1968 it was moved to a safer location. It now stands about 10 km inland at Kampung Nilam Puri, a local centre for religious study.

Pantai Cinta Berahi
Kota Bharu's best-known beach has a name that's hard to forget. Pantai Cinta Berahi, the 'Beach of Passionate Love', is 10 km north of the town, only 30 minutes by bus from Kota Bharu. It's actually just a wide, sandy beach with a few casuarinas and hardly lives up to its exotic name. It is becoming quite a popular resort, but there are better beaches on the east coast. It's pleasant enough if you are staying in town and want some sun and sand.

Places to Stay & Eat The only budget accommodation is the run-down, pokey A-frame huts at the *Long House Beach Motel*

(tel 09-740090). They cost M$13, or air-con singles/doubles cost M$32/42. *HB Village* (tel 09-744993), 1½ km from the village, is better and has a few M$14 A-frame huts and more comfortable bungalows with attached bath for M$25 and M$50 with air-con. The *Cinta Motel* (tel 09-781307) has bungalows with attached bath for M$40 to M$60. The top place by far is the *Perdana Resort* (tel 09-785000) with swimming pool, tennis courts, restaurant, etc. Pastel-coloured designer bungalows cost M$103 to M$172. The No 10 bus from Kota Bharu stops at the Perdana Resort and terminates at HB Village.

Pantai Irama

Pantai Irama ('Beach of Melody') at Bachok has landscaped gardens along the foreshore and is popular with day-trippers. Like most of the beaches around Kota Bharu, it's pleasant but nothing special.

Places to Stay You can stay at *Pantai Irama Chalets* (tel 09-93148), which is half a km north of the bus station; good chalets cost M$30.

Other Beaches

Pantai Dasar Sabak, 13 km from Kota Bharu and three km beyond the Pengkalan Chepa Airport, is a beach with a history. On 7 December 1941 the Pacific Theatre of WW II commenced there when Japanese troops stormed ashore, a full hour and a half before the rising sun rose over Pearl Harbor.

Other beaches close to Kota Bharu include **Pantai Dalam Rhu** near the fishing village of Semerak, 19 km from Pasir Puteh, near Kuala Besut. It's sometimes known as Pantai Bisikan Bayu, the 'Beach of Whispering Breeze'. North of Kota Bharu there's **Pantai Kuda**, 'Horse Beach', 25 km away in the Tumpat area, and **Pantai Seri Tujuh** (see the following Tumpat District section).

Tumpat District

Tumpat District is a major agricultural area bordering Thailand, and the Thai influence is very noticeable. Small villages are scattered among the picturesque rice fields, and there are a number of interesting Thai Buddhist temples, such as Wat Prothivihan. Other places of interest include the beach resort at Pantai Seri Tujuh, and Pengkalan Kubor is an exit point for Thailand. Tumpat town is at the end of the railway line, but it has no hotels.

Temples Wat Phothivihan, a Buddhist temple with a 40-metre-long reclining Buddha statue, is claimed to be one of the largest in South-East Asia. It was built in 1973. There is a resthouse available for use by sincere devotees for a donation.

To get to Wat Phothivihan, take bus Nos 19 or 27 to Chabang Empat for M$1. Get off at the crossroads and turn left. Walk 3½ km along this road, through interesting villages and paddy fields, until you reach Kampung Jambu and the reclining Buddha (takes about one hour).

The region is dotted with Thai-influenced temples or 'wats', and the Wesak Festival (usually held in August) is a particularly good time to visit them. At Chabang Empat, if you take the turn to the right past the police station there is another wat one km away. There are wats on the main road two km south of Tumpat and if you continue past Chabang Empat on bus No 19 you reach Wat Phikulthong.

Pantai Seri Tujuh Resort This downmarket beach resort is on a long spit of land, with a sweeping stretch of beach facing the sea and a quiet bay behind. It is popular during holidays, but otherwise very quiet. The resort is government-run and rooms start from M$20 and go up to M$60 for chalets with air-con. Contact 09-757963 for bookings.

Pengkalan Kubor Right on the Thai border, Pengkalan Kubor is the immigration checkpoint for this little used back route into Thailand. During the day a large car ferry crosses the river to busy Tak Bai in Thailand for 50 sen per person. From Kota Bharu take bus Nos 27, 27A or 43.

Don't take the small long-propeller boats that cross in the evening. These cater to Malaysians looking for Thai girls and they return in the early morning before the immigration checkpost opens.

Kuala Krai

Kuala Krai, 65 km south of Kota Bharu, used to be the end of the road but now it continues on to Gua Musang. On the way to Kuala Krai you can stop at Labok, a natural hot springs five km off the road. Kuala Krai has a small zoo specialising in local wildlife, including native bears and musang (large long-haired wildcats). It's open every day except Friday from 9 am to 6.30 pm, closed from 12.30 to 2 pm. Admission is M$1.

Places to Stay The *Hotel Keow Sin* is on the main road 50 metres from the railway station. Basic rooms cost from M$8. Further along the street, the *Hotel Joo Mui* is similar. The *Hotel Krai* has better rooms for M$12, if you bargain.

Waterfalls

There are a number of waterfalls in the Pasir Puteh area. Jeram Pasu is the most popular; to reach it you have to follow an eight-km path from Kampung Padang Pak Amat, about 35 km south of Kota Bharu en route to Pasir Puteh. Other falls in this same area include Jeram Tapeh, Cherang Tuli and Jeram Lenang.

River Trips

You can make a number of river trips from Kota Bharu. A short trip takes you downriver to Kuala Besar and you can then return on bus No 28. Longer trips can be made from Kuala Krai.

From Kota Bharu, take bus No 5 to Kuala Krai at 7.45 am and then a boat from Kuala Krai to Kuala Balah (M$5) at around 11 am – no boat on Fridays. It's a two-hour trip through dense jungle.

From Kuala Balah you can hitch or pay for a ride (around M$4) to Jeli, near the Thai border, then bus to Tanah Merah (M$2) and from there back to Kota Bharu (approxi-

mately M$2). Buses on the new east-west highway also pass through Tanah Merah.

It's worth staying in Kuala Balah overnight so you have time to look around. You can catch a boat back to Kuala Krai very early the next morning.

Another alternative is to get off the boat at Dabong, before you reach Kuala Balah. Dabong is on the railway line and you can get a train back to Kota Bharu at around 1.45 pm. The train takes three long hours to reach Kuala Krai and a further two hours from there to Wakaf Baru. From Wakaf Baru, take bus Nos 19 or 27 into Kota Bharu. It's much easier to leave the train at Kuala Krai and to catch a taxi from there to Kota Bharu for M$5 – the taxi trip takes about one hour.

From Dabong, it's a one-hour walk to some caves. Ask locals for directions to the caves and to the waterfall which is in the same area (maybe 30 minutes further on).

Places to Stay Kuala Balah has recently been rebuilt a km or so away from its previous flood-prone site. You can stay at the *Rest House*.

Coast to Coast

With the completion of the northern east-west highway there are now three routes from coast to coast, apart from the crossing in the south between Ayer Hitam and Jemaluang, a little south of Mersing.

East-West Highway

The east-west road starts near Kota Bharu and runs roughly parallel to the Thai border, eventually meeting the little-used road north from Kuala Kangsar to Keroh on the Thai border at Grik. The views from the highway are often superb.

Hitching is fairly easy along this stretch if you're on the road early. The road may be subject to closure during the monsoon.

The east-west road was a massive undertaking. As well as battling the harsh jungle terrain and monsoon washouts, communist guerrillas also launched regular attacks. The last remnants of the guerrillas finally gave themselves up a couple of years ago, but the road still has its hazards and travel is restricted at night.

Grik

Grik was once just a logging 'cowboy town' but the east-west highway and the huge Temengor Dam hydropower scheme has really put it on the map. Tasik Temengor is now one of Malaysia largest lakes. For WW II buffs the area has many associations with the exploits of Force 136.

Places to Stay The *Rest House* has ancient but spacious doubles with attached bath for M$15 and is probably the best place to stay. The much more central *Sin Wah Hotel* has basic but large rooms for M$10.

Getting There & Away There are buses from Ipoh or Kuala Kangsar to Grik every two hours or so. Taxis to or from Kota Bharu cost about M$18. See the Kota Bharu section for Butterworth-Kota Bharu buses.

Kota Bharu to Kuala Lumpur

The Jungle Railway

The central railway line goes largely through aboriginal territory. It's an area of dense jungle offering magnificent views.

Commencing near Kota Bharu, the line runs to Kuala Krai, Gua Musang, Kuala Lipis, Jerantut (access point for the Taman Negara National Park), and eventually meets the Singapore-KL railway line at Gemas. Unless you have managed to book a sleeping berth right through, you'll probably find yourself sharing a seat with vast quantities of agricultural produce, babies and people moving their entire homes. Allow for at least a couple of hours delay, even on the expresses.

The line's days are probably numbered as

roads are rapidly being pushed through. The road now goes all the way from Singapore, through Kuala Lipis to Kota Bharu. The train is a lot slower but definitely more interesting.

See the introductory Getting Around section for timetable and fares on the jungle railway. Taxis from Kota Bharu to Gua Musang cost M$14, from Kuala Krai M$12.

GUA MUSANG

This former logging camp is now rapidly on its way up and planners see it as the centre of a huge new development area carved from the jungle. Logging is still a major industry, and the town has a frontier feel to it, but the massive new administrative buildings on the outskirts of town point to its future.

Gua Musang (Musang Cave) owes its name to the caves in the limestone outcrop that towers above the railway station. The superb-looking musang is a native animal that looks like a cross between a large cat and a possum, with long fur and a long curling tail, but unfortunately hunters have killed off these former inhabitants of the caves.

It is possible to explore the caves but it is a very steep, hazardous climb to the entrance. The entrance is above the kampung next to the railway line, a few hundred metres from the station. Take a torch – a guide is recommended if you want to venture far into the caves. Young boys will offer to guide you for a few dollars.

Places to Stay

The *Rest House* is a run-down, rambling old place that costs M$16 for a room with shared bathroom. It's friendly and from the verandah you can watch the whole life of swinging Gua Musang – you are, in fact, right opposite the volleyball court.

Other Chinese hotels in the main street are a little cheaper but equally basic and less colourful. The top place is the *Kesada Inn* (tel 09-901229) just outside town.

KUALA LIPIS

The road from Fraser's Hill through Raub meets the railway line at this town. Kuala Lipis is a well-maintained pretty town with fine rows of colonial shops down the main street. There's not much to do in Kuala Lipis, though it's a pleasant place.

Some visitors make jungle treks from Kuala Lipis and most people who go on these treks enjoy them. Unfortunately, we have had a number of letters from female travellers making serious complaints about treks organised by Johnny Tan Bok. None of these visitors appear to have raised their concerns with the Malaysian authorities but we strongly recommend that female travellers should not take his treks. We have had good reports of other treks organised out of Kuala Lipis, but the best advice is to use registered guides such as those at Taman Negara National Park.

Places to Stay There are several cheap hotels in Kuala Lipis. Near the railway station are the *Hotel Paris, Hotel Central* and *Hotel Tiong Kok*, where you can get a room for around M$14. Johnny Tan Bok has a traveller's place above the Wangli Restaurant, 100 metres from the bus station, which again female travellers should treat with caution.

A little better than the cheapies is the *Hotel Seri Pahang*. The *Rest House* has the best rooms around.

Getting There & Away Kuala Lipis is on the railway line. There is a morning express train to Kota Bharu and a night train to Singapore. There are also buses from Kuala Lipis to Kota Bharu, Kuala Lumpur and Kuantan.

If you want to go to Taman Negara, take the train, a bus or a taxi to Jerantut and then a bus from Jerantut to Kuala Tembeling. You can also catch a bus or a local train to Tembeling Halt, near Kuala Tembeling, but you may well miss the early morning boats to Taman Negara.

To and from Kuala Lipis there are also buses to Kota Bharu, KL and Kuantan.

JERANTUT

Jerantut is the gateway to Taman Negara National Park. Most visitors to the park spend at least one night here, but the town itself has no real attractions. You can stock up on supplies in Jerantut at the large emporium on the main road towards Temerloh.

Places to Stay

The cheapest hotels are near the railway station on the main road. The dismal *Hotel Tong Heng* has rooms for M$8 while the slightly better *Hotel Wah Hing* has rooms from M$9 to M$14. The *Hotel Jerantut* has rooms from M$12 to M$17 and is definitely worth the extra money.

Right opposite the bus station, the brand new *Hotel Chett Fatt* is a friendly place that welcomes travellers. The rooms are spotlessly clean but a little soulless. It is good value at M$15 for a fan room, M$20 with air-con. Near the bus station, the *Hotel Bunga Raya* costs from M$16 for a fan room up to M$23 for air-con rooms.

The *Resthouse*, across the railway line on the way to Kuala Lipis, is the top place in town. Pleasant motel-style rooms cost M$26 with fan or M$36 with air-con.

Places to Eat

There are food stalls near the bus station and plenty of cheap coffee shops along the main road. The liveliest area at night is on the road to Taman Negara past the emporium, where you can find plenty of Chinese restaurants and a couple of Karaoke bars. *Restaurant Liang Fong* has good food and is reasonably priced.

Getting There & Away

Jerantut is on the Kota Bharu-Gemas railway line. From Jerantut, buses to Kuantan leave every hour until 4 pm and cost M$6.40 (M$7.70 air-con). A bus to Kota Bharu leaves at 10 am and costs M$18. For buses to KL you have to go via Temerloh – buses to Temerloh leave every half hour and cost M$2.25. Taxis cost M$5. Taxis to KL cost M$14.

For Kuala Tembeling and the boats to Taman Negara, the Jelai company's blue and white buses leave approximately every two hours from 8 am and cost M$1.10. The buses will drop you at the jetty, 500 metres past the township. A taxi to Kuala Tembeling costs M$3 per person. To catch the 9 am boat to Taman Negara you have to get the first bus at 8 am, as it takes about 45 minutes to reach Kuala Tembeling.

TAMAN NEGARA NATIONAL PARK

Peninsular Malaysia's great national park covers 4343 sq km and sprawls across the states of Pahang, Kelantan and Terengganu. The part of the park mostly visited, however, is all in Pahang but other access points are being developed.

Reactions to the park depend totally on the individual's experience. Some people see lots of wildlife and come away happy, others see little more than leeches and find the park hardly worth the effort.

The park headquarters are at Kuala Tahan. There are a number of jungle walks to hides and salt licks from the headquarters where you may see animals.

Getting well away from it all requires a few day-long treks and/or expensive trips upriver by boat. The 60-km boat trip from Kuala Tembeling to Kuala Tahan (park headquarters) takes three to four hours, depending on the level of the river. You reach the park boundary near Kuala Atok, 35 km from Kuala Tembeling.

Along the river, you'll see several Orang Asli kampungs, domestic water buffalo and the local fishing people. Other animals you might see from the boat include monkeys, otters, kingfishers and hornbills. It's a beautiful journey.

Accommodation and transport in Taman Negara has gone through a number of changes in the past few years. The government keeps handing the responsibility over to private enterprise and then taking it over again. Check with the tourist office in KL about bookings.

Information & Orientation

Make arrangements for your visit to Taman Negara at the Malaysia Tourist Information Complex (tel 03-2434929), 109 Jalan Ampang, Kuala Lumpur. You have to make advance bookings for the park boat and the accommodation at Kuala Tahan. A deposit of M$30 is usually requested, but you may be able to make bookings over the phone and pay on arrival. An entry permit costs M$1, a camera licence is M$5 and a fishing licence is M$10.

The park headquarters has a reception centre, a couple of restaurants, a hostel, some chalets and two shops selling a small range of tinned foods, toiletries, batteries, local cakes and snacks. You can rent camping and hiking gear from the shop near reception. Every night at 8.45 pm, a free slide show is shown during which a free map of Taman Negara and its trails is handed out.

The best time to visit the park is between March and September. It's closed in the rainy season from mid-November to mid-January and also during Hari Raya for about one week.

Although everyday clothes are quite suitable around Kuala Tahan, you'll need heavy-duty gear if you're heading further afield. Jungle attire is a good idea both as protection and to make you less conspicuous to the wildlife you want to see. River travel in the early morning hours can be surprisingly cold. Mosquitoes can be annoying but you can buy repellent at the park shop if you're not already prepared.

Leeches are generally not a major problem, although they can be a real nuisance after heavy rain. There are many ways to keep these little blood-suckers at bay –

Hornbill

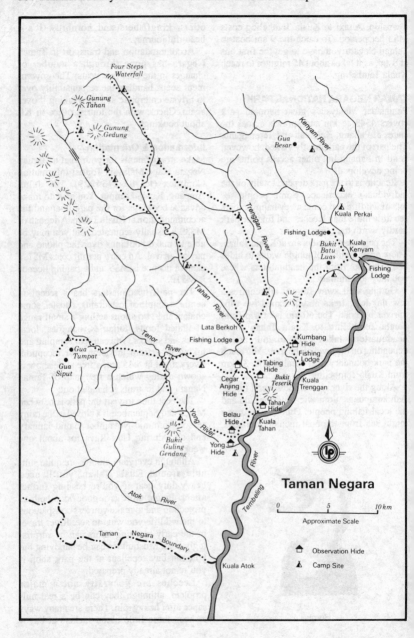

Four Steps Waterfall

Gunung Tahan

Gunung Gedung

Kenyam River

Gua Besar

Trengganu River

Tahan River

Kuala Perkai

Fishing Lodge

Bukit Batu Luas

Kuala Kenyam

Fishing Lodge

Tenor River

Lata Berkoh

Fishing Lodge

Kumbang Hide

Fishing Lodge

Gua Tumpat

Gua Siput

Tabing Hide

Cegar Anjing Hide

Bukit Teserik

Kuala Trenggan

Tahan Hide

Belau Hide

Kuala Tahan

Bukit Guling Gendang

Yong River

Yong Hide

Tembeling River

Atok River

Taman Negara Boundary

Kuala Atok

Taman Negara

0   5   10 km

Approximate Scale

🏠 Observation Hide

▲ Camp Site

Top: Mount Kinabalu, Sabah (GC)
Bottom: Mountain Views, Sabah (HF)

VB, GC, Flora & Fauna, Kinabalu National Park
TW, ST,
ST, HF

mosquito repellent, tobacco, salt, toothpaste and soap can all be used with varying degrees of success. A liberal coating of Baygon insect spray over shoes and socks works best.

The shop next to the reception centre will hire out tents, day packs, water bottles, small cookers, cooking utensils and even light boots (small sizes). Fishing equipment can be hired.

Some of the Orang Asli live close to park headquarters. Locals say that the Orang Aslis are supplied with free food to encourage them to settle in the park headquarters area.

If you're overnighting in a hide you'll need a powerful torch (flashlight). The camp office has a couple for hire, but don't count on there being one available at the time you need it.

Hides & Salt Licks

There are several hides and salt licks in the park which are readily accessible. A number of them are close to Kuala Tahan and Kuala Trenggan, but your chances of seeing wildlife will increase if you head for the hides furthest from park headquarters. All hides are built overlooking salt licks and grassy clearings. If you're staying overnight, you need to take your own sleeping bag, or some sheets from Kuala Tahan (lent free of charge); you won't need blankets.

Each hide costs M$5 per person per night. Even if you're not lucky enough to see any wildlife, the fantastic sounds of the jungle are well worth the time and effort taken to reach the hides. The 'symphony' is at its best at dusk and dawn.

A powerful torch is necessary to see any animals that wander into the salt-lick area. It's probably best to arrange shifts where one person stays awake, searching the clearing with a torch every 10 to 15 minutes, while everyone else sleeps until it's their turn to take over.

Rats can be a problem at some of the hides. They search for food during the night and have been known to move whole bottles of cooking oil (one of their favourite treats) from hides to their nests. Either hang food high out of reach, or, as one traveller suggested, leave some in the centre of the floor

so you can see them – some of the rats are gigantic.

Jenut Tahan This is an artificial salt lick less than five minutes' walk from the reception building. It's a clearing which has been planted with pasture grass and there's a waterhole nearby. There's room in the hide for about eight people to sit and watch the salt lick but there are no facilities for sleeping overnight.

Jenut Tahan is often packed with noisy locals who find this hide a convenient venue for all-night parties – no chance of seeing any animals there!

Jenut Tabing The hide at this natural salt lick, about a one-hour walk from Kuala Tahan, is equipped with eight beds, a toilet and *tempat mandi* (bathing area). Nearby, there's a river with fairly clean water (though it should be boiled before drinking). Animals seen at Tabing include wild boar, tapir and deer.

Jenut Belau This is about 1½-hour's walk from headquarters and there's no clean water supply at the hide itself. Tapir, deer and civet cats are reported to frequent Jenut Belau.

Jenut Kumbang You can either walk to Jenut Kumbang (about five hours from Kuala Tahan) or take the 9 am boat (around M$10) to take you up the Tembeling River to Kuala Trenggan. The boat goes when demand is sufficient and returns at 3.30 pm, otherwise you have to hire one for around M$60. The boat journey from Kuala Tahan takes about 45 minutes, and then it's a 45-minute walk to the hide.

Jenut Kumbang has six bunk beds, a toilet and basin and there is a clear stream nearby. The most common animals seen there are tapir, rats, monkeys and gibbons but tigers and elephants have been seen.

Jenut Cegar Anging Once an airstrip, this is now an artificial salt lick established to attract wild cattle and deer. There are four bunk beds, a toilet and tempat mandi (no

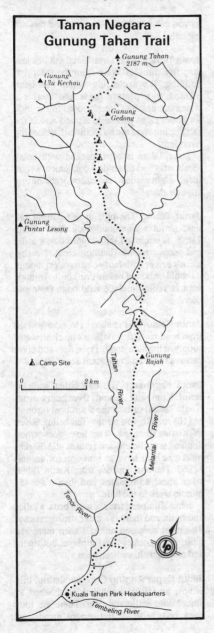

Taman Negara – Gunung Tahan Trail

water of course!). A nice, clear river runs a few metres from the hide. Jenut Cegar Anging is 1½ hours' walk from Kuala Tahan.

Mountains & Walks

Trails around park headquarters are well marked, though some of the paths are hard going. Trails are signposted and have approximate walking times marked clearly along the way. If you're interested in birdlife, it's best to start walking before 8 am.

There are two daily walking tours conducted by park officials. The first walk commences at Kuala Tahan and continues to Bukit Teserik and then on to Tabing Hide. From there, you take a boat to Lata Berkoh (minor rapids) and then walk back to Kuala Tahan from Lata Berkoh. The cost is around M$40 per person – the guide won't go unless there are at least four people lined up – and lunch is included.

The second organised walk starts from Kuala Tahan, stops at Bukit Indah where you take a boat through major rapids to Kuala Trenggan and then walk back to Kuala Tahan. This walk costs M$40 per person (minimum of four people) and includes lunch. Both trips begin at 9 am and finish between 3 and 4 pm.

Gunung Tahan at 2187 metres is the highest mountain in Peninsular Malaysia, but to climb to the summit requires a 2½-day trek from Kuala Tahan to Kuala Teku at the foot of the mountain and another 2½ days to the summit. A guide is not compulsory but is a good idea if you're not familiar with Gunung Tahan. Guides cost M$400 per week. You can climb 590-metre Gunung Gendang in a day trip from Kuala Tahan.

Rivers & Fishing

Lubok Simpon, only 10 minutes on foot from the park headquarters, has a good natural bathing pool. Anglers will find the park a real paradise. Fish found in the park rivers include the superb fighting fish (known in India as the Mahseer but here as the Kelasa).

Popular fishing rivers include the Tahan River, the Kenyam River (above Kuala

Trenggan) and the remote Sepia River. The best fishing months are from February, March, July and August. A fishing permit costs M$10 and hiring a rod costs M$5 per day.

Boat Trips

Several boat trips can be arranged at park headquarters but they're all expensive. Expect to pay at least M$60 return for the shortest trip in a four-seater.

From Kuala Tahan you can hire a boat to Lata Berkoh, a powerful set of rapids on the Tahan River. There's a natural swimming hole below the rapids and there's a Visitors' Lodge 185 metres downstream. The boat trip takes around one hour.

Another trip takes you from Kuala Tahan to Kuala Trenggan. It's a really spectacular journey through virgin jungle, gorges and rapids. There are seven sets of major rapids to be negotiated by highly skilled boat operators – this is why it costs so much to hire the boat in the first place. The trip takes about 45 minutes and everyone gets wet. There's a Visitors' Lodge at Kuala Trenggan.

A 1½-hour boat trip will take you from Kuala Trenggan to Kuala Kenyam. There are plenty of fruit trees at Kuala Kenyam. From there, you can walk inland to Bukit Batu Luas (130 metres of limestone) where there is a marked trail to the top of the rock. It takes around two hours to walk to the rock. There are some caves you can explore at the rock.

Places to Stay

If you have your own tent, you can camp at park headquarters for M$1 per person per night, otherwise, you can hire a tent for M$5. Beyond park headquarters, you can camp anywhere in Taman Negara.

The park hostel, *Asrama*, has nine rooms, each clean and comfortable with four bunk beds, overhead fans and personal lockers. Men and women share the dormitory rooms but there are separate toilets and showers. No toilet paper is provided. The hostel costs M$10 per person.

There are 12 older chalets that cost M$30 per night and a long block of a dozen or more

new chalets that cost M$40. Mosquito nets are provided and you get your own bathroom. Further into the park, you'll find *Visitors' Lodges* at Kuala Atok, Kuala Trenggan and Kuala Kenyam which cost M$8 per person. At Kuala Perkai and Lata Berkoh, there are two *Fishing Lodges*.

Places to Eat

There are two restaurants at Kuala Tahan with similar menus and prices. The food is ordinary, though they do have Western-style breakfasts for those who can't face pork and fish porridge in the morning.

You can get delicious mee soup and other local dishes at the food stalls set up at night; prices are much less than those at the restaurants. The ais batu kacang is excellent at these stalls. There are two shops in Kuala Tahan where you can buy basic supplies.

Getting There & Away

The entry point into the park is Kuala Tembeling, 18 km from Jerantut. Boats leave from the jetty, 500 metres west of the turn-off to the small village of Kuala Tembeling. Boats leave at 9 am and 2 pm. You should definitely try to book in advance in KL, but travellers have fronted up at the jetty and been lucky enough to get on a boat. The telephone number at the jetty office is 09-262284.

It's a three-hour boat trip from Tembeling to the park headquarters at Kuala Tahan. The trip costs M$30 return. Leaving the park, boats also leave at 9 am and 2 pm and take 2½ hours.

See Jerantut for details of buses and taxis to Kuala Tembeling. From KL to Jerantut you have to go via Temerloh if you take the bus. Kuala Tembeling can also be reached by train, though it is less convenient. The station is at Tembeling Halt, 2½ km from the jetty. Tembeling Halt is the station between Jerantut and Kuala Lipis and you must make arrangements in advance if you want the train to stop there. When leaving the park, trains pass Tembeling Halt and Jerantut for Kota Bharu at approximately 6 am, to Singapore at around 8 pm.

Kuala Lumpur to Kuantan

This busy road runs 275 km from KL past Bentong and through Temerloh, an important junction town. As an alternative to the direct KL-Kuantan route, you can start north from KL on the Ipoh road and turn off to Fraser's Hill. Continuing from The Gap you reach Raub, a busy gold-mining area where the hunt for gold continued right up to 1955, and eventually Kuala Lipis.

You can turn off the road just before Raub and rejoin the main KL-Kuantan road at Bentong or, turn off at Benta Seberang for Jerantut, en route to the national park. At Jerantut you can turn south to Temerloh or continue on to rejoin the KL-Kuantan road midway between Temerloh and Kuantan.

RAUB

This town, between Fraser's Hill and Kuala Lipis, has a few cheap hotels including the very basic *Raub Hotel* and the *Dragon Hotel* where singles cost about M$10.

MENTAKAB

This railway station town is where the jungle railway crosses the KL-Kuantan road. It is a thriving town but has little of interest for the visitor. There are plenty of hotels if you have to spend the night.

TEMERLOH

A bustling Chinese town, Temerloh has several cheap hotels and a good resthouse. There's also an active and colourful market there each Saturday afternoon.

The town is on the wide Pahang River and you can sometimes find boats going downriver to Pekan on the coast. You can also use Temerloh as a starting point for trips south to Tasik Bera. It's normally approached through Bahau and Ladang Geddes, which can also be reached from Seremban through Kuala Pilah.

Places to Stay

There are a number of cheap Chinese hotels in Temerloh. Next to the bus station, the *Ban Hin* is clean and well-run but a little expensive at M$16 for a room with fan and bath, M$24 with air-con. *Hotel Isis* around the corner has better rooms for a couple of dollars more.

The *San Lin* near the taxi station is the best cheapie with big rooms for M$10. The *Rest House*, on a hill overlooking the river, has the best accommodation is town.

Getting There & Away

Temerloh is a junction town and buses go to all parts of the peninsula. Buses to Jerantut leave every half an hour between 6 am and 6.45 pm and cost M$2.25. Buses to KL leave every hour between 7 am and 6 pm and cost M$5.50.

TASIK BERA

Tasik Bera is the largest lake in Malaysia and around its shores are five Orang Asli kampungs. Around 800 people live at Tasik Bera and it's worth visiting.

You have to get government permission at the district office in Temerloh to visit the area.

Once you have the permit, the problem is getting to Tasik Bera. There are no buses and very few cars visit the area. Most of the Orang Asli people get about on motorcycles. Taxis are a little reluctant to go to the lake and will ask a hefty price (about M$50) to cover their return journey. They're not interested in bargaining. Hitching is possible but traffic is scarce.

The easiest way to get to Tasik Bera is by bus or share-taxi from Temerloh to Triang and then chartered taxi from Triang to Tasik Bera. The most accessible kampung is Kota Iskandar, where there's a Government Rest House.

Unfortunately, unless you can arrange a lift to Temerloh or Triang on the back of someone's motorcycle, the only way out of the kampung is to hitch or walk the 30 km.

East Malaysia – Sarawak

Sarawak's period as the personal kingdom of the Brooke family of 'White Rajahs' ended with the arrival of the Japanese in WW II. When the Japanese forces capitulated in August 1945 Sarawak was placed under an Australian military administration until April 1946 when the third White Rajah Vyner Brooke, who had been exiled in Sydney during the war, made it known that he wanted to cede Sarawak to the British. The Bill of Cession was debated in the State Council (Council Negeri) and was finally passed in May 1946. On July 1 Sarawak officially became a British Crown Colony, thus putting Britain in the curious position of acquiring a new colony at the same time they were shedding others. Cession was followed by a brief but bloody anti-cession movement supported chiefly by Anthony Brooke, Vyner Brooke's nephew and heir apparent to the White Rajah title, and about 300 government officers who had resigned in protest at being excluded from the political process. The conflict climaxed in late 1949 when the Governor of Sarawak, Mr Duncan Stewart, was murdered by a Malay student. By 1951 the movement had lost its momentum and Anthony Brooke urged them to give it up.

Along with Sabah (then North Borneo) and Brunei, Sarawak remained under British control when Malaya gained its independence in 1957. In 1962 a British inquiry concluded that the people of the Borneo territories wished to become part of the Malay Federation. At the last minute Brunei pulled out as it didn't want to see the revenue from its vast oil reserves channelled to the peninsula. At the same time Malaya also had to convince the United Nations that Filipino claims to North Borneo were unfounded, as were Indonesia's claims that the formation of Malaysia was a British neo-colonialist plot. The final agreement was finally hammered out in July 1963 and in September of the same year the Federation of Malaysia was born. The so-called Confrontation with

Indonesia continued right up until 1966 and at its height 50,000 British, Australian and New Zealand forces were deployed in the Malaysian-Indonesian border area.

Although the Emergency over the Communist insurgency in the peninsula was declared over in 1960, things were still on the boil in Sarawak. The state had a large population of impoverished Chinese peasant farmers and labourers and it was these people who found appeal in the North Kalimantan Communist Party which supported guerrilla activity. Communist aspirations in Borneo were killed however, after the collapse of the Indonesian Communist Party in 1965, after which time the Indonesians and Malaysians combined forces to drive them out of their bases in Sarawak.

Today, with its oil production plus timber, pepper and some rubber, Sarawak is of great economic importance to the nation. For the visitor, Sarawak's interest is in its diversity of tribes and, for the moment, the areas of untouched jungle, although these are falling rapidly to the loggers' chainsaws. Many of the tribes up the major rivers of Sarawak (the Rejang, Balleh, Belaga, Balui, Baram and Skrang) live in longhouses – 'villages' where the entire population live under one roof with separate rooms leading on to one long communal verandah. Hospitality to visitors is a way of life in these longhouses and many travellers in Sarawak stay overnight at one during their travels.

The Politics of Logging

No matter what you do or where you go in Sarawak, one thing that you can't fail to notice is the extent of the logging industry – enormous log-laden barges moving slowly down the rivers are likely to be some of the most enduring images of your trip. It is the main source of revenue for the state government as royalties derived go straight to the state rather than the federal government.

It is worth taking a little peep at how this

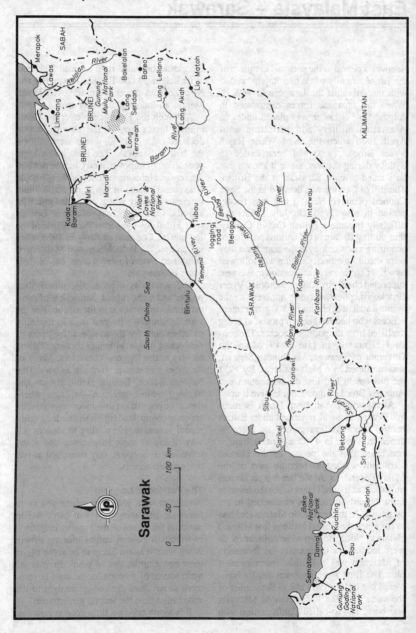

industry works in Sarawak – the further you look the more unbelievable it all seems. The insults and gross injustices heaped upon the indigenous tribes are nothing short of atrocious. Perhaps the whole situation is best summed by looking at James Wong. This man pioneered many of the techniques for extracting logs from virgin rainforest in the early days of logging in Sarawak, and at the moment is a large concession holder. Nothing extraordinary about that perhaps, but what is extraordinary is that, up until the 1990 elections, this man was also the state's Minister for Tourism & the Environment! He saw no conflict of interest, and claimed that 'logging in Sarawak will go on for ever and ever'.

As can be imagined there's plenty of money to be made from logging. Unfortunately it's only a very few who make this money and become extremely rich while the forests are decimated and the local people have their lifestyle, culture and environment destroyed. Equally obvious is the fact that whoever is responsible for awarding (or denying) logging licences is in an extremely powerful position. This power lies with the state Minister for Forestry, who is directly responsible to the Chief Minister. For years this position of power has played a central role in the abuses that have occurred in the logging industry. Evidence of these abuses of power are widespread, and during the 1987 state election the people were treated to an amazing public display of internecine squabbling within the ruling coalition. The Chief Minister's uncle (himself an ex-Chief Minister) formed a breakaway party and declared a loss of confidence in the Chief Minister.

A snap election was called and the Chief Minister, in a move against his uncle, froze 25 logging licences valued at billions of ringgit. Not long after, there were accusations in the press that the Chief Minister had granted logging concessions to himself and his family and nominees, and was accused by the opposition of dishing out licences to gain political favours. After counter allegations the ex-Chief Minister was forced to admit that he had also given out concessions to all state assembly members and each of his eight daughters. Lists of names of people and companies who held logging licences appeared in the press and the names of prominent politicians and their families appear regularly.

What is perhaps most surprising is that the whole sordid episode did not bring any cries of outrage from the community that such things should not go on.

The other unpleasant side of the industry is the shoddy treatment meted out to the Dayak tribes – the people most profoundly affected by logging activities. These people still rely to a large extent on wild game animals to meet their nutritional needs. The logging operations wreak havoc on the animals' habitat and per capita meat consumption has fallen drastically in the last 30 years. The rivers are also badly affected by siltation and pollution and fish stocks have also fallen alarmingly.

The state and federal governments are quick to point the finger at the Dayak practice of swidden (or shifting) agriculture using slash-and-burn techniques, claiming that it is largely responsible for widespread forest depredations (up to 60,000 hectares annually). Such claims are clearly nonsense. Although the local tribes are responsible for 25% of the areas clear-felled annually, all but 5% of this is carried out on land which has been cleared by them for agriculture in the past and has been left for seven to 30 years to regenerate before they reclear and replant it. Of the estimated 270,000 hectares of primary forest logged in Sarawak annually (40% of the national total), it is estimated that only around 3600 hectares of that is cleared by the local people for agricultural uses.

Numerous applications for logging licences have been made by various longhouse communities in the past, in the hope they would be able to generate some income to benefit the longhouses and at the same time control the way the timber was extracted. None received a reply. Another scheme was proposed by one group of longhouse leaders and this entailed the logging company working in a particular area contributing a small royalty per ton of timber extracted into a fund and the money could be used to improve the living conditions in some of the longhouses in that area. The company was not prepared to discuss the matter.

Another interesting aspect of the logging issue is that of Communal Forests. These are areas of primary forest gazetted under the Sarawak Forest Ordinance and set aside for use by the local tribes for hunting, gathering wood, rattan and traditional herbal medicines. Not only have at least 18 applications by communities for new Communal Forest Reserves been turned down (none have been approved, although some have been let out as logging concessions), but the total area set aside as Communal Forest Reserves has shrunk from 303 sq km in 1968 to a mere 56 sq km in the 1980s – 0.06% of the total estimated forest area in the state!

If there was anything to be gained by the local people from logging as it is currently practised it would be that employment opportunities would be created in the industry for longhouse people, but even here they are exploited. Wages are pitifully low, working hours long and safety precautions minimal in what is already a dangerous activity.

The logging practices used in Sarawak also leave a lot to be desired. Although it is supposedly 'sustained yield forestry' with only minimal trees being removed, the damage to the rest of the forest sustained in extracting these few logs is enormous. A report by the World Wildlife Fund estimates that 'forest logging in Sarawak removes about 46% of the natural cover'. This takes into account the land taken up by logging roads and camps. Not only that, but once a forest has been logged it is supposed to be left to regenerate for at least 25 years before being logged again, in Sarawak a forest may have been logged as many as three times in that period.

The Dayak tribes have not taken all these abuses lying down. In 1987 barricades were erected along at least 25 logging roads in the Baram and Limbang valleys, bringing

logging to a halt. A delegation of 12 representatives of the various native communities, along with Harrison Ngau (the Sarawak representative of Sahabat Alam Malaysia – Malaysia's Friends of the Earth), went to Kuala Lumpur and met with government ministers and the press. In the months that followed, many Penan and Kayan villagers were arrested and Harrison Ngau was placed under house arrest under the pernicious Internal Security Act (ISA). After legislation in Sarawak's parliament was passed making it an offence to obstruct any logging road, the barricades were pulled down and it was full steam ahead for the loggers. Further barricades were erected, and mass arrests made in 1988, '89 and '90.

Despite pleas from local, national and international bodies, including the United Nations, the USA, the European Parliament and others that logging be much more strictly controlled, it continues apace. In 1990 the pace was stepped up with logging continuing under lights 24 hours a day. Current estimates give the forests a life of five years, 10 years maximum, before it has all been logged over.

All in all it's a depressing situation and one can only hope that the Malaysian and Sarawak governments finally see the light – a vain hope judging by current trends – before the forests are totally logged out, the native customs and traditions destroyed, and the environment devastated.

Politically the Dayak people themselves are represented by the PBDS (Parti Bansa Dayak Sarawak) and are starting to gain some popular support. In the 1990 elections Harrison Ngau won a parliamentary seat and, while his will be just one voice in the corridors of power on the peninsula, hopefully it's the start of a better deal for the rainforests and those whose livelihood depends on them.

Further Reading For a deeper insight into the problems of logging and its effects on the tribal people of Sarawak, there are a few small booklets by various publishers which deal with the problem admirably. What is surprising is that these booklets are on sale all over Malaysia. The best of them are:

Pirates, Squatters & Poachers (Survival International, London, 1989, M$9). This is an excellent introduction to the subject with good background material.

Logging Against the Natives of Sarawak (INSAN, Petaling Jaya, 1989, M$10). A case study of the effect of logging on longhouse communities in the Belaga district, as well as some accounts of the shocking injuries and paltry compensation paid to some local logging workers.

Solving Sarawak's Forest & Native Problem (Sahabat Alam Malaysia, Penang, 1990, M$2.50). As the title suggests, some proposals for a solution to the problems in Sarawak, including a draft of the UN Universal Declaration on Rights of Indigenous Peoples which is to be presented to the UN General Assembly for discussion and, hopefully, adoption.

The Battle for Sarawak's Forests (SAM, Penang, 1989, M$12). A large format paperback chronicling the events in the struggle up until early 1989.

Visas & Permits

Even though Sarawak is a part of Malaysia it has its own immigration controls which are designed, in theory, to protect the indigenous tribal people from being swamped by migrants from the peninsula and elsewhere. They are also in place to restrict the access of foreigners to the same tribal people – the last thing the government wants is another Bruno Manser alerting the world to the shoddy treatment these people are getting as logging continues apace. If you're flying into Kuching or Miri from the peninsula or Sabah you will have to go through immigration again even though the flight is officially an internal one.

On arrival you will probably be granted a two-month stay if you ask for it. If you get a shorter permit it can be extended at immigration offices in Kuching or Miri. The Sarawak state government is very touchy about unannounced researchers, journalists, photographers and the like so remember, you're a tourist, nothing more.

Travel in the interior is relatively straightforward although permits are required to go almost anywhere away from the coast.

If you plan to visit any of the longhouses above Kapit on the Rejang or Balleh rivers then you'll need a special permit. These are obtainable in Kapit without fuss or fee. Officially, you need an international cholera vaccination certificate for these permits but usually no one checks this.

For travel to Gunung Mulu and elsewhere in the Kelabit Highlands (Bareo and the upper reaches of the Baram River) a permit from the District Officer in Marudi is required, unless you are flying direct from Miri, in which case get the permit in Miri itself. If you are travelling to Gunung Mulu you also need a permit from the National Parks & Wildlife office in Miri.

From Bareo it's possible to trek north to Bakelalan, but as this trail crosses the Indonesian border at one point you need a Border Permit from the army in Bareo (the army staffs the border checkpoint).

You also need a special permit if you intend to visit the 'Painted Cave' (but not the main cave) in Niah National Park. These permits are issued as a matter of course when you check in at the park headquarters so there's no point in trying to get one in advance, although this can be done from National Parks & Wildlife offices in Kuching and Miri. The same office in Kuching issues permits for the Semenggoh Wildlife Rehabilitation Centre and for Bako National Park, while the Miri office is the place to go for bookings and permits for Gunung Mulu National Park.

A special permit is also required from the immigration office in Kuching in order to cross the land border between Sarawak and Kalimantan, Indonesia (eg if heading for Pontianak) and it's unlikely you'll get it. An Indonesian visa is also required. Indonesian visas are issued without fuss in Kota Kinabalu but are more problematical at the Kuching and Tawau consulates.

General Costs

Although accommodation in East Malaysia is generally not cheap, in Sarawak there is usually one affordable option in each town – either a hotel with a dormitory or a hostel of some description. The same thing cannot be said for Sabah where the cheap hotels are almost without exception brothels and you'll be looking at around M$25/30 for a reasonable room in a straight hotel.

National Parks

The Malaysian jungles are some of the oldest undisturbed areas of rainforest in the world. It's estimated that they've existed for about 100 million years since they remained largely unaffected by the far-reaching climatic changes brought on elsewhere by the Ice Ages. In recent years, however, vast areas of this virgin forest – particularly in Sarawak and Sabah – have been devastated by the uncontrolled and thoughtless activities of timber and mineral concerns.

Fortunately, quite large areas of some of the best and most spectacular of these rainforests have been made into national parks in which all commercial activities are banned. These parks are, in effect, the essence of a trip to Borneo, other than visits to longhouses. A lot of effort goes into maintaining them and making them accessible to visitors, and you cannot help but be captivated by the astonishing variety of plant and animal life to be found.

In Sarawak itself at the moment there are seven such parks:

Gunung Gading National Park – at the extreme western tip near Sematan (61 sq km)
Bako National Park – north of Kuching (27 sq km)
Similajau – on the coast, north-east of Bintulu (75 sq km)
Niah National Park – of Niah caves fame, about halfway between Bintulu and Miri (31 sq km)
Lambir National Park – just south of Miri (69 sq km)
Gunung Mulu National Park – east of Marudi near the Brunei border (529 sq km), and only gazetted in 1990
Lanjak-Entimau Park – straddles the border and is contiguous with a national park in Kalimantan.

The Lambir National Park is for day use only; there's no overnight lodging or camping. Due to the limited and often primitive road system in Sarawak, Gunung Gading and Similajau are difficult to reach for those without their own 4WD transport.

Getting Around

Air MAS has a comprehensive network of domestic flights served by its fleet of 12-seater Twin Otter aircraft. Fortunately domestic flights are a real bargain, which is just as well as often the only viable access into the interior is by plane. If you have plans to visit places such as Bareo and Long Lellang in the highlands, then chances are you'll be going at least one way by plane. Kuching and Miri are connected to each other and to Sabah by regular flights on 120-seater 737s, while Sibu and Bintulu are served by 50-seat Fokker F50s.

Places in Sarawak served by MAS flights are: Belaga, Kapit, Long Lellang, Long Seridan, Sibu, Mukah, Kuching, Bintulu, Bareo, Marudi, Miri, Bakelalan, Long Semado, Limbang and Lawas. The new airstrip at Gunung Mulu, commenced in June 1990, may also be open by now.

The hassle with taking the Twin Otter flights in the interior is that they are very much subject to the vagaries of the weather. In the dry season (April to September) this is usually not a problem but in the wet season, especially in Bareo, it can rain continuously for a few days at a time. If you are relying on these flights make sure you have some time up your sleeve to allow for delays. Overbooking is another problem, and during school holidays (mid-May to mid-June, late October to early December) it is virtually impossible to get a seat on *any* Twin Otter flight into the interior at short notice. The only hope is to turn up at the airport and hope for a cancellation.

The free baggage allowance on the Twin Otters is only 10 kg per person, but excess baggage only costs from 40 sen to M$1.30 per kg, depending on the distance flown.

With the cost of accommodation in Brunei many people find themselves flying straight over that country, although it is possible to transit overland in a day without having to stay overnight. The cheapest and most convenient option is the flight from Miri to

Labuan (M$57), a duty-free island off the south coast of Sabah, from where there are plane and boat connections with the mainland and Kota Kinabalu. It's also possible to fly from Miri to Lawas ($59) or Limbang ($45) but the transport connections onward into Sabah are not as good.

Road Travel by road in Sarawak is improving rapidly as the trunk road from Kuching to the Brunei border is well on the way to being surfaced all the way. There may still be some sections of dirt between Sibu and Miri, and if that's the case you'll get a taste of what travel in Sarawak used to be like – roads that in the dry season are rough and dusty beyond belief and in the wet season are rough and treacherously slippery.

Between Sibu, Bintulu and Miri there are plenty of buses daily in each direction. At the moment Sibu to Bintulu takes four hours (M$15 air-con, M$12 without air-con), Bintulu to Niah Caves takes 2½ hours (M$10), Niah Caves to Miri two hours (M$10 air-con) and Miri to Kuala Baram (Brunei border) one hour (M$11.50). The travel times should decrease as the condition of the road improves. The road between Kuching and Sibu is still not completed and even when it is, the high-speed passenger launches which can do the trip in a very smart 3½ hours will be hard to beat.

There are also buses west from Kuching to Bau, Lundu and Sematan and north to Bako (for the Bako National Park).

Boat Sarawak is the home of incredibly fast passenger launches known by the generic term *expres*. These are long, narrow riverboats which carry around 100 people in aircraft-type seats. All the boats have air-conditioning, video screens which show non-stop wrestling and kung-fu movies and powered turbo-charged V12 diesel engines which generate speeds of up to 60 kmh! The newest boats are very sleek and streamlined – looks very much like an aircraft in fact – but the curved 'fuselage' rules out travelling on the roof, which is often far more pleasant than the supercool interior and the movies.

Unfortunately these new boats are a disaster waiting to happen as the windows are all sealed and the only exits at the front are often obstructed by baggage. From 1990 all new boats have to be fitted with proper emergency exits but there will still be many boats which don't have them. The older boats have a much squarer profile and so riding on the roof is possible, although you do need to have some protection from the sun as it's pretty fierce, and the noise from the exhaust can be deafening.

The riverboats provide regular connections between Sibu and Kapit (two to three hours, M$15), Bintulu and Tubau (three hours, M$40) and Kuala Baram and Marudi (two hours, M$12). In the wet season when there is more water in the rivers there are also services from Kapit to Belaga (six hours, M$20), from Marudi to Kuala Apoh (two hours, M$10) and Long Panai (two hours, M$12), and to Long Terrawan from Kuala Apoh (M$7) and Long Panai (M$5).

As well as the river *expres* boats there are at least four companies which run services between Kuching and Sibu (four hours, M$25). These are larger, ocean-going versions of the river *expres* boats – still with the aircraft seats, air-con and violent videos.

Kuching

Kuching is without doubt one of the most pleasant and interesting cities you'll come across in East Malaysia. Built principally on the southern bank of the Sarawak River (Sungai Sarawak), it was known last century as Sarawak and was where James Brooke chose to settle. Prior to this the capital had been at Lidah Tanah and Santubong. The city was given its name (which means 'cat' in Malay) by the second Rajah in 1872. There is much speculation as to how the city got its name. Two of the more likely theories are that it was named after the Kuching River, which in turn was named after the fruit tree *mata kuching*, or that it was so called because

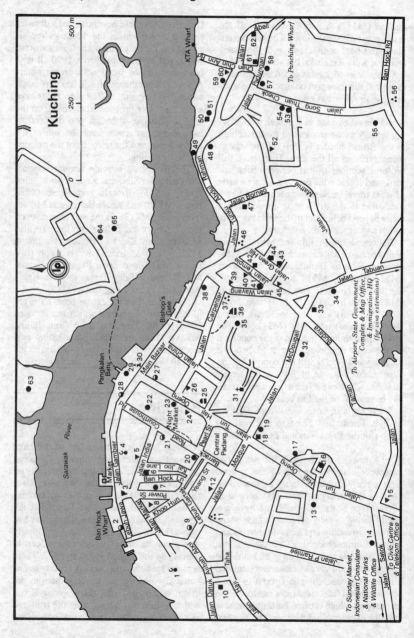

Kuching

■ PLACES TO STAY

6	Kiaw Hin Hotel
10	Arif Hotel
18	Aurora Hotel
33	Fata Hotel
36	Anglican Hostel
42	Kuching Hotel, Sin Hwa Travel
43	Green Mountain Lodging House, Orchid Inn, Furama Inn
44	Mandarin Lodging House
47	Hilton Hotel
50	Holiday Inn
61	Kapit Hotel
62	Longhouse Hotel

▼ PLACES TO EAT

5	Madinah Cafe, Jubilee & Malaya Restaurants
8	Food Centre
12	New Hawkers Centre
15	Food Stalls
24	Fook Hoi Restaurant
26	National Islamic Cafe
39	Food Stalls
40	Food Stalls
45	Hua Jang Cafe
52	Permata Food Centre
60	Pizza Hut

OTHER

1	Masjid Negara
2	STC Buses
3	Taxis
4	Indian Mosque
7	Electra House
9	Bus Stop

11	Sikh Temple
13	New Museum Buildin
14	RTM
16	Sarawak Museum
17	Curator's Office
19	Kuching Plaza
20	Police
21	Bus Stop
22	Law Courts
23	Pavilion
25	GPO
27	Bus Stop
28	Bus Stop
29	Square Tower
30	Tourist Office
31	Anglican Cathedral
32	St Thomas' School
34	Cat City Art Shop, Long House Native Art
35	Bishop's House
37	Hong San Temple
38	Yeo Hing Chuan, Sarawak House
41	Rex Cinema
46	Tua Pek Kong Temple
48	Chartered Bank
49	Singapore Airlines, British Council Library
51	Sarawak Plaza
53	MAS
54	TDC Office
55	Lee Huo Theatre
56	Indian Temple
57	Express Bahagia
58	Tan Brothers
59	Eeze Trading
63	Istana
64	Police Museum
65	Fort Margherita

of the many wild cats found along its banks in the time of the Rajahs.

Although quite a large city, the centre of Kuching is very compact and seems isolated from the suburbs by the river and parks. The city contains many beautifully landscaped parks and gardens, historic buildings, an interesting waterfront, colourful markets, one of Asia's best museums, and a collection of Chinese temples, Christian churches and the striking state mosque. The city also has a totally over-the-top civic centre with its outrageously futuristic design – it bears more resemblance to some type of spacecraft, and with a price tag of $35 million ringgit one can only wonder at the folly of the state's planners – how many longhouses in the interior still don't have a reliable water supply.

There's plenty in and around Kuching to keep you busy for a few days, and it makes an ideal base from which to visit Bako National Park.

If you're looking for somewhere pleasant to relax, try either the grounds of the Anglican cathedral or the Sarawak Museum gardens, at the back of the museum itself.

Orientation

By comparison with the state capitals of Peninsular Malaysia, the centre of Kuching is small and compact and almost all places of interest or importance to travellers are within easy walking distance of each other.

You should only need to use public buses or taxis when travelling to and from the airport (about 12 km); to the wharfs at Pending for boats to Sibu (about six km); to the state government complex to buy maps for trekking purposes or make an international phone call; or to visit the National Parks & Wildlife office for a permit for the Semenggoh Wildlife Rehabilitation Centre or Bako National Park.

Information

Tourist Information Kuching has two tourist offices. By far the better of the two is the Sarawak Tourist Association office (tel 082-242218) on Main Bazaar in the centre of town. It is housed in the old godown of the Sarawak Steamship Company and includes a historical display and very expensive souvenir shop. The people who work in this office are very helpful and should be able to answer any specific enquiries you have. The office is open Monday to Thursday from 8 am to 12.45 pm and 2 to 4 pm, Friday from 8 to 11.30 am and 2.30 to 4.15 pm, and on Saturday from 8 am to 12.45 pm. There is also an STA office at the airport but they have a limited range of brochures.

The federal Tourist Development Corporation (TDC) office (tel 082-246575) is on the 2nd floor of the AIA building on Jalan Song Thian Cheok. They stock a wide range of printed information but are otherwise fairly ineffectual.

For information on the national parks, including permits for Semenggoh Wildlife Rehabilitation Centre and bookings for Bako National Park, head for the National Parks & Wildlife office (tel 082-248088), on the 7th floor of the Satok building on Jalan Satok, about a km west of the centre. The office is open Monday to Thursday from 8 am to 12.45 pm and 2 to 4.15 pm, Friday from 8 to 11.30 am and 2.30 to 4.45 pm and on Satur-

day from 8 am to 12.45 pm. To get there, take a blue bus Nos 1, 7, 15 or 19 from outside the GPO, or a taxi for $3.

Visas & Permits The immigration office (tel 082-240301) is in the state government offices on Jalan Simpang Tiga about three km south of the centre on the way to the airport. The office is open the same hours as the National Parks & Wildlife office. To get there, catch a CCL bus Nos 6 or 17 from near the state mosque.

For Indonesian visas, take a CCL bus Nos 5A or 6 from near the state mosque to the Indonesian Consulate at 5A Pisang Rd. It is open Monday to Friday from 8 am to 1 pm and 1.30 to 4 pm, closed Saturday and Sunday. Tourist visas are not generally given but it may be worth a try.

Money For changing money (travellers' cheques) the best place to go is the Hong Kong & Shanghai Bank on Jalan Tun Haji Openg near the junction with Main Bazaar. It has a dedicated Bureau de Change on the 1st floor and transactions are completed with the minimum of fuss. Banking hours are 9.30 am to 3 pm on weekdays and 9.30 to 11 am on Saturdays.

On Sundays and public holidays, you can change money at the bookstore in the Holiday Inn or at the Hilton Hotel.

Post & Telecommunications The GPO is right in the centre on Jalan Tun Haji Openg. International calls have to be made from the Telekom building on Jalan Batu Lintang about 10 minutes south of the centre; take a blue bus Nos 14 or 14A from outside the GPO. The office is open from 8 am to 6 pm Monday to Saturday and 8 am to 12 noon on Sunday.

Travel Agencies Sarawak Travel Agencies (tel 082-243708), 70 Padungan Rd, is a well-established agency with a variety of tours available. Borneo Transverse (tel 082-257784) at 10B Jalan Wayang and Interworld Travel (tel 082-252344) at 110 Green Rd have been recommended by travellers. Borneo Adventure Travel (tel 082-416223) on Jalan Pisang south of the city centre is a helpful company. None of the travel agencies in Kuching are cheap.

Bookshops & Libraries The Yahia bookshop has an interesting range of books on Malaysia and neighbouring regions. Another good bookshop is the Berita Book Centre on Jalan Haji Taha, not far from the state mosque. There are other bookshops in town, but most only stock books in Bahasa Malaysia.

If you're thinking of trekking in Sarawak and need good maps the best place to go to is H N Mohd Yahia & Son bookshop inside the Holiday Inn on Jalan Tunku Abdul Rahman. This shop stocks copies of the maps put out by the Sarawak Lands & Surveys Department which cover Sarawak, Sabah and Peninsular Malaysia as well, and is open until 10 pm.

If you want more detailed sectional maps, take a taxi ($3) or a local bus to the State Government offices near the end of Jalan Simpang Tiga; take a blue CCL bus Nos 6, 14 or 18 (fare is about 50 sen). The map sales office (Bahagian Katografi) is on the 2nd floor on the left.

Excellent large-scale maps – 1:1,000,000 and 1:500,000 of the whole of Sarawak, plus 1:50,000 of various parts of the state are available, but you need security clearance from the police headquarters in the centre of town for the sectional maps. If you intend buying any of these ask for the relevant forms and a form of recommendation at the map sales office. The people there are very friendly and will help you fill in the forms. Security clearance takes a day. Take your passport with you to the maps sales office.

The British Council Library (tel 082-242632) is on the 2nd floor of the Ang Chang building on Jalan Tunku Abdul Rahman, above Singapore Airlines. It is open on Monday from 2 to 6 pm, Tuesday to Friday from 10 am to 6 pm, and Saturday from 10 am to 5 pm.

The Istana
Sometimes spelt Astana, this shingle-roofed palace, set amid rolling lawns on the northern bank of the Sarawak River, was built by the second White Rajah, Charles Brooke, in 1870. During the Japanese Occupation, prisoners were interned in the basement of the building. It's no longer open to the public as it's now the Governor of Sarawak's residence. It looks very grand and is plainly visible from the small park (Pangkalan Batu) on the opposite side of the river.

Fort Margherita
Built by Charles Brooke in the mid-19th century and named after his wife, the fort was designed to guard the entrance to Kuching in the days when piracy was commonplace. It is now a police museum (Muzium Polis) which houses a collection of weapons, uniformed dummies, memorabilia of the Japanese Occupation and the Communist insurgency as well as currency-forging equipment seized at various times.

It's well worth a visit and is open every day, except Fridays and public holidays, from 10 am to 6 pm. There's no entry charge but you have to leave your passport at the guard's room at the entrance.

To get there take one of the small *tambangs* (ferry boats) which ply back and forth all day until late in the evening between the landing stage behind the Square Tower and the bus stop below the fort. The fare is 30 sen each way, and this you should have in exact change and leave on the seat as you leave the boat – an unusual local custom. If you want to hire a tambang to take you up or down the river for a cruise, the standard fare is $15 for 1½ hours.

Sarawak Museum
This is one of the best museums in Asia and should not be missed. It consists of two segments, the old and new, connected by a footbridge over Jalan Tun Haji Openg. Built in the style of a Normandy town house, the old part was opened in 1891, and was strongly influenced by the anthropologist Wallace, a contemporary of Darwin, who

spent two years there at the invitation of Charles Brooke. The original section was expanded in 1911. The new section was opened towards the end of 1983 and is large, modern and air-conditioned. Together they house an incredible collection of tribal artefacts, stuffed animals and birds from the Borneo jungles, a shell collection, whale skeletons, a recreation of a longhouse complete with head-hunting skulls, wild photographs of even wilder tribal people from the beginning of the century and a whole section on the exploration and processing of oil.

Also included are ceramics, brassware, Chinese jars and furniture and a great section on some of the tribal peoples – their arts, tools, clothes and so on. There's a cave replica and a description of gathering birds' nests for soup. Through the day, various video and slide shows are offered in the new section. On the ground floor of the new section is a huge cat display. There's also a souvenir and gift shop with some interesting items which should have reopened after recent renovations.

In the old section, look for the python that was killed in Kuching – it's strung up on the wall. The gable ends of the upper floor in this section are painted with beautiful motifs inspired by those found in a longhouse at Long Nawang.

You can easily spend a few hours there and to top it all, it's free. The museum is open Saturday to Thursday from 9.15 am to 6 pm, closing for lunch between 12 noon and 1 pm. It's closed all day Friday.

Court House & Brooke Memorial

The Court House was built in 1871 and was the seat of the White Rajahs' government. It was used until 1973 when the new government complex on Jalan Tun Haji Openg opened. The clock tower was added in 1883. Also at the Court House is a memorial to Charles Brooke, the second White Rajah.

Temples, Mosques & Churches

The most interesting of these are the Chinese temples and the best of these is perhaps the

Hong San Temple at the junction of Jalan Carpenter and Jalan Wayang at the back of the Rex Cinema. It was built in 1897 in honour of Kuek Seng On, a native of Hokkien province in mainland China who was deified about 100 years ago.

Others include the **Tua Pek Kong Temple** at the junction of Jalan Temple and Jalan Tunku Abdul Rahman, which was built in 1876 and is the oldest in Kuching. The **Kwan Yin Temple** on Jalan Tabuan was built in 1908 in honour of the goddess of mercy. Visitors are welcome at any of these temples.

The **Masjid Negara** (state mosque), completed in 1968, is visually impressive, particularly from across the river, but otherwise uninteresting. There is no admission for non-Muslims from Thursday 3 pm to Friday 3 pm, Saturday 4 to 6 pm and Sunday 2 to 5 pm.

Of the Christian churches perhaps the most interesting is the futuristic, single-roofed Roman Catholic **Cathedral** past the Sarawak Museum on Jalan Tun Haji Openg.

Other Interesting Buildings

Kuching has many other buildings worthy of note. The **Square Tower** on Main Bazaar, opposite the end of Jalan Tun Haji Openg, was built in 1879 as a prison. Right on Jalan Tun Haji Openg itself near the GPO is the curious three-storey building known as the **Pavilion**. Built in 1907 the building has been home to various government bodies including the general hospital and the education department (the present occupant). The **GPO** itself is an unusual sight with its Corinthian columns in the facade.

At the top of the hill behind the Padang is the **Bishop's House**, the oldest dwelling in Sarawak. It was built in 1849 and was occupied by Dr McDougall, the first Anglican Bishop of Borneo. It is now part of a school.

The outrageous **Civic Centre** is about one km south of the centre along Jalan Tun Haji Openg. It has, among other things, a planetarium which has shows in English at 3 pm daily, with an extra show at 7.30 pm on Tuesdays and Thursdays; entry is $2.

Markets

The site of the former bus station has now become Kuching's open-air market. It's small and not particularly interesting unless you hit a good day and some villagers are in town. At the waterfront, there is an outdoor area and a clothes and hawkers' centre in a large white building. Along Jalan Gambier are open-air food stalls and fresh vegetables and foodstuff can also be bought there.

The Sunday morning market is sometimes very busy and can be well worth the walk. It's along Jalan Satok; turn away from the museum at the corner of Jalan Satok and Jalan Tun Haji Openg. The Dayaks bring all their produce and livestock to this area late on Saturday afternoon – so the Sunday market actually begins on Saturday night. The Dayaks sleep at their stalls overnight and resume trading around 5 am on Sunday. You may see all manner of food including some vegetables and herbs you probably haven't seen before. Wild boars are butchered, and chopped-up turtles are on display. You may also see fantastic orchids, live fish hanging

Basket Seller

in suspended plastic bags of water, cassowaries, monkeys, bats, lizards – you name it, it's for sale. There are all kinds of live birds, plastic toys, clothes and other odds and ends usually reserved for Woolworths.

Jalan Carpenter

This street (signposted as Jalan Ewe Hai at its eastern end) is interesting to wander through, with its many little shops, businesses and laneways. There are also a couple of restaurants and a bakery. Sundays are pleasant for strolling as the streets are remarkably quiet – good for taking pictures. It seems a day for those eternal Chinese pastimes – mahjong and card playing.

Hero's Grave

The Hero's Grave commemorates Allied soldiers from WW II who died in and around Kuching at the hands of the Japanese who controlled the area in 1944.

Organised Tours There is an incredible array of travel agents and tour operators in town. Besides the usual day trips in and around Kuching town, many travel agents offer longer trips out to national parks or to longhouses along the Skrang and Rejang rivers.

Places to Stay – bottom end

One of the most popular places is the *Anglican Cathedral Hostel* (tel 082-414027), on the hill at the back of St Thomas's church. A 'donation' of M$20/25 for a singles/doubles gets you a large, spotlessly clean room with fan, polished wooden floors, comfortable beds, cane chairs, clean toilets and showers and good views. There are a couple of cheaper, smaller rooms on the upper level but these cop the heat. If a conference or something is on it could well be booked out but otherwise, a room for a traveller is no problem. There are also a couple of self-contained flats for rent which cost M$30 per night and four or five people can stay in each flat. The hostel has a fridge for communal use as well as an area for washing clothes. The man to see is a friendly chap named

Pulin Kantul who lives next to the hostel. The hostel is not registered as a hotel, so be a little discreet about using it. The easiest way to get there is to take the steps at the end of the lane off Jalan Carpenter between Nos 68 and 70. Access by car is from Jalan Mc-Dougall.

There are no real bargains amongst the hotels. About the best of them is the *Kuching Hotel* (tel 082-413985), opposite the Rex Cinema on Jalan Temple. Rooms are M$16/20 for singles/doubles and all are equipped with fan and sink. The communal bathrooms and toilets are kept acceptably clean, and the manager and staff are very friendly and helpful.

The *Arif Hotel* is a friendly hotel not far from the state mosque. It's a good place and pretty good value at $20 for a room with fan, $25 with fan and bath, $28 with air-con, and $33 with air-con and bath.

Places to Stay – middle

The *Kapit Hotel* (tel 082-244179) at 59 Jalan Padungan, has rooms for $32/42. All rooms have air-con, bath, TV and phone but they are definitely on the small side. The only drawback with this place is it's distance from the centre – about 15 minutes' walk. At the time of writing the *Longhouse Hotel* (tel 082-421563) was offering discount rates of $38/44, making it very good value.

On Jalan Green Hill there's a whole group of mid-range 'lodging houses'. All have air-con rooms with attached bath, TV, etc. There's little to choose between them – they are all quite acceptable. The *Green Mountain Lodging House* (tel 082-246952) at No 1 is about the cheapest of them and has some rooms with fan and bath at $25/28, or $32 with air-con and bath. For the cheapest air-con rooms go to the *Mandarin Lodging House* (tel 082-418269) at No 6. It has rooms for $30 with bath and TV. The *Orchid* (tel 082-411417) at No 2 costs $35/40 with air-con and bath while the *Furama* (tel 082-413561) at No 4 charges $28/42, also with air-con and bath.

Also on Jalan Green Hill is the *Metropole Inn Hotel* (tel 082-412561) at No 22. This is a much larger hotel with rooms for $38/57 with air-con and bath, and is also the place to book Concorde boats to Sibu.

At the end of Jalan McDougall is the *Fata Hotel* (tel 082-248111) which has very good value rooms in its old section for $36/42 with bath, air-con and TV while rooms in the new building cost $52. Just around the corner on Jalan Tabuan is the *Borneo Hotel* (tel 082-244122) which charges $57/73 for air-con rooms with breakfast.

Up the scale a notch is the *Aurora Hotel* (tel 082-240l281) on the corner of Jalan Mc-Dougall and Jalan Tun Haji Openg. 'Standard' rooms go for $55 single or double while 'deluxe' (bigger) rooms cost $70.

Places to Stay – top end

During quieter periods, many of Kuching's top-end hotels reduce rates drastically, sometimes by as much as 40%, to attract customers. If you usually stay in middle-range hotels, it's worth checking out some of the top-end prices.

Top of the range is the *Hilton Hotel* (tel 082-248200) which dominates the river skyline at the eastern end of town. Single/ double rooms cost $225/251 and have all the mod-cons. A little further along Jalan Tunku Abdul Rahman is the older *Holiday Inn* (tel 082-423111) with rooms ranging from $167/202 to $190/225 depending on the view, and suites from $248 up to a mere $1150.

At Santubong, on the coast about 30 km from Kuching, the *Holiday Inn Damai Beach Resort* (tel 082-411777) has rooms from $110.

Places to Eat

The best food you'll come across in Sarawak is in Kuching, so make the most of it. There are many excellent restaurants, hawker centres and small food stalls around town serving all manner of food.

For tasty Malay food, head for Jalan India and eat at any of the restaurants there. The *Jubilee, Madinah* and *Malaya* restaurants are all next to each other here and although there's little to choose between them, I found the Jubilee the best. Not far away on Jalan Carpenter you'll find the *National Islamic Cafe* which also serves tasty, cheap Malay food, and has excellent rotis and murtabak. The Sunday market is another good place for Malay food. There are all sorts of interesting food stalls and an amazing variety of local cakes and sweets − the peanut pancakes are delicious.

You can get excellent satay and laksa (and other dishes) at the food centre on Jalan Market, and at the food stalls on the corner of Jalan Mosque and Jalan Datuk Ajibah Abol.

There are a couple of very small hawker centres which seem to operate from in front of old Chinese temples. There's one on Jalan Wayang opposite the end of Jalan Carpenter (Rex Cinema Hawker Centre), and another on Jalan Carpenter itself, near Jalan China. At these stalls you can get all the usual Chinese dishes (mee, rice, etc) as well as beer and other drinks. Despite the abundance of fish at the market the price of seafood in Kuching is way over the top, although at the cheaper end of the scale, the *Hua Jang Cafe* serves very good prawns. At the small *Permata Food Centre*, on Jalan Padungan behind the MAS building, you can sample excellent local, Indonesian and Filipino food.

At the time of writing a new hawkers' centre and multistorey car park was under construction on the corner of Jalan Mosque and Lebuh Gartak. If this is now open the hawkers' food scene in Kuching may have changed considerably.

Fast-food freaks won't go hungry either − there's a *Pizza Hut* on Jalan Tunku Abdul Rahman out past the Holiday Inn, a *Kentucky Fried Chicken* in the Sarawak Plaza next to the Holiday Inn, and a *Sugar Bun* outlet in the Kuching Plaza on Jalan McDougall.

For Chinese food, one of the best places is the *Meisan Restaurant* in the Holiday Inn. It specialises in dishes from the Sichuan province and is expensive but worth the splurge. The *Fook Hoi Restaurant*, opposite the GPO, serves decent Chinese food and is popular with local people. The *Supersonic Coffee House*, also opposite the GPO, serves fairly plain Chinese food and assorted Western dishes but it's not cheap. Most of the larger hotels have their own expensive restaurants which serve a mixture of Malaysian and Western food. There's a nice Japanese restaurant in the *Aurora Hotel* as well as the usual coffee shop, which also serves a reasonable Western breakfast for $8.50. For a full-on breakfast splurge dip into the breakfast buffet at the *Holiday Inn*. It's not cheap at $16.50 but you won't need to eat again for hours.

Things to Buy

Kuching is one of the best centres in Sarawak for buying tribal artefacts. Shops selling arts and crafts are scattered around the city but be warned that prices are outrageously high.

Hog charm sticks go for M$80 to M$100; larger, crudely carved totems for M$400 to M$1000 and intricately patterned baskets for up to M$800 depending on quality, source and age. Another very fine item is the woven textiles. The older ones go for about M$200 and up. Jewellery is likewise expensive. It's best to spend some time browsing before you commit yourself to a purchase. Sibu is in fact a cheaper place to buy artefacts but the range is far smaller.

The best area to try is along Main Bazaar at the Jalan Wayang end. Shops along here include Yeo Hing Chuan at No 46, the very flashy and expensive Sarawak House (tel 082-252531) at No 67, and the Thian Seng Goldsmith at No 48.

On Jalan Tunku Abdul Rahman just past the Holiday Inn is Eeze Trading (tel 082-254941) which has a whole stack of bird's nests and mounted scorpions, spiders and other insects but little else. In the same area is Tan Brothers on Jalan Padungan. The range here is good and the prices about as reasonable as you'll find in Kuching.

Getting There & Away

Air The MAS office (tel 082-244144) is near the TDC on Jalan Song Thian Cheok. It is open Monday to Friday from 8 am to 5 pm,

Saturday from 8 am to 4.30 pm and Sunday from 8 am to 4 pm. Singapore Airlines (tel 082-240266) is in the Ang Chang building on Jalan Tunku Abdul Rahman.

The Indonesian airline Merpati, which has weekly flights to Pontianak (Kalimantan) is handled by the Sin Hwa Travel agency on Jalan Temple opposite the Rex Cinema, two doors from the Kuching Hotel. This office can also handle MAS bookings.

To/From Singapore & Peninsular Malaysia The regular MAS fare between KL and Kuching is M$231. There are early morning flights, economy fare, at M$162. From Singapore to Kuching the fare is S$170, but in the opposite direction it's only M$170.

Skipping over to JB from Singapore drops the fare to M$147. To get this fare, however, you have to buy the ticket in Malaysia. In Singapore it will cost you S$147. To encourage people to fly from JB, MAS has a direct bus service from their Singapore office to the JB airport for S$10. The absurd aspect of this arrangement is that you have to go through Malaysian immigration when entering from Singapore, and again a couple of hours later when entering Sarawak from the peninsula! MAS also has a 14-day (sometimes more) advance purchase fare which can lower prices even further.

From Kuching the economy fare to Bandar Seri Begawan is M$192. The same rules apply with the Brunei and Singapore dollars, so the fare from Bandar to Kuching is B$192.

To/From Indonesia Merpati operates one flight per week on Fridays from Kuching to Pontianak (Kalimantan) and Jakarta. It also flies the same route in the opposite direction on the same day. The fare is M$123 to Pontianak and M$323 to Jakarta. MAS also has a weekly return flight to Pontianak only on Mondays.

The ticket agent in Kuching is Sin Hwa Travel (tel 082-246688), 8 Jalan Temple, opposite the Rex Cinema. Pontianak is not a 'no visa' entry point to Indonesia, so you must have a visa before you arrive.

Around Sarawak & Sabah Although MAS has a very extensive provincial network, none of the flights to the interior operate out of Kuching. You have to go to Sibu or Miri for those. From Kuching you can fly to Sibu (five flights daily, M$60), Bintulu (seven flights daily, M$97), Miri (10 flights daily, M$136), Labuan (daily, M$173) and Kota Kinabalu (three flights daily, M$198).

Bus Long-distance STC green bus depart from the terminus on Lebuh Jawa which is a continuation of Jalan Gambier. Destinations include:

Destination	Fare	Frequency	Route No	Distance
Bau	M$2.05	every 20 minutes	No 2	35 km
Lundu	M$5.60	3 times daily	No 2B	98 km
Serian	M$3.60	every 20 minutes	No 3, 3A	65 km
Sri Aman	M$12.20	3 times daily	No 15	195 km
Airport	M$0.80	every 40 minutes	No 12A	11 km

If you're heading east from Kuching by bus you cannot reach Sibu in one day since you will not arrive in Sarikei until the early evening and will have to spend the night there. As there's precious little of interest in Sarikei itself, and as the road from Sri Aman to Sarikei and Sarikei to Sibu is one hell of a bone shaker, most travellers prefer to take a launch or boat from Kuching to Sibu.

The alternative is to stopover in Sri Aman and to explore the surrounding area since it's possible to reach Sibu from Sri Aman in one day. Where there are only a few buses each day to a certain destination it's advisable to book in advance at the ticket office on Jalan Jawa.

Boat – Kuching-Sarikei-Sibu You have a choice on this run of express boat or cargo/passenger boat. The express is considerably faster as the cargo boats have to load and unload at the various ports of call (Sarikei and Bintangor). If you have the time, the cargo/passenger boats are the more interesting way to cover this part of the journey. The trip takes at least 16 hours.

There are about four operators running express boats between Kuching and Sibu. There is little to choose between them, although departure times differ. They all take around four hours, a change of boat (from a sea-going boat to a smaller riverboat) is required at Sarikei, and of course they have violent videos for your entertainment. Expres Bahagia, Expres Pertama and Follow Me all charge M$25, while Concorde Marine charges M$28. Concorde is perhaps the best as you can sit outside on the ocean leg of the trip. All companies also offer 1st class seats for around M$30 but there is little difference in classes. All boats should be booked at least a day in advance to be on the safe side.

All boats leave from the one of the wharfs in the horribly industrial suburb of Pending, about six km east of the city centre. Catch a bus Nos 17 or 19 from outside the market on Main Bazaar and tell the driver which boat you are catching. A taxi costs M$8.

The addresses of boat operators and the departure times from Kuching are as follows:

Expres Pertama (tel 082-414735), 196 Padungan Rd; 12.30 pm
Follow Me, Wong Kah Chin Brothers (tel 082-423507), No 13, Lot 264 Jalan Song Thian Cheok; 11.45 am
Expres Bahagia (tel 082-421948), 50 Padungan Rd; 8.45 am, 1 pm
Concorde Marine, Metropole Inn Hotel (tel 082-412551), Jalan Green Hill; 8.30 am

Boat – Kuching-Sibu-Miri There are a few companies which operate cargo/passenger boats to Sibu and even further along the coast. The Sarawak Tourist Association is quite helpful with information about these cargo boats.

Southern Navigation Sdn Bhd (tel 082-242613), in the Metropole Inn Hotel on Jalan Green Hill, is an agent for the MV *Soon Bee II* which departs Kuching for Sarikei and Sibu every Tuesday and Saturday at 6 pm.

The trip takes about 18 hours and costs M$10.

South East Asia Shipping (tel 082-336220), Lot 8686, Section 64 Pending Rd, operates the MV *Rajah Mas*. This boat departs Kuching every Monday and Thursday at 6 pm and takes about 18 hours to reach Sibu. There are no cabins available and the fare is M$10 on deck.

Another cargo boat making regular trips between Kuching and Sibu via Sarikei is the MV *Hong Lee* operated by the Rajah Ramin Shipping Sdn Bhd (tel 082-335488), Lot 1378, Section 66 Jalan Buroh, Bintawa Industrial Estate. It leaves Kuching for Sibu every Wednesday and Saturday at 6 pm.

Boat – Kuching-Bintulu-Miri Cargo boats depart Kuching fairly regularly, but there is no fixed schedule. Ask at the STA office for more details. One company operating boats along the coast is the Siam Company (tel 082-242832) at the back of the shop at 28 Main Bazaar. They have boats sailing irregularly to Bintulu, Miri and Limbang but no connections between these places.

Getting Around
To/From the Airport A taxi between Kuching Airport and the city centre costs M$12 and 50% more after midnight. Buses are available between the airport and the centre of town for about 80 sen and they operate every 40 minutes from 6 am to 6 pm. The only bus going to the airport is STC green bus No 12A; No 12 goes to the *old* airport.

Bus At first, bus transport around Kuching may seem chaotic as there's no bus terminal. There are at least four types of buses – the most common being the blue Chin Lian Long buses (tel 082-32766), which leave from Lebuh Gartak, near the state mosque; the green Sarawak Transport Company buses (tel 082-242967); and white with blue and orange stripes of the Petra Jaya Co.

You'll probably only need to take buses to the airport, immigration, the National Parks & Wildlife office or to the wharfs where launches to Sibu depart from. Most local bus fares are under 60 sen. The tourist offices can supply you with exact routings.

Some useful routes covered by CLL buses are: Jalan Mosque to the state government complex (bus Nos 6, 11, 14 or 14A – fare 40 sen); Jalan Satok to the Holiday Inn (bus Nos 1, 19 or 23A – fare 35 sen); Jalan Satok to the wharfs (bus Nos 17 or 19 – fare 60 sen). A useful route covered by STC buses is city to Kuching Airport (No 12A – fare 80 sen). The STC deals mainly with long-distance travel.

Taxi Taxis wait around the market and the area where long-distance buses drop passengers. A taxi to the wharf costs M$8, to the international airport M$12.

Car Rental Avis (tel 082-411370) has an office in the Holiday Inn on Jalan Tunku Abdul Rahman, while Mahana Rent a Car (tel 082-423435) is on Jalan Borneo opposite the Hilton Hotel.

Boat Small boats and express boats ply the Sarawak River, connecting the small villages around Kuching. You can also charter boats. Ask other passengers what the fare should be

and be prepared to bargain. Make sure you agree on the fare before you take the ride.

AROUND KUCHING
Semenggoh Wildlife Rehabilitation Centre
This is where you'll find Sarawak's answer to the orang-utan sanctuary at Sepilok in Sabah. The Semenggoh sanctuary, 32 km south of Kuching, is a rehabilitation centre for orang-utans, monkeys, honey bears and hornbills which have either been orphaned or kept illegally by locals.

Unfortunately the centre is not really set up for tourism and it's hard to find anyone who speaks English well if you want to ask questions. The semi-wild orang-utans are fed at 8.30 am and again at 2.30 pm so it's best to time your visit to coincide with one of these feeding sessions. If you have visited (or intend to visit) the Sepilok Rehabilitation Centre in Sabah you'll find Semenggoh a bit of a disappointment.

The centre is reached from the Forest Department Nursery along a plankwalk through the forest – a very pleasant walk. There are also a couple of signposted jungle trails behind the nursery – the Southern Trail can be used as an alternative to the plankwalk but would be slippery and muddy in the wet season.

A permit is required in order to visit the sanctuary and can be arranged, free of charge, at the National Parks & Wildlife office (tel 082-248088), on the 7th floor of the Satok building on Jalan Satok, about a km west of the Kuching city centre. You need

An Iban man

to tell them the day you intend visiting the centre.

Getting There & Away To get to the centre and Forest Department Nursery, take a STC Penrissen bus No 6 from Kuching. The trip takes about 40 minutes, costs M$1.20 and there are departures at 8.15, 11 and 11.50 am, and 2 pm. Unfortunately the centre is closed from 12 noon to 2 pm but it's still possible to wander around and inspect the cages. If you are driving, there is a new gravel road which has been pushed through the forest to the rehabilitation centre from the Botanical Research Station, 500 metres before the Forest Department Nursery.

Santubong

North of Kuching on the coast, this is the nearest beach 'resort' to Kuching, other than the beaches in the nearby Bako National

Park, and is very popular with local people on the weekends. It is 32 km from Kuching and there is a small village. Nearby at Sungai Jaong, about 1½ km upriver from the coast, rock carvings can be seen.

Close to the Holiday Inn Damai Beach Resort is Kampung Budaya Sarawak, a Malay 'cultural village'. There are examples of various types of longhouses as built by the different peoples of the interior, as well as a Chinese and a Malay house, all built around an artificial lake. At the different longhouses there are daily demonstrations of local arts and crafts such as basketry, sugar cane crushing, blowpipe making, may weaving, sago processing and others. It's a good opportunity to see a variety of activities from differing cultures all in the one spot but as you might expect it is something of a tourist trap; entry is M$10, and the centre is open daily from 9 am to 7.30 pm. For more information phone 082-422411.

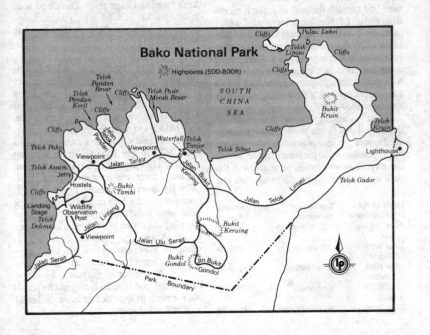

Places to Stay The only accommodation at Santubong is the expensive *Holiday Inn Damai Beach Resort* (tel 082-411777), which has rooms from M$110 up to M$700, although discounts are offered in the off-season. There are a few shuttle buses daily between the Holiday Inn Kuching and this place, although they charge like wounded bulls – M$15!

Bako National Park

This park is at the mouth of the Bako River, north of Kuching, and contains some 27 sq km of unspoilt tropical rainforest. The coastline has many fine sandy beaches, rocky headlands and mangrove swamps while the interior sports seven distinctive types of vegetation. Due to the different vegetation types many animals – notably the rare and protected species of hornbill and the proboscis monkey – have made their homes in this park. It's a very beautiful area and is well worth a visit.

Over 30 km of well-marked trails have been laid through the park to make it accessible and all of them are colour coded with a paint mark on trees adjacent to the path. On some of the longer walks you should plan your route before leaving and aim to be back at the hostels at Telok Assam before dark at 6.45 pm. Although you may be told that a guide is necessary it's easy to find your way around without one.

If you're thinking of walking to the end of the longest trail (Jalan Telok Limau) you will need to arrange transport to collect you since it's impossible to do the return trip on foot in one day. Transport can be arranged with the park warden. The main trails in the park are:

Name of Path	Destination	Time Required
Jalan Lintang	circular path	3-4 hours
Jalan Tanjung Sapi	cliffs/viewpoint	½ hour
Jalan Telok Delima	mangroves	¾ hour
Jalan Telok Pandan	cove beaches	1½ hours
Jalan Telok Paku	cove beach	¾ hour
Jalan Serait	park boundary	1½ hours
Jalan Tanjor	waterfalls	2 hours
Jalan Tanjung Rhu	cliffs/viewpoint	2½ hours
Jalan Bukit Keruing/ Jalan Bukit Gondol	mountain path	7 hours
Jalan Ulu Serait/ Jalan Telok Limau	Pulau Lakei (island)	8 hours

A permit is needed to visit the park, and this, along with accommodation bookings, must be made in advance at the National Parks & Wildlife office (tel 082-248088) in Kuching. Telephone bookings are accepted but must be confirmed and paid for at least three days before your intended departure. It's actually a lot easier to go to the national parks office in person. People have been known to turn up at the park without any bookings and as far as we know they haven't been turned away. It's best to avoid weekends if possible as the park gets more crowded then.

The park canteen has a variety of goods for sale (mainly tinned food) but there is also fresh bread and vegetables. There's no need to bring a lot of food with you, although prices are higher at the park than they are elsewhere.

Places to Stay There are resthouses, hostels and a camping site at the park. Resthouses include a fridge, gas burners, all utensils and bed linen. It costs M$60 per resthouse or M$30 per double room in the new resthouse, and M$40 and $20 in the old resthouse. Hostel cabins sleep six to a room and a bed costs M$2.10 per person. Linen, cooking utensils, a few cups and plates are provided.

Lastly, there are permanent tents (basically fly sheets) on raised platforms with open fireplaces which cost M$2 each. Bring your own supplies/utensils and sheets or sleeping bags. Two or three people can sleep under these. The problem here is that monkeys prowl around and will pinch anything that is not firmly secured – be careful.

From November to February, the sea is often rough and at times it may not be possible for boats to approach or leave the hostel area at Telok Assam.

Getting There & Away The park is 37 km from Kuching and can be reached by bus and boat. To get there, take bus No 6 from near the Sikh temple in Kuching town; the fare is M$2.10 one way (M$3 for a return ticket, valid for a week). The trip to Kampung Bako takes about 45 minutes and buses depart hourly from about 7 am to 5 pm.

From Kampung Bako, you must charter a private boat to the national park for about M$25 for up to 10 people, or M$3 per person if there are more than 10. The journey takes about 30 minutes.

Dayak Longhouses

As you might expect, the most interesting and unspoilt longhouses are found furthest from the main urban centres, in particular, along the upper reaches of the Skrang, Rejang, Balleh, Belaga, Balui and Baram rivers.

If you're not planning on going that far, or would like a preview, then the nearest longhouse to Kuching is at Kampung Segu Benuk which is a 35-km bus ride south of the city, followed by a short walk. Don't expect too much of this place as all the package tours include it on their itinerary so it's very commercialised. A better choice would be the one on the banks of the Kayan River reached by boat from Lundu.

Lundu & Sematan

Sematan is a tiny coastal village near the extreme western end of Sarawak. It has a very laid-back and relaxing atmosphere with a good deserted beach, warm sea and safe swimming. Many years ago it was a bauxite mining area, but that's all long since gone. A tourist hotel complex is planned, based around the lake left by the bauxite mine, but it will be years before that gets anywhere.

Between Lundu and Sematan is the Gunung Gading National Park but it doesn't have any facilities for visitors, although these may come in the future; check with the National Parks & Wildlife office in Kuching.

In addition to the national park there is a longhouse about 15 minutes by car from Sematan. Try hitching a ride, or asking people around town if they know anyone going to the longhouse – a taxi would be expensive as you'd have to hire the whole vehicle and pay the return fare. If you don't mind walking, the round trip will take you about three hours.

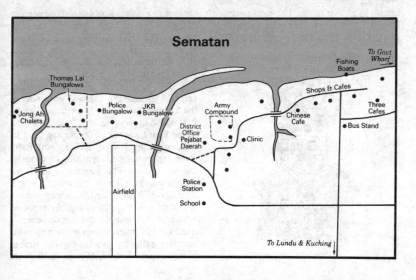

Places to Stay & Eat The people are friendly and you may well be offered a free room at Sematan, but you can rent a room at the *Thomas Lai Bungalows*. There are seven of these altogether, set in a coconut palm grove next to the sea. The cheapest unit has two rooms, kitchen and bathroom and costs M$40 a night (maximum of 10 people). The most expensive units have three rooms, kitchen and bathroom and cost M$100 a night (maximum of 15 people). Naturally, at these prices you'd need to get a small group together before setting out from Kuching.

You can either rent them from the caretaker on arrival in Sematan or book in advance through Mrs Doris Lai (tel 082-45174) or through the tourist office. The best food in Sematan is served at the *Muslim restaurant* – try their seafood and omelettes. If you have to wait around in Lundu and would like to eat, excellent Chinese meals are available at the *Siong Kee Restaurant*, close to the bus stand – look for the large Guinness sign.

Getting There & Away The bus fare from Kuching is about M$14. First take an STC bus No 2B from Kuching to Lundu for M$5. There are three buses daily and the journey takes 1½ to two hours. The road is sealed from Kuching to Bau, but quite rough from Bau to Lundu. From Lundu there are 10 daily

Iban Woman

STC buses to Sematan (route No 17); it's a one-hour journey on a rough road at a cost of M$2.

Serian

Serian is a very small town 65 km south-east of Kuching. There is a series of rock pools and a waterfall at the river, a short distance from the village itself. On weekends it's a very popular destination for locals who come to Serian to swim and to escape from the heat for a while.

Places to Stay If you want to stay overnight there's the *Kota Semarahan Serian Hotel* (tel 082-874118) at 47B Serian Bazaar, which has just five rooms from M$15.

Getting There & Away From Kuching take an STC express bus to Serian; the journey takes about an hour and the fare is M$4. There are also slower (and cheaper) non-express buses. If you go on a weekend, try hitching as there's lots of traffic.

Up the Rejang River

Other than a visit to Kuching and one or more of the national parks, the Rejang is the principal travel destination in Sarawak. Scattered along this river and its tributaries, particularly the upper reaches, are the longhouses of the Iban and other tribes.

The Rejang is the main 'highway' of central and southern Sarawak and most of the trade in the interior is carried out along it. It is also the way the logs from the forests in the upper reaches of the Rejang (and its tributaries the Balleh, Belaga and Balui rivers) are brought down to Sibu for processing and export. The number of log-laden barges on the river is astounding – and depressing. What is most disturbing perhaps is that the vast majority of logs are exported whole, so not only are the forests severely damaged to extract the logs, there's no value added locally by processing the timber before export. Instead, 65% of the logs are exported to Japan, where the majority are used to make plywood, formwork for cement on building sites and to make the millions of disposable chopsticks the Japanese get through each day. Before the loggers arrived the river was a clear green; these days it's a muddy brown from all the topsoil which has washed out of the forests.

The best time for a visit up the Rejang is in late May and early June, as this is the time of the Dayak harvest festival, so there is plenty of movement on the rivers and the longhouses welcome visitors. There's also plenty of celebrations, which usually involve the consumption of copious quantities of *arak* and *tuak* (rice wine).

On the river there is hotel accommodation only in Song, Kanowit, Kapit and Belaga.

Visiting a Longhouse

Most people head off up the river with the intention of visiting a longhouse, and certainly this is well worth doing. It does, however, require a bit of effort on your part. It's not just a matter of rolling up on the doorstep of a longhouse and expecting to be welcomed with open arms. The Dayak certainly are hospitable people but you do need

to have an introduction to visit one – turning up announced, except during the harvest season, is not good manners.

To arrange a visit the most important commodity to have on hand is time. The best place to head for is Kapit, a small administrative town upriver. It's the last big settlement on the river and here the longhouse people come in for supplies. The best strategy for finding someone to take you to a longhouse is to make yourself known around the town – sit in the cafes and get talking to people, and, even better, talk to the guys who pump fuel on the fuel barges in the river. Ask them if they know of anyone going to a longhouse in the area. They usually know who is in town and who's going where. The Petronas barge seems to get the most longboats refuelling and is a good place to start.

Before heading upriver from Kapit you need to get a permit from the state office. It takes only a few minutes but is not available on Saturday afternoon or Sunday. The permit is merely a formality and the chances are you'll never be asked for it. On the top floor of the same building is the Lands & Surveys Department office and they have excellent maps of Sarawak, and for M$1.50 will

A Longhouse

photocopy sections of the most detailed ones. This gives good detail of the Rejang and Balleh rivers, including many longhouse names.

Many travellers head for the stretch of the Rejang River between Kapit and Belaga. This area is easily accessible as there are express boats operating between the two towns, in the wet season at least. Perhaps a more interesting river is the Balleh River, which branches off to the east a short distance upstream from Kapit. Both these rivers have dozens of small tributaries and its up these that you really want to go. At Belaga the Balui and Belaga rivers merge and become the Rejang River. To travel up either of these rivers from Belaga requires permission from the Resident in Belaga, and this is generally not given, although it seems there's little to stop you if you are determined. The Katibas River joins the Rejang at Song (between Sibu and Kapit) and this is also a good river to explore, and no permits are required.

Some people have reported that some of the longhouse inhabitants between Kapit and Belaga are decidedly unfriendly towards visitors. No doubt they're sick to death of strangers turning up out of the blue and expecting to be welcomed with open arms, fed and entertained. One traveller was stuck for words when an old Iban lady asked: 'Where in Europe can I go and be welcomed into a stranger's house?' Don't let this put you off, as generally, the Iban are very friendly, hospitable people who welcome foreigners and are pleased to invite you into their homes. If you want to get a real feel for life in the longhouses then you should plan on staying at least one night. Staying at a longhouse is one of the highlights of any trip to Sarawak. You will most likely have to sleep with the chief's family, or the family of the person who brings you to the longhouse.

Having found someone to take you, you'll need to stock up with gifts with which to 'pay' for your visit. Forget any qualms you may have about giving people things that might be bad for them – cigarettes and alcohol are the gifts most appreciated. Sweets always go down well too, and not just

with the kids. Of course if you can give something original, especially from your own country, it will be well received. A carton of cigarettes and a few bottles of arak will go down well.

On arrival at the longhouse ask for the *tuai rumah* (chief). You'll then probably be offered a place to stay for the night and you'll be invited to join them for a meal.

Longhouse Etiquette

Longhouse etiquette is fairly formal and there are a number of important customs you need to be aware of so you don't make a fool of yourself. Firstly, never enter a longhouse without permission; always wait to be invited. If there is a *pemali* (ritual prohibition) in force (usually after a death or some misfortune), indicated by a bunch of branches tied to the rail at the bottom of the ladder or by a white flag near the entrance, you won't be invited in – find another longhouse.

Once inside, always remove your shoes; it's extremely bad form to wear footwear inside a longhouse. Chances are you'll be given a welcome drink of tuak; drink it, or at least some of it. Accept food and drinks with both hands rather than just one.

Meals are usually taken with the tuai rumah and are served on the floor and are eaten with both hands. Don't stretch your legs when sitting on the mat; this applies at any time, not just during meals. Don't spit or blow your nose during a meal. Chances are the food will be fairly bland and uninteresting but, again, eat some of it or at the very least touch the food and then touch your mouth. Vegetarians may find it difficult as meat is usually used in local cooking. It's not a bad idea to take along some food of your own.

When washing or bathing in the river, men are expected to wear at least underpants while women should stay covered with a sarong. Nudity is not on – this is not Europe.

In the evenings there'll probably be a lot of tuak drinking and you may well be expected to sing and dance. Join in and don't be afraid to make an idiot of yourself, the locals will love it! Tuak usually tastes weak but it is pretty potent stuff and although it doesn't give hangovers it is a fairly safe bet that you'll find yourself going to the toilet frequently the following day. The accepted way to drink it is from the glass in a single shot.

Make an effort to speak at least a few words of Iban. Although there's always someone who speaks Malay, any attempt at communication in the local lingo is warmly appreciated. Your conversations will be limted if you speak only English.

What to Take

Apart from gifts, other indispensable items include a torch, mosquito repellent, a medical kit with plenty of aspirin and panadol (you'll probably be seen by all and sundry as the local healer), and some Lomotil, Imodium or other anti-diarrhoeal.

Some Iban Words & Phrases

I	*aku*
you	*nuan*
drink	*ngirup*
eat	*makai*
thank you	*terima kasih*
day	*hari*
night	*malam*
where	*dini*
what	*nama*
good	*manah*
not good	*jai also enda manah*
I'm sorry	*aku minta ampun*
go	*bejalai*
today	*saharitu*
tomorrow	*pegila*

Good morning
  Salamat pagi
Good afternoon
  Salamat tengah-hari
Good night
  Salamat malam
Good bye
  Salamat tinggal
How are you?
  Gerai nuan?

Pleased to meet you
  Rindu amat betemu enggau nuan
See you again
  Arap ke betemu baru
Who is the chief?
  Sapa tuai rumah kita ditu?
What is your name?
  Sapa nama nuan?
Where do we bathe/wash?
  Dini endor kitai mandi?
Can I take a photograph of you?
  Tau aku ngambi gambar nuan?

SIBU

Sibu is the main port city on the Rejang River and will probably be your first stop on the river. Situated 60 km upstream from the ocean, its bustling waterfront sports all manner of craft from motorised dugouts to ocean-going cargo boats. It's here that the raw materials of the interior – logs, gravel, minerals and agricultural produce – are brought for transhipment and export. Manufactured goods from Peninsular Malaysia and abroad also arrive here for distribution to the interior.

There's not a lot to do in Sibu itself unless you like hanging around waterfronts or vegetable markets, and although both these are quite entertaining, most travellers only stay overnight and head off up the Rejang the next day. It's worth climbing the tower of the Chinese temple as there are great views of the river. At the other end of the waterfront, just past the bus station, is a clock tower, donated by the Orient Clock Co, complete with clock that plays different tunes on the hour – very tacky!

Information

At the Sarawak Hotel a man named Johnny Wong acts as a representative for the Sarawak Tourist Association. He's helpful if there's anything you need to know about Sibu and the surrounding area.

The GPO is right in the centre of town, as are the major banks. The MAS office (tel 083-326166) is at 61 Jalan Tuanku Abdul Rahman, a few minutes' walk from the centre of town. It is open Monday to Friday from 8 am to 5 pm, Saturday from 8 am to 12 noon and Sunday from 9 to 11 am.

There is an excellent swimming pool about 30 minutes' bus ride from the centre. Take a bus No 10 from the bus station. The pool is open Monday to Thursday from 2 to 6 pm, Friday from 2 to 5 and 7 to 9 pm, Saturday from 9 to 11 am and 2 to 5 pm, and on Sunday from 9 to 11 am, 2 to 5 and 7 to 9 pm; entry is M$1.

The express boat wharf is right in the centre of town by the Chinese temple, and the bus station is also on the waterfront. Everything (apart from the swimming pool and the airport) is within walking distance of these two places.

Places to Stay – bottom end

The majority of budget hotels in Sibu are pretty seedy places and there's not a lot to choose between them. By far the best place to stay is the Methodist guest house, *Hoover House*, next to the church on Jalan Pulau. It's excellent value at M$10 per person for clean, well-kept rooms with polished wooden floors, fan and attached Western-style bathroom. There are also air-con rooms available for M$25 per person – not such great value. Fresh drinking water, guest towels and soap are brought to your room. The only problem is that it's often full.

All over town you'll see signs saying *bilik untuk sewa* (or variations on that), which means 'rooms for rent' but these places are often brothels. Of the regular hotels, one of the better places is the friendly *Hoover Lodging House* (tel 084-334490), not to be confused with the Methodist guest house. You'll probably be given one of their cards as you step off the express boat. It's at 34 Jalan Tan Sri, in a fairly seedy area just a few minutes' walk from the bus station. The rooms are a bit on the small side and many don't have windows, but at M$10/15 for a

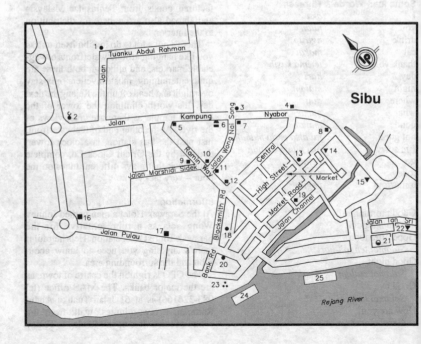

single/double what do you want? There are more expensive rooms with air-con and bath for M$18/25. There are a few other 'lodging houses' in the same street – such as the *Holiday, Royal Park, 88* and *Lena*.

Cheaper is the *Sibu Hotel* (tel 084-330784) on Jalan Marshidi Sidek. The rooms are good value at M$12/15 with fan or M$20/26 with air-con, bath and TV, but the walls *and* window panes have been painted a sickly shade of green! The *Hotel Malaysia* (tel 084-332298) on Jalan Kampung Nyabor is a friendly place with rooms with fan and common bath for M$15, or with air-con and bath for M$30/35.

Another reasonable place is the *Mandarin Hotel* (tel 084-339177) at 183 Jalan

Kampung Nyabor, although you need to get a room at the back as it's a noisy road. Doubles with fan and bath go for M$16, while singles/doubles with air-con and bath are M$31/34. At No 24 on the same road is the *Federal Hotel* (tel 084-333086) which has a variety of rooms ranging from M$17 for a single with fan to M$32 for a double with air-con, bath and TV. Once again the cheapest rooms are also the hottest.

The *Miramar Hotel* (tel 084-332433) at 47 Jalan Channel is quite popular with travellers. Fan-cooled rooms with private bathrooms cost M$21; with air-con it's M$30 and towels and soap are provided. As is the case with most hotels, the fan-cooled rooms are on the upper floors and can be viciously hot. From the windows you get a great view of the night market stalls which are set up in the street below.

Places to Stay – middle

A good hotel in this price range is the *New World Hotel* (tel 084-310311) on the corner of Jalan Wong Nai Song and Cross Rd. All rooms have air-con, bath and TV and go for M$35/40. Across the road is the *Sarawak Hotel* (tel 084-333455) which is slightly cheaper at M$30/43 for rooms with similar facilities.

Places to Stay – top end

The *Hotel Zuhra* (tel 084-310711) at 103 Jalan Kampung Nyabor is one of the cheaper top-end hotels with air-con rooms from M$55/65 singles/doubles. The staff are very friendly and helpful. There's a coffee shop downstairs and a clean, airy Chinese cafe next door.

The *Li Hua Hotel* (tel 084-324000) at the Longbridge Commercial Centre past the bus station has 77 fully air-conditioned single rooms from M$60 and doubles from M$95.

The top of the range is the enormous *Premier Hotel* (tel 084-323222) on Jalan Kampung Nyabor. All rooms have air-con and private facilities, and prices range from M$74 to M$200 per night. This hotel has its own nightclub, bars and coffee lounges and although these were gutted by fire in

---

■ PLACES TO STAY

4	Mandarin Hotel
5	Malaysia Hotel
7	Federal Hotel
8	Premier Hotel
9	Sibu Hotel
10	New World Hotel
11	Sarawak Hotel
12	Rex Hotel
16	Government Rest House
17	Hoover House
19	Miramar Hotel
22	Hoover Lodging House

▼ PLACES TO EAT

| 14 | New Capitol Restaurant |
| 15 | Sugar Bun |

OTHER

1	MAS
2	Mosque
3	Police
6	GPO
13	Palace Cinema
18	Expres Bahagia Office
20	Concorde Office
21	Bus Station
23	Chinese Temple
24	Sarikei Boat Jetty
25	Kapit Boat Jetty

mid-1990 they should be back in operation by now.

Places to Eat

The best cheap food in Sibu is found at the various hawker centres and food stalls. On the ground floor of the *New World Hotel* is a cafe with a few food stalls selling a variety of foods, and there is an excellent bakery at one end.

For hawker food there's a small two-storey food centre at the end of Market Rd, at the rear of the Palace Cinema. Here you'll find stalls selling Malay curries and roti, laksa as well as Chinese food and ais kacang. There are also food stalls on the 2nd floor of the market.

In the late afternoon stalls set up near the market, mainly outside the Miramar Hotel, and these are great for picking up snack foods such as *pau* (steamed dumplings), barbecued chicken wings and all manner of sweets.

The *Sugar Bun*, diagonally opposite the church on the large roundabout, not far from the bus station, is OK for breakfast or Western-style fast-food snacks. For those with the inclination there's a *Kentucky Fried Chicken* outlet on Jalan Wong Nai Song.

For a full-on sit-down Chinese meal at a proper restaurant try the *New Capitol Restaurant* near the Premier Hotel. It's expensive but the food is reportedly the best in Sibu.

Getting There & Away

Air If you're travelling by boat from Sibu to Kapit and Belaga and want to fly back, book your flight as far in advance as possible because the Sibu-Kapit-Belaga (and return) sector is only covered twice a week by a 12-seater Twin Otter. The fare is M$48 to Kapit, M$76 to Belaga. There are also Twin Otter flights to Marudi three times a week (M$100).

To Kuching there are five flights daily (M$60) and to Bintulu four daily for M$53. Some of these flights go on to Miri (M$93) and Kota Kinabalu (M$156).

Road – To/From Bintulu & Miri The 220-km road from Sibu to Bintulu should be close to being surfaced all the way. What was once an incredibly rough and dusty (or rough and slippery, depending on the season) ride, should now be a breeze. The Lanang Bus Co has buses to Bintulu at 6 and 8.30 am, and 12 noon; the 8.30 bus is not air-conditioned. The fare is $14.80 (M$18 air-con) and the trip takes around four hours, although this will be less if the road is surfaced all the way. Syarikat Bus Express also has air-con buses to Bintulu at 6.15 am and 12.15 pm for M$18. They also have one departure for the eight-hour trip to Miri at 6.45 am. It's an air-con bus and the fare is M$35. Tickets for all buses should be bought half a day or so in advance.

Road – To/From Kuching See the Kuching Getting There & Away section for details about road transport between Kuching and Sibu.

Boat – To Sibu-Sarikei-Kuching All express boats to Sarikei and Kuching (change at Sarikei) leave from the Sarikei Wharf in front of the Chinese temple. There are four companies operating to Kuching; the trip takes around four hours and costs M$25 to M$28 depending on the company.

Although it's best to buy tickets in advance you should have no difficulty getting one on the boat. Ticket outlets and departure times from Sibu are:

Expres Pertama (tel 084-335055), 14 Khoo Peng Loong Rd; 7 am
Follow Me (tel 084-324184), 23 Jalan Maju; 6.30 am
Exspres Bahagia (tel 084-319228), 20A Blacksmith Rd; 7.30, 11.30 am
Concorde Marine (tel 084-331593), 1 Bank Rd; 11.30 am

Several cargo boats make trips from Kuching to Sibu to Bintulu and beyond. See the Kuching section for further details.

Boat – To Kapit-Belaga Getting to Kapit is the first leg of the journey up the Rejang River. The newest *expres* launches which do

State Mosque, Kota Kinabalu (HF)

Top: Sandakan, Sabah (HF)
Bottom: Poring Hot Springs, Sabah (HF)

this trip cover the 130 km or so from Sibu to Kapit in a shade over two hours! The older boats do it in 2½ to three hours. The first launch from Sibu leaves at 5.45 am, and when there's enough water in the river this boat goes on to Belaga. Other launches leave approximately hourly up until 12 noon or sometimes 1 pm. Just go down to the Kapit Wharf and ask which is the next boat. People are very helpful and the boats usually have a 'clock' displaying intended departure time. The fare to Kapit is M$15.

All launches call at Kanowit and Song, while the slower ones will also stop at a number of smaller settlements and logging camps en route.

Getting Around

If you arrive in Sibu by launch (from Kuching or Sarikei) or by cargo/passenger boat (from Kuching, Sarikei, Bintulu or Miri) then you will dock at Sarikei or Kapit wharves, which are both only a few minutes' walk from all the main hotels and restaurants.

If you arrive by air take either a taxi or bus No 1 to the bus station in the centre of town. This is also where the Bintulu and Miri buses leave from.

KAPIT

This small town on the eastern bank of the Rejang River dates from the days of the White Rajahs and still sports an old wooden fort built by Charles Brooke. To anyone from outside it's just a sleepy riverside village tucked into the rainforest, but to upriver people it's the 'big city' to which they come to buy, sell and exchange goods as well as for entertainment – there are pool halls and a few of the cafes have video machines.

The bank of the river here is quite steep, so in the dry season when the water level falls it's quite a drop to the river. For an idea of how high the water can get check out the flood markers on the front of the old fort.

If you are looking for a lift and introduction to a longhouse ask at the Petronas or Shell fuel barges.

There are two longhouses about seven km

from town along Jalan Selerik but they're thoroughly urbanised and nothing like the more traditional ones you'll find further upriver.

Information

If you need to change money (ie travellers' cheques) there are two banks in town – one in the same block as the Kapit Longhouse Hotel overlooking New Bazaar and the other right next door to the Hotel Meligai. You can get good maps of the area at the Lands & Survey Department office on the top floor of the government complex. The MAS agent is Hua Chiong Co (tel 084-796988) one block back from the waterfront.

Permits for Travel Beyond Kapit Go to the Pejabat Am office on the 1st floor of the State Government Complex and collect the necessary forms. Fill them in and take them next door to the office of the Residen and the permit will be issued in a couple of minutes. One question in the form asks when your cholera vaccination expires but this is not checked. The permit is valid for either five or 10 days, depending on which you specify, and is valid for travel up the Rejang as far as Belaga and up the Balleh River for an unspecified distance. If you get up the river and find your permit is going to expire, don't lose any sleep as it seems the only people who want to have anything to do with the permit is the office that issues them.

These government offices are only open normal office hours so if you arrive on a weekend you'll have to wait until Monday morning for them to open.

Things to See

There isn't a great deal to do or see in Kapit though the waterfront and the market are interesting and the Chinese temple works up a sweat on the big drums some evenings.

The brand new municipal library opposite the Federal Government Complex on the bypass road has a good local collection and is air-conditioned, although the opening hours are limited: Monday to Friday from 4.15 to 8.30 pm; Saturday from 9 to 11.15

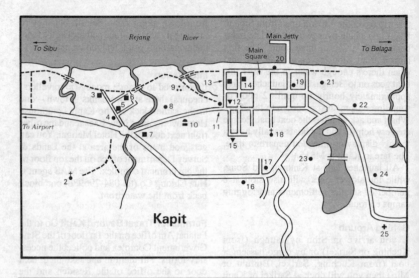

Kapit

■ PLACES TO STAY

3 Kapit Longhouse Hotel
5 Rejang Hotel
6 Hiap Chiong Hotel
7 Hotel Meligai & Bank
13 Ark Hill Hotel
14 Well Inn

▼ PLACES TO EAT

12 Ung Tong Bakery
15 Food Stalls

OTHER

1 Chinese Cemetery

2 Catholic Church
4 Bank
8 School
9 Temple
10 Post Office
11 Market
16 Federal Government Complex
17 Library
18 Church
19 MAS Agent
20 Shell Station
21 Old Fort
22 Police Headquarters
23 State Government Complex
24 Civic Centre
25 Hospital

am and 2 to 4.30 pm; and Sunday from 9 to 11 am and 2 to 6.30 pm.

Also worth a look is the museum in the lavish new civic centre (another incredible waste of money – 2½ million ringgit were spent on this one). It's supposedly open from 9 am to 12 noon and 2 to 4 pm daily except Friday and Sunday. In practice it seems it's locked all the time until a visitor comes along. There is an interesting relief map of the area showing all the longhouses, as well as displays on what the government is doing in the way of developing the infrastructure. There's also a couple of cultural displays.

Places to Stay – bottom end

The place to head for is the *Rejang Hotel* (tel 084-796709) which has cheap (and hot) single rooms on the top floor for M$10, or fan-cooled doubles with bath for M$18, and air-con doubles with bath for M$24 – good value, although the decor in some of the rooms is a bit radical.

The other two cheap hotels are brothels first and hotels second, and are not particularly pleasant places to stay. The *Hiap Chiong Hotel* (tel 084-796213) has some rooms on the top floor for M$18 with fan and bath and these seem to escape the worst of the noise and general seedy atmosphere. The *Kapit Longhouse Hotel* (tel 084-796415) is not recommended but if you have no option, rooms are M$20 with fan and bath, M$30 with air-con and bath.

Places to Stay – middle

Kapit has two very pleasant mid-range hotels, both of them new and quite good value. In the *Ark Hill Hotel* (tel 084-796168) all rooms are air-con and have attached bath and TV and cost M$35. The *Well Inn* (tel 084-796009) is also new and has similar rooms and prices.

Places to Stay – top end

The top-end offering is the *Hotel Meligai* (tel 084-796611) which has 40 rooms for M$52/75.

Places to Eat

Far and away the best place to eat is the *River View (Ming Hock) Restaurant* on the top floor of the market building. As well as regular Chinese food they also have a variety of local foods including venison, frogs legs and prawns although these are not available every day. There are views of the river from the balcony and it's a pleasant place to sit in the evenings and sip a beer.

The *Kah Ping Cafe* on the main square has good pork dishes and is popular among the locals. The food stalls back from the main street are not that popular but stall No 12 does traditional Iban food while No 29 does an unusual murtabak.

The *Ung Tong Bakery* next to the market has excellent buns and coffee – a good bet for breakfast. It's run by a friendly Chinese family.

Entertainment

For entertainment in the evenings Kapit has at least three snooker halls and one surprisingly sophisticated Karaoke lounge if you fancy yourself as a singer.

Getting There & Away

Air When the river is really low you will not be able to get a launch or boat to Belaga, so if this is your intended destination the only way of getting there is to fly. MAS flies to Sibu, Kapit, Belaga and back on Thursdays and Sundays. The fare to Belaga is M$47 and M$48 to Sibu.

Road The only local road transport are taxis and there are very few of these. It isn't surprising since there's hardly anywhere you can go by road. If you arrive by air you'll have to take a taxi the two km into town.

Boat – To/From Sibu There are frequent *expres* launch departures to Sibu from 8 am up until around 3 pm. Just go down to the jetty when you're ready and hop on. The Kapit to Sibu fare is M$15 and the journey takes from 2½ to 3½ hours, depending on the age of the launch.

Boat – To/From Belaga During the wet season *expres* launches leave for Belaga daily from the main jetty. The trip takes up to six hours and costs M$20. During the dry season when the river is low the *expres* boats can't get through the Pelagus Rapids about an hour upstream of Kapit. This is mainly because there is no protection for the propeller, and at M$2000 each the boat owners are not surprisingly unwilling to risk damage. Small cargo boats still do the run, however. They are slow and uncomfortable, take around eight hours and charge M$40. If you catch one of these boats make sure you wear clothes that give you protection from the sun as there may be no shade.

There are also cargo boats heading up the Balleh River on a daily basis as far as Interwau – ask at the fuel barges in Kapit.

If you want to charter a longboat to take you upriver you're looking at around M$150 per day (which includes the services of the operator and someone who keeps an eye out for obstructions, especially when the river is low) excluding fuel – so the all-up charge is around M$200.

BELAGA

Belaga is just a small village and government administration centre on the upper reaches of the Rejang where the river divides into the Belaga and Balui rivers.

Along these rivers are many interesting Kayan and Kenyah longhouses. If you start talking to a friendly local on the boat, you may well be invited to stay at their longhouse. Don't forget to offer food, cigarettes, or some small gift as a contribution towards your keep. There is a Kayan longhouse within walking distance from Belaga town.

You cannot travel beyond Belaga without official permission and unless you have a written invitation from someone living further up the river, it's highly unlikely that you'll be granted permission. Travellers have been known to go ahead without a permit, however, if you do this it might be an idea to let someone else know where you are heading, in case any problems arise. Permits are not required to use the logging road to Tubau.

Places to Stay

The *Sing Soon Hing Hotel* (tel 084-461257) is a reasonable Chinese cheapie with fan-cooled rooms from M$18 and rooms with air-con at M$27.

The *Belaga Hotel* (tel 084-461244) is the cheapest in town with rooms at M$15 with fan or M$25 air-con. The manager is a friendly man who can arrange for boats up the river, etc. There's also the *Huan Kilah Lodging House* (tel 084-461259) with rooms from M$30.

Getting There & Away

In the dry season it's possible to travel from Belaga to Bintulu on the Rejang River making use of the logging vehicles and then down the Jelalong, Labang and Kemena rivers. The journey is far from easy, mainly because you have to rely on getting lifts with logging company vehicles, and this can take a couple of days. The first step is to take a boat up the Belaga River about half an hour to the head of the logging road at the Kastima Camp. To hire a longboat costs about M$60 for this. Once at the road it's a matter of sitting and waiting for a vehicle. You should get on the same day, but it's not guaranteed. This vehicle takes you to the logging camp (known as Centre Camp), a trip of about two hours along a road through the forest. There is a canteen at the camp where you can buy food and there's also some basic accommodation.

From the logging camp a Landcruiser leaves at 1 pm daily for the trip to Tubau. From Tubau there are frequent *expres* boats to Bintulu (the last leaves at 12 noon) which cost M$14 and take about 3½ hours. It may also be possible to hitch a ride on a timber barge – a slow but interesting 18-hour trip. If you are stuck in Tubau there is accommodation for M$10. The trip is just as viable in the opposite direction.

The Coast

BINTULU

Bintulu is a modern, air-conditioned boom town which is best to pass through as quickly as possible, unless you want holes burned in every pocket. There's absolutely nothing of interest in the town, although you do get good sunsets by the river, and with the transport connections there's no need to stay overnight. If you are heading for Niah Caves Bintulu is a good place to stock up with provisions, although the little town of Batu Niah near the national park has an adequate selection.

The MAS office (tel 086-31554) is on Jalan Masjid and is open Monday to Friday from 8.30 am to 4.30 pm, Saturday from 8.30 am to 3.30 pm, and Sunday from 8.30 am to 12.30 pm. There's a cinema on Keppel Rd if you're stuck for some entertainment in the evening.

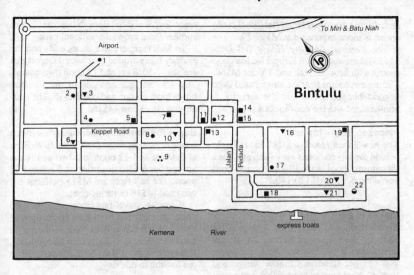

■ PLACES TO STAY	10 Food Stalls
	16 Glory Cake House
5 Capitol Hotel	20 Abidaa Cafe
7 Kamena Lodging House	21 Seaview Restoran
11 Hoover Hotel	
13 New Capitol Hotel	OTHER
14 Royal Hotel	
15 Sunlight Hotel	1 Terminal
18 Rumah Tumpangan Ah Ping	2 Telekom
19 Plaza Hotel	4 Chartered Bank
	8 Market
▼ PLACES TO EAT	9 Chinese Temple
	12 Sky Cinema
3 Honey Bun	17 MAS
6 Chicken Delight	22 Bus Station

Places to Stay – bottom end

Accommodation at this end of the market is pretty grim. There are a few mostly nameless *rumah tumpangan* (guest houses) along the waterfront road not far from the bus station. They just have partitioned rooms with fans and common bathrooms – basic but adequate for a night if you're stuck. The average charge is M$15 per double room.

A better bet is the *Capitol Hotel* (tel 086-34667) just off Keppel Rd in the centre. Big scruffy rooms with fan cost M$15, or

M$25/35 gets you a room with air-con and bath. It's certainly seen better days this place, but is habitable.

Places to Stay – middle

The best place in this range is the *Sunlight Hotel* (tel 086-32577) on the corner of Jalan Abang Galau and Jalan Pedada. All rooms have air-con and attached bath, and there are a few cheaper ones on the top floor for M$35, otherwise you're looking at M$48/55 for a largish room with shabby bathroom. Right next door is the *Royal Hotel* (tel 086-32166) which is more expensive at M$69/79.

The *Kamena Lodging House* (tel 086-31533) at the back of 78 Keppel Rd has good rooms with air-con, bath and TV for M$60. The annexe rooms near the airport used to be a good budget option but the security is non-existent and the door locks a joke.

Places to Stay − top end

The new *Plaza Hotel* (tel 086-35111) right behind the bus station is very flash and has a swimming pool and all other mod-cons you'd expect for M$120/140.

Places to Eat

The best place to eat in the evenings is the stalls by the market on Keppel Rd. By the bus station is the *Seaview Restoran* where you can get standard Chinese tucker, and they do good toasted sandwiches and coffee at breakfast.

For good Malay food, there's the *Abidaa Cafe* on Jalan Masjid near the bus station, while close to the airport entrance there's *Honey Bun*, a fast-food place with mediocre and expensive food and juices. If you're after this kind of food *Chicken Delight* is a better bet.

On Jalan Abang Galau the *Glory Cake House* has various cakes and other sticky things.

Getting There & Away

Air MAS has four flights daily to Sibu (M$53), six daily to Kuching (M$97), three daily to Miri (M$57) and one to Kota Kinabalu (M$110). The airport is smack in the middle of town.

Bus − To/From Batu Niah & Miri There are two daily buses which go directly to Batu Niah from Bintulu. The first departs at 7.30 am and the other at 12.15 pm. Return buses (without air-con) depart Batu Niah daily at 6 and 7 am, 12 noon and 3 pm. The trip takes about 2½ hours and the fare is M$10.

You can take the Miri bus and get off at the Batu Niah junction, but from there it's an eight-km walk to Batu Niah itself, and another three km to the national park.

To Miri there are five buses daily and the journey takes around four hours. Departures are at 7, 7.30, 8 am and 12 noon (two buses). The 7.30 am bus and one of the 12 noon buses have air-con and cost M$18. The non-air-con buses cost M$15.

Bus − To/From Sibu There are non-air-con buses departing daily from Bintulu to Sibu at 6, 9 am and 12 noon and two additional air-con buses also departing at 6 am and 12 noon. The bus fares are M$15 (without air-con) and M$18 (with air-con).

If you're travelling from Sibu to Batu Niah, the early bus from Sibu hooks up with the 12.15 pm bus to Batu Niah, so there's no need to stay in Bintulu overnight. Similarly, if travelling from Batu Niah it's possible to get to Sibu in one day.

Boat It's sometimes possible to find cargo/passenger boats from Bintulu to either Sibu or Miri. The fare to either place is M$35 and the journey takes about 18 hours. Check with the agents along the waterfront.

If you're trying to get to Belaga there are *expres* launches up the Kemena River as far as Tubau. The journey takes about 3½ hours and costs M$14. They leave from the jetty, just a few minutes' walk from the bus station.

NIAH NATIONAL PARK & NIAH CAVES

A visit to the Niah Caves is one of the most memorable experiences in East Malaysia. The Great Cave, also one of the largest in the world, is in the centre of the Niah National Park which is dominated by the 394-metre-high limestone massif of Gunung Subis, visible from far away.

Since 1958, when archaeologists discovered evidence that humans have been living in and around the caves for some 40,000 years, they have been under the protection of the Sarawak Museum.

The rock paintings found in the 'Painted Cave' were the only ones known to exist in Borneo at the time and were associated with several small canoe-like boats which were

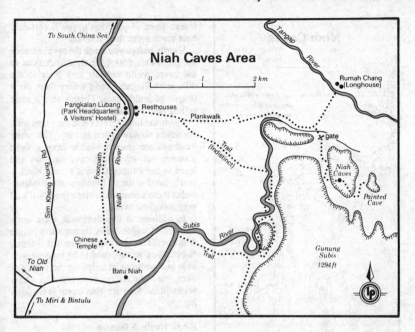

used as coffins, indicating that this part of the caves was used as a burial ground. A reconstruction of this cave together with some of the remains found there can be seen in the Sarawak Museum in Kuching.

Pangkalan Lubang

The park headquarters and hostel resthouses are on the Niah River at Pangkalan Lubang, about four km from Batu Niah. The park headquarters Visitors' Centre has some interesting and informative displays on the geology of the caves, archaeology and other aspects. It's worth spending half an hour or so here.

The area around the headquarters itself is not without interest. While you're relaxing in the cane chairs on the hostel verandah four km from Batu Niah and about 17 km from the sea, keep an eye on the river. The river level can change by over a metre depending on the strength of the tides out to sea, and the current varies from static to quite strong. Logging is widespread in this area and you may see large, log-laden barges chug their way downstream. These barges are almost as wide as the river. Once at the river mouth the logs are loaded onto ships and exported to Japan, South Korea, Taiwan and the Philippines.

Wildlife occasionally seen in the river include monitor lizards (up to two metres long), crocodiles and snakes, but they're all extremely shy and, for the benefit of those who are thinking of swimming in the river, rarely seen around the hostel area.

The Caves

To get to the caves from the hostel and headquarters you first have to take the longboat across the river. The standard charge is 50 sen per person. Once across the river there's a three-km-long plankwalk to the caves. It is made of Belian wood, which is very durable and so heavy that it cannot be transported by

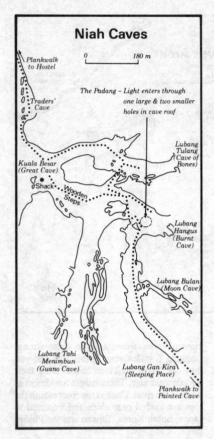

Niah Caves

0   180 m

Plankwalk
to Hostel

Traders'
Cave

The Padang – Light enters through
one large & two smaller
holes in cave roof

Kuala Besar
(Great Cave)

Lubang
Tulang
(Cave of
Bones)

Shack

Wooden
Steps

Lubang
Hangus
(Burnt
Cave)

Lubang Bulan
(Moon Cave)

Lubang Tahi
Menimbun
(Guano Cave)

Lubang Gan Kira
(Sleeping Place)

Plankwalk to
Painted Cave

water since it doesn't float. This plankwalk passes through some very pretty primary rainforest all the way to the caves. If you do the trip in the rainy season take care because the plankwalk gets very slippery.

Unfortunately, most visitors are so intent on reaching the caves that they miss out on the life in the forest around them. If you break your trek and spend some time just watching and listening you may be lucky enough to see such animals as the long-tailed macaque monkeys, hornbills, squirrels and flying lizards, as well as the many hundreds of species of butterflies which inhabit this

forest. Even if you don't, you'll certainly hear much more than you see.

Shortly before you reach the cave entrance the plankwalk forks; the right fork goes to the caves while the left fork goes to the village of Rumah Chang where there are a couple of longhouses. There's also a store selling cold beer and soft drinks!

Inside the huge Great Cave the plankwalk continues so navigation is easy. The white handrails are usually visible from a short distance but where the cave narrows and leads to the Painted Cave it's pitch black – you'll need a torch. Because of the plank-walks there's no need to hire a guide – it's all very straightforward.

In addition to the plankwalk there are a number of vague trails through the jungle which will take you to the summit of Gunung Subis. They're supposed to be marked with blue and white paint strips on the trunks of trees, but these are not at all obvious. Other walks in the area are also worth investigating.

Birds' Nests & Guano

More recent human activity in the caves has centred around the fact that they are the home of three species of swiftlet, numbering some four million, and 12 species of bat, of which there are also several million.

The swiftlets construct their nests in crevices in the roof of the Great Cave and it's these nests which are used in the preparation of that famous Chinese dish, bird's nest soup.

The collection of these nests, which are sold for M$250 to M$550 a kg, is supposed to be limited to certain times of the year, but is apparently carried out quite regularly. Scattered throughout the Great Cave are many flimsy poles, up which the collectors have to scramble to get to the nests. The poles stretch from the floor to the roof and some are well over 30 metres high. One can only marvel at the agility and nerve of the those who undertake this extremely dangerous activity. Inevitably there are a few serious accidents each year – and a fall from the ceiling is usually fatal. In order to regulate this lucrative market, the government has nationalised the industry and so all the collecting is in fact illegal. The huge gates protecting the cave entrance are there not to keep tourists out but to keep out the moonlighters who want a piece of the action. At the time of writing, however, there were not enough staff in the national park to enforce the policy and gathering was continuing apace.

Another activity which has been going on since 1928 is the collection of guano – the bird and bat excrement which is used as a fertiliser. The guano is collected each week on Mondays, Tuesdays and Wednesdays and carted laboriously along the plankwalk to the depot at Pangkalan Lubang where it is weighed, rebagged and boated down to Batu Niah for sale. If you're heading up to the caves on these days you may well have to give way to the collectors sweating it out down the plankwalk, with huge bags of guano on their back.

The millions of winged inhabitants of the caves provide an unforgettable spectacle as evening comes along. Swiftlets are day flyers and bats are nocturnal animals, so if you arrange to be at the mouth of the cave around 6 pm you can watch the shift change as the swiftlets return home and the bats go out for the night. You might even be lucky enough to see one of the large predatory birds, such as the bat hawks, swoop into the cave for a meal.

If you go up to the caves at this time be sure to bring a strong torch for the return trip. It's an exciting night-time jungle experience, but made easy by the plankwalk. Though you are certain to hear and see plenty on the way you'll probably remember most the many luminous mushrooms that grow beside the plankwalk.

Permits & Information

No permit is needed to visit the Great Cave but if you wish to visit the Painted Cave then you need a permit but it's really just a formality and is issued as a matter of course when you check in at the park headquarters at Pangkalan Lubang.

You can book accommodation for Niah at the national parks offices in Miri or Kuching (see the relevant sections) but make sure you get a receipt to show you've paid as the information doesn't necessarily get passed on to the park headquarters. It's usually not a problem to just turn up at the caves without a booking, especially during the week. If your luck is out and there's no accommodation the worst you'd have to do is sleep on the office floor or head back the four km to Batu Niah where there are a few hotels.

Places to Stay

Pangkalan Lubang The *Visitors' Hostel* at the park headquarters is a great place to stay. It can sleep 36 people in fairly crowded 12-bed dorms but has an excellent wide verandah looking out over the Niah River and the forest beyond. Cooking facilities are provided and there's electricity from 6 pm to midnight. On checking in you are issued with a set of crockery and cutlery, a sheet and a blanket, all of which you have to account for when leaving. You need to bring your own food with you, although there is a small store at the park gate which sells basic provisions – mostly canned goods. A bed costs M$3 per night. In the dry season the rainwater tanks often run out so the water is drawn from the river and must be boiled before drinking.

On the opposite side of the river are four two-bedroom resthouses which are completely self-contained. The charge is M$30 for a double room, or M$60 for the whole resthouse.

Batu Niah If for some reason you don't want to stay at the Visitors' Hostel or your time of arrival prevents you from getting there that night, there are a couple of hotels in Batu Niah. The *Niah Caves Hotel* (tel 086-737726) is clean, reasonably cheap at M$15/26 for a single/double and has good basic food in the restaurant downstairs. All rooms are air-con and have common bath.

The *Hock Seng Hotel* is cheaper at M$15/18 for a single/double with bath and fan, and M$30 with air-con and bath.

Getting There & Away

Batu Niah to Pangkalan Lubang (headquarters & Visitors' Hostel) Whether you come from Bintulu or Miri you will end up at Batu Niah. From there the best way to get to the Visitors' Hostel (or the start of the plankwalk if you're not staying at the hostel) is to ask around for a lift. Private cars often double as taxis, and the rate is M$4 per person, or M$8 for the whole vehicle if you are alone.

An alternative is to hire a longboat from behind the market. The trip takes just a few minutes and costs M$10 for the boat, and these can usually carry four to six people.

Lastly you can walk along the track by the river but this takes about an hour.

Bus – To/From Bintulu There are two direct buses daily from Bintulu to Batu Niah – the first departs at 7.30 am and the other at 12.15 pm. The fare is M$10 and the journey takes about 2½ hours. It is possible to take a Bintulu-Miri bus but you'll get dropped at the junction, about eight km from Bintulu and will have to hitch or walk. There are also

other buses which charge M$1 from the junction to Batu Niah. From Batu Niah to Bintulu, there are four buses daily leaving at 6 and 7 am, 12 noon and 3 pm.

Bus – To/From Miri There are four daily buses from Miri direct to Batu Niah. They depart at 7, 10.30 am, 12 noon and 2.30 pm (air-con), cost M$9 and the trip takes about two hours. From Batu Niah to Miri there are departures at 6.45, 7.45 (air-con) and 10.45 am and 1 pm.

On the way to Batu Niah you can stop at Lambir Hills National Park, 19 km from Miri. There's a pleasant waterfall about 20 minutes' walk in from the park buildings on the road. At the waterfall there's an empty house where you can stay for free – no beds or cooking facilities. Check with the forest officer in Miri or at the park.

MIRI

Miri is just another boom town based on oil money which has managed to attract a large number of expatriates, prostitutes and transvestites. Much of the town is being

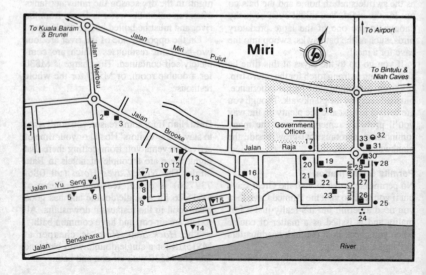

redeveloped and only the old centre remains. It's a pleasant enough town though there's precious little of interest to keep you there and, as in Bintulu, everything is air-conditioned and expensive.

Most travellers stay only overnight when heading to Brunei, to the Niah Caves, to Gunung Mulu or Bareo. The only real point of interest in the town is the Chinese temple down by the waterfront at the end of Jalan China.

■ PLACES TO STAY

2 Fatimah Hotel
3 Hotel Plaza Regency
11 Gloria Hotel
16 Fully Inn
19 Fairland Inn
21 South East Asia Lodging House
23 Borneo Hotel
26 Tai Tong Lodging House
27 Thai Foh Inn
29 Malaysia Lodging House
30 Mulu Inn
31 Park Hotel

▼ PLACES TO EAT

4 The Cottage
5 The Ranch
6 The Pub
7 Danish Hot Bread Bakery
10 Maxim Restaurant
12 Hungry Horse
14 Kentucky Fried Chicken
15 King Hua Restaurant
28 Aseanika Restoran

OTHER

1 GPO
8 MAS
9 Malang Sisters Travel Agency
13 Sin Liang Supermarket
17 Majlis Islam
18 National Parks & Wildlife Office
20 Chartered Bank
22 Taxis
24 Chinese Temple
25 Food Stalls
32 Bus Station
33 Wisma Pelita

Information & Orientation

If you're heading for Gunung Mulu, call at the national parks office for a permit and to book accommodation. A permit from the Resident's office is also required for visits to Gunung Mulu and to Bareo and the interior, although these are best obtained from the District Officer in Marudi. You can also book accommodation for Niah National Park. The national parks office (tel 085-36637) is in Jalan Raja behind the Majlis Islam building. Opening hours are 8 am to 12.45 pm and 2 to 4.15 pm Monday to Friday and 8 am to 12.45 pm on Saturdays.

The MAS office (tel 085-414144) is on Jalan Yu Seng about 10 minutes' walk from the centre. It is open Monday to Friday from 8.30 am to 4.30 pm, Saturday from 8.30 am to 4 pm and Sunday from 8.30 am to 12.30 pm. The post office and the Telekom office are about 15 minutes' walk from the town centre along Jalan Brooke.

For changing money there is a branch of the Standard Chartered Bank on Jalan Raja, and there are moneychangers which are open longer hours.

Everything in Miri is within easy walking distance of everywhere else so there's no need to take taxis or local buses to get anywhere, except the airport.

If you want to organise a trip to Gunung Mulu or elsewhere in the interior, there are plenty of travel agents in Miri. Two of them which travellers have used and found to be reliable are: Seridan Mulu Tours & Travel Services Sdn Bhd, Lot 140, 2nd floor, Jalan Bendahara (tel 085-416066); and Malang Sisters' Travel Agency, Lot 255, 1st floor, Beautiful Jade Centre, Halaman Kabor (tel 085-38141).

On the 1st floor of Wisma Pelita is the Pelita Book Centre which has quite a good local collection as well as English novels and other publications.

Places to Stay – bottom end

Miri is a fairly lively town, not only because of the oil and development, but also because Bruneians in search of a bit of action flock here on weekends.

Finding a cheap room is almost impossible. Everything is air-conditioned – even the brothels – and expensive. The only remotely cheap option is the dorms in a couple of the Chinese hotels, although these have little privacy. The *Tai Tong Lodging House* (tel 085-34072) at 26 Jalan China is about the best deal with dorm beds for M$6, although there's little privacy, the noise and cigarette smoke can make for a restless stay and it's not really a friendly place. Other rooms in this Chinese cheapie go for M$27/35 with fan and common bath, or M$45 for a double with bath and air-con, and most rooms have windows – another rare feature of Miri hotel rooms.

Another place with dorm beds is the *South East Asia Lodging House* (tel 085-416921) on the square behind the Cathay Cinema. Dorm beds in the corridor are M$5, but the rooms, although they have windows, are poor value at M$30 with fan, or M$38 with air-con, all with common bath.

For a private room your best bet is the *Fairland Inn* (tel 085-4138981), also on the square behind the Cathay cinema. Although the rooms in this friendly hotel are small, they are clean, have windows, air-con, attached bath and TV for M$30/35 – a relative bargain.

The *Red Crescent Society* is perhaps the best bet with a mattress on the floor of a big breezy room for a donation of M$3 – and the money goes to a worthy cause.

Places to Stay – middle

Most of the hotels in this category are middle range in price only; what they provide differs little from the bottom-end places. The *Thai Foh Inn* (085-418395) on Jalan China has dark cell-like rooms for M$45 with bath and air-con.

The *Malaysia Lodging House* (tel 085-34300) is similar but cheaper at M$25 for a glorified cell or M$50 with air-con and bath.

Better value is the *Fully Inn* (tel 085-412541) near the market. All rooms are air-con with attached bath and go for M$40 with a bit of bargaining.

Places to Stay – top end

The *Park Hotel* (tel 085-414555) on Jalan Raja quotes rates of M$98/113 but offers a discount of 30% as a matter of course. It's one of the best places in Miri.

Also of a high standard is the *Hotel Plaza Regency* (tel 085-414458) at 47 Jalan Brooke. Room rates are M$125/140 but a 40% discount applies. At 27 Jalan Brooke is the *Gloria Hotel* (tel 085-416699) which is also in the top bracket with rooms at M$110/128.

The newish *Million Inn* (tel 085-41552) opposite the Beautiful Jade Centre has singles/doubles for M$78/88 but there's a discount of 30%. Another new place is the *Rinwood Inn* (tel 085-415888) at Lot 579 Jalan Yu Seng, about half a km from The Pub.

Places to Eat

Other than hotel restaurants there are plenty of good food places in Miri, especially in the new blocks between Jalan Brooke and the waterfront.

For hawker food there's a small food centre near the Chinese temple and here you can choose between Malay food and the usual Chinese dishes. There's also a small fruit and vegetable market here. On the other side of this market is the *Aseanika Restoran* which does superb rotis and also serves Indonesian food. For tasty food try the *Seaview Cafe* on the corner of Jalan China, near the Chinese temple.

On Jalan Yu Seng there're quite a few more upmarket and fast-food places. One of the best restaurants in Miri is the *Maxim Restaurant* which serves superb Chinese food including a variety of seafood and steamboat. Prices are surprisingly reasonable but you need to get here early in the evening to get a table – it's a very popular place, both with locals and expatriates. On the same street is the *Danish Hot Bread Bakery* with a good selection of cakes and pastries.

For a good value set-menu meal the *Cafe de Hamburg* on Jalan Brooke near the Gloria

Hotel charges M$10 for its four-course lunch.

In Wisma Pelita you'll find a branch of the local *Sugar Bun* fast-food chain, where you'll find a selection of pastries, cakes and buns, plus the usual fast-food hamburger and fried chicken section. It's very Americanised right down to the squeaky clean kids behind the counter who'll tell you to 'have a nice day'. In the same building is the Pelita Supermarket if you need to stock up with supplies before heading for Niah Caves.

Entertainment

Miri has a surprisingly good live entertainment scene in the evenings – discos, live bands and the inevitable Karaoke lounges. Most places are along Jalan Yu Seng. Take a wander along in the evening and see what's on, although things don't really get going until after 10 pm. There is no cover charge at any of these places but expect to pay around M$9 for a large beer.

The Cottage is a small pub which has some interesting local bands, while across the road the flashier *Pub* has bigger acts from KL and elsewhere. *The Ranch* is a similar place, and others include the *Strawberry Lounge*, *Rupan Lounge* and the *Q-Ta Steakhouse*. There're also a number of snooker halls along this stretch of road.

Getting There & Away

Air MAS has Twin Otter services to Marudi (twice daily, M$29), Bareo (daily via Marudi, M$70), Long Lellang (twice weekly, M$66), Limbang (three daily, M$45), Lawas (three daily, M$59) and Labuan (weekly, M$57).

Bigger aircraft fly to Bintulu (three daily, M$57), Kota Kinabalu (two flights daily, M$90), Kuching (10 flights daily, M$136) and Sibu (five daily, M$93).

Bus – To/From Bintulu & Batu Niah Syarikat Bas Suria operates buses to Bintulu at 7, 7.30 (air-con) and 8 am, 12 noon (air-con) and 12.30 pm. The trip takes about 4½ hours and the fare is M$15 or M$18 (air-con).

There are four daily buses from Miri direct to Batu Niah. They depart at 7, 10.30 am, 12 noon and 2.30 pm (air-con), cost M$9 and the trip takes about two hours. From Batu Niah to Miri there are departures at 6.45, 7.45 (air-con) and 10.45 am and 1 pm.

Bus – To/From Sibu There are two air-con buses daily going all the way to Sibu which take eight hours and cost M$35.

Bus – To/From Brunei The Miri Belait Transport Company (office at the main bus stand) operates six buses daily to Kuala Belait – the first town in Brunei – from 7 am to 3 pm. The fare is M$12 and the trip takes about 2½ hours. The road is sealed from Miri to Kuala Baram where a river crossing is made. Vehicles often have to queue for some time before reaching the ferry, so most passengers get out and wait for their bus/car by the edge of the water. You can leave your bags on the bus.

Just across the river you go through the Malaysian immigration checkpoint and reboard the same bus for the two-minute ride to the Brunei immigration checkpoint. You must take all your belongings off the bus and go through passport control and customs.

Once through customs, you board a Brunei bus which takes you to the Belait River for another ferry crossing. The queues here are often horrendous but this is not a problem if you are travelling by bus as the driver and passengers leave the bus on one side, cross on the ferry (free) then board another bus parked on the other side. Your ticket from Miri takes you all the way to Kuala Belait.

At Kuala Belait you are dropped at the Belait United Traction Company bus stand, from where you can take another bus to Seria. This is preferable to staying in Kuala Belait overnight as the cheapest hotel in Kuala Belait charges B$100 for a single room!

Buses depart Kuala Belait for Seria frequently throughout the day and cost B$1. The last bus goes at 7.30 pm and taxis cost between B$3 and B$4. The journey takes about 30 minutes.

If you need to change money – no one is interested in the Malaysian ringgit – the Hong Kong & Shanghai Banking Corporation is opposite the bus stand in Kuala Belait.

From Seria, you must take another bus to Bandar Seri Begawan, the capital of Brunei Darussalam. Several bus companies do the run and there are many buses daily. The fare is B$4 and the journey takes about 1½ hours. It's a good sealed road all the way. From Kuala Belait or Seria to Bandar Seri Begawan it's easy to hitch.

Early in the morning, you can also get taxis from the bus station in Miri to Kuala Belait for about M$30 per person.

LIMBANG

This town is the divisional headquarters of the Limbang District, sandwiched between Brunei and Sabah. There is nothing of interest in the town itself but you may well find yourself coming through on the way to or from Brunei or to Gunung Mulu.

You can buy MAS tickets at Mah Moh Hin (tel 085-21881) at 15 Cross St.

Places to Stay

One of the cheapest places in town is the *Bunga Raya Hotel* (tel 085-21181) opposite the wharf. Basic dormitory accommodation costs M$10 per night and there are rooms from M$30. As is the case at most hotels, you are provided with soap and a towel.

Other hotels include the *Muhibbah Hotel* (tel 085-22488), with rooms from M$44, and the *South-East Asia Hotel* (tel 085-21013) which has reasonable rooms from M$20, and the *Borneo Hotel*.

Places to Eat

The *Cita Rasa Restoran* in the Limbang Recreation Club has breakfasts for M$7, and meals for M$2 to M$11. There is a very pleasant verandah looking out over the river. It's about 10 minutes' walk from the town centre, following the river upstream.

Getting There & Away

Air MAS has three-times-daily Twin Otter flights to Miri (M$45), weekly flights to Labuan (M$30), twice daily flights to Lawas (M$25) and twice weekly flights to Kota Kinabalu (M$60).

Road There is a local road network but it doesn't connect with either Sabah or Brunei.

Boat There are several boats daily to Bandar Seri Begawan, the capital of Brunei. The trip takes about 30 minutes and costs M$7 from Limbang, B$7 from Brunei.

There are also boats to Punang, further up the coast, from where it's just a short minibus ride to Lawas.

LAWAS

Like Limbang, there is very little to do in Lawas but once again you may find yourself here while en route to or from Brunei, on your way up to the Kelabit Highlands and Bakelalan, or in order to take the short flight to Miri skipping clean over Brunei.

The MAS agent is the Eng Huat Travel Agency (tel 085-5570) at 2 Jalan Lian Siew Ann.

Places to Stay

The cheapest place to stay is the *Government Rest House* on the airport road – if you can get in. Failing that there's the *Federal Hotel* (085-85115) which is expensive with rooms from M$40.

Getting There & Away

Air Lawas is well served by MAS Twin Otters. There are twice weekly flights to Kota Kinabalu (M$47), three times daily flights to Miri (M$59), twice daily flights to Limbang (M$25), five times weekly to Bakelalan (M$46) and Long Semado (M$40).

Bus You can take a bus to Merapok, on the Sarawak/Sabah border, which will cost M$3.50 and take about 40 minutes. The road to Beaufort and Kota Kinabalu connects down to Merapok, but there is not a lot of traffic. You can apparently get lifts with trucks.

MERAPOK

Merapok is a strange one-street hamlet in the middle of nowhere and you get the distinct impression that you could be there forever trying to get out. At least that's the case if you arrive by somewhat unorthodox methods – as we did. But there are two billiard halls, with beautiful tables made in Australia, and a cafe while you wait!

Sabah immigration is a few hundred metres out of town and you're supposed to report there for immigration formalities. If you happen to drive past it, like most people do, it doesn't really matter. Sabah immigration is pretty easygoing and you can report to another office in Sabah, such as Sipitang or Kota Kinabalu (but not Tenom or Beaufort) even several days later.

Getting There & Away

Bus From here it's a question of hassling for a lift to Sipitang (the usual price is M$2 per person for the half-hour journey) which isn't difficult – *someone* will be going there so long as you don't arrive too late in the day.

If you take the 11 am launch from Brunei to Lawas then you'll arrive in Sipitang too late for any scheduled transport (taxis or buses) out of there and, if you want to get to Beaufort or Kota Kinabalu that night, you'll have to hitch – which is not easy as there's very little traffic.

The Kelabit Highlands

If you're heading out for a long trek into the interior to such places as Bareo, Lio Matoh and Long Lellang the first step is to get a permit from the Resident in Miri. It's straightforward but does take a day or so. You can also get these permits from the District Officer in Marudi.

From Miri the first stage of the journey is by road to Kuala Baram, on the Baram River near the Brunei border. The fare is M$2.10 and buses depart Miri hourly (at least) from 6 am to 5.30 pm.

If you're heading for Gunung Mulu Nation-

al Park take the 6 am bus if you want to get there in one day. From Kuala Baram you can take an *expres* launch up the Baram River to Marudi for M$12 and the journey takes about three hours. The first launch leaves Kuala Baram at 7.15 am and the launches go at least hourly up until 2 pm.

For Gunung Mulu National Park, take the express boat from Marudi to Long Terrawan (if the river is high) for M$18, or to Kuala Apoh (if there's less water) for M$10, from where you can get another launch to Long Terrawan for M$7. There's only one departure from Marudi per day at 12 noon.

From Long Terrawan a longboat meets the 12 noon boat from Marudi and leaves for Mulu around 3.30 pm, arriving at around 6 pm. The cost is set at M$35 per person if there are more than four people, or M$150 for the whole boat for three or less people.

There are regular boats from Marudi to Long Lama. From Long Lama to Long Akah reckon on about M$25 and one to 1½ days, and from there to Lio Matoh about the same. In the dry season when the river is low this trip costs considerably more as you have to hire a boat, operator and guide.

MARUDI

Marudi is devoid of attractions but you will probably find yourself coming through here on your way to or from the interior, and unless you fly from Miri to Bareo, you need to get a permit from the District Office here to head further upstream or to Mulu. This is not a problem, unless of course you are a Swiss man called Bruno.

There are good views of the river from the hilltop Fort Hose, built in 1901. There are two banks for changing foreign currency.

There is a road network around Marudi and you can visit longhouses at Long Selaban and Long Moh – you can either hitch or take a taxi.

Places to Stay & Eat

The popular *Grand Hotel* (tel 085-55712), Marudi Bazaar, is a good place four or five blocks from where the *expres* launches dock. The cheapest room (single or double) is

M$13.50 and for that you get your own bathroom and toilet as well as clean sheets. It's about the tallest building in town so the sunset views from the roof are good. There are also air-con rooms.

The *Mulu Air-Con Inn* (tel 085-55905) and the *Hotel Zola* close by have both been recommended. There is also the *Mayland Hotel* (tel 085-55106), Kampung Dagang, which has single rooms from M$30 and doubles from M$45.

Ah Jong's is a good place for breakfast as they have fresh bread and doughnuts. For Chinese food the *Rose Garden* has been recommended.

Getting There & Away

Air MAS operates daily Twin Otter flights to Miri (M$29) and Bareo (M$55), three times weekly flights to Sibu (M$100) and twice weekly flights to Long Lellang (M$46). The airstrip at Gunung Mulu may be finished by now, in which case there'll be flights there from Miri and probably Marudi.

The airstrip is within walking distance from town.

Boat The *expres* boats from Kuala Baram to Marudi operate hourly, cost M$12 and there's no extra charge for Kung Fu or American wrestling videos.

Heading upriver there is an *expres* boat to Kuala Apoh or Long Terrawan (depending on the water level) daily at 12 noon for M$18 and the trip takes about three to 3½ hours.

BAREO

Bareo sits on a beautiful high valley floor in the Kelabit Highlands, close to the Indonesian border. It makes an ideal base for treks in the highlands. On arrival you will be asked for your permit and probably be told you have to stay in Bareo, but it's not a problem to go straight out to one of the nearby Kenyah or Kelabit longhouses.

Bareo has shops where you can stock up on supplies and gifts to take to the longhouses, as does Bakelalan.

The MAS agent is the Bareo Co-operative Society.

Places to Stay

The *Bareo Lodging House* is M$8 per person but it's nothing special and you may want to head straight out to the longhouses.

Getting There & Away

MAS flies Twin Otters from Bareo to Miri daily (M$70), usually via Marudi (M$55). The flights are very much dependent on the weather and it's not uncommon for flights to be cancelled, so make sure your schedule is not too tight. These flights are also fully booked well in advance during school holidays.

TREKS AROUND BAREO

Bareo-Pa Lungan

A four-hour walk on a wide trail takes you to Pa'Lungan, a friendly longhouse with a pleasant river to swim in. The chief has a room for visitors with mats, blankets, pillows and mosquito net.

From there you can hire guides and bearers to climb Gunung Murud, at 2423 metres (7946 feet) the highest peak in Sarawak.

Bareo-Bakelalan-Long Semado

Another possibility is to walk to Bakelalan and then fly to Lawas (five times weekly, M$46), or continue walking to Long Semado, which is also connected to Lawas by Twin Otter flights (five times weekly, M$40). Walks in this area are not a picnic – you need to be self-sufficient in food and shelter and be prepared for some hard walking. It's a very good idea to hire a local guide. This costs around M$30 per day and they can usually carry some of your gear. As well as a guide you also need a Border Permit from the army in Bareo as the route takes you into Kalimantan.

Bareo-Lio Matoh

You can also walk to Lio Matoh, and this takes seven to nine days depending on how fast you go. It's a great trek as you stay in longhouses most nights (in basic jungle huts the others) but you must take a guide.

Top, Left, Right: Kampung Ayer, Brunei (HF)

Top: Omar Ali Saifudin Mosque, Bandar Seri Begawan, Brunei (HF)
Bottom: Stilt Village from Omar A.S. Mosque, Bandar Seri Begawan, Brunei (ML)

The nightly stops and walking times on a nine-day walk are as follows:

Day 1	Long Danau	9 hours
Day 2	Ramudi	5 hours
Day 3,4,5	Jungle Huts	15 hours total
Day 6	Long Palawan	7 hours
Day 7	Long Banga	3 hours
Day 8	Jungle hut	6 hours
Day 9	Lio Matoh	7 hours

The guest books in the longhouses are full of good information. Lots of the Kelabits are hard-core Christians and don't smoke so bring sugar, seeds, tea, kerosene or anything imaginative for the chief.

GUNUNG MULU NATIONAL PARK

Since Gunung Mulu National Park reopened in late 1985 it has become one of the most popular travel destinations in Sarawak. Unfortunately it's also one of the most expensive places to visit. Reports from travellers vary; some feel the expense worthwhile, others don't.

Gunung Mulu National Park is Sarawak's largest national park covering 529 sq km of peat-swamp, sandstone, limestone and montane forests. The two major mountains are Gunung Mulu (2377 metres of sandstone) and Gunung Api (1750 metres of limestone).

The park contains hundreds of species of flowering plants, fungi, mosses and ferns. It has around 10 different species of pitcher plants, which attract botanists and scientists from around the world.

Gunung Mulu has a variety of mammals, birds (eight different types of hornbill), frogs, fish and insects, but it's not the place to head for if you want to see loads of exotic wild animals.

The park is noted for its many underground caves. Cave explorers recently discovered the largest cave chamber in the world, the Sarawak Chamber, and the 51-km-long Clearwater Cave, one of the longest in the world. At present, only the Deer Cave and the Clearwater Cave are open to the public, but, if you're lucky, you may be able to find a guide who will take you to see others.

Many of the caves closed to the public are inaccessible, or considered dangerous while some contain fragile formations that park authorities want to preserve and protect from further deterioration.

Permits & Information

Permits for Gunung Mulu National Park can be obtained at the national parks office (tel 33361) in Miri. The staff at this office don't seem to know much about Gunung Mulu.

For better information, visit one of the travel agents in Miri. The Malang Sisters' Travel Agency or Seridan Mulu Tours & Travel – see the Miri section for locations. Neither place is cheap (no agent in Miri is) and it's much cheaper to do it yourself and of course it gives you greater flexibility.

Besides getting a permit for the park, visitors must book (and, if in a group, pay a deposit of M$20 per group) for accommodation. On arrival at the park you must report to the head ranger. It's unlikely that you would be sent away if you turned up without confirmed reservations but as facilities at park headquarters are very limited, it's better to book in advance.

There are no walking trails around park headquarters and, unfortunately, you cannot go anywhere without taking a guide which is annoying as you often don't need one. Guides' fees vary between M$20 and M$30 per day. If you are hiring a guide for a few days, make sure you agree on the total price before you start off.

The Caves

The Deer Cave, 2160 metres long and 220 metres deep, has the world's largest cave passage. Most of the passage is illuminated, though a strong torch is useful for the darker areas. Water cascades from openings in the roof after very heavy rain.

You enter the cave on one side of the mountain, exit from the other and it takes about 30 minutes to walk the entire length.

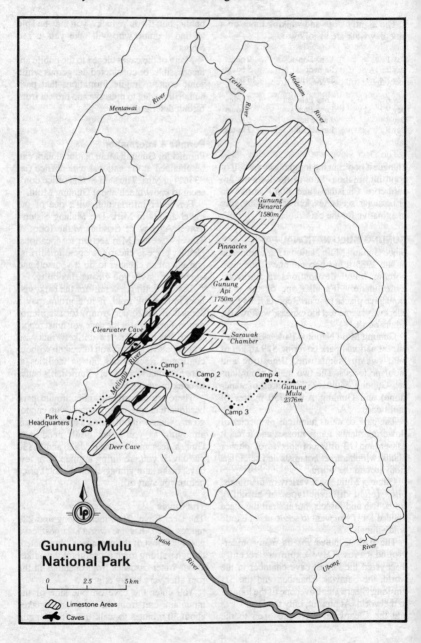

Mentawai River

Mentawai River

Terikan River

Medalam River

Gunung
Benarat
1580m

Pinnacles

Gunung
Api
1750m

Clearwater Cave

Sarawak
Chamber

Camp 1

Camp 2

Camp 4

Camp 3

Gunung Mulu
2376m

Melinau River

Park
Headquarters

Deer Cave

Tutoh River

Ubong River

Gunung Mulu
National Park

0   2.5   5 km

Limestone Areas

Caves

Guides are compulsory and charge M$20 to take you through the cave, but they don't care how many people there are in a group, so round up as many as you can.

The Deer Cave's biggest attraction is the spectacular black cloud of free-tailed bats which emerges from the entrance between 5 and 6 pm each night and returns early in the morning. If you want to see this incredible sight, camp overnight at the entrance to the cave.

The Deer Cave is a pleasant, easy walk from the park headquarters through some beautiful forest. It's worth spending a couple of hours in the forest areas around the cave.

The Clearwater Cave is 51 km long (the longest cave passage in South-East Asia) and 355 metres deep. It's very dark inside and you need a really strong torch to see the finer details of its various features and limestone formations. There are several river crossings and you should be prepared to wade through waist-deep water at times.

To get to the Clearwater system, you must hire a boat to take you about two hours up the Melinau River – if the river is running low, you might have to help the boat along for most of the way. It costs about M$80 to hire the boat, operator and a guide, but then you have to consider the extra costs like petrol (about M$25) and wear and tear of the engine (about M$15). It all adds up so once again try to get a few people together to make things easier money-wise.

Make sure you wear strong walking shoes inside the cave and keep an eye on the ground. There are some dangerous-looking jagged points jutting out from the limestone floor. There is a swimming hole at the entrance to the cave where you can spend an enjoyable afternoon. You can camp overnight if you like.

According to tourist literature, the Sarawak Chamber is the largest cave in the world and 'is about the size of 16 football fields'. At present, it remains closed to the public.

There are several other caves in the park, many are still being 'prepared' by the national parks organisation. They estimate that the number of caves already explored represents only 30% of the total number present in Gunung Mulu National Park.

The Pinnacles

Gunung Api is the highest limestone mountain in Malaysia and its great attraction is its towering limestone Pinnacles – an incredible stone forest standing 45 metres high, halfway up the side of the mountain. If you want to see the Pinnacles – unless you're part of a small group – you're in for a very expensive three-day trek by boat and foot. However, you will see some spectacular scenery.

The trek to the Pinnacles starts with a three to four-hour boat trip (depending on the level of the river) from park headquarters, then a two-hour walk to a camp with a shelter by the Melinau River. You can sleep overnight at this picturesque spot before climbing Gunung Api.

The ascent is very steep in parts and it takes a good three to four hours to reach the Pinnacles. It's best to start out early in the morning as it's not only a lot cooler then but it's more likely that you'll see interesting animal and birdlife along the way.

On the way back to park headquarters, you can follow the river to the Melinau Gorge which lies north-east of the Pinnacles. The Gorge is at the end of the walking track, about 1½ hours' walk from the previously mentioned camp.

If you have the time (and money) you can also stop at the Clearwater Caves on the way back. If you do this, you need at least a day to look around. Members of the Punan tribe live along the banks of the Melinau River. The Punans are very friendly and hospitable people who enjoy the company of visitors – they are also very poor, so make sure you have your own food supplies.

Count on M$100 to M$120 per group per day for the guide's fees, boat operators' fees, boat hire, petrol, etc. Obviously the more people there are, the cheaper it gets. Ask for a breakdown of the total price, so you know exactly what costs what.

The Gunung Mulu Trail

The climb to the summit of this 2376-metre mountain takes three to five days and is the highlight of many a traveller's visit to the national park.

If you are reasonably fit and healthy, three days is adequate for the ascent and descent of Gunung Mulu. If you have time, take an extra day or two so you can relax more along the way. For any star athletes pressed for time it is possible to do the whole thing in two days. A guide costs M$20 per day, plus M$10 for a night. However long you take they still charge M$110.

You should carry enough food for the entire trip, as well as your own cooking utensils and a sleeping bag (it gets quite cold at night). It's not unusual for it to rain every day and as the tracks are not maintained, you'll often find yourself wallowing knee-deep in mud – nothing will save you from the leeches there! Take something to keep out the rain and wear good walking shoes.

There are several camps along the trail. Most consist of a wooden platform with a roof – it's free to sleep overnight at any of these camps in the national park.

If you leave park headquarters very early in the morning, you can reach Camp 1 in about three hours – plenty of leeches for company. This camp is beside a beautiful river. A further four to five hours' walk will take you as far as Camp 3 which is where most people sleep overnight. A simple canvas roof over a rough floor provides shelter but the water is very brown and should be boiled before use.

On the second day, you're faced with an extremely steep climb from this camp to Camp 4. The walk to Camp 4 takes four or five hours and there's a shed you can sleep in. If it hasn't rained, there won't be any water at Camp 4, so try to remember to carry some muddy water up from Camp 3.

On the third day, leave your pack at Camp 4 and climb to the summit. You can either sleep at the camp another night, or descend the mountain in the one day. The latter is quite tough on the legs, but at least you can cool down in the river along the way.

Here is one traveller's recent account of the Gunung Mulu ascent:

On the first day, we walked from park hardquarters to Camp 3. We started out on a flat trail, walking through a great forest with huge trees. It took about two hours to reach Camp 1, then 40 minutes to reach Camp 2 (not really a camp, just a clearing).

From there, the trail becomes almost vertical and, after rain, it's just a mud chute in places. It gets so steep that you have to pull yourself up by grabbing tree roots, but if you make an early start you can have frequent rests – it was a two-hour slog for us, but I've heard of people taking at least twice that time.

The other handicap is the leeches; I counted 54 of them from headquarters to Camp 3 and my socks were stained red. Try to pull them off as soon as you feel them – the trek is hard enough without having to give blood. Check your shoes often, they get in through the holes for your laces and have a feast.

The second day, Camp 3 to Camp 4, is easier and takes about 2½ hours. The forest changes from tall trees to moss-covered, stunted growth. Look out for the many varieties of pitcher plants and stop and listen for any wildlife – you might see monkeys and birds. When we were climbing the mountain, it was cloudy, damp and humid – it must be like that for most of the year as everything is covered in moss.

Have a rest at Camp 4 and then start the 1½-hour walk to the top. There are a few steep areas with ropes and then you'll find yourself amongst colourful bushes, scrambling over roots. At the top, you can wander around and look for orchids.

Sleep at Camp 4 again overnight and climb up to the helipad to see the sunrise in the morning. You can walk all the way to park headquarters in one day, but you'll wonder how you made it up some of the steeper parts. You can swim in the river down by Camp 1.

Places to Stay

There are four six-bed dorm rooms at the park, and a bed in one of these costs M$6 per person. There's also a resthouse with a six-bed room for M$60, and deluxe double rooms for M$150. You can cook your own food as there are gas stoves, and you can use the cutlery, crockery, pots and pans. There is a small canteen at park headquarters selling basic tinned foods, bread, milk, eggs and margarine. The prices are not too expensive when you consider all the hassle of transporting goods to the park.

There are also a number of guest houses at the park but these seem to be owned by the tour companies. It's possible to stay with the family in the house next to the Mulu Canteen.

Getting There & Away

Air The new airstrip at the national park may be open by now, in which case there'll be flights from Miri and probably Marudi. If it's still not open you can take an MAS flight from Miri to Marudi (daily, M$29), but then it's still boats only from there.

Road/Boat Miri is the starting point for the journey to Gunung Mulu as this is where you book your accommodation. From Miri take a bus to Kuala Baram for M$2.10. Buses depart Miri regularly but if you want to get to the national park in one day, take the 6 am bus. Alternatively, you can stay in Marudi for the night.

From Kuala Baram there are express boats to Marudi for M$12; the first departure is at 7.15 and they leave at least hourly until around 2 pm. The trip takes about three hours and you'll be subjected to some horrible Kung Fu videos. From Marudi, you can take the daily 12 noon *expres* launch to Kuala Apoh for M$12. There is only one departure per day. If the river is high this boat should go on to Long Terrawan. If not you'll have to take another launch from Kuala Apoh to Long Terrawan (M$7). From Long Terrawan there is a longboat which leaves daily at 3.30 pm for the trip to the national park. The cost is M$150 for the entire boat if there are less than five people, or M$35 per person for five or more. The trip takes around 2½ hours.

For the return trip from the park you need to be up at 5 am to get the boat to Long Terrawan (or Kuala Apoh/Long Panai) in time to get the connecting boat to Marudi.

It's also possible to approach Gunung Mulu from Limbang on the northern side of Brunei. It involves going by road from Limbang to Kuala Medamit, and then hiring a longboat up the Mendalam River and staying overnight at the Rumah Lasong longhouse. The next stage is again up the river to Terikan, from where you start jungle trekking to Camp 5 near Gunung Api in the national park. You would need to hire a guide for this trip, and be prepared to hire longboats to get up the Mendalam River.

East Malaysia – Sabah

Prior to independence Sabah was known as North Borneo and operated by the British North Borneo Company. After WW II, both Sabah and Sarawak (which had been ruled by the Brooke family) were handed over to the British government and they both finally gained their independence when they merged with Malaysia in 1963.

There was some trouble after independence as Sabah's existence was disputed not only by Indonesia but also by the Philippines. There are close cultural ties between the people of the Sulu Archipelago of the Philippines' Mindanao province and the neighbouring people of Sabah. To this day there is a busy smuggling trade operated from Sabah into Mindanao and

Mindanao's Muslim rebels often retreat down towards Sabah when pursued by government forces.

Post-independent Sabah was governed for a time by Tun Mustapha who ran the state almost as a private fiefdom and was often at odds with the central government in Kuala Lumpur. In 1976 he slipped from power and since then Sabah has moved closer to the central government. Sabah's economic strength is based on timber and agriculture.

For the visitor Sabah offers scenic grandeur, Mt Kinabalu and some fascinating wildlife. Unfortunately it's an expensive place to travel around compared to the peninsula. The population of Sabah is just over one million.

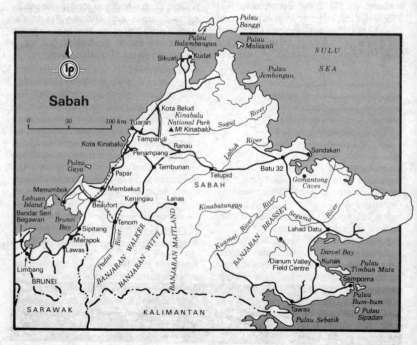

Tamus

The local weekly markets (known as *tamus*) held at various small towns all over Sabah are a colourful local attraction. Tamu days are:

Babagon	Saturday
Beaufort	Saturday
Keningau	Thursday
Kinarut	Saturday
Kiulu	Tuesday
Kota Belud	Sunday
Kota Kinabalu	Sunday
Kuala Penyu	1st Wednesday of month
Kundasang	20th of month
Manggis	Thursday
Matunggong	Saturday
Membakut	Sunday
Mesapol	Friday
Papar	Sunday
Penampang	Saturday
Putatan	Sunday
Ranau	1st of month
Simpangan	Thursday
Sindumin	Saturday
Sinsuran	Friday
Sipitang	Thursday
Tambunan	Thursday
Tamparuli	Wednesday
Tandek	Monday
Telipok	Thursday
Tenghilan	Thursday
Tenom	Sunday
Tinnopok	15th & 30th of month
Toboh	Sunday
Topokon	Tuesday
Tuaran	Sunday
Weston	Friday

Visas & Permits

Sabah is semi-autonomous and, like Sarawak, has its own immigration controls, On arrival you are likely to be given a month's stay permit and it's rare to be asked to show money or onward tickets.

Permits can be quickly and easily renewed at an immigration office, which can be found at most points of arrival, even at small riverine places like Merapok near Beaufort. If you miss them it's no problem, you simply report to another immigration office, even several days later, and explain the situation.

No further permits are required to visit the interior.

General Costs

Sabah is an expensive place to travel around. Only at Kinabalu National Park and Poring Hot Springs will you find accommodation that could be classed as 'budget'. Elsewhere it's the familiar story of at least M$20 per night and often much more.

Lodging is also complicated by the fact that virtually all of the cheaper places are brothels, which means you may have to stay in places which would normally be outside the range of budget travel.

The alternative to budget accommodation in Sabah is the series of government resthouses which cost M$12 per person per night. There are resthouses in Keningau, Kota Belud, Kudat, Kuala Penyu, Lahad Datu, Papar, Ranau, Semporna, Sipitang, Tambunan and Tuaran. Generally, the resthouses are for government officials and their families, but if a place is not full, travellers are *sometimes* permitted to stay. Bookings are made through the district officer of the appropriate town and there are listings in the government pages of the telephone directory.

Getting Around

As in Sarawak, the road system has undergone major improvement in the last few years. The only unsurfaced sections from Beaufort/Tenom all the way around to Tawau now are between Ranau and Telupid on the road to Sandakan, and between Batu 32 and the Kinabatangan River (between Sandakan and Lahad Datu), and even on these stretches the contracts have been awarded so work should be under way.

Kota Kinabalu

Known as Jesselton until 1963, Kota Kinabalu was razed during WW II to prevent the Japanese using it as a base. Nowadays it's just a modern city with wide avenues and tall buildings without any of the historical charm of Kuching. All the same, KK, as the locals call it, is a pleasant city, well landscaped in

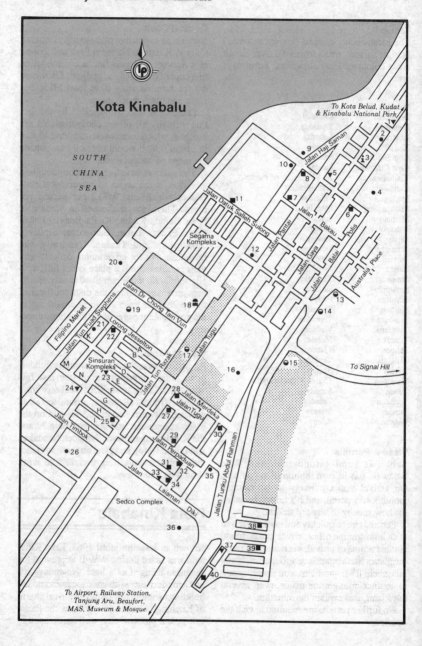

Kota Kinabalu

SOUTH
CHINA
SEA

To Kota Belud, Kudat
& Kinabalu National Park

To Signal Hill

To Airport, Railway Station,
Tanjung Aru, Beaufort,
MAS, Museum & Mosque

parts, and its coastal location gives it an equable climate.

■ PLACES TO STAY

6   Hotel Jesselton
7   Ang's Hotel
8   Hotel Capital
11 Hyatt Kinabalu International
22 Travellers Rest Hostel
25 Hotel Rakyat
27 Central Hotel
28 Hotel Nam Tai
29 Pine Bay Hotel
30 Putera Hotel
31 Full On Resthouse
32 Islamic Hotel
34 Ruby Inn
38 Hotel Pertama
39 Hotel Mutiara
40 Hotel Shangrila

▼ PLACES TO EAT

1   XO Steakhouse
5   Kentucky Fried Chicken
23 Kedai Kopi Seng Hing
24 Night Food Stalls
25 New Arafat Restaurant
33 Sri Melaka Restoran
37 Restoran Tioman

OTHER

2   Hong Kong & Shanghai Bank
3   TDC Tourist Office
4   Sarawak Tourist Promotion Corporation
9   Wisma Sabah
10 Wisma Merdeka
12 KK Supermarket
13 Minibuses to Kota Belud, Kudat
14 Minibuses to Beaufort, Keningau, Tenom
15 Minibuses to Mt Kinabalu, Ranau, Sandakan
16 Council Offices & Library
17 City Buses
18 GPO
19 Minibuses to Airport, Penampang, Likas, Beaufort
20 Central Market
21 Sabah Parks
26 Centrepoint
35 Immigration Office
36 Cinemas

One of Asia's fastest growing cities, with a population of around 200,000, KK is an interesting blend of European, Malay and Chinese cultures. It's worth spending a few days in KK if only to sample the excellent variety of cuisines – something which is sadly lacking elsewhere in the state. You must also go to KK to book accommodation for the trip to Mt Kinabalu – Sabah's number one attraction.

Orientation

Although the city sprawls for many km along the coast from the international airport at Tanjung Aru to the new developments at Tanjung Lita, the centre itself is quite small and most places are within easy walking distance of each other. This includes the bulk of the hotels and restaurants, banks, travel agents, the tourist office, the national parks office and the GPO.

There is no bus station in town, instead there are two or three areas in central KK where you can find the bus you want, or at least be directed to the right area by the runners who accost you as you walk along. Taxis are all over town, but seem to conglomerate in the area between the GPO and the council offices.

Information

Tourist Offices The tourist office (tel 088-211732) of the TDC is in the Wing Onn Life Building on Jalan Segunting at the northern end of the city centre. It is staffed by two knowledgeable and helpful staff, and is open Monday to Friday from 8 am to 12.45 pm and 2 to 4.15 pm, and on Saturday from 8 am to 12.45 pm.

The Sarawak Tourist Promotion Corporation should by now have moved into its new premises in the old post office on Jalan Gaya, close to the TDC tourist office. They also have an office on Level 1 of the airport building.

Sabah Parks Office The Sabah Parks office (tel 088-211585) is very conveniently situated in Block K of the Sinsuran Kompleks on Jalan Tun Fuad Stephens. Before going to

Mt Kinabalu, Tunku Abdul Rahman National Park or Poring Hot Springs you must go to this office to make reservations for accommodation (and guides, if required).

The further ahead you do this the more chance you have of being able to go there when you want. Mt Kinabalu is a very popular place both with overseas visitors and local people, and accommodation at the park headquarters is often booked up a week in advance.

The office is open Monday to Thursday from 8 am to 12.45 pm and from 2 to 4.15 pm; on Fridays from 8 to 11.30 am and 2 to 4.15 pm; and again on Saturdays from 8 am to 12.45 pm. The staff are helpful and in addition to handling reservations they stock a range of guidebooks and information pamphlets on Mt Kinabalu National Park and Tunku Abdul Rahman National Park. They also sell postcards and T-shirts.

Other Offices The Sabah Foundation has its offices in the much-vaunted Sabah Foundation building at Likas, a few km north of the city centre. The Forestry Division office here (tel 088-34596) is the place to make bookings to visit the Danum Valley Field Centre near Lahad Datu in eastern Sabah. Bookings can also be made at the office in Lahad Datu although they then have to be referred to KK.

The immigration office is on the 4th floor of the tall government building, near Jalan Tunku Abdul Rahman and around the corner from the Diamond Inn. As long as your entry permit is still valid, they don't seem to mind if your passport lacks the official entry stamp for Sabah. Permits can be easily extended in less than an hour, though you may be asked for your onward ticket.

Money If you're staying in the Sinsuran Kompleks the most convenient bank is the branch of the Sabah Bank right next door to the Sabah Parks office. There are plenty of others around the central town area.

Post & Telecommunications The GPO is right in the centre of town and has an efficient poste restante counter.

For international calls, the Telekom office in Block B of the Kompleks Kuwara about 15 minutes' walk south of the centre of town is open daily from 8 am to 10 pm. It is about 40% cheaper to ring after 9 pm. Collect (reverse charge) calls cannot be made from this office. There is also an office on Level 1 at the airport which is open the same hours.

Foreign Embassies The Indonesian Consulate (tel 088-54100) is on Jalan Karamunsing, south of the city centre. This office reportedly issues one-month visas without any fuss.

Travel Agencies There are plenty of travel agencies in KK, all of them expensive. For scuba diving expeditions to Sipadan Island off the south-east coast of Sabah, contact Borneo Divers & Sea Sports Sdn Bhd (tel 088-425080) at Lot 529, Mile 3½, Tuaran Rd. Diving trips are *very* expensive but are all inclusive – US$475 for a four day/three night trip from KK.

For white-water rafting, try Api Tours Sdn Bhd (tel 088-221230) on Jalan Tunku Abdul Rahman just north of the Hotel Shangrila. Typical charges for a rafting day-trip from KK is around M$150, but with travelling and preparation time you'll be lucky to have two hours actual rafting. Longer trips can also be arranged.

Borneo Wildlife Adventure Sdn Bhd at Lot 4, Block L of the Sinsuran Kompleks also arrange rafting and other trips.

Bookshops & Libraries Good bookshops are hard to find in KK. The best one is the Rahmat Bookstore in the Hyatt Hotel. It's very small, but it has a good selection of books on Sabah and other parts of Malaysia. The next best choice is probably the Arena Book Centre in Block L of the Sinsuran Kompleks. There are other bookshops in town which stock new and secondhand books written in English, but they sell little more than second-rate novels.

The British Council Library (tel 088-54056) is in the Wing Onn Life Building above the TDC tourist office.

Sabah Museum

The museum is next to the State Legislative Assembly Hall on Jalan Tunku Abdul Rahman. The main building is a four-storey structure built in the longhouse style of the Rungus and Murut tribes. Inside are good collections of tribal and historical artefacts, including ceramics. Another section has flora & fauna exhibits from around the country. There's also a souvenir shop in the main building.

The Science Centre, next to the main building, sometimes holds temporary exhibitions and demonstrations of the latest in computer technology. Next to the Science Centre is the Art Gallery & Multivision Theatre. There is also a restaurant and coffee shop with views over the gardens and man-made lakes in the grounds out to Mt Kinabalu on a clear day. Definitely worth a visit. Hours are 10 am to 6 pm Monday to Thursday; closed Friday; and from 9 am to 6 pm on Saturday, Sunday and public holidays. Catch a red bus along Jalan Tunku Abdul Rahman for 35 sen and get off just before the mosque. The museum is on a hill on the left side of the road.

State Mosque

As an example of contemporary Islamic architecture at its best, this mosque is well worth a visit. It's on the outskirts of town and you'll see it if you're on your way to or from the airport. It's much more interesting than the mosque at Kuching.

The mosque can accommodate 5000 male worshippers and has a balcony where there's room for 500 women to pray.

Visitors are allowed inside though, naturally, shoes must be removed before entering and you should be appropriately dressed.

Things to See & Do

If you'd like a view over the city go for a stroll up Signal Hill at the eastern edge of the city centre above the former GPO. It's best at sunset. You'll often see tourist literature in Sabah adorned with photographs of the Sabah Foundation's cylindrical, mirror-fronted, 31-storey building at Likas Bay,

with its revolving restaurant and ministerial suites. The literature gushes breathlessly about this landmark and insists that you include it in your programme but it isn't worth the effort. Anyway it can be seen from a distance, en route to Kinabalu National Park, standing in the middle of a vast, devastated landscape.

There is also the market which is in two sections – the waterfront area for fish and an area in front of the harbour for fruit and vegetables. Next to the main market on the waterfront is a market known locally as the Filipino Market, mainly because all the stalls are owned by Filipinos and they sell a wide variety of handicrafts made in the Philippines.

Places to Stay

After Kuching and Brunei, KK seems positively overflowing with hotels but most of them are fairly expensive. Sometimes, you'll find mid-range hotels with cheaper fan-cooled rooms on the higher floors – it's worth asking.

Places to Stay – bottom end

Finding a decent budget hotel in KK is not easy as most of the likely looking places are brothels. Essentially to get a good room you have to pay for it. There are, however, a couple of travellers' hostels which fill the gap.

The *Travellers Rest Hostel* (tel 088-231892) is on the 3rd floor, Block L of the Sinsuran Kompleks. It's a popular place and the dorm beds at M$15 including breakfast are not bad value. The spartan rooms, however, are overpriced at M$28/32 with fan, or M$34/38 with air-con.

The other hostel option is *Cecilia's Bed & Breakfast* (tel 088-35733) at 413 Jalan Saga, Kampung Likas six km north of the centre of town. The prices are M$18 per person in a shared room or M$30/40 for a single/double room, and this includes a good-value breakfast.

Of the regular hotels, the cheapest non-brothel is the *Islamic Hotel* (tel 088-54325), above the restaurant of the same name on

Jalan Perpaduan. Rooms with fan and common bath go for M$21. Another cheapie is the *Central Hotel* (tel 088-53522) on Jalan Tugu. The rooms are very shabby but would do for a night at M$26 for a double with fan, or M$26/28 for a single/double with air-con, all with common facilities.

The *Putera Hotel* (tel 088-53940) on Jalan Merdeka, near the corner with Jalan Tunku Abdul Rahman, is a fairly clean Chinese hotel with large single/double rooms for M$20/25 with fan, or M$35 for a double with air-con. All rooms have common bath.

Another place which is better value than most is the *Hotel Mutiara* (tel 088-54544) on Jalan Bandara Berjaya, not far from the Hotel Shangrila. The rooms are clean and quiet and cost M$25 for a single/double with fan, or M$37 for a double with air-con and bath attached.

For just a little more the *Hotel Rakyat* (tel 088-21100) Block I of the Sinsuran Kompleks is streets ahead of the competition. Rooms in this clean, friendly, Muslim-run place cost M$30/35 for a single/double with fan and bath, M$35/42 with air-con and bath.

Places to Stay – middle

The *Full On Resthouse* (tel 088-219321) next to the Islamic Hotel has good rooms for M$44/48, all with air-con and bath attached. Just around the corner is the *Diamond Inn* (tel 088-225222), about the best place in this price range, with rooms for M$45/57 with air-con, bath, TV and fridge. The *Ruby Inn* (tel 088-213222) in the same street is run by the same people but is more expensive at M$60/70 with the same facilities.

The *Sinsuran Inn* (tel 088-211158) almost next door to the Hotel Rakyat is not bad value at M$42/45 for small rooms with air-con and attached bath.

Up the scale a notch, *Ang's Hotel* (tel 088-55433) on Jalan Bakau has good rooms with air-con for around M$70. Don't bother with the restaurant downstairs though, unless you eat nothing but pork. Back on Jalan Merdeka, near Jalan Tugu, you'll find the *Hotel Nam Tai*. It's fairly clean and has double rooms for around M$40.

The *Winner Hotel* (tel 088-52688) at 9-10 Jalan Haji Saman, has 35 rooms single/ double rooms for M$55/65.

Places to Stay – top end

KK has a number of hotels with prices right up there with the leading hotels in Singapore, Kuala Lumpur and Penang. The top hotels are the *Hotel Capital*, the *Hotel Jesselton*, the *Hyatt Kinabalu International*, and the big and very expensive beachfront *Tanjung Aru Beach Hotel*.

The *Hotel Shangrila* is a level below these places and is good value.

Hotel Capital (tel 088-53433), 23 Jalan Haji Saman, 102 rooms, from M$150
Hyatt Kinabalu International (tel 088-219888), Jalan Datuk Salleh Sulong, 350 rooms from M$200 to M$1250.
Hotel Jesselton (tel 088-55633), 69 Jalan Gaya, 27 rooms from M$80 to M$100
Sabah Inn (tel 088-53322), 25 Jalan Pantai, 40 rooms from M$50 to M$100
Hotel Shangrila (tel 088-212800), Bandara Berjaya, 126 rooms from M$103/138 including breakfast
Tanjung Aru Beach Hotel (tel 088-58711), Tanjung Aru, 300 rooms from M$200 to M$1100

Places to Eat

For the variety of restaurants and the quality of food available, KK is probably the best city in Borneo. There are Chinese, Indian, Malay, Indonesian, Spanish, Filipino, Japanese, Korean and Western restaurants right in the centre of town.

For Malay food try the *New Arafat Restaurant* in Block I of the Sinsuran Kompleks. This 24-hour place is run by very friendly Indians and serves excellent curries, rotis and murtabaks.

In Block E of the Sinsuran Kompleks is the *Kedai Kopi Seng Hing*, an unremarkable Chinese cafe which serves remarkable prawn mee soup at lunch time – recommended.

For hawker food, there's a lively night market which sets up in the evenings in the vacant lot at the southern end of the Sinsuran Kompleks. Many of the stalls sell second-hand clothes and are run by Filipinos, but there's a good variety of food stalls; you can even get that Indonesian delicacy *coto Makassar* (buffalo-gut soup) if you're feeling adventurous.

For something a little more upmarket there's the *XO Steakhouse* at 54 Jalan Gaya at the northern end of town. It serves excellent 'air chilled' steaks which have been flown in from Australia and the USA. You can expect to pay around M$20 for an Australian steak, or M$30 to M$40 for an American one. The meat is beautifully tender but at these prices a little more creativity could be used in the salads department – frozen chips and coleslaw aren't very exciting. They also have bottles of Californian wines.

If you're down at the Kompleks Kuwasa at the Telekom office in Block B, the *Gardenia Atrium Lounge* is right below it and has good coffee and pastries. In Block D of the same complex is the *Avasi Cafeteria*, a very popular lunchtime hangout for local office workers. In the Karamunsing Kompleks on the opposite side of the roundabout from the Kompleks Kuwasa there's a non-smoking *Kentucky Fried Chicken* outlet.

Back on Jalan Tunku Abdul Rahman near the Hotel Shangrila there's the *Restoran Tioman* which serves good Chinese and Malay food. A similar place is the *Noodle Inn* on Jalan Sepuluh.

In the Segama Kompleks, down at street level, is *Sat's Ice Cream Parlour* where you can get freshly-squeezed fruit juices and local-style ice-cream desserts. Some of the middle to top-end hotels have Western restaurants; the *Wishbone Cafe & Restaurant* on Jalan Gaya, is not bad – it's downstairs in the Hotel Jesselton and serves both Western and Asian food. The *Tivoli Restaurant* in Hotel Shangrila has an evening Malay buffet for M$18.50.

Entertainment
KK has three or four cinemas around the corner of Jalan Sepuluh and Jalan Tunku Abdul Rahman. Karaoke freaks are equally well catered for.

On the 11th floor of the Wisma Merdeka there's a 10-pin bowling alley!

Things to Buy
Though a major centre, KK isn't a great place for handicrafts. There is a small shop in the Tanjung Aru Beach Hotel which has some fairly expensive handicrafts and souvenirs for sale. The Hyatt's bookshop has a range of books on various parts of Malaysia and some of them are excellent.

Unfortunately, the weekly tamus don't seem to have much to offer in the way of tribal handicrafts, though occasionally you may find something. You can sometimes buy handicrafts from tribal people when you visit longhouses. Some of the Filipino refugees on Pulau Gaya sell their handicrafts for reasonable prices.

About 10 km out of town on the Penampang road there is a new cultural centre specialising in articles made by the Kadazan people. Take any Penampang minibus from KK.

Getting There & Away
Air The MAS office (tel 088-51455) is on the ground floor of the Karamunsing Kompleks, about five minutes' walk south of the Hotel Shangrila along Jalan Tunku Abdul Rahman, and off to the left at the huge roundabout. It is open Monday to Friday from 8.30 am to 5.30 pm, Saturday from 8.30 to 3.30 pm and Sunday from 9 am to 1 pm. They also have an office at the airport which is open from 5 am to 7 pm daily.

Philippine Airlines (tel 088-239600) is also in the Karamunsing Kompleks, while Cathay Pacific (tel 088-54733) is in the Kompleks Kuwara. British Airways (tel 088-58511) has an office at 19 Jalan Haji Saman. Royal Brunei Airlines (088-240131) is handled by an agent in Wisma Sabah.

To/From Peninsular Malaysia & Singapore The cheapest way of getting from Peninsular Malaysia to KK is by purchasing an advance purchase ticket from Johore

Bahru; the regular fare is M$301. There are also economy night flights from Kuala Lumpur for M$266; the regular fare is M$380. Advance purchase tickets must be paid for 14 days in advance while the night fares only apply to certain flights.

The KK-Singapore fare is M$346 (S$346 if you buy it in Singapore); it is far cheaper to take the flights to or from Johore Bahru and cross the causeway on the MAS bus which takes you right into Singapore for M$10.

To/From Hong Kong MAS and Cathay Pacific each have two flights weekly between KK and Hong Kong. The fare is approximately M$660, but you will probably find cheaper tickets on Philippine Airlines. The flight time is a little under four hours.

To/From the Philippines MAS flies to Manila five times a week. Philippine Airlines also operates on this route; the fare is US$189 and flight time is just under two hours.

From time to time there have been flights between KK or other towns in Sabah and Zamboanga in the southern Philippines' island of Mindanao. At present they are, once again, out of operation.

Around Sabah & Sarawak KK is the hub of the MAS network in Sabah and there are regular flights to Brunei (three times weekly, M$65), Bintulu (daily, M$110), Kuching (three daily, M$198), Labuan (four daily, M$43), Lahad Datu (three daily, M$88), Miri (three daily, M$90), Sandakan (seven daily, M$69) and Tawau (seven daily, M$80).

There are also 12-seater Twin Otter flights from KK to: Limbang (twice weekly, M$60), Lawas (weekly, M$47) and Kudat (twice weekly, M$50).

Bus There is no main bus station in KK; instead, there are a few places from where buses, minibuses and taxis depart. These areas are marked on the map.

The area east of the council offices is the departure point for taxis and minibuses to everywhere north, south and east.

The large open plot of land behind the GPO is a very busy minibus park. Most buses from here are local but some also go to Beaufort and Penampang.

As you approach the long-distance minibus area you'll be accosted by touts drumming up business. Don't commit yourself to any minibus until you get there and see how many people they have; there'll often be more than one minibus going and the one you're getting on may have no people, in which case it will be a long wait while it fills up. If you get to the bus stand and there's no minibus with even one passenger going your way, hang back for a few minutes; chances are there's one nearly full doing a lap of the town trying to fill the last couple of seats.

All minibuses leave when full and there are frequent early morning departures. There are fewer departures later in the day and for some destinations, such as Ranau, the last bus departs around lunch time. For long-haul trips, like KK to Sandakan, the last bus may leave as early as 8 am, so unless you're up at the crack of dawn you could find yourself stuck for another night. Some examples of minibus fares from KK are:

Beaufort (90 km), regular departures up to about 3 pm, two hours on a very good road, M$7

Kota Belud (77 km), departures up to 2 pm daily, two hours on a road that is sealed all the way for M$5

Kudat (122 km), departures to about 1 pm, four hours on a road which is partially sealed for M$12

Sandakan (386 km), minibus departures early morning only, about eight hours for M$35. A large bus make the same trip for M$35. The road is sealed as far as Ranau but it's a pretty rough ride from there to Telupid, and around Batu 32. It's paved in and around Sandakan

Keningau (128 km), regular departures to about 1 pm, about 2½ hours on a road which is surfaced all the way

Ranau (156 km), early morning departures, the last bus leaves at 12.30 pm and takes about two hours. All buses pass Kinabalu National Park. The road is very good

Tenom, regular departures on a good sealed road, M$25 by taxi, M$20 by minibus

If you're heading for Kinabalu National Park from KK you can get there by taking the minibuses for Ranau or Sandakan and getting off at the park headquarters, which is right by the side of the road. Ask the driver to drop you off there. The fare to the park headquarters costs M$10 and takes about 1½ hours.

Train The railway station is five km south of the city centre at Tanjung Aru, close to the airport. There are daily trains to Beaufort and Tenom at 8 and 11 am, and the trip takes four hours to Beaufort, seven hours to Tenom. Although the stretch between Beaufort and Tenom is very spectacular and well worth the ride, it is easier and quicker to get to Beaufort or Tenom from KK by road.

Taxi Besides the minibuses, there are share-taxis to most places. They also go when full and their fares are at least 25% higher than the minibuses. Their big advantage is that they are much quicker and more comfortable.

Boat There are twice daily boats to Labuan from the jetty behind the Hyatt Hotel. The *Duta Muhibbah Dua* leaves at 8 am taking 2¾ hours, while the *Labuan Express* leaves KK at 2 pm and takes 2¼ hours. In the opposite direction they leave Labuan at 1 pm and 8.30 am respectively. The fare is M$28 economy class and M$33 in 1st class.

There's usually no need to book in advance but if you want to, contact the Rezeli Murai Travel Agency, Lot 3, 1st floor, Block D, Segama Kompleks.

Getting Around
To/From the Airport One of the few occasions in which you'll need to use local public transport is to get to the airport at Tanjung Aru, south-west of the centre. To get there take a 15-minute taxi ride for M$10, or a red 'Putatan' bus for 65 sen from Jalan Tunku Abdul Rahman and ask to be dropped at the airport. This bus stops opposite the road which leads to the airport and from there it's a 10-minute walk to the terminal. Alter-

natively, take a 'Putatan' minibus right into the airport for about M$1.50.

Heading into town from the airport, there's a bus stop to the right as you leave the airport. Taxis operate on a coupon system and prices are listed at the airport desk. It's quite easy to hitch into town from the airport.

The airport is new and modern, with an efficient MAS office, post office, Telekom office, a bank, a small bookshop and a cafe and an overpriced restaurant upstairs.

Taxi Local taxis are plentiful in the extreme. They are not metered so it's a matter of negotiating the fare before you set off. Taxi stands are all over town, but most can be found in the large area between the council offices and the GPO.

Car Rental There are a few car rental operators including:

Ais (no, not Avis)
    Lot 1, Block A, Ground Floor, Sinsuran Kompleks (tel 088-238953)
Kinabalu Rent a Car
    Hyatt Kinabalu International (tel 088-232602)
Adaras Rent a Car
    Lot G07, Ground Floor, Wisma Sabah (tel 088-222137)

AROUND KOTA KINABALU
Tunku Abdul Rahman National Park
The park has a total area of nearly 4929 hectares and is made up of the offshore islands of Gaya, Mamutik, Manukan, Sapi and Sulug. Only a short boat ride from the centre of the city, they offer good beaches, crystal-clear waters and a wealth of tropical corals and marine life.

To book any accommodation on the islands you must go through the Sabah Parks office in KK (see Information in Kota Kinabalu section in this chapter).

Pulau Manukan You'll find the park headquarters on Pulau Manukan, the second largest island of the park. With an area of 20 hectares, the island offers good beaches with coral reefs on the southern and eastern coasts, and there are walking trails around the perimeter.

This island is also undergoing extensive development with the construction of chalets, restaurant, jetty and swimming pool.

There are 20 chalets which are fully furnished but don't have cooking facilities and there is a restaurant on the island.

Pulau Gaya With an area of about 1465 hectares, Pulau Gaya is by far the largest island in the park and is the one just offshore from Kota Kinabalu.

This island is inhabited by about 500 Malaysians and 4700 Filipino refugees who live in stilt villages on the water. The water village, actually outside the park boundaries, is quite interesting, but as there are few walkways, you may have to take one of the local boats which ferry people about.

There are about 20 km of marked hiking trails and the well-known Police Beach at Bulijong Bay. If you're lucky, you may see monkeys, pangolins or even what's known as the bearded pig.

Pulau Sapi Pulau Sapi (Cow Island) lies just off the south-western tip of Pulau Gaya and is the most visited island in the park. With an area of just 10 hectares, the island has good beaches and trails and day-use facilities. There's a three-km nature trail on the island and apparently there are some monkeys living in the forest and they sometimes go down to the beach to swim and look for crabs. You may also see the white-bellied sea eagle around this island.

Pulau Mamutik This is the smallest island in the park with an area of just six hectares.

There are good beaches right around the island and some good coral reefs, particularly on the eastern side.

There is a resthouse for up to eight people on the island which costs M$60 per night.

Pulau Sulug This island, covering eight hectares, is the least visited island of this group, probably because it's the furthest away from KK, and is being pushed as a 'Robinson Crusoe experience'. It has some beautiful coral reefs and tropical fish, but only one beach, on the eastern shore.

Getting There & Away
Coral Island Cruises have boats from behind the Hyatt Hotel to the islands at 9, 10 and 11 am and 1.30, 2.30 and 3.30 pm. To Mamutik, Manukan or Sapi it's M$12, to Sulug or Police Beach it's M$18. For more information contact the office in the ground floor of Wisma Sabah.

If you just want to go across to the water village, boats shuttle back and forth from the Filipino Market and from near the Hyatt. You may be able to find local boats willing to take you out to the other islands but they won't be cheap.

Tanjung Aru Beach
Several km south-west of KK centre is Tanjung Aru Beach, adjacent to Prince Philip Park and close to the international airport. It's not bad as beaches go and the area is dotted with open-air food and drink stalls and the occasional pile of rubbish. You can find much better beaches as well as Rungus longhouses at Kudat way up near the northern tip of Sabah.

To get to Tanjung Aru Beach, take a red bus displaying 'beach' from Jalan Tunku Abdul Rahman. It costs 55 sen and will drop you near the yacht club, a pleasant 500 metres from the international hotel at the other end of the beach.

Penampang
Home of the popular Kadazan people, Penampang is a pretty village about 13 km from KK. Some handicrafts can be found and if you're lucky, you might catch the local dancers performing the *Sumazau* (harvest dance). Occasionally, these young dancers perform in KK.

Take a look at St Michael's Church, the largest and oldest church in Sabah, or visit the Kadazan graveyards where you'll see some burial jars.

There is an authentic Kadazan restaurant called the *Yun Chuan Restaurant* in Block L,

Penampang Newtownship. Prices are reasonable and the food is good.

To get to Penampang, take a minibus from the bus stand behind the GPO for 70 sen.

South of Kota Kinabalu

PAPAR
Situated 38 km south of KK, this is a coastal Kadazan village where they make coconut wine. There's a beach in Papar and the Papar River where you can take a boat ride. It's worth going on a Sunday so you can experience the weekly tamu. To get there, take a minibus for M$2 from the area behind the GPO.

TAMBUNAN
Across the Crocker Range from Penampang, Tambunan is an agricultural service town about 90 km from KK. This was the stamping ground of Mat Salleh, who rebelled against the British late last century.

The main reason for visiting Tambunan today is to see the Tambunan Village Resort

Centre. It is built totally out of bamboo and was constructed by the kids on the Operation Raleigh expedition in 1987.

Places to Stay
The *Tambunan Village Resort Centre* charges M$25 for a double room in the long-house, and also has chalets for M$35 and motel rooms for M$30.

Getting There & Away
There are regular minibuses plying between Tambunan and KK, Ranau, Keningau and Tenom.

KENINGAU
The provincial capital of the Interior Residency, Keningau is a lumber and agricultural town deep in the heart of Murut country, though it's most unlikely you'll see anyone dressed in traditional tribal wear. Attracted by the prospects of well-paid employment, migrants have flocked there from neighbouring districts and the town's population has doubled since the 1960s.

Keningau is a mini-boom town which is being torn apart to provide new business

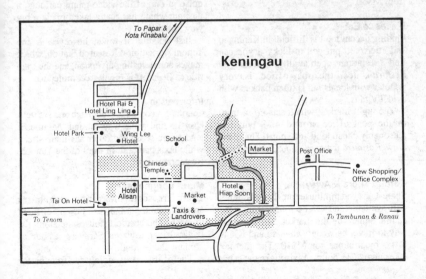

premises, shops, hotels, administrative offices and the like. If you enjoy sport there's a large sports complex with a good swimming pool opposite the Hotel Perkasa Keningau.

Other than that, the only worthwhile experience Keningau offers is the journey there over the forested Crocker Mountains. Get there soon though, if you want to see any trees because they're logging at an alarming rate.

Places to Stay
Like other boom towns in East Malaysia, accommodation is expensive and the price you pay for a room doesn't necessarily reflect the facilities it offers.

The best value is the *Government Rest House* (tel 089-31525) which costs M$12 per night if it's not full with government officials. The *Hotel Hiap Soon* (tel 089-31541) has nice staff and clean rooms with air-con from M$30.

Mass Lodging has overpriced rooms from M$40. The *Hotel Alisan* and *Hotel Rai* have better, cheaper rooms. The *Hotel Perkasa Keningau* (tel 089-31044) is the most expensive hotel in town, with 75 air-con rooms from M$50.

Places to Eat
Finding decent food is difficult in Keningau and after 6.30 pm you're lucky if you can find a restaurant open at all. The *Keningau Restoran*, near the post office, is very popular with locals but is often packed with avid TV fans.

The night market, which sets up in front of the post office around 4.30 pm, has reasonably cheap food and soups. The *Mandarin Restaurant* serves good Chinese food.

Getting There & Away
Share-taxis and minibuses are the only transport available and can be found around the central square by the market. The cheapest way to travel between Keningau and KK is to go by minibus for M$10. The journey takes about 2½ hours. Taxis make the same

trip but charge M$20. There are some great views as the road cuts through the spectacular Crocker Range. Occasionally, you pass small areas devastated by logging, fire or both. The best scenery is between Tambunan and KK.

Keningau to Tenom costs M$4 by minibus and takes about one hour along a good bitumen road through forest and rubber plantations. A taxi costs about M$5. There are also taxis and minibuses to Tambunan and Ranau. From Ranau you can go either to Sandakan or Kinabalu National Park.

TENOM
Tenom is the home of the friendly Murut people, most of whom are farmers. Soyabeans, maize and a variety of vegetables are grown in this fertile area and there are several cocoa plantations.

It's a very pleasant rural town, with much more old world charm than Beaufort, and is also the railhead on the line from Tanjung Aru (KK).

But despite the peaceful setting, there's absolutely nothing to do in the town itself, except of course play snooker or get assaulted by the horrendous cacophony of noise in one of the video-game parlours, a pastime which has really taken off in a big way in Sabah.

Just outside of town, however, is the Tenom Agricultural Research Station, which makes an interesting diversion, and the train ride to Beaufort is highly recommended.

Information
Tenom is a compact little place and it's very easy to find your way around. Minibuses tend to cruise up and down the main street, while taxis hang out in front of the Yun Lee Restaurant.

Murut Longhouses
There are some interesting longhouses around Tenom but they can be a bit difficult to reach. The best longhouses are along the Padas River towards Sarawak, as far as Tomani and beyond.

There are buses going to Tomani for

around M$4 or you may be able to get a boat there.

Agricultural Research Station

This research station run by the Department of Agriculture is at Lagud Sebrang, about 15 km north-east of Tenom. There are on-going research programmes into cocoa, food crops, coffee, fruit trees and apiculture (bees).

The main point of interest for the casual visitor is the Orchid Centre which has been established over a period of years by a British man, Anthony Lamb, who has spent many years in Borneo. To visit the Orchid Centre you should report to the Administration office on the far side of the sports field at the research station. It is only open during business hours so Saturday afternoon and Sundays are out. If you want a meal while you're out there there's a canteen in the grandstand of the sports field and it sells basic rice and mee meals.

To reach the centre take a Lagud Sebrang minibus from beside the sports field in Tenom. They run about every hour or so throughout the morning (M$2), but things dry up in the early afternoon so go early so as not to get stranded out there, although it is possible to hitch.

If you have a deeper interest and want to make a more formal visit, contact the Director, Department of Agriculture Headquarters in Kota Kinabalu (tel 088-735651) in advance.

Places to Stay

The cheapest hotel in town is the *Hotel Lam Fong* near the railway station. It's about as basic a place as you'll ever find; it's clean, if shabby, and costs M$10/15 with a bit of bargaining.

If you can't face the Lam Fong, the next best place is the *Hotel Syn Nam Tai* on the main street. It's also a basic Chinese cheapie and has rooms for M$15/20 with common bath.

Probably the best value in town is the *Hotel Kim San* (tel 087-735485) in the new group of shops set back from the main road. The friendly, pipe-sucking Chinese owner, Michael Wong, is a good source of information on things to do in the area. The rooms cost M$25 with air-con and TV and you can have up to three people in a room.

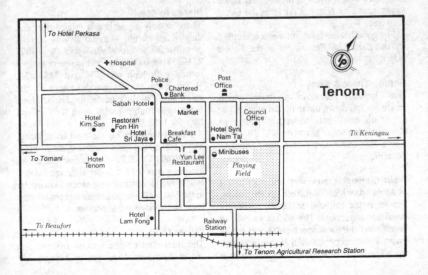

Right across the road is the *Hotel Tenom* (tel 087-736378) which has huge, airy, carpeted rooms with air-con, bath and TV for M$28 single/double – for two it's a bargain by expensive Sabah standards.

There are quite a few other hotels in Tenom, including the *Hotel Sri Jaya* on the main street and the Indian-run *Sabah Hotel*. Avoid the *Lucky Lodge* – it's the town brothel.

At the top of the scale is the *Hotel Perkasa Tenom* (tel 087-73581) sited on a hill overlooking the town and the surrounding district. With 70-odd fully air-con rooms it seems totally over the top for sleepy Tenom and in fact has very low occupancy rates. Rooms cost M$69/80 with bath attached. If you want to check in, or have a reservation, ring from the town and they'll come down and collect you; otherwise take a taxi for M$2.

Places to Eat

As usual there are plenty of Chinese kedai kopis all over town selling basic Chinese food. The *Yun Lee Restaurant* on the main street is popular with the locals, but it closes very early in the evening, as do most of them. One place that is open in the evening is the *Restaurant Fon Hin*, not far from the Hotel Kim San.

For good Malay food, rotis and murtabak try the *Bismillah Restaurant* in the Sabah Hotel.

Getting There & Away

Bus There are dozens of minibuses which cruise up and down the main street trying to drum up business. Most are going to Keningau, but some also go to KK. There are also a few minibuses which head south to Tomani.

Train Although the railway line goes as far as Melalap, which is further up the valley, Tenom is the railhead as far as passenger trains are concerned. The 46-km journey to Beaufort is the most spectacular part of the journey and recommended if you've come from Tambunan or Keningau and are on your way to Sarawak or Brunei. For more information on this service see the Beaufort section below.

Taxi Taxis also make the run to Keningau (M$5) and on to KK (M$25), usually with a wait in Keningau for passengers.

BEAUFORT

Beaufort is a quiet little provincial town on the Padas River with a fair amount of charm, although there's absolutely nothing to see or do so it's unlikely you'll stay more than one night.

If you're heading to or coming from eastern Sarawak through Brunei, Labuan and Menumbok or through Lawas, Merapok and Sipitang then you will pass through Beaufort. The railway line from Tanjung Aru (Kota Kinabalu) to Tenom also passes through Beaufort so you can take the train in either direction.

Information

There's a branch of the Hong Kong & Shanghai Banking Corporation in Beaufort which will change travellers' cheques. There is no bank at Sipitang.

Places to Stay

There're only a few hotels in Beaufort and they're not cheap, so avoid staying there if possible. The *Hotel Beaufort* (tel 087-211911) is the cheapest option where air-con rooms with bath and TV cost M$30/36, although the singles are definitely on the small side. By the cinema, the *Padas Hotel* has single/double rooms with air-con and bath for M$37/42.

Across the river on the road to Sipitang, about 500 metres from the centre, the *Mandarin Inn* (tel (087-212798) is a newer place with air-con rooms for M$30/36, although the distance from the centre is a nuisance. Downstairs in the hotel is Karaoke lounge and next door a huge noisy video-game parlour.

Places to Eat

The restaurant on the ground floor of the *Hotel Beaufort* does pretty reasonable

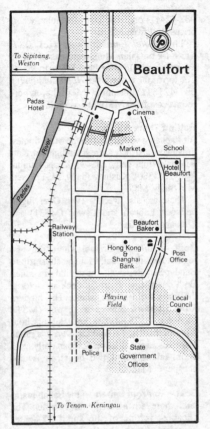

Beaufort

To Sipitang, Weston

Padas River

Padas Hotel

Cinema

Market

School

Hotel Beaufort

Railway Station

Beaufort Baker

Hong Kong & Shanghai Bank

Post Office

Playing Field

Local Council

Police

State Government Offices

To Tenom, Keningau

For Menumbok (for Labuan) there are plenty of minibuses until early afternoon. The trip, along a reasonable gravel road, takes one hour at a cost of M$8.

Train Sabah is the only place in East Malaysia where you will find railways and even here there's only one line. The 154-km track connects Tenom to KK (Tanjung Aru) via Beaufort.

It's a spectacular trip between Beaufort and Tenom, where the train follows the Padas River through steamy jungle. At times the dense jungle forms a bridge over the narrow track. The ride from Beaufort to KK is not so exciting and takes too long for the trip to be convenient or worthwhile.

There are two types of passenger trains available. The railcars are the best for comfort, speed and views, and the ordinary diesel trains are the ones to take if you want a slower, more colourful journey packed in with the local people and their produce.

The railcar is basically an overgrown minibus with just 13 seats. Make a booking as soon as you arrive in Beaufort (or Tenom, if travelling in the opposite direction) as it's sometimes fully booked, although even if it is, it's worth going to the station at departure time as last-minute cancellations are frequent. Sit in the front seat on the right going from Beaufort, on the left from Tenom, as you get the best views of the river and there's a clear view of the narrow track unfolding in front of you. The car has been designated '1st class' and therefore gets a 1st-class price. The diesel trains are cheaper and slower. The schedule is:

Chinese food. Otherwise, there are numerous Chinese coffee shops around town offering the standard rice or mee dishes.

For cakes, buns and other pastries the *Beaufort Baker* has a good selection.

Getting There & Away

Bus The minibuses gather near the Hotel Beaufort, but there's absolutely no way you'll miss one as they cruise round town honking hopefully at any pedestrian. There are frequent departures for Kota Kinabalu (two hours, M$7), and less frequently to Sipitang.

Beaufort-Tenom

Diesel Train	Mon-Sat	10.50 am, 1.55 pm
	Sun	6.45 am, 2.30 pm
Railcar	Mon-Sat	8.25 am, 3.50 pm
	Sun	9.10 am, 3.40 pm

Tenom-Beaufort

Diesel Train	Mon-Sat	7.30 am, 1.40 pm
	Sun	7.55 am, 3.05 pm
Railcar	Mon-Sat	6.40 am, 3.10 pm
	Sun	7.20 am, 1.55 pm

The fares are more expensive on Sundays. On weekdays the railcar costs M$10, the diesel train M$4; on Sundays the fares are M$14 and M$6 respectively.

If you want to go all the way to KK, the route is only covered by diesel trains which take five hours, leaving Beaufort at 9.50 am, and in the opposite direction from KK at 11 am.

PULAU TIGA NATIONAL PARK

Off coastal Kuala Penyu, which sits on a peninsula, is the Pulau Tiga National Park with an area of nearly 15,864 hectares. There is still volcanic activity in the way of bubbling mud and methane gas.

There is little in the way of facilities and the islands are expensive to get to. Contact the Sabah Parks office in KK if you are interested in going there.

LABUAN ISLAND

Off the coast from Menumbok, Labuan is one of the departure points for the trip to Brunei. Labuan is a Federal Territory and is governed directly from Kuala Lumpur. The island acts as a duty-free centre and as such attracts many of Brunei's population, as well as Malaysians, for quick shopping sprees.

Victoria is the main town and it is the place where the ferries tie in. There really isn't anything to see unless you're into the bloody Sunday cockfights, though there are some nice beaches.

Labuan is the place where the Japanese forces in north Borneo surrendered at the end of WW II; there's an appropriate memorial on the island. It was also here that the Japanese officers responsible for the Death Marches from Sandakan were tried by an Australian War Crimes Court.

Places to Stay

Accommodation is expensive. A good bet is the *Dahlia Hotel* near the bus station, which has rooms for M$26 with fan, M$32 with air-con. There are several hotels in this range in the same area.

More expensive is the *Victoria Hotel* (tel

087-42411) on Jalan Tun Mustapha, where prices start from M$70.

The *Hotel Emas-Labuan* (tel 087-413966), on Jalan Muhibbah, has about 40 rooms ranging in price from M$50 to M$60. The top of the range is the *Hotel Labuan* (tel 087-421311) on Jalan Merdeka, where rooms cost from M$160 to M$500.

Getting There & Away

Air Labuan is well served on the MAS domestic network and there are regular flights to: Kota Kinabalu (four daily, M$43), Kuala Lumpur (daily, M$380), Kuching (daily, M$173) and Miri (daily, M$57).

There are also weekly Twin Otter flights between Labuan and Lawas (M$31) and Limbang (M$30).

Boat – To/From Brunei There are two regular departures daily for the short trip to Bandar Seri Begawan, the capital of Brunei. Both boats leave from the dock at Victoria, the main town in the island. The modern *Ratu Samudra* leaves at 2 pm (M$18 economy, M$25 1st class) and takes one hour 20 minutes. The *Sri Labuan Dua* is a much older vessel and it leaves Labuan daily at 12 noon, taking about two hours. It is also cheaper at M$15.

Boat – To/From Sabah To the Sabah mainland there are a couple of options. The cheapest is one of the small 12-seater launches which shuttle back and forth between Victoria and Menumbok, which is really nothing more than a jetty, a restaurant and a few houses. The crossing takes about 30 minutes and costs M$10. They leave when full (roughly hourly) throughout the day. The alternative to the launches is the much slower, less frequent (and cheaper) car ferries which operate between the same two places. These take an hour or so and depart Menumbok at 10.30 am and 4 pm, and from Labuan at 8 am and 1 pm. From Menumbok there are frequent minibuses to Beaufort (one hour, M$8) and Kota Kinabalu (two hours, M$15).

The small launches also connect Labuan

and Sipitang. They also operate throughout the day when full (about one hour, M$20).

There are also two launches connecting Labuan and Kota Kinabalu. The *Duta Muhibbah Dua* leaves Labuan at 1 pm, arriving in KK around 4.40 pm, while the *Labuan Express* departs at 8.30 am, arriving at 10.15 am. In the opposite direction they leave KK at 8 am and 2 pm respectively.

Boat – To/From Sarawak It is possible to travel between Labuan and Lawas in Sarawak although the boats are infrequent and you may have to wait around for a day or two to find something that's going – be patient.

SIPITANG
Sipitang is the closest Sabah town to the Sabah/Sarawak border. There is an immigration office but everything is fairly relaxed.

Places to Stay
If you have to stay in Sipitang for the night there's a *Government Rest House*, about a km from the centre on the Merapok road, which costs M$12 per person. A more basic flea-pit in the centre of the village costs less than this.

Getting There & Away
Minibuses and share-taxis depart for Beaufort every day around 7 to 8 am and cost M$7 per person. From Beaufort there are buses, taxis and trains to KK or Tenom.

To the Sarawak border at Merapok it's a half-hour trip. There's not much traffic but you shouldn't have to wait too long; the cost is M$2.

Small 12-seater launches leave when full for the one-hour trip to Labuan.

North of Kota Kinabalu

MENGKABONG WATER VILLAGE
About halfway along the coast from Kota Kinabalu to Kota Belud is the beautiful little Bajau water village of Mengkabong where the houses are built on stilts in the sea. Transport around the village is by canoe or sampan. It's well worth making a detour to see this place if you're passing by, although it is something of a tourist trap.

First head for Tuaran and then take local transport from there. There is a tamu held in Tuaran on Sundays which is also worth visiting – you might be able to pick up some local handicrafts.

Getting There & Away
Transport to Tuaran from either Kota Kinabalu or Kota Belud is no problem. From Tuaran it's a short taxi ride to Pantadalit Beach.

KOTA BELUD
The town is the venue of Sabah's largest and most colourful tamu and as such is a magnet for travellers. The tamu takes place every Sunday – get there as early as possible.

Tamus are not simply open-air markets where tribal people gather to sell their farm products of fruit and vegetables and to buy manufactured goods from the Chinese and Indian traders; they are also social occasions when news and stories are exchanged.

The tamu at Kota Belud attracts all manner of traders from quasi-medical commercial travellers selling herbal remedies and magic pills to water buffalo owners who haggle all morning over the price of a cow or a calf.

For keen photographers the tamus provides a never-ending procession of colourful characters and situations and, if you're lucky, the Bajau 'cowboys' may turn up on their caparisoned horses looking like mediaeval knights at a tournament.

Unfortunately, those looking for tribal handicrafts will be disappointed. You may have more luck in that department at the Sunday tamu at Sikuati, 23 km from Kudat, which is attended by the Rungus people who live in longhouses in the surrounding area.

Kota Belud itself is just a small, sleepy rural town with a vegetable and meat market;

a town where everything except for the pool halls and video-game parlours closes down very early and bored adolescents roam the streets looking for something to do. Once a week on Sunday it comes to life as people from many km around flock to the tamu.

If you're in desperate need of cash at the Sunday tamu local Chinese traders will often change travellers' cheques at a poor rate of exchange. Ask in shops and offices.

Places to Stay

There are only two hotels in town. The *Hotel Tai Seng*, which has 20 rooms from M\$20 upwards, and the *Hotel Kota Belud* (tel 088-976576) on Jalan Francis which has clean air-con rooms from M\$28.

If you can't afford to stay at the hotels you can sleep free at the school near the police station – ask for the school teacher. Your 'bed' will be a table tennis table.

There is also a faint possibility of staying at the *Government Rest House* (tel 088-67532) which costs M\$12 per person per night, but it's officially for government offi-

cers only. The police station can be most helpful if you're stuck for accommodation.

Places to Eat

Most of the restaurants, and there are very few, close at the latest by 5.30 pm and unless you've eaten by then you're up for a 'meal' of peanuts, confectionery and beer bought from the stalls on the sports ground side of the central square/market.

Even the restaurant on the ground floor of the *Hotel Kota Belud* closes by 5.30 pm, regardless of how many people are staying in the hotel! They do serve good mee soup but asking for anything else is useless.

An exception to the early closing hours is the popular *Indonesia Restoran*, in the gravel car park behind the Kota Belud Hotel, which does simple dishes like nasi goreng and is open until 8 pm. The standard of hygiene in other food stalls leaves much to be desired. All in all, Kota Belud has very little to offer in terms of good food.

Getting There & Away

All the minibuses and share-taxis operate from the central square and most of these

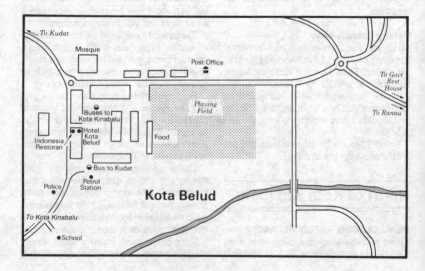

serve the Kota Belud-Kota Kinabalu route which costs M$5 and takes about 1½ hours. The road is sealed all the way. On Sundays – tamu day – the number of minibuses and taxis has to be seen to be believed. On other days it's much quieter.

If you're heading up the coast to Kudat there is one bus daily which departs about 10 am from outside the petrol station, costs M$10 and takes about two to 2½ hours.

If you want to get to Kinabalu National Park then take any of the minibuses or share-taxis which are going to Kota Kinabalu and get off at Tamparuli, about halfway there. The trip takes about half an hour and costs M$4. From Tamparuli there are several minibuses and taxis to Ranau every day up to about 2 pm. The taxis cost M$12 and the minibuses M$6, although bargaining may be necessary. The journey to the National Park headquarters takes about an hour along a good sealed road. Tell the driver to drop you off there.

KUDAT

Kudat, near the north-eastern tip of Sabah, has some of the best beaches in Sabah. The beaches are definitely for those who want tranquillity and who expect little in terms of facilities; very few people find their way up to this part of Sabah. For unspoilt beauty, the beaches to head for are north of Bak Bak.

The Kudat area is the home of the Rungus people, tribal cousins of the Kadazans, and they continue to live in their traditional manner. The older women wear black sarungs and colourful, beaded necklaces. On festive occasions, heavy brass bracelets are worn as well. The Rungus tribes produce some excellent, elaborate beadwork and you can sometimes buy their handicrafts at the Sunday tamu held at Sikuati, a town 23 km from Kudat.

More and more Rungus people are building their own houses in preference to living in a traditional longhouse. There are still some interesting longhouses around Kudat and, if you visit one, it's polite to take a few small gifts of food or cigarettes. It's also better to be invited to a longhouse by a friendly local, than to invite yourself – but this is easier said than done.

Places to Stay

If you're planning on staying in Kudat there are three main hotels. At the bottom of the heap is the *Hasba Hotel* (tel 088-61959) with basic rooms from M$16 to M$25. The rooms are stuffy, hot and dirty.

The *Hotel Sunrise* (tel 088-61517) is the largest and best with 16 rooms and its own good restaurant. Rooms cost from M$30 up to M$58 with air-con and attached bathroom. The *Kudat Hotel* (tel 088-616379), Little St has just eight rooms, all with air-con, from M$30 to M$35.

There is also a *Government Rest House* (tel 088-61304) with seven rooms at M$12 per person, but the usual warning about 'government workers' only applies.

If you're stuck for somewhere to sleep it's worth asking if you can stay at one of the Christian churches in Kudat – but remember to leave a reasonable donation.

Getting There & Away

Air There are MAS Twin Otter flights from Kudat to: Sandakan (six weekly, M$54) and Kota Kinabalu (twice weekly, M$50).

Bus Several minibuses a day make the three to four-hour trip from Kota Kinabalu for M$10. Bak Bak Beach is 11 km from Kudat and difficult to get to without your own transport – count on M$6 for a taxi out there, M$12 to be picked up!

MT KINABALU

Towering 4101 metres above the lush tropical jungles of North Borneo and the centrepiece of the vast 750-sq km Kinabalu National Park, Mt Kinabalu is the major attraction in Sabah. It is the highest mountain between the snow-capped peaks of the Himalaya and those of New Guinea and, although 50 km inland, its jagged granite peaks are visible most mornings from many places along the coast.

Yet, despite its height, it is one of the easiest mountains in the world to climb. No

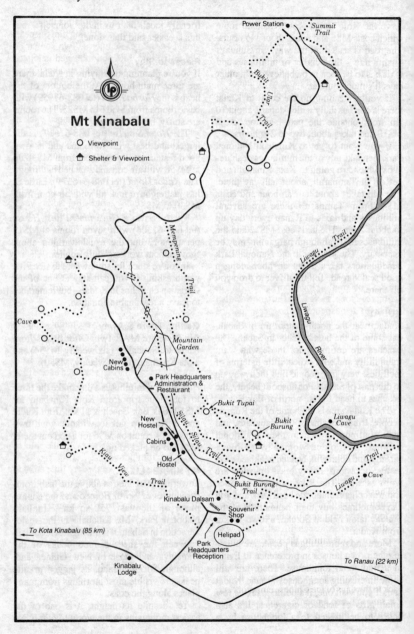

Mt Kinabalu

○ Viewpoint
⛫ Shelter & Viewpoint

Power Station

Summit Trail

Bukit Ular Trail

Mempening Trail

Liwagu Trail

Liwagu River

Cave

Mountain Garden

New Cabins

Park Headquarters Administration & Restaurant

Bukit Tupai

Bukit Burung

Liwagu Cave

New Hostel

Cabins

Old Hostel

Sigut Sigut Trail

Kiau View Trail

Bukit Burong Trail

Cave

Liwagu Trail

Kinabalu Dalsam

Souvenir Shop

Helipad

Park Headquarters Reception

To Kota Kinabalu (85 km)

Kinabalu Lodge

To Ranau (22 km)

special skills or equipment are required. All you need is a little stamina, and you do need to be equipped with gear to protect you from the elements – it gets very cold and wet up there. Given this, you will be rewarded with one of the most memorable experiences of your life. The views – even before you get to the top – are magnificent and the sunsets equally incredible. Where else could you see the rays of the setting sun shining *up* through the clouds below you?

History
The first recorded ascent of the mountain was made in 1851 by Sir Hugh Low, the British colonial secretary on the island of Labuan. The highest peak is named after him as is the mile-deep 'gully' on the other side of the mountain.

In those days the difficulty of climbing Mt Kinabalu lay not in the ascent itself, but in getting to the base of it through the trackless jungles and finding local porters willing to go there. None of the Dusun (now called Kadazan) tribespeople who accompanied Low had ever climbed the mountain before, believing it to be the dwelling place of the spirits of their dead.

Low was therefore obliged to take along with him a guide armed with a large basket of quartz crystals and teeth to protect the party. The ceremonies performed by the guides to appease the spirits on reaching the summit gradually became more elaborate as time went on so that by the 1920s they had come to include the sacrifice of seven eggs, seven white chickens, loud prayers and gunshots, but in recent times the custom appears to have died out.

These days you won't have to hack through the jungle for several days to get to the foot of the mountain like the early explorers did as there's a sealed road all the way from Kota Kinabalu to the park headquarters.

There's a colourful local Kadazan legend as to how the mountain got its name. It goes back to the days of the Chinese emperors and it is said that one emperor heard that on this mountain there was a fabulous pearl,

guarded by a dragon. He told his three sons that whichever one could bring him the pearl would be the next emperor. Two sons tried and failed; the third son managed to snatch the pearl but just as he was sneaking away the dragon woke and gave chase. The prince managed to hide in the jungle, with the pearl, while the rest of his party went on, with the dragon in hot pursuit. They jumped back in their boat and hightailed it for China. The dragon still followed so they fired their cannons at it, and it eventually sank, having swallowed numerous cannon balls, thinking that they were the pearl. Meanwhile the prince back in the jungle took a local wife and raised a family, but after some years decided that it was time to return to China and claim the throne. He promised his wife that he would come back to fetch her, but of course he never showed up. In despair she climbed to the top of the mountain to pray for his return, and died in the process. Hence 'Kina', meaning China, and 'balu', widow.

Geology
From its immense size you might imagine that Mt Kinabalu is the ancient core of the island of Borneo but in fact the mountain is a relatively recent arrival. Its origins go back a mere nine million years to when a solidified core of volcanic rock began swelling up from the depths below, pushing its way through the overlying rock. This upward movement is apparently still going on and a team of Japanese geologists have estimated that the mountain continues to grow at the rate of about five mm per year.

On account of its youth, very little erosion has occurred on the exposed granite rock faces around the summit, though the effects of glaciers which used to cover much of Kinabalu can be picked out by the trained eye. The glaciers have disappeared but, at times, ice forms in the rock pools near the summit – it gets pretty cold up there at nighttime so you need warm clothing to make the final ascent.

Flora
Exhilarating though it undoubtedly is,

merely being able to climb to the top of this mountain isn't the only experience which awaits you. Mt Kinabalu is a botanical paradise stocked with a phenomenal number of different plants, many of which are unique to the area.

Some of the more spectacular flowers belonging to the orchid family are found there – almost 1000 species have been discovered so far with many more blooming unnamed among still-unexplored gullies and ridges. There are many unusual rhododendrons and the giant red blossoms of the *rafflesia* which, at more than 70 cm in diameter, are one of the largest flowers in the world.

Even if you don't manage to catch sight of a *rafflesia* you will certainly see one or more of the many types of insectivorous pitcher plants which grow in profusion there. You may well come across them elsewhere in Borneo – particularly in Gunung Mulu National Park, Sarawak – but there's nowhere else they grow in such numbers.

They come in all manner of elaborate shapes, sizes and colours, although you probably won't be as lucky as the late-19th century botanist, Spencer St John who found one that was 30 cm in diameter. He reported finding a *nepenthes rajah* pitcher of this size which contained 2½ litres of watery fluid and a drowned rat!

Orchid

Most, however, are only large enough to catch unwary insects which are attracted to nectar which the plants secrete, but then find themselves unable to escape up the slippery inner surface of the pitcher. While on your way to the summit, try exploring a few metres in the undergrowth on either side of the trail – you're bound to come across a pitcher plant sooner or later.

Further Reading

Before you go to the park you might like to read a little about what's in store for you on the mountain by purchasing a copy of the national parks publication, *A Guide to Kinabalu National Park* by Susan Kay Jacobson, which is on sale at the office in Kota Kinabalu for M$5.

Another book which is worth reading even if you're not a botanist is *Nepenthes of Mount Kinabalu* by Shigeo Kurata which sells for the same price. ('Nepenthes' is the botanical name for pitcher plants.)

Hugh Low's experiences on the mountain are recounted in a book called *Experiences in the Forests of East Asia*, written by Spencer St John. It was originally published in London in 1864 but a reproduction paperback is available locally.

Permits

A M$10 climbing permit is required for Mt Kinabalu, M$2 for students and free for children under 13. There are also vehicle entry charges to the park: M$5 for a large bus, M$2 for a minibus, M$1 for a car or jeep, 50 sen for a motorcycle.

Scientists and botanists wanting to collect specimens for research must first apply for a permit on form A1, available at the Sabah Parks office. You are then issued with a form A2 permit which costs M$50 and is valid for a single visit to the national park.

Park Headquarters

The accommodation and catering at the park headquarters is excellent and well organised. It's built in a beautiful setting with a magnificent view of Mt Kinabalu when the clouds are not obscuring the slopes and summits.

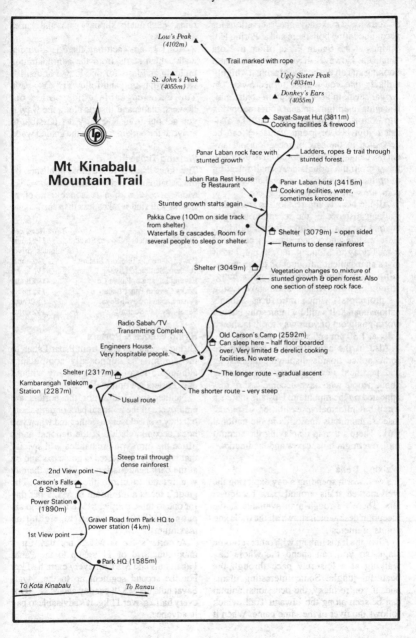

Low's Peak
(4102m)

Trail marked with rope

St. John's Peak
(4055m)

Ugly Sister Peak
(4034m)

Donkey's Ears
(4055m)

Sayat-Sayat Hut (3811m)
Cooking facilities & firewood

**Mt Kinabalu
Mountain Trail**

Panar Laban rock face with
stunted growth

Ladders, ropes & trail through
stunted forest.

Laban Rata Rest House
& Restaurant

Panar Laban huts (3415m)
Cooking facilities, water,
sometimes kerosene.

Stunted growth starts again

Pakka Cave (100m on side track
from shelter)
Waterfalls & cascades. Room for
several people to sleep or shelter.

Shelter (3079m) – open sided

Returns to dense rainforest

Shelter (3049m)

Vegetation changes to mixture of
stunted growth & open forest. Also
one section of steep rock face.

Radio Sabah/TV
Transmitting Complex

Old Carson's Camp (2592m)
Can sleep here – half floor
boarded over. Very limited & derelict cooking
facilities. No water.

Engineers House.
Very hospitable people.

Shelter (2317m)

The longer route – gradual ascent

Kambarangah Telekom
Station (2287m)

The shorter route – very steep

Usual route

Steep trail through
dense rainforest

2nd View point

Carson's Falls
& Shelter

Power Station
(1890m)

Gravel Road from Park HQ to
power station (4 km)

1st View point

Park HQ (1585m)

To Kota Kinabalu   To Ranau

You should make advance reservations for accommodation both there and at Poring Hot Springs at the Sabah Parks office in Kota Kinabalu. However, if you arrive without a booking and all the beds are taken, it's highly unlikely that you will be turned away. On arrival check in at the reception centre and, if staying overnight, present your reservation slip from Kota Kinabalu and you'll be allocated your bed or room. Valuables can be deposited in the safe at reception and any excess baggage can be stored there until you return from the mountain. A small selection of crafts and books is also available. Prices compare well with those elsewhere.

All the hostels and resthouses are within walking distance of the reception and just beyond them is the administration building. Here a slide and video show is presented from Friday to Monday at 7.30 pm, and it gives an excellent introduction to the mountain. Also shown here is a whiz-bang, 15-minute, 'multivision' slide show (using 14 projectors!) which introduces Sabah's national parks. It's mildly interesting but not worth going out of your way for. It is shown daily at 1.30 pm and admission is M$1.

Also in the administration building are some notice boards displaying interesting and pertinent newspaper cuttings, mostly about people who have become lost or disappeared on the mountain. Upstairs there's a small but informative exhibition of plants, insects, mammals and birds in the national park. There's a map displaying the summit trail, overnight huts, caves and landmarks.

Walking Trails

It's well worth spending a day exploring the well-marked trails around park headquarters. There's a rough map available at the reception desk which shows all the trails and points of interest.

All of the trails link up with others at some stage, so you can spend the whole day walking at a leisurely pace through the beautiful jungle. Some interesting plants and, if you're lucky, the occasional animal can be seen along the Liwagu Trail, which follows the river of the same name. When it

rains, watch out for slippery paths and armies of leeches.

At 11.15 am each day there is a guided walk which starts from the administration building and lasts for one to two hours. It's well worth taking and follows an easy path. The knowledgeable guide points out flowers, plants and insects along the way. If you set out from KK early it's possible to arrive at the park in time for the guided walk.

Walking Times

The times listed here are those published by the Sabah Parks and are fairly conservative. Most people with a reasonable level of fitness will find it takes less than this.

Path	Time Required
Park Headquarters to Power Station	1½ hours
	(15 minutes' drive)
Power Station to Telekom Station	1½ hours
Telekom Station to Layang Layang	1½ hours
Layang Layang to Pakka Cave	1½ hours
Pakka Cave to Panar Laban	1½ hours
Panar Laban to Sayat-Sayat	1 hour
Sayat-Sayat to Summit	1½ hours

Hiring Guides & Porters

Hiring a guide (at least from Panar Laban to the summit) is supposedly compulsory although a lot of people get away without one. Porters are optional.

Neither the guides nor the porters are employees of the national park organisation, but they work closely together and when you book accommodation at the national parks office the form you are handed will specify that you have 'requested' a guide to stand by at the park headquarters at 7 am on the day you intend to climb the mountain. The guide's fee is a minimum of M$25 per day for one to three people, M$28 for four to six people, M$30 for seven to eight (the maximum).

A porter's fee is M$25 per day for a maximum load of 11 kg up to the Panar Laban huts and M$1 for every extra half kg. For the second segment up to the Sayat-Sayat huts it's M$28 per day and M$1.20 for every half kg over 11 kg. It's advisable to pay in advance.

Local guides and porters are usually members of the Kadazan tribe. Generally, older guides are more efficient, reliable and knowledgeable than younger guides.

There are many conflicting opinions about the use of guides. The national parks organisation says they're compulsory because climbers can 'easily lose their way on the rock surface when the fog and mist start covering the upper part of the mountain', which is probably true if you've never climbed mountains before.

Another theory is that in making it compulsory to hire a guide, the chances of people stealing pitcher plants and smuggling them out of the country are drastically reduced.

There's a guarded gate at the power station to keep people from going without guides, but if you start early you pass the gate before the ranger starts his shift. It's an expensive nuisance if you can't share the cost of a guide with other people.

The best compromise you can make is to tell the Sabah Parks office that you intend to share a guide with other people when you get there – this is no problem. Some travellers say that you can try tagging on to the end of a group as they pass the gate with their guide, then break away and climb on your own.

Booking Accommodation

Overnight accommodation is provided at the park headquarters itself on the Ranau road, at Poring Hot Springs, in the new resthouse on the mountain and in mountain huts at 3360 metres and at 3750 metres on the summit trail.

Try to book as far in advance as possible (at least several days to a week) and note that on weekends, school and public holidays all the accommodation may be taken up.

You can, if you like, make your reservations by post or phone, but they will not be confirmed until fully paid for. The postal address is Sabah Parks (Reservations), PO Box 626, Kota Kinabalu, Sabah. In Kota Kinabalu you can contact the reservation clerk on 088-211585 and the administrative clerk on 088-211652.

Most travellers, however, make their reservations by calling at the Sabah Parks office, Jalan Tun Fuad Stephens, which is centrally located and is open Monday to Thursday from 8 am to 12.45 pm and 2 to 4.15 pm; on Fridays from 8 to 11.30 am and 2 to 4.15 pm, and on Saturdays from 8 am to 12.45 pm.

In making up your mind on how long you want to stay at Mt Kinabalu you should bear in mind that the weather on the mountain is very unpredictable. You can be in bright sunshine one minute and soaked to the skin the next. Just after dawn is the best time to catch the summit free of clouds. You might be lucky and get a clear dawn the first morning you go to the summit, but if you don't, or it's raining, you'll see absolutely nothing and will feel bitterly disappointed at having to go back down. If at all possible, book for four nights with two of them in the mountain huts.

Most people shorten the walk by well over an hour by taking the minibus from the park headquarters up as far as the power station. It leaves every day around 7.30 am (check-in at 7 am) and takes only about 15 minutes. The cost varies on the number or people: from one to five people it's M$10 per head, for six to 13 people it's just M$2.

One super-fit traveller wrote that he walked from the park headquarters to the summit and back down again in one day – but I wouldn't recommend it as you get to the top in the afternoon when it's likely to be cloudy. In any case Mt Kinabalu is quite high enough for altitude sickness problems to occur; some acclimatisation is recommended.

Places to Stay & Eat

Park Headquarters There's a variety of excellent accommodation at the park headquarters. The cheapest place is the 46-bed *Old Fellowship Hostel* which costs M$10 per person, or M$3 for students with official ID.

The 52-bed *New Hostel* is more expensive at M$15 (M$4 for students). Both hostels are clean and comfortable, have cooking facilities and a dining area with an open fireplace.

Blankets and pillows are provided free of charge. In the early hours of the morning you get a brilliant view of Mt Kinabalu from the balcony of the New Hostel.

The rest of the accommodation at park headquarters is very expensive. The twin-bed cabins are M$50 and annexes for up to four people are M$100. On weekends and during school holidays these rates jump to M$80 and M$160 respectively. There are two-bedroom chalets which can sleep up to six people and they cost M$150 (M$200) per night. Then there are the deluxe cabins, single storey for five people and double storey for seven people, costing M$150 (M$200) and M$180 (M$250) respectively.

At the top of the range, there's the *Kinabalu Lodge*, outside the park on the main road, where one unit costs M$360 per night and sleeps eight people. The *Hotel Perkasa Kundasang* (tel 088-79511) is a few km along the main road towards Ranau, and has 74 rooms which start from about M$70.

There are two places where you can buy meals at park headquarters. The cheaper and more popular of the two is the restaurant known as *Kinabalu Dalsam*, down below reception, which offers Malay, Chinese and Western food at reasonable prices. There's also a small shop which sells a limited range of tinned foods, chocolate, beer, spirits, cigarettes, T-shirts, bread, eggs and margarine.

The other restaurant is in the main administration building just past the hostels. It's more expensive than the Dalsam though the food is quite good. Both restaurants are open from 7 am to 9 pm.

On the Mountain On your way up to the summit you will have to stay overnight at one of the mountain huts or the 54-bed *Laban Rata Rest House* at Panar Laban which costs M$25 per person in four-bed rooms. Surprisingly it has both electricity and a restaurant.

The mountain huts are equipped with wooden bunks and mattresses, gas stoves, cooking facilities and some cooking utensils. You can hire sleeping bags for M$2, so there's no point in lugging your own all the way to the top of the mountain. Take a torch and your own toilet paper. Don't expect a warm Swiss-type chalet with a blazing fire at these huts. They're just tin sheds with the absolute minimum of facilities.

There are three huts at 3300 metres: the 12-bed *Waras* and *Panar Laban* huts and the 44-bed *Guntin Lagadan Hut*; and there's also the 10-bed *Sayat-Sayat Hut* is at 3750 metres. A bed in any of these huts costs M$4 per person, M$1 for students and, if the huts are full, M$1 for anyone sleeping on the floor.

The huts at 3300 metres are the most popular as it's as far as most people can comfortably get in one day, and there's a canteen in the nearby Laban Rata Rest House which is not only open for regular meals but also opens from 2 to 3 am so you can grab some breakfast before attempting the summit.

On the other hand, if you stay overnight in the Sayat-Sayat Hut you don't have to get up in the middle of the night in order to reach the summit by dawn. Possibly the extra effort on the first day is worth the reward of a slightly easier day on the next. The key for the Sayat-Sayat Hut is kept by the guy who rents the sleeping bags at the Panar Laban huts, so make sure you collect it (and a sleeping bag) on the way through if you intend staying at Sayat-Sayat.

As far as sleep is concerned, it doesn't make much difference where you stay; unless you've spent a lot of time in the mountains recently you'll probably sleep quite fitfully – the air is quite thin up there. It's *very* cold in the early mornings (around 0°C!), so take warm clothing with you!

Getting There & Away

Bus – To/From Kota Kinabalu There are several minibuses daily from KK to Ranau which depart up to about 1 pm. The 85-km trip as far as park headquarters takes about 1½ to two hours and the fare is around M$8.

If you're heading back towards KK, minibuses pass the park headquarters between about 8 am and 12 noon to 1 pm daily. Stand by the side of the main road and

Top, Bottom: Chinese Temple, Bandar Seri Begawan, Brunei (HF, ST)

Omar Ali Saifudin Mosque (BH)

wave them down. If you can't be bothered to wait, hitching is quite easy.

Bus – To/From Kota Belud & Tamparuli
Tamparuli is where the road up the coast to Kudat branches for Kota Belud and Ranau. If you've been visiting Mengkabong Water Village or Kota Belud and are heading for Kinabalu National Park, then first go to Tamparuli.

From Tamparuli there are several minibuses and share-taxis daily to Ranau which, like the ones from KK, pass right by the park headquarters. The minibuses cost about M$4 and a taxi will cost you at least double. The journey to the park headquarters takes about two hours from Kota Belud, one hour from Tamparuli.

Bus – To/From Ranau & Sandakan
To get from the park headquarters to Ranau, wait at the side of the main road for a minibus going to Ranau or Sandakan, or hitch. There is a large bus to Sandakan which passes park headquarters around 9 am and there are other minibuses which pass Kinabalu National Park on their way to Ranau, but the last one goes by before 2 pm.

The 22-km journey to Ranau takes about half an hour and costs M$3, while the trip to Sandakan takes at least six hours and costs M$27, although it will become quicker as the road is improved.

RANAU
Ranau is just a small provincial town halfway between Kota Kinabalu and Sandakan. Nothing much ever happens yet it has some remarkably friendly people. Few travellers stay overnight since the big attraction is Poring Hot Springs about 19 km north of the town. If you arrive late in the afternoon during the week, however, you may be forced to stay overnight, as the only transport available to Poring would be chartered taxis which are far from cheap. Although it's usually quiet, Ranau does have a very

colourful and busy tamu on the first of each month.

Places to Stay
Hotel Ranau (tel 088-875531) is the first place you see when entering the town opposite the petrol stations. Rooms start at M$23 for a single without air-con.

There is also a *Government Rest House* (tel 75534) which costs M$12 per person for rooms with attached bathroom and air-con. It's a little way from the centre and you may not get a room if there're government officials in the area.

People have been known to stay at the Catholic church which has one guest room, but it's not really for travellers. If you do stay there, make sure you offer a donation to the priest.

Places to Eat
Probably the best place to eat is the Chinese restaurant around the corner from Hotel Ranau on the top side of the first block. The food is good, the menu varied and prices very reasonable.

The *Leang Leang Restaurant* is also very

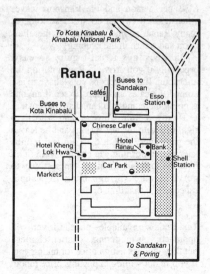

good and there are at least half a dozen others, but most close early.

Getting There & Away

Bus – To/From Kota Kinabalu Minibuses and taxis depart daily up to about 2 pm, cost M$10 and take about three hours.

Bus – To/From Sandakan Minibuses leave Ranau for Sandakan from around 7.30 am, cost M$25 and take at least six hours, although this should decrease as the road is gradually improved. The most comfortable vehicle is probably the large bus which leaves KK for Sandakan at 6.30 am, arriving in Ranau around 9.30 am. The last minibus to Sandakan leaves Ranau around 2.30 pm and if there are no spare seats you can sit on your pack in the aisle – not exactly comfortable.

Bus – To/From Poring Hot Springs On weekends it's easy and cheap to get to the hot springs from Ranau. Drivers in pick-ups cruise round the blocks shouting, 'Poring, Poring!'. The price is more or less fixed at M$3 per person and the transport leaves when it's full (which doesn't take long, as many Ranau people go there for the afternoon and return in the evening).

On weekdays it isn't quite so easy, especially if you arrive in Ranau during the afternoon. If this happens you'll have to ask around the cafes and shops to see if anyone is going there and you can share the cost.

There's a little Chinese man who lives right opposite the hot springs and he leaves the park every day at 6.30 am and returns later in the morning. He charges M$5 (a bit over the top) but it's about the best way to get from the springs back to Ranau, especially at that time of day.

Taxi Taxis *are* available – and the drivers will approach you muttering, 'charter, charter', but they will ask a high price for taking you. If you're not willing to pay this price (about

M$15) then you'll have to stay in Ranau overnight and try again the next morning when your chances of reasonably priced transport are much better. The road to Poring is a dead-end so hitching a ride is difficult.

PORING HOT SPRINGS

The Poring Hot Springs are also part of the Kinabalu National Park but are 43 km away from the park headquarters and 19 km north of Ranau.

Developed by the Japanese during WW II, the steaming, sulphurous water is channelled into pools and tubs which attract people who go there to relax tired muscles after the trek to the summit. The tubs are of varying sizes and can fit from two to eight people, and have hot and cold water taps so you can mix your ideal temperature. As one traveller put it, 'Where else could you take a hot bath in the night with the stars above and the sounds of the jungle around?'

As at Kinabalu park headquarters, there are several km of forest trails around the springs which lead to some attractive waterfalls and dark caves. You can swim in the pool at the base of one waterfall, a 35-minute walk. There's also a swimming pool set among gardens, flowers, trees and hordes of butterflies.

A recent addition to the facilities here, and a very worthwhile and unusual one at that, is the 'Jungle Canopy Walkway'. It consists of series of rope walkways suspended in the trees well above the jungle floor (up to 30 metres at its highest) and it offers a unique chance of a monkey's-eye view of the surrounding forest. It's totally safe and great fun – well worth the M$5 entry (payable at the entrance to the hot springs). The only problem is that it's only open from 10 am to 4 pm so the best times for a sighting of some jungle wildlife is missed. Let them know at the office that the opening times are wrong – if they're lobbied enough they may change this.

No permit is required to visit the springs but if you intend staying overnight, as is the case at Mt Kinabalu it is important to reserve accommodation at the Sabah Parks office in

Kota Kinabalu in advance. This is especially true on weekends; during the week it's not usually a problem to roll up without a booking. See the Mt Kinabalu section for full reservation details.

Places to Stay & Eat

The 24-bed *Poring Hostel* costs M$8 per person (M$2 for students) and blankets and pillows are provided free of charge. Each room contains eight beds and there is a clean, spacious kitchen with gas cookers. There's a camping ground which costs M$2 per night; pillows and blankets can be hired for 50 sen each.

There are more expensive cabins; the *New Cabin* costs M$60 per night (M$80 on weekends and school holidays) and has two twin-bed rooms, while the *Old Cabin* costs M$75 (M$100) per night and has three twin rooms. The mosquitoes at Poring are vicious but thankfully all the rooms have netting.

There are cooking facilities at Poring but you should take your own food from Ranau as there's only one small, expensive shop outside the park and it has a very limited range. If staying overnight in the hostel you'll be issued with a set of crockery, cutlery and as many saucepans as you want but you must account for these on leaving.

Getting There & Away

Access is by minibus, taxi or hitching the 19 km along the bitumen road from Ranau – see Getting There & Away in the Ranau section for details.

Eastern Sabah

SANDAKAN

The former capital city of Sabah, Sandakan, is today a major commercial centre where the products of the interior – rattan, timber, rubber, copra, palm oil and even birds' nests from the Gomantong Caves – are brought to be loaded onto boats for export.

The city lies at the entrance to a huge bay and its docks sprawl along the waterfront for many km. The bay itself is dotted with islands, some of them with excellent beaches. There is always the hustle and bustle of boats, large and small.

The main attractions are well outside the city, however. At Sepilok is one of the world's three orang-utan sanctuaries. There's another one in Sumatra, west of Medan, and one in Semenggoh, Sarawak. The Sepilok sanctuary is well worth visiting.

There's also the Gomantong Caves across the other side of the bay, where edible birds' nests are collected for that famous Chinese delicacy, and offshore there's one of the world's few turtle sanctuaries where giant turtles come to lay their eggs.

Orientation

The centre of Sandakan is very compact and consists of three main blocks built between the seafront and the wooded hills on which the Governor's residence sits. In these blocks you'll find many of the hotels and restaurants, banks, MAS office, the local bus stand and the long-distance minibus stands. Confusion arises when you are trying to find a certain address here though, because you have Lebuh Dua (2nd St), then Lorong Dua (2nd Lane) and so on for Jalan Tiga (3rd) and Empat (4th) which all run parallel. For good measure Jalan Lima (5th St) cuts across the lot of them!

The minibus stand for local blue buses (Labuk Bus Co) is squashed in by the waterfront. All other local minibuses leave from the stand just past the old Port Authority building. The long-distance minibuses go from the bus stand just by the Sandakan Community Centre at the western end of the centre.

The Sabah Parks office is in the centre, but the immigration and forestry departments are close to the airport, about 11 km from the centre along the Ranau road.

Information

The post office is on Jalan Leila at the western end of town, just past the Shop & Save Supermarket. The Sabah Parks office (tel 089-273453) is on the 9th floor of Wisma

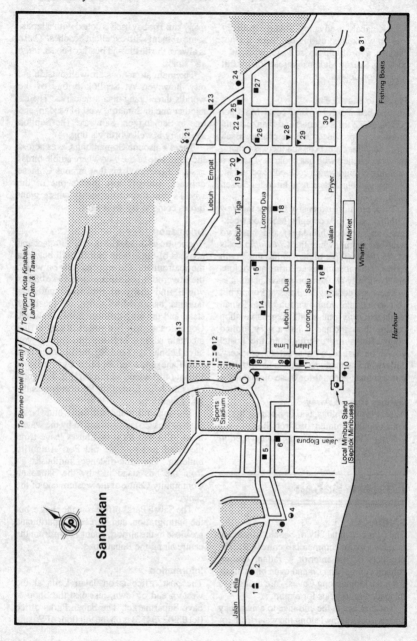

Sandakan

To Airport, Kota Kinabalu, Lahad Datu & Tawau

To Borneo Hotel (0.5 km)

Sports Stadium

Jalan Elopura

Local Minibus Stand (Sepilok Minibuses)

Jalan Leila

Lebuh Empat

Lebuh Tiga

Lorong Dua

Lebuh Dua

Lorong Satu

Jalan Pryer

Jalan Lima

Market

Wharfs

Harbour

Fishing Boats

Khoo Siak Chew at the end of Lebuh Tiga. This is where you need to come to make a reservation to visit the Turtle Islands National Park (Taman Pulau Penya). The office is open Monday to Thursday from 8 am to 12.45 pm and 2 to 4.15 pm, Friday from 8 to 11.30 am and 2 to 4.15 pm, and Saturday from 8 am to 12.45 pm.

The immigration office is in the secretariat building, just past the roundabout at Batu 7 on the Ranau road, 11 km from the centre of town. Take any Batu 7 or higher bus (ie, Batu 8, 12, 19, 30, etc).

For a permit for Gomantong Caves you need to pay a visit to the Urban Forest & Forest Recreation Division of the Forestry Department, housed in a flash new building at Batu 7, about 500 metres past the 11-km peg on the Ranau road. The white two-storey building is on the left, set in a spacious garden. If you come to the golf course you've come too far. While you're out there pay a visit to the Forestry Department museum in the same building.

The MAS office (tel 089-273966) is on the ground floor of the Sabah Building, right in the centre of town. It is open Monday to Friday from 8 am to 4.30 pm, Saturday from 8 am to 3 pm and Sunday from 8 am to 12 noon.

Things to See & Do

The **waterfront** at Sandakan, with its motley collection of fishing boats, barges, ferries and ocean-going container ships as well as the vegetable and fish markets, is worth wandering around for a morning or afternoon, but apart from this there isn't a great deal to see in Sandakan itself – the points of interest are all out of town.

Sandakan also has a **Buddhist temple** in the suburb of Sibuga which is worth a look, and from there you can get an excellent view over Sandakan Bay. Take a Leila bus to Sibuga and ask for the temple.

Another interesting place is the **floating village** of Tanjung Aru, on an island in Sandakan Bay. There's a government resthouse on the island or you can just day trip from Sandakan. To get there, charter a boat from the wharf behind the bus stand for around M\$12, or hitch a ride on a fishing boat for a couple of ringgit.

Places to Stay – bottom end

It's difficult to find a reasonable, cheap hotel in Sandakan. Many are overpriced and very poor value; the cheaper ones are generally short-time places. Most travellers seem to head straight for *Uncle Tan's* (tel 089-669516) out at Batu 7 near the airport. Tan is

---

- ■ **PLACES TO STAY**

  5   Hotel Gaya
  6   Hotel New Sabah
  11 Hotel Nak
  14 Hotel Paris
  15 Hotel City View
  16 Mayfair Hotel
  18 Malaysia Hotel
  23 Hotel London
  25 Hotel En Khin
  26 Merlin Hotel
  27 Hotel Hung Wing

- ▼ **PLACES TO EAT**

  11 Apple Fast Food Restaurant
  17 Habeeb, Aysha & Buhari Restaurants
  19 Fairwood Fastfood
  20 Superman Ice Cream Parlour
  22 Emas Seafood Restoran
  28 Fat Cat Restaurant
  29 Hong Kong Fast Food
  30 Restaurant Taj

  OTHER

  1   Post Office, Night Market
  2   Shop & Save Supermarket
  3   Sandakan Community Centre
  4   Bus Stand
  7   Hong Kong & Shanghai Bank
  8   Chartered Bank
  9   MAS
  10 Old Port Authority Building
  12 Town Hall
  13 Police
  21 Mosque
  24 Wisma Khoo Siak Chew
  31 Shopping Complex

a friendly retired schoolteacher who takes travellers into his house. He charges M$15 for a dorm bed, which includes a huge breakfast and free tea and coffee throughout the day, and also serves evening meals, usually of excellent local dishes, for a bargain M$5. There is room for a dozen or so people and the atmosphere is very friendly. As a sideline Tan runs very low-key and exceedingly cheap trips to both the Turtle Islands and to a jungle camp he has on the lower Kinabatangan River. To get there from town take a Batu 7 Airport bus and get off at Taman Khong Lok, the first street on the right after the roundabout. Tan's house is at the top of the rise, about 500 metres along on the right. From the airport it's an easy walk. If you are arriving by bus from Ranau, some of the drivers know Tan's and will let you off right outside if you tell them.

All the other so-called cheap accommodation is in the centre of town and is no great bargain. One of the better places is the *Hotel Hung Wing* (tel 089-218895) on Jalan Tiga. It's a middle-range hotel with some cheaper rooms which are great value. Generally, the higher the floor, the cheaper the room. If you're willing to climb to the 6th floor, you'll find clean, spacious rooms with attached bathroom and fan for M$20/30. Air-con rooms range from M$40/50 on the 5th and 6th floors to M$55/65 on the lower floors.

Also on Jalan Tiga is the *Hotel Paris* (tel 089-218488) which has clean rooms from M$25/30 with fan and bath, or M$38/48 with air-con and bath. The *Mayfair Hotel* (tel 089-219855) at 24 Jalan Pryer only air-con rooms and these go for M$32/40 with bath attached. The *Hotel New Sabah* (tel 089-218711) on Jalan Singapura is similarly priced.

A good, clean Chinese place is the *Hotel En Khin* (tel 089-217377) at 50 Lebuh Tiga, almost opposite the Hung Wing; all rooms are air-con with bath attached and cost M$32/40.

Places to Stay – middle

The middle-range hotels are all similar in standard and their cheaper rooms go quickly.

The *Federal Hotel* (tel 089-219611) on Jalan Tiga has rooms with air-con and own bathroom from M$38 on the upper floors, and more expensive rooms lower down.

The *Hotel London* (tel 089-216371) on Jalan Empat is a clean air-con place with rooms from M$40/50 with attached bath.

Places to Stay – top end

At the top of the range there's the new *Hotel City View* (tel 089-271122) on Jalan Tiga. Rooms cost M$120/140, although a 35% discount was being offered when I checked it out.

Another place is the *Hotel Nak* (tel 089-216988) on Jalan Edinburgh, which has rooms with air-con, bath and TV for M$83/103.

Further out of town there's the *Sabah Hotel* (tel 089-213299) which has rooms from M$150. It is on the hill out of town and has a considerable amount of old world charm. There is also an Indonesian and a Chinese restaurant there.

Places to Eat

Sandakan is full of cheap Chinese restaurants and coffee houses serving the standard rice or noodles with fried vegetables, so if that's what you're after you'll be well satisfied.

For good Malay food try the *Habeeb Restoran* on Jalan Pryer. They do excellent murtabak, and also have an air-con room upstairs. There's a couple of similar places close by including the *Aysha* and *Buhari*.

For a Western breakfast or snack there're a few choices. The best is probably *Fairwood Fastfood* on Jalan Tiga, which is open from 7 am and has a good value set breakfast. Another possibility is the *Apple Fast Food* restaurant in the ground floor of the Hotel Nak on Jalan Edinburgh. Wisma Sandakan is the multistoreyed peach-coloured office block which backs onto the hill behind town. On the 2nd floor there are a few fast-food possibilities including *Fat Cat Restaurant* and *Satay Ria*, and the *Restoran Gili Padi* which serves good local dishes.

For absolutely no-frills tucker try one of

the stalls upstairs in the central market. A couple of ringgit will get you a decent meal although choose your stall carefully as the hygiene standards are a bit rough. There's more market food at the night market which sets up outside the post office each evening.

The *Superman Ice Cream Parlour* on Jalan Tiga serves very good ice creams and juices.

Getting There & Away

Air Sandakan is on the MAS domestic network and there are regular flights to: Kota Kinabalu (seven daily, M$69), Kudat (daily, M$54), Lahad Datu (twice daily, M$40), Semporna (three weekly, M$50) and Tawau (twice daily, M$61).

Road All long-distance minibuses leave from the area next to the footbridge over Jalan Tiga; local minibuses leave from the area next to the old Port Authority building. Most long-distance minibuses depart for their destinations between 5 and 6 am.

There are buses to Kota Kinabalu which cost about M$35 and take eight hours. You can take the same transport to Kinabalu National Park headquarters for M$27. Minibuses to Ranau cost M$25 and the journey takes up to six hours. The road as far

as Batu 32 (where the Lahad Datu roads heads off to the south-east) and on to Telupid should now be surfaced all the way.

There is one large Bungaraya Co bus which departs Sandakan for Lahad Datu and Tawau daily at 5.30 am, but there are also many minibuses which leave throughout the morning to Lahad Datu, some going on to Tawau. The trip to Lahad Datu takes about three hours and costs M$15. The road from Batu 32 to the Kinabatangan River is still not made and is in a pretty terrible state, but from the river to Lahad Datu it's in very good condition.

The contracts for making the road from the Batu 32 to Kinabatangan River, and from Ranau to Telupid, have been awarded so work should be under way.

Getting Around

If you're arriving or leaving by air, the airport is about 11 km from the city. There are minibuses throughout the day connecting the two which leave from the local minibus stand. To get to the airport from the centre take a Batu 7 Airport minibus. A taxi to or from the airport costs M$10. Taxis can be found in the side streets which run off Jalan Tiga and Lorong Dua.

The Sandakan Death Marches

Sandakan was the site of a Japanese POW camp and in September 1944 there were 1800 Australian and 600 British troops interned here. What is probably not widely known is that more Australians died here than on the building of the infamous Burma Railway.

Early in the war, food and conditions were not too bad, and the death rate was only around three per month, but as it became clearer to the Japanese officers that they didn't have enough staff to guard against any rebellion in the camps, and that the Allies were closing in, they decided to cut the rations to the prisoners to weaken them. The death rate started to rise and disease spread. It was also decided to move the prisoners inland, 250 km through the jungle to Ranau.

On 28 January 1945, 470 prisoners set off; 313 made it to Ranau. On the second march 570 started from Sandakan; 118 reached Ranau. The third march consisted of the last men in the camp and numbered 537. Conditions on the marches were deplorable; many men had no boots, rations were less than minimal and many men fell by the wayside. Those who couldn't walk when the camp was evacuated by the Japanese were disposed of.

Once in Ranau the men who had survived were put to work carrying 20 kg sacks of rice over hilly country 40 km to Paginatan. Disease and starvation took a horrendous toll and by the end of July 1945 there were no prisoners left in Ranau; the only survivors from the 2400 at Sandakan were six Australians who had escaped either from Ranau or during the marches.

AROUND SANDAKAN
Australian War Memorial

There's an Australian War Memorial just past the government buildings at Batu 8 on the road to Ranau. This was the site of the Japanese POW camp and was the starting point for the 'death marches' to Ranau. There's just a couple of bits of rusting machinery around, but the place has an eerie air, and local ghost stories abound.

To get there take any Batu 8 or higher bus and get off at the Esso station about one km on the right past the government buildings at the airport roundabout. Walk along Jalan Rimba for about 10 minutes; the camp is on the right about 100 metres after it turns to gravel.

Sepilok Orang-Utan Rehabilitation Centre

Located at Sepilok, about 25 km from Sandakan, this is one of only three orang-utan sanctuaries in the world. It was established in 1964 and now covers 4000 hectares.

Apes are brought here to be rehabilitated to forest life and so far the centre has handled about 80 of them, but only about 20 still return regularly to be fed. It's unlikely you'll

Orang-Utans

see anywhere near this number at feeding time – three or four is a more likely number.

The apes are fed from two platforms, one in the middle of the forest (platform B) about 30-minute walk from the centre, and the other close to the headquarters (platform A). The latter platform is for the juvenile orang-utans and they are fed daily at 10 am and 2.30 pm. At platform B the adolescent apes which have been returned to the forest are fed daily at 11 am. They are just fed milk and bananas, and there's no guarantee they'll show up as this feeding is purely supplementary to what they can find for themselves in the jungle. For this feeding the rangers leave from outside the Nature Education Centre at 10.30 am daily.

Of the ones which have returned to the wild, females often come back to the feeding platforms when they're pregnant and stay near the sanctuary centre until they've given birth, after which time they go back to the forest.

You are allowed to wander through the forest at your own pace and risk. Although the orang-utans are not aggressive animals, the proboscis monkeys, who live in the mangrove swamps, have been known to attack humans. It's not uncommon to see snakes and lizards in the forest.

Don't be in so much of a hurry to see the orang-utans that you miss the forest and if it's been raining watch out for leeches! If you're taking photographs you'll need to have ASA 400 film available (it's quite dark in the forest).

The reserve also has a Nature Education Centre which is open to the public. Some information is displayed about the animals of the reserve and there is a daily video presentation.

Peace Corps and CUSO (Canadian University Services Overseas) volunteers have helped to establish a small museum as well as a library and film theatre. They have also set up a self-guided nature trail and longer trails, one leading to a good spot for swimming.

As well as the orang-utans, there is a couple of Sumatran rhinos at the centre, and the rhino 'stockade' is open from 9.30 to 10.30 am and 2.30 to 3 pm.

Visiting hours at the centre are Saturday to Thursday from 9 am to 12 noon and 2 to 4 pm, and on Friday from 9 to 11.30 am and 2 to 4 pm.

Don't miss this place; it's well worth a visit.

About 500 metres before the rehabilitation centre is a Forest Research Centre which has, among other things, a good library and entomology museum and may be worth a look.

Getting There & Away To get to the centre take the blue Labuk bus marked 'Sepilok Batu 14' from the local bus stand next to the central market on the waterfront. The fare is M$1.20 and the journey takes about 45 minutes. There are departures at 9.20 and 11.20 am and 1 and 3 pm. There are also other minibuses which make the trip every hour or so.

TURTLE ISLANDS NATIONAL PARK

The Pulau Penyu National Park comprises three small islands which lie 32 km north of Sandakan. Pulau Selingan, Pulau Bakungan Kecil and Pulau Gulisan are visited by marine turtles which come ashore to lay their eggs, mostly between the months of August and October each year.

The green turtle is a strong, slow-moving creature, commonly found on Pulau Selingan and Pulau Bakungan Kecil. It weighs between 50 and 90 kg and lays around 180 eggs. The hawksbill turtle lays it's eggs on Pulau Gulisan. It's much smaller than the green turtle, weighing between 25 and 55 kg.

Places to Stay

It's not possible to visit the turtle islands on a day trip, so any excursion involves staying overnight. The only accommodation is at a *Sabah Parks Chalet* on Pulau Selingan, which costs M$30 per person per night. Good cooking facilities are provided but you need to bring all your own provisions. Bookings must be made in advance at the Sabah

Parks office in Sandakan as facilities are limited.

Getting There & Away

Unfortunately, getting out to the islands is not an easy task. There are no regular services so you'll probably have to charter an expensive boat to take you there. If you can manage to round up a few people who also want to visit the sanctuary, it's well worth chartering a boat.

Uncle Tan in Sandakan organises trips out to the islands and it's about as cheap as you'll get it. He charges M$200 per person for a two-day trip, and this includes the chalet accommodation, meals and transport, so is not bad value. Travel agent prices are much higher.

GOMANTONG CAVES

These caves are across the other side of the bay from Sandakan and about 20 km inland. They are famous as a source of swiftlets' nests, which are the raw material for that famous Chinese delicacy, birds' nest soup.

You can watch the nests being collected from the roof of the cave, as they are at Niah in Sarawak, by men climbing long, precariously placed bamboo poles.

Permits to visit the caves are required and you need to get these in advance from the Forest Department headquarters in Sandakan.

Getting There & Away

The problem with the caves is their inaccessibility. Travel agencies will arrange a trip, but their costs are high and outside the range of most travellers' budgets. If you're heading for Sarawak visit the Niah Caves as they are easily accessible and there is good budget accommodation available. If you still want to visit Gomantong then, again, Uncle Tan in Sandakan is probably the best person to see.

It is possible to visit the caves using public transport but it may involve a lot of walking. First, take any Lahad Datu minibus and ask for the Sukau turn-off, then hitch or walk the six km to the park headquarters. On the return trip there is a bus from Sukau to KK which passes the park around 4.30 pm.

KINABATANGAN RIVER

The Kinabatangan River is one of the main rivers in Sabah and flows generally northeast to enter the sea east of Sandakan. Although logging is widespread along the upper reaches of the river, below the Sandakan to Lahad Datu road the jungle is relatively untouched. It is an ideal place to observe the wildlife of Borneo, and sightings of the native proboscis monkeys are common along the banks in the morning and evening. Orang-utans are also seen from time to time.

This area is virtually inaccessible but Uncle Tan (see the Sandakan section) has a jungle camp about an hour downstream from the Sandakan to Lahad Datu road, and while it is extremely basic, it does give the traveller the opportunity to get out of the towns and stay in the jungle. He charges M$15 per person per day for accommodation and meals. It's not the Hilton but is perfectly adequate. The only other charge is M$130 for transport from Sandakan to the camp and return, so obviously it's better if you have a few days to spare. Many travellers come to the camp with the intention of staying a couple of days, and stay much longer. It's well worth a visit.

LAHAD DATU

Lahad Datu is a busy little plantation and timber service town of 20,000 people. There are very few tourists and probably the only reason for visiting is if you are en route to or from the excellent Danum Valley Field Centre, 80 km west of Lahad Datu, run by the Sabah Foundation.

The town is full of Filipino and Indonesian migrants/refugees and the streets are full of women trying to make a few ringgit selling cigarettes.

Information

The Sabah Foundation office (tel 089-81092) is on the 2nd floor of the Hap Seng building on the main street, in front of the fancy new 'mini secretariat' building. You can't miss this building as it's the tallest in town and has the name across the top in three-metre high letters. It's here that you need to report to before heading off for Danum. It is possible to make reservations from here but as these have to be referred to KK anyway, it's better to do them in KK yourself. The office in Lahad Datu is open normal office hours.

The MAS office is on the ground floor of the Hotel Mido on the main street.

Places to Stay

The budget accommodation scene here is a disaster – there isn't any. Try not to get marooned here, and this should be easy enough as the transport to and from Danum Valley goes at such a time that you can make onward connections the same day.

The cheapest place that isn't a brothel is the *Rumah Tumpangan Malaysia* (tel 089-83358) just off the main street on a side street between the Ocean Hotel and the cinema. It's basic but clean enough with rooms with fan and common bath for M$26/31.

Next up the scale is the *Ocean Hotel* (tel 089-81700) on the main street opposite the Hap Seng building. It's a very good hotel with good sized rooms, all with air-con and attached bath, for M$38/48. Similar in price and facilities is the *Hotel Perdama* (tel 089-81400) in the same area, while the *Hotel Full Wah* (tel 089-83948), opposite the Chinese temple behind the cinema, charges M$43/51 with air-con, bath and TV.

The top place in town is the *Hotel Mido* (tel 089-81800), right on the main street. Rooms here start at M$52/66.

Places to Eat

Fortunately the lack of accommodation options doesn't spill over into the eating department; there are plenty of cheap restaurants and food stalls in Lahad Datu.

One of the best places for Muslim Malay food is the *Restoran Kabir* near the mini-Secretariat and the minibuses. They serve excellent curries, rotis and murtabak, and there is an air-con room upstairs.

In the evenings the hawkers set up their

stalls in the area behind the Hotel Mido and a couple of ringgit will get you a decent feed.

Getting There & Away

Air MAS operate services between Lahad Datu and Kota Kinabalu (three daily, M$88), Sandakan (twice daily, M$40) and Tawau (four times weekly, M$40).

Bus The long-distance minibuses leave from outside the buildings near the mini-Secretariat. There are frequent departures for Sandakan (3½ hours, M$10), Semporna (2½ hours, M$8) and Tawau (2½ hours, M$15). There are plenty of departures to all places up until around 3 pm. The road to Semporna and Tawau is one of the best in the state.

The Sabah Foundation vehicle to the Danum Valley Field Centre leaves from the Han Seng building on Monday, Wednesday and Friday at around 3 pm.

AROUND LAHAD DATU
Danum Valley Field Centre

Located on the Segama River 85 km west of Lahad Datu, this field centre has been set up by the Sabah Foundation and a number of private companies to provide facilities for research, education and recreation in an untouched rainforest area. It's curious that a number of the private companies are involved in logging in Sabah.

There are currently a number of local and foreign scientists carrying out research projects at the centre, and there are walking trails and other activities to keep you busy. It's a beautiful place and well worth a visit if you can afford it. Although not outrageously expensive the costs do mount up.

It's necessary to get a permit (M$15) and make bookings in advance, preferably with the Sabah Foundation office in Kota Kinabalu but, failing that, at the office in Lahad Datu. This is mainly because the vehicle which serves the centre has limited seating capacity and they need to know in advance how many passengers there'll be. See the Lahad Datu and KK sections for details of the offices.

A guide is obligatory on your first walk in

the forest from the centre and for this you have to pay M$20 for half a day.

Places to Stay & Eat There are two places to stay – a self-catering, 30-bed *hostel*, and a *rest house*. A bed in the hostel costs M$30, while the resthouse rooms go for M$45 per person.

Cooking facilities and utensils are provided in the hostel, but you need to bring all your own food. Resthouse guests, and anyone staying at the hostel, can get good meals at the resthouse at the rate of M$30 per day.

Getting There & Away A Sabah Foundation vehicle leaves the centre on Monday, Wednesday and Friday at 9 am, and returns from Lahad Datu on the same days at around 3 pm; the one-way cost is M$30. If you have to arrange your own transport from Lahad Datu it costs around M$130 to charter a vehicle to take you in.

SEMPORNA

Semporna, between Lahad Datu and Tawau, has a large stilt village and there's a cultured pearl farm off the coast there. About the only time you're likely to come through here is if you are on an organised diving trip to Sipadan Island, off the coast to the south-east. To travel to the island independently you have to catch the weekly boat from Tawau.

Semporna has a beautiful setting around a small bay, with picturesque islands not far offshore, but with the horrendous cost of accommodation here it's not worth coming just for that.

The MAS agent is Today Travel Services (tel 089-781077).

Places to Stay & Eat

The only hotel in Semporna is the very nice, but also expensive, *Dragon Inn Hotel*. It is part of the Semporna Ocean Tourism Centre (SOTC), which is a complex built in traditional floating village style over the water. The hotel itself is excellent and the rooms are tastefully decorated and furnished. The charge is M$68/78 for a room with bath, air-con and TV, and it includes a light breakfast. The SOTC is about 100 metres out in the bay, and is connected to the shore by a causeway which leads to the small port.

There is a *Government Rest House* out of town near the hospital but you'd be very lucky to get a bed.

The *Pearl City Chinese Restoran* forms the other part of the Semporna Ocean Tourism Centre. The food is excellent but this is definitely not a cheap restaurant. A cheaper option is the *Floating Restoran & Bar*, halfway along the short causeway which connects the town to the SOTC. For M$7 you can get an excellent meal of local fish.

In the town itself there are numerous Chinese kedai kopis as well as the popular *Restoran Kinabalu* which serves good Malay food.

Getting There & Away

Air MAS operates Twin Otter flights between Semporna and Sandakan (thrice weekly, M$50).

Bus There are plenty of minibuses between Semporna and Lahad Datu (2½ hours, 160 km, M$8) and Tawau (1½ hours, 110 km, M$4). There are also taxis to Tawau for M$10.

Boat If you are trying to get to Sipadan the only public boat is the MV *Sasaran Muhibbah Express* which leaves once a week from Tawau.

SIPADAN ISLAND

This island 36 km off the south-east coast of Sabah offers excellent diving, mainly because it is an oceanic island, ie it is the tip of a limestone pinnacle which rises from the ocean floor. This means that on the eastern side of the island the water drops away to around 600 metres and you are diving on the 'wall'.

The only problem with Sipadan is that visiting is pretty much limited to day trips, or to those people with bundles of cash. Borneo Divers in Kota Kinabalu offer all-inclusive trips to Sipadan which cost US$350 per person for a two-day trip ex KK,

up to US$700 for a seven-day trip. These prices include everything – transport, diving equipment, three dives per day, food and drinks and beach-hut accommodation.

Getting There & Away

For the day-trippers the MV *Sasaran Muhibbah Express* leaves Tawau on Sundays at 7.30 am, returning from the island the same day at 2 pm; the round-trip fare is M$35.

TAWAU

A mini-boomtown on the very south-east corner of Sabah close to the Indonesian border, Tawau is a provincial capital and centre for export of the products of the interior – timber, rubber, manila hemp, cocoa, copra and tobacco.

There's precious little to do or see in Tawau – it's just a town you pass through on the way to or from Tarakan in Kalimantan. Like Lahad Datu, Tawau has large numbers of Filipino and Indonesian refugees and immigrants.

Tawau is still a small, compact town with virtually everything in or near to the centre. The only time you may need to use public transport is to get to the airport which is a km out of town.

Information

The MAS office (tel 089-772703) is in the Wisma SASCO, close to the centre of town. It is open from 8 am to 4.30 pm Monday to Friday, from 8 am to 3 pm Saturday and 8 am to 12 noon on Sunday. Bouraq, the Indonesian feeder airline, uses Merdeka Travel at 41 Jalan Dunlop as its agent. The Indonesian Consulate is on Jalan Kuharsa, some distance from the centre of town, but at last report it wasn't issuing visas.

For bookings for the boat to Sipadan and Indonesia, the Sarasan Tinggi Co (tel 089-772455) has its office in the centre of town near the local bus stand.

Places to Stay – bottom end

So-called budget hotels in Tawau are, like

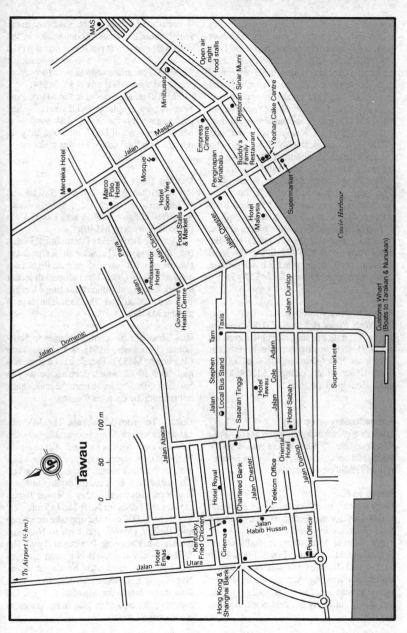

398 East Malaysia – Sabah – Eastern Sabah

those elsewhere in Sabah, outrageously priced and poor value for money. The best value is definitely the *Ambassador Hotel* (tel 089-772700) at 1872 Jalan Paya, just out of the centre. Rooms in this hotel are fairly large, have air-con and bath attached, and cost M$23 – for one, two or three people.

The clean and friendly *Hotel Soon Yee* (tel 089-772447) next to the market is not bad value at M$20 for a single with fan, and M$28/34 for singles/doubles with air-con and bath attached, although the rooms are definitely a bit on the small side.

The *Penginapan Kinabalu* is an older style lodging house and although the rooms are clean it is overpriced at M$20/30 for a single double with fan and common bath.

Two other more expensive places are the *Oriental Hotel* (tel 089-761602) and the *Hotel Tawau* (tel 089-771100) at 73 Jalan Chester; both these places have air-con rooms with attached bath for M$37/45.

Places to Stay – middle

The *Hotel Royal* (tel 089-773100) near the Empire Cinema has single/double rooms for M$69/81, all with air-con and bath. A similar place is the *Hotel Emas* (tel 089-762000) on Jalan Utara which charges M$69/80 for single/double rooms.

Places to Stay – top end

Tawau's top-end offering is the *Marco Polo Hotel* (tel 089-777988) where rooms go for M$89/108 on weekdays, and a very reasonable M$79/89 on weekends.

Places to Eat

There's plenty of choice in Tawau. For good Malay food try the *Restoran Sinar Murni* – good chicken curry here.

For hawker food, there're stalls in the Central Market, and the Tawau Food Plaza on the 2nd floor of the otherwise empty multistorey building. At night the food stalls along the road near the waterfront get going, and this is definitely the best place to eat at this time.

For a bit of a splurge, the restaurant in the *Hotel Emas* has a steamboat buffet in the evenings, and this is not bad value at M$16 per head. It also offers a Western breakfast for M$8. The coffee shop in the *Marco Polo Hotel* has a breakfast buffet for M$14.

The *Kublai Restaurant* in the Marco Polo Hotel is a major splurge and if you really feel extravagant try the bird's nest soup – at M$120 for a small bowl, although they do require 24 hours' notice for this dish.

Getting There & Away

Air MAS has flights between Tawau and Kota Kinabalu (seven daily, M$80), Sandakan (twice daily, M$61) and Lahad Datu (five times weekly, M$40).

There are also weekly international flights (on Sundays) to Tarakan in Kalimantan (Indonesia). It's just a 35-minute flight on a 12-seater Twin Otter. The Indonesian feeder airline, Bouraq, also flies three times weekly between Tawau and Tarakan. The fare is around M$180.

Bus There are frequent minibuses to Semporna (1½ hours, M$4) and Lahad Datu (2½ hours, M$15). There's also a large bus daily at 5.30 am which goes all the way to Sandakan. They all leave from the main street, not far from the Empress Cinema.

Boat – To/From Indonesia The MV *Sasaran Muhibbah Express* operates between Tawau and Nunukan and Tarakan in Kalimantan. It leaves from the customs wharf around the back of the large supermarket. The schedule is a bit complicated. On Monday, Wednesday and Friday it leaves Tawau at 9 am and heads for Nunukan (45 minutes, M$25, or 15,000 rp in the opposite direction) and Tarakan (M$60) and back to Nunukan the same day, leaving Tarakan at 3 pm. The following day it departs Nunukan at 1 pm and returns to Tawau. On Sunday it leaves Nunukan at 5.30 am instead of 1 pm so it can then leave Tawau for Sipadan at 7 am. On Saturday the boat sails just from Tawau to Nunukan and return.

If travelling to Nunukan or Tarakan, it's worth noting that visas cannot be issued on arrival; you must get one before crossing into Indonesia.

Boat – To/From Sipadan Island The same vessel that serves the Tawau-Tarakan run goes to Sipadan Island on Sundays for a day trip. It leaves Tawau at 7 am, returning from the island at 2 pm. The trip takes about two hours and costs M$35 return.

Getting Around

Probably the only time you'll need to use local transport is if you're going to or coming from the airport, which is one km from the centre. The best thing to do is take one of the hotel buses into town. They are provided by the Royal Hotel, Hotel Emas, Tawau Hotel and the Marco Polo Hotel. They're all free and you're under no obligation to stay at the hotel which runs the bus.

If you want to go from town to the airport, it may not be so easy. Hitching is very easy, or you can take a taxi for M$3.

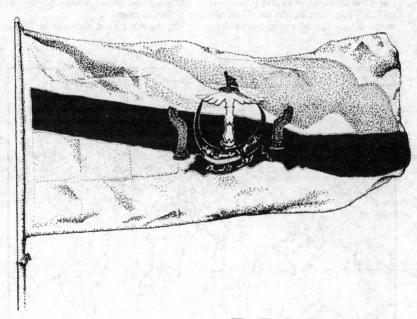

BRUNEI

Brunei Darussalam

Brunei is a tiny Islamic Sultanate lying in the north-eastern corner of Sarawak. It falls into that category of small states, remnants of empires, colonies and quirks of history that seem to captivate the imagination.

It is neither tradition nor romantic exoticism that makes this country fascinating – it is astounding wealth. The Sultan's gargantuan spending is the stuff of legends. In this skinflint world of penny-pinching it is unheard of, some would say sinful, to expend money as lavishly as this man does. It is also refreshing and few complain, for this population of only 250,000 is the second wealthiest per capita on earth. In 1990 it was estimated that the Sultan was worth a shade over US$25 billion – making him the richest man in the world. The oil comes mainly from offshore wells at Seria and Muara. Inland, the country remains almost as it has always been – undeveloped, unexploited and relatively untouched by the outside world.

The enormous wealth is displayed in various ways, most obviously in the ostentatious public buildings of the capital, Bandar Seri Begawan. The airport is suitable for a country 10 times the size of Brunei. Everything is done big here.

Perhaps more outlandish are the Sultan's personal buys: a US$350 million palace; a fleet of Italian exoticars said to be serviced by a mechanic flown in from Italy; and his grand passion – a fabulous polo farm with 200 Argentine ponies, some enjoying air-conditioned stalls.

On the other hand everyone in Brunei

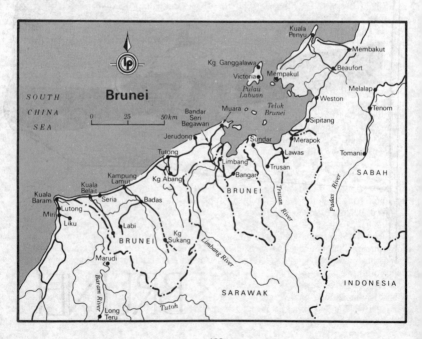

benefits from oil money. There are no taxes, there are pensions for all, free medicare, free schooling, free sports and leisure centres, cheap loans, subsidies for many purchases including cars and the highest minimum wages in the region.

Facts

HISTORY
In the 15th and 16th centuries Brunei Darussalam, as it's formally known, was a considerable power in the area and its rule extended throughout Borneo and into the Philippines.

The Spanish and the Portuguese were the first European visitors, arriving in the 16th century. The Spanish actually made a bid to take over but were soon ousted.

The arrival of the British in the guise of James Brooke, the first White Rajah of Sarawak, in the early 19th century, spelt the end of Brunei's power.

A series of 'treaties' were forced onto the Sultan as James Brooke consolidated his hold over Kuching with the aim of developing commercial relationships and suppressing piracy – a favourite Bruneian and Dayak occupation.

The country was gradually whittled away until, with a final dash of absurdity, Limbang was ceded to Sarawak, thus dividing the country in half.

In 1929, just as Brunei was about to be swallowed up entirely, oil was discovered. The Sultan's father, who abdicated in 1967, kept Brunei out of the Malaysian confederacy, preferring that the country remain a British protectorate, which it had been since 1888.

Since the 1960s, when there was a failed coup attempt, the country has been under emergency laws, but you'll see little evidence of this.

In early 1984 the popular Sultan, Yang Maha Mulia Paduka Seri Beginda Muda Hassanal Bolkiah Mu'izzaddin Waddaulah, the 29th of his line, led his tightly-ruled country somewhat reluctantly into complete independence from Britain. The 37-year-old leader rather enjoyed the English umbrella and colonial status and independence was almost unwanted.

GEOGRAPHY
Brunei consists of two separate areas, bordered by the South China Sea to the north and bounded on all other sides by Sarawak.

It covers an area of 5765 sq km and other than the capital, Bandar Seri Begawan, the oil town of Seria and the commercial town of Kuala Belait, Brunei is mainly jungle.

CLIMATE
From November to January, during the north-east monsoon, temperatures are somewhat lower than the 28°C average. With an average humidity of 82% it's a pretty warm place.

ECONOMY
Oil. The country is virtually dependent on it, although some diversification plans for the economy are now being instituted for that fearsome day when the pump runs dry. These plans include more rice farming, some forestry and eventual self-sufficiency in beef production.

To this latter goal the government purchased a cattle station in Australia's Northern Territory which is larger than Brunei itself! Fresh beef is flown into Bandar Seri Begawan daily.

Brunei is also one of the world's largest exporters of liquefied natural gas. A small amount of rubber is also exported.

The government with Brunei Shell Petroleum (the only oil company there in any substantial way) is by far the country's largest employer. All government workers get subsidised holidays and trips to Mecca. All in all, not too shabby an arrangement. When there is any criticism, the government-owned newspaper stifles it.

The traditional pattern of agriculture in Brunei is that of shifting cultivation, which continues in the more remote areas. Farming is largely a part-time occupation and there are no large estates. About 80% of the country's food requirements have to be imported.

POPULATION

The total population of Brunei is about 250,000 and is composed of Malays (78%), Chinese (18%), Indians and around 25,000 Iban, Lun Bawang and other tribal people of the interior. There are also around 20,000 expatriate workers from Europe and elsewhere in Asia.

Brunei is quite a strict Muslim country; there is little alcohol and apparently government men prowl the streets after dark looking for unmarried couples standing or sitting too close to each other. Getting nailed for this crime, known as *khalwat*, can mean imprisonment and fine. For the traveller just passing through, this makes Bandar Seri Begawan an incredibly dull place after dark.

The official language is Malay but English is widely spoken.

VISAS

For visits of up to 14 days, visas are not necessary for citizens of France, Switzerland, Canada, Japan, Thailand, Philippines, Indonesia, the Netherlands, Luxembourg, Belgium, Germany and the Republic of Korea. British, Malaysian and Singaporean citizens do not require a visa for visits of 30 days or less.

All other nationalities, including British overseas citizens and British dependent territories citizens must have visas to visit Brunei. If entering from Sarawak or Sabah there's no fuss on arrival – no money showing, no requirement for an onward ticket and it's unlikely your bags will even be looked at – and a one-week stay permit is more or less automatic. If you ask you can usually get two weeks; it might be useful, you never know. Two-day transit visas are reportedly available on the land borders if you don't have a visa but this is not official; it seems to depend largely on the whim of the immigration official at the time – some people get them, others are knocked back.

EMBASSIES

Brunei has diplomatic offices in the following countries:

Australia
    PO Box 74, Manuka, Canberra 2603 (tel (062) 3964321)
Indonesia
    Bank Central Asia Building, Jalan Jenderal Sudirman, Jakarta (tel (021) 5782180)
Japan
    5-2 Kitashinagawa 6-chome, Shinagawa-ku, Tokyo 141 (tel (03) 4477997)
Malaysia
    Plaza MBF, Jalan Ampang, Kuala Lumpur (tel (03) 4574149)
Philippines
    Bank of Philippine Islands Building, Ayala Ave, Paseo De Roxas, Makati, Manila (tel (02) 8162836)
Singapore
    7A Tanglin Hill, Singapore (tel 4743393)
Thailand
    Orakarn Building, 26/50 Soi Chitlon, Ploenchit Rd, Bangkok 10500 (tel (02) 515766)
UK
    49 Cromwell Rd, London SW7 2ED (tel (01) 5810521)
USA
    Watergate, Suite 300, 2600 Virginia Ave NW, Washington DC 20037 (tel (202) 3420158)

MONEY
Currency

The official currency is the Brunei dollar but Singapore dollars are equally exchanged and can be used. There's about a 40% difference between the Brunei dollar and the Malaysian ringgit. Banks give around 10% less for cash than they do for travellers' cheques.

Costs

Brunei is fiercely expensive, mainly because the cheap accommodation options are limited and unreliable. For budget travellers Brunei is a bit of a disaster and many people travelling overland between Sabah and Sarawak find it economical to take one of the MAS flights between Miri and Labuan (M$57) or Lawas (M$59).

Transport and food within the country are comparable with prices in the rest of East Malaysia – ie, more expensive than Peninsular Malaysia but not outrageously expensive.

TOURIST INFORMATION

There is an information desk in the capital, Bandar Seri Begawan, but there is little in the way of printed tourist information.

If you want an exhaustive analysis of everything to do with Brunei, including statistics on just about everything, the 160-page, glossy, government publication entitled *Brunei Darussalam in Profile* is what you need. It is available on request from Brunei diplomatic missions.

HOLIDAYS & FESTIVALS

Holidays and festivals in Brunei are mostly religious celebrations or festivities which mark the anniversary of various important events in the history of the country.

As is the case with Malaysia and Singapore, the dates of most religious festivals are not fixed as they are based on the Islamic calendar.

Fixed holidays:

New Year's Day
  1 January
National Day
  23 February
Anniversary of the Royal Brunei Armed Forces
  31 May
Sultan's Birthday
  15 July
Christmas Day
  25 December

Variable holidays include:

Chinese New Year
  February
Isra Dan Mi'Raj
  February
Ramadan
  March
Good Friday
  March-April
Anniversary of the Revelation of the Koran
  April
Hari Raya Puasa
  April
Hari Raya Haji
  June
Muslim New Year
  July
Moulud (Prophet's Birthday)
  July

Bandar Seri Begawan

The capital, Bandar Seri Begawan, abbreviated to Bandar, is the only town of any size and really one of the few places to go in the country. It's a neat, very clean and modern city with some fine, overstated buildings.

You won't see any bicycles, trishaws or even motorcycles there. Everybody has an air-conditioned car and they're nearly all new; you'll notice the quietness, because they all have working mufflers.

The historical water villages surrounding the city are quite fascinating and offer some contrasting tradition. A big plus is the friendly people; even young women will smile and say hello. There are a few things to see and do around town but, unless you stay at the youth centre (if it's open), the city can be expensive to linger in.

Information

Tourist Information There is a tourist information booth (tel 31794) at the airport which isn't bad and has maps but, although they are helpful, they can't answer questions about the rest of the country.

Post & Telecommunications The post office is on the corner of Jalan Sultan and

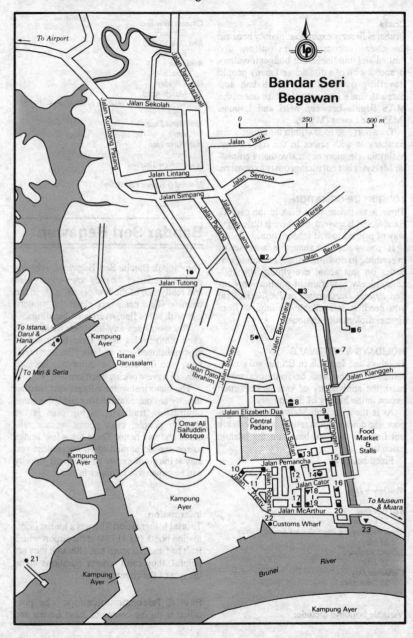

To Airport

Jalan Dato Marshall

Jalan Sekolah

Jalan Kumbang Pasang

Bandar Seri
Begawan

0   250   500 m

Jalan Tasik

Jalan Lintang

Jalan Sentosa

Jalan Simpang

Jalan Tereja

Jalan Padang

Jalan Tasik Lama

Jalan Berita

1

2

Jalan Tutong

3

To Istana,
Darul &
Hana

4

Kampung
Ayer

5

6

7

Istana
Darussalam

Jalan Stoney

Jalan Bendahara

To Miri & Seria

Jalan Dato
Ibrahim

Jalan Kianggeh

Jalan Elizabeth Dua

8

Omar Ali
Saifuddin
Mosque

Central
Padang

9

Jalan Sungai

Jalan Sultan

Jalan Kianggeh

Food
Market
&
Stalls

Kampung
Ayer

13

Jalan Pemancha

15

10

Jalan Roberts

12 14

16

Kampung
Ayer

11

Jalan Cator

17   18
19

To Museum
& Muara

Jalan Pretty

20

Jalan McArthur

Kampung
Ayer

22

Customs Wharf

23

21

Brunei   River

Kampung Ayer

■ PLACES TO STAY

2 Ang's Hotel
3 Sheraton Hotel
6 Capital Hostel
15 Brunei Hotel

▼ PLACES TO EAT

18 Express Fast Food
23 Food Centre

OTHER

1 Immigration
4 High Court
5 Churchill Museum
7 Pusat Belia
8 Post Office
9 Chinese Temple
10 MAS
11 Malayan Bank
12 Oriental Travel
13 Hong Kong & Shanghai Bank
14 Bus Station
16 Borneo Leisure Travel
17 Teck Guan Complex
19 Darussalam Complex
20 Harrisons
21 Makam Di-Raja (Mausoleum)
22 Boats to Labuan, Limbang, Lawas

Jalan Elizabeth Dua. This building also houses a 24-hour telephone office. You can dial international calls yourself here (expensive at B$8 per minute) or at any public phone that accepts telephone cards. Cards are available from the post office in denominations ranging from B$2 to B$100.

The telephone system is in the process of changing to six-digit numbers, so if you're not getting through, add a 2 to the start of the number.

The Hash A good way to meet some of the resident expat population is to take part in one of the Hash House Harrier runs. Ask at the British Council for details, or any expats you see in the streets should be able to help – they're generally a friendly bunch.

Foreign Embassies Countries with diplomatic representation in Brunei include:

Australia
    4th Floor, Chop Teck Guan Complex (tel 02-229435)
France
    Kompleks Jalan Sultan, Jalan Sultan (tel 02-220960)
Germany
    UNF Building, Jalan Sultan (tel 02-225547)
Indonesia
    Lot 4498, Kamping Sungau Hanching (tel 02-230180)
Malaysia
    Lot 12-15 Tingkat 6 Bang (tel 02-228410)
Philippines
    Badiah Complex (tel 02-241465)
UK
    Hong Kong Bank Building (tel 02-226001)
USA
    3rd Floor, Chop Teck Guan Complex (tel 02-229670)

Cultural Centres The British Council is on the 5th floor of the Hong Kong Bank Building. It is open Monday to Thursday from 8 am to 12.15 pm and 1.45 to 4.30 pm, on Friday and Saturday from 8 am to 12.30 pm.

Bookshops For books and magazines try the 3rd floor of the Teck Guan Plaza Building, on the corner of Jalan Sultan and Jalan McArthur. There are also STP distributors on the corner of Jalan Pemancha and Jalan Sultan and the Rex Bookstore around the corner on Jalan Sungai Kianggeh.

Omar Ali Saifuddin Mosque
Named after the 28th Sultan of Brunei, the mosque was built in 1958 at a cost of about US$5 million. Designed by an Italian architect, the golden-domed structure stands close to the Brunei River in its own artificial lagoon and is the tallest building in Bandar Seri Begawan. It's one of the most impressive structures in the East.

As is customary, the interior is simple but tasteful although certainly no match for the stunning exterior; but which other mosque anywhere has an elevator and an escalator?

The floor and walls of the mosque are made from the finest Italian marble, the stained-glass windows were handcrafted in England and the luxurious carpets were flown in from Saudi Arabia. The small pools and quadrants surrounding the main building are beautiful. The ceremonial stone boat sitting in the lagoon/moat is used for special occasions.

You can sometimes take the elevator to the top of the 44-metre minaret or walk up the long, winding staircase without charge. The view over the city and nearby Kampung Ayer or water village is excellent.

The mosque is closed to non-Muslims on Thursdays and on Friday mornings. From Saturday to Wednesday you may enter the mosque between the hours of 8 am and 12 noon, 1 and 3 pm or 4.30 and 5.30 pm. Remember to dress appropriately and to remove your shoes before entering. Muslim travellers can enter the mosque to pray at any time.

Winston Churchill Memorial Museum

This museum was built by Sultan Omar Ali Saifuddin and houses a collection of articles which once belonged to Churchill. To anyone with an interest in 20th-century history it's quite an interesting place and worth a browse for an hour or two. It's open from 9.30 to 11.30 am and 2.30 to 5 pm daily, except Tuesdays when it's closed all day. Admission is free.

Aquarium Hassanal Bolkiah Brunei

Adjacent to the Churchill museum is the aquarium which has a total of 47 exhibition tanks, both fresh and seawater, one of them nearly eight metres long. There's an interesting and colourful collection of tropical fish from the local reefs. The aquarium is open from 9 am to 12 noon and 1.15 to 7 pm daily except Mondays when it's closed all day and Fridays when it's closed from 11.30 am and 2.15 pm. Admission is 30 sen.

Constitutional History Gallery

On the other side of the aquarium is the history museum, created to mark the independence of Brunei in 1984. The history of Brunei is traced from the 1800s to the present

day. There are even action scenes set up where buttons may be pressed to light up part of the scene and start off a recorded commentary describing the 'action' – typically, none of these buttons work. This museum is rather dull, and is not helped by the fact that there's very little in English.

Opening hours are 9 to 11.30 am and 2.30 to 5 pm daily, except for Mondays when the museum is closed. Admission is free.

The Library

There is a general reference library in the Churchill complex which houses a fairly good collection of books on South-East Asia and, of course, several books written by Sir Winston Churchill.

Brunei Museum

Located at Kota Batu, six km from the centre of Bandar Seri Begawan, the museum is housed in a beautifully constructed building on the banks of the Brunei River. When combined with a visit to the Malay Technology Museum on the riverbank below, it's well worth the short trip out of town.

The museum has a collection of historical treasures from the 15th century together with artefacts of the cultural heritage of Brunei. It also has a natural history section with exhibits of stuffed and mounted animals, birds and insects.

There is an extensive section on oil with an amusing vignette showing local life with and without the 'benefits' that oil brings. Best is the ethnography section with good examples of musical instruments, baskets and brassware. Also check the coffins of the Kenyah people's chiefs. There is a large collection of Chinese ceramics from 1000 AD to more recent times. The museum is open Tuesday, Wednesday, Thursday, Saturday and Sunday from 9.30 am to 5 pm; Friday from 9.30 to 11.30 am and 2.30 to 5 pm; and is closed on Mondays.

City buses depart from the downtown depot; the fare is 50 sen, but buses are not that frequent. Taxis cost B$6, but you can hitch quite easily. After visiting the museum, you can continue in the same direction to the bottom of the hill and the turn-off to the Malay Technology Museum.

Malay Technology Museum

This new and very impressive museum is built right on the edge of the river directly below the National Museum. It's a 15-minute walk as you have to go well past the Brunei Museum to get to the road leading to this museum.

A lot of time and effort has been lavished on this place and there are three galleries with various exhibits. Gallery 1 is based on water village architecture and has reconstructions of how the houses have evolved over the last 150 years or so. Gallery 2 has exhibits of handicrafts and fishing techniques practised by the people of the water villages. These include weaving, silver-smithing and brass casting. The theme of Gallery 3 is the tools and techniques used by the indigenous tribes of the interior for food gathering, agriculture and hunting. It is an excellent display although the light-coloured mannequins in striped pyjamas hardly look like Penans or Kedayans or any other indigenous Bruneian!

Brunei's first gunboat is on display under a traditional roof by the riverbank in front of the museum.

Opening hours are the same as the Brunei Museum.

Tomb of Sultan Bolkiah

Near the museum, about one km closer to town, is the tomb and mausoleum of the fifth Sultan of Brunei, known as the 'Singing Admiral' who died returning from a voyage to Java. He lived from 1473 to 1521, during a period when Brunei was the dominant power in the region.

Kampung Ayer

This collection of 28 water villages, built on stilts out in the Brunei River, has been there for centuries and at present houses a population of around 30,000 people. It's a strange mixture of ancient and modern; old traditions and ways of life are side by side with modern plumbing, electricity and colour TVs. A visit to one of the villages is probably the most rewarding experience you'll have in Brunei, though the garbage which floats around them has to be seen to be believed. The villages are at their best at high tide.

To get there, go down to any of the wharfs either at the path to the west of the mosque, near the end of the Limbang and Lawas boat wharf or by the food stalls on the other side of the canal from the Information Office building. Hail one of the many outboard launches which act as water taxis and shuttle people back and forth between early morning and late evening. The fare across the river should be no more than B$1, although locals pay less.

All the houses in each area are connected by a maze of wooden planks and once there you can just wander at random. It's fascinating to wander around for an hour or so – even if you do keep finding yourself in the middle of someone's kitchen.

When Bandar Seri Begawan was being modernised, it was suggested that the people from the water villages be relocated to the mainland. These people refused to move and in enlightened fashion were permitted to stay. Schools and hospitals, of cement rather than wood, were then built on the water for the villagers.

There are all sorts of shops and businesses amongst the houses in Kampung Ayer. If you're lucky, you might come across handicraft shops selling silverware, brass, woven cloth and baskets. If not, you can always ask the boat operators to take you to these places.

A boat trip right around Kampung Ayer takes at least 30 minutes and the boat operators will probably want B$30 for their efforts – bargain hard.

Handicraft Centre

The preposterously large and grandiose handicraft centre was built to help develop local craftwork. It's along the waterfront toward the museum, visible from town and an easy walk. However, if you are interested in traditional crafts, it is disappointing. Only new silverwork and weaving are available and everything is very expensive; you can pay hundreds of dollars for some pieces. There's not much variety either. You can visit workshops upstairs.

Around Town

From town it's a short walk to a small waterfall and a view. Past the Ang's Hotel, going away from the town centre, after two sets of traffic lights take the next right turn, Jalan Tasek Lama. Go up the road to the parking lot, through the gate by the parking lot and continue for about 15 minutes. Continuing past the flowers and picnic tables follow the stream to the falls. They are best in the wet season when the water is deeper; you can swim there. Another road by the gate leads to a 15-minute walk uphill to a view over the water reservoir.

The Sheraton Hotel has 'jogging maps' which can also be used for walks.

Chinese Temple

There is a Chinese temple on the corner of Jalan Elizabeth Dua and Jalan Sungai Kianggeh with some colourful, pictorial tilework and plenty of carved, gilded wood. It's a busy place on Saturday evenings.

Istana Nurul Iman

The Istana Nurul Iman, the magnificent Sultan's palace, larger than the Vatican Palace, is an impressive sight, especially when illuminated at night, and you can be sure no expense has been spared in its construction. Unfortunately, the istana is open to the public only three days a year during Hari Raya Puasa, the end of the fasting month of Ramadan.

The istana is four km out of town on the Tutong road. You can either spend a leisurely hour walking to it or you can try hitching. The Tutong and Seria buses pass the istana but they run infrequently. On the hill opposite the istana are homes belonging to other members of the royal family.

Other Interesting Buildings

All over town you'll notice uniquely designed, oversized federal buildings – the Government complex opposite the youth centre, the Royal Ceremonial Hall, the Arts and Handicrafts Centre, the National Museum and Technology museums and the Supreme Court. Try to see the Royal Ceremonial Hall (Lapau) where traditional events are held and the Sultan's golden throne sits. The Legislative Assembly (Dewan Majlis) has been moved to the istana.

Visitors are welcome to attend traditional Malay weddings; ask the Public Relations Officer for more information.

Places to Stay – bottom end

Pusat Belia (tel 02-229423), the youth centre on Jalan Sungai Kianggeh, a short walk from the town centre, was the only cheap place to stay in town but it now houses the homeless after a fire destroyed a large part of the water village. It might be reopened to travellers at a future date.

There is a *Government Rest House* (tel 02-223571) on the corner of Jalan Sungai Kianggeh and Jalan Cator, behind the Brunei Hotel. It costs around B$8 per night and the rooms are in much better condition than the youth centre's dorms. It's reserved exclusively for government workers or guests of the government, but you can try your luck.

If you draw a blank at this place and can't afford the Capital Hostel then you are really in strife, although I have heard of travellers sleeping out in the parks and getting away with it. One traveller reported that there was cheaper accommodation available on the 4th floor of the Giok Tee Building at 66 Jalan McArthur at Jalan Roberts end, with doubles for B$40.

Places to Stay – middle

The jump in price from bottom to middle-range accommodation is enormous.

The *Capital Hostel* (tel 02-223561), off Jalan Tasik Lama just behind the Pusat Belia, is the one you'll have to use if you're on a budget and cannot get into the youth centre or the Rest House. Rooms cost B$70/85 single/double and all have air-con, TV and fridge. The restaurant and bar downstairs serve reasonably priced meals. The continental breakfast is B$5 or B$8 with eggs and is handy if you're at the youth centre.

A more recent middle to top addition is the *National Inn* (tel 02-221128) but it's on Jalan Tutong, out of the town centre, across the Brunei River behind the mosque. It features fine, modern rooms, all with air-con and prices from B$70. The hotel offers free transport to the airport and a regular shuttle service into town. The restaurant serves expensive meals.

Places to Stay – top end
There are more hotels in this category than in any other. The *Sheraton Hotel* (tel 02-244272) is the country's top hotel and has all the modern amenities, including a pool. It is centrally located on Jalan Bendahara. There are 170 rooms with singles/doubles from B$215/225.

Ang's Hotel (tel 02-243553) on Jalan Tasik has its own restaurant and bar and is fully air-conditioned, of course. The 84 rooms start at B$118/128 for singles/doubles.

On the corner of Jalan Sungai Kianggeh and Jalan Pemancha is the *Brunei Hotel* (tel 02-242372). Each room has air-con, a private bath and TV and the hotel has a restaurant and bar. Rates are B$140/165 for singles/doubles.

Places to Eat
All the hotels and the youth centre have their own restaurants. The meals at the *Capital Hostel* are pretty good and quite cheap. You can get tasty Hokkien noodles and other noodle dishes for B$4.50. There's not much of a menu at the canteen in the youth centre; basically, what you see is what you get and the choice is very limited.

The food centre on the riverfront just over the canal from the Customs Wharf is not a bad place to eat, although as is the case all over Bandar, there's not much going in the evenings.

Another place to head for is the food stalls by the river, across the footbridge near the intersection of Jalan Sungai Kianggeh and Jalan Pemancha. You can get excellent food of all descriptions here including satay, bar-becued fish and chicken wings. In the evenings only another group of stalls springs up in the car park behind the Chinese temple, opposite the post office. The only trouble with both these sets of food stalls is that they are take-aways only, so you have to find somewhere to sit down and eat your food.

Along the main street, Jalan Sultan, you'll find a few places to eat. The *Express Fast Food* on the corner of Jalan Sultan and Jalan Cator is an American-style fast-food place with typically bland food. Of the other restaurants, two which stand out, if only because they are open in the evenings, are the *Hua Hua* and *Al Hilal* which serve basic Chinese and Malay food respectively.

On Jalan McArthur the *Sri Indah Restoran* has decent roti and murtabak, good for grabbing a quick breakfast before catching a boat. On the same street, the *Chop Jing Chew Bakery*, opposite the customs building on Jalan McArthur sells cakes, bread and ice cream. On the corner of Jalan McArthur and Jalan Sultan there's the *Carnation Country Bake Corner* which, as you might expect, has various cakes and pastries. Across the road in Darussalam Complex, you'll find the busy *Chin Lian Restaurant* where you can get cheap, tasty Malaysian food, although at lunch time only.

Jalan Roberts has a few Chinese cafes but after about 6.30 pm the place is deserted.

There's an English-style pub in Ang's Hotel as well as a Chinese restaurant which serves excellent laksa – not cheap but definitely worth the splurge.

The sale of liquor was banned in early 1991.

Getting There & Away
Air Airlines which fly into Brunei include Royal Brunei, MAS, SIA and Cathay Pacific.

Airlines with offices or general sales agents in Bandar Seri Begawan include:

British Airways (GSA)
    Harrisons, corner of Jalan Kianggeh & Jalan McArthur (tel 02-243911)

MAS
    144 Jalan Pemancha (tel 02-224141)
Qantas (GSA)
    Freme Travel, Hong Kong Bank Building (tel 02-228852)
Royal Brunei Airlines
    RBA Plaza, Jalan Sultan (tel 02-242222)
Singapore Airlines
    Jalan Sultan (tel 02-227253)
Thai International
    51 Jalan Sultan (tel 02-242991)

Royal Brunei flies to Bandar Seri Begawan from Singapore, Hong Kong, Manila, Darwin and other destinations. It's actually cheaper to fly Manila-Bandar Seri Begawan than Manila-Kota Kinabalu, even though it's further. Being a Muslim airline, Royal Brunei does not serve alcohol on its flights.

None of the airline offices offer student or other discounts but some of the travel agents will offer small discounts.

The standard economy fare to Singapore is B$320 one way. To Kuching the airfare is B$192, Kota Kinabalu B$65 and Kuala Lumpur B$372 (but when coming *from* any of these cities the fare is in Malaysian ringgit not Brunei dollars, so is around 30% cheaper). To Bangkok the fare is about B$500 and to Manila B$450.

Road The only roads which exist in Brunei are the ones linking Bandar Seri Begawan to Seria, Kuala Belait and the Sarawak border near Kuala Baram. The only way to reach Lawas or Limbang is by launch. It has been said that the government purposely keeps the roads out of Brunei in such miserable condition to make any invasion by land difficult!

The bus station in Bandar Seri Begawan is on Jalan Cator, near Britannia House, at the back of the Brunei Hotel. There are many buses every day to Seria. The fare is B$4 and the journey takes 1½ to two hours.

From Seria to Kuala Belait there are frequent buses daily, the fare is B$1 and the journey takes about 30 minutes. It's very easy, to hitch from Bandar Seri Begawan to Seria or Kuala Belait because there are plenty of air-conditioned cars and very few hitch-hikers. Alongside the road around

Seria, and right in the middle of the town itself, you'll see plenty of the 'nodding donkey' oil wells.

If you want to reach Miri in one day from Bandar Seri Begawan, start out early in the day. There are now four or five buses daily from Kuala Belait to Miri. These are operated by the Miri Belait Transport Company. The fare is B$11 and the journey takes about 2½ hours and involves river crossings.

From Kuala Belait it's a five-minute bus ride (20 minutes' walk) to the Belait River where the car ferry plies back and forth. Although the queue for cars can be incredibly long here, especially on weekends, bus passengers and the driver cross the river on the ferry and pick up another bus parked on the other side, thus avoiding the queues.

Once you cross the river it's a short ride to the Brunei immigration checkpoint. After going through Brunei customs you board a Malaysian bus which takes you to the Malaysian immigration checkpoint. From there it's a very short ride to the queue at the next river which usually takes 15 to 30 minutes to cross.

From Kuala Baram to Miri, the road is sealed all the way and is in fairly good condition.

Launches & Boats Unless you are going to fly to Labuan or Kota Kinabalu, the only way to get to Sabah or the isolated eastern Sarawak outposts of Limbang or Lawas is to use launches or launch/taxi combinations.

All international boats leave from the dock at the end of Jalan Roberts, where Brunei immigration formalities are taken care of.

Boat – To/From Limbang There are several private *expres* boats which do this run at various times of the day – departure times depend on demand. The fare is B$7 and the trip takes about 30 minutes; ask around at the dock.

There isn't much to see or do in Limbang and the town has a bit of a reputation as a sin spot. You can either stay at Limbang overnight, take another boat to Punang (further up the coast) or fly to Miri, Lawas or Kota Kinabalu. See the Limbang section in the Sarawak chapter for further details.

Boat – To/From Labuan Labuan is a duty-free island off Brunei from which you can get ferries to Sabah and then a bus into Kota Kinabalu, ferries direct to Kota Kinabalu, or flights to Sabah, Sarawak or Peninsular Malaysia. For more details, see the Labuan Island Getting There & Away section in the Sabah chapter.

From Bandar there are two daily services to Labuan. The more comfortable boat is the new air-con *Ratu Samudra*. It leaves Bandar daily at 8 am, the trip takes one hour 20 minutes and tickets cost (B$18 economy class) and B$25 (1st class). Economy class is perfectly adequate. On the return journey it leaves Labuan at 2 pm. Tickets for the *Ratu Samudra* should be bought a day or so in advance. The ticketing agent is Borneo Leisure Travel (tel 02-23407) on the ground floor of Brittania House, on the corner of Jalan Sungai Kianggeh and Jalan Cator.

The *Sri Labuan Dua* is a much older vessel and takes about two hours to cover the distance between Bandar and Labuan. It is also cheaper than the *Ratu Samudra* at B$15. It leaves Labuan daily at 12 noon, and from Bandar for the return journey at 3 pm. The ticket agent in Bandar is Oriental Travel Service (tel 02-26464), mezzanine floor, Haji Ahmad Laksamana Othman Building on the corner of Jalan Sultan and Jalan Pemancha.

You can also get private boats to take you; they'll probably settle for B$15 or so, but will ask for more. With triple outboard engines they are very fast and not particularly safe. Just stand around the dock area and touts and boat owners will approach you or call out.

Boat – To/From Lawas There are usually one or two launches daily between Bandar and Lawas which cost B$25 (or M$25 from Lawas) and take about two hours. The one which most travellers take departs at 11 am daily. Runners will accost you as you enter the wharf area at the end of Jalan Roberts – no problem finding a boat.

See the Lawas Getting There & Away section in the Sarawak chapter for details of onward transport to Sabah and Labuan and flights into the Kelabit Highlands.

Getting Around
To/From the Airport Although the taxi drivers would have you believe otherwise, there are minibuses between the city bus station and the airport. From the bus station look for the minibuses with the words 'Lapangan Terbang Antarabangsa' (International Airport) painted on the side.

Taxis charge a hefty B$20 – welcome to Brunei! The big, modern airport is only eight km from the city.

Bus Local buses around Bandar Seri Begawan are few and far between and only leave when full. The bus station is beneath the central market, behind the Brunei Hotel.

To get to the museums take a Muara or Kota Batu bus (50 sen). There are also regular buses to Seria.

Car Rental There's not really anywhere to drive to, but there are a couple of companies that rent cars:

Avis
    Sheraton Hotel (tel 02-227100)
National
    Sheraton Hotel (tel 02-224921)
Roseraya
    Brittania House (tel 02-241442)

Around Brunei

MUARA
This is a small town north of Bandar Seri Begawan at the top of the peninsula. It's a new oil centre with not much to see but there is a pretty decent beach.

The *World Wide Club* is basically for expats and is a good place to meet someone who lives in the country. The *Tropicana Seafood Restaurant*, Block 1, ground floor of Pang's building is a nice place to eat. There are also a lot of yachts in Muara, for you opportunists.

Getting There & Away

The bus from Bandar Seri Begawan takes about 40 minutes and costs B$2 or you can try hitching. There are other beaches on the north coast, but these are not as pleasant and the buses are less frequent.

BANGAR

Bangar is another small town, but it is reached only by boat. You can get launches there from Bandar Seri Begawan. Bangar is the district centre and is on the Temburong River south-east of the capital. The town has a couple of shops and a market.

Places to Stay & Eat

There is a *Government Rest House* which travellers can use at a cost of B$8 per night. Apparently you can organise some sleeping arrangements in town, perhaps through the information office in Bandar Seri Begawan.

There are several Iban longhouses along the upper reaches of the river. While there are basic cafes in Bangar, take food with you if you're going upstream. You can get one of the three taxis in town or a private car to take you to longhouses. The fare should be no more than B$1 per km.

The nearest longhouse to Bangar is about 13 km away, and, as you'd expect, the further up the river you go, the more 'authentic' the longhouses become. You might even find a nice new Volvo parked outside the more urban longhouses! Most of the longhouses in this area are homes of the friendly Murut people.

Getting There & Away

There's one road going inland from Bangar to Limbang and another follows the river upstream for a distance to the village of Batang Duri.

Between 7 am and 3 pm daily you can get launches to Bangar from Bandar Seri Begawan. Go to the customs wharf and bargain – the fare should be B$6 to B$7 and

the journey less than one hour. It is also possible to catch an early boat to Bangar (7.30 am) and a late boat back to Bandar Seri Begawan (4 pm) but unless you have access to private transport or can afford expensive taxis to take you about, you'll be rushed.

SERIA

Seria is the main town on the north coast, situated between Tutong and Kuala Belait, quite close to the Malaysian border. There are at least three banks in town and a few interesting cafes and cake shops.

Before Seria a road branches off inland to Labi. About halfway to Labi is Luagan Lalak with good views and a lake. From Labi there are several Iban longhouses which you can go to. The main one is called Rumah Panjang Mendaram Besar and it's worth visiting. There is a road but, as very few cars use it, you may have to walk. Take a few small gifts. On the way, you'll pass Rampayoh where there is a waterfall.

Places to Stay

The *Hotel Seria* has fan-cooled singles for B$35 and doubles for B$40. If you're just passing through Brunei from Sabah to Sarawak, and can't stay in the Pusat Belia in Bandar, then it's quite a saving to spend your last Brunei night here rather than at the extremely expensive Bandar Seri Begawan hotels.

At the other end of Seria's price scale the *Sea View Hotel* is completely modern at B$85 for singles and B$90 for doubles.

Getting There & Away

The road from Bandar Seri Begawan is good; there are about 10 buses daily taking two hours. The last one leaves Seria at 4 pm. From Seria there are frequent minibuses to Kuala Belait for B$1.

KUALA BELAIT

The last town before Malaysia, Kuala Belait is where you get buses for Miri in Sarawak. There are two banks in town and an efficient post office.

You can hire a motor launch by the market for trips up the river to Kuala Balai, a small river village. The 45-minute trip (one way) goes by good, jungle vegetation at the river's edge. Near Kuala Balai you'll see sago palms growing. Along the way ask the driver to stop at the wooden case of skulls mounted on stilts, left over from the head-hunting days.

Places to Stay

At the cheap end of the scale there's a *Government Rest House* where, if you're permitted to stay, rooms are about B$12. Rooms are generally reserved for government officials, but occasionally travellers may be allowed to stay.

Otherwise, there's the *Sentosa Hotel* at 92 Jalan McKerron which is all air-conditioned and has single rooms from B$100 and a Chinese restaurant downstairs which serves excellent seafood. The *Seaview Hotel* by the beach has rooms for well over B$100.

Getting There & Away

For Malaysia there are quite a few buses daily, mostly in the morning, and the fare is just under B$11 for the 30-minute trip. Just out of town the road ends and you take a ferry over the Belait River. The road then continues along the coast to the border. At the border you change to a Malaysian bus and head to the Baram River, from where there's another ferry crossing. From there to Miri it's a good road.

Index

ABBREVIATIONS

MAPS

TEXT

Map references are in **bold** type.

THANKS

Writers (apologies if we've misspelt your names) to whom thanks must go include:

Airpower Travel (Mal), Andre (USA), Elfaaz Lodge (Mal), Jill & Mick (Aus), Julie & Jon (UK), Aad Vredenbregt (Nl), Abdul Kadir (I), Adam Rojenthal (UK), Adrian Allan (UK), Alan Hannaford (Aus), Alexander Wettstein (UK), Alex Stewart (Aus), Andrea Aemenbeager (Swit), Andrea Davies (UK), Andrea McLaughlin (C), Andrew Douglas (UK), Andrew Zeluk (Aus), Andy Ellis (UK), Andy Frame (Aus), Andy Kew (S), Anna Ahlen (Sw), Anna Bindschedler, Anne Marsden Thomas (UK), Ann Holdsworth, Ass. Youth Clb Malaysian (M), Azizah Harharah (Sin), AA Windham (Mal), Ah Tee Lim (Mal), Barbara & Dad Rout (Aus), Barry I Clements (Aus), Bernard & Joy Holland (UK), Bernie Hodges, Bera A E MacClement (In), Betty Malang (Mal), Bill Hunt (Aus), Bill & Carol Mackinnon Little (UK), Bob Aitken (UK), Brenda Koo (UK), Briana Lawrie (USA), Brian Adams (Aus), P O Adler (Sw), Brian Kliesen (USA), Burhanuddin Ghazali (Mal), Buster & Kitty Tacklebox (Aus), BW Perkins (Aus), Callum Whyte (Thai), Carla Rufelds (C), Caroline Evans (UK), Carolyn Earle (Aus), Carol Ketley (UK), Carol Rubenstein (S), Cathy & Jeff Rippin-Sisler (C), Charles Cottell (UK), Charles Krimminger (USA), Choy Wong (Mal), Christine Moulet (Sin), Christophe Lavenant (Fr), Chris Perez (Aus), Claire Jones (Aus), Clare Walbridge (UK), Cloud Hoogland (Nl), Colette Ozanne (F), Collin Belcher (UK), Craig & Gillian McHaffie (C), Cybele Rico (Bra), Cydia Broakman (Nl), Daniel Bodis (NZ), Darren Ian Unen (C), David Park (USA), David Rumsey (NZ), David Stephenson (UK), Dave & Nanci Bramsen (USA), Dawn Lock (UK), Daymar Hahn, Dan Caplan (USA), Mark Caprio (J), Dan Fineman, Deborah Koons (USA), Diego Marconi (It), Dinah Scott (UK), Douglas Lattey (UK), Doug & Jenny Moss-Newport (Aus), Doug Bills (Aus), Duncan Dominic, De Lee Leo (Bel), Edward van Steijn (Nl), Elaine Williams (Aus), Elizabeth & Ken Rae (Aus), Elsie Lee (Mal), Eluise Marvin (USA), Els Pouke (Nl), Els van Dam, Emin Demirji (G), Eric Telfer (USA), Evert Bouws (Mal), Evert Bouws (Nl), Eva Bolander (Sw), Fabrizio Bartaletti (It), Finn Houmark (Dk), Frank Bye (NZ), Frank Kriz (C), Frank Teneralli (USA), Fred Ameling (Nl), Gabi Heise (D), Gareth Clark (UK), Gary Jerome, Geoff Mercer, Georgina Wisbey (UK), Gerard Wyfjes (Nl), Gerelle Gordon (NZ), Glenn Hoetken (USA), Gordon Bonin (UK), Gordon Mott (C), Graham Riding, Grey Eaves (UK), Hamidah Bte Hussain (Mal), Hamirudin Hashim (Mal), Hans & Joke van Egmond (Nl), Harnet Blake (UK), Harry Atkinson (SL), Heidi A Fassbind (CH), Helen Richardson (UK), Henrik Eriksson (Sw), Henry van Gael (Bel), Honor Gay (UK), Hotel Jesselton (Mal), HP & Olga Wagner (CH), Ian Lowe (Aus), Ir. D. Wiersma (Nl), Ivan Wainewright (UK), Jackie Reason (UK), Jack & Shirley Castle (Aus), James Fontamilla (USA), James Simpson (UK), James Taylor (UK), Janet Powell Pinci (It), Jane Harland (UK), Jane Sutcliffe (UK), Jane & Alan Fowler (UK), Jane & Mike Driscoll (UK), Jan de Graat (Aus), Jan Willem (Nl), Jay Lasner (USA), Jean & Sylvaine Siau (F), Jennifer & Derek Clark-Ward (UK), Jennifer Macleod (USA), Jenny Mills (Aus), Jill Sheppard (UK), Jill Strudwick (UK), John Anderson (Aus), John Carrier (Sw), John Daley (NZ), John Fouquet (Mal), John Kasteel (Aus), John Morrow (Thai), John Walsh (NZ), Selwyn Weiss (Aus), John & Rhonda Scarlett (Aus), Jonathan Mosel (C), Jong Lee Keng (Mal), Jorg Tiedemann (Thai), Jude Bondini (C), Judy Rochlin (USA), Judy Vanderryn (USA), Julian Price (NZ), Justin Mansley (UK), JK & F Aitken (Aus), Kalid Puteh (S), Karen Hedderman, Karen Snyder (UK), Karin & Kim Luciano (A), Petter Lundgren (Sw), Katherine Liddell (UK), Keith Liddicoat (In), Keith Rakow (USA), Kent Hellberg (Sw), Kerry & Melanie Underwood (UK), Ken Tan (Mal), Kim Kelly (C), Kumar K Pardip (Mal), Kym Henkee-Poole (S), Larry & Sandra Davidson (USA), Leena Tuhkanen (Fin), Legrand Blomme (C), Leonie Muffett (Aus), Linda Bishpam (UK), Lisbeth Djurhuus (Dk), Lisa Haggblom (USA), Lisa Kazlauskaj, Loring Lawrence (USA), Lucy King (NZ), Lucy Stone (Mal), Lynn Bates, M.G. McCulloch (Aus), Mabel MacDonald (USA), Major Robert Burnham (USA), Marilyn Feorino (USA), Maria A. Teodori (It), Marie Cazaurang (F), Marlies de Zeeuw (Nl), Martina Beckmann (D), Martine Bidault (F), Martin Heseltine (Aus), Martin Minderlein (D), Marc Legrand (USA), Mary Campbell (Aus), Maureen McFarlane (Thai), Maureen Mcfarlane (C), Maurice Little (UK), Max Nankervis (Aus), Mette Heide (Dk), Michael Bordan (C), Michael Dillon (C), Michael James Dover, Michael & Sarah McCambridge (UK), Michael J Szkolny (UK), Michelle Van Hove (C), Michel Martineau (C), Michel Mortineau (C), Mieke Verger (Nl), Mike Guest (C), Mike Lee, Mike Nalenko (Aus), Mike Papesch (NZ), Miss Henny Pootjes (Nl), Miss Siew Choo Lim (Mal), Miss L W Poon Poon (HK), Mrs. Florence Tan (S), Mrs Bearcae (UK), Mrs Jan Buchanan (Aus), Mrs B MacClement (NZ), M, P, K & W Sonne (Nl), Mr Gan (Mal), Mr A J Worsdale (C), Mr G O'Shea (UK), Mr H Kaasjager (Nl), Mr R Ford (UK), Mrs. Larysa Foty, Mr T K Hillier (UK), Ms Spijkerbosch (NZ), Ms E Hurst (UK), Navjot Bedi (UK), Neale Cunningham (D), Neil Teplitz (USA), Neoh Ah Kow (Mal), Nerissa David (Aus), Nicholas Martland (UK), Nicholas Murray (Aus), Nicole Iszak (UK), Nicole van Doorn (B), Nick Roberts (UK), Nigel Miles (UK), Nikki Broun (D), Nils Villumser (Dk), Otto Ulc (USA), Palle Frese (Dk), Paradis B&B Breakfast (Mal), Patrick Chan Bayview Inn (S), Paul Basintal (Mal),

Paul Downer, Paul Greening, Paul Miller (Aus), Paul Newcomb (UK), Pat Firby (UK), Pat Yale (UK), Peter Alex (UK), Peter Dymoke (Aus), Peter Morgan (HK), Peter O'Connell (Aus), Peter Schouten (Nl), Peter Walsh (Aus), Peter & Flo Shaw (Aus), Peter J Callaghan (Aus), Per Rahbek (Dk), Philip Crolin (UK), Philip Ting (Mal), Phil Hurst (UK), Phyllis Keenan, Rachel Fancy (UK), Rab Albertson (UK), Ray Hayley-Barker, Rene Frandsen (Mal), Richard Cooper (USA), Richard Gregory Smith (A), Rick Dubbeldam (Nl), Rixt Riegstra (UK), Robert Gunnersson (Ice), Robert Legier (C), Robert Markow (C), Robert Minter (Aus), Robt J Motz (UK), Rolf Vogler (CH), Ronnie Chen (S), Rosamund Vallings (NZ), Roslyn Jones (UK), Ross Doyle (NZ), Roy Vinnicombe (Aus), Rob Gable (Mal), Rob V Duppen (Nl), Russell Hancock (Aus), Ruth Cakebread (UK), Sarah Frost, Sarah Maxim (USA), Sarah Willmer (UK), Saskia Cox (UK), Sam C T Sartain (USA), Scott Walker, Shahriza bin A Shuker (Mal), Sheila K. Singhal (C), Paul Skidmore (UK), Shelley Endenburg (C), Siang Piow Liu (Mal), Sian Loftus (Aus), Simon Lamplugh (A), Simon Vallings (NZ), Stanley T Malang (Mal), Stanley T Malang (Mal), Stan Cory (Aus), Stephen Meredith (Aus), Stephen Morey (Aus), Stephen Pinfield, Stephen Reid (NZ), Steven Bammel (USA), Steve Lustgarden (USA), Stewart Olney (UK), Bert Oolders (Nl), Stuart Greif (NZ), Susan Perry (UK), Sue King (UK), Sue Oliver (UK), Tey Roberts (USA), Thina Bergman (Sw), Thomas Guest (UK), The Low Budget Traveller, Tim Pinos (C), Tommy Aerts (B), Ton Starrenburg (Nl), Tracy Kelly (UK), Travellers Inn (Mal), Ahmad Zailani Ismail (Mal), Trisha Doran (UK), Trish McPherson (UK), Trudie Bosma (Nl), Unot Norten (N), Vernon Weitzel (Aus), Wahono Goncalo (Mac), Wayne Richards (Aus), Wayne & Dagmar Hughes (C), Zac Lee (Mal), ? Haythorpe, A & C Peers/Taylor (UK), A Devota (USA), A Hancock (UK), A J Dodd (UK), B K Darby (Aus), C Mulroney (UK), C & A Scerri (Aus), C A Briggs (UK), D Langley (Aus), F Gali (C), J Basheer (Aus), J Pogacinik (Yug), J Vas (Nl), J A J van de Laar (Nl), J B Anderson (NZ), J R Tippett, K Bin T P Tengku (S), K van Lohuizen (Nl), M Kerkhoven (Nl), N Rajan (S), N C Morgan (UK), N D Otto (Aus), P Barker (UK), P Cheong, P Lippevelt (B), P Speer, R Brenner & N Cunningham (D), R Walker, R W Hatfield (UK), S Clarke (UK), S Donovan (UK), S Evans (UK), S Jewitt (UK), S Olney (NZ), T Hovenkamp (Nl), W Peters (Nl), W Sutcliffe (UK), Z Lee (Mal)

A – Austria, Aus – Australia, B – Belgium, Bra – Brazil, C – Can, CH – Switzerland, D – West Germany, Dk – Denmark, F – France, Fin – Finland, G – Greece, HK – Hong Kong, I – India, In – Indonesia, It – Italy, J – Japan, Mal – Malaysia, N – Norway, Nl – Netherlands, NZ – New Zealand, S – Singapore, SL – Sri Lanka, Sw – Sweden, Thai – Thailand, UK – United Kingdom, USA – United States of America

Guides to South-East Asia

South-East Asia on a shoestring
The well-known 'yellow bible' for travellers in South-East Asia covers Brunei, Burma, Hong Kong, Indonesia, Macau, Malaysia, Papua New Guinea, the Philippines, Singapore, and Thailand.

Bali & Lombok - a travel survival kit
This guide will help travellers to experience the real magic of Bali's tropical paradise. Neighbouring Lombok is largely untouched by outside influences and has a special atmosphere of its own.

Burma - a travel survival kit
Burma is one of Asia's most interesting countries. This book shows how to make the most of a trip around the main triangle route of Rangoon–Mandalay–Pagan, and explores many lesser-known places such as Pegu and Inle Lake.

Philippines - a travel survival kit
The friendly Filipinos, colourful festivals, and superb natural scenery make the Philippines one of the most interesting countries in South-East Asia for adventurous travellers and sun- seekers alike.

Indonesia - a travel survival kit
Some of the most remarkable sights and sounds in South-East Asia can be found amongst the 7000 islands of Indonesia — this book covers the entire archipelago in detail.

Hong Kong, Macau & Canton - a travel survival kit
A comprehensive guide to three fascinating cities linked by history, culture and geography.

Thailand - a travel survival kit
This authoritative guide includes Thai script for all place names and the latest travel details for all regions, including tips in trekking in the remote hills of the Golden Triangle.

Vietnam, Laos & Cambodia - a travel survival kit
This comprehensive guidebook has all the information you'll need on this most beautiful region of Asia – finally opening its doors to the world.

Also available:
Thai phrasebook, *Burmese* phrasebook, *Pilipino* phrasebook, and *Indonesia* phrasebook.

Lonely Planet Guidebooks

Lonely Planet guidebooks cover every accessible part of Asia as well as Australia, the Pacific, South America, Africa, the Middle East and parts of North America and Europe. There are four series: *travel survival kits*, covering a single country for a range of budgets; *shoestring guides* with compact information for low-budget travel in a major region; *walking guides*; and *phrasebooks*.

Australia & the Pacific
Australia
Bushwalking in Australia
Islands of Australia's Great Barrier Reef
Fiji
Micronesia
New Caledonia
New Zealand
Tramping in New Zealand
Papua New Guinea
Papua New Guinea phrasebook
Rarotonga & the Cook Islands
Samoa
Solomon Islands
Sydney
Tahiti & French Polynesia
Tonga
Vanuatu

South-East Asia
Bali & Lombok
Burma
Burmese phrasebook
Indonesia
Indonesia phrasebook
Malaysia, Singapore & Brunei
Philippines
Pilipino phrasebook
Singapore
South-East Asia on a shoestring
Thailand
Thai phrasebook
Vietnam, Laos & Cambodia

North-East Asia
China
Chinese phrasebook
Hong Kong, Macau & Canton
Japan
Japanese phrasebook
Korea
Korean phrasebook
North-East Asia on a shoestring
Taiwan
Tibet
Tibet phrasebook

West Asia
Trekking in Turkey
Turkey
Turkish phrasebook
West Asia on a shoestring

Indian Ocean
Madagascar & Comoros
Maldives & Islands of the East Indian Ocean
Mauritius, Réunion & Seychelles

Mail Order

Lonely Planet guidebooks are distributed worldwide and are sold by good bookshops everywhere. They are also available by mail order from Lonely Planet, so if you have difficulty finding a title please write to us. US and Canadian residents should write to Embarcadero West, 112 Linden St, Oakland CA 94607, USA and residents of other countries to PO Box 617, Hawthorn, Victoria 3122, Australia.

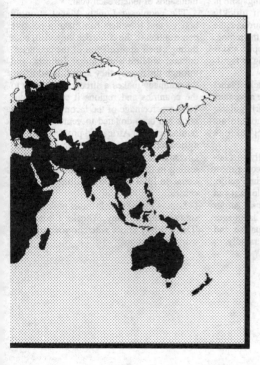

Europe
Eastern Europe on a shoestring
Iceland, Greenland & the Faroe Islands
Trekking in Spain

Indian Subcontinent
Bangladesh
India
Hindi/Urdu phrasebook
Trekking in the Indian Himalaya
Karakoram Highway
Kashmir, Ladakh & Zanskar
Nepal
Trekking in the Nepal Himalaya
Nepal phrasebook
Pakistan
Sri Lanka
Sri Lanka phrasebook

Africa
Africa on a shoestring
Central Africa
East Africa
Kenya
Swahili phrasebook
Morocco, Algeria & Tunisia
Moroccan Arabic phrasebook
West Africa

North America
Alaska
Canada
Hawaii

Mexico
Baja California
Mexico

South America
Argentina
Bolivia
Brazil
Brazilian phrasebook
Chile & Easter Island
Colombia
Ecuador & the Galápagos Islands
Latin American Spanish phrasebook
Peru
Quechua phrasebook
South America on a shoestring

Middle East
Egypt & the Sudan
Egyptian Arabic phrasebook
Israel
Jordan & Syria
Yemen

The Lonely Planet Story

Lonely Planet published its first book in 1973 in response to the numerous 'How did you do it?' questions Maureen and Tony Wheeler were asked after driving, bussing, hitching, sailing and railing their way from England to Australia.

Written at a kitchen table and hand collated, trimmed and stapled, *Across Asia on the Cheap* became an instant local bestseller, inspiring thoughts of another book.

Eighteen months in South-East Asia resulted in their second guide, *South-East Asia on a shoestring*, which they put together in a backstreet Chinese hotel in Singapore in 1975. The 'yellow bible' as it quickly became known to backpackers around the world, soon became *the* guide to the region. It has sold well over ½ million copies and is now in its 6th edition, still retaining its familiar yellow cover.

Today there are over 80 Lonely Planet titles — books that have that same adventurous approach to travel as those early guides; books that 'assume you know how to get your luggage off the carousel' as one reviewer put it.

Although Lonely Planet initially specialised in guides to Asia, they now cover most regions of the world, including the Pacific, South America, Africa, the Middle East and Eastern Europe. The list of *walking guides* and *phrasebooks* (for 'unusual' languages such as Quechua, Swahili, Nepalese and Egyptian Arabic) is also growing rapidly.

The emphasis continues to be on travel for independent travellers. Tony and Maureen still travel for several months of each year and play an active part in the writing, updating and quality control of Lonely Planet's guides.

They have been joined by over 50 authors, 40 staff — mainly editors, cartographers, & designers — at our office in Melbourne, Australia, and another 10 at our US office in Oakland, California. Travellers themselves also make a valuable contribution to the guides through the feedback we receive in thousands of letters each year.

The people at Lonely Planet strongly believe that travellers can make a positive contribution to the countries they visit, both through their appreciation of the countries' culture, wildlife and natural features, and through the money they spend. In addition, the company makes a direct contribution to the countries and regions it covers. Since 1986 a percentage of the income from each book has been donated to ventures such as famine relief in Africa; aid projects in India; agricultural projects in Central America; Greenpeace's efforts to halt French nuclear testing in the Pacific and Amnesty International. In 1990 $60,000 was donated to these causes.

Lonely Planet's basic travel philosophy is summed up in Tony Wheeler's comment, 'Don't worry about whether your trip will work out. Just go!'